Sex Differences and Similarities in Communication

Critical Essays and Empirical Investigations of Sex and Gender in Interaction

LEA's COMMUNICATION SERIES
Jennings Bryant/Dolf Zillmann, General Editors

Selected titles include:

Canary/Dindia • *Sex Differences and Similarities in Communication: Critical Essays and Empirical Investigations of Sex and Gender in Interaction*

Cupach/Spitzburg • *The Dark Side of Interpersonal Communication*

Daly/Wiemann • *Strategic Interpersonal Communication*

Frey • *Group Communication in Context: Studies of Natural Groups*

Hewes • *The Cognitive Bases of Interpersonal Communication*

Kalbfleisch • *Gender, Power, and Communication in Human Relationships*

Leeds-Hurwitz • *Semiotics and Communication: Signs, Codes, Cultures*

Noor Al-Deen • *Cross-Cultural Communication and Aging in the United States*

For a complete list of other titles in LEA's Communication Series, please contact Lawrence Erlbaum Associates, Publishers

Sex Differences and Similarities in Communication

Critical Essays and Empirical Investigations of Sex and Gender in Interaction

Edited by

Daniel J. Canary
Pennsylvania State University

Kathryn Dindia
University of Wisconsin–Milwaukee

 LAWRENCE ERLBAUM ASSOCIATES, PUBLISHERS
1998   Mahwah, New Jersey   London

Lawrence Erlbaum Associates, Inc., Publishers
10 Industrial Avenue
Mahwah, New Jersey 07430

Cover design by Kathryn Houghtaling Lacey

Library of Congress Cataloging-in-Publication Data

Sex differences and similarities in communication : critical essays
and empirical investigations of sex and gender in interaction /
edited by Daniel J. Canary, Kathryn Dindia.
   p.   cm.
  Includes bibliographical references and index.
  ISBN 0-8058-2333-6 (alk. paper). — ISBN 0-8058-2334-4 (pbk. :
alk. paper).
   1. Communication—Sex differences. I. Canary, Daniel J.
II. Dindia, Kathryn.
P96.S48S49 1997
155.3'3—dc21   97-49098
                                     CIP

Books published by Lawrence Erlbaum Associates are printed on acid-free paper,
and their bindings are chosen for strength and durability.

Printed in the United States of America
10 9 8 7 6 5 4 3 2 1

Contents

Preface   ix

Prologue: Recurring Issues in Sex Differences and
Similarities in Communication   1
   Daniel J. Canary and Kathryn Dindia

1   What's the Difference? A Dialogue About Differences
    and Similarities Between Women and Men   19
    Julia T. Wood and Kathryn Dindia

2   Toward an Expanded Orientation to the Study of Sex
    Differences in Friendship   41
    Paul H. Wright

3   Gender Differences in Interaction: A Reexamination   65
    Elizabeth Aries

4   Researching Sex Differences Within Sex Similarities:
    The Evolutionary Consequences of Reproductive
    Differences   83
    Peter A. Andersen

 5 Social Support and the Emotional Lives of Men and
    Women: An Assessment of the Different Cultures
    Perspective   101
    Adrianne W. Kunkel and Brant R. Burleson

 6 The Gender-Linked Language Effect: Do Language
    Differences Really Make a Difference?   127
    Anthony Mulac

 7 How Big Are Nonverbal Sex Differences? The Case of
    Smiling and Sensitivity to Nonverbal Cues   155
    Judith A. Hall

 8 Gender as a Culturally Determined Construct:
    Communication Styles in Japan and the United States   179
    Vincent R. Waldron and Lesley Di Mare

 9 Gender Differences in Intimacy and Related Behaviors:
    Context and Process   203
    Harry T. Reis

10 An Evolutionary View on Understanding Sex Effects
    in Communicating Attraction   233
    Melanie R. Trost and Jess K. Alberts

11 Gender Differences in Being Influential and/or
    Influenced: A Challenge to Prior Explanations   257
    Michael Burgoon and Renee S. Klingle

12 Theoretical Approaches to Understanding Sex
    Differences and Similarities in Conflict Behavior   287
    *Lynda M. Sagrestano, Christopher L. Heavey,
    and Andrew Christensen*

13 A Comparison of Topics and Objectives in a Cross
    Section of Young Men's and Women's Everyday
    Conversations   303
    Ruth Anne Clark

14 Expressing Emotion: Sex Differences in Social Skills
    and Communicative Responses to Anger, Sadness, and
    Jealousy   321
    Laura K. Guerrero and Reneé L. Reiter

15 Sex Differences in Presenting and Detecting Deceptive
        Messages   351
        Judee K. Burgoon, David B. Buller, Joseph R. Grandpre,
        and Pamela Kalbfleisch

16 Conversational Maintenance Behaviors of Husbands
        and Wives: An Observational Analysis   373
        Elizabeth B. Robey, Daniel J. Canary, and
        Cynthia S. Burggraf

17 Perceptions of Men and Women Departing From
        Conversational Sex Role Stereotypes During Initial
        Interaction   393
        A. Elizabeth Lindsey and Walter R. Zakahi

18 First Date Initiation and Enactment: An Expectancy
        Violation Approach   413
        Paul A. Mongeau, Colleen M. Carey, and
        Mary Lynn M. Williams

19 Methodological Considerations When Examining a
        Gendered World   427
        Mike Allen

Author Index   445

Subject Index   461

Preface

Scholarly opinions about the differences between men and women are more than academic; opinions about sex differences have personal, professional, and political implications. Given the seriousness of the implications, it is no wonder that scholars often advocate their academic positions on the issue of sex differences with passion and zeal.

Of course, men and women differ in many ways. Some biological differences, for instance, are undeniable in that no one seriously considers an examination of sex differences in reproductive roles (pregnancy, childbirth, and breast-feeding). In addition to sex differences, sex inequalities are clearly evident in the division of labor, economic security, and national offices of government. For instance, women in paid jobs continue to struggle to achieve a fair division of labor in the home. Less clear, however, are the differences in men's and women's communication in professional, social, and personal relationships.

This book examines the social scientific literature regarding how men and women communicate. Readers who are interested in the scientific literature in communication, psychology, and related fields should find this anthology an important resource. Students in advanced undergraduate classes and graduate classes, and practitioners interested in research-based conclusions regarding sex differences in communicative behavior, should be especially informed. People who seek support for a particular point of view—especially one that divides men and women in a dichotomous or polarized fashion—will probably want to look elsewhere.

As the title implies, the chapters in this book present sex similarities as well as sex differences in communication. The primary reason we examine sex similarities in addition to sex differences stems from our desire to present a balanced scientific anthology on the topic. In our view, another book that polarizes men and women would move the corpus of knowledge backward, making us less informed than we should be at this point in time. Instead, this book advances the idea that, with respect to communicative behavior, men and women are similar in some domains and different in others. The task, then, is to juxtapose similarities and differences.

A contemporary and popular view presents men and women as members of different cultures, such that men and women speak different languages and hold alternative meanings for the terms they do share in common. On this view, the intersection between similarities and differences represents at best an illusion. One may think one understands members of the opposite sex, when in fact one cannot understand members of the opposite sex.

A much less popular, though still contemporary, view is that men and women act as if they come from the same culture. That is, men and women behave in similar ways virtually all of the time. Obviously, men and women eat similar foods with identical tools, drink similar beverages much the same way, and sleep in similar positions. Central to the present volume is the claim that men and women similarly use and understand the same verbal and nonverbal messages.

We believe that sex similarities provide a context, a backdrop, for sex differences. Importantly, this backdrop offers ways to contrast communicative differences between men and women. Yet, the backdrop metaphor represents more than an ideological frame of reference. More precisely, using similarities to contextualize and clarify differences between men and women allows researchers to look for differences only in places where we theoretically and empirically hypothesize them to be, as opposed to everywhere or nowhere.

Critically, the chapters in this volume vary in terms of the authors' positions. Most of the authors theoretically and/or empirically combine sex similarities and sex differences, whereas a few take positions on either end of the similarity–difference continuum. These alternative points of view provide a sense of freedom not found in other books that aim to limit views about men's and women's communication; one does not have to presume sex differences or sex similarities to be politically correct (PC) or scientifically correct (SC) in this book. Thus, we think this book provides various models regarding how scholars can recalibrate categorical thinking to discover where sex differences and similarities lie. In doing so, many of the authors may have erred on the side of being SC (vs. PC).

Most of the chapters provide innovative alternatives to categorical thinking about men and women. As editors, we were pleased by the variation in scope and evidence used to develop ideas. Contributors characteristically offer in-depth, state-of-the-art reviews of the scientific literature, and several authors also present original empirical research results to make their points. We all will benefit from the massive amount of effort that these chapters represent.

The reader might be interested to learn that most of the chapters in this book were selected on a competitive basis. After reading announcements in national and international newsletters, potential contributors submitted chapter proposals and papers, and we then decided which chapters should be included. Each of us voted independently, with two "thumbs up" required for each chapter included in the present volume. Thus, less than half of the proposals/papers submitted were accepted. The result is a multidisciplinary reflection on how men and women communicate in various contexts and domains of behavior.

As the reader might anticipate, the present volume required cooperation and help from many people. At the outset, we want to thank all of the people who submitted proposals or papers that we did not select for inclusion. Many of these people are friends, and we were genuinely torn in the process of selection. We rely on their understanding and professionalism regarding the competitive selection process; we can only offer our honest appreciation in return.

Of course, we thank each and every one of the chapter contributors. Over the span of two years, this project has come to fruition due to their efforts. In all instances, the contributors offered excellent first drafts. And following our comments, editing, and margin notes, the contributors worked in a timely, professional manner to polish their prose and extend their chapters in ways they had not anticipated. We have no doubt that their contributions to this book will constitute required reading in courses and seminars for years to come.

Next we must thank the people who linked this project to Lawrence Erlbaum Associates. At the top of this list is Dennis Gouran. His encouragement and editorial advice helped us to shape our proposal. Moreover, his endorsement as advisory editor for the Communication Series (advised by Jennings Bryant and Dolf Zillmann) was critical. We also wish to thank Michelle Mattrey, a Ph.D. student at Penn State University, for constructing excellent indexes. In addition, we thank Kathleen O'Malley, who initially served as Acquisitions Editor for LEA. Kathleen has now moved on to another position, but we still remember her early efforts on our behalf.

Of those people who made the move to Mahwah, we extend our sincere thanks to Linda Bathgate. Linda helped to smooth out the transition of editors, led us through the reorganization of the book, and was resourceful in balancing the overall cost of the book (which we are sure the reader will appreciate). In addition, Lane Akers was most flexible in renegotiating the book title. We also want to thank Barbara Wieghaus for her excellent supervision during the production stage of the book, including copyediting and typesetting.

We sincerely hope that you find this anthology as intriguing as we have. We think that the chapters will interest you and kindle new ways to think about sex differences and similarities in communicative behavior. We believe that scholarly interest in sex differences in communicative behavior will continue to be advanced by also paying attention to sex similarities.

—*Daniel J. Canary*
—*Kathryn Dindia*

Prologue: Recurring Issues in Sex Differences and Similarities in Communication

Daniel J. Canary
Pennsylvania State University

Kathryn Dindia
University of Wisconsin–Milwaukee

The study of how sex differences might affect the way that people communicate presents a difficult research undertaking. A thorough literature review appears impossible because hundreds of books and articles have been written on the topic. Within this literature, authors present differing views with skill and passion and employ alternative methods to reflect most favorably on the theoretical position taken. The scientific study of how sex similarities might contextualize and inform the study of differences is largely a novelty. Most of the time, researchers want to see differences, not similarities; researchers seek confirmation of the research hypothesis, not support for the null. Only when no significant differences are found do scientists tend to admit that similarities appear plausible.

This book specifically aims to uncover sex and gender differences within the context of similarities. Neither of the editors presume that omnipresent sex differences exist. Our view is that men and women are different. But it is possible that men and women are more alike than different, and focal points that connect similarities to differences theoretically as well as methodologically constitute a critical juncture for speculation and study.

The goal of this prologue is to provide the reader with an overview of the major issues emerging in this anthology. Our prologue certainly does not exhaust the many important issues that each of the chapters addresses. Instead, the following pages point to themes that recur in the chapters. These themes are discussed to foreshadow some of the exciting developments found here as well as in the larger scholarly debate on sex and gender differences occurring in communication, psychology, linguistics, family studies, and other fields. Following a discussion of recurring themes, we briefly preview the excellent chapters that were contributed to this volume by experts in the field. The intent here is only to summarize these fine works because the reader will find much more information and insight in each of the chapters.

ISSUE 1: DIFFERENCES OR SIMILARITIES

Researchers have experience being men or women (and earlier, boys or girls). Hence, researchers must somehow deal with "biased beliefs" they have derived through lived experiences about a major component of their own personal identities. As Tannen (1994) recently indicated, "Entering the arena of research on gender is like stepping into a maelstrom. What it means to be female or male, what it's like to talk to someone of the other (or the same) [sex], are questions whose answers touch people where they live, and when a nerve is touched, people howl" (p. 3). In a similar manner, one cannot escape one's ideological frame of reference when researching how sex differences might affect communication between people. Crawford (1995) put it this way:

> Sex difference findings can never enter the scientific discourse neutrally. Rather, they are interpreted within the context of deeply held beliefs about women's [and men's] natures. In accounting for their results, researchers cannot avoid being influenced by the sociocultural discourse of gender, because "facts" about sex differences have no meaning outside that discourse. What "counts" as an interesting or important result, and what "makes sense" as an interpretation, are always ideological matters. (p. 32)

Most people appear to believe that men and women are fundamentally different. Hare-Mustin and Marecek (1988) argued that people who assume pervasive sex differences in social behavior have an "alpha bias" or "the exaggeration of differences" (p. 457). Researchers (like us) who presume that few if any differences exist between men and women adopt a "beta bias." According to Hare-Mustin and Marecek, more researchers suffer from alpha bias than beta bias, and more scholars presume sex and gender differences than similarities.

Several contributors to this volume appear to have an alpha bias. For example, Reis (chap. 9) provides a model that helps explain why men and women differ in their experience and expression of intimacy. According to Reis, studies using the Rochester Interaction Record (RIR; a diary method for self-reporting daily interactions) reveal a large sex difference regarding intimacy in same-sex friends, although sex differences disappear in the RIR studies of cross-sex friendships. Other authors who appear to adopt the predominant alpha bias include Hall (chap. 7), Mulac (chap. 6), Trost and Alberts (chap. 10), among others.

Several contributors to this volume appear to adopt the view that similarities rather than differences characterize men and women (perhaps as a result of our cues and comments). For instance, Kunkel and Burleson (chap. 5) find that "some noteworthy differences between men and women exist, when both within- and between-gender comparisons are made; the similarities are as important—if not more important—than the differences." Other contributors who appear to adopt a similar beta bias include Andersen (chap. 4); Aries (chap. 3); Robey, Canary, and Burggraf (chap. 16); and Wright (chap. 2). But even when such similarities are granted, authors often remain eager to explore and elaborate on sex differences more than similarities. For example, Andersen's (chap. 4) excellent chapter on sex differences in nonverbal cues begins with a statement that celebrates similarities; it then develops an explanation for sex differences in communication behavior.

The debate regarding sex differences versus sex similarities is a hotly contested one. Recently, an issue of *American Psychologist* was devoted to the issue of sex differences. In that issue, Eagly (1995) argued that, although sex difference effect sizes are small to moderate, they still account for as much of the variance as one should expect from virtually any psychological construct. Thus, she argued that, relatively speaking, sex differences are not small. In contrast, Hyde and Plant (1995) noted that sex differences are most typically small (i.e., they reported that 25% of the research reports a close to zero effect due to sex, 35% reports a small effect, 27% reports a moderate effect, and only 13% reports large to extremely large effect sizes). Based on these figures, Hyde and Plant argued that more similarities than differences exist between men and women.

Whereas *American Psychologist* focused on the general domain of psychological processes, the present volume concentrates on communication behavior between people and how sex or gender differences, including psychological processes, translate into symbolic actions between people. Indicating the centrality of the sex difference versus similarity debate to communication research, Wood and Dindia (chap. 1) offer a dialogue that addresses several issues related to the debate. These authors consider three related questions: Are men and women different? If so, what are the sources of their differences (biological or social)? What should the focus of research on sex and gender differences and similarities entail? Obviously, one chapter (or edited volume) cannot address each of these important questions to every reader's satisfaction. Nevertheless, these fundamental questions underscore that the issue of sex differences versus similarities is open to debate.

ISSUE 2: DEFINING SLIPPERY TERMS

Providing definitions is a rudimentary—and sometimes boring—academic exercise. Yet without definitions, writers can confuse readers without the slightest intentions of doing so. Such confusion is especially apparent in the literature concerned with sex and gender. One does not have to read far to notice that scholars often use the term *gender* in lieu of *sex* in part because *gender* does not carry connotations of sexuality or sexual intercourse. Other scholars prefer *gender* to *sex* because the former term conveys their interest in examining the psychological and social processes of gender construction (e.g., Beall, 1993). Other scholars prefer to reserve *gender* for instances of behavior that convey one's social/pscyhological/cultural understanding of self as a man or a woman and to reserve *sex* to reference biological distinctions between men and women (Deaux, 1985).

We adopt the position that *sex* refers to the genetic, biological differences between boys and girls, between men and women; *gender* refers to the psychological and social manifestations of what one believes to be male and/or female, which might—or might not—reflect one's biological sex. Some contributors to this volume focus more on sex differences, including Andersen (chap. 4) and Trost and Alberts (chap. 10), among others. These authors make a case for studying sex as opposed to gender (i.e., their theoretical explanations cast the issue of differences between men and women as stemming from a biological origin that plays out in social behavior). Other authors stress gender. This group includes Kunkel and Burleson (chap. 5), Lindsey and Zakahi (chap. 17), and Wood and Dindia (chap. 1), among others.

One needs to be aware of the manner in which sex and/or gender differences are inferred. For example, scholars can cogently argue for the examination of gender differences instead of sex differences. However, some of the research studies cited to support such arguments in fact examine biological differences between men and women (i.e., the independent variable is measured by a question indicating the participant's biological sex), so such studies can only indirectly support a gender difference approach (see Allen, chap. 19). Similarly, researchers might insist that they study socially defined gender when in reality they sometimes operationally define *gender* using the standard dichotomy that represents biological sex.

A second critical term that varies considerably among authors is *communication*. As part of the "Erlbaum Series on Communication," this volume is dedicated to the examination of theories and research that directly entreat symbolic behaviors. Some of the authors explore verbal communication behavior, whereas others discuss findings concerning nonverbal behavior. Even the verbal–nonverbal distinction does not unpack a variety of other issues that impinge on what is meant by the term *communication*. The research presented and represented in this volume variously and most often implicitly defines *communication*. Accordingly, the reader must remain vigilant to the nuances in how communication is portrayed.

One important question concerns the level of abstraction from actual behavior. Many researchers examine microscopic forms of communication behavior. This group would include the research represented in the chapter by Judee Burgoon and colleagues (chap. 15), as well as in the works of Aries (chap. 3), Hall (chap. 7), Mulac (chap. 6), and Robey, Canary, and Burggraf (chap. 16). At issue in these studies is whether one's biological sex or psychological/sociological gender affects the performance or perception of discrete verbal or nonverbal behaviors. Other researchers investigate more macroscopic levels of communication. For instance, recall that Reis (chap. 9) reports large sex differences in studies of intimacy. In these studies, intimacy was measured with a single item that had participants rate their conversations on a 7-point scale, from *superficial* (1) to *meaningful* (7). In this manner, Reis assesses global assessments of behavior. Other authors who assess communication globally include Clark (chap. 13), Waldron and Di Mare (chap. 8), and Trost and Alberts (chap. 10). Whether sex/gender differences more clearly emerge in the macroscopic or microscopic analyses remains open to speculation.

ISSUE 3: MODERATING, CONTEXTUAL FACTORS

Few scholars adopt the view that effects due to sex or gender operate independently of social context. A recent trend in the literature is to move away from monolithic characterizations of men and women to theoretical models that combine moderating, contextual factors. Perhaps Aries (chap. 3) makes the clearest case in this volume for integrating situational factors when discussing sex differences in communication. Her analysis shows that in some situations some of the time, men and women verbally communicate in ways that might conform to the generally held stereotype of men as primarily instrumental and women as primarily communal. Similarly, Wright (chap. 2) argues that structural, rather than dispositional, variables account for many of the existing differences between men's and women's friendships.

Other scholars contrast individual sex differences against situational or relational factors. Illustrating this approach, Sagrestano, Heavey, and Christensen (chap. 12) review their program of research on the demand–withdrawal pattern. Most of the research on the demand–withdrawal pattern has shown both a main effect for sex as well as a weaker, although higher ordered interaction effect that actually reverses the main effect. More precisely, wives demand and their husbands withdraw in most situations. However, when one focuses on issues that the men want to change, husbands demand more and their wives withdraw. Sagrestano et al. interpret these findings as evidence of two processes at work: a social structural effect (i.e., a pattern developed over time) and an individual, sex difference effect.

In addition, Reis (chap. 9) reports sex differences in intimacy. However, such differences do not involve a main effect; they involve an interaction effect (sex of subject by sex of target), indicating that situational factors (i.e., dyadic composition) are present. Similarly, Waldron and Di Mare (chap. 8) studied sex, culture, and the interaction of sex and culture and found an interaction effect. Sex differences manifested themselves differently in Japan than in the United States. In contrast to Sagrestano et al., Reis, and Waldron and Di Mare, Mulac's (chap. 6) program of research indicates stable gender differences across a variety of situations. Mulac examines naturally occurring language from a broad range of communication tasks and settings. Across these contexts, the pattern of results has been consistent (cf. Aries, 1996).

The point so clearly made by Aries in this volume has been argued in the past (e.g., Deaux, 1984; Eagly, 1987): One should not expect to find sex differences in every behavior all the time. As Wood and Dindia (chap. 1) ask, must we examine sex differences in each and every domain of communication behavior? Instead of presupposing that sex or gender predicts every behavior all the time, the more promising question concerns how we can theoretically explain the effects due to sex and/or gender as they occur in context.

ISSUE 4: THEORETICAL EXPLANATIONS

In 1993, Canary and Hause lamented that too few theories existed to explain sex differences in communication. Although theory still lags behind descriptive research, researchers have made advances in theoretical explanations of sex and gender differences. A number of theoretical explanations are postulated for differences in men and women's communication in this volume (e.g., Andersen, chap. 4; Trost & Alberts, chap. 10). The problem confronting us in this volume concerns how sex and/or gender is manifested in communication behavior. As Deaux and Major (1987) noted, "the enactment of gender primarily takes place within the context of social interaction, either explicitly or implicitly" (p. 370). Accordingly, we ask how theories that concern people's biological sex or social gender precisely explain how sex and/or gender is reflected in or affects communication behavior. At least three answers can be found.

For a large group of people, the ready-made answer lies in stereotypes (Crawford, 1995). That is, stereotypic views of men and women are said to provide sufficient explanation of sex differences in communication behavior. The argument typically goes like this: (a) People hold sex role stereotypes that prescribe general orientations toward behavior (i.e., men are instrumental, women are communal); (b) people are socialized to live up to stereotypic expectations, even if they personally do not adopt them; and (c) therefore, relatively speaking, women will be communal and men will be instrumental. Such reasoning often leads to rather obvious predictions concerning various forms of communication behavior. For example, reasoning from stereotypes would lead to the prediction that women (who are more communal than men) are more likely to use cooperative conflict tactics, whereas men (who are more instrumental) are more likely to use competitive conflict tactics.

Although conventional stereotypes may resonate with some people, they do not accurately represent how people communicate in their personal relationships. For instance, the research (especially observational research) shows that women are more likely to be confrontational and hostile during conflict, whereas men are more likely to avoid conflict and be cooperative when in conflict (Schaap, Buunk, & Kerkstra, 1988; Sagrestano et al., chap. 12, this volume). Other reviews have shown that stereotypes are poor predictors of how men and women communicate (e.g., Aries, 1996). However, stereotypes can predict behavior in certain circumstances (especially those involving strangers or acquaintances) and indicate when conventional norms are violated (Aries, chap. 3; Lindsey & Zakahi, chap. 17; Mongeau, Carey, & Williams, chap. 18).[1]

A second answer to the question regarding the theoretical link between sex/gender and communication can be found in the development and testing of predictions derived from theories that focus on communication rather than sex or gender. In these theories, sex or gender defers to communicative processes as the primary phenomenon of interest, although sex or gender are implicated. For instance, language expectancy theory (see Burgoon & Klingle, chap. 11, this volume) presents eight propositions that specify how message persuasiveness depends on violations of social expectations. Only the last proposition specifies sex differences, and

---

[1]Stereotypes may predict behavior in situations involving college students and gender-stereotypical tasks. Adolescents and young adults (vs. older adults) more often adhere to stereotypes of men and women and thus stereotypes. Accordingly, one should consider how subjects' age might moderate sex differences attributed to everyone (which is also related to the previous theme, moderating/contextual factors). Another way to say this is that much of the research on sex differences involves college undergraduates, who are more likely than older adults to adopt conventional views of men and women interacting (e.g., men are good decision makers, women are high self-disclosers). To the extent that stereotypic views of men and women subside due to individual development and experiences, studies involving undergraduates may not generalize to older adults. Coincidentally, the tendency for younger adults to behave stereotypically associates with topics that often occupy researchers' interests (e.g., courtship behavior, expression of intimacy, etc.).

this proposition relies on the development of the previous seven statements. Similarly, Mongeau, Carey, and Williams (chap. 18, this volume) use expectancy violation theory to explain gender differences in perceptions of and behavior during female-initiated first dates.

A third answer to the question regarding the link between sex/gender and communication concerns how sex as a biological factor directly affects communication behavior. This approach argues that biological characteristics of the sexes, such as X and Y chromosomes and the hormonal activities they activate, affect communication behavior. With regard to evolutionary approaches, Andersen's (chap. 4) and Trost and Alberts' (chap. 10) chapters deserve mention. These authors carefully articulate how thousands of years of genetic development lead men and women to engage in different forms of courtship behavior (Trost & Alberts) as well as different nonverbal capacities (Andersen).

A fourth answer to the question regarding the link between sex/gender and communication is that male–female differences in communication are the result of sociological gender rather than biological sex. That is, social, historical, and cultural forces underlie the apparent behavioral differences between men and women (Kahn & Yoder, 1989; Sagrestano et al., chap. 12, this volume). These authors conceptualize gender as a social construction, almost divorced from concerns that stem from one's genetic code (e.g., Wood, & Dindia, chap. 1, this volume).

A fifth answer to the questions regarding the link between sex/gender and communication concerns how sex as a biological factor translates into gender as a social construction. Recently, Canary, Emmers-Sommer, and Faulkner (1997) argued that biological sex implicitly affects gender as communicated. In other words, a person can convey gender as it reflects one's biological sex largely without one's awareness of the connections between sex and gender. For instance, the physical development of the male adolescent (but not the female adolescent) associates with increased assertiveness on the part of the male adolescent, and such assertiveness is linked to a decrease in the female parent's power (but not the male parent's power; e.g., Steinberg & Hill, 1978). Accordingly, we can see how one's biological sex acts as a direct but implicit influence on one's gendered interaction behavior. Of course, researchers hypothesize other communication behaviors that reveal how gender is affected by biological sex.

ISSUE 5: INSTRUMENTAL AND COMMUNAL ORIENTATIONS

One final issue concerns *where* one looks for sex and gender differences (and similarities). Contributors to this volume focus on two general areas: instrumentality and communality. These foci correspond to general orientations that people have toward each other and represent current theory and research on sex differences (e.g., Wright, chap. 2, this volume).

Several of the chapters appear to divide along the instrumental–communal distinction. Chapters that appear to focus more on communality than instrumentality include nonverbal expressions of intimacy (Hall, chap. 7), self-reported intimacy (Reis, chap. 9), attraction (Trost & Alberts, chap. 10), first date initiation and enactment (Mongeau, Carey, & Williams, chap. 18), and social supportiveness (Kunkel & Burleson, chap. 5). Chapters that focus more on instrumentality than communality entreat such topics as deception (J. Burgoon, Buller, Grandpre, & Kalbfleisch, chap. 15), conflict management (Sagrestano, Heavey, & Christensen, chap. 12), conversational norm violations (Lindsey & Zakahi, chap. 17), conversational maintenance (Robey, Canary, & Burggraf, chap. 16), and persuasibility (Burgoon & Klingle, chap. 11). However, the authors of these chapters do not necessarily distinguish between instrumental and communal foci.

Indeed, as Wright (chap. 2, this volume) indicates, the dichotomy is not mutually exclusive; some behaviors that we see as communal might be categorized by authors as instrumental or vice versa, and some chapters focus on both communal and instrumental domains. For instance, Andersen (chap. 4) appears to consider both domains. He argues that, due to biological evolution, women possess greater ability to read nonverbal behaviors (a communal skill), whereas men possess greater ability to navigate territory (an instrumental skill). Guerrero and Reiter (chap. 14) discuss how people respond to anger, sadness, and jealousy, and it appears that such responses can reflect both communal and instrumental needs. In her examination of the conversational objectives of young men and women, Clark (chap. 13) reports sex similarities in topics that relate to both communality and instrumentality; she reports a few differences that reflect a greater communal orientation of women versus men.

CHAPTER PREVIEWS

The chapters presented in this volume represent a wide array of research concerning sex differences and similarities in communication behavior. But the current collection is more than a broad set of reviews; this book also contains challenging, new insights made by blue ribbon experts on the topic (as one reviewer put it) as well as emerging scholars. The chapters address many contemporary theoretical issues, and several offer original empirical data to support their claims. All of the chapters discuss current trends in theory and research regarding how sex/gender affects communication behavior or how communication behavior reflects sex/gender.

We organize the contributions in order of abstraction in discussing domains of behavior. The more general, inclusive chapters are presented first (e.g., sex differences in language use). These are followed by chapters that discuss midrange domains of behavior (e.g., mating behavior), which are followed by chapters that report empirical examinations of specific sex differences and similarities (e.g., first date requests). The exception to this rule was the chapter by Allen (chap. 19), which discusses methodological issues (vs. a type of behavior).

In chapter 1, Wood and Dindia engage in a dialogue on sex/gender differences and similarities in communication. They each respond in turn to three key questions implicated in scholarship on women's and men's communication: Are women and men different? If so, what are the sources of differences? What should be the focus of research on sex/gender differences and similarities in communication? This chapter presents arguments from both sides of the continuum on sex/gender similarities and differences. However, as the authors discovered in writing their dialogue, their views are not as diametrically opposed as they originally anticipated—a statement that applies generally to both the communication of men and women *and* researchers' views on men and women as reflected in this volume.

In chapter 2, Wright takes to task the traditional notion that women's friendships are communal and men's friendships are agenic. Relying on a detailed review of the relevant literature, Wright argues that women's friendships are more communal than men's, but that women's and men's friendships are similar in agency. However, Wright qualifies this conclusion by indicating that the difference in communality in women's and men's friendships may be due to structural rather than dispositional variables (i.e., roles and obligations impose greater restrictions on men developing communal friendships). In addition, Wright presents an expanded view of communality, which includes both intimate verbal communication (such as self-disclosure) and shared activities.

Aries acknowledges in chapter 3 that research on conversational interaction reveals many gender differences. However, Aries calls into question the dominant interpretation of this research (i.e., that sex differences are large and pervasive) discussing five rival hypotheses of gender differences found in the research: (a) gender differences are based on White middle-class samples and may not be generalizable beyond this group; (b) the magnitude of gender differences are small and there is much within-sex variability; (c) gender differences are not manifested in all situations (e.g., the effects of task, length of interaction, etc.); (d) variables that co-vary with gender may be responsible for many gender differences (e.g., status and social roles); and (e) gender differences (and perceived gender differences) are sometimes the result of sex stereotypes and self-fulfilling prophecies. Aries argues that we need to know something about people's role and status, the type of conversation in which they are engaged, the sex of their conversational partners, and the goals they are trying to achieve to predict a person's communication behavior. Knowledge of the speaker's sex alone offers little predictive power, according to Aries.

In chapter 4, Andersen (as well as Trost & Alberts, chap. 10) elaborates an overlooked explanation for sex differences in communication behavior that has been around for over 100 years—Darwin's theory of human evolution. Andersen (and later Trost & Alberts) emphasizes how evolutionary theory only explains sex differences for those tasks for which men and women face different evolutionary pressures, such as reproduction. Andersen argues that men and women are similar in most respects, that the small differences that exist between men and women have a biological basis, and that the search for biological differences should begin with reproduction (the most fundamental difference between men and women). Andersen reviews research indicating that men and women are more similar than different; that sex (not gender) differences exist in communication (and noncommunication) behavior—in particular, women's superior social and nonverbal sensitivity and men's superior spatial ability; and that men's and women's different evolutionary reproductive roles constitute the source of these differences. Andersen provides some convincing speculations to explain sex differences that would cause most readers to (re)consider biological explanations of sex differences.

Kunkel and Burleson critique the different cultures perspective in chapter 5. They first present an overview of the sources and claims of the different cultures perspective. Next they derive several predictions from the different cultures view pertaining to emotional support processes. Specifically, they predict that men and women should differ in: (a) their criteria for what counts as sensitive comforting strategies, (b) their preferences for the sex of a comfort provider, (c) the value they place on comforting skills, and (d) their liking for those who comfort in gender-typical versus gender-atypical ways. Kunkel and Burleson then discuss the results of several studies they have conducted to evaluate these predictions. The results of these studies provide virtually no support for any of the predictions derived from the different cultures perspective. The final section of the chapter discusses an alternative perspective to the different cultures perspective—the skill deficit or skill specialization account—which appears capable of explaining the results of their research.

Mulac provides convincing evidence for male–female language differences and that these differences make a difference (chap. 6). Mulac reviews his program of research on female–male differences in language use and the effects of these differences on observer judgments. This program of research indicates that when the communication of both sexes is transcribed and presented to college students, the students are unable to guess better than chance the sex of the communicators. Similarly, when linguistic variables are analyzed independently, one by one, no large differences were found in how much male and female speakers use particular language features. However, using multivariate procedures, communicator sex can be determined with 70%–100% accuracy. In addition, these same language differences have judgmental consequences (hence the term *gender-linked language effect*). Observers (male and female, young and old) perceived female and male speakers differently based on their language use. Women were rated higher in sociointellectual status (social status and literate) and aestheic quality (nice and beautiful), and men were rated higher on dynamism (strong and aggressive). More important, Mulac shows that the gender-linked language differences predict the variance in psychological ratings. Finally, the gender-linked language effect is independent of gender stereotypes, although the two effects are similar. That is, women were rated higher in sociointellectual status and aesthetic quality and men were rated higher on dynamism based on both their gender-linked language differences and knowledge of speaker sex (or gender stereotypes). Thus, gender stereotypes resemble actual gender language differences, and Mulac suggests that a causal relationship exists between gender-linked language and gender stereotypes.

In chapter 7, Hall argues for a comparative approach (Eagly, 1995) to interpreting the size of sex differences (e.g., compare them to the effects in other domains of social-personality psychology) rather than an absolute approach to judging the size of sex differences (e.g., calculating the proportion of variance accounted for by sex). As a demonstration of the comparative approach to assessing the magnitude of effect sizes, Hall compares the size of nonverbal sex differences in smiling and sensitivity to nonverbal cues to (a) other psychological sex differences, and (b) other correlates of smiling and nonverbal sensitivity. Hall finds that sex differences for smiling and nonverbal sensitivity are larger than most other psychological sex differences that have been subjected to meta-analysis, and they are comparable to the effect of other psychological variables on smiling and nonverbal sensitivity. Thus, Hall concludes that sex differences for smiling and nonverbal sensitivity are relatively large.

Although most people would agree that culture affects sex differences, researchers seldom review how culture and sex combine to affect communication behavior. In chapter 8, Waldron and Di Mare review the literature on sex differences in Japan and the United States to determine whether sex, culture (i.e., nationality), or the interaction of sex and culture best accounts for differences in communication in men and women in Japan and the United States. Among other things, they conclude that there are no major differences in communicative styles between Japanese men and women. Accordingly, studies do not support Western stereotypes of sex differences in Japanese communication styles (e.g., Japanese women are submissive). Similarly, when studies compared the effects of culture and sex, culture was the more important variable. The authors conclude that sex differences manifest themselves differently in Japan than in the United States (interaction effect of sex and culture or nationality).

In chapter 9, Reis reviews research using the RIR (a diary method used to examine interaction), which overwhelmingly finds that men's same-sex interaction is perceived as substantially less intimate than women's same-sex interaction, whereas opposite-sex interaction yields no consistent sex difference. Reis uses the interpersonal process model, which posits that the perception of intimacy is closely linked to certain characteristics of social interaction. He also reviews research on intimacy-related phenomena including sex differences in self-disclosure, nonverbal communication, social support, loneliness, and friendship style, which, taken together, explain why men perceive their same-sex interaction as less intimate than do women. Reis reviews alternative explanations of the findings of sex differences in same-sex intimacy—in particular, those that have tried to minimize sex differences or posit alternative explanations for the differences (other than sex or gender) concluding that men do in fact interact with one another less intimately than do women. Reis ends the chapter by arguing that these differences have to do with something about the nature of male–male relationships (e.g., socialization) rather than anything intrinsic to the nature of men (e.g., physiology) because the differences only pertain to same-sex and not opposite-sex relationships.

In chapter 10, Trost and Alberts describe how an evolutionary perspective explains sex differences and similarities in courtship behaviors, especially flirting. The authors briefly review explanations of mate preferences and then move to an in-depth discussion of how differential parental investment explains existing research on sex differences in mate-seeking behaviors, courtship, and (more specifically) flirting. Trost and Alberts' review coincides with an evolutionary explanation of sex differences showing how differential parental investment can be a useful perspective for predicting and explaining some sex differences in behavior—in particular those tasks for which men and women face different selection pressures, such as finding a suitable mate.

Burgoon and Klingle (chap. 11) examine the proffered explanations for gender differences in persuasion and influenceability (i.e., men are more persuasive than women and women are more persuadable than men) and provide evidence from their program of research on physician–patient compliance gaining that challenges past explanations of these differences. Burgoon and Klingle use language expectancy theory and reinforcement expectancy theory to argue that men are more persuasive than women. They argue that the interaction effect of communicator sex and persuasive message strategy (in addition to the main effect of communicator sex) should be examined to predict persuasive success. In discussing the issue of gender differences in susceptibility to persuasion, Burgoon and Klingle first discuss deficit interpretations of female influenceability (e.g., deficits of the research or deficits in women) and instead posit a male deficit model (being more influenceable is a virtue rather than a problem) in interpreting the results that women are more susceptible to influence than men. Relying on their research, the authors contend that there is a subset of men who are unwilling to change their attitudes and/or behaviors regardless of the situation. This subset of men explains the main effect for gender and persuasibility, rather than viewing women as more influenceable than men.

In chapter 12, Sagrestano, Heavey, and Christensen begin their analysis of the demand–withdrawal pattern in marital conflict by elaborating two perspectives in the psychological literature on sex differences: the individual difference approach and the social structural approach. The individual difference approach uses characteristics of the individual, biological sex or personality (differences in personality that are formed at an early age and are hard to change), to explain differences between women and men. The social structural approach uses characteristics of the social context, at both the situational and the broader sociocultural level (e.g., power, social roles), to explain sex differences. The authors provide empirical evidence from their own research program for and against these approaches in the area of conflict in marriage and the use of social influence techniques in peer and marital relationships. They conclude with a discussion of the importance of identifying sex/gender differences and similarities and, when there are differences, understanding the underlying causal mechanisms.

As Clark indicates in chapter 13, some literature indicates sex differences in the topics discussed by women and men (e.g., Bischoping's conclusion that women talk more about members of the opposite sex and appearances than do men, and that men talk more about sports than do women). Based on this premise of difference, Clark examined topics and objectives of college-age men and women in a cross section of everyday conversations with same-sex friends and acquaintances. The results of the study revealed substantial similarity in the topics and objectives of men's and women's everyday conversations. However, there were some differences that supported Bischoping's conclusion.

In chapter 14, Guerrero and Reiter examine sex differences in expressing emotion. The authors review literature on the biological and socialization bases for sex differences in encoding and decoding socioemotional communication and for sex differences in individuals' communicative responses to emotion (i.e., the specific types of messages that people use to communicate or avoid communicating various emotional states to others). The authors report original research on sex differences in self-reported socioemotional expressivity, sensitivity, and control and in communicative responses to anger, sadness, and jealousy. Overall, the authors report more similarities than differences between men and women and a few significant (albeit small) sex differences.

In chapter 15, Burgoon, Buller, Grandpre and Kalbfleisch review literature on sex differences in encoding and decoding deception. First, they review research on encoding deception. Despite evidence that men's and women's nonverbal expressions differ in many ways (Hall, 1984, chap. 7, this volume), they find few differences in women's and men's verbal and nonverbal deception message displays, and the differences are small. Second, they review research on sex differences in decoding deception. Despite women's general superiority at judging nonverbal behavior and greater social sensitivity (see also Hall, chap. 7; Guerrero & Reiter, chap. 14; Andersen, chap. 4), J. Burgoon and colleagues (chap. 15) find little evidence for women's superior ability at decoding deception. Rather, the sex differences they do find are small and moderated by sex composition. Thus, women's (vs. men's) greater skill at encoding and decoding emotion does not necessarily transfer to encoding and decoding deception.

As Robey, Canary, and Burggraf report in chapter 16, conversational maintenance research has long relied on a dominance perspective (i.e., men's dominance over women can be seen in the way that women work harder to maintain conversations with men). For example, women are said to offer more back channel messages to encourage the male partner to talk. Unfortunately, this research is limited to a few studies and has largely relied on anecdotal evidence from small samples. To directly examine whether women engage in more conversational maintenance work, Robey et al. analyze married couples' discussions that are best typified as small talk. The authors find that husbands and wives are more similar than different in their conversational maintenance behaviors. Robey et al. conclude that the dominance perspective must be replaced with one that is more sensitive to the manner in which people construct their gender roles in interaction.

In chapter 17, Lindsey and Zakahi review the literature on sex role stereotypes and sex role violations; they discuss two theoretical approaches to provide a framework for understanding how agenic and communal stereotypical behaviors become manifest during interaction. The authors report two experiments designed to examine perceptions and evaluations of sex role norm violations, with an emphasis on the violation of two conversational behaviors in initial interaction—women asking questions and men talking about themselves. Their results indicate that responses to persons violating sex role norms differ from responses to individuals who conform to norms. Also, gender schematicity of the person may influence his or her responses to norm violations. Responses to norm violations, however, are both more and less positive, depending on the dimension of evaluation. Although this chapter focuses on two sex role conversational norms and their violations, it has implications for sex role normative behavior in general.

Next, Mongeau, Carey, and Williams (chap. 18) discuss first date initiation and explain it from a social psychological perspective. Mongeau and colleagues review research on sex differences in (female) first date initiation and sexual expectations and enactment on the (female initiated) first date. Their results reveal that men perceive women who initiate dates (vs. women who do not initiate dates) as more sexually interested, and that men enter first dates initiated by women with heightened sexual expectations. However, data from actual first dates indicate that participants evaluate women as communicating less intimacy than do men and that less sexual intimacy occurs on female-initiated (as opposed to male-initiated) first dates. In clarifying the gap between perception and behavior, Mongeau and Carey use expectancy violation theory.

Finally, Allen (chap. 19) concludes this volume by stressing the link between theoretical and methodological issues in studying sex/gender differences. Allen discusses the consequences of using sex (i.e., "please indicate your sex, male ___ female ___") as a marker variable for gender. Allen discusses the generalizability of research on sex/gender differences conducted on college student samples and how the generalizability of college student samples depends on whether one assumes sex (biological) or gender (sociological) differences. Allen also argues that, although sex differences are small and inconsistent, they should be compared to theoretical expectations regarding size of differences and theoretical expectations regarding conditions in which differences should occur. Allen points out how small mean differences in men and women can translate into large differences at the extreme ends of the distributions of men and women. He then discusses the impact of large but extreme sex differences on sex stereotypes. Allen reminds us that examining sex/gender is "not a simple case of saying men and women are similar or men and women are different" and that our theories and methodologies need to be sophisticated enough to determine the extent and basis of similarities and differences between men and women.

In brief, the chapters herein represent the latest research on sex differences (and similarities) in communication. Various points of view (e.g., the magnitude of sex differences, how one defines *sex* vs. *gender*, where one should look for sex differences, and the manner in which sex differences are contexualized) are reflected in the excellent chapters. These chapters summarize existing literature and present a strong case for continued, rigorous, and theoretical research on sex and gender differences—and similarities—in communication behavior.

REFERENCES

Aries, E. (1996). *Men and women in interaction: Reconsidering the differences.* New York: Oxford University Press.

Beall, A. E. (1993). A social constructionist view of gender. In A. E. Beall & R. J. Sternberg (Eds.), *The psychology of gender* (pp. 127–147). New York: Guilford.

Canary, D. J., Emmers-Sommer, T. M., & Faulkner, S. (1997). *Sex differences in personal relationships.* New York: Guilford.

Canary, D. J., & Hause, K.S. (1993). Is there any reason to research sex differences in communication? *Communication Quarterly, 41,* 129–144.

Crawford, M. (1995). *Talking difference: On gender and language.* Thousand Oaks, CA: Sage.

Deaux, K. (1984). From individual differences to social categories: Analysis of a decade's research on gender. *American Psychologist, 39,* 105–116.

Deaux, K. (1985). Sex and gender. *Annual Review of Psychology, 36,* 49–81.

Deaux, K., & Major, B. (1987). Putting gender into context: An interactive model of gender-related behavior. *Psychological Review, 94,* 369–389.

Eagly, A. H. (1987). *Sex differences in social behavior: A social-role interpretation.* Hillsdale, NJ: Lawrence Erlbaum Associates.

Eagly, A. H. (1995). The science and politics of comparing women and men. *American Psychologist, 50,* 145–158.

Hall, J. A. (1984). *Nonverbal sex differences: Communication accuracy and expressive style.* Baltimore: The Johns Hopkins University Press.

Hare-Mustin, R. T., & Marecek, J. (1988). The meaning of difference: Gender theory, postmodernism, and psychology. *American Psychologist, 43,* 455–464.

Hyde, J. S., & Plant, E. A. (1995). Magnitude of psychological gender differences: Another side to the story. *American Psychologist, 50,* 159–161.

Kahn, A. S., & Yoder, J. D. (1989). The psychology of women and conservatism: Rediscovering social change. *Psychology of Women Quarterly, 13,* 417–432.

Schaap, C., Buunk, B., & Kerkstra, A. (1988). Marital conflict resolution. In P. Noller & M. A. Fitzpatrick (Eds.), *Perspectives on marital interaction* (pp. 203–244). Philadelphia, PA: Multilingual Matters.

Steinberg, L. D., & Hill, J. P. (1978). Patterns of family interaction as a function of age, the onset of puberty, and formal thinking. *Developmental Psychology, 14,* 683–684.

Tannen, D. (1994). *Gender and discourse.* New York: Oxford University Press.

Chapter 1

What's the Difference?
A Dialogue About Differences and
Similarities Between Women and Men

Julia T. Wood
University of North Carolina

Kathryn Dindia
University of Wisconsin–Milwaukee

Over the past few years, the two of us have disagreed in our published statements regarding differences between women and men. When we talked in person, however, we discovered that we agree more than our published work might suggest. This chapter is an opportunity to explore our perspectives to clarify what each of us thinks are differences and similarities between women's and men's communication and to collaborate in suggesting an appropriate research agenda for the future. The chapter is organized into answers each of us gives to key questions implicated in scholarship on women's and men's communication. We respond, in turn, to three questions: (a) Are women and men different? (b) If so, what are the sources of differences? and (c) What should be the focus of research on sex and gender differences and similarities in communication?

ARE WOMEN AND MEN DIFFERENT?

Julia

Sex differences are relatively minor in view of the overwhelming genetic-biological similarities between women and men. Further, some differences generally attributed to biology, such as brain lateralization, may reflect environmental influences. Neuroscientist Bleier (1986) asserted that re-

19

ported sex differences in brains predominantly reflect environmental factors—a matter of gender, not sex.

Gender Differences Are Pervasive. Gender differences are not so minor. Gender is a social, symbolic construction that expresses the meanings a society confers on biological sex. Gender varies across cultures, over time within any given society, and in relation to the other gender. There are gender differences that are real, persisting, and significant by any measure. Communication-related differences between women and men that have been repeatedly reported by researchers include: (a) male childhood and adolescent communication involves more interruptions, self-displays, challenges, strong assertions, and direct judgments than female childhood and adolescent communication (Maccoby, 1990); (b) women rely more than men on verbal communication, including personal disclosures, to build and maintain intimacy with friends and romantic partners (Johnson, 1996; Riessman, 1990); (c) men rely more than women on shared activities and doing things for others to build, sustain, and express intimacy with friends and romantic partners (Inman, 1996; Swain, 1989; Wood & Inman, 1993); (d) women generally find talking about relationships satisfying, whereas men generally find talking about relationships satisfying only when there is some tension or problem requiring attention (Acitelli, 1988, 1992); (e) women are more sensitive to and perceptive of others' nonverbal cues than are men (Gottman & Carrere, 1994; Hall, 1984); and (f) women are more involved in caring for others than are men (Okin, 1989; Ruddick, 1989; Wood, 1994).

Each of these differences is a matter of degree versus dichotomy (Duck & Wright, 1993; Wright, 1988). In other words, differences between women's and men's communication styles are general only, which implies that both sexes pursue instrumental and expressive goals, although each sex may emphasize one objective more than the other. Yet the difference in degree is sometimes consequential. For instance, in heterosexual relationships, female and male partners may be frustrated by each other's preferences for talking and doing, respectively, as primary paths to intimacy. The deferential, relationship-enhancing style of communication emphasized in feminine communication cultures and the instrumental, aggressive communication promoted in masculine communication cultures may contribute to some men's sexual harassment of women and to some women's reluctance to object (Bingham, 1996). In professional settings, men and women may misunderstand each other's styles of requesting, listening, questioning, and offering assistance (Murphy & Zorn, 1996).

Unlike sex differences, gender differences are cultivated, but not determined, by the distinct conditions of the lives of women and men as groups. Social ideologies prescribe that each group be allowed some and not other experiences (football and cheerleading; hunting and ballet), roles (damsel in distress, knight in shining armor; president, first lady; mother, father), personal appearances (grow a beard, shave legs; pectoral implants, breast augmentation), and professional options (human relations, executive; mommy track, no daddy track). Both underlying and reflecting these differences are profound asymmetries in the social, economic, and political power and the income and economic security that are enjoyed (or not enjoyed) by women and men. The distinct circumstances of women's and men's lives account for the majority of current differences (but not necessarily differences that existed historically in Western cultures or historically or currently in other cultures) in women's and men's behaviors, including communication.

Differences attributed to individuals' gender may actually be reflections of socially structured inequities in the power accorded to and experienced by women and men as groups (Janeway, 1971; Tavris, 1992). According to Epstein (1988), "the past decade of research on gender supports the theory that gender differentiation . . . is best explained as a social construction rooted in hierarchy" (p. 88). In other words, gender is less useful than power in explaining many general differences between men and women.

Power Differences Underlie Gender Differences. Asymmetrical power and the disparities to which it gives rise explain a number of differences between women and men. Power disparity also explains with stunning accuracy the differences between other groups of unequal social standing, including slaves and masters, prisoners and guards, children and parents, and subordinates and superiors in the workplace (Bettelheim, 1943; Freud, 1946; Henley, 1977; Jennings, Kilkenny, & Kohlberg, 1983; Puka, 1990; Sanford, 1955).

Many, if not most, differences between the sexes reflect women's and men's unequal social power and the disparate behavioral and attitudinal tendencies their respective degrees of power promote. People who have less power—whether women, minorities, prisoners, or members of the poverty class—learn coping skills (Puka, 1990) that reduce the likelihood of suffering the displeasure of those who are more powerful. Thus, those who hold subordinate social roles learn to interpret subtle nonverbal behaviors; defer, please, notice, and attend to others' needs; speak tentatively and indirectly; be nonthreatening; and make others comfortable. These skills are not dictated by sex; rather they are responses to the lesser power accorded to women and other socially subordinate groups (Wood, 1994).

Dissimilar material, social, and symbolic circumstances made available to women and men are created, upheld, and naturalized by intimately imbricated cultural practices and structures. Constructed differences between women and men are likely to continue as long as there remain real and consequential inequities in the opportunities, status, and roles that society prescribes for women and men, minorities and majorities, and subordinates and superiors.

Consider one example: Women's careers often follow a less linear route than do men's careers. Compared with men, women are overwhelmingly more likely to delay, interrupt, reroute, and/or downsize their careers to care for children and/or elderly parents, in-laws, and other relatives (Blair, Brown, & Baxter, 1994; Tavris, 1992). The career path pursued by many women is often attributed to women's "natural" tendencies to care for others and/or the jarring buzz of women's biological clocks. The fact that the career path pursued by many women does not conform to prevailing views of professionalism is often used to justify dissimilar career opportunities, advancement, and salaries for women and men. Yet the career path typical of many women is not the inevitable result of being women, not men. Instead, it reflects social prescriptions that define women and not men as primary caregivers, men and not women as primary breadwinners, and professionalism as unwavering and undiluted commitment to work. Thus, the different career paths of many women and men are best explained by social structures and practices, not by anything innate or enduring in the sexes' natures.

There is nothing innate about women's disproportionate involvement in family life. Despite relentless efforts to document a maternal instinct consistent with the Western views of women, research has failed to confirm any innate nurturing capacity in women. In fact, several studies have shown that when men are involved in caregiving roles they become as nurturing, attentive to others, and emotionally supportive as women generally are believed to be and more so than most men are (Kaye & Applegate, 1990; Risman, 1989). Experiments that could not ethically be conducted on humans revealed that male rats and female virgin rats, some with normal hormones and others that were surgically deprived of hormones and sex organs, developed equal "parenting" inclinations and skill when put into contact with baby rats (Rosenblatt, 1967; Rosenblatt & Siegel, 1981).

Like men, women have been shown to develop abilities not socially prescribed for their gender when they are situated in positions that promote those skills. Women become more ambitious, confident, competitive, and assertive than women in general and as much so as their male peers when they are in professional roles that promote the development of these inclinations (Epstein, 1981, 1988). To keep this discussion parallel, just as male rats develop "maternal" skills when placed in parenting roles, female monkeys are competitive and sexually aggressive in contexts that foster these qualities (Haraway, 1986). This suggests that personal identity and behavioral repertoires are not fixed with super glue at any time, but evolve continuously as individuals enter new social contexts that entail new opportunities and demands.

My hunch is that if we equalized the conditions of women's and men's lives, most current gender differences would virtually disappear. Men would develop greater skill in nurturing, cooperating, and being emotionally expressive because they would more frequently find themselves in roles and situations that cultivate those tendencies; women would enhance their skills in asserting themselves, competing, and being instrumental because they would more frequently find themselves in situations and roles that cultivate those inclinations. Also, if the social world remade itself so that the sexes had equal power, institutional cultures would shift to accommodate what are today considered "women's issues."

Kathryn

A number of scholars and lay persons have argued that women and men are different. Julia differentiates between biologically based (sex) differences and culturally based (gender) differences and argues that biological differences between women and men are relatively minor but that gender differences are "real, persisting, and significant by any measure." In contrast, I argue that gender differences are relatively minor and that although there are "real, persisting, and significant" sex differences that have major effects on anatomy and physiology, these sex differences have little effect on personality and social behavior (however, see Andersen, chap. 4, this volume; Trost & Alberts, chap. 10, this volume). I am a minimalist. I believe that differences in women's and men's personality traits and social behaviors are minimal by any measure and that these minimal differences do not warrant labeling men and women as different.

Gender Differences Are Small. Research indicates that there are small differences between women and men in their communication behaviors. Canary and Hause (1993) reviewed 15 meta-analyses of sex differences in communication-related variables and concluded that sex differences are small and moderated by a number of factors. Canary and Hause found an average weighted effect size of $d = .24$, which indicates that sex or gender accounts for about 1% of the variance in communication-related variables. In addition, all the meta-analyses reported significant moderating variables (sex interacts with another variable to affect the dependent variable).

Canary and Hause's review is not exhaustive; most notably it excludes the meta-analyses of nonverbal behavior conducted by Hall (1984), which found a number of effect sizes larger than the average weighted effect size found by Canary and Hause. (I recalculated the mean weighted effect size for sex differences in communication-related variables, including the 15 meta-analyses reviewed by Canary and Hause and the meta-analyses of nonverbal behaviors conducted by Hall, 1984. I found a slightly higher average weighted effect size of $d = .28$.) Similarly, Canary and Hause's review is limited to communication-related variables and ignores the broader domain of social personality psychology (see Ashmore, 1990; Hyde & Frost, 1993; Hyde & Plant, 1995, for reviews of meta-analyses of sex differences in psychology). Hyde and Plant (1995) analyzed effect sizes found in meta-analyses of psychological gender differences and found that 25% of the effects sizes were near zero ($d = .00 - .10$), 35% were in the small range ($d = .11 - .35$), 27% were in the moderate range ($d = .36 - .65$), 10% were in the large range ($d = .66 - 1.00$), and 3% were in the vary large range ($d > 1.00$). The researchers concluded that there are many small gender differences but also some large ones.

Cohen (1969) offered the following guidelines for interpreting d: $d = .20$ is small, $d = .50$ is moderate, and $d = .80$ is large. Thus, according to Cohen, the average weighted effect size for sex differences in communication would be considered small. As stated by Allen (chap. 19, this volume):

> If one states that the average man is not different from the average woman, this is accurate. The average woman, when comparing a man and woman with a difference between groups of $d = .20$, is not that dissimilar from her counterpart. The difference is slight because the average value of each distribution is similar. (p. 436)

Employing the criterion of mean differences, the average difference between women and men is small by most assessments (but see Reis, chap. 9, this volume).

Similarly, there is substantial within-sex variability in women's and men's communication behaviors and a high degree of overlap in the distributions of women's and men's communication behaviors. Cohen (1969) showed that, for a small effect size ($d = .20$), there is an 85% overlap in the distributions of scores in the two groups compared. Using the average effect size found by Canary and Hause (1993), we see that approximately 85% of women's and men's scores across the various communication variables overlap, whereas approximately 15% of women's and men's scores do not overlap. Employing the criterion of overlap in distributions, the average difference between women and men is also small by most assessments. Thus, the differences between women and men in communication are small, and we are not justified in labeling women and men as different.

This conclusion is drawn based on the results of quantitative research on sex differences fully realizing that this research is imperfect. Among other things, quantitative research on sex differences relies on perceptual data (Ragan, 1989)—when observational data are employed, research generally occurs in artificial laboratory situations—and college student samples, which may or may not generalize to the population (see Allen, chap. 19, this volume). Thus, quantitative research on sex differences is flawed in a number of ways and meta-analyses of this research are only as valid as the original studies. Regardless of these limitations, the preponderance of empirical evidence suggests that sex differences are small.

Although some others interpret the results of the quantitative research on sex differences as I do (Aries, 1996, chap. 3, this volume), some others do not (cf. Eagly, 1995; Hall, chap. 7, this volume; Hyde & Frost, 1993). In particular, it has been pointed out that a similar amount of variance is accounted for by other variables in social/personality psychology. Eagly (1995; see also Hall, chap. 7, this volume) argues that judging the magnitude of sex differences or any research finding is a relative matter. An effect size should be compared with effect sizes that have been obtained in other meta-analyses, either for related studies in the same field or for studies in other fields (Hyde & Frost, 1993). The logic is that if the effect size is similar to or greater than other effect sizes, then it is large relatively speaking.

Hyde and Plant (1995) compared effect sizes for psychological gender differences to effect sizes for various psychological, educational, and behavioral treatments. They found that the distribution of effect sizes for gender was significantly different from the distribution of effect sizes for treatments. In particular, there were more close to zero effect sizes for gender (25%) than for treatments (6%). Treatment effect sizes probably are not representative of psychological effect sizes in general. Nonetheless, the results did not support the assertion that sex differences are similar in size to other psychological variables.

Even if effect sizes for gender were similar to effect sizes for other psychological variables, I do not agree with the relativity argument for two reasons. First, ultimately we are interested in absolute differences not relative differences. The question we want to answer is, "How big are the differences between women and men?" not "How big are the differences between women and men relative to other effects in social psychology?" Sex or gender may account for as much of the variance in personality and social behavior as any other variable. However, none of these variables may account for much of the variance in personality and social behavior. Human behavior may be so complex that we cannot predict much of the variance in it by reference to any single independent variable, including sex or gender.

Second, Cohen's (1969) admittedly arbitrary designations of *small, medium,* and *large* effect sizes are relative. A large effect accounts for 14% of the variance in the dependent variable, which he argued is a reasonable definition of a large effect size in the social sciences. Thus, a large effect size is not absolutely large in terms of how much of the variance it accounts for; it is relatively large in comparison to what can be expected in the social sciences. Again, there is little evidence of large effect sizes, relative to other effects in the social sciences, for sex/gender differences in personality and social behavior (Hyde & Plant, 1995).

Differences of Degree Versus Kind.   Women and men differ in kind if women either have certain characteristics or perform certain behaviors that are not present in men or vice versa (Adler, 1975). For example, if all men are agentic and no women are agentic, men and women differ in kind with respect to agency. Similarly, if all women are communal and no men are communal, men and women differ in kind with respect to communion.

Women and men differ in degree if both possess the same trait or display the same behavior but one possesses or displays more of it (Adler, 1975). Thus, if both women and men are agentic and communal, but men are more agentic and women are more communal, then with respect to agency and communion they differ in degree.

I would argue that where differences between women and men exist, they are differences of degree not kind. For example, rather than arguing that men are agentic and women are communal (Bakan, 1966), I would argue that men may be slightly more agentic than women and women may be slightly more communal than men (see Wright, chap. 2, this volume). As indicated in the preceding paragraphs, the empirical research indicates that, although statistically significant mean differences exist between women and men in a number of communication behaviors, the small effect sizes and the overlap in distributions of women and men on these variables are not consistent with the kind of difference that would be expected if women and men were different in kind. If women and men were different in kind, we would expect large effect sizes and no overlap in the distributions of women and women.

Why Women and Men Are Polarized.   If differences are small and reflect differences of degree rather than kind, why are women and men portrayed as dichotomous groups (Thorne, 1993)—two separate and homogeneous categories (Crawford, 1995) that are polarized (Canary & Hause, 1993)? In my opinion, this is the result of gender stereotypes that are reinforced by the scholarly and popular press.

One cause of this false dichotomy is the failure to report effect sizes in the scholarly literature. Thousands of studies have been published that report statistically significant results for sex differences. The authors of these studies conclude that women and men differ with respect to the dependent variable. Similar to placing individuals into dichotomous groups labeled *women* and *men,* researchers dichotomize statistical results into significant or nonsignificant, failing to realize the variability within groups.

As stated by Hunter (1996a, 1996b), "The conventional significance test provides NO direct information about effect size." Conventional significance tests indicate only whether women and men differ; they do not indicate the size of the difference. The difference needs to be measured quantitatively and the magnitude of the difference reported. We should not just ask, "does sex have an effect?" We should also ask, "How large is the effect?" Unfortunately, few studies on sex differences report effect sizes. This practice is inexcusable. Cohen's (1969) book on power analysis was published almost 30 years ago. It is time researchers stopped dichotomizing research results on sex differences into significant and nonsignificant and instead started reporting the magnitude of these effects.

Fortunately, research on sex differences is popular and meta-analyses have been performed on a number of different dependent variables (there are at least 171 meta-analyses on psychological sex differences; see Hyde & Plant, 1995). Meta-analysis provides a remedy for the failure to report effect sizes. When multiple studies that examine sex differences on a common dependent variable have been conducted, a meta-analysis can be performed to provide an estimate of effect size. One of the major benefits of meta-analysis is that it indicates whether a significant difference exists, as well as how large it is (Hyde & Frost, 1993).

Nonetheless, the magnitude of sex differences should be reported in all empirical studies that report significant results. To ensure that this happens, journal editors should require that effect sizes be reported when statistically significant results regarding sex differences are found. However, as noted by Eagly (1995), if this is done, it should be done for all effects. Reporting effect sizes for sex differences alone would trivialize sex differences because most readers are unaware that the percentage of variance accounted for by any one variable is typically small in psychological research.

The popular press is also responsible for why women and men are portrayed as fundamentally different. Gender stereotypes are pervasive in this culture. As stated by Kahn and Yoder (1989), "one of the core beliefs of our society is that women and men are basically different—the 'opposite' sexes" (p. 422). The stereotype that men are *masculine*—strong, ambitious, successful, rational, and nonemotional—and women are *feminine*—attractive, deferential, unaggressive, emotional, nurturing, and concerned with people and relationships—(Wood, 1996) is propagated by the popular press.

John Gray, author of the decade's best-selling book *Men Are From Mars, Women Are From Venus,* is selling the message that women and men are different. According to Gray (1990), "men and women differ in all areas of their lives. Not only do men and women communicate differently but they think, feel, perceive, react, respond, love, need, and appreciate differently. They almost seem to be from different planets, speaking different languages and needing different nourishment" (p. 5). Gray has written several best sellers that capitalize on sex differences; thousands of people attend his seminars and buy his audio- and videotapes. He is currently on a world tour promoting his videos, Web sites, counseling centers, and upcoming movie and TV shows. He would not be popular if he were saying that women and men were both from the same planet, earth. Not only does sex sell, sex differences sell; sex similarities do not.

However, Gray does more than just reflect gender stereotypes—he reproduces them. Gray propagates the myth that men and women are fundamentally different (e.g., that men love technology and women love shopping, that men want to be alone and women want to talk). Gray portrays all problems between the sexes as the result of these differences. The *New York Times* called Gray inept but harmless. I disagree.

ARE DIFFERENCES BETWEEN WOMEN AND MEN MATTERS OF SEX OR GENDER?

Julia

The question "Are women and men different?" appears deceptively simple, yet the answer is not simple at all. As groups, women and men differ in a number of ways, yet most prevailing differences between women and men are neither innate nor necessary.

Interpretations of the degree and meaning of differences between the sexes vary widely among feminist theorists. *Feminist theory* is one of those collective nouns that house a range of not-always-similar phenomena (Wood, 1995, 1997). Distinct and sometimes conflicting forms of feminist theory include radical difference, Marxist, ecofeminism, womanism, existentialism, psychodynamism, and revalorism. Like most scholars, I claim allegiance to only some branches of feminist thought and find others irrelevant, insufficiently substantiated, and/or misguided.

I do not align myself with radical difference feminists who claim that women and men differ in essential, innate ways. For some difference feminists, including many in France, the enduring essence of Woman is a biology that irrevocably links her with nature. For others, the enduring essence of woman is located in her psyche, which is usually assumed to develop in the early mother–child bond (see Chodorow, 1978, 1989). In either case, radical difference feminists assume that there is a basic nature of Woman that persists across time, space, and experience. Elsewhere (Wood, 1993, 1994) I have argued that this position mistakenly conflates historically and socially contingent embodiments of womanhood with an essential, enduring, immutable nature of Woman.

I also do not embrace the related position of revalorism, which asserts that women are innately special, or virtuous, due to their essential nature as women. According to this line of thinking, unlike men, women are naturally cooperative, loving, supportive, nurturing, peaceful, kind, gentle, and—well—nice. The credit or blame for injecting revalorism into modern feminist theorizing belongs largely to Carol Gilligan. Her immensely popular 1982 book, *In a Different Voice*, resuscitated the 18th-century view of women as domestic angels endowed with moral purity (Kerber, 1986; Noddings, 1984, 1990).

I appreciate the revalorist effort to disrupt androcentric logic and champion women's traditional roles and preoccupations, which have been devalued in Western culture. In my judgment, many qualities and priorities historically associated with women deserve greater respect than they have generally received. Yet I reject the excesses, essentialist foundations, and substitution of female for male superiority that saturate most revalorist work. I am not convinced that the qualities praised by difference and revalorist feminists are essential to all women, absent in all men, constant across time and space, or cause for unmitigated celebration and advocacy.

Standpoint Theory. The theoretical label that best describes my position is *standpoint* (Haraway, 1988; Harding, 1991; Wood, 1993). Standpoint theory claims that the material, social, and symbolic circumstances of women's and men's lives differ in ways that are epistemologically significant. The disparate circumstances typical of most women's and men's lives promote distinctive identities, perspectives, priorities, views of social life, and ways of interacting.

Standpoint theory draws on research concerned with speech communities or communication cultures (Maltz & Borker, 1982). The pronounced tendency for sex segregation in childhood (Maccoby, 1990) means that boys and girls tend to be socialized in relatively discrete contexts that emphasize different goals, rules, forms, and meanings of communication, in particular, and social life, in general. Findings indicate that masculine communication cultures accentuate instrumental goals, linear organization, individualistic orientations, and monologic, competitive forms of speech. Feminine communication cultures generally accord greater priority to expressive goals, fluid organization, collective or communal orientations, and interactive, cooperative forms of speech (Aries, 1987; Cancian, 1987; D. Hall & Langellier, 1988; Johnson, 1989). Research on communication cultures does not, as is sometimes mistakenly thought, imply that there are essential difference between the sexes, nor does it imply that early socialization in communication cultures absolutely and forever determines identity and behavior.

Standpoint theory only claims that women and men, like people every-where, learn rules, meanings, and norms of communication and social life through interaction with others in particular contexts and that different social groups, or communication cultures, inculcate distinct styles of being, knowing, and communicating. By extension, individuals may learn new rules, meanings, and forms of communication if they participate in com-munication cultures that foster skills and perspectives different than those they learned previously. In summary, I regard gender as positional, not enduring; constructed, not innate; a matter of degree, not absolute dichot-omy; and fluid, not fixed.

For the most part, differences between women and men involve gender, which is constructed by social ideologies. Actual sex differences are limited to primary and secondary sex characteristics and resulting physical char-acteristics and capabilities. Biological qualities (the province of sex) are less important than the meanings that society attributes to them and the distinctive roles, opportunities, experiences, and constraints that society assumes are and should be linked with each biological sex (the province of gender).

Unlike sex, gender is constructed. On entrance into the world, boys and girls are more alike than not. This is the only reasonable conclusion to draw from the fact that, of the 23 pairs of chromosomes that serve as the blueprint for human nature, only 1 pair governs sex. Yet the meager 1/23rd of genetic influence has been elaborated by cultural views of what women and men are and should be and, especially, by the entrenched cultural assumption that men and women are different—opposite (Bem, 1993; Tavris, 1992).

All known societies have ensconced gender ideologies that are imposed, in varying degrees, on individuals and that construct most girls in ways considered feminine and most boys in ways considered masculine at a particular time and place (Epstein, 1988; Fox-Genovese, 1991; Wood, 1995). Western gender ideology is reflected in cultural practices such as blue and pink blankets at birth, dolls and trucks in child play, and primary caregiver and breadwinner roles for adults. Not biology, but gender pre-scriptions for women and men account for most differences in priorities, behaviors, attitudes, feelings, and self-concepts of the sexes.

So powerfully do socially constructed gender ideologies affect individuals' perceptions and behaviors that they have repeatedly and radically altered ideas of what is and is not masculine and feminine. Witness that today Marilyn Monroe would be considered too fat to be a star, much less a sex idol, and Kate Moss' waif look would never have catapulted her to super-model status in the 1940s. Likewise, John Wayne would be an unlikely cultural icon today, and Tom Hanks would have been insufficiently mascu-line in Wayne's time. Before and after the world wars, factory work for pay was considered unfeminine and inappropriate for middle and upper class women, but the same work was considered appropriate, feminine, and laudably patriotic during the world wars when the United States needed women's labor. Earlier in this century, Western women bound their breasts because large breasts were considered unattractive and unfeminine. In recent decades, breast augmentation surgery has ascended to be the leading form of plastic surgery undergone by women. What women and men are, what they can/should do and look like, what is/is not feminine and masculine are beliefs crafted by social structures and practices that reflect and serve the interests of a particular society at a given time.

Social gender ideologies and individual embodiments of gender influence one another: Individuals' performances of gender are constrained by the alternatives that society makes available to them; in turn, individuals' enactments of socially approved options reproduce the social order that defined alternatives in the first place (Epstein, 1988). Although many individuals reject or modify some gender prescriptions, few radically resist basic gender ideologies. Thus, cultural foundations of gender are a primary concern.

Kathryn

I do not agree with the different cultures perspective (see Kunkel & Burleson, chap. 5, this volume, for a critique of the different cultures viewpoint). According to the different cultures perspective, children primarily play in sex-segregated groups. Boys and girls play different kinds of games (e.g., boys play football, baseball; girls play school, house, jump rope) that cultivate different rules and norms of communication. Consequently, girls and boys develop different styles of communication, which carry over into adulthood. As Tannen (1990) stated, "boys and girls grow up in what are essentially different cultures, so talk between women and men is cross-cultural communication" (p. 18).

Indeed, children between the ages of 5 and 15 may play primarily with children of their own sex; girls' play may be more dyadic, cooperative, and egalitarian, and boys' play may be more group oriented, competitive, and status oriented. But the bottom line is that, in this society, girls and boys are raised together—a point Maccoby (1988) made at the end of her review of the sex segregation hypothesis. Crawford (1995) made the common culture of girls and boys clear:

> They share the use of common space in their homes; eat, work and play with their siblings of both sexes; generally attend co-educational schools in which they are aggregated in many classes and activities; and usually participate in religious meetings and activities together. Both sexes are supervised, cared for, and taught largely by women in infancy and early childhood, with

male teachers and other authority figures becoming more visible as children grow older. (pp. 87–88).

Aries (1996) made the same point:

> The two-cultures approach has minimized the importance of the fact that boys and girls have daily interactions with members of the opposite sex, with siblings, parents, relatives, friends in the neighborhood, or teachers at school. While people of different classes or racial groups may have little opportunity to interact with people outside their group, this is not true for males and females. Although boys and girls tend to select same-sex peers as their primary companions, their daily interactions are by no means limited to people of the same sex. (p. 141)

Some gender differences between women and men do indeed exist. These differences result from their differential same-sex interactions and the distinct social contexts in which girls and boys are often situated. However, women and men are overwhelmingly similar because they are raised in the same culture.

Thus, contrary to Gray's (1992) metaphor, "men are from Mars, women are from Venus," I have used the metaphor, "men are from North Dakota, women are from South Dakota" (Dindia, 1997a, 1997b) to represent the degree of differences between women and men. Although I am a minimalist, I would argue that the minimal differences that exist between women and men are primarily the result of gender not sex. They are affected by everything from our parents, our peers, our teachers, the media, sexist language, and so on, including sex-segregated childhood play. Like Kahn and Yoder (1989), I think that the source of differences lies in external, societal, and structural factors (social, historical, political, and cultural forces that shape and reinforce certain patterns of behavior in women and men) rather than in something about women and men (biology, early socialization). In our theory and research, however, we have ignored the social context, instead focusing almost exclusively on the individual. Thus, I agree with Julia about the cause but not the extent of sex differences.

WHAT IS THE VALUE OF STUDYING SEX DIFFERENCES?

Julia

Kathryn and I share the view that researchers have spotlighted differences between the sexes, often at the cost of neglecting substantial similarities between them. I am also sympathetic to arguments that highlighting differences fosters falsely dichotomous thinking, risks reinforcing gender stereotypes that can be detrimental to both sexes, and fuels division between women and men. Most of all, I am aware and wary that, historically, claims of sex and gender differences consistently have been used against women: Women should not be sullied by owning property, ruined for motherhood by higher education (Clarke, 1873), or jeopardized by dangerous jobs that, by coincidence, pay more than jobs that are safe for women.

These caveats notwithstanding, it would be a mistake to ignore or give scant attention to differences between the lives—but not the capacities, personalities, natures, and potentialities—of women and men. The reason we must give special attention to differences, which are less abundant than similarities between the sexes, is that differences are the lynchpin of persistent and painful inequities in the lives of women and men. As a critical scholar, my goals are to understand and work toward changing cultural structures and practices that create these differences and their derivative injustices.

Kathryn

Julia and I agree that we need to study sex and gender differences. It is important to discover the truth regardless of its political implications. Traditionally, social science seeks to know the truth. The goals of science are to describe, predict, explain, and control phenomena. We must be able to describe the quality and quantity of differences between women and men before we can begin to explain them. The kinds and degree of differences indicate a variety of potential explanations. For example, evolutionary theory (see Andersen, chap. 4, this volume; Trost & Alberts, chap. 10, this volume) only explains some differences, not others. Evolutionary theory does not account for declining differences over a short period of time. Thus, we must identify the differences and their extent before we can begin to explain them.

I, too, recognize that highlighting differences may foster discrimination against women. However, if differences are large we need to know this. There are dangers in minimizing or ignoring real differences (Hyde & Frost, 1993). Similarly, if differences are large, then differential treatment, as long as it is justified by actual abilities and behaviors, may be justified. However, in the past, differential treatment has been based on stereotypes rather than scientific research.

It is also important to know if there are no differences or if the differences are inconsequential. If passed beyond the boundaries of academia to the public, this information can further reduce gender stereotypes, sex role behavior, and sexism. Thus, it is important to study sex and gender differences. However, our research's undue attention to sex differences—to the exclusion of sex similarities—has perpetuated stereotypes of women and men and, consequently, inequities between women and men. The emphasis on gender differences has blinded us to gender similarities (Hyde, 1985). The bottom line, as Julia points out, is that we have studied sex differences and ignored sex similarities. It is time to start studying sex differences and similarities. This is the reasoning behind this book.

Similarly, the undue attention to describing sex and gender differences—to the exclusion of explaining them—has created a theoretical vacuum in the literature on sex and gender. There are too many studies of sex differences in which there is no theoretical rationale for testing sex differences. Is it necessary to examine every variable ever studied in communication and psychology for sex differences? It is time that scholarship on sex and gender differences moved beyond description to explanation. Studying sex and gender differences and similarities is secondary to explaining whatever differences and similarities we find in women's and men's communication.

Similarly, as social scientists, we should not ignore the issue of application. Ultimately, the test of any theory is whether it works in practice. Gray (1992) made differential prescriptions to women and men based on presumed differences between the sexes. For example, one of the many stereotyped differences discussed in his book is that "men go to their caves and women talk" (p. 29). (As if women don't have caves!) Gray told women that they "need to learn that when a man is upset or stressed he will automatically stop talking and go to his 'cave' to work things out" (p. 69). He advised women to let a man hide in his cave. In contrast, he told men that, "when a woman is stressed she instinctively feels a need to talk about her feelings and all the possible problems that are associated with her feelings" (p. 36). He advised men to listen when a woman wants to talk. Thus, Gray prescribed different and stereotyped responses to women and men. Prescriptions such as these are doomed to failure and perform a disservice to lay persons because they are not based on theory supported by empirical research. As social scientists, we need to generate theory that can be used by lay persons to understand and improve their relationships. For all we know, women and men are too similar and that is why their relationships do not work.

CONCLUDING STATEMENTS

Julia

Differences between women and men exist not because of essential, innate differences between women and men, but rather because of social structures and practices that create and normalize disparate power and correspondingly disparate opportunities, experiences, and socially approved identities and activities for the sexes. Historically and currently, many scholars look to personal qualities in women and men to explain differences and justify unequal treatment of women and men. This is a badly flawed investigatory focus because it ignores social structures and practices that produce and promote differences between women and men. Only by understanding and changing the cultural wellsprings of gender can we diminish embodied differences and their social and material consequences.

In an analysis of popular and academic insistence on endemic differences between women and men, Tavris (1992) suggested that,

> if women's daily behavior, like men's, is more influenced by the roles they play, the ideologies they believe in, and they work they do than by anything fundamental to their gender, then we need to transform roles, ideologies, and work so that humane qualities can be encouraged in both sexes. (p. 62)

Tavris' conclusion suggests that the most urgent priorities for gender and feminist inquiry and teaching are to identify, critique, and change structural and material circumstances that create inequities in the roles, activities, opportunities, and experiences of women and men. This focus does not make the mistake of conflating malleable social constructions with unalterable personal and biological/psychological qualities.

A major focus of my research, theorizing, and teaching is how constructed differences are perpetuated and used to define and constrain women and men. Social prescriptions for women and men reflect the ideology that women are naturally better than men at taking care of others, cleaning homes, cooking, and, in general, taking care of the range of things necessary for all of us to exist. This is a very convenient belief for those who benefit by women's invisible and largely unpaid caregiving service (Okin, 1989).

I align myself more with critical scholarship than with social science research—a position that inclines me to focus on understanding more than description and on social change more than explanation and prediction. Thus, Kathryn and I associate ourselves with different research traditions that encourage us to endorse sometimes different, although not incompatible, research goals and methods. *Cui bono?*, a Latin phrase that translates to "Who benefits?", is germane to any serious analysis of gender. The answer to this question explains why issues of gender and gender differences are not only empirical but also resoundingly political.

Kathryn

Julia is correct: We represent different research traditions. But we are both scholars, feminists, women, and human beings. Thus, according to standpoint theory, our views should overlap considerably and they do. We both agree that differences exist, that the differences are differences of degree not kind, and that the differences are primarily the result of culture; they are not essential and unalterable. We differ only on the issue regarding size of the differences. We both believe sex and gender differences should be studied along with sex and gender similarities, and we both think we need to focus more on theory and application. Although I am not a critical theorist, I too would like to change the circumstances that create gender inequalities and discrimination against women (and men, in such matters as divorce and child custody). In fact, my purpose in co-editing this book is to contribute to a more balanced approach to sex and gender differences. An approach that studies differences *and* similarities will reduce gender stereotypes, sex role behavior, and sexism.

REFERENCES

Acitelli, L. (1988). When spouses talk to each other about their relationship. *Journal of Social and Personal Relationships, 5,* 185–199.

Acitelli, L. (1992). Gender differences in relationship awareness and marital satisfaction among young married couples. *Personality and Social Psychology, 18,* 102–110.

Adler, M. J. (1975). The confusion of the animalists. In R. M. Hutchins & M. J. Adler (Eds.), *The great ideas today 1975* (pp. 72–89). Chicago: Encyclopaedia Britannica.

Aries, E. (1987). Gender and communication. In P. Shaver & C. Hendrick (Eds.), *Sex and gender* (pp. 149–176). Newbury Park, CA: Sage.

Aries, E. (1996). *Men and women in interaction: Reconsidering the differences.* New York: Oxford University Press.

Ashmore, R. D. (1990). Sex, gender, and the individual. In L. A. Pervin (Ed.), *Handbook of personality: Theory and research* (pp. 486–526). New York: Guilford.

Bakan, D. (1966). *The duality of human existence: Isolation and communion in Western man.* Boston, MA: Beacon.

Bem, S. L. (1993). *The lenses of gender.* New Haven, CT: Yale University Press.

Bettelheim, B. (1943). Individual and mass behavior in extreme situations. *Journal of Abnormal and Social Psychology, 38,* 417–452.

Bingham, S. (1996). Sexual harassment on the job, on the campus. In J. T. Wood (Ed.), *Gendered relationships: A reader* (pp. 233–252). Mountain View, CA: Mayfield.

Blair, C., Brown, J., & Baxter, L. (1994). Disciplining the feminine. *Quarterly Journal of Speech, 80,* 383–409.

Bleier, R. (1986). Sex differences research: Science or belief? In R. Bleier (Ed.), *Feminist approaches to science* (pp. 147–164). New York: Pergamon.

Canary, D. J., & Hause, K. S. (1993). Is there any reason to research sex differences in communication? *Communication Quarterly, 41,* 129–144.

Cancian, F. (1987). *Love in America.* Cambridge, MA: Cambridge University Press.

Chodorow, N. (1978). *The reproduction of mothering; Psychoanalysis and the sociology of gender.* Berkeley: University of California Press.

Chodorow, N. (1989). *Feminism and psychoanalytic theory.* New Haven, CT: Yale University Press.

Clarke, E. (1873). *Sex in education: A fair chance for girls.* Boston: J. R. Osgood.

Cohen, J. (1969). *Statistical power analysis for the behavioral sciences.* San Diego, CA: Academic Press.

Crawford, M. (1995). *Talking difference: On gender and language.* London: Sage.

Dindia, K. (1997a, March). *"Men are from North Dakota, Women are from South Dakota."* Paper presented at the Marquette University's 3rd Annual Women's Studies conference, Milwaukee, WI.

Dindia, K. (1997b, November). *"Men are from North Dakota, Women are from South Dakota."* Paper presented at the Speech Communication Association convention, Chicago.

Duck, S., & Wright, P. (1993). Reexamining gender differences in same-gender friendships: A close look at two kinds of data. *Sex Roles, 28,* 709–727.

Eagly, A. H. (1995). The science and politics of comparing women and men. *American Psychologist, 50,* 145–158.

Epstein, C. F. (1981). *Women in law.* New York: Basic Books.

Epstein, C. F. (1988). *Deceptive distinctions.* Hillsdale, NJ: Lawrence Erlbaum Associates.

Fox-Genovese, E. (1991). *Feminism without illusions: A critique of individualism.* Chapel Hill, NC: University of North Carolina Press.

Freud, S. (1946). *The ego mechanisms of defense.* New York: International University Press.

Gilligan, C. (1982). *In a different voice: Psychological theory and women's development.* Cambridge, MA: Harvard University Press.

Gottman, J. M., & Carrere, S. (1994). Why can't men and women get along? Developmental roots and marital inequities. In D. J. Canary & L. Stafford (Eds.), *Communication and relational maintenance* (pp. 203–227). New York: Academic Press.

Gray, J. (1992). *Men are from Mars, Women are from Venus: A practical guide to improving communication and getting what you want in your relationships.* New York: HarperCollins.

Hall, D., & Langellier, K. (1988). Storytelling strategies in mother-daughter communication. In B. Bate & A. Taylor (Eds.), *Women communicating: Studies of women's talk* (pp. 107–126). Norwood, NJ: Ablex.

Hall, J. A. (1984). *Nonverbal sex differences: Communication accuracy and expressive style.* Baltimore, MD: The Johns Hopkins University Press.

Haraway, D. (1986). Primatology is politics by other means. In R. Bleier (Ed.), *Feminist approaches to science* (pp. 77–118). New York: Pergamon.

Haraway, D. (1988). Situated knowledges: The science question in feminism and the privilege of partial perspective. *Signs, 14,* 575–599.

Harding, S. (1991). *Whose science? Whose knowledge? Thinking from women's lives.* Ithaca, NY: Cornell University Press.

Henley, N. (1977). *Body politics:- Power, sex, and nonverbal communication.* Englewood Cliffs, NJ: Prentice-Hall.

Hunter, J. (1996a). *Significance tests.* Debate at American Psychological Society, San Francisco.

Hunter, J. (1996b). *Significance tests.* Debate at American Psychological Association, Toronto.

Hyde, J. S. (1985). *Half the human experience: The psychology of women* (3rd ed.). Lexington, MA: D. C. Heath.

Hyde, J. S., & Frost, L. (1993). Meta-analysis in the psychology of women. In F. Denmark & M. Paludi (Eds.), *Psychology of women: A handbook of issues and theories* (pp. 67–103). Westport, CT: Greenwood.

Hyde, J. S., & Plant, E. A. (1995). Magnitude of psychological gender differences: Another side to the story. *American Psychologist, 50,* 159–161.

Inman, C. (1996). Closeness in the doing: Male friendship. In J. T. Wood (Ed.), *Gendered relationships: A reader* (pp. 95–110). Mountain View, CA: Mayfield.

Janeway, E. (1971). *Man's world, woman's place.* New York: Dell.

Jennings, W. S., Kilkenny, R., & Kohlberg, L. (1983). Moral development theory and practice for youthful and adult offenders. In W. S. Laufer & J. M. Day (Eds.), *Personality theory, moral development, and criminal behavior* (pp. 281–355). Lexington, MA: Lexington Books.

Johnson, F. L. (1989). Women's culture and communication: An analytical perspective. In C. Lont & S. A. Friedley (Eds.), *Beyond boundaries: Sex and gender diversity in communication* (pp. 301–316). Fairfax, VA: George Mason University.

Johnson, F. L. (1996). Closeness in the doing: Women's friendships. In J. T. Wood (Ed.), *Gendered relationships: A reader* (pp. 79–94). Mountain View, CA: Mayfield.

Kahn, A. S., & Yoder, J. D. (1989). The psychology of women and conservatism: Rediscovering social change. *Psychology of Women Quarterly, 13,* 417–432.

Kaye, L. W., & Applegate, J. S. (1990). Men as elder caregivers: A response to changing families. *American Journal of Orthopsychiatry, 60,* 86–95.

Kerber, L. K. (1986). Some cautionary words for historians. *Signs, 11,* 304–310.

Maccoby, E. E. (1988). Gender as a social category. *Development Psychology, 24,* 755–765.

Maccoby, E. E. (1990). Gender and relationships: A developmental account. *American Psychologist, 45,* 513–520.

Maltz, D., & Borker, R. (1982). A cultural approach to male-female miscommunication. In J. J. Gumpertz (Ed.), *Language and social identity* (pp. 196–216). Cambridge: Cambridge University Press.

Murphy, B. O., & Zorn, T. E. (1996). Gendered interaction in professional relationships. In J. T. Wood (Ed.), *Gendered relationships: A reader* (pp. 213–232). Mountain View, CA: Mayfield.

Noddings, N. (1984). *A feminine approach to ethics and moral education.* Berkeley: University of California Press.

Noddings, N. (1990). Ethics from the standpoint of women. In D. L. Rhode (Ed.), *Theoretical perspectives on sexual difference* (pp. 160–173). New Haven, CT: Yale University Press.

Okin, S. M. (1989). *Justice gender, and the family.* New York: Basic Books.

Puka, B. (1990). The liberation of caring: A different voice for Gilligan's different voice. *Hypatia, 5,* 59–82.

Ragan, S. L. (1989). Communication between the sexes: A consideration of sex differences in adult communication. In J.F. Nussbaum (Ed.), *Life-span communication: Normative processes* (pp. 179–193). Hillsdale, NJ: Lawrence Erlbaum Associates.

Riessman, C. K. (1990). *Divorce talk: Women and men make sense of personal relationships.* New Brunswick, NJ: Rutgers University Press.

Risman, B. (1989). Can men mother? Life as a single father. In B. J. Risman & P. Schwartz (Eds.), *Gender in intimate relationships* (pp. 155–164). Belmont, CA: Wadsworth.

Rosenblatt, J. S. (1967). Nonhormonal basis of maternal behavior in the rat. *Science, 156,* 1512–1513.

Rosenblatt, J. S., & Siegel, H. I. (1981). Factors governing the onset and maintenance of maternal behavior among nonprimate animals: The role of hormonal and nonhormonal factors. In D. J. Gubernick & P. H. Klopfer (Eds.), *Parental care in mammals* (pp. 12–76). New York: Plenum.

Ruddick, S. (1989). *Maternal thinking: Towards a politics of peace.* Boston: Beacon.

Sanford, N. (1955). The dynamics of identification. *Psychological Review, 62,* 106–118.

Stier, D. S., & Hall, J. A. (1984). Gender differences in touch: An empirical and theoretical review. *Journal of Personality and Social Psychology, 47,* 440–459.

Swain, S. (1989). Covert intimacy: Closeness in men's friendships. In B. J. Risman & P. Schwartz (Eds.), *Gender in intimate relationships* (pp. 71–86). Belmont, CA: Wadsworth.

Swim, J. K. (1994). Perceived versus meta-analytic effect sizes: An assessment of the accuracy of gender stereotypes. *Journal of Personality and Social Psychology, 66,* 21–36.

Tannen, D. (1990). *You just don't understand: Women and men in conversation.* New York: William Morrow.

Tavris, C. (1992). *The mismeasure of woman.* New York: Simon & Schuster.

Thorne, B. (1993). *Gender play: Girls and boys in school.* New Brunswick, NJ: Rutgers University Press.

Wright, P. (1988). Interpreting research on gender differences in friendship: A case for moderation and a plea for caution. *Journal of Social and Personal Relationships, 5,* 367–373.

Wood, J. (1993). Gender and moral voice: From woman's nature to standpoint theory. *Women's Studies in Communication, 15,* 1–24.

Wood, J. (1994). *Who cares?: Women, care, and culture.* Carbondale, IL: Southern Illinois University Press.

Wood, J. (1995). Feminist scholarship and the study of relationships. *Journal of Social and Personal Relationships, 12,* 103–120.

Wood, J. (Ed.). (1996). *Gendered relationships: A reader.* Mountain View, CA: Mayfield.

Wood, J. (1997). *Gendered lives: Communication, gender and culture* (2nd ed.). Belmont, CA: Wadsworth.

Wood, J., & Inman, C. (1993). In a different mode: Masculine styles of communicating closeness. *Journal of Applied Communication Research, 21,* 279–295.

Chapter 2

Toward an Expanded Orientation to the Study of Sex Differences in Friendship

Paul H. Wright
University of North Dakota

C. S. Lewis, a literary scholar of acknowledged depth and versatility, once observed that women and men enjoy laughing at one another (Lewis, 1960). Among other things, women often exchange comments of bemusement and amusement about the golf games, fishing trips, car talk, sports talk, and shoptalk that they assume to form the core of men's activity-centered, goal-directed, and wholly depersonalized friendships. Men, likewise, exchange comments of bemusement and amusement about the phone conversations, coffee dates, personal talk, relationship talk, soul baring, and mutual uplifting that they assume to form the core of women's relationship-centered, emotionally supportive, and wholly personalized friendships. These polarized conceptions of women's and men's friendships are, of course, caricatures. The essence of a caricature is that, while recognizing it as a gross exaggeration, most people see in the exaggeration highlights of the distinctive features of the subject portrayed. In other words, good caricatures embody significant elements of truth.

But how good are the caricatures people draw of the typical friendships of women and men? Literally scores of studies indicate that the caricatures embody large elements of truth, leading some scholars to say that the caricatures do not exaggerate at all but provide valid portrayals of women's and men's friendships. Other scholars disagree. For this latter group, a discerning look at the same studies reveals a sufficient number of exceptions and qualifications; hence, they question whether differences between women's and men's friendships are notably large or pervasive. Carried to

41

its logical extreme, the controversy over the nature of sex differences in friendship suggests a basic question: Should relationship scholars be working toward one model or theory of friendship, or do we need two—one applicable to women's and another applicable to men's friendships? This admittedly hyperbolic question provides the point of departure for the present chapter.

This chapter argues that it is time to reexamine our observations about differences in women's and men's friendships, and to look for answers to the questions those observations raise in a variety of places. What is proposed in the conclusion is a modest beginning toward conceptualizing women's and men's friendships in a more contextualized manner. First, the chapter considers three different implicit orientations that scholars adopt in viewing research on sex differences in friendships. Limitations in each of these orientations suggest that, for all our research, we still do not understand those differences very well. Second, it undertakes a review of key studies comparing women's and men's friendships. This review will involve, in some cases, a closer than usual look at the data presented. The purpose of the review will be to (a) demonstrate that the similarities in women's and men's friendships outweigh the differences, and (b) highlight the need for a contextualized orientation in understanding the differences that clearly exist. Third, it outlines an expanded orientation to the study of women's and men's friendships that proposes a shift in the way we define and assess *communality* (intimacy, expressiveness, self-disclosure) and some initial steps toward incorporating potentially influential structural as well as dispositional factors into our analyses and explorations.

BACKGROUND: THREE ORIENTATIONS
AND THEIR VICISSITUDES

Sex Differences in Friendship: Legion and Dichotomous

In 1981, Bell asserted broadly and boldly, "When we look at friendship in society, we can see many variations. But there is no social factor more important than that of sex in leading to friendship variations" (1981a, p. 55). A great deal of research conducted both before and since 1981, taken as a whole and more or less uncritically, seems to substantiate Bell's claim. Just what are those important sex-linked variations? The traditional consensus holds that: (a) women's friendships are affectively richer than those of men (Booth, 1972); (b) women's friendships emphasize reciprocity, whereas men's emphasize agreement and similarity (Weiss & Lowenthal, 1975); (c) women's friendships are reciprocal, men's associative (Reisman, 1981); and (d) women have complex and holistic friendships with partners who have relevance for many areas of experience, whereas men have focused and circumscribed friendships with special purpose partners who have relevance for limited areas of experience (Barth & Kinder, 1988; Block, 1980; Weiss & Lowenthal, 1975; Wright, 1982a).

The foregoing litany of sex differences in friendship is by no means exhaustive. Several investigators have undertaken reviews of the voluminous literature on this problem (e.g., Fehr, 1996; Sherrod, 1989; Winstead, 1986; Wright, 1989). It is clear from these reviews that the interrelated matters of intimacy, self-disclosure/expressiveness, and mere talk versus nonintimacy, inexpressiveness, and activity-centeredness remain pivotal. Women's friendships are characterized by the former, men's by the latter. At one time, I epitomized these differences metaphorically, describing women's friendships as *face to face* and men's friendships as *side by side* (Wright, 1982a). On a more conceptual (and more useful) level, the entire pattern of differences is encapsulated in Bakan's (1966) distinction between *communion* and *agency*. Scholars now commonly characterize women's friendships as communal and men's friendships as agentic. Up to a point, researchers seldom question the orientation implicit in this polarized view of women's and men's friendships; women's friendships were regarded as communal but not agentic, whereas men's friendships were regarded as agentic but not communal.

A Challenge to the Dichotomy, a Response, and an Altered Orientation

In the course of preparing a review of sex differences in friendship across stages of adulthood, I was compelled to look carefully at a large number of studies. This examination led to a reconsideration of the frequency, strength, and ubiquity of the modal pattern of differences between women's and men's friendships (Wright, 1988). Whereas my review generally supported the overall robustness of the modal pattern, there was an appreciable number of studies in which the usual sex differences were not found. Moreover, when sex differences were found, they were often quite small (despite statistically significant comparisons) and generally characterized by considerable within-sex variance and widely overlapping distributions. In addition, in focusing on female–male differences, investigators often overlooked indications that women's and men's friendships were similar in more ways or to a greater degree than they were dissimilar. Finally, sex differences in friendship were sometimes attenuated or overridden by organismic or subject variables other than the sex of the respondent (e.g., sex role orientations, intimacy, and power motivation).

Considerations of the foregoing kind have not gone unnoticed by scholars, some of whom nonetheless maintain that differences in the friendships of women and men are strong and dichotomous. In what we might call "weight of the evidence" assessments, some scholars acknowledge but minimize findings that fail to show the usual sex differences in friendship. They treat those findings as exceptions to be granted but not taken too seriously. For example, Brehm (1992) concluded a discussion of the respective personalized versus activity-centered nature of women's and men's friendships as follows:

> There are exceptions to the rule, and all close friendships involve some of both elements (Wright, 1988). Nevertheless, Wright's (1982) terms remain pithy and accurate descriptors of two different, gender-related approaches to friendships: Women's are "face-to-face," while men's are "side-by-side." (p. 365)

In a similar *weight of evidence* vein, Fehr (1996) devoted a book chapter to a painstaking review of the issue of sex differences in friendship, coming down rather heavily in favor of large and pervasive differences.

The preceding challenge to a clear communal–agentic dichotomy, and the response to it, amounts to an alteration of scholars' implicit orientation to women's and men's friendships. Rather than viewing women's and men's friendships as falling into separate communal versus agentic categories, researchers began to view them as varying bimodally (with minimal overlap) along a communal–agentic continuum, with women's friendships concentrated toward the communal pole and men's toward the agentic pole. Figure 2.1 illustrates the hypothetical distribution of women's and men's friendships implied in this orientation. This orientation, although less categorical, remains essentially dichotomous and still leaves the question, Should we be working toward one model of friendship or two?

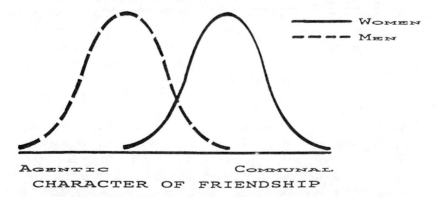

FIG. 2.1. Hypothetical distribution of women's and men's friendships along an agentic–communality continuum as implied in Orientation 2.

**Further Considerations and Yet Another (Still Inadequate)
Orientation**

The accumulation of further studies, as well as a continued scrutiny of the literature as a whole, suggested yet another, more radical alteration of our implicit communal versus agentic orientation. This orientation is discussed in greater detail in due course. For now, suffice it to say that there is little compelling evidence that the friendships of women are appreciably less agentic than those of men. The evidence does indicate that women's friendships are somewhat more communal than they are agentic and that—as currently conceptualized—they are somewhat more communal than those of men.

The orientation implicit in this view, illustrated in Fig. 2.2, underlies discussions of findings reported by Duck and Wright (1993) and Wright and Scanlon (1991). It regards communality and agency as two separate continua each ranging from *none* to *very much*. For the agentic continuum, the hypothetical distributions of women's and men's friendships would be quite similar. For the communal continuum, the hypothetical distributions would overlap appreciably, but would show the central tendency to be higher for women's than for men's friendships.

Although I regard this third orientation as an accurate summary of what we now know (or believe) about differences in women's and men's friendships, it is nonetheless woefully inadequate as a sound framework within which to organize further research and theorizing. Basically, it maintains the centrality of the communal–agentic dichotomy even as it disavows the importance and ubiquity of that dichotomy in characterizing women's and men's friendships. Thus, relationship scholars strongly committed to either the second or third of our three implicit orientations persist in exchanges of the *yes, but* kind, with each side conducting research (and interpreting that of the other side) in ways that support their respective positions. The

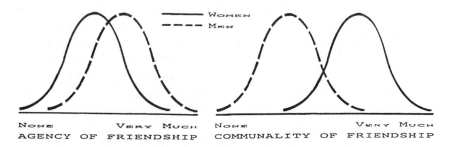

FIG. 2.2. Hypothetical distributions of women's and men's friendships along separate agentic and communal continua as implied in Orientation 3.

narrow focus of this controversy appears to be hypnotic. Advocates of neither side seem to be considering the possibility that we might reconceptualize the issue in a way that enhances our understanding of what it means to be communal and agentic in the conduct of friendships and of the possible role of "structural" factors in influencing similarities and differences between women and men in this regard.

Problems of Operationalization and Dispositional Bias

Two basic problems stand in the way of a broader and more contextualized way of conceptualizing sex similarities and differences in friendship. One of these reflects the lopsided manner in which researchers conceptualize and operationalize communality and agency. The other is a strong tendency to interpret observed differences in women's and men's friendships in dispositional terms to the exclusion of possibly strong structural influences.

Lopsided Operationalization. Researchers have assessed communality (generally under the essentially synonymous but less generic term *intimacy*) in detailed and differentiated ways, whereas they have assessed agency (*nonintimacy*) in starkly simple ones. Communality is variously operationalized in terms of globally described intimacy, personal/emotional expressiveness, amount of self-disclosure, quality of self-disclosure (e.g., intimate or nonintimate, personal or impersonal), confiding, and emotional supportiveness. Agency is operationalized in terms of activity-centeredness. That is, if interaction partners focus primarily on a shared activity, they are *ipso facto* agentic (nonintimate) rather than communal (intimate).

This predilection overlooks the fact that activities, as well as different kinds of talk and emotional sharing, vary widely in intimacy. Hays (1984, 1985) recognized this point in his useful distinction between intimate and nonintimate companionship to parallel the distinction between intimate and nonintimate communication. In an application of this point to the issue of sex differences in friendship, a number of critics (e.g., Wood, 1994; Wood & Inman, 1993) have argued that studies in which women show higher levels of intimacy than men are biased. That is, investigators have defined and explored intimacy in stereotypically feminine terms. However, masculine as well as feminine ways of expressing and experiencing intimacy exist. Thus, men (on the average) may be just as intimate in their friendships as women, but men express intimacy differently.

The Dispositional Bias. Relationship scholars exhibit a strong propensity to explain differences in women's and men's friendships in terms of differing internalized and presumably stable characteristics (such as the motives underlying friendship) and the individually adaptive or adjustive functions provided to or sought from friendships (Fischer & Oliker, 1983; Wright, 1989). The de facto quality of dispositional explanations surfaces in the readiness with which researchers assume that sex differences in friendship are ultimately understandable in terms of sex role socialization and developmental patterns (e.g., Fehr, 1996).

In contrast to this dispositional emphasis, Fischer and Oliker (1983) argued that structural factors influence differences in both the number and kinds of friendships that women and men establish. Structural explanations emphasize "the different positions women and men typically occupy in the social system, and their differing access to economic, political, and ideological sources of power or privilege" which represent the "direct, uninternalized effects of social structure" (p. 124) and include normative constraints, role demands, and the availability of certain kinds of potential partners. It is encouraging to note that cross-cultural studies exploring (or including) sex differences in friendship appear to be increasing (Aukett, Ritchie, & Mill, 1988; Berman, Murphy-Berman, & Pachauri, 1988; Reisman, 1990; Uhl, 1991; Wheeler, Reis, & Bond, 1989). However, regardless of whether such studies indicate support for the usual female–male differences, most investigators fall back on dispositional or (sometimes) ambiguous explanations. That is, they interpret their results, if at all clearly, in terms of internalized personal characteristics that differ for women and men presumably due to cultural differences in socialization practices.

In any case, studies comparing women's and men's friendships rarely (if ever) identify structural variables and use them to equate groups or match female and male subjects. Is it not possible, then, that some (perhaps many) of the friendship differences we typically attribute to what women versus men are like might be diminished or negated if we take into account specific features of the social context in which those friendships are embedded?

A Modest Beginning Toward a More Contextualized Orientation

The pages that follow examine findings from some of the key studies of sex differences in friendship. Due to the sheer volume of studies available, this chapter is selective but representative. The outcome of the review will put to rest the hyperbolic question posed earlier—that is, whether we need separate theories/models of friendship for women and men or if one will do for both. The answer is that one model will do nicely because differences in women's and men's friendships emerge in a context of more fundamental similarities. With this point as a backdrop, this chapter outlines an emerging orientation to the study of sex differences in friendship. This new orientation consists of two simple shifts in focus: one toward a more inclusive way of conceptualizing communality (intimacy) in friendships and another toward a means of conceptualizing the impact of structural variables—à la Fischer and Oliker (1983)—on friendships.

DIFFERENCES EMBEDDED IN SIMILARITIES

In developing the argument that sex differences in friendship are embedded in a context of broader similarities, this section first touches on what appears to be a point of demonstrable similarity (i.e., conceptions and values of friendship). Then it deals with various aspects of communality and agency in friendships. Finally, it highlights sex differences and similarities in holistic (vs. circumscribed) friendships.

Conceptions and Values of Friendship

A number of studies point to the conclusion that women and men do not differ in their conceptions of friendship nor in what they value about them. Sapadin (1988) concluded from her comparison of professional women and men that, despite differences in the actual experience of friendship, "both sexes viewed the characteristics of an ideal friendship in similar ways" (p. 400). Several investigations of conceptions of a best friend among university undergraduates and college-educated adults (Ashton, 1980; Tesch & Martin, 1983; Wall, Pickert, & Paradise, 1984) found that both women and men emphasized communication, intimacy, trust, and interpersonal sensitivity in a manner generally considered characteristic of the modal pattern for women. Similarly, Monsour (1992) found that, despite on-the-average differences in magnitude, women and men agreed on the ordering of characteristics indicating intimacy in friendship, ranking *self-disclosure* and *emotional expressiveness* highest on the list and *activities* near the bottom. Caldwell and Peplau (1982) reported that a large majority of both women and men indicated a preference for having a few intimate friends rather than many good but less intimate friends. Finally, Parker and de Vries (1993) found strong agreement between women and men on what they value in friendship, with *trust* and *authenticity* being most highly rated by both.

Communion and Agency in Friendship

According to my own data (Duck & Wright, 1993, Study 2; Wright & Scanlon, 1991), the widely accepted generalization that women's friendships are, on the average, both more communal and less agentic than those of men appears to be only half valid. In these studies, women (vs.

men) regarded their same-sex friends to be higher in ego-supportiveness, self-affirmation, and security value—clearly communal characteristics. However, women and men did not differ in the degree to which they regarded their same-sex friends as providing concrete, practical forms of cooperation and assistance (utility value) or as being a source of new ideas, activities, and ways of doing things (stimulation value). This suggests that women's friendships do tend to be more communal than those of men but they are no less agentic.

A less obvious implication of the foregoing findings is that thinking of communal versus agentic emphases in friendship in terms of talking versus participating in activities is probably overdrawn. Each of the friendship values listed earlier may be expressed through either verbal interaction or activities. Usually it is both. Nevertheless, pitting merely talking against engaging in activities constitutes a popular focus for exploring sex differences in friendship.

Talk Versus Activities

Women friends talk; men friends do. This conclusion seems to be supported by scores of studies. A close look at some of the work, however, may raise doubts as to whether women pursue talk (and shun activities) and men pursue activities (and shun talk) so much as to permit a broad generalization.

In a study often cited as attesting to women's talk-centered and men's activity-centered friendships, Caldwell and Peplau (1982) found that more women than men preferred just talking with friends than doing some activity. The opposite held for men. (For a cross-cultural replication, see Aukett et al., 1988.) But what did Caldwell and Peplau really find? Fifty-seven percent of the women preferred talk, leaving 43% who preferred an activity. Is a figure this close to 50–50 enough to support the generalization that women friends talk? The comparison for the men was more impressive, with 84% of the men preferring an activity. Caldwell and Peplau also reported that, given an either–or choice, more women than men (61% vs. 43%) preferred a friend who feels the same way about things over one who likes to do the same things. At $p < .11$, however, the chi-square comparison for this difference was not significant at a generally accepted level. Taken by themselves, these findings indicate, at most, that men more likely emphasize activities with their friends, whereas women are more evenly divided in their preferences for talk versus activities. In other words, women do not greatly emphasize talk at the expense of activities.

The work of Caldwell and Peplau does not, of course, stand alone. Numerous studies utilizing interviews and self-report measures exploring either partners' experiences of friendship in general or their experiences with a particular friend (or sometimes a set of friends) generally confirm the typical talk versus activity sex differences. Within this literature, however, researchers often tacitly and sometimes explicitly recognize that women friends do, in fact, participate in varied activities and that men friends do, in fact, talk to one another quite a bit (e.g., Aries & Johnson, 1983; Johnson & Aries, 1983a, 1983b; Pukalos, 1989). Whereas this latter observation should raise some doubts about the generality of the talk–activity dichotomy, it does not. Women's activities are regarded as vehicles for interaction in which talk remains focal (Johnson & Aries, 1983a; Pukalos, 1989). Men's talk centers on impersonal topics such as sports, work, hobbies, and shared activities (Johnson & Aries, 1983b), presumably (for this reason) leaving the talk–activity dichotomy undisturbed.

Amid uncertainties raised by variations in methodology, empirical focus, and interpretive bent, the body of work on the talk–activity issue, as a whole, leaves me convinced that both women and men friends talk a lot and do a lot. Probably they most often talk while doing. However, when reflecting on their friendships, as in responses to interview questions and self-report items, women more often talk about talking and men more often talk about doing. This impression finds support in two different kinds of studies, one utilizing in-depth interviews and another utilizing diary records of actual meetings with friends. In the interview study (Walker, 1994), women and men responded to broad questions about friendship with the usual talk versus activity difference. When asked more focused questions about specific friendships, however, women's reports of involvement in activities increased, as did men's reports of involvement in significant talk. The diary study (Duck & Wright, 1993, Study 1) involved three data sets, with women and men in each set recording interactions with a friend. With some minor variation across data sets, both women and men rated *talk* highest as the purpose of the interaction and *working on a task* as second highest.

Intimacy

Women's friendships are characterized by high levels of intimacy; men's are not. This generalization expresses what many researchers consider the core distinction between women's communal and men's agentic friendships. Numerous studies do indeed support the conclusion that women's friendships are, on the average, more intimate than those of men (see also Reis, chap. 9, this volume). These supportive studies constitute, at base, an elaboration of the talk–activity distinction covered in the previous section; *intimacy* is defined in terms of self-disclosure, confiding, personal affirmation, and emotional support. As with other conclusions about sex differences in friendship, the intimacy–nonintimacy generalization is not universally accepted (see Fehr, 1996).

My own impression from the accumulated research is that, for both women and men, interpersonal intimacy constitutes a strong and valued aspect of close friendships. This represents an overriding similarity. However, embedded in this similarity is a noticeable tendency for women (vs. men) to express higher levels of intimacy. In support of this impression, this section touches on four issues: (a) potentially confounding variables, (b) the size and consistency of sex differences in self-disclosure, (c) the expression of intimacy through shared activities, and (d) the levels of intimacy of men's closer friendships.

Potentially Confounding Variables.   The status of the sex of the participant as a subject variable (as opposed to one that is exerimentally manipulable) raises questions about how basic sex differences in friendship intimacy really are and, consequently, how confidently we can apply findings indicating such differences to women and men in general. For instance, we might find that women score higher, on the average, than men in nurturance and that people who score high on nurturance tend to form more intimate friendships. Thus, any sex differences we find in friendship intimacy may be accounted for by the relatively small proportion of women who score very high and/or the relatively small proportion of men who score very low on nurturance. Indeed, researchers have found that controlling for various kinds of personal dispositions such as sex role orientations (Barth & Kinder, 1988; Narus & Fischer, 1982; Wright & Scanlon, 1991), social motives (McAdams, Healy, & Kraus, 1985), and personal orientations (Bell, 1981b) sometimes reduces and sometimes (but less often) eliminates sex differences in friendship intimacy. Such findings constitute a tiresomely made (e.g., Wright, 1988) and tiresomely acknowledged (e.g., Fehr, 1996) caution to refrain from overgeneralizing the stronger tendency of women than men to express intimacy in their friendships. However, the caution is a tune that has been badly overplayed. Although participant sex is a subject variable, it is strongly associated with a number of different sex-linked predispositions. It accounts for more of the variance in friendship intimacy, as currently conceptualized, than any potentially attenuating variable (or combination of such variables) associated with it.

Sex Differences in Self-Disclosure.   Virtually any review of work on sex differences in friendship will note convincingly that, according to most relevant studies, women, on the average, self-disclose more broadly and more intimately than do men. The key phrase is "on the average," leaving open the possibility that a majority of women and men self-disclose in a similar manner. Dindia and Allen (1992) concluded from a meta-analysis of 205 studies that there are sex differences in self-disclosure but that such differences are so small as to be of questionable theoretical or practical importance.

One study in particular (Hacker, 1981) is often cited as evidence that women are "blabbermouths" and men "clams." Hacker did find some sex differences in self-disclosures to friends, but one has to dig through a veritable mountain of similarities to find them. First, and most important, she reported little difference in the proportions of women and men classified as high, moderate, and low self-disclosers in their friendships. Second, 78% of the women and 86% of the men reported that they would reveal both strengths and weakness to same-sex friends, and 50% of the women and 62% of the men reported that they would reveal both strengths and weakness to cross-sex friends. It was only among participants who would reveal only strengths or only weaknesses to a friend that she found notable differences. None of the women would reveal only strengths to either a female or male friend, whereas 18% and 33% of them would reveal only weaknesses to a female or male friend, respectively. None of the men would reveal only weaknesses to either a female or male friend, whereas 31% and 9% of them would reveal only strengths to a female or male friend, respectively—interesting perhaps, but hardly a sound basis for a blabbermouths–clams dichotomy.

Intimacy Through Shared Activities. Several relationship scholars (e.g., Wood, 1994; Wood & Inman, 1993) claimed that women's friendships appear to be more intimate than those of men only because research is biased toward feminine ways of expressing intimacy—that is, through self-disclosure and face-to-face socioemotional interaction. Men also develop intimate friendships, but express their intimacy in masculine ways—that is, through shared activities.

The similarity of women's and men's conceptions and values of friendship cited earlier, combined with apparent sex differences in the experience of intimacy in friendship, suggest two possibilities. One possibility is that men want the same kind of intimacy from their friendships as women but are not as successful in achieving it. This possibility coincides with the finding that men (vs. women) report less satisfaction with their friendships (e.g., Reisman, 1990). A second possibility is that both men and women express varying levels of intimacy through correspondingly intimate actions and shared activities but, having accepted the stereotypic *feminine* definition, may not label (or recognize) any interaction other than confiding or self-disclosure as intimate (cf. Walker, 1994). This implies, of course, that actions and shared activities as well as confiding, self-disclosure, and the like vary in levels of intimacy—an implication clearly supported in Hays' (1984, 1985) work on nonintimate and intimate companionship. My own position (developed more fully later) is that friends express intimacy through acts and activities as well as in confiding, self-disclosure, and so on, but that it makes little conceptual sense to differentiate among these forms of expression.

Intimacy in Closer Friendships.   When considering whether sex differences in the intimacy of friendships diminish as friendships grow closer in other respects, one again encounters the problem of mixed findings. My own work has shown that, in deeper and long-standing friendships, differences between women and men on communal characteristics are reduced and sometimes nullified (e.g., Wright, 1982b). Candy-Gibbs (1982) reached the same conclusion from a study of elderly widows and widowers. Moreover, in a longitudinal study, Hays (1985) found that women's and men's close friendships grew to similar levels of both intimate communication and intimate companionship as the relationships developed over a 12-week period.

However, Barth and Kinder (1988) reported that women indicated greater depth and involvement at all levels of friendship than did men. Similarly, Reis and his associates (Reis, 1986; Reis, Senchak, & Solomon; 1985), using a composite measure of *overall meaningfulness,* consistently found that women score their interactions as higher than those of men regardless of whether the comparison involves best friends only or other relationships, including lesser friends.

A common procedural shortcoming of studies of closeness and intimacy concerns the absence of an assessment of closeness apart from the participant's global self-identification of, for example, a best friend. It is entirely possible, then, that when women and men in such studies respond to their best friends, they are not necessarily responding to friends of the same kind or at the same level of closeness. For example, studies utilizing an instrument that includes separate measures of friendship strength (e.g., the Acquaintance Description Form; Lea, 1989; Wright, 1985) consistently show that women's self-identified best friendships tend to be stronger than those of men. When levels of friendship are co-varied out, differences between women and men on intimacy variables (self-affirmation, ego-support, security, emotional expression) are markedly reduced, although usually not eliminated completely (e.g., Duck & Wright, 1993).

Holistic and Circumscribed Friendships

Several scholars have identified yet another overall difference in women's and men's friendships: More women than men react to their friends in global and multifaceted ways, whereas more men than women react to their friends with respect to distinct, relatively isolated attributes (Wright, 1982a). For example, women tend to perceive more complexity in their friendships than do men (Weiss & Lowenthal, 1975). Furthermore, women more likely have one or a few all purpose friends, whereas men more likely have several special purpose friends (Barth & Kinder, 1988; Block, 1980).

This difference, too, occurs within a context of broad similarity. Both women and men can generally identify not just one but several friends and acknowledge that the friendships they form differ in both kind and intensity. De facto evidence for this point derives from the large number of studies that compare women's and men's friendships at differing levels. More directly, Gouldner and Strong (1987) found that a sample of upper-middle-class women ages 30 to 65 years made a clear distinction among talk friends, activity friends, work friends, and close friends. Truly close friendship was important to the women they interviewed, but so relatively rare as to be designated the extraordinary relationship.

The latter observation raises a question: If both women and men develop some holistic friendships and some circumscribed friendships, why do studies indicate that women's friendships are more often holistic and men's more often circumscribed? One possibility is that the difference may simply comprise another manifestation of women's predisposition to form communal friendships and men's predisposition to form agentic friendships. Another possibility is that the pattern of structural factors for most women (vs. men) promotes the development of friendships that are holistic, whereas the pattern of structural factors for most men is more conducive to the development of circumscribed friendships.

The foregoing considerations contain a potentially important implication for studies comparing women's and men's friendships. Women and men enjoy some friendships that are circumscribed and presumably situational. At the same time, women are more likely than men to have friendships that are holistic. Thus, when asked to identify a friend or best friend for research purposes, it is likely that more women than men will select a holistic friend. If researchers asked women and men to identify friends of the same kind or within a specified context (e.g., work friends), would the usual sex differences be found? There is some evidence that they would not, at least not consistently. Furman (1987) gathered data from professors in several universities concerning their best friendships within their academic departments. She found no differences between the women and men in these departments with respect to their same-sex friendships. These findings differ from those of Sapadin (1988), who found the typical female–male differences in the way professional women and men experience friendship. A major difference in the two studies is that Sapadin explored friendships in general, whereas Furman explored friendships within a work setting.

Summary

I have argued that friendship is, first and foremost, just that—friendship. As concluded a number of years ago (Wright, 1988), "The same kinds of experiences and interactions take place to some degree in virtually all close friendships regardless of whether those friendships are composed of fe-

male, male, or mixed dyads" (p. 370). Embedded within this overall same-
ness, however, some on-the-average differences between women and men
emerge. It is interesting to note that, with one possible exception, sex
differences in friendship involve aspects that women experience more or
more strongly than do men. Thus, women tend to place somewhat more
emphasis on mere talk and (more noticeably) to engage in more confiding
and intimate self-disclosure. Women tend to be more personalized, secure,
and emotionally supportive in their same-sex friendships, and women tend
to respond to their friends more holistically. If there is anything about
men's friendships that exceed those of women it is a greater emphasis on
shared activities.

The preceding summary suggests a broader and more mundane difference than the usual communal–agentic distinction: Women, on the average, are more inclined to form very close friendships than are men.
Whether one attributes women's closer friendships to greater attractiveness
or greater workability will depend largely on his or her preference for
dispositional or structural explanations. As noted previously, dispositional
explanations have been more highly favored. It is possible, however, that
close friendships are no less attractive and important to men, but that
structural factors make the development of such friendships more difficult
and less workable for the average man than for the average woman. This
possibility is a part of the expanded orientation to sex differences in friendship to which this chapter now turns.

TOWARD AN EXPANDED ORIENTATION

Some time ago (Wright, 1978), I proposed a perspective on the nature of
friendship and its course of development that was built, in part, on two
propositions. First, friendship growth involves increasing amounts of
contact between partners in a growing variety of settings and activities.
Second, such growth takes place within a relationship that is preferential,
nonobligatory, and relatively unstructured with respect to specific role
requirements and normative regulations. The first of these points has
implications for the experience and expression of communality in
friendships; the second has implications for the impact of structural
variables on the formation and maintenance of friendships. Ultimately,
each has implications for the study of sex differences in friendship.

An Expanded View of Communality in Friendships

Communality and Friendship in General. Interaction that increases in both
amount and variety in a developing friendship carries with it the opportunity,
if not the inevitability, that each partner will be exposed to more facets of

the other. In addition, with growing familiarity and security, the partners likely become increasingly spontaneous (i.e., less guarded and less self-monitoring) in how they act and what they say. Such behavioral self-exposure and (usually implicit) verbal self-disclosure will normally enhance each partner's awareness of what the other regards as important and self-involving as well as enabling each to see the other with respect to what is genuine rather than superficial or insincere. To the degree that each partner in a friendship considers the other unfeigned and genuine, and responds to that partner with respect to what the partner regards as important and self-involving, they are, in a basic sense, expressing communality.

From this point of view, explicit and self-conscious verbal expressions of communality are no more important in friendship than expressions of communality implicit in the kinds of activities close friends often share and in the ways friends engage in those activities. Both flow from the familiarity, trust, and personalized interest and concern that are characteristic of partners in close friendships. Thus, if we distinguish between communality expressed through talk and communality expressed through activity, we should note that they likely unfold in a closely parallel fashion in developing friendships. In fact, in light of findings indicating that explicit self-disclosures make up an extremely small percentage of the talk that people exchange in everyday interactions (Dindia, Fitzpatrick, & Kenney, 1989; Duck, Rutt, Hurst, & Strejc, 1991), intimacy expressed through activities may be a more sensitive index of friendship closeness.

Implications for Women's and Men's Friendships. If researchers were to define and measure friendship communality in a way that included communal acts and activities along with confiding and self-disclosure, would they still find women, on the average, scoring higher than men? The answer to this question, of course, awaits the outcome of relevant research. The relevancy of such research would hinge on the use of procedures that tap intimacy levels of different acts and activities with as much differentiation and precision as those used to assess the intimacy levels of verbal self-disclosure and confiding.

Studies should give due recognition to three points concerning intimacy levels of activities. First, some activities are intrinsically more intimate than others. Hays (1984, 1985) addressed this point directly, noting, for example, that visiting one's relatives with a friend is more intimate than attending a party together. Second, a given reported activity may involve more or less intimacy depending on its broader setting. To use a hackneyed example, two men may report going fishing together. A fishing trip that entailed canoeing into the deep woods for a 3-day camp-out would be more intimate than one that entailed a short drive to a nearby lake for an hour or so of angling. Third, a given activity may involve more or less intimacy depending on the way the partners interact and, especially, their primary reason for participating in it. Two people may play chess simply because they love the game and welcome any and all comers. However, they may be good friends who use their mutual enjoyment of chess as one of perhaps several arenas for expressing their friendship. The game just wouldn't be the same with anyone else.

What would such relevant research show about the comparative communality of women's and men's friendships? The extant evidence suggests that women's friendships would still show higher average levels of overall communality than those of men, but the difference would be reduced in size and observed somewhat less consistently. This impression, however, presupposes research that, like most, does not equate women's and men's friendships with respect to such variables as friendship settings or situational constraints. In other words, controlling for the influence of structural factors may eliminate sex differences in friendship communality.

Structural Factors in Friendship

Although scholars have emphasized dispositional factors in the study of friendship, they have not altogether ignored the influence of structural factors. For example, Adams and Blieszner (1994; Blieszner & Adams, 1992) proposed an integrative model of friendship that focuses on the complex interplay of individual (dispositional) characteristics with opportunities and constraints stemming from social structures. A detailed examination of the relevant social structures remains beyond the scope of this chapter. My own efforts to articulate the direct impact of sociobehavioral environments on friendship have been sporadic and incomplete (Wright, 1982b, 1989, 1995), but even these call for considerably more elaboration and documentation than one can render here.

In brief, my present position is this: Friendship is largely preferential and nonobligatory (i.e., the least normatively regulated, role-bound, legalistic, and programmed of any important personal relationship; Paine, 1974; Suttles, 1970; Wright, 1978). Two implications follow. First, the impact of structural factors is predominantly permissive rather than promotive. That is, friendships probably will not flourish in sociobehavioral environments with strong normative restraints against free, unstructured interaction. They may or may not flourish in those without such restraints. Second, even in the absence of normative restraints, friendship carries with it much less requiredness and urgency than do involvements in more clearly regulated personal and social relationships. Therefore, friendships are relatively easy to put on hold, and sometimes to forego completely, in the face of expectations from more structured relationships and other role obligations.

The preceding considerations suggest the usefulness of analyzing the general impact of structural factors on friendships in terms of the individual's overall pattern of roles and obligations. Some time ago, Hess (1972) provided a starting point for such an analysis. Starting with the observation that structural factors determine the individual's total cluster of roles, she proposed that this cluster of roles, in turn, influences the number and kinds of friendships an individual can establish. At an operational level, however, one may bypass a delineation of the cluster of roles and identify the broad characteristics of a given friendship in terms of the primary type of connection that exists between that friendship and the person's other roles. Hess specified four such connections.

In the connection labeled *fusion*, a friendship is contingent on the performance of one or more other roles. Examples are coworker associations, mentor–protégé relationships, mutual involvement in civic and interest groups, and the like, when that mutual involvement extends beyond participation in the primary roles into the voluntary and personalized interaction definitive of friendship.

In *substitution*, a friendship allows a person to actualize relationship functions when she or he lacks the opportunity to actualize those functions through "major" (sic) social roles. For example, a person bereft of appropriate kin may interact in a motherly, fatherly, sisterly, or brotherly way with an individual who, in all other respects, is just a friend.

In *complementarity*, a friendship enhances an individual's performance of one or more other roles that are otherwise unrelated to the friendship. The advice, support, encouragement, and sometimes technical assistance of a friend, for example, may help an individual interact more effectively with his or her spouse or children or perform more productively on the job.

In *competition*, a friendship and other roles impose conflicting demands on the individual's time and/or value allegiances. For instance, a person's commitment to career development may be so intense as to limit the time and resources he or she has available to devote to his or her friendships.

Implications for Communal and Agentic Friendships. Because of her focus on overall friendship possibilities at different life stages, Hess (1972) restricted her typology to global aspects of friendship. For example, she noted that the number and kinds of roles associated with the younger and middle adult years normally permit the individual less flexibility with respect to both discretionary time and patterns of activity than those associated with either adolescence or older adulthood. Therefore, although the pattern of roles characteristic of young or middle adulthood provide an individual with opportunities for numerous friendships connected through fusion, those friendships often stand in a competitive connection with his or her total role cluster. However, the relatively greater flexibility of adolescence and older adulthood generally provides fewer opportunities for fused friendships, but the friendships the individual does form less often stand in a competitive connection with the total cluster.

Two points beyond those that Hess highlighted are relevant to the present chapter. First, the four connections do not necessarily exclude one another, particularly in cases where friendships and other roles are connected through fusion. Second, the type of connection or combination of connections between a friendship and other roles can have a bearing on the communal or agentic character of that friendship. Specifically, fused connections often associate with conditions imposing restraints against the development of communal friendships. There are three reasons for this.

First, fused friendships most often occur with respect to roles structured around specific time constraints, relatively well-defined tasks, and often performance standards or tangible output. Examples are involvement in work and career pursuits, political activism, clubs and lodges, civic/philanthrophic associations, religious organizations, and the like. In friendships fused with such roles, the partners must divide their efforts between enacting the roles and pursuing the friendships. This, of course, constitutes a competitive connection, limiting both the time and flexibility necessary for the development of communal friendships.

Second, on a similar but more general point, the greater the number of roles one adopts and the more effort one expends on them, the less time and energy one has to devote to any friendships, including those that are fused with the roles. Therefore, busy people may (or may not) have a relatively large number of fused friendships, but it is unlikely that many of those friendships will be communal in nature.

Third, roles that are structured around specific time constraints and clearly circumscribed activities often (but by no means always) encourage competition in its more general connotation. In friendships fused with such roles, the partners may find themselves vying for unshareable resources or outcomes, such as raises, promotions, a place on the starting lineup, the political party's endorsement of candidacy, or the choice roles in dramatic productions. We would normally expect this kind of competitive situation to constitute a further obstacle to developing communal friendships.

Implications for Sex Differences in Friendship. From the present point of view, the overall greater communality of women's than men's friendships may be due partly, perhaps mostly, to the total clusters of roles and obligations that impose greater restraints against men's developing communal friendships. The issue of concern is the degree to which differences in the friendships of women and men—or, for that matter, girls and boys through childhood and adolescence—are influenced by differences in the number and kinds of activities in which they are permitted, encouraged, or pressured to participate. More specifically, do such patterns of activity relate to roles that are more conducive to the development of fused friendships for men than for women and to the development of freestanding friendships for women than for men? Do those roles, either in number or their combined degree of preemptiveness, encourage more competitive connections between friendships and other roles for men than for women? Do men's total clusters of roles, more often than those of women, involve competition in the more general sense—that is, competition with others for unshareable resources or outcomes?

Summarizing the impact of structural variables in terms of differing types of connections between friendships and other roles may not provide a complete answer to questions of the foregoing kind, but it provides a workable place to start. Pertinent research would entail developing techniques for assessing connections between a given friendship and the individual's other roles, especially with respect to fusion and competition. Such techniques would enable investigators to augment participants' reports of the more immediate dyadic characteristics of a given friendship with data concerning an important aspect of the overall structural context of that friendship. Then researchers could easily use matching or regression procedures to examine the extent to which the sex difference in friendship communality is due to structural versus dispositional influences and possibly interactions of these influences. Such an approach would provide valuable information about friendship and sex differences as well as sex differences in friendship.

CONCLUSION

Some time ago (Wright, 1988), I capped a plea for moderation and caution in the way we interpret sex differences in friendship as follows: "Our research should move us toward more valid and increasingly applicable conceptualizations of personal relationships. Let us avoid stereotypes or, worse yet, caricatures" (p. 372). The present chapter has made it clear that I now accord this *should* even greater urgency. However, I no longer agree with the implication that caricatures are worse than stereotypes. *Au contraire,* people who hold and act on stereotypes are seldom aware that they do so and are insidiously affected by them. People who create and respond to caricatures are aware that they are exaggerations and generally enjoy them. Therefore, it is probably healthy that women and men sometimes laugh at not only one another's friendships but their own as well—as when comedienne Rita Rudner described her husband's response to her plea that he get in touch with his feminine side. "I tried," he said, "but she was always on the phone talking to her friend." Lewis (1960) opined that "No one ever really appreciated the other sex—just as no one really appreciates children or animals—without at times feeling them to be funny. For, indeed, both sexes are" (p. 111).

Granted, the goal of our research is to arrive at increasingly valid insights into sex differences and similarities in friendship. But our increased understanding is unlikely to make whatever differences exist disappear or make them seem any less funny. So perhaps we should expect healthy laughter. Although women and men laugh at their own and each other's friendships, with hope our increased understanding will keep us from taking our laughter too seriously.

REFERENCES

Adams, R. G., & Blieszner, R. (1994). An integrative conceptual framework for friendship research. *Journal of Social and Personal Relationships, 11*, 163–184.

Aries, E. J., & Johnson, F. L. (1983). Close friendships in adulthood: Conversational content between same-sex friends. *Sex Roles, 9*, 1183–1196.

Ashton, N. L. (1980). Exploratory investigation of perceptions of influences on best-friend relationships. *Perceptual and Motor Skills, 50*, 379–386.

Aukett, R., Ritchie, J., & Mill, K. (1988). Gender differences in friendship patterns. *Sex Roles, 19*, 57–66.

Bakan, D. (1966). *The duality of human existence.* Boston: Beacon.

Barth, R. J., & Kinder, B. N. (1988). A theoretical analysis of sex differences in same-sex friendships. *Sex Roles, 19*, 349–363.

Bell, R. R. (1981a). *Worlds of friendship.* Beverly Hills, CA: Sage.

Bell, R. R. (1981b). Friendships of women and men. *Psychology of Women Quarterly, 5*, 402–417.

Berman, J. J., Murphy-Berman, V., & Pachauri, A. (1988). Sex differences in friendship patterns in India and the United States. *Basic and Applied Social Psychology, 9*, 61–71.

Blieszner, R., & Adams, R. G. (1992). *Adult friendship.* Newbury Park, CA: Sage.

Block, J. D. (1980). *Friendship: How to give it, how to get it.* New York: Macmillan.

Booth, A. (1972). Sex and social participation. *American Sociological Review, 37*, 183–192.

Brehm, S. S. (1992). *Intimate relationships* (2nd ed.). New York: McGraw-Hill.

Caldwell, M. A., & Peplau, L. A. (1982). Sex differences in same-sex friendships. *Sex Roles, 8*, 721–732.

Candy-Gibbs, S. E. (1982, November). *The alleged inferiority of men's close relationships: An examination of sex differences in the elderly widowed.* Paper presented at the annual scientific meeting of the Gerontological Society of America, Boston.

Dindia, K., & Allen, M. (1992). Sex differences in self disclosure: A meta-analysis. *Psychological Bulletin, 112*, 106–124.

Dindia, K., Fitzpatrick, M. A., & Kenney, D. A. (1989, May). *Self disclosure in spouse and stranger interactions: A social relations analysis.* Paper presented at the annual convention of the International Communication Association, New Orleans, LA.

Duck, S., Rutt, D. J., Hurst, M. H., & Strejc, H. (1991). Some evident truths about everyday conversation: All communication is not created equal. *Human Communication Research, 18*, 228–267.

Duck, S., & Wright, P. H. (1993). Reexamining gender differences in friendship: A close look at two kinds of data. *Sex Roles, 28*, 709–727.

Fehr, B. A. (1996). *Friendship processes.* Newbury Park, CA: Sage.

Fischer, C. S., & Oliker, S. J. (1983). A research note on friendship, gender and the life cycle. *Social Forces, 62,* 124–133.

Furman, L. G. (1987). *Cross-gender friendships in the work place: Factors and components.* Unpublished doctoral dissertation, Fielding Institute.

Gouldner, H., & Strong, M. S. (1987). *Speaking of friendship: Middle-classwomen and their friends.* New York: Greenwood.

Hacker, H. M. (1981). Blabbermouths and clams: Sex differences in self-disclosures in same-sex and cross-sex dyads. *Psychology of Women Quarterly, 5,* 385–401.

Hays, R. B. (1984). The development and maintenance of friendship. *Journal of Social and Personal Relationships, 1,* 75–98.

Hays, R. B. (1985). A longitudinal study of friendship development. *Journal of Personality and Social Psychology, 48,* 909–924.

Hess, B. B. (1972). Friendship. In M. W. Riley, M. Johnson, & A. Foner (Eds.), *Aging and society* (pp. 357–393). New York: Russell Sage.

Huston, T. L., & Levinger, G. (1979). Interpersonal attraction and relationships. In M. R. Rosenszweig & L. W. Porter (Eds.), *Annual Review of psychology* (Vol. 29, pp. 115–156). Palo Alto, CA: Annual Reviews.

Johnson, F. L., & Aries, E. J. (1983a). The talk of women friends. *Women's Studies International Forum, 6,* 353–361.

Johnson, F. L., & Aries, E. J. (1983b). Conversational patterns among same-sex pairs of late-adolescent close friends. *Journal of Genetic Psychology, 142,* 225–238.

Lea, M. (1989). Factors underlying friendship: An analysis of responses to the Acquaintance Description Form in relation to Wright's friendship model. *Journal of Social and Personal Relationships, 6,* 275–292.

Lewis, C. S. (1960). *Four loves.* New York: Harcourt Brace.

McAdams, D. P., Healy, S., & Kraus, S. (1985). Social motives and patterns of friendship. *Journal of Personality and Social Psychology, 47,* 828–838.

Monsour, M. (1992). Meanings of intimacy in cross- and same-sex friendships. *Journal of Social and Personal Relationships, 9,* 277–295.

Narus, L. R., & Fischer, J. L. (1982). Strong but not silent: Reexamination of expressivity of the relationships of men. *Sex Roles, 8,* 159–168.

Paine, R. (1974). An exploratory analysis in "middle-class" culture. In E. Leyton (Ed.), *The compact: Selected dimensions of friendship* (pp. 117–137). St. John's NFLD: Institute for Social and Economic Research.

Parker, S., & de Vries, B. (1993). Patterns of friendship for women and men in same- and cross-sex friendships. *Journal of Social and Personal Relationships, 10,* 617–626.

Pukalos, J. (1989). Young adult relationships: Siblings and friends. *Journal of Psychology, 123,* 237–244.

Reis, H. T. (1986). Gender effects in social participation: Intimacy, loneliness, and the conduct of social interaction. In R. Gilmour & S. Duck (Eds.), *The emerging field of personal relationships* (pp. 91–105). Hillsdale, NJ: Lawrence Erlbaum Associates.

Reis, H. T., Senchak, M., & Solomon, B. (1985). Sex differences in intimacy of social interaction: Further examination of potential explanations. *Journal of Personality and Social Psychology, 48,* 1204–1217.

Reisman, J. M. (1981). Adult friendships. In S. Duck & R. Gilmour (Eds.), *Personal relationships: Vol. 2. Developing personal relationships* (pp. 205–230). London: Sage.

Reisman, J. M. (1990). Intimacy in same-sex friendships. *Sex Roles, 23,* 65–82.

Sapadin, L. A. (1988). Friendship and gender: Perspectives of professional men and women. *Journal of Social and Personal Relationships, 5,* 387–403.

Sherrod, D. (1989). The influence of gender on same-sex friendships. In C. Hendrick (Ed.), *Review of personality and social psychology: Vol. 10. Close relationships* (pp. 164–186). Newbury Park, CA: Sage.

Suttles, G. D. (1970). Friendship as a social institution. In G. J. McCall (Ed.), *Social relationships* (pp. 95–135). Chicago: Aldine.

Tesch, S. A., & Martin, R. R. (1983). Friendship concepts of young adults in two age groups. *Journal of Psychology, 115,* 7–12.

Uhl, S. (1991). Forbidden friends: Cultural veils of female friendship in Andalusia. *American Ethnologist, 18,* 90–105.

Walker, K. (1994). Men, women, and friendship: What they say, what they do. *Gender and Society, 8,* 246–265.

Wall, S. M., Pickert, S. M., & Paradise, L. V. (1984). American men's friendships: Self-reports on meanings and changes. *Journal of Psychology, 116,* 179–186.

Weiss, L., & Lowenthal, M. F. (1975). Life-course perspective on friendship. In M. Thurnher & D. Chiraboga (Eds.), *Four stages of life* (pp. 48–61). San Francisco: Jossey-Bass.

Wheeler, L., Reis, H. T., & Bond, M. H. (1989). Collectivism-individualism in everyday social life: The middle kingdom and the melting pot. *Journal of Personality and Social Psychology, 57,* 79–86.

Winstead, B. A. (1986). Sex differences in same-sex friendships. In V. J. Derlega & B. A. Winstead (Eds.), *Friendship and social interaction* (pp. 81–97). New York: Springer-Verlag.

Wood, J. T. (1994). *Gendered lives: Communication, gender and culture.* Belmont, CA: Wadsworth.

Wood, J. T., & Inman, C. C. (1993). In a different mode: Masculine styles of communicating closeness. *Journal of Applied Communication Research, 21,* 279–295.

Wright, P. H. (1978). Toward a theory of friendship based on a conception of self. *Human Communication Research, 4,* 196–207.

Wright, P. H. (1982a). Men's friendships, women's friendships and the alleged inferiority of the latter. *Sex Roles, 8,* 1–20.

Wright, P. H. (1982b, February). *The development and selected applications of a conceptual and measurement model of friendship.* Paper presented at the Texas Tech University Conference on Families and Close Relationships, Lubbock, TX.

Wright, P. H. (1985). The Acquaintance Description Form. In S. Duck & D. Perlman (Eds.), *Understanding personal relationships: An interdisciplinary approach* (pp. 39–62). London: Sage.

Wright, P. H. (1988). Interpreting research on gender differences in friendship: A case for moderation and a plea for caution. *Journal of Social and Personal Relationships, 5,* 367–373.

Wright, P. H. (1989). Gender differences in adults' same- and cross-gender friendships. In R. G. Adams & R. Blieszner (Eds.), *Older adult friendships: Structure and process* (pp. 197–221). Newbury Park, CA: Sage.

Wright, P. H. (1995). Friendship. In D. Levinson (Ed.), *Encyclopedia of marriage and the family* (Vol. 1, pp. 315 320). New York: Macmillan.

Wright, P. H., & Scanlon, M. B. (1991). Gender role orientations and friendship: Some attenuation but gender differences abound. *Sex Roles, 24,* 551–566.

Chapter 3

Gender Differences in Interaction: A Reexamination

Elizabeth Aries
Amherst College

The study of gender differences in interaction has drawn the attention of numerous researchers from the disciplines of psychology, sociology, linguistics, communication, women's studies, and organizational behavior. Across a wide variety of subject populations, interaction settings, and research methodologies, researchers typically report that men are more likely than women to emerge as leaders, to be directive and hierarchical, to dominate in groups by talking more and interrupting more, and to be oriented toward solving problems. In contrast, women are found to be more expressive, supportive, facilitative, egalitarian, and cooperative than men, and to focus more on relationships and share more personally with others (Aries, 1987, 1996).

By taking a different perspective on these data, however, these well-established truths about men and women in interaction may be called into question. The prevailing picture that has emerged is based on the fact that we have not paid careful attention to five important questions:

1. Do our stereotypes describe most men and women or only selected samples of men and women?
2. What is the magnitude of the differences we have found?
3. To what extent does the appearance of gender differences depend on the situational context?
4. Are the gender differences we have found attributable to other variables that co-vary with gender like status and social roles?

5. To what extent are gender differences in conversation due to stereotype effects?

If we reframe our thinking around these five questions, we come to see
that knowledge of a person's gender gives us little ability to make an
accurate prediction about how a person will behave and that variables that
co-vary with gender may be responsible for many of the gender differences
observed.

RELIANCE ON WHITE MIDDLE-CLASS SAMPLES

Research findings regarding sex differences in interaction are based primarily on White middle-class samples. What we have taken to be the characteristics of men and women in interaction may pertain only to the
selected samples we have studied. Neither men nor women form homoge-
nous groups. Members of the same sex differ from one another in age,
race, ethnicity, social class, sexual orientation, variables that affect self-defi-
nition, and patterns of interaction. Because we have based our findings
on men and women who are White and middle class, we have exaggerated
the coherence within male and female styles of communication and failed
to appreciate the extent to which members of the same sex differ, thereby
making comparisons between men and women problematic.

The extension of research to diverse subject populations has already
begun to challenge the accuracy of traditional gender stereotypes. Sex role
prescriptions that hold for mainstream Americans may not be identical
for minority groups (De Leon, 1995). African-American subjects report
masculine characteristics (e.g., assertiveness, independence, self-reliance)
to be as desirable for women as for men (Harris, 1994). Black women
attribute more masculine traits to themselves than do White women (Binion, 1990; De Leon, 1995). Black women, in their capacity as wives, mothers,
providers, and heads of households, have had to exhibit more masculine
qualities to be successful in the performance of their multiple roles (De
Leon, 1995). When describing the communication style that characterized
their friendships with people of their own race, Black friends used terms
like *quick-tempered* and *confrontive*, whereas White participants' terms included *nonconfrontive*, *tactful*, and *withdrawn* (McCullough, 1987; cited in
Kramarae, 1990).

As we begin to pay attention to the differences that exist in communication styles among members of the same sex who differ in race, ethnicity,
class, or sexual orientation, the clarity of our conception of gender differences diminishes. What we see instead is that there may be multiple sex
role systems that differ in their prescriptions for the behavior of men and
women.

THE MAGNITUDE OF GENDER DIFFERENCES

One criterion that has been widely used to determine whether men and women differ is statistical significance. Several limitations exist to the use of statistical significance as the sole criterion for the interpretation of research evidence. A statistically significant difference may not be a large or substantial difference. When sample sizes are large, a small mean difference can be statistically significant (at $p < .05$).

To take a research example from the literature on role differentiation in mixed sex groups, Anderson and Blanchard (1982) examined the extent to which men and women differed in their focus on task behavior and the socioemotional aspects of interaction. They assessed the magnitude of the differences found in studies of gender and role differentiation and found that men on average were eight percentage points higher than women on the use of task behavior and women were eight percentage points higher than men on the use of positive socioemotional behavior. These differences were statistically significant yet small in magnitude. We describe men as task-oriented and women as socioemotional in orientation when in fact both devote the majority of their behavior to the task and the difference in their behavior is not even moderate (see also Wright, chap. 2, this volume). We have tended to overlook the considerable overlap between the behavior of men and women and to misrepresent small differences as mutually exclusive.

Researchers have begun to look to other criteria to assess research findings, such as the percentage of variance in behavior that can be accounted for or explained by knowledge of a person's sex. Sex generally accounts for less than 10% of the variance in social behavior and typically less than 5% (Canary & Hause, 1993; Eagly, 1987; Hyde & Linn, 1986). For example, in a study of interruptions, Natale, Entin, and Jaffe (1979) found that in dyads the speaking time of the conversational partner predicted 63% of the variance in interruptions, whereas the sex of the speaker accounted for only 7% of the variance. Thus, to make an accurate prediction of how frequently a person will interrupt, knowledge of the speaker's sex has relatively little predictive value in comparison with other variables. As Unger (1990) argued, sex is not "particularly important in comparison to all the independent variables that influence any particular human behavior" (p. 115).

A related piece of information that can be used to assess research findings is the magnitude of the difference or the effect size (i.e., the degree to which gender differences are manifested). Effect size can be conceptualized in terms of how much overlap there is between the distributions for men and women: The smaller the overlap between the distributions for men and women, the larger the effect size. An effect size of 0, as measured by Cohen's d (Cohen, 1977), reflects a 100% overlap between the distributions of men and women. Cohen considers an effect of $d = .20$ to be small (with an 85% overlap between the distributions for men and women), an effect of $d = .50$ to be moderate (with a 67% overlap), and an effect of $d = .80$ to be large (with a 53% overlap). A small effect accounts for 1% of the variance in behavior, a medium effect for 6% of the variance, and a large effect 14% of the variance.

Effect sizes can be used to assess the results of single studies as well as whole domains of research through a statistical technique called *meta-analysis*. Meta-analysis enables researchers to combine effect sizes found in individual studies to assess the overall magnitude of effect size across all studies in a given area.

Let us review some of the effect sizes that have been found for meta-analyses carried out in the area of gender and communication. Dindia and Allen (1992) did a meta-analysis of self-disclosure covering 205 published studies and 51 dissertations. They found women to be more disclosing than men but the effect size to be small ($d = .18$). They concluded that, "Whether the magnitude of sex differences in self-disclosure is theoretically meaningful and practically important is debatable. . . . It's time to stop perpetuating the myth that there are large differences in men's and women's self-disclosure" (p. 118).

Two meta-analyses have been carried out in the area of gender and leadership behavior. Eagly and Johnson (1990) carried out a meta-analysis of 162 studies of gender differences in leadership style. Male leaders did not differ from female leaders on task orientation ($d = .00$), nor did female leaders show more of an interpersonal orientation than male leaders ($d = .04$). Women showed a more democratic style than did men ($d = .22$) but the effect size was small. In this meta-analysis, gender differences were found in the laboratory studies but not the field studies. Eagly and Johnson concluded that the criteria used by organizations to select and socialize managers into their roles minimizes any tendencies that men and women might bring to lead or manage with distinctly different styles. Eagly and Karau conducted a meta-analysis of 58 studies of leadership emergence in mixed-sex, initially leaderless, task-oriented groups (Eagly & Karau, 1991). Men emerged more frequently than women when task leadership was assessed ($d = .41$) and women emerged more as leaders when social leadership was assessed ($d = -.18$).

Although there are numerous narrative reviews of the literature on gender differences in language, the magnitude of these differences has not been assessed. Initial analyses from a meta-analysis of gender and language, which aggregated results from studies using different language forms, revealed no consistent gender differences in language use (Smythe & Schlueter, 1989).

Thus, effect sizes found for gender differences in communication style range from *very small* to *moderate*, accounting for less than 6% of the variance in behavior at best and generally less than 1% of the variance in communication behavior. Canary and House's (1993) review of meta-analyses on sex differences in communication activities suggests that only 1% of variance is accounted for by sex. When we look beyond statistical significance and attend to effect size or percent of variance explained, the data suggest that the overlap in the behavior of men and women is considerable and that polarized depictions of interaction styles are not warranted.

THE SITUATIONAL CONTEXT OF INTERACTION

Gender differences are not manifested in all situational contexts. As Deaux and Major (1987) argued,

> Because perceivers, individual selves, and situations all vary in the content and salience of gender-linked expectations, we expect a wide range in observed female and male behaviors, from virtual identity of the sexes in some circumstances to striking differences in others. (p. 382)

A review of the literature on gender differences in interaction reveals that the appearance of gender differences is inconsistent from one study to the next. In a review of the literature on interruptions, James and Clarke (1993) reported that in the majority of studies no significant sex differences were found. In an analysis of 64 data sets looking at power and prestige in mixed-sex task groups, Lockheed (1985) found that 70% showed more male activity, influence, or leadership; 17% showed no gender difference; and 12.5% favored women. In a review of sex differences in amount of talk, James and Drakich (1993) found men to talk more in 43% of the studies, no gender differences in 28.6% of the studies, 27% of the studies to have equivocal results, and women to talk more than men in 3.6% of studies. In a review of 28 studies of task behavior, Wheelan and Verdi (1992) found men to be more task-oriented than women in 19 studies, whereas 9 studies showed no sex difference. In their review of 20 studies of socioemotional behavior, Wheelan and Verdi also found that 16 reported women to be higher than men and 4 reported no sex difference.

Although many studies find gender differences that fit the stereotypes, numerous studies report no gender differences and some report findings in the opposite direction. We may not even be aware of all the findings of no gender difference for two reasons. Findings of no difference are often considered to be unworthy of publication. In addition, in studies that use multiple dependent variables, the lack of gender differences on many of those variables is rarely cited by later reviewers while only the few significant differences are highlighted.

We must look to the situational context of the interaction in each study to explain why it is that gender differences are manifested in some studies but not in others. How people behave depends on such moderating variables as the demands of the task, the length of the interaction, the sex composition of the group, and the relationship between the participants—variables that may affect the salience of gender-linked expectations for behavior.

Task

If tasks draw on roles, interests, or expertise assumed to be more typically acquired by men, men are more likely to show higher levels of task activity than women in groups (Aries, 1996). For instance, when the task was taken into consideration in Eagly and Karau's (1991) meta-analysis of gender and leadership emergence, men were found to be much more likely to emerge as leaders in initially leaderless task groups when tasks were masculine ($d = .79$) than when tasks were feminine ($d = .26$) or when tasks required greater social complexity (e.g., interpersonal problem solving, extensive sharing of ideas, negotiation; $d = .23$).

Women are found to be more self-disclosing to same-sex partners than are men (Dindia & Allen, 1992; Hill & Stull, 1987). However, whether men are disclosing depends on the context. When men and women were asked to bring a same-sex best friend to the laboratory to have an intimate conversation and reveal thoughts and feelings, no gender differences were found in self-disclosure (Reis, Senchak, & Solomon, 1985). Thus, when self-disclosure was legitimized between men, their behavior was similar to that of women.

Length of the Interaction

Gender differences tend to be greater in groups that are engaged in brief or one-time encounters than in groups that meet over time. As members get to know the relative task-relevant competencies and attributes of other members, sex becomes less important as a determinant of behavior. Because so many of our studies involve short encounters, the tendency for men to emerge as leaders has been exaggerated. The meta-analysis of gender and leadership emergence by Eagly and Karau (1991) shows that men were more likely to emerge as leaders when groups lasted less than 20 minutes ($d = .58$) than when interaction lasted more than a single session ($d = .09$). In their review of the literature on gender and role differentiation, Wheelan and Verdi (1992) found few studies of groups that met for extended periods. In their own study of a 4-day group relations conference, Wheelan and Verdi found that gender differences emerged initially in expressive and goal-directed activity but these differences disappeared over time.

Sex Composition of the Speakers

Another factor that affects the expression of gender differences is the sex composition of the speakers. In many cases, gender differences have been found to be greater in single-sex than in mixed-sex interaction (Aries, 1996). The sex of one's conversational partner has been found to affect the amount a person is willing to disclose. The highest levels of self-disclosure are found to occur between women and the lowest between men, whereas cross-sex disclosure falls between the two. Meta-analytic findings reveal gender differences in self-disclosure to be greater in single-sex ($d = .31$) than in mixed-sex interaction ($d = .08$; Dindia & Allen, 1992). Men's lower level of disclosure to other men does not mean that men cannot be self-disclosing; rather, men may be more likely to choose women as the target for their disclosures. Indeed, Dindia and Allen found equal disclosure to men by men and women ($d = 0.00$).

When comparisons are made of all-male and all-female groups, men are found to place a greater emphasis on displays of dominance (Aries, 1976; Ellis, 1982; Miller, 1985). However, men are found to place less emphasis on dominance in their interactions with women than with other men (Aries, 1976; McCarrick, Manderscheid, & Silbergeld, 1981).

The sex composition of the group has been found to affect leadership behavior. In studies of dominance and leadership behavior involving interaction with strangers, women who are high in dominance assumed leadership over women low in dominance but not over men low in dominance (Carbonell, 1984; Davis & Gilbert, 1989; Megargee, 1969; Nyquist & Spence, 1986). Leadership is associated with masculinity and women are aware of gender-linked expectations for their behavior, making them reluctant to assume overt leadership over men. Some evidence suggests that women use more qualifications of speech in mixed-sex task groups than in single-sex groups (Carli, 1990; McMillan, Clifton, McGrath, & Gale, 1977). Carli found that women in mixed-sex dyads who prefaced remarks with such phrases as, "I'm no expert, I may be wrong," frequently had greater influence over their male partners. Thus, women may adopt stereotypic deferent behavior with men to be effective.

It can be seen from these studies that men and women do not display a single style of interaction; interaction style varies with the social context. Situations place different pressures on individuals to display gender-stereotypic behavior (Deaux & Major, 1987). Contextual variables play an important role in determining the magnitude of gender differences found in our studies.

STATUS AND SOCIAL ROLES

For decades, feminists have argued that the differences attributed to gender can be accounted for by differences in social roles and social status (Henley, 1973–1974, 1977; Kramarae, 1981; Spender, 1980; Thorne & Henley, 1975; Unger, 1976, 1979). Despite the profound social change that has occurred in American society in the past 25 years, men and women are still positioned differently in society: Men hold more power and status than women. Women have indeed entered the labor force in greater numbers, but they are still paid less for the same work and on average hold jobs with lower status than men.

A great deal of evidence demonstrates that the dominance and leadership attributed to men is displayed more often by high-status than low-status individuals; when status is controlled for, sex differences are diminished. For example, in a study of dominance displayed at work, dominance was predicted by participants' social roles. Less dominance was displayed toward coworkers and supervisors than toward people being supervised (Moskowitz, Jung Suh, & Desaulniers, 1994). However, dominance was not predicted by the sex of the participant. High-status and powerful individuals have been found to interrupt more than low-status, less powerful individuals (Eakins & Eakins, 1983; Greif, 1980; Kollock, Blumstein, & Schwartz, 1985; West & Zimmerman, 1977; Woods, 1988). In discussions among intimate heterosexual couples, speaking time was related to the amount of power each person held in the relationship in decision making. The more powerful person spoke more in discussions. When men and women enjoy equal power, men do not speak significantly more than their female partners in discussions (Kollock et al., 1985). When men and women are placed in equal status positions, sex differences are reduced. When dominance and leadership are legitimized for women in organizational settings, the behavior of male and female leaders is quite similar (Eagly & Johnson, 1990).

Similarly, many of the characteristics attributed to women—interpersonal sensitivity, politeness, use of "women's language" (e.g., tag questions, qualifications of speech), and so on—are found more often in low-status than in high-status individuals. In two studies of interaction in dyads in which one person was the leader and the other the follower, subordinates showed more sensitivity to the way the leader felt about them than the leader showed to the subordinate's feeling; but there were no gender differences (Snodgrass, 1985, 1992). People who hold power show less politeness than do those with low power (McLachlan, 1991). People mitigate their requests when speaking to superiors (Baxter, 1984; P. Johnson, 1976; Sagrestano, 1992; Steil & Hillman, 1993). "Women's language" appears to be used more frequently by people who are unemployed, housewives, or hold lower status jobs than by well-educated and professional people (O'Barr & Atkins, 1980). Subordinates have shown higher rates of speech associated with women than managers (C. Johnson, 1994). Risman (1987) found that the behavior of men who were single fathers and had primary responsibility for the care of young children was more similar to the behavior of working or single mothers than it was to married fathers. Men are capable of providing nurturance and do so when placed in the traditionally female role.

We have not always given sufficient attention to the importance of social, political, and economic contexts in examining gender differences. The gender differences we observe are produced in a context in which men hold positions of power over women. Many have argued that gender is not simply a matter of difference but must be understood as a matter of power and dominance (Henley, 1977; Kramarae, 1981; Spender, 1980; Thorne & Henley, 1975; Torres, 1992). Our reliance on laboratory studies masks the effect of these variables by taking people out of their current roles and context. When status and social roles are built into our studies as independent variables along with gender, gender differences are mitigated.

STEREOTYPE EFFECTS AND SELF-FULFILLING PROPHECIES

In interaction, we immediately recognize the sex of our conversational partners based on discernable visible cues. To the extent that we hold stereotyped beliefs about men and women, these beliefs can lead us to differential expectations about how people will behave based on their sex and can cause us to perceive gender differences even when they are not present (Aries, 1996).

Broad consensus has existed about the characteristics presumed to be typical of each sex. Men are described as leaders—as dominant, aggressive, independent, and competitive. Women are described as emotional, subjective, and aware of the feelings of others (Broverman, Vogel, Broverman, Clarkson, & Rosenkrantz, 1972). These stereotypes have remained relatively stable over the past 20 years (Bergen & Williams, 1991; Werner & LaRussa, 1985). Male speakers are believed to be louder, more forceful, dominating, and aggressive, whereas female speakers are believed to be more friendly, open, self-revealing, emotional, and polite, and to show more concern for the listener (Kramer, 1977). Women (vs. men) are thought to use more indirect influence strategies (Johnson, 1976) and more tag questions

(Siegler & Siegler, 1976), whereas men are thought to interrupt more than women (Hawkins, 1988).

Stereotypes are probably not always accurate depictions of group members. Research shows that Black American and Puerto-Rican women attribute more masculine characteristics to themselves than do White women, and the former do not fit traditional stereotypes of femininity (Binion, 1990; De Leon, 1995). In a similar manner, men are perceived as leaders. Yet in a test of the accuracy of people's beliefs, Swim (1994) found the perceived effect size for leadership emergence by men to be quite large ($d = 1.04$), whereas actual meta-analytic findings were much smaller ($d = .49$). Women are believed to use tag questions more than men do, but women have not consistently been found to do so (Aries, 1996).

Studies show that even when men and women behave in an identical manner they may be perceived differently. Listeners bend their perceptions in the direction of expectation. When participants heard tape recordings of conversations in which male and female speakers used tag questions and qualifiers equally, women were perceived to use these speech forms more frequently than were men (Newcombe & Arnkoff, 1979). When participants read transcripts of speech believed to be spoken by a woman, speech was rated higher on aesthetic quality (pleasing, nice, sweet, and beautiful); when speech was believed to be spoken by a man, it was rated higher on dynamism (strong, active, aggressive, and loud; Mulac, Incontro, & James, 1985). This occurred regardless of whether the actual speaker from whom the transcript was based was male or female or whether there were actual speech differences. In a follow-up study, when participants believed a speaker to be male they rated speakers higher on dynamism than if the speaker was believed to be female, but the effect held for only two out of four conversations (Lawrence, Stucky, & Hopper, 1990). Thus, stereotype effects, like gender differences, may be evoked to different degrees depending on specific speakers or specific conversational contexts.

Male and female speakers may not only be perceived differently, but they may be evaluated differently when displaying identical behavior. Bradley (1981) observed 24 experimental groups with a male or female confederate in each who posed as a subject. The confederates were instructed to argue a position contrary to the other group members. Half the confederates advanced their cases without proof while the other half advanced arguments by giving evidence and factual data. Half the confederates in each condition used tag questions and disclaimers and half did not. Women who advanced arguments without support were evaluated as less intelligent, knowledgeable, and influential than men who argued without support. Women who used tag questions and disclaimers were rated as less intelligent and knowledgeable than men who used these speech forms. Whether men used tag questions or disclaimers hardly affected their ratings, whereas women were perceived as less intelligent and knowledge-able when they used tag questions and disclaimers. Thus, the sex of the speaker contributes to the impression the speaker makes beyond actual behavior differences, if any. Similarly, women who used forceful language in job interviews were seen as more aggressive than men who used similar language (Wiley & Eskilson, 1985).

In a meta-analysis of 61 studies of gender and the evaluation of leaders, Eagly, Makhijani, and Klonsky (1992) found a small tendency for female leaders to be evaluated less favorably than male leaders ($d = .05$), but the effect was more pronounced for leaders using an autocratic style ($d = .30$). The further women departed from sex role expectations the more nega-tively they were evaluated. Women are caught in a double bind: When they use behavior associated with women, they are perceived as lacking in instrumental competency; when they use behavior associated with men, they are seen as aggressive.

Two theories put forth to account for gender differences in interaction emphasize the importance of stereotypes in shaping these differences. The theory of status characteristics and expectation states holds that when direct information about the relative competency of group members is not avail-able, members will rely on external status to form expectations (Berger, Cohen, & Zelditch, 1972; Berger, Fisek, Norman, & Zelditch, 1977). Higher expectations will be formed for men because of their higher status in society and these expectations will become self-fulfilling prophecies for behavior. Men will be given more opportunities to participate and their contributions will be more highly valued. Research shows that when no expectations are given about the competency of group members, men are believed to be more competent than women. These gender differences are reduced when women are believed to possess more task-related com-petency than men (Pugh & Wahrman, 1983, 1985; Wood & Karten, 1986).

Social role theory contends that because men and women are assigned to different roles in work and in the family, men and women will be expected to possess different characteristics that suit them for those roles. Men will be expected to be more agentic and task-oriented, women to be more communal and emotionally expressive in accordance with their social roles (Eagly, 1987). These expectations furnish guidelines for how men and women should behave; people are expected to behave in a manner consistent with their roles.

Thus, gender stereotypes have both a descriptive and a prescriptive component. They indicate what group members are like, but also what group members *should* be like—that is, what behavior is appropriate for members of the group. People do not necessarily perform gender-related behaviors because they are internalized in personality. Eagly (1987) con-tended that,

People often conform to gender-role norms that are *not* internalized, because of the considerable power that groups and individuals supportive of these norms have to influence others' behavior through rewards and punishments of both subtle (e.g., nonverbal cues) or more obvious (e.g., monetary incentive, sexually harassing behavior) varieties. (p. 19)

As both expectations states theory and social role theory predict, gender stereotypes have the power to become self-fulfilling prophecies for behavior. In a study of West Point cadets, Rice, Bender, and Vitters (1980) demonstrated that the attitudes that group members held about women's roles could affect the behavior of women leaders. In all-male groups where members held liberal attitudes toward women, women leaders initiated more structure and played a more important role than they did in groups where men held traditional attitudes toward women's roles. Thus, men's attitudes toward women were reflected in their behavior toward women, which in turn affected the ability of those women to be effective leaders.

In summary, research shows that gender stereotypes play an important role in setting expectations for our own behavior and that of others. Stereotypes dictate what we notice. They may cause us to see gender differences even when they are not present and to respond differently to individuals on the basis of sex. Gender stereotypes also have the power to become self-fulfilling prophecies for behavior. However, it is important to note that stereotype effects are evoked to a different degree depending on the situational context and are most pronounced when gender is a salient issue in an interaction (Aries, 1996). Gender stereotypes have a larger impact in shaping the expectations and perceptions of speakers in initial encounters when more personal information about participants is not yet available. The magnitude of gender stereotypes has not been assessed. Like gender effects, it is likely that stereotype effects are statistically significant but not large.

CONCLUSIONS

A review of the research on conversational interaction reveals many gender differences. A polarized depiction of men and women has emerged from these findings that has been widely popularized by best sellers such as Tannen's (1990) *You Just Don't Understand: Women and Men in Conversation* and Gray's (1992) *Men Are From Mars, Women Are From Venus.* Gray went so far as to claim, "Not only do men and women communicate differently but they think, feel, perceive, react, respond, love, need, and appreciate differently. They almost seem to be from different planets, speaking different languages" (p. 5).

The research evidence, however, permits multiple interpretations. We have tended to focus on men and women as groups, overlooking individual differences between members of the same sex. The findings for samples that are not White and not middle-class do not always support popular stereotypes. We have tended to polarize differences misrepresenting small differences as mutually exclusive. We have failed to pay sufficient attention to situational variability in behavior—to the fact that gender differences do not appear consistently across situational contexts and are not found in many studies. We have overlooked the importance of social roles, status, and gender stereotypes as alternative explanations for gender differences.

Those who take an essentialist position have argued that the differential socialization of men and women leads to the development of contrasting styles of communication. Women learn to be polite and expressive and to assume an interpersonal orientation, whereas men learn to be assertive and direct. These differences need not be biologically based, but they are assumed to reside within the individual. However, the data reviewed in this chapter suggest that we must move beyond the essentialist model to explain why there is so much within-gender variability, why the appearance of gender differences in interaction is situationally variable, why no gender differences are found in many contexts, and why people use behaviors associated with the opposite sex in certain roles and contexts. We can only begin to make an accurate prediction of the particular behaviors speakers will choose if we know something about their role and status, the type of conversation in which they are engaged, their conversational partners, and the goals they are trying to achieve. Knowledge of the speaker's sex will give us little predictive power.

Many researchers are beginning to move toward an understanding of gender as something that people do in social interaction (West & Zimmerman, 1987). West and Zimmerman argued that, "A person's gender is not simply an aspect of what one is, but, more fundamentally, it is something that one *does*, and does recurrently, in interaction with others" (p. 140). The display of feminine or masculine behavior depends on the situational context. As Bohan (1993) contended, "Thus, none of us is feminine or is masculine or fails to be either of those. In particular contexts, people do feminine; in others, they do masculine" (p. 13).

We need to move beyond the conception that the interaction styles of men and women reside within individuals. We should return gender to its larger social context, taking into consideration other social forces that shape the expression of gendered behavior. We must weigh carefully how we choose to understand the gender differences we have found as well as how much importance we choose to give to these gender differences. Our construction of polarized conceptions of men and women in interaction helps sustain current realities and keep inequalities in place.

REFERENCES

Anderson, L. R., & Blanchard, P. N. (1982). Sex differences in task and social-emotional behavior. *Basic and Applied Social Psychology, 3*(2), 109–139.

Aries, E. (1976). Interaction patterns and themes of male, female, and mixed groups. *Small Group Behavior, 7*(1), 7–18.

Aries, E. (1987). Gender and communication. In P. Shaver & C. Hendrick (Eds.), *Sex and gender* (pp. 149–176). Newbury Park, CA: Sage.

Aries, E. (1996). *Men and women in interaction: Reconsidering the differences.* New York: Oxford University Press.

Baxter, L. A. (1984). An investigation of compliance-gaining as politeness. *Human Communication Research, 10*(3), 427–456.

Bergen, D. J., & Williams, J. E. (1991). Sex stereotypes in the United States revisited: 1972–1988. *Sex Roles, 24*(7/8), 413–423.

Berger, J., Cohen, B. P., & Zelditch, M. (1972). Status characteristics and social interaction. *American Sociological Review, 37*, 241–255.

Berger, J., Fisek, M. H., Norman, R. Z., & Zelditch, M. (1977). *Status characteristics and social interaction.* New York: Elsevier.

Binion, V. J. (1990). Psychological androgyny: A Black female perspective. *Sex Roles, 22*(7/8), 487–507.

Bohan, J. S. (1993). Regarding gender: Essentialism, constructionism, and feminist psychology. *Psychology of Women Quarterly, 17*, 5–21.

Bradley, P. H. (1981). The folk-linguistics of women's speech: An empirical examination. *Communication Monographs, 48*, 73–90.

Broverman, I. K., Vogel, S. R., Broverman, D. M., Clarkson, F. E., & Rosenkrantz, P. S. (1972). Sex-role stereotypes: A current appraisal. *Journal of Social Issues, 28*, 59–78.

Canary, D. J., & Hause, K. S. (1993). Is there any reason to research sex differences in communication? *Communication Quarterly, 41*(2), 129–144.

Carbonell, J. L. (1984). Sex roles and leadership revisited. *Journal of Applied Psychology, 69*, 44–49.

Carli, L. (1990). Gender, language, and influence. *Journal of Personality and Social Psychology, 59*(5), 941–951.

Cohen, J. (1977). *Statistical power analysis for the behavioral sciences.* New York: Academic Press.

Davis, B. M., & Gilbert, L. A. (1989). Effect of dispositional and situational influences on women's dominance expression in mixed-sex dyads. *Journal of Personality and Social Psychology, 57*(2), 294–300.

Deaux, K., & Major, B. (1987). Putting gender into context: An interactive model of gender-related behavior. *Psychological Bulletin, 94*, 369–389.

De Leon, B. (1995). Sex role identity among college students: A cross-cultural analysis. In A.M. Padilla (Ed.), *Hispanic psychology: Critical issues in theory and research* (pp. 245–256). Thousand Oaks, CA: Sage.

Dindia, K., & Allen, M. (1992). Sex differences in self-disclosure: A meta-analysis. *Psychological Bulletin, 112*(1), 106–124.

Eagly, A. H. (1987). *Sex differences in social behavior: A social-role interpretation.* Hillsdale, NJ: Lawrence Erlbaum Associates.

Eagly, A. H., & Johnson, B. T. (1990). Gender and leadership style: A meta-analysis. *Psychological Bulletin, 108*(2), 233–256.

Eagly, A. H., & Karau, S. J. (1991). Gender and the emergence of leaders: A meta-analysis. *Journal of Personality and Social Psychology, 60*(5), 685–710.

Eagly, A. H., Makhijani, M. G., & Klonsky, B. G. (1992). Gender and the evaluation of leaders: A meta-analysis. *Psychological Bulletin, 111*(1), 3–22.

Eakins, B., & Eakins, R. G. (1983). Verbal turn-taking and exchanges in faculty dialogue. In B. L. Dubois & I. Crouch (Eds.), *Proceedings of the conference on the Sociology of the Languages of American Women* (pp. 53–62). San Antonio, TX: Trinity University Press.

Ellis, D. G. (1982). Relational stability and change in women's consciousness-raising groups. *Women's Studies in Communication, 5*, 77–87.

Gray, J. (1992). *Men are from Mars, women are from Venus: A practical guide to improving communication and getting what you want in your relationships*. New York: HarperCollins.

Greif, E. B. (1980). Sex differences in parent–child conversations. *Women's Studies International Quarterly, 3*, 253–258.

Harris, A. C. (1994). Ethnicity as a determinant of sex role identity: A replication study of item selection for the Bem Sex Role Inventory. *Sex Roles, 31*(3/4), 241–273.

Hawkins, K. (1988). Interruptions in task-oriented conversations: Effects of violations of expectations by males and females. *Women's Studies in Communication, 11*(2), 1–20.

Henley, N. (1973–1974). Power, sex, and nonverbal communication. *Berkeley Journal of Sociology, 18*, 1–26. Reprinted in B. Thorne & N. Henley (Eds.). (1975). *Language and sex: Difference and dominance* (pp. 184–203). Rowley, MA: Newbury House.

Henley, N. M. (1977). *Body politics: Power, sex and nonverbal communication*. Englewood Cliffs, NJ: Prentice-Hall.

Hill, C. T., & Stull, D. E. (1987). Gender and self-disclosure: Strategies for exploring the issues. In V. J. Derlega & J. H. Berg (Eds.), *Self-disclosure: Theory, research, and therapy* (pp. 81–100). New York: Plenum.

Hyde, J. S., & Linn, M. C. (Eds.). (1986). *The psychology of gender: Advances through meta-analysis*. Baltimore: Johns Hopkins University Press.

James, D., & Clarke, S. (1993). Women, men, and interruptions: A critical review. In D. Tannen (Ed.), *Gender and conversational interaction* (pp. 231–280). New York: Oxford University Press.

James, D., & Drakich, J. (1993). Understanding gender differences in amount of talk: A critical review. In D. Tannen (Ed.), *Gender and conversational interaction* (pp. 281–312). New York: Oxford University Press.

Johnson, C. (1994). Gender, legitimate authority, and leader-subordinate conversations. *American Sociological Review, 59*, 122–135.

Johnson, P. (1976). Women and power: Toward a theory of effectiveness. *Journal of Social Issues, 32*, 99–110.

Kollock, P., Blumstein, P., & Schwartz, P. (1985). Sex and power in interaction: Conversational privileges and duties. *American Sociological Review, 50*, 34–46.

Kramarae, C. (1981). *Men and women speaking*. Rowley, MA: Newbury House.

Kramarae, C. (1990). Changing the complexion of gender in language research. In H. Giles & W. P. Robinson (Eds.), *Handbook of language and social psychology* (pp. 345–361). Chichester, England: Wiley.

Kramer, C. (1977). Perceptions of female and male speech. *Language and Speech, 20*, 151–161.

Lawrence, S. G., Stucky, N. P., & Hopper, R. (1990). The effects of sex dialects and sex stereotypes on speech evaluations. *Journal of Language and Social Psychology, 9*(3), 209–224.

Lockheed, M. E. (1985). Sex and social influence: A meta-analysis guided by theory. In J. Berger & M. Zelditch (Eds.), *Status, rewards and influence* (pp. 406–429). San Francisco: Jossey-Bass.

McCarrick, A. K., Manderscheid, R. W., & Silbergeld, S. (1981). Gender differences in competition and dominance during married-couples group therapy. *Social Psychology Quarterly, 44*(3), 164–177.

McLachlan, A. (1991). The effects of agreement, disagreement, gender and familiarity on patterns of dyadic interaction. *Journal of Language and Social Psychology, 10*(3), 205–212.

McMillan, J. R., Clifton, A. K., McGrath, D., & Gale, W. S. (1977). Women's language: Uncertainty or interpersonal sensitivity and emotionality. *Sex Roles, 3*(6), 545–559.

Megargee, E. I. (1969). Influence of sex roles on the manifestation of leadership. *Journal of Applied Psychology, 53*(5), 377–382.

Miller, J. B. (1985). Patterns of control in same-sex conversations: Differences between women and men. *Women's Studies in Communication, 8,* 62–69.

Moskowitz, D. S., Jung Suh, E., & Desaulniers, J. (1994). Situational influences on gender differences in agency and communion. *Journal of Personality and Social Psychology, 66*(4), 753–761.

Mulac, A., Incontro, C. R., & James, M. R. (1985). Comparison of the gender-linked language effect and sex role stereotypes. *Journal of Personality and Social Psychology, 49*(4), 1098–1109.

Natale, M., Entin, E., & Jaffe, J. (1979). Vocal interruptions in dyadic communication as a function of speech and social anxiety. *Journal of Personality and Social Psychology, 37*(6), 865–878.

Newcombe, N., & Arnkoff, D. B. (1979). Effects of speech style and sex of speaker on person perception. *Journal of Personality and Social Psychology, 37*(8), 1293–1303.

Nyquist, L., & Spence, J. T. (1986). Effects of dispositional dominance and sex role expectations on leadership behaviors. *Journal of Personality and Social Psychology, 50*(1), 87–93.

O'Barr, W., & Atkins, B. (1980). "Women's language" or "powerless language"? In S. McConnell-Ginet, R. Borker, & N. Furman (Eds.), *Women and language in literature and society* (pp. 93–110). New York: Praeger.

Pugh, M. D., & Wahrman, R. (1983). Neutralizing sexism in mixed-sex groups: Do women have to be better than men? *American Journal of Sociology, 88*(4), 746–762.

Pugh, M. D., & Wahrman, R. (1985). Inequality of influence in mixed-sex groups. In J. Berger & M. Zelditch (Eds.), *Status, rewards, and influence* (pp. 142–162). San Francisco: Jossey-Bass.

Reis, H. T., Senchak, M., & Solomon, B. (1985). Sex differences in the intimacy of social interaction: Further examination of potential explanations. *Journal of Personality and Social Psychology, 48*(5), 1204–1217.

Rice, R. W., Bender, L. R., & Vitters, A. G. (1980). Leader sex, follower attitudes toward women, and leadership effectiveness: A laboratory experiment. *Organizational Behavior and Human Performance, 25,* 46–78.

Risman, B. J. (1987). Intimate relationships from a micro-structural perspective: Men who mother. *Gender and Society, 1,* 6–32.

Sagrestano, L. (1992). Power strategies in interpersonal relationships. *Psychology of Women Quarterly, 16,* 481–495.

Siegler, D. M., & Siegler, R. S. (1976). Stereotypes of males' and females' speech. *Psychological Reports, 39,* 167–170.

Smythe, M., & Schlueter, D. W. (1989). Can we talk?? A meta-analytic review of the sex differences in language literature. In C. M. Lont & S. A. Friedley (Eds.), *Beyond boundaries: Sex and gender diversity in communication* (pp. 31–48). Fairfax, VA: George Mason University Press.

Snodgrass, S. E. (1985). Women's intuition: The effect of subordinate role on interpersonal sensitivity. *Journal of Personality and Social Psychology, 49*(1), 146–155.

Snodgrass, S. E. (1992). Further effects of role versus gender on interpersonal sensitivity. *Journal of Personality and Social Psychology, 62*(1), 154–158.

Spender, D. (1980). *Man made language.* London: Routledge & Kegan Paul.

Steil, J. M., & Hillman, J. L. (1993). The perceived value of direct and indirect influence strategies: A cross-cultural comparison. *Psychology of Women Quarterly, 17,* 457–462.

Swim, J. K. (1994). Perceived versus meta-analytic effect sizes: An assessment of the accuracy of gender stereotypes. *Journal of Personality and Social Psychology, 66*(1), 21–36.

Tannen, D. (1990). *You just don't understand: Women and men in conversation.* New York: William Morrow.

Thorne, B., & Henley, N. (1975). Difference and dominance: An overview of language, gender and society. In B. Thorne & N. Henley (Eds.), *Language and sex: Difference and dominance* (pp. 5–42). Rowley, MA: Newbury House.

Torres, L. (1992). Women and language: From sex differences to power dynamics. In C. Kramarae & D. Spender (Eds.), *The knowledge explosion: Generations of feminist scholarship* (pp. 281–290). New York: Teacher's College Press.

Unger, R. K. (1976). Male is greater than female: The socialization of status inequality. *Counseling Psychologist, 6*(2), 2–9.

Unger, R. K. (1979). *Female and male: Psychological perspectives.* New York: Harper & Row.

Unger, R. K. (1990). Imperfect reflections of reality: Psychology constructs gender. In R. T. Hare-Mustin & J. Marecek (Eds.), *Making a difference: Psychology and the construction of gender* (pp. 102–149). New Haven, CT: Yale University Press.

Werner, P. D., & LaRussa, G. W. (1985). Persistence and change in sex role stereotypes. *Sex Roles, 12*, 1089–1100.

West, C., & Zimmerman, D. H. (1977). Women's place in everyday talk: Reflections on parent–child interaction. *Social Problems, 24*, 521–529.

West, C., & Zimmerman, D. H. (1987). Doing gender. *Gender and Society, 1*(2), 125–151.

Wheelan, S. A., & Verdi, A. F. (1992). Differences in male and female patterns of communication in groups: A methodological artifact? *Sex Roles, 27*(1/2), 1–15.

Wiley, M. G., & Eskilson, A. (1985). Speech style, gender stereotypes and corporate success: What if women talk more like men? *Sex Roles, 12*(9/10), 993–1007.

Wood, W., & Karten, S. J. (1986). Sex differences in interaction style as a product of perceived sex differences in competence. *Journal of Personality and Social Psychology, 50*(2), 341–347.

Woods, N. (1988). Talking shop: Sex and status as determinants of floor apportionment in a work setting. In J. Coates & D. Cameron (Eds.), *Women in their speech communities: New perspectives on language and sex* (pp. 141–157). New York: Longman.

Chapter 4

Researching Sex Differences Within Sex Similarities: The Evolutionary Consequences of Reproductive Differences

Peter A. Andersen
San Diego State University

The popular media perpetuates the belief that men and women are from different planets. In his best-selling book, *Men Are From Mars, Women Are From Venus*, Gray (1992) promoted a metaphor that men, who are Martians, and women, who are Venusians, cannot communicate because of their different planetary origins. Dindia, in her opening dialogue in this volume, states that she would prefer to advocate books and seminars entitled "Men are from South Dakota, Women are from North Dakota." The actual research on sex differences has led to one major, overall conclusion: Men and women are far more similar than different. They are not from different metaphoric planets or cultures. They are all earthlings with goals, hopes, dreams, emotions, fears, and communication behaviors that are a whole lot more similar than they are different.

Of course, South Dakotans probably believe that North Dakotans are from another planet. From close range, differences are more obvious than similarities and they are certainly more newsworthy and sensational! From any vantage point other than Dakota, North and South Dakotans look pretty similar. This does not deny that differences exist between men and women. Some differences are due to societally induced sex roles and some are due to genetically conveyed biological differences between men and women.

This purpose of this chapter is to debunk two central myths about sex differences in social and communication behavior. The first myth is that substantial sex differences exist between men and women. The reality is that men and women are probably about 98% to 99% similar in most abilities, skills, and behaviors. The second myth is that these small differences between men and women have no biological basis. As demonstrated here, sex-linked biological differences do exist.

SEXUAL SIMILARITY IN COMMUNICATION

Hundreds of studies have examined sex differences in communication. Recent cumulative reviews and meta-analyses of this research suggest huge communicative similarities between men and women and relatively small differences. In their recent review of meta-analyses of over 1,200 studies of differences in communication, Canary and Hause (1993) concluded:

> The hundreds of studies represented in the meta-analyses indicate that sex differences in social interaction are small and inconsistent; that is about 1% of the variance is accounted for and these effects are moderated by other variables. Given this research, we should not expect to find substantial sex differences in communication. (p. 140)

The Canary and Hause summary includes meta-analyses of sex differences in self-disclosure, influencibility, conformity, helping behavior, leadership, aggression, verbal skill, competence, and group behavior. Although significant differences in communication between the sexes are observed, the differences are uniformly small or moderate, vary from study to study, and are influenced by other intervening variables. These studies, nicely summarized in the Canary and Hause article, are not reviewed here. Rather, this chapter provides some additional evidence that supports their conclusion.

In the early 1990s, Brenda Wilkins and I published a meta-analysis of gender differences and similarities in management communication with results highly consistent with those summarized by Canary and Hause (see Wilkins & Andersen, 1991). The results of 174 published tests of sex differences in managerial communication revealed significant sex effects that collectively accounted for less than one half of one percent (.05%) of the variance in communication behavior. In no subset of managerial communication behavior did sex differences account for 2% of the variance. Another way to conceptualize this finding is that there is about a 98% or greater probability that, based on communication behavior, you cannot tell a female manager from a male manager.

Another area not included in the Canary and Hause (1993) review concerns tactile communication behavior. In their comprehensive review of literature, Stier and Hall (1984) reported no overall tendency for men to touch women more than vice versa. The review did find that women engage in more same-gender touch than do men. Stier and Hall concluded: "In general touch in opposite-gender dyads did not appear to be strongly asymmetrical" (p. 456). Similarly, Hall and Veccia (1990) found that, over all ages and body parts, men touched women with the same frequency that women touched men. Similarly, Guerrero and Andersen (1994) reported that touch within male–female relational dyads in public places is almost completely symmetrical. Among all couples a .89 intradyadic correlation was observed for touch. For casual daters, the intradyadic correlation for touch was .81, for serious daters .88, and for married couples .98. These results suggest that, insofar as tactile behavior is concerned, men and women definitely inhabit the same planet.

BIOLOGY AND COMMUNICATION

Within the considerable similarities in communication between men and women, differences do exist. Years ago, Birdwhistell (1970) discussed primary sexual characteristics that relate to basic reproduction via ova or spermatozoa, secondary sexual characteristics that are anatomical, such as differences in body hair or muscle mass; and tertiary characteristics that represent patterned social behaviors that are learned and situationally produced.

Because reproductive or primary differences are the least amenable to change (even sex-change operations do not give the patient the ability to produce eggs or sperm) and least influenced by the sociocultural climate, the search for sex differences should begin there. As Halpern (1986) stated: "The different roles that men and women play in reproduction are incontrovertible" (p. 68). Because human beings have spent hundreds of thousands of years evolving as men and women, a fruitful place to search for the most stable differences in communication would be in behaviors most closely associated with reproductive roles.

The textbooks on sex (or gender) and communication could be characterized as being in biological denial. Not one book has a forthright discussion of genetic or biological differences in the communication behavior of men and women.

Unfortunately, there is considerable political pressure to avoid discussion of biologically based differences. In a recent *Newsweek* article, Begley (1995) provided the following account:

> When Raquel Gur gave a talk to M.D.–Ph.D. students in Illinois about sex differences in brains, a group of women asked her to stop publicizing the work: they were afraid women would lose 20 years of gains if word got out that the sexes weren't the same. (p. 51)

Suppressing such information, of course, only leads to outrageous claims that cannot be countered. Academics should not suppress findings that fail to meet current standards for political correctness. Realizing the political minefield that any author discussing this topic walks, I begin my discussion of biological differences with one of the most consistent differences in communication research: the superior social and nonverbal sensitivity of women.

SOCIAL AND NONVERBAL SENSITIVITY

Folk wisdom and a considerable body of current communication research indicates that women are more engaged, sensitive, and skilled communicators than are men. Although some of these differences no doubt emerge from differences in the socialization of men and women, these differences are too geographically, historically, and developmentally pervasive to be primarily social. Indeed, as Hall (1979) suggested, "If there is a key feature of women's mystique, it is probably some kind of special social sensitivity or social ability that they are believed to possess . . . detection of emotional cues is surely a part of what is called 'women's intuition' " (p. 32). Similarly, women are better able to express themselves particularly in the realms of emotional and nonverbal communication (see Burgoon, Buller, Grandpre, & Kalbfleisch, chap. 15; Guerrero & Reiter, chap. 14; Hall, chap. 7, this volume). As a male communication scholar, it is somewhat difficult to summarize this body of research without feeling a degree of envy for the communication skill and connection that women experience.

Studies have shown that women are better decoders and encoders of nonverbal and emotional communication (see Hall, chap. 7, this volume); they also have generally superior verbal skills that emerge in female infants (Collaer & Hines, 1995; Halpern, 1986), are more skillful and connected listeners (Ivy & Backlund, 1994; Tannen, 1990), and are more engaged, empathic communicators (see Pearson, West, & Turner, 1995). In the area of social sensitivity, and of nonverbal sensitivity in particular, women earn their deserved reputation for enhanced social skill and intuition (see Hall, chap. 7, this volume).

Differences in Nonverbal Sensitivity

One of the clearest and most consistent sex differences in communication concerns women's superior nonverbal receiving ability. Women's superior decoding ability is detected for people at a variety of ages and across numerous cultures (Knapp & Hall, 1992).

Some of the research has employed the Profile of Nonverbal Sensitivity (PONS; Rosenthal et al. 1979), a test with notoriously poor reliability (e.g., Buller & Aune, 1992). Despite the insensitivity of the PONS, it consistently reveals sex differences. Rosenthal et al. (1979) found that females have approximately a half standard deviation advantage in nonverbal sensitivity. This was true of the short PONS, the long PONS, and the still photo PONS, and it was relatively consistent across age. However, the size of the effect was slightly larger for grade school children, which suggests either early developmental or biological differences.

Rosenthal et al. (1979) pondered: "Are females biologically programmed to have or to develop superior nonverbal skill (perhaps because such skill enhances the survivability of offspring) or do female children develop superior skill as a result of social learning?" (p. 165). Rosenthal et al. did not take a position on this issue but cited research studies which have shown that for infants 1 to 3 days old, girls tended to cry more than boys in response to another infants' cries but not to other sounds, suggesting a biological difference. Additionally, Rosenthal and DePaulo (1979) reported meta-analytic research across 11 nations showing consistently higher scores for women on the PONS.

Meta-analyses of sex differences using a variety of measures of nonverbal sensitivity also demonstrate the superior skill of women in this domain. Hall (1978) summarized 75 studies on this topic and found 80% of them showed a female advantage. The effect size across all of the studies was moderate ($d = .40$) or slightly less than a half of a standard deviation. The combined probability of all of the studies was 3 in 10,000, suggesting chance can be ruled out as an explanation. Hall (1979) also showed that these results are stable across the decades when the study was conducted. Moreover, Hall (1978) showed no effect for the sex or age of the senders or the age of the receivers, suggesting this is a highly stable phenomenon. Given that other factors have so little impact on this phenomenon, biological forces would seem to be indicated. Hall (1979) concluded: "Even at the youngest ages tested, the female advantage is at least what it is among older groups. If females' advantage is learned it must be learned very early indeed" (p. 42).

Alternatives to a biological hypothesis seem somewhat implausible. It has been suggested that sex differences really reflect gender differences in sex role orientation. If so, the masculinity or femininity scores of individuals, regardless of biological sex, should better predict nonverbal sensitivity than does biological sex. This is not the case. Based on a meta-analysis of 11 studies that associated masculinity and femininity with nonverbal sensitivity, Hall (1979) concluded: "Overall the correlations of masculinity or femininity measured on unipolar scales with nonverbal decoding ability were small and nonsignificant" (p. 52). Greater femininity does not result in greater nonverbal sensitivity. Indeed, according to Hall (1979), when masculinity and femininity were partialed out, the effects for sex differences in decoding were not appreciably changed. In her commentary on Hall's results nearly 20 years ago, Weitz (1979) concluded:

> Hall says she does not wish to speak about the possible biological roots of what has been loosely termed "women's intuition," but perhaps it is time that we did speak of this factor. The difficulty of doing so without an excess of political baggage is the problem, but should not blind us to the need for discussion. (p. 135)

Unfortunately, political motivations have caused a collective denial of probable biological explanations.

Similarly, it has been frequently proffered that women are more socially sensitive because they live in an oppressive, patriarchal society where sensitivity to subtle cues is necessary for survival. No serious student of sex roles can deny that many women have lived and continue to live in an oppressive patriarchal society. But little support exists for the hypothesis that oppression causes sensitivity. Hall (1978) demonstrated that there is no age effect for sex differences in nonverbal sensitivity. She concluded, "That young girls should be better judges of nonverbal communication than young boys are is inconsistent with this hypothesis, unless one seriously believes that young girls as well as women are oppressed in our society" (p. 354). Early oppression of girls is, of course, a possibility but other evidence suggests that oppression is not linked to sensitivity. Hall (1979) reported results which show that when equalitarian attitude scales were correlated with nonverbal sensitivity no significant association was obtained for men. For women, equalitarianism was *positively* associated with nonverbal decoding. Hall summarized: "These positive correlations indicate that females with more equalitarian, 'liberated' views on women's role in society were better decoders than more conservative females, over two age levels" (p. 5–D). This is exactly the opposite result predicted by the oppression hypothesis. Similarly, Hall (1979) found that women who subscribed to traditional sex roles had lower sensitivity scores than more liberated women.

Theories of Biological Sex Differences in Social Sensitivity

One possibility for sex differences in social sensitivity is that women are genetically predisposed to greater sensitivity. Hall (1978) reluctantly concluded:

> Another kind of explanation in its simplest form, would hold that females are "wired" from birth to be especially sensitive to nonverbal cues or especially quick learners of such cues. This would make evolutionary sense, be-

cause nonverbal sensitivity on a mother's part might enable her to detect distress in her youngsters or threatening signals from other adults, thus enhancing the survival chances of her offspring. (p. 854)

In fact, several sets of studies show that females are particularly sensitive to negative affective cues (Hall, 1978; Rosenthal et al., 1979). Similarly, increased nonverbal sensitivity might help both in selecting a nurturant mate of her choice and enhancing her social interaction with her mate, perhaps ensuring bonding and male involvement in childrearing. But what are the specific mechanisms that could impart superior social sensitivity to women?

One explanation is based on sex differences in brain lateralization. Considerable research has shown that men have more specialized, lateralized brain functions, whereas women have more symmetrical, integrated brain functions (Andersen, Garrison, & Andersen, 1979; Halpern, 1986). Hall (1979) summarized research that suggests that the more efficient communication between the brain hemispheres of women enable logical, verbal information to be coordinated with nonverbal information to produce greater intuition and social sensitivity. In their review of literature examining the brain and communication, Stacks and Andersen (1989) suggested that interhemispheric cooperation (or intrapersonal communication) has a number of benefits including enhanced processing of complex information and analysis of emotional content and imagery.

A second explanation for gender-linked differences in social sensitivity may be a sex-linked difference at a chromosomal level. Sensitivity, as is discussed in greater detail later, has greater benefits for women because women have significantly greater parental investment (Goldsmith, 1991; Symons, 1987; Trost & Alberts, chap. 10, this volume). Women have a finite number of reproductive opportunities due to relatively long periods of gestation and lactation compared with men who have large potential reproductive opportunities because their only necessary biological role in reproduction is insemination. Thus, skills that result in child protection, mate retention, and successful parenting, such as social sensitivity and other communication skills, would be relatively more important from a genetic standpoint for women than for men. Eagly (1987) suggested that the centrality of childrearing in women fosters communal orientation, affectional qualities, interpersonal sensitivity, emotional expressiveness, and social orientation.

A third mechanism that may produce sex differences is based on the presence of hormones at critical stages of development. Little evidence directly links hormone levels to greater or lesser social sensitivity. However, girls exposed to prenatal male hormones are described as *tomboyish*—more interested in so-called male activities and less interested in female activities that are arguably more social in nature (Serbin & Sprafkin, 1987).

SPATIAL SKILLS

The research reviewed earlier paints a clear picture of women possessing genetically superior social skills, particularly in the important area of non-verbal communication. Before the reader concludes that men are right hemispherically retarded, an equally robust sex difference that favors males should be noted in spatial ability, which is also a right-hemisphere function. Literally scores of studies show a moderate to large ($d = .45-.96$), probably innate, difference in the spatial skills of men compared with women (see Buffery & Gray, 1972; Gaulin, 1992; Hyde, 1990). Even in the communication literature, which is normally oblivious to genetics as a field, communication scholars Stewart, Cooper, and Friedley (1986) listed male excellence in visuospatial ability as one of only four well-established primary sex differences. In a major review of the evolution of sex differences in spatial ability, Gaulin (1992) noted that, among well-documented psychological sex differences, a male advantage on spatial tasks is the most reliable. He stated "Such explanations can only be evolutionary. When the psychological features under study are widely distributed across human societies and are also present in nonhuman mammals the argument that they are cultural epiphenomena is substantially weakened" (p. 127).

Evidence From Spatial Tests

The male advantage for spatial perceptions is observed across scores of studies and numerous types of tests. The largest male advantage is for mental rotation and visualization of objects (Linn & Petersen, 1985). Men excel at tasks involving rotation of solid objects, unfolding of solid objects, and folding of flat objects (Halpern, 1986). Halpern concluded:

> Males score considerably higher on novel tests that require spatial visualization. The largest between sex differences are found on tests that require subjects to mentally rotate a two-dimension representation of a three-dimensional object in space. It is highly unlikely that anyone of either sex would have any experience with three-dimensional mental rotations. (p. 152)

Recent meta-analyses conclude that, by conventional status standards, the advantage for men on three-dimensional rotation tasks constitutes a large ($d = .96$) effect size (Collaer & Hines, 1995; Hyde, 1990; Linn & Petersen, 1985).

Similar male advantages appear for other spatial tasks. Halpern (1986) reviewed research that men have an advantage on an orientation factor that includes the ability to detect spatial relationships among objects and to perceive spatial patterns accurately. This ability may have evolved as a navigational skill to locate mates (Gaulin, 1992) or to detect movement of enemies or predators.

Men also excel at field independence—the ability to separate a stimulus from its environmental setting in a surrounding visual field and in various tests of adjusting objects to their vertical position (Buffery & Gray, 1972). These results have been confirmed in the United States, England, Holland, Italy, France, Hong Kong, Sierra Leone, and others (Buffery & Gray, 1972). Men exceed women at a host of related spatial perception tasks where they display a moderate to large effect size in the available meta-analyses ($d = .50–.96$; Collaer & Hines, 1995; Hyde, 1990; Linn & Petersen, 1985).

Men exceed women across numerous studies of water-tipping tasks where participants are shown a bottle or glass of water and asked to predict where the water will be when the glass is tipped (Halpern, 1986; Hyde, 1990; Linn & Petersen, 1985). Boys' ability exceeds girls' at every grade throughout childhood and as adults on water-tipping tasks. Moreover, as Halpern (1986) concluded:

> It does not seem likely that males have more or better experience with a tipped glass of water. In fact, one could argue that females, the primary cooks and dishwashers in many homes, might have more related experience with tipped glasses of water and other liquids than males. (p. 151)

Male advantage is observed across these and numerous other spatial tasks, motor skills, tracking tests, and spatial memory measures.

Interestingly, men and women employ different mental strategies in attempting to perform spatial tasks. Men often attempt to visualize the entire pattern, whereas women seem more likely to use verbal labels (Halpern, 1986). When finding directions or solving mazes, women seem to employ landmarks, whereas males are more sensitive to overall spatial geography and geometry (Gaulin, 1992). Interestingly, just as women appear to be better able to see the entire picture or gestalt in social relations, men seem to be able to visualize the entire pattern or geography in spatial tasks. It is as if the right brain hemisphere has developed different specializations for which each sex is predisposed. Of course, all of these generalizations are based on group means, and any individual of either sex may have relatively poor or excellent spatial abilities or nonverbal abilities.

What is particularly striking about spatial ability research is how consistent the findings are across the developmental life span and across diverse cultural groups (Hyde, 1990; Linn & Petersen, 1985). In her meta-analytic studies, Hyde (1990) showed that prior conclusions of the emergence of sex differences in spatial abilities at adolescence is incorrect. Instead, "where gender differences were present, they were present throughout the lifespan" (p. 65). Similarly, the findings show remarkable cross-cultural consistency (Buffery & Gray, 1972; Gaulin, 1992; Halpern, 1986). Halpern maintained that, "even in countries with more equal participation between the sexes with respect to higher education it is rare to find a study that does not report a male advantage on spatial ability tests" (p. 148).

Theories of Biological Sex Differences in Spatial Perception

Several theoretical explanations have been offered for these robust sex differences in spatial ability reported in the literature. Research tends to support three explanations all of which may play some role as explanations of biological sex differences in spatial ability.

A primary explanation is based on hemispheric lateralization in the brain. It has been known for some time that women have more symmetrical, integrated hemispheric function, whereas males are more lateralized or specialized for each function (Andersen et al., 1979; Halpern, 1986). Success at some types of tasks such as spatial navigation may be enhanced by extreme lateralization that minimizes linear cognition from the left hemisphere, which may actually interfere with successful, holistic processing. Other tasks such as human conversation abilities may benefit from integration of information from the verbal, left hemisphere and the nonverbal, right hemisphere. Biologically, men are left-hemispherically lateralized for language, whereas their nondominant, right hemisphere is more specialized for spatial tasks (Andersen et al., 1979; Halpern, 1986). Moreover, complex sex-by-handedness interactions on various tasks tend to bolster lateralization explanations (Halpern, 1986).

A second explanation is that gender-linked differences in spatial ability are transmitted through sex-linked chromosomes. Studies have shown that spatial abilities are highly heritable (Linn & Petersen, 1985). Men's superior spatial abilities are probably a sex-linked characteristic transmitted through sexual selection. "Sexual selection is a type of disruptive selection that favors one phenotype in females and a different phenotype in males" (Gaulin, 1992, p. 125). Of course physical traits like hemophilia and color blindness represent precisely this type; they virtually always appear in males but only rarely in females. According to Buffery and Gray (1972),

> There is good reason to believe that the human sex difference in visuo-spatial abilities is under the control of the sex chromosomes. More particularly, there is evidence to suggest that a recessive gene determining superior visuo-spatial ability is carried on the x chromosome. (p. 127)

A daughter receives two x chromosomes, one from each parent. A son receives only one, from his mother; the y chromosome from his father carries little information. According to genetic theory, "the high spatial ability gene is recessive; therefore this trait will occur more frequently in males than in females because males have no other gene to mask the effects of the recessive gene" (Halpern, 1986, p. 71). Empirical results testing this model have been highly supportive (see Buffery & Gray, 1972; Halpern, 1986).

A third process that could produce sex-linked differences in spatial abilities is based on hormones. A number of studies have shown that increased androgen levels produce greater spatial ability in both males and females (Gaulin, 1992). Sex hormones influence the development of numerous adaptive sex differences including secondary sexual characteristics at puberty. Hormones, acting during critical developmental periods, have a major effect on spatial abilities (see Gaulin, 1992, for a review). Women who are masculinized with increased androgens from their own adrenal glands show superior visuospatial skills on a variety of tests (Collaer & Hines, 1995). Similarly, men with chronic androgen deficiencies show deficient visuospatial skills on a variety of tasks such as object rotation and navigation (Collaer & Hines, 1995).

Thus, three separate but interrelated mechanisms—the degree of hemispheric lateralization, recessive sex-linked chromosomes, and hormonal abnormalities—have each been shown to produce sex-linked variation in spatial ability. What forces in the evolutionary history of humankind have produced females with such superior social abilities and males with such superior spatial abilities? In the next section, some educated speculations are offered to explain these sexual asymmetries.

THE ORIGINS OF BIOLOGICAL SEX DIFFERENCES

Human beings evolved from our biological predecessors over the past several million years. Genetic changes proceeded very slowly across many generations (Jacquard, 1984). Humans have experienced relatively little genetic change over the last few hundred generations or so. Thus, we share a genetic endowment and biological heritage with people who lived thousands of years ago. Culturally, the rate of change is extremely rapid and geometrically accelerating; genetically we are pretty much like our Stone Age ancestors. Thus, our biological traits evolved under environmental circumstances very different than the present. As Archer (1991) stated:

> Behavior will be adapted to the environment in which it evolved; behavior favored by selection will be that which led to an increase in individuals' reproductive success or fitness. However, that environment may not be the same as the present environment, so it is important to distinguish between ways that selection led to adaptive behavior in the past and the maintenance of behavior in its present form today. (p. 12)

Thus, women who may have evolved superior social skills as caregivers need not use those skills as caregivers in today's cultural setting but may use those social skills creatively as managers, teachers, or doctors. Men no longer need their superior spatial skills for hunting or mate location but may find them useful in navigational tasks, professional sports, or engineering. Biology is not destiny. However, as suggested previously, our evolutionary past has produced some sex-linked group differences in certain abilities.

During thousands of years of human evolution, most of which took place before industrialism, cities, literacy, or even agriculture, humans developed sex-linked roles that differentially favored men's and women's survival. These changes reflect biological sex role differentials based on two causal relationships: mating and childbirth.

Human Mating Patterns

Humans are a moderately dimorphic species; that is, most human characteristics are possessed by both men and women. When a trait occurs in different frequencies between males and females, the species is said to be *dimorphic* (Gaulin, 1992; Goldsmith, 1991; Whicker & Kronenfeld, 1986). In species where there is no competition for mates and animals are monogamous, no dimorphism typically occurs. In species that compete for mates, sexual dimorphism typically occurs with males becoming larger and more aggressive because these qualities are selected over many generations of competition for mates. According to Goldsmith (1991), in some species females:

> frequently become the object of competition between males. This competition expresses itself in various ways, often in aggressive interaction between males, by trends toward sexual dimorphism—with males becoming larger and more aggressive than females. (p. 51)

Dimorphism likely occurs in species where males seek multiple opportunities to mate with females. "In most species of primates, including *Homo Sapiens*, the sexes differ in the maximum reproductive rates. In these species sexual dimorphism in anatomy, physiology, and behavior is the norm" (Gaulin, 1992, pp. 125–126).

Despite our own cultural values that monogamy and marriage are desirable qualities, the human species is generally polygamous—most humans in most cultures mate with more than one person. In his review of literature, Gaulin (1992) maintained that, among 1,154 societies described by ethnographers, 980 (84.9%) practice polygamy. Gaulin maintained:

> Many independent sorts of evidence argue that *Homo Sapiens* is a mammal of polygynous ancestry. Certain sex differences are typical of polygynous

species but are absent in monogamous species. Relative to female conspe-
cifics, males of polygynous species tend to be larger, more active in courtship,
more aggressive, and more susceptible to various perturbations of development. They tend to reach sexual maturity later, to have higher metabolic
rates and to be more prone to death at all ages. All of these sex differences
are characteristic of human populations. (p. 144)

Considerable evidence suggests that male primates, including humans,
are nonmonogamous. Gaulin (1992) concluded "Given the patterns of
dimorphism that characterized our hominid ancestry, disruptive selection
arising out of polygyny has probably operated for at least four million years
in the human lineage" (p. 146). Their genetic potential throughout history
was maximized by mating with as many fertile females as possible. Although
today's males may mate for other reasons than reproduction (e.g., pleasure,
intimacy, bonding, etc.), the biology from which contemporary males
evolved remains largely intact. Relational communication researchers
should examine this biological difference to enhance their understanding
of human sexual interaction.

> Following this line of thinking to its logical conclusion provides an expla-
> nation for the promiscuous, adulterous male. However despicable his be-
> havior is in social terms, biologically he is just doing what comes naturally.
> By impregnating as many females as possible with his sperm, his genes stand
> the best possible chance of survival. (Lewis, 1985, p. 73)

Symons (1987) argued that if a male hunter–gatherer could have four
children with his wife during their short life spans, he would increase his
reproductive success by 25% if he sired just one child by another woman
during his lifetime. For women, the reproductive reality is different: She
would bear the same number of children whether she has one mate or
several (unless of course her primary mate is infertile). Nonmonogamy
has low reproductive or genetic value for females.

Males who could travel greater distances and navigate well would have
a better opportunity to encounter other groups and potentially sire offspring with females of that group. Size, speed, and increased bone structure
of the skull, along with spatial ability would be selected for males who
might encounter other protective males in their ventures, have to navigate
long distances, and find their way back. Contemporary males have inherited
all such qualities via natural selection from our long genetic past. According
to Gaulin (1992),

> Under some kinds of polygynous mating systems, females have small, rela-
> tively exclusive ranges while males travel much more widely. In essence,

males in these systems compete to increase their access to potential mates
by overlapping as many female ranges as possible. (Gaulin, 1992, p. 129).

Indeed, this is the typical pattern among many primate species (Gaulin,
1992; Gray, 1985). Men pay a price for their size, strength, and mobility.
Throughout history, male mortality has been high. Nonetheless, according
to a biological view, males have been left with the legacy of their ancestors—a legacy that includes superior spatial ability.

According to a biological view, females would be relatively more monogamous, although if they became pregnant by another man they might dupe
an unsuspecting mate into raising another man's biological offspring.
Nonetheless, females can be choosier in finding a mate—one who provides
resources, is sexually attractive, and a good genetic, physical specimen. As is
the case with humans, "the sex investing most in offspring (typically females)
should be more resistant to, and discriminating about, sexual overtures prior
to mate selection" (Buss, 1987, p. 339). Men are attracted worldwide to
nubile, healthy women. Females are attracted to somewhat older males with
more resources (Kenrick & Keefe, 1992a). To find mates who are depend-
able and provide resources, women with superior social nonverbal sensitivity
increase their survival advantage if their female offspring inherited their
qualities. Males merely had to recognize fertile, healthy females, so nonverbal sensitivity presented little advantage. Of course, as is elaborated on in
the conclusion, none of this argues that sociocultural forces or education
are less powerful than our genetic, biological endowment.

Parental Investment and Role Differentiation

For most members of the human species, growing old was a luxury few
enjoyed. For hundreds of thousands of years, mean life expectancy was less
than 30 years (Kenrick & Keefe, 1992b; Swedlund & Armelagos, 1976). Even
by the 17th century, life expectancy barely climbed over 30. As Whicker and
Kronenfeld (1986) reported: "Life in the agrarian period was indeed short,
nasty, and brutish. Life expectancy was short and stresses were great,
especially on women. Average life expectancy in England in 1690 was 32" (p.
24). Except for the last several generations, throughout the thousand
generations of human history, the typical adult female had no more than a
dozen years to bear children. Given the high infant mortality rate and
maternal mortality rates, high fertility levels were necessary simply to replace
the human population each generation.

As we are well aware of today, the human population did indeed grow.
Under 1,000,000 humans populated the earth in 35,000 B.C., to perhaps
4 to 8 million in 10,000 B.C., to 80 million during the agrarian revolution
in 5,000 B.C., to nearly a billion by the end of the 18th century (Jacquard,

1984). To compensate for high mortality, high fertility was required. Stevens (1992) summarized: "Throughout most of human history, people lived in small societies, often hunting and gathering societies typified by high rates of mortality and high rates of fertility" (p. 112). Although women's reduced fertility while nursing and postpartum taboos against sexual intercourse may have decreased fertility (Swedlund & Armelagos, 1976), overall fertility was high for most groups throughout human history. Likewise, women nursed their babies for several years up until the modern era. The result was this: Women spent most of their short lives pregnant, nursing, and carrying small infants.

Women's excessively high investment in parenting is a historic fact. Buss (1987) stated: "In our species, for example, a male copulation that is trivial in terms of investment can produce a nine-month investment by the female that is substantial in time, energy and foreclosed alternatives" (p. 339). Nursing and child care add to that investment.

Obviously, pregnant or lactating mothers, particularly with one or more children, have major constraints on their physical activities. Activities like foraging, hunting, scouting, and combat were more likely to have been male activities. Once again, this does not mean that in contemporary society women are relegated to such domestic roles nor are men precluded from being the primary caregivers.

Women spent their time close to the group interacting with the sick, aphasics with head injuries, and preverbal children. Many adults experienced head injuries and were nonlinguistic aphasics. Women were leaders of the domestic group and had to develop superior social skills, particularly nonverbal communication skills, or the primary group failed and no genes survived to be passed along to later generations. Similarly, the strength and spatial abilities of male hunters, explorers, and combatants became critical for the species to survive and these became sex-linked skills. In contemporary society, culture and education can compensate for these biological characteristics. Nonetheless, as groups, women have retained superior social skills, especially nonverbal skills, and men have maintained superior visuospatial abilities.

SOME FINAL CAVEATS

Two primary points have been suggested in this chapter: (a) Men and women are quite similar in most respects but the search for biological differences has been ignored by most researchers and textbook writers; and (b) our search for biological differences should begin with reproduction—the most fundamental difference between men and women. The biological difference between men and women will be a function of our separate, evolutionary, reproductive roles.

Biological Determination

The model presented here is distinctly nondeterministic or what is sometimes called *weak determinism*. Although evolution has produced biological
tendencies that represent slightly different predispositions for men and
women, no point made in this chapter justifies excluding any human from
any role to which they might aspire.

Weak determinism suggests that biology may underlie some predispositions but not that we are completely inevitable by-products of our biology.
Halpern (1986) stated, "A weak force of biological determinism allows the
possibility that females and males may, by self-determination or some other
means, overcome sex-related biological predictions or tendencies" (p. 68).
As Archer (1991) explained, "In recent years a middle ground has emerged,
in which Darwinian thinking is no longer characterized in terms of genetic
determinism . . . the emphasis [is] on flexible adaptive mechanisms rather
than fixed behavioral responses" (p. 12). Biological sex differences create
behavioral tendencies—they do not determine individuals' behavior.

Of course a thorough review of the evidence on sex differences reveals
that they are a function of culture, biology, and their interaction. As
Rosaldo (1974) pointed out, "anything so general as the universal asymmetry of sex roles is likely to be the result of a constellation of different
factors, factors that are deeply involved in the foundation of human societies. Biology may be one of these" (p. 23).

Finally, there are those who maintain that we should never investigate
or discuss biological differences among human beings, particularly among
ethnic groups or between the sexes. Of course such an attitude in biology
would have annihilated research on hemophilia or Tay-Sachs disease. Na-
zism and its cousins, racism and sexism, have cast a long shadow over the
social sciences. They have led to a kind of academic McCarthyism—where
certain ideas are censored or criticized because of fear they will be used
as justifications for sexism or racism. Psychological denial of biological
mechanisms is fundamentally unhealthy for an academic discipline. Writing about racial differences in the *Chronicle of Higher Education*, anthropolo-
gist Shipman (1994) stated:

> The time has come to know the truth about ourselves, our species. We must
> muster the courage to find out the truth and face it. Now when an unpleasant
> accusation is leveled at a racial group we have no solid evidence with which
> to rebut it. (p. 133)

Moreover, the forces of learning, remediation, and compensation mean
that no person should be a victim of her or his biological inherence. Every
man can be taught to be socially, emotionally, and nonverbally sensitive

and every woman can be taught to mentally rotate an object or find her way home.

REFERENCES

Andersen, P. A., Garrison, J. P., & Andersen, J. F. (1979). Implications of a neurophysiological approach for the study of nonverbal communication. *Human Communication Research, 6,* 74–89.

Archer, J. (1991). Human sociology: Basic concepts and limitations. *Journal of Social Issues, 47,* 11–26.

Begley, S. (1995, March 27). Gray matters. *Newsweek,* pp. 48–54.

Birdwhistell, R. L. (1970). *Kinesics and context.* Philadelphia: University of Pennsylvania Press.

Buffery, A. W. H., & Gray, J. A. (1972). Sex differences in the development of spatial and linguistic skills. In C. Ounsted & D. C. Taylor (Eds.), *Gender differences: Their ontogeny and significance* (pp. 123–158). London: Churchill Livingston.

Buller, D. B., & Aune, R. K. (1992). The effects of speech rate similarity on compliance: Application of communication accommodation theory. *Western Journal of Communication, 56,* 37–53.

Buss, D. M. (1987). Sex differences in human mate selection criteria: An evolutionary perspective. In C. Crawford, M. Smith, & D. Krebs (Eds.), *Sociobiology and psychology: Ideas, issues, and applications* (pp. 335–352). Hillsdale, NJ: Lawrence Erlbaum Associates.

Canary, D. J., & Hause, K. S. (1993). Is there any reason to research sex differences in communication? *Communication Quarterly, 41,* 129–144.

Collaer, M. L., & Hines, M. (1995). Human behavioral sex differences: A role for genabal hormones during early development. *Psychological Bulletin, 118,* 55–107.

Eagly, A. H. (1987). *Sex differences in social behavior: A social role interpretation.* Hillsdale, NJ: Lawrence Erlbaum Associates.

Gaulin, S. J. C. (1992). Evolution of sex differences in spatial ability. *Yearbook of Physical Anthropology, 359,* 125–151.

Goldsmith, T. H. (1991). *The biological roots of human nature.* New York: Oxford University Press.

Gray, J. (1992). *Men are from Mars, women are from Venus: A practical guide to improving communication and getting what you want in your relationships.* New York: HarperCollins.

Gray, J. P. (1985). *Primate sociobiology.* New Haven, CT: HRAF Press.

Guerrero, L. K., & Andersen, P. A. (1994). Patterns of matching and initiation: Touch behavior and touch avoidance across romantic relationship stages. *Journal of Nonverbal Behavior, 18,* 137–153.

Hall, J. A. (1978). Gender effects in decoding nonverbal cues. *Psychological Bulletin, 85,* 845–857.

Hall, J. A. (1979). Gender, gender roles, and nonverbal communication skills. In R. Rosenthal (Ed.), *Skill is nonverbal communication* (pp. 31–67). Cambridge, MA: Oelgeschlager, Gunn & Hain.

Hall, J. A., & Veccia, E. M. (1990). More "touching" observations: New insights on men, women, and interpersonal touch. *Journal of Personality and Social Psychology, 59,* 1155–1162.

Halpern, D. F. (1986). *Sex differences in cognitive abilities.* Hillsdale, NJ: Lawrence Erlbaum Associates.

Hyde, J. S. (1990). Meta-analysis and the psychology of gender differences. *Journal of Women in Culture and Society, 16,* 55–73.

Ivy, P. K., & Backlund, P. (1994). *Exploring gender speak: Personal effectiveness in gender communication.* New York: McGraw-Hill.

Jacquard, A. (1984). *In praise of difference: Genetics and human affairs*. New York: Columbia University Press.

Kenrick, D. T., & Keefe, R. C. (1992a). Age preferences in human reproductive strategies. *Behavioral and Brain Sciences, 15*, 75–133.

Kenrick, D. T., & Keefe, R. C. (1992b). Sex differences in age preference: Universal reality or ephemeral construction. *Behavioral and Brain Sciences, 15*, 119–133.

Knapp, M. L., & Hall, J. A. (1992). *Nonverbal communication in human interaction* (3rd ed.). Forth Worth, TX: Hacourt Brace Jovanovich.

Lewis, D. (1985). *Loving and loathing: The enigma of personal attraction*. London: Constable.

Linn, M. D., & Petersen, A. C. (1985). Emergence and characterization of sex differences in spatial ability. *Child Development, 56*, 1479–1498.

Pearson, J. C., West, R. L., & Turner, L. H. (1995). *Gender and communication*. Madison, WI: Brown & Benchmark.

Rosaldo, M. Z. (1974). Women, culture and society: A rhetorical overview. In M. Z. Rosaldo & L. Lamphere (Eds.), *Women, culture, and society* (pp. 17–42). Stanford, CA: Stanford University Press.

Rosenthal, R., & DePaulo, B. M. (1979). Sex differences in accommodation in nonverbal communication. In R. Rosenthal (Ed.), *Skill in nonverbal communication: Individual differences* (pp. 68–103). Cambridge, MA: Oelgeschlager, Gunn & Hain.

Rosenthal, R., Hall, J. A., DiMatteo, M. R., Rogers, P. L., & Archer, D. (1979). *Sensitivity to nonverbal communication: The PONS test*. Baltimore, MD: Johns Hopkins University Press.

Serbin, L. A., & Sprafkin, C. H. (1987). A developmental approach: Sexuality from infancy through adolescence. In J. H. Geer & W. T. O'Donahue (Eds.), *Theories of human sexuality* (pp. 163–196). New York: Plenum.

Shipman, P. (1994, August 3). Facing racial differences—together. *Chronicle of Higher Education*, pp. BI–B3.

Stacks, D. W., & Andersen, P. A. (1989). The modular mind: Implications for intrapersonal communication. *The Southern Communication Journal, 54*, 273–293.

Stevens, G. (1992). Mortality and age-specific patterns of marriage. *Behavioral and Brain Sciences, 15*, 112–113.

Stewart, L. P., Cooper, P. J., & Friedley, S. A. (1986). *Communication between the sexes: Sex differences and sex-role stereotypes*. Scottsdale, AZ: Gorsuch Scarisbrick.

Stier, D. S., & Hall, J. A. (1984). Gender differences in touch: An empirical and theoretical review. *Journal of Personality and Social Psychology, 47*, 440–459.

Swedlund, A. C., & Armelagos, G. J. (1976). *Demographic anthropology*. Dubuque, IA: W. C. Brown.

Symons, D. (1987). An evolutionary approach: Can Darwin's view of life shed light on human sexuality? In J. H. Geer & W. T. O'Donahue (Eds.), *Theories of human sexuality* (pp. 91–126). New York: Plenum.

Tannen, D. (1990). *You just don't understand: Women and men in conversation*. New York: William Morrow.

Weitz, S. (1979). Commentary: Interactional aspects. In R. Rosenthal (Ed.), *Skill in nonverbal communication: Individual differences* (pp. 135–138). Cambridge, MA: Oelgeschlager, Gunn & Hain.

Whicker, M. L., & Kronenfeld, J. J. (1986). *Sex role changes: Technology, politics, and policy*. New York: Praeger.

Wilkins, B. M., & Andersen, P. A. (1991). Gender-differences and similarities in management communication: A meta-analysis. *Management Communication Quarterly, 5*, 6–35.

Chapter 5

Social Support and the Emotional Lives of Men and Women: An Assessment of the Different Cultures Perspective

Adrianne W. Kunkel
Brant R. Burleson
Purdue University

An explosion of research has occurred over the last two decades examining sex and gender differences in interpersonal behaviors, such as emotional expression, social support, and intimacy, especially as these behaviors are displayed in close personal relationships. One general conclusion drawn from this research is that women tend to be more emotionally sensitive and expressive than men; that is, women tend to be more affectively oriented, whereas men tend to be more instrumentally oriented (Aries, 1996; Balswick, 1988; Gilligan, 1982; Hoffman, 1977; Vaux, 1985; Winstead, 1986). This general conclusion has been particularly buttressed by research on emotional support processes (see Cutrona, 1996). Studies of sex differences in comforting and other forms of emotional support have consistently found that women are more willing and likely to: (a) inquire about upsetting situations (e.g., Mickelson, Helgeson, & Weiner, 1995); (b) provide emotional support (e.g., Trobst, Collins, & Embree, 1994); (c) seek support (e.g., Ashton & Fuehrer, 1993); (d) feel confident about their support-providing efforts (e.g., Clark, 1993); (e) value support-giving skills (e.g., Burleson, Kunkel, Samter, & Werking, 1996); (f) employ supportive strategies that directly confront emotions (e.g., Barbee et al., 1993; Barbee, Gulley, & Cunningham, 1990; Derlega, Barbee, & Winstead, 1994); and (g) use comforting messages that explicitly acknowledge, elaborate, and legitimize the feelings of others (e.g., Borden, 1979; Burleson, 1982; Samter, 1989). Thus, men and women clearly differ in their propensity to provide and seek support as well as in the strategies they employ when attempting to provide support.

101

Numerous explanations have been offered for the observed gender differences in emotional support behaviors, including biologically based accounts (Fausto-Sterling, 1985; Levine & Hoffman, 1975) and social role accounts (Deaux & Major, 1987; Gerson & Peiss, 1985). One account, the different cultures perspective, sees differences in socialization patterns leading to the articulation and perpetuation of two distinct cultures—one male and the other female. The different cultures perspective asserts that men and women inhabit and are socialized into different emotional worlds or cultures, with members of each sex developing distinct, but equally valid and effective ways of dealing with emotional experiences, including expression of emotional support and intimacy (Wood, 1994a). Further, proponents of the different cultures perspective argue that men and women have different languages that are thought to develop out of the differential socialization and communication experiences of boys and girls (Wood, 1993).

The idea that men and women are so different that they should be regarded as members of different cultures is a perspective that has become widespread in both scholarly circles and the popular press. For example, mega-best sellers advocating the different cultures position include John Gray's (1992), *Men Are From Mars, Women Are From Venus*, and its provocatively entitled sequel, *Mars and Venus in the Bedroom* (1995). Then there is Deborah Tannen's (1990), *You Just Don't Understand: Women and Men in Conversation*, as well as her more recent *Talking from 9 to 5—Women and Men in the Workplace: Language, Sex and Power* (1994). Articles in the *Utne Reader* ask: "Men and women: Can we get along? Should we even try?" (January 1993), while best-selling self-help books (*He and She Talk: How to Communicate with the Opposite Sex*, Schloff & Yudkin, 1993) offer advice on how to cross the cultural chasm and communicate effectively with members of the opposite sex.

The notion that men and women constitute members of different gender cultures (Wood, 1995) is equally prevalent in scholarly literature. Scholars representing many of the humanities and virtually all of the social sciences—including anthropology, communication, family studies, linguistics, psychology, and sociology—have proclaimed that men and women literally live in different worlds:

> It is clear that men and women do come from different cultures, [and] the crucial difference between those cultures is that men come from a culture that emphasizes status and power, whereas women come from a culture that emphasizes relative closeness rather than relative power. (Noller, 1993, p. 148)

> American men and women come from different sociolinguistic subcultures, having learned to do different things with words in a conversation. (Maltz & Borker, 1982, p. 200)

Numerous studies and reviews of research demonstrate that distinct gender cultures exist and that they differ systematically in some important respects. (Wood, 1995, p. 245)

Boys and girls grow up in what are essentially different cultures, so talk between women and men is cross-cultural communication. (Tannen, 1990, p. 18)

Husbands and wives, especially in Western societies, come from two different cultures with different learned behaviors and communication styles. They are "intimate strangers" with the potential for many gendered misunderstandings. (Bruess & Pearson, 1996, p. 60)

The idea that men and women come from, constitute, and perpetuate different cultures seems to be winning ever wider endorsement, especially in social science textbooks (Galvin & Cooper, 1996; Wood, 1994a). Indeed, the idea that men and women live in different emotional worlds is increasingly being accepted—and taught—as a fact (see Borisoff & Hahn, 1995). We believe this has serious implications for theory, research, and pedagogy. For example, if men and women come from different cultures, this suggests that theories of, say, close relationships need to be developed independently for men and women because each sex presumably seeks different things in their relationships, develops their relationships differently, acts differently in those relationships, and manages relationship issues and problems differently. The different cultures view also has important methodological consequences. If men and women are from different cultures, then we need to use culturally sensitive methods in conducting research. Consistent with this view, Cancian (1986) argued that most research on intimacy and emotional support processes suffers from a feminine bias because researchers have inappropriately used an exclusively feminine yardstick to evaluate emotion-related behaviors in relationships. Moreover, if men and women inhabit different cultures, then educators will need to develop different programs directed at enhancing the distinct emotional and intimacy skills of males and females. That is, men and women will need to be taught to respect the differences in each other's culture and how to communicate across the cultural divide (Maltz & Borker, 1982; Swain, 1989; Tannen, 1986, 1990; Wood, 1993, 1994a). In essence, men and women will need multicultural diversity training. For example, women need to be taught how to provide emotional support to men and vice versa.

Although the different cultures view is increasingly popular and accepted in both lay and scholarly circles, this perspective has not yet received the careful scrutiny and critical examination that it deserves. Some feminist scholars (e.g., Crawford, 1995; Henley & Kramarae, 1991) have criticized the different cultures view for providing unwitting legitimation and rein-

forcement of gender-based communicative practices grounded in patriarchal privilege and hegemony. These critiques, however, tend to accept the
major claims of the different cultures view as factually accurate (i.e., that
men and women do communicate in fundamentally different ways), at-
tacking this viewpoint primarily on ideological and political grounds.

Our concern in this chapter is chiefly with the factual accuracy of the
claims made by proponents of the different cultures perspective. Little
systematic empirical evidence supportive of the different cultures view has
been reported. Moreover, we find a disturbing tendency in some literature
for one writer to cite the speculative claims of another writer as if those
claims were empirical fact. Much of the data cited to support the different
cultures perspective is anecdotal in nature. Although anecdotes provide
compelling illustrations, they can only suggest hypotheses, not test them.
Claims about how men and women generally behave represent empirical
generalizations, and therefore they need to be substantiated (or refuted)
by evidence appropriate to the logical character of the claims made.

Because of the serious consequences of the different cultures view, and
the fact that this view has not yet received the critical examination it
deserves, we have undertaken a program of research designed to assess
key claims of the different cultures position. The purpose of our research
has been to empirically evaluate the different cultures viewpoint with respect to its analysis of close personal relationships and the modes of communication that occur in those relationships. In particular, we have examined the extent of gender-related differences in various aspects of
emotional support. The current chapter presents a summary of our critique
of the different cultures viewpoint and related research. It begins by presenting a more detailed overview of the sources and claims of the different
cultures perspective. Next it derives several predictions from the different
cultures view pertaining to emotional support processes. Then it discusses
the results of several studies carried out to evaluate those predictions. A
final section presents some implications of our research, discusses alternatives to the different cultures view, and suggests some guidelines for future
research on gender and communication.

THE DIFFERENT CULTURES PERSPECTIVE

There are several sources for the notion that males and females constitute
different cultures, including research on socialization processes, language
use, personal relationships, and feminist theory (see Wood, 1993). The
literature concerning the different cultures perspective, although varied in
purpose and scope, contends that men's and women's ways of communicating are strikingly different and, thus, constitute different cultural styles.

Socialization Research

Much socialization research maintains that, in contemporary Western societies, women are socialized into a culture that emphasizes interdependence, cooperation, and the pursuit of socioemotional concerns, whereas men are socialized into a culture organized around independence, competition, influence, and the pursuit of shared activities (Maccoby, 1990; Wood, 1993, 1994a). Each culture is believed to instill in its members a different, although equally valid, set of assumptions concerning the functions of communication in close relationships (Wood, 1994a).

The sociolinguistic research of Maltz and Borker (1982) has been particularly influential. These researchers suggest that boys and girls are socialized within different speech communities (Gumperz, 1982). The origin of gender-related cultural differences is traced to the ways in which young boys and girls learn to use communication as they interact, play, and relate with others—mostly in sex-segregated play groups. According to Maltz and Borker, the world of boys is hierarchically organized and competitive, with dominance and assertiveness being particularly valued. In contrast, the world of girls is nonhierarchically organized and cooperative; thus, equality and emotional closeness are valued. These features of social relationships lead to and sustain distinct patterns of language use, with the world of boys encouraging them to utilize self-assertion, boasting, storytelling, and factual reports, whereas the world of girls encourages them to express and respond to the feelings of others, share personal perspectives, and commune through conversation. The adult extension of these childhood differences is that men's speech within friendships tends to be characterized by storytelling and verbal aggressiveness, whereas women's speech with friends tends to be characterized by the sharing of feelings and expressions of emotional support (see Bruess & Pearson, 1996; Henley & Kramarae, 1991; Tannen, 1990; Wood, 1994a). On this view, the psychological and behavioral differences observed between men and women reflect and constitute basic cultural differences.

Language Research

Early work by language researchers such as Lakoff (1975) attempted to explain how societal and interpersonal power differentials affected the speech of men and women. Lakoff contended that women have been discriminated against in society and are thus disadvantaged (relative to men) in terms of the functional and powerful communication forms to which they have access (see also Johnson, 1989). Specifically, Lakoff maintained that, in the process of socialization, women learn to use language in ways that are seemingly deficient in comparison with the ways that men use language. For example, women who make use of women's language (i.e., language that deviates from the masculine norm) are typically thought of as weak and uncertain, which ultimately situates women (relative to men) in a position of less power (Lakoff, 1975). Thus, research by linguists (e.g., Lakoff, 1975; West & Zimmerman, 1977, 1983; Zimmerman & West, 1975) initiated the notion that men and women have different life experiences that lead them to form distinct language communities—with women being constitutive of the less powerful community.

Relationships Research

Research on personal relationships has also been influential in the development and articulation of the different cultures perspective. Considerable research has examined gender differences in the same-sex friendships of both adults (e.g., Aries & Johnson, 1983; Caldwell & Peplau, 1982) and children (e.g., Lever, 1976), as well as gender differences in men's and women's orientations to romantic relationships (see Noller, 1993; Wood, 1993). Typically, it has been found that men and women hold different values concerning what is important in close relationships, and these values reflect distinct patterns of behavior. Women are taught that talk is the primary vehicle through which people create and maintain intimacy and connectedness (Ashton & Fuehrer, 1993; Derlega, Metts, Petronio, & Margulis, 1993). In contrast, men are socialized to view talk as a mechanism for getting things done, accomplishing instrumental tasks, conveying information, and maintaining one's autonomy (Mazur & Olver, 1987; Rawlins, 1992). Interaction between members of masculine and feminine cultures is thus believed to proceed along the same lines as interaction between members of any two cultures whose experiences and social milieus differ (see Henley & Kramarae, 1991; Maltz & Borker, 1982; Noller, 1993).

Feminist Theory

Research from a feminist perspective has also been important in the development of the different cultures point of view. Traditional feminist theory contends that "society differentially evaluates women's and men's speech . . . and [this] must be taken into account in any theory of difference and miscommunication" (Henley & Kramarae, 1991, p. 23). Understanding how society consistently privileges men's experience and language usage is paramount to the feminist agenda. Feminist theorists have suggested that understanding and recognizing the differences between men and women may provide a more thorough understanding and articulation of women's culture, which has often been privatized and marginalized in relation to men's culture (Crawford, 1995; Johnson, 1989). Further, understanding the differences in men's and women's cultures, especially modes of speaking, has been viewed as a prerequisite for the critique and subsequent change of societal power structures.

In summary, there are several sources that have helped contribute to the idea that men and women constitute different cultures. The theoretical, methodological, and pedagogical implications of the different cultures view warrant the critical evaluation and assessment of this perspective.

EVALUATING THE DIFFERENT CULTURES ANALYSIS OF EMOTIONAL SUPPORT

The different cultures thesis has been applied to a broad variety of communicative genres (e.g., supporting, informing, persuading, gossiping, managing conflict; see Tannen, 1990; Wood, 1994a). Our research has focused on implications of the different cultures view for communication processes and preferences in contexts where emotional support is sought and provided. Emotional support represents a significant form of communication in close relationships. Considerable research indicates that people—both men and women—regularly seek emotional support from friends and family members and expect those relationship partners to provide support when called on to do so (Burleson, 1990). Moreover, as an important (and perhaps distinctive) provision of close relationships, emotional support facilitates coping processes and benefits both physical health and psychological well-being (Burleson, Albrecht, Goldsmith, & Sarason, 1994).

As noted at the outset of this chapter, there are noteworthy behavioral differences in how men and women express care and convey emotional support. Generally, research has found that women are more likely than men to seek and provide emotional support; women also are more likely to employ supportive forms of communication that explicitly address feelings, perspectives, and subjective interpretations (Ashton & Fuehrer, 1993; Barbee et al., 1990; Rosario, Shinn, Morch, & Huckabee, 1988; Trobst et al., 1994; Vaux, 1985; see also Cutrona, 1996).

Both sociolinguists (e.g., Kluckholm, 1951) and anthropologists (e.g., Geertz, 1973) suggested that a culture is defined by practices (especially those pertaining to communicative behaviors), artifacts, and abstractions (e.g., beliefs, attitudes, values, perceptual schemes). Abstractions pertaining to significant social activities, such as supportive communication, are an especially important component of a cultural system (Johnson, 1989). Because abstractions are a central part of what defines a culture, members of different cultures are usually regarded as adhering to different systems of abstractions (i.e., having different beliefs, attitudes, values, and perceptual schemes). Hence, if men and women constitute distinct cultures, this should be reflected in sharp gender differences in abstractions as well as correspondent differences in behaviors.

Moreover, the different cultures view maintains that behavioral differences are indicative and constitutive of a cultural difference. This implies that behavioral differences (differences in practices) are undergirded by cognitive differences (differences in abstractions). Thus, behavioral differences in how emotional support is enacted are held to be reflective of these underlying cognitive differences as well as constitutive of them (Johnson, 1989; Wood, 1993). More specifically, the behavioral differences to which boys and girls are exposed and enact during the course of socialization are held to create cognitive differences in these boys and girls—differences in the content of cognition. These cognitive differences lead to different gender-based patterns of behavior, which then further reinforce and stabilize the differences in cognitive content. The differences in cognitive content are crucial to the claim of cultural difference. That is, it is assumed that men and women differ in what they think and feel, as well as in how they behave. If they do not think and feel differently, it is difficult to maintain that men and women are members of different cultures.

The logic of the different cultures perspective suggests that men and women should differ with respect to at least four classes of cognitive variables. First, men and women should differ with regard to the criteria or standards they use in deciding whether something is caring, comforting, and supportive, or how much something is caring, comforting, and supportive. Second, men and women should differ with respect to the preferred gender of a partner in various circumstances and interactions (e.g., receiving comfort). Third, men and women should differ in their values (what is good, important, or desirable in a relationship), especially in the importance attached to emotional support in the context of close relationships. Finally, men and women should differ in their preferences for behavioral styles of same-sex peers; these preferences can often be inferred from the outcomes experienced by men and women when they provide support and comfort in either gender-typical or gender-atypical ways.

The different cultures view predicts the same pattern for each of these four sets of variables: Each gender should be biased toward its own form of doing emotional support. In other words, the different cultures view maintains that the masculine and feminine ways of caring and providing support are equally competent and desirable for members of their respective cultures and are generally preferred by them. Men do not experience feminine comforting as supportive and vice versa. Advocates of the different cultures perspective argue that researchers often miss this fact because of the use of biased, feminine rulers (Cancian, 1986). In particular, masculine ways of expressing care and support have been devalued, delegitimized, and ignored by both the popular culture and scholars (especially by researchers in social psychology and communication; see Wood & Inman, 1993). These claims are explicitly made by several proponents of the different cultures view:

> From a masculine perspective, talking about feelings and self-disclosing are not preeminent ways to show care and may be unsatisfying, uncomfortable, and not particularly contributory to feelings of closeness. . . . Feminized views of caring not only devalue the ways masculine people show care but also diminish the likelihood they will get the kind of caring they value. Research indicates that masculine individuals particularly appreciate instrumental demonstrations from others. (Wood, 1993, pp. 41, 42)

> If women are often frustrated because men do not respond to their troubles by offering matching troubles, men are often frustrated because women do. Some men not only take no comfort in such a response, they take offense. . . . Women and men are both often frustrated by the other's way of responding to their expression of troubles. And they are further hurt by the other's frustration. If women resent men's tendency to offer solutions to problems, men complain about women's refusal to take action to solve problems they complain about. (Tannen, 1990, pp. 51, 52)

In summary, the different cultures point of view predicts that men should: (a) see masculine forms of comforting as more supportive than feminine forms, (b) prefer other men as sources of support when they are distressed, (c) place a lower value on the activities of comforting and emotional support than women, and (d) like men who engage in masculine forms of comforting while disliking men who engage in more feminine modes of providing comfort. The same pattern is predicted for women in that they should: (a) see feminine forms of comforting as more supportive than masculine forms, (b) prefer women as sources of emotional support, (c) place a comparatively high value on the activities of comforting and supporting, and (d) like peers who engage in feminine rather than masculine styles of comforting. Each of these predictions has been examined in the research program summarized in the next section.

TESTS OF HYPOTHESES DERIVED FROM THE DIFFERENT CULTURES PERSPECTIVE

Criteria for Effective Comforting Messages

The first general hypothesis examined in our research program is that men and women have different standards for what counts as sensitive, effective, or good comforting messages. From the different cultures point of view, men should view masculine messages as more sensitive and effective than feminine messages, whereas the reverse should be true for women. This hypothesis has been examined in several different studies (Burleson & Samter, 1985b; Kunkel, 1995; Samter, Burleson, & Murphy, 1987).

All of these studies have employed similar methods. In each study, comforting messages varying in the quality of person-centeredness have been constructed for several different hypothetical situations. Groups of men and women have then been asked to rate these messages for their sensitivity and effectiveness. At a theoretical level, person-centered comforting messages acknowledge, elaborate, legitimize, and contextualize the feelings and perspective of a distressed other (Burleson, 1987). In contrast, less person-centered messages tend to deny or ignore the distressed other's feelings or deal with those feelings only implicitly by attempting to distract attention from the negative feelings. Considerable research has found that women use more person-centered comforting strategies than men (e.g., Burleson, 1982; Samter, 1989), thus person-centered comforting messages can be viewed as feminine while comforting messages low in person-centeredness can be viewed as masculine in character. Consequently, the different cultures account predicts that women should prefer highly person-centered comforting messages and should evaluate them as most sensitive and effective, whereas men should prefer less person-centered messages and view them as more sensitive and effective.

The first study to examine this hypothesis (Burleson & Samter, 1985b) had college-age men and women rank order for their overall quality nine comforting messages that systematically varied in person-centeredness. A significant, but small sex effect ($r = .19$, $p < .05$) was found: Women viewed highly person-centered messages as better ways to comfort than did men, although this effect accounted for less than 4% of the variance in ratings of message quality. Subsequent analyses of these data revealed that over 80% of variance in ratings of message quality was accounted for by the degree of message person-centeredness (Burleson & Samter, 1985a). Thus, both men and women viewed highly person-centered comforting messages as better than messages low in person-centeredness.

Taking a somewhat different approach, Samter et al. (1987) had participants evaluate the sensitivity of comforting messages embedded in conversational dialogues. Participants in this study (230 men and 180 women) read dialogues containing comforting messages displaying low, moderate, or high levels of person-centeredness. Samter et al. also systematically varied the sex of the support provider. Participants completed scales providing evaluations of the sensitivity of the messages used in the dialogues as well as the sensitivity of the provider. Analyses for evaluations of message sensitivity detected only a significant main effect for the person-centered quality of the comforting messages; this effect explained over 46% of the variance in message ratings. No significant effect for participant sex was observed, nor was there any interaction between participant sex and level of message person-centeredness. Thus, both men and women viewed highly person-centered messages as more sensitive than less person-centered strategies. Analyses for evaluations of provider sensitivity detected a small, significant effect for provider sex ($eta^2 = .01$) and a large, significant effect for level of message person-centeredness ($eta^2 = .44$). Participants viewed women providers as behaving slightly more sensitively than males providers, regardless of the quality of the messages used; this result may reflect cultural stereotypes of women as nurturers. Providers using highly person-centered messages were viewed as more sensitive than providers using less person-centered messages. Again, the effect for degree of message person-centeredness was not qualified by participant sex. Hence, the results of this study provide no support for predictions derived from the different cultures account.

Kunkel (1995) carried out the most thorough examination of the effects of sex on criteria used to evaluate the sensitivity and effectiveness of comforting messages. To validate the notion that highly person-centered comforting messages are viewed as feminine while less person-centered messages are viewed as masculine, Kunkel had her participants (165 men and 127 women) rate 36 preformulated comforting messages for their masculinity or femininity; these messages varied systematically in degree of person-centeredness. Consistent with expectations, both males and females viewed messages low in person-centeredness as very masculine while viewing messages high in person-centeredness as very feminine. Kunkel also asked her participants to rate messages for sensitivity and effectiveness. Level of message person-centeredness explained 80% of the variance in sensitivity and effectiveness ratings, whereas participant sex explained a small, but significant, 2% of the variance in message ratings. Women evaluated highly person-centered messages somewhat more favorably than did men. These results were replicated in two subsequent studies (Jones & Burleson, in press; Samter, Whaley, Mortenson, & Burleson, in press).

The results of studies examining message perceptions are quite consistent and provide little support for the different cultures perspective. Men and women appear to use virtually the same standards in evaluating the sensitivity and effectiveness of comforting messages. Both men and women see person-centered messages as more sensitive and effective than less person-centered strategies, although men and women clearly see less person-centered messages as more masculine and likely to be used by men. Sex occasionally accounts for a small amount of variance (2%–4%) in how messages are perceived.

Preference for Gender of Comfort Provider

Men and women appear to evaluate comforting messages similarly when responding to a rating task, but who do they want to talk to when they are emotionally upset? The different cultures perspective strongly suggests that members of each gender will prefer seeking comfort from their own kind. Men should prefer men as support providers, whereas women should prefer women. This is the second general hypothesis examined in our research program.

This hypothesis was examined by Kunkel (1995). First, participants (165 men and 127 women) were simply asked to indicate who, during a time of emotional stress, they would be most likely to communicate with for support—a close same-sex friend or a close opposite-sex friend. Results indicate that 71% of the men and 76% of the women indicated they would prefer receiving support from a female friend. Thus, both men and women expressed a clear (and statistically significant) preference for female comfort providers.

Kunkel also presented her participants with descriptions of five emotionally stressful situations (e.g., a parent coming down with cancer; discovering unfaithfulness on the part of one's dating partner); for each situation, she had them indicate how comfortable they would feel when talking about the problem to a friend of each gender and how supportive they thought a friend of each gender would be in responding to the situation. Both male and female participants reported they would feel more comfortable discussing their troubles with female friends; sex of support provider explained 17% of the variance in comfortableness ratings. Participants of both sexes also reported that they anticipated that their female friends would be more supportive than their male friends; sex of support provider explained 34% of the variance in anticipated supportiveness.

Kunkel's results are consistent with those of a growing number of studies: Both men and women see females as generally more supportive than males (e.g., Burda & Vaux, 1987; Hays & Oxley, 1986) and experience interactions with females as more intimate, supportive, and meaningful than interactions with males (e.g., Reis, Senchak, & Solomon, 1985; Wheeler, Reis, & Nezlek, 1983). More important, several other studies have found that both sexes are more likely to seek emotional support from female providers than male providers (e.g., Aukett, Ritchie, & Mill, 1988; Buhrke & Fuqua, 1987; Clark, 1994; Flaherty & Richman, 1989; Lowenthal & Haven, 1968), although one study (Barbee et al., 1990) found that men and women preferred receiving support from members of their own sex.

In summary, results of studies examining people's preferences for the gender of support providers contradict hypotheses derived from the different cultures perspective. Contrary to the different cultures view, both males and females strongly prefer receiving support from females and report being more likely to actively seek support from females during emotionally troubling times. These findings make sense given that both men and women evaluate highly person-centered messages as more comforting and see women as more likely to use these messages than men.

The Value Placed on the Provision and Receipt of Comfort

The third general hypothesis derived from the different cultures view is that men and women should hold different values pertaining to emotional support and its provision in close personal relationships. More specifically, women should place a premium on the affectively oriented qualities of their relationship partners, whereas men should view the instrumental skills of their partners as more important.

We have examined this general hypothesis in the context of three different relationships: same-sex friendships, cross-sex friendships, and opposite-sex romances (Burleson, Kunkel, Samter, & Werking, 1996; Griffiths & Burleson, 1995). In these studies, we have used an instrument developed by Burleson and Samter (1990) called the Communication Functions Questionnaire (CFQ) to obtain evaluations of the importance of several different communication abilities in the context of specific interpersonal relationships. The evaluated communication abilities have included both affectively oriented skills (e.g., comforting, ego support) and instrumentally oriented skills (e.g., persuasion, giving information).

Our findings have been consistent across relationship type. Specifically, some small sex differences consistent with the two cultures view have been found: Women tend to view the affectively oriented skills of their partners as slightly more important than do men, whereas men tend to value the instrumentally oriented skills of their partners as more important than do women (Burleson et al., 1996). However, contrary to predictions derived from the different cultures view, both men and women value the affectively oriented skills of their partners much more than they do the instrumentally oriented skills of these partners. That is, both men and women assess communication skills such as comforting and ego support as much more important than skills such as persuasion and giving information. Type of communication skill typically explained about half (50%) of the variance in participants' ratings of skill importance. In contrast, participant sex typically explained only about 5% of the variance in skill ratings (Burleson et al., 1996; Griffiths & Burleson, 1995).

Kunkel (1995) developed a second way to examine similarities and differences in people's priorities for emotional support situations. To determine the priority assigned to affective and instrumental goals in emotional support contexts, Kunkel asked participants to rate the importance of six different goals when dealing with an upset person. Three of these goals were primarily affective in nature (e.g., helping the other work through his or her feelings, allowing the other to blow of steam, and letting the other talk about feelings and perspectives). The other three goals were more instrumental in character (solving the problem, getting the right advice about the situation, and finding ways to put the problem behind them). The different cultures view suggests that, in emotional support situations, men will give greater priority to instrumental goals (solving the problem), whereas women will give greater priority to affective goals (working through feelings). However, contrary to the predictions of the two cultures view, Kunkel found that both men and women assigned significantly greater priority to affective goals than to instrumental goals. Men and women did not differ in the priority given to instrumental goals, although women did place greater emphasis on affective goals than did men. Type of goal accounted for substantially more variance in participants' ratings (42%) than did sex of the participants (8%).

Our research on people's communication values and their priorities in emotional support situations provides little support for hypotheses derived from the different cultures view. Men and women are much more similar than different, with both men and women placing greater value or priority on the affective dimension of relationships than the instrumental dimension.

Outcomes of Gender-Typical Comforting Behaviors

A fourth general hypothesis derived from the two cultures view stipulates that members of each sex should like or be most attracted to others who engage in gender-typical forms of comforting behavior. One empirically testable consequence of this notion is that males who exhibit masculine (less person-centered) forms of comforting behavior should be well liked by other men, whereas males who engage in feminine (highly person-centered) modes of comforting should be rejected by same-sex peers. This general hypothesis has been examined in two different studies—one using children and one using an adult sample.

Burleson et al. (1986) obtained assessments of several different communication skills, including comforting skill, from first- and third-grade school children. These researchers used sociometric methods to assess the extent to which each child was accepted or rejected by his or her same-sex classmates. The different cultures view suggests that boys who are most likely to use masculine (i.e., less person-centered) comforting messages should be more accepted by their peers, whereas boys most likely to use more feminine, highly person-centered comforting messages should be rejected by same-sex peers. In this study, no relationship between peer acceptance and comforting skill was found for either sex. However, contrary to the different cultures viewpoint, person-centered comforting skill was negatively associated with peer rejection for both boys and girls. That is, boys who exhibited feminine, person-centered comforting skill were less rejected by other boys than those who exhibited more masculine, less person-centered comforting skill.

A similar design was employed by Samter and Burleson (1990) in a study of the communication skills predicting peer acceptance of young adults residing in college fraternities and sororities. Assessments of person-centered comforting skill and peer acceptance and rejection were obtained from participants (approximately 100 male and 100 female college students). Once again, a significant negative association was found between person-centered comforting skill (a feminine approach to comforting) and peer rejection. Moreover, contrary to the two cultures view, sex did not moderate the association between person-centered comforting skill and peer acceptance: The magnitudes of the negative associations for the male and female groups did not significantly differ. Both the results observed with elementary school children and college students are inconsistent with the hypothesis derived from the two cultures view. Males with stereotypically masculine comforting skills are not better liked by same-sex peers—indeed, they are more likely to be rejected by these peers.

A different line of research has focused on the communication skills predicting marital satisfaction and commitment. In a recent study, Sprecher, Metts, Burleson, Hatfield, and Thompson (1995) had 94 married, engaged, or cohabiting heterosexual couples complete measures of relationship satisfaction and relationship commitment, as well as assessments of partners' expressive interaction skills including skill at supportive communication. Sprecher et al. found that a partner's perceived competence at supportive communication was an equally important correlate for men and women of satisfaction with the relationship ($r = .66$ and $r = .67$ for males and females, respectively) and commitment to that relationship ($r = .56$ and $r = .45$ for males and females, respectively). These findings suggest that the supportive communication skills of partners are equally important for men and women in the context of long-term romantic relationships.

The Sprecher et al. (1995) results are consistent with a growing body of research indicating that, for both sexes, partners' feminine qualities—especially empathy and emotional support—predict marital satisfaction (e.g., Antill, 1983; Ickes, 1985; Lamke, 1989). These results also coincide with the findings of Reis and his colleagues, who have repeatedly found that interactions with women are experienced as more intimate and meaningful by both males and females (e.g., Reis, 1986; Reis et al., 1985; Wheeler et al., 1983). Moreover, Reis and his associates found that, for both sexes, the percentage of interactions involving males is positively associated with loneliness, whereas the percentage of interactions involving women is negatively associated with loneliness.

In summary, it appears that both males and females are more attracted to the members of both sexes that exhibit more feminine modes of behavior, especially feminine modes of providing comfort and emotional support. Further, both males and females appear to be repelled by those who engage in highly masculine forms of emotional support. These findings appear to be quite inconsistent with the different cultures view.

CONCLUSION

The different cultures perspective maintains that there should be substantial cognitive and behavioral differences between men and women. In particular, the different cultures viewpoint suggests that men and women should differ in (a) their criteria for what counts as sensitive comforting strategies, (b) their preferences for the gender of a comfort provider, (c) the value they place on comforting skills in the context of close relationships, and (d) their liking for those who comfort in gender-typical versus gender-atypical ways. We reviewed several studies empirically evaluating these predictions. Virtually no support was found for any of the predictions derived from the different cultures perspective.

Men and women are quite similar in their criteria, preferences, values, and patterns of interpersonal liking. Both men and women view highly person-centered comforting messages as most sensitive and effective; both see messages low in person-centeredness as relatively insensitive and ineffective. Both sexes indicate that they viewed highly person-centered comforting messages as feminine (i.e., as most likely to be utilized by women). Both men and women indicated that they prefer seeking comfort from women in times of trouble and distress. Both sexes viewed comforting skills as important in the context of various personal relationships and as substantially more important than instrumentally focused communication skills. Finally, both men and women are less likely to reject same-sex peers who possessed highly person-centered comforting skills and are more likely to reject peers who had less person-centered comforting skills.

A few statistically significant effects for sex differences were observed in the studies summarized earlier. However, these sex differences were uniformly small in magnitude, rarely accounting for more than 4% of the variance in a dependent variable. The occasional character and small size of observed sex differences is obviously not consistent with the degree of difference that would be expected if men and women really constituted different cultural groups. As Thorne (1993) suggested, the notion of different cultures implies a sense of dichotomous difference. Yet the largely overlapping distributions for men and women observed in the studies reviewed here certainly do not suggest any such dichotomous difference.

Although few differences were found between men and women in the cognitive variables examined in our studies, it must be remembered that there are important differences between the sexes in aspects of their comforting behavior. As noted at the outset of this chapter, women are more likely than men to provide emotional support to others, seek emotional support from others, focus on emotions while providing support, and use highly person-centered comforting messages in the effort to relieve distress. These differences—whose discovery provided part of the motivation for the articulation of the different cultures view—cannot be ignored. Indeed, the observed gender differences in behavior are comparatively substantial and robust, often accounting for more than 10% of the variance in the examined dependent variables. There is, then, a complex pattern of gender-related similarities and differences with respect to varied features of emotional support. In essence, with respect to comfort and emotional support, men and women both value the same things, see the same things as providing comfort, and prefer seeking comfort from females. Women, however, are more likely than men to provide comfort and use the message forms experienced as comforting.

A coherent theory must systematically account for both the observed similarities and differences in men and women with respect to varied aspects of emotional support. The different cultures perspective obviously is not such a theory; it emphasizes and can explain only sex-related differences. An alternative perspective, the skill deficit or skill specialization account (Burleson et al., 1996; Kunkel, 1995), appears capable of explaining both the observed similarities and differences.

Like the different cultures perspective, the skill specialization account sees gender-related differences in social skills as originating in the socialization experiences of children. According to this view, all cultures are partially composed of a dynamic, but fragmented, stock of knowledge (Berger & Luckmann, 1966). All cultures also recognize different types of persons or social categories, with sex or gender being one of the most important distinctions made in any society. Over the course of socialization, different types of persons are differentially exposed to various segments of the cultural stock of knowledge. Some portions of the knowledge stock are distributed to all members of the culture (e.g., the linguistic system, certain values), whereas other portions of the knowledge stock are distributed quite narrowly and specifically (e.g., certain skills). For example, in contemporary American culture, children of both sexes are exposed to many of the same communication practices, cultural artifacts, and value orientations by socialization agents such as parents, siblings, neighbors, teachers, and the mass media (see Golombok & Fivush, 1994; Thorne, 1993). However, to a greater extent than boys, girls in American society are encouraged to express and manage emotions. Greater practice at expressing emotions and dealing with the emotions of others leads women to develop more sophisticated skills for nurturing, comforting, and providing support. In contrast, to a greater extent than girls, boys are encouraged to influence others, direct the activities of others, and amuse others. Greater practice in these activities leads men to develop more sophisticated persuasive, informative, and narrative skills. Thus, members of each sex tend to specialize in some skills while having comparative deficits in other skills. However, what counts as skill in a particular domain (e.g., comforting, persuading) remains the same for both sexes.

Thus, the skill specialization account suggests that men and women seek similar things from their intimate relationships, conduct their intimate relationships through similar forms of behavior, and value the same sorts of communicative skills and abilities in their partners. However, this account also holds that there will be differences in the specific communication skills of men and women as a function of cultural norms that encourage differential patterns of skill development and use. Consequently, the skill specialization account can make sense out of the specific patterns of gender-related similarities and differences observed with respect to comforting and other forms of emotional support.

The skill specialization account also has virtue in encouraging researchers to adopt a rhetorical perspective, rather than a sociolinguistic perspective, on comforting behavior and similar communication skills. Researchers with backgrounds in linguistics and sociolinguistics (such as Maltz & Borker, 1982; Tannen, 1990) tend to treat group-based differences in communicative behaviors as a matter of style. For example, Tannen consistently referred to gender differences in problem talk (i.e., comforting) as a matter of conversational style, arguing that men and women have "different *but equally valid* styles" (1990, p. 15; italics original) and that "each style is valid on its own terms" (p. 47). Wood (1993, 1994a) also used the *style* terminology in her discussion of male and female differences in emotional support. Moreover, Wood (1993) specifically criticized works that "attach unequal value to masculine and feminine styles, and strive to teach students or clients the 'better' mode" (p. 53). Urging scholars to resist "being 'goaded by hierarchy,' " Wood (1993, p. 53) advocated a neutral evaluative stance with respect to gender differences in patterns of emotionally supportive behaviors.

Taking a neutral evaluative stance toward what is characterized as a matter of conversational style remains fully consistent with linguistic and sociolinguistic approaches to communicative phenomena. After all, many—if not most—differences at the linguistic and sociolinguistic levels of analysis are neutral: It obviously makes no sense to say that the morpheme *tree* is a better representation of a tree than the morpheme *arbor* or that the adjective–noun syntactic pattern is superior to the noun–adjective syntactic pattern. However, many of the communicative phenomena examined by Tannen, Wood, Maltz and Borker, and others are not exclusively subject to analysis at the linguistic and sociolinguistic levels; indeed, they may not be best analyzed at these levels.

Many communicative phenomena, especially functionally directed behaviors such as comforting, are fruitfully considered at the rhetorical level of analysis. For over 2,500 years, a constitutive assumption of the rhetorical tradition has been that there are not merely different ways of doing things with words; rather, some ways of doing things with words are better than other alternatives—more effective, more convincing, more efficient, more sensitive—whatever the particular criterion. Hence, a rhetorical approach to the analysis of gender-linked communication practices, especially functionally directed uses of language such as comforting, diverges significantly from linguistic and sociolinguistic approaches in fundamental assumptions. From a rhetorical perspective, the researcher is interested in identifying different strategic options and determining which of these options is better or more effective for the task undertaken. By viewing comforting and related behaviors as social skills, the skill specialization account encourages researchers to adopt a rhetorical perspective.

Some important methodological and pedagogical implications follow from our critique of the different cultures view. Recent scholarship by proponents of the different cultures account (Swain, 1989; Wood, 1993, 1994a; Wood & Inman, 1993) argued that the way intimacy and emotional closeness have been evaluated by social scientists has been biased by usage of a feminine ruler and that many theories of intimacy are "flawed by their exclusion of masculine styles of creating and expressing closeness" (Wood, 1993, p. 45). These scholars contended that men and women possess separate rulers with which they measure intimacy and emotional closeness. However, as most of the findings reported in this chapter strongly suggest, men and women tend to use similar, if not identical, rulers in evaluating the sensitivity and effectiveness of emotional support. Thus, assessments of comforting behavior in terms of emotion focus (Barbee et al., 1993) or person-centeredness (Burleson, 1982) do not unduly rely on an exclusively feminine standard but rather employ standards that men and women consensually share. Indeed, findings summarized in this chapter provide additional validation for methods used to evaluate comforting message quality (e.g., Applegate, 1980).

Second, the findings summarized in this chapter stand as a critique of research designs commonly used by proponents of the different cultures account—designs that exclusively focus on the examination of between-group differences. There is a growing literature in the fields of communication and personal relationships suggesting that, although some noteworthy differences between men and women exist, when both within- and between-gender comparisons are made, the similarities are as important—if not more important—than the differences (Aries, 1996; Burleson et al., 1996; Canary & Hause, 1993; Duck & Wright, 1993; Thorne, 1993; Wright, 1988, chap. 2, this volume). The results reported in this chapter thus emphasize that between-gender differences must be viewed against the backdrop of what are often substantial similarities. Future research should permit the assessment of both similarities and differences. Moreover, the magnitudes of these similarities and differences should be reported and used in interpreting results.

Finally, our findings call into question some of the pedagogic advice offered by advocates of the different cultures account. Supporters of the different cultures view (e.g., Maltz & Borker, 1982; Tannen, 1986, 1990; Wood, 1993, 1994a) have suggested that men and women need to become bilingual to avoid miscommunication. Our results suggest that men and women speak the same language, although each sex may have certain specialties in the use of that language. The empirical findings summarized in this chapter suggest that it would be counterproductive to teach men and women to value comforting efforts frequently produced by men (i.e., messages low in person-centeredness). Simply because men typically use less person-centered comforting strategies does not mean that this masculine mode of behavior is—or should be—valued and advocated. In fact, the research findings suggest quite the contrary: More needs to be done to enhance men's abilities in the comforting realm—both in schools and in the home. The enhancement of men's comforting skills might help alleviate some of the pressure associated with women's traditional and culturally assigned role of caregiver (Ferguson, 1984; Wood, 1994b).

In concluding, we find ourselves in agreement with Thorne (1993), who contends that:

> The separate-cultures story has lost its narrative force. . . . To move our research wagons out of the dualistic rut, we can, first of all, try to start with a sense of the whole rather than with an assumption of gender as separation and difference. If we begin by assuming different cultures, separate spheres, or contrastive differences, we will also end with a sharp sense of dichotomy rather than attending to multiple differences and sources of commonality. (p. 108)

In dragging our research wagons from the dualistic mud, we should give ongoing attention to the similarities *and* differences that characterize the sexes, and we should always remember that degrees of similarity and difference are empirical matters that need to be ascertained by carefully examining the worlds we inhabit and create.

REFERENCES

Applegate, J. L. (1980). Adaptive communication in educational contexts: A study of teacher's communicative strategies. *Communication Education, 29,* 158–170.

Antill, J. K. (1983). Sex role complementarity versus similarity in married couples. *Journal of Personality and Social Psychology, 45,* 145–155.

Aries, E. (1996). *Men and women in interaction: Reconsidering the differences.* New York: Oxford University Press.

Aries, E. J., & Johnson, F. L. (1983). Close friendship in adulthood: Conversational content between same-sex friends. *Sex Roles, 9,* 1183–1196.

Ashton, W. A., & Fuehrer, A. (1993). Effects of gender and gender role identification of participant and type of social support resource on support seeking. *Sex Roles, 28,* 461–476.

Aukett, R., Ritchie, J., & Mill, K. (1988). Gender differences in friendship patterns. *Sex Roles, 19,* 57–66.

Balswick, J. (1988). *The inexpressive male.* Lexington, MA: Lexington.

Barbee. A. P., Cunningham, M. R., Winstead, B. A., Derlega, V. J., Gulley, M. R., Yankeelov, P. A., & Druen, P. B. (1993). Effects of gender role expectations on the social support process. *Journal of Social Issues, 49,* 175–190.

Barbee, A. P., Gulley, M. R., & Cunningham, M. R. (1990). Support seeking in personal relationships. *Journal of Social and Personal Relationships, 7,* 531–540.

Berger, P. L., & Luckmann, T. (1966). *The social construction of reality: A treatise in the sociology of knowledge.* New York: Doubleday.

Borden, A. W. (1979). *An investigation of the relationships among indices of social cognition, motivation, and communicative performance.* Unpublished doctoral dissertation, University of Illinois, Champaign.

Borisoff, D., & Hahn, D. (1995). From research to pedagogy: Teaching gender and communication. *Communication Quarterly, 43,* 381–393.

Bruess, C. J. S., & Pearson, J. C. (1996). Gendered patterns in family communication. In J. Wood (Ed.), *Gendered relationships* (pp. 59–78). Newbury Park, CA: Sage.

Buhrke, R. A., & Fuqua, D. R. (1987). Sex differences in same- and cross-sex supportive relationships. *Sex Roles, 17,* 339–352.

Burda, P. C., & Vaux, A. C. (1987). The social support process in men: Overcoming sex-role obstacles. *Human Relations, 40,* 31–44.

Burleson, B. R. (1982). The development of comforting communication skills in childhood and adolescence. *Child Development, 53,* 1578–1588.

Burleson, B. R. (1987). Cognitive complexity. In J. C. McCroskey & J. A. Daly (Eds.), *Personality and interpersonal communication* (pp. 305–349). Newbury Park, CA: Sage.

Burleson, B. R. (1990). Comforting as everyday social support: Relational consequences of supportive behaviors. In S. Duck (Ed.), *Personal relationships and social support* (pp. 66–82). London: Sage.

Burleson, B. R., Albrecht, T. L., Goldsmith, D., & Sarason, I. G. (1994). Introduction: The communication of social support. In B. R. Burleson, T. L. Albrecht, & I. G. Sarason (Eds.), *The communication of social support: Messages, interactions, relationships, and community* (pp. xi–xxx). Newbury Park, CA: Sage.

Burleson, B. R., Applegate, J. L., Burke, J. A., Clark, R. A., Delia, J. G., & Kline, S. L. (1986). Communicative correlates of peer acceptance in childhood. *Communication Education, 35*, 349–361.

Burleson, B. R., Kunkel, A. W., Samter, W., & Werking, K. J. (1996). Men's and women's evaluations of communication skills in personal relationships: When sex differences make a difference—and when they don't. *Journal of Social and Personal Relationships, 13*, 201–224.

Burleson, B. R., & Samter, W. (1985a). Consistencies in theoretical and naive evaluations of comforting messages. *Communication Monographs, 52*, 103–123.

Burleson, B. R., & Samter, W. (1985b). Individual differences in the perception of comforting messages: An exploratory investigation. *Central States Speech Journal, 36*, 39–50.

Burleson, B. R., & Samter, W. (1990). Effects of cognitive complexity on the perceived importance of communication skills in friends. *Communication Research, 17*, 165–182.

Caldwell, M. A., & Peplau, L. A. (1982). Sex differences in same-sex friendship. *Sex Roles, 8*, 721–732.

Canary, D. J., & Hause, K. S. (1993). Is there any reason to research sex differences in communication? *Communication Quarterly, 41*, 129–144.

Cancian, F. (1986). The feminization of love. *Signs, 11*, 692–708.

Clark, R. A. (1993). Men's and women's self-confidence in persuasive, comforting, and justificatory communicative tasks. *Sex Roles, 28*, 553–567.

Clark, R. A. (1994). Children's and adolescents' gender preferences for conversational partners for specific communicative objectives. *Journal of Social and Personal Relationships, 11*, 313–319.

Crawford, M. (1995). *Talking difference: On gender and language.* Thousand Oaks, CA: Sage.

Cutrona, C. E. (1996). *Social support in couples.* Thousand Oaks, CA: Sage.

Deaux, K., & Major, B. (1987). Putting gender into context: An interactive model of gender-related behavior. *Psychological Review, 94*, 369–389.

Derlega, V. J., Barbee, A. P., & Winstead, B. A. (1994). Friendship, gender, and social support: Laboratory studies of supportive interactions. In B. R. Burleson, T. L. Albrecht, & I. G. Sarason (Eds.), *The communication of social support: Message, interactions, relationships, and community* (pp. 136–151). Newbury Park, CA: Sage.

Derlega, V. J, Metts, S., Petronio, S., & Margulis, S. T. (1993). *Self-disclosure.* Newbury Park, CA: Sage.

Duck, S., & Wright, P. H. (1993). Reexamining gender differences in same-gender friendships: A close look at two kinds of data. *Sex Roles, 28*, 709–727.

Fausto-Sterling, A. (1985). *Myths of gender: Biological theories about women and men.* New York: Basic Books.

Ferguson, K. E. (1984). *The feminist case against bureaucracy.* Philadelphia, PA: Temple University Press.

Flaherty, J., & Richman, J. (1989). Gender differences in the perception and utilization of social support: Theoretical perspectives and an empirical test. *Social Science and Medicine, 28*, 1221–1228.

Galvin, K., & Cooper, P. (Eds.). (1996). *Making connections: Readings in relational communication.* Los Angeles, CA: Roxbury.

Geertz, C. (1973). *The interpretation of cultures.* New York: Basic Books.

Gerson, J. M., & Peiss, K. (1985). Boundaries, negotiation, consciousness: Reconceptualizing gender relations. *Social Problems, 32*, 317–331.

Gilligan, C. (1982). *In a different voice: Psychological theory and women's development.* Cambridge, MA: Harvard University Press.

Golombok, S., & Fivush, R. (1994). *Gender development.* Cambridge, England: Cambridge University Press.

Gray, J. (1992). *Men are from Mars, women are from Venus: A practical guide for improving communication and getting what you want in your relationships.* New York: HarperCollins.

Gray, J. (1995). *Mars and Venus in the bedroom: A guide to lasting romance and passion.* New York: HarperCollins.

Griffiths, K., & Burleson, B. R. (1995, April). *Gender and communication values in friendships: A comparison of gender-related similarities and differences in same-sex and cross-sex friendships.* Paper presented at the Central States Communication Association convention, Indianapolis, IN.

Gumperz, J. J. (1982). *Discourse strategies.* Cambridge, England: Cambridge University Press.

Hays, R. B., & Oxley, D. (1986). Social network development and functioning during a life transition. *Journal of Personality and Social Psychology, 50,* 305–313.

Henley, N. M., & Kramarae, C. (1991). Gender, power, and miscommunication. In N. Coupland, H. Giles, & J. M. Wiemann (Eds.), *"Miscommunication" and problematic talk* (pp. 18–43). Newbury Park, CA: Sage.

Hoffman, M. L. (1977). Sex differences in empathy and related behaviors. *Psychological Bulletin, 84,* 712–722.

Ickes, W. (1985). Sex-role influences on compatibility in relationships. In W. Ickes (Ed.), *Compatible and incompatible relationships* (pp. 187–208). New York: Springer-Verlag.

Johnson, F. L. (1989). Women's culture and communication: An analytical perspective. In C. M. Lont & S. A. Friedley (Eds.), *Beyond boundaries: Sex and gender diversity in communication* (pp. 301–316). Fairfax, VA: George Mason University Press.

Jones, S. M., & Burleson, B. R. (in press). The impact of situational variables on helpers' perceptions of comforting messages: An attributional analysis. *Communication Research.*

Kluckholm, C. (1951). Values and value orientations in the theory of action. In T. Parsons & E. A. Shils (Eds.), *Toward a general theory of action.* Cambridge, MA: Harvard University Press.

Kunkel, A. W. (1995, November). *Assessing the adequacy of explanations for gender differences in emotional support: An experimental test of the different cultures and skill deficit accounts.* Paper presented at the Speech Communication Association convention, San Antonio, TX.

Lakoff, R. (1975). *Language and woman's place.* New York: Harper & Row.

Lamke, L. (1989). Marital adjustment among rural couples: The role of expressiveness. *Sex Roles, 21,* 579–590.

Lever, J. (1976). Sex differences in the games children play. *Social Problems, 23,* 478–483.

Levine, L. E., & Hoffman, M. L. (1975). Empathy and cooperation in 4-year-olds. *Developmental Psychology, 11,* 533–534.

Lowenthal, M. F., & Haven, C. (1968). Interaction and adaptation: Intimacy as a critical variable. *American Sociological Review, 33,* 20–30.

Maccoby, E. E. (1990). Gender and relationships. *American Psychologist, 45,* 513–520.

Maltz, D. N., & Borker, R. A. (1982). A cultural approach to male-female miscommunication. In J. J. Gumperz (Ed.), *Language and social identity* (pp. 196–216). Cambridge, England: Cambridge University Press.

Mazur, E., & Olver, R. R. (1987). Intimacy and structure: Sex differences in imagery of same-sex friendships. *Sex Roles, 16,* 539–558.

Mickelson, K. D., Helgeson, V. S., & Weiner, E. (1995). Gender effects on social support provision and receipt. *Personal Relationships, 2,* 211–224.

Noller, P. (1993). Gender and emotional communication in marriage: Different cultures or differential social power? *Journal of Language and Social Psychology, 12,* 132–152.

Rawlins, W. K. (1992). *Friendship matters: Communication, dialectics, and the life course.* New York: Aldine DeGruyter.

Reis, H. T. (1986). Gender effects in social participation: Intimacy, loneliness, and the conduct of social interaction. In R. Gilmour & S. Duck (Eds.), *The emerging field of personal relationships* (pp. 91–107). Hillsdale, NJ: Lawrence Erlbaum Associates.

Reis, H. T., Senchak, M., & Solomon, B. (1985). Sex differences in the intimacy of social interaction: Further examination of potential explanations. *Journal of Personality and Social Psychology, 48*, 1204–1217.

Rosario, M., Shinn, M., Morch, H., & Huckabee, C. B. (1988). Gender differences in coping and social supports: Testing socialization and role constraint theories. *Journal of Community Psychology, 16*, 55–69.

Samter, W. (1989). *Communication skills predictive of interpersonal acceptance in a group living situation: A sociometric study.* Unpublished doctoral dissertation, Purdue University, West Lafayette, IN.

Samter, W., & Burleson, B. R. (1990). Evaluations of communication skills as predictors of peer acceptance in a group living situation. *Communication Studies, 41*, 311–326.

Samter, W., Burleson, B. R., & Murphy, L. B. (1987). Comforting conversations: The effects of strategy type on evaluations of messages and message producers. *The Southern Speech Communication Journal, 52*, 263–284.

Samter, W., Whaley, B. B., Mortenson, S. R., & Burleson, B. R. (in press). Ethnicity and emotional support in same-sex friendship: A comparison of Asian-Americans, African-Americans, and Euro-Americans. *Pesonal Relationships.*

Schloff, L., & Yudkin, M. (1993). *He & she talk: How to communicate with the opposite sex.* New York: Plume Books.

Sprecher, S., Metts, S., Burleson, B., Hatfield, E., & Thompson, A. (1995). Domains of expressive interaction in intimate relationships: Associations with satisfaction and commitment. *Family Relations, 44*, 1–8.

Swain, S. (1989). Covert intimacy: Closeness in men's friendships. In B. Risman & P. Schwartz (Eds.), *Gender in intimate relationships: A microstructural approach* (pp. 71–86). Belmont, CA: Wadsworth.

Tannen, D. (1986). *That's not what I meant! How conversational style makes or breaks relationships.* New York: Random House.

Tannen, D. (1990). *You just don't understand: Women and men in conversation.* New York: William Morrow.

Tannen, D. (1994). *Talking from 9 to 5—Women and men in the workplace: Language, sex and power.* New York: Avon Books.

Thorne, B. (1993). *Gender play: Girls and boys in school.* New Brunswick, NJ: Rutgers University Press.

Trobst, K. K., Collins, R. L., & Embree, J. M. (1994). The role of emotion in social support provision: Gender, empathy and expressions of distress. *Journal of Social and Personal Relationships, 11*, 45–62.

Utne Reader. (1993, January). Men and women: Can we get along? Should we even try?

Vaux, A. (1985). Variations in social support associated with gender, ethnicity, and age. *Journal of Social Issues, 41*, 89–110.

West, C., & Zimmerman, D. H. (1977). Women's place in everyday talk: Reflections on parent-child interaction. *Social Problems, 24*, 521–529.

West, C., & Zimmerman, D. H. (1983). Small insults: A study of interruptions in conversations between unacquainted persons. In B. Thorne, C. Kramarae, & N. Henley (Eds.), *Language, gender and society* (pp. 102–117). Rowley, MA: Newbury House.

Wheeler, L., Reis, H., & Nezlek, J. (1983). Loneliness, social interaction, and sex roles. *Journal of Personality and Social Psychology, 45*, 943–953.

Winstead, B. A. (1986). Sex differences in same-sex friendships. In V. J. Derlega & B. A. Winstead (Eds.), *Friendship and social interaction* (pp. 81–99). New York: Springer-Verlag.

Wood, J. T. (1993). Engendered relations: Interaction, caring, power, and responsibility in intimacy. In S. Duck (Ed.), *Social context and relationships* (pp. 26–54). Newbury Park, CA: Sage.

Wood, J. T. (1994a). *Gendered lives: Communication, gender, and culture.* Belmont, CA: Wadsworth.

Wood, J. T. (1994b). *Who cares? Women, care, and culture.* Carbondale, IL: Southern Illinois University Press.

Wood, J. T. (1995). *Relational communication: Continuity and change in personal relationships.* Belmont, CA: Wadsworth.

Wood, J. T., & Inman, C. C. (1993). In a different mode: Masculine styles of communicating closeness. *Journal of Applied Communication Research, 21,* 279–295.

Wright, P. H. (1988). Interpreting research on gender differences in friendship: A case for moderation and a plea for caution. *Journal of Social and Personal Relationships, 5,* 367–373.

Zimmerman, D. H., & West, C. (1975). Sex roles, interruptions, and silences in conversations. In B. Thorne & N. Henley (Eds.), *Language and sex: Difference and dominance* (pp. 105–129). Rowley, MA: Newbury House.

Chapter 6

The Gender-Linked Language Effect: Do Language Differences Really Make a Difference?

Anthony Mulac
University of California–Santa Barbara

There are two abiding truths on which the general public and research scholars find themselves in uneasy agreement: (a) Men and women speak the same language, and (b) men and women speak that language differently. So we have, at one and the same time, gender-linked (or *sex-linked* as they are sometimes called) similarities and differences in language use. What this means for communication between and among men and women, and in fact whether it means anything at all, is the topic of this chapter.

PROGRAM OF RESEARCH

My observations on women's and men's language are based on the program of research conducted at the University of California–Santa Barbara over the past 15 years. During this time, colleagues and I have collaborated on 15 empirical investigations of female–male differences in language use and the effects of those differences on observer judgments. Because we have assessed women's and men's language for possible differences, we have also tested for similarities. This is the case because any language variables that fail, in a given communication context, to distinguish between women and men may be viewed as representing similarities of language use.

From the beginning, our research approach has involved a series of theoretical assumptions: First, if men and women differ in their communication behavior, such differences would likely be found in microscopic language behaviors. The logical consequence is to look at their word choice. Second, because language is spoken and understood as combinations of language features, rather than individual features, analyses that seek gender-linked differences should assess linguistic features in combination, not one at a time. Accordingly, look at combinations of language. Third, because different communication contexts might lead to shifts in gender differentiators, investigations should be conducted in a variety of communication settings. That being the case, sample language under various circumstances. Fourth, to increase the power and generalizibility of research findings, relatively large numbers of communicators should be assessed. Therefore, sample a lot of people. Fifth, to be meaningful from a communication standpoint, the transcribed language of men and women should lead to differences in psychological judgments rendered by observers. Consequently, see if people judge them differently. Sixth, it should be shown that transcript raters cannot determine the sex of communicators to guard against their judgments being influenced by gender stereotypes. Therefore, check whether judges can guess communicator sex. Finally, a predictive link should be demonstrated between raters' judgments of speakers' psychological characteristics, on the one hand, and the speakers' gender-differentiating language use, on the other. Accordingly, check whether language differences play a part in judgments.

For our program of research, we implemented a paradigm that was consistent with these theoretical assumptions: Speakers of a particular age group (e.g., fifth graders, university students, or senior citizens) were asked to engage in a particular communication task (e.g., to describe a landscape photograph or solve a problem with a partner). Their spontaneous speech samples were recorded on audiotape and transcribed for later analysis. The following are examples of transcripts of two speakers, between 30 and 35 years of age, describing the same landscape photograph[1]:

SPEAKER NUMBER: 5

This picture I like very much, with the mountains—they dominate the picture—and the yellow trees. There's a lot of . . . there's color in this picture without really having color. There's, there's a force in this picture; it . . . draws you to it, like you really want to be there. And, uh, let's see . . . there's something so removed from the city about it—peaceful and cool—and you'd really like to be there. Uhm, again there's something about the colors—they, they're icy colors and yet the yellow in the forefront, in the foreground, uhm give, or lend, a certain kind of warmth to the picture.

SPEAKER NUMBER: 11

Okay. It looks like a beautiful winter scene, in which we've got lots of very . . . probably fall, maybe the first snowfall of the year. Large groups of tall

---

[1]These transcripts were taken from the 12 whose effects were analyzed in Mulac, Incontro, and James (1985).

mountains and partially covered with snow . . . and perhaps some lower hogbacks and such forth . . . and covered with various types of coniferous and deciduous trees. Probably morning time with a low layer of fog just kind of . . . between the ground and the tops of the mountains. Beautiful blue sky up above. Reminds me a lot of the Sierra Nevada's perhaps, maybe the west side.

In several of our investigations, individuals were asked to write essays or descriptions of landscape photographs and these were printed for assessment. The number of speakers or writers whose language we sampled in various studies has ranged from 12 to 108 individuals, with an average of 40 or more. By assessing a relatively large number of actual language samples, we increased our ability to generalize to other individuals. Linguistic analyses were then conducted by trained coders who assessed the transcripts for linguistic features previously found to distinguish the speech or writing of women (e.g., intensifiers ["really"] or references to emotion ["I felt sad"]) or men (e.g., references to quantity ["30 feet tall"] or elliptical sentences ["Great picture."]). In each study, the actual sex of the speakers or writers was not made available to the language coders. The language data were aggregated across coders and analyzed, using discriminant analysis procedures, to determine whether the female and male communicators had used language differently.

Next, untrained observers were asked to guess the sex of the speakers or writers. Their ability, or inability, to accurately identify the sex of the individuals on the basis of language use provided important information on the degree of similarity of men's and women's language. These data also indicated whether other observers could be influenced by gender stereotypes.

In addition, other untrained observers were asked to rate psychological characteristics of each of the speakers (or writers) as a person, based on the transcripts of what those individuals had said. Ratings were done using a 12-item semantic differential, the Speech Dialect Attitudinal Scale (SDAS; Mulac, 1975, 1976), which was designed to assess the effects of dialect differences. Factor analysis of the SDAS ratings has consistently yielded the following three-factor solution: (a) *Socio-Intellectual Status* (e.g., rich/poor, literate/illiterate), (b) *Aesthetic Quality* (beautiful/ugly, nice/awful), and (c) *Dynamism* (strong/weak, aggressive/unaggressive). Our analyses of these ratings showed whether the male and female communicators were judged differently.

Finally, we determined, by means of multiple-regression analysis, whether gender-differentiating language could explain the judgments of psychological characteristics. To the extent that male/female language differences could predict psychological ratings, such results demonstrated that language was implicated in the effect.

SIMILARITIES IN LANGUAGE

Sex-Guess Accuracy

Our research has shown that the language used by U.S. women and men is remarkably similar. In fact, it is so indistinguishable that native speakers of American English cannot correctly identify which language examples were produced by women and which were produced by men. Support for this claim comes from our empirical investigations of female–male language differences and the effects of those differences. We felt there was a need to learn whether readers could determine the sex of the speakers because, if they could, other respondents might be influenced by gender stereotypes when they rated the speakers. In other words, if raters could determine that a given speaker was a man, they might rate him higher on strength and aggressiveness purely because of their stereotypical view that men exhibit these attributes, without regard to how his language use made him appear. However, if they could not correctly identify speaker sex, they could not be influenced by stereotypes.

In our first study that measured sex-guess accuracy (Mulac & Lundell, 1980), we recorded brief landscape photograph descriptions by 48 speakers from four age groups (six males and six females from each group): (a) public school fifth graders, (b) university freshmen and sophomores, (c) university teaching assistants and instructors, and (d) people in their 50s and 60s. One-minute segments from these recordings were transcribed orthographically and printed, one-to-a-page, with arbitrary speaker numbers (e.g., "Speaker Number 24"). We then asked beginning communication students at the University of California–Santa Barbara, for whom English was the first language, to guess the sex of the speakers from each of the age groups. Results show that they were not able to do so with anything better than chance accuracy.

Mulac and Lundell (1982) recorded 30 students giving their first speech in a university public speaking class. On the basis of 1-minute transcripts, university students were unable to guess the sex of the speakers. The third study (Mulac, Incontro, & James, 1985) involved recording 12 secondary teachers and college instructors from across the country describing landscape photographs. Once again, university students were unable to distinguish male from female speakers. The same result was found for the essays of 96 4th-, 8th-, and 12th-grade students writing on the topic, "Is it ever all right to tell a lie?" (Mulac, Studley, & Blau, 1990). Finally, Mulac and Lundell (1994) reported a similar finding for 40 university students' impromptu essays describing landscape photographs.

University students were able to guess speaker sex accurately in one study, but it dealt with the language of characters in children's television programs rather than that of actual female and male individuals (Mulac, Bradac, & Mann, 1985). In that investigation, respondents could correctly identify the sex of over 68% of the 168 characters, all of whom were speaking in carefully scripted dialogues. Therefore, native speakers of American English are able to detect gender-linked differences when those differences have been produced by television writers who presumably employ gender-stereotypical language. However, these same respondents cannot identify actual women and men who are communicating in an impromptu fashion. These consistent results provide clear evidence that the spoken and written language used in everyday communication by women and men, as well as girls and boys, displays a high degree of similarity.

Average Language Feature Use

Results of our studies also point to the high degree of comparability of language in another way. If we view the actual language use in a given investigation, one variable at a time, we are struck more by the similarity of men's and women's language than by the difference. For example, in Mulac, Wiemann, Widenmann, and Gibson (1988), we assessed the language of university students (63 men and 79 women) as they worked to solve problems in same-sex or mixed-sex dyads. Table 6.1 shows the average male and female use of 12 variables per 100 words of speech.

If we average across same-sex and mixed-sex dyads, we see that men interrupted their partner an average of 1.15 times per 100 words of their speech, whereas women interrupted 0.78 times per 100 words. Men used directives (e.g., "Write that down") 0.31 times per 100 words and women used directives 0.22 times. In addition, women employed questions an average of 2.06 times per 100 words versus 1.60 times for the men. Women averaged 0.70 intensive adverbs ("really") per 100 words, whereas men averaged 0.46 intensive adverbs. Other variables demonstrate even smaller discrepancies between women and men in these problem-solving interactions. This evidences a substantial degree of comparability in their selection of linguistic elements. However, despite the obvious similarity of language use, we did find significant differences in a later phase of this study by employing a powerful, multivariate statistical procedure.

Based on the prior discussion, it appears that similarities in language use are consistently found in the sex-guess phase of our investigations and in the average use of specific language features. Both of these results seem to indicate that similarity of language constitutes the rule regarding the communication behavior of women and men in our society. The question remaining is this: If their language use is so similar why is there so much heated discussion about differences in their linguistic performance? Do women and men *really* use language differently?

TABLE 6.1

Means and Standard Deviations for 12 Linguistic Variables[a] Used by Male and Female Interactions in Same-Sex and Mixed-Sex Dyads (Mulac et al., 1988)

Variables	Means				Standard Deviations			
	Male/Same	Female/Same	Male/Mixed	Female/Mixed	Male/Same	Female/Same	Male/Mixed	Female/Mixed
Fillers	2.85	2.57	2.38	2.91	1.63	1.61	0.94	1.03
Interruptions	1.18	0.72	1.12	0.84	0.99	0.65	0.83	0.85
Adverbials begin S.	0.35	0.47	0.40	0.39	0.25	0.43	0.29	0.23
Conj./filler begin S.	2.00	1.38	1.69	1.66	1.12	0.61	0.97	0.55
Directives	0.37	0.21	0.25	0.22	0.42	0.26	0.29	0.25
Negations	0.60	0.56	0.85	0.85	0.54	0.40	0.64	0.52
Questions	1.47	1.85	1.74	2.26	0.88	1.20	1.25	1.71
Hedges/softeners	0.33	0.50	0.42	0.27	0.40	0.74	0.57	0.27
Intensive adverbs	0.52	0.67	0.40	0.73	0.44	0.57	0.35	0.90
Justifiers	0.21	0.33	0.20	0.21	0.22	0.33	0.19	0.23
Action verbs	4.21	4.16	3.99	4.15	1.27	1.32	1.22	1.77
Personal pronouns	11.88	13.17	11.81	12.57	2.96	3.77	3.37	3.72

[a]Statistics given per 100 words.

DIFFERENCES IN LANGUAGE

Summary of Research on Differences

The answer to the prior question is an unrestrained "Yes!"—meaningful differences in language behavior do exist. This conclusion is supported by a substantial number of empirical investigations of actual male–female language use conducted in a variety of communication contexts with communicators of different ages. In 1993, we summarized the results of over 30 studies, including our own experimental studies referenced earlier; all found statistically significant differences in the use of language features by male and female communicators (Mulac & Gibbons, 1993).[2] Twenty-one linguistic features were found to distinguish gender in two or more investigations. Table 6.2 summarizes the results of this analysis, indicating 6 variables used more by men, 10 used more by women, and 5 whose use was equivocal. Next to each variable, an *M* or *F* is printed for each study that found that variable to be employed more by males or by females. For example, we discovered four studies that reported references to quantity used more by males (hence *M* was printed four times next to it) and six that indicated intensive adverbs employed more by females. The appendix provides descriptions and examples of the 21 features along with the research context and citation for each finding (see appendix).

We located six features that were generally used more by male communicators. They include the following, with examples drawn from our research transcripts: references to quantity (". . . an 81% loss in vision"), judgmental adjectives ("Reading can be a drag"), and elliptical sentences ("Nice photo."). Men were also more likely to use directives ("Think of some more"), locatives ("The sun is off to the left side"), and "I" references ("I have a lot of meetings").

In addition, we found 10 language features that were generally used more by women and girls. Among them were intensive adverbs ("He's really interested"), references to emotions ("If he really loved you"), and dependent clauses ("which is the type that produces slightly more fuel than it uses"). Women were also more likely to use sentence-initial adverbials ("When the material is too difficult, studying with someone can be beneficial"), uncertainty verbs ("It seems to be . . ."), oppositions ("The tone of it is very peaceful, yet full of movement"), and negations ("Preparation will make you not sound like a fool"). Finally, this analysis showed that women were more likely to use hedges ("We're kind of set in our ways"), questions ("Do you think so?"), and longer mean length sentences.

---

[2]Although the number of linguistic comparisons undertaken in these studies varied, roughly one half of the features assessed across them evidenced gender differences.

TABLE 6.2
Mulac and Gibbons (1993) Results Showing 21 Gender-Differentiating
Language Features Supported by Two or More Empirical Studies

Gender	Language Features	Gender/Study Findings						
Male[a]	References to quantity	M[b]	M	M	M			
	Judgmental adjectives	M	M	M				
	Elliptical sentences	M	M					
	Directives	M	M					
	Locatives	M	M					
	"I" references	M	M					
Female	Intensive adverbs	F	F	F	F	F	F	
	References to emotions	F	F	F	F	F		
	Dependent clauses	F	F	F	F	F		
	Mean length sentence	F	F	F	F	F	M[c]	
	Sentence-initial adverbials	F	F	F	F			
	Uncertainty verbs	F	F	F				
	Oppositions	F	F					
	Negations	F	F					
	Hedges	F	F					
	Questions	F	F					
Equivocal	Personal pronouns	F	F	F	F	F	M	M
	Tag questions	F	F	F	F	M	M	
	Fillers	F	F	F	M	M		
	Progressive verbs	F	F	M				
	Justifiers	F	M					

[a]Where the pattern is consistent across studies, the variable is listed under the gender making greater use of it. Variables are listed in decreasing order of gender-predicting effectiveness.

[b]Each letter (M = male or F = female) represents one study that found a given language feature to be indicative of the males or females whose communication was analyzed.

[c]Fourth-grade boys' use of run-on sentences seems to explain this single conflicting result.

The remaining five features were found to be equivocal predictors of gender. That is, some studies showed these five to be used more by men and others more by women. These included personal pronouns ("Before we go on, do you . . . ?"), tag questions ("That's right, isn't it?"), fillers ("It's, you know . . . , it's"), progressive verbs ("watching him"), and justifiers (". . . because that's what I saw").

Our review indicated that 16 language features distinguish communicator gender with a high degree of reliability across a substantial number of investigations. These findings demonstrate that clear-cut differences are present and must be acknowledged. However, it is obvious that no Gilesian markers of gender exist (Giles, Scherer, & Taylor, 1979)—no linguistic forms that clearly and unerringly point to the gender of the speaker. Instead we have, as Smith (1985) observed, only gender-linked tendencies to favor certain linguistic features over others. If we use these 16 features to analyze the two language samples presented earlier of speakers describing a landscape photograph, we can begin to see some of the subtle tendencies indicated in the literature review.

SPEAKER NUMBER: 5 (A women)

This picture I *like* (reference to emotion) *very* (intensive adverb) much, with the mountains—they dominate the picture—and the yellow trees. There's a lot of . . . there's *color in this picture without really having color* (opposition). There's, there's a force in this picture; it . . . *draws you* (reference to emotion) to it, like you *really* (intensive adverb) *want* (reference to emotion) to be there. And, uh, let's see . . . there's something *so* (intensive adverb) removed from the city about it—peaceful and cool—and you'd *really* (intensive adverb) *like* (reference to emotion) to be there. Uhm, again there's something about the colors—they, *they're icy colors and yet* (opposition) the yellow in the fore-front, in the foreground, uhm give, or lend, a certain kind of warmth to the picture.

A summary of the female indicators found in this woman's description is as follows: four intensive adverbs, four references to emotion, and two oppositions. Although she also used some male features—for example *a lot of* (reference to quantity) and *in the foreground* (locative), these were left unmarked for the sake of clarity of presentation.

SPEAKER NUMBER: 11 (A man)

Okay. It looks like a *beautiful* (judgmental adjective) winter scene, in which we've got *lots of* (reference to quantity) very . . . probably fall, maybe the *first* (reference to quantity) snowfall of the year. *Large groups* (reference to quantity and clliptical sentence) of *tall* (reference to quantity) mountains and *partially* covered (reference to quantity) with snow . . . and perhaps some *lower* (reference to quantity) hogbacks and such forth . . . and covered with various types of coniferous and deciduous trees. *Probably morning time* (elliptical sentence) with a *low* (reference to quantity) layer of fog just kind of . . . *between the ground and the tops* (locative) of the mountains. *Beautiful* (judgmental adjective) *blue sky* (elliptical sentence) *up above* (locative). *Reminds me* (elliptical sentence) a lot of the *Sierra Nevada's* (locative) perhaps, maybe the *west side* (locative).

This man's description includes the following male variables: seven references to quantity, two judgmental adjectives, four elliptical sentences, and four locatives. As indicated earlier, the gender-indicative features noted should be viewed as linguistic tendencies of male and female communicators. They are not gender markers because both men and women use them.

Pattern of Gender-Linked Differences

The 16 gender-distinguishing language features can be seen to form a coherent pattern when viewed from the perspective of verbal styles that distinguish national cultures (e.g., Germans vs. French). But what do intercultural style differences have to do with understanding gender differences? Because of the theoretical claim that men and women grow up in separate subcultures and therefore learn to use language differently (Maltz & Borker, 1982; Tannen, 1994), it seemed reasonable to test the utility of this intercultural perspective. Gudykunst and Ting-Toomey (1988) proposed four dimensions of language style that are useful in describing differences between cultures: The first dimension, *Direct Versus Indirect,* represents the extent to which speakers reveal their intentions through explicit verbal reference. The second, *Succinct Versus Elaborate,* focuses on the quantity of talk and the extent to which rich, expressive language is used. *Personal Versus Contextual* style emphasizes personhood as opposed to role relations. Finally, *Instrumental Versus Affective* represents the extent to which a speaker focuses on things as opposed to people.

We tested this perspective experimentally on the basis of reader judgments of parallel sentences with and without each language feature (Mulac & Gibbons, 1993). The results indicate that the 6 features of men's style fit on one end of these dimensions and 9 of the 10 features of women's style fit on the opposite end. For example, men's higher use of directives ("Think of some more") exemplifies direct style, in contrast to women's indirectness shown by their use of uncertainty verbs ("It seems like I don't have enough time") and questions ("Do you know what I'm saying?"). In addition, men's use of elliptical sentences ("Gorgeous!") represents succinct style, whereas women's intensive adverbs ("The sky is very blue") and longer mean length sentences indicate elaborate style. Furthermore, men's use of "I" references can be seen as exemplifying personal style as opposed to contextual style; however, no women's features appear to denote contextual style. Finally, men's greater use of references to quantity ("The view is from out at sea, about a football field away") represents instrumental style, and women's references to emotion ("It seems to be eerie and depressing") represents affective style.

Therefore, men's language can be seen as relatively direct, succinct, personal, and instrumental, and women's features are indirect, elaborate, and affective. It is significant that our experimental results indicate that none of the 6 male language features were located at the women's end of any cultural dimension, nor were any of the 10 female language features located at the men's end (Mulac & Gibbons, 1993). Thus, gender-linked language differences exhibit a coherent pattern that is consistent with intercultural expectations.

Multivariate Assessment of Differences

Compared with the majority of the 31 studies discussed earlier, we have employed a somewhat different method to determine whether speakers or writers use language in gender-differentiating ways. Like many investigators, we have used trained observers to code language variables (such as intensive adverbs and directives) appearing in the transcripts of naturally occurring language. However, after aggregating across coders, we have analyzed these language data by means of stepwise discriminant analysis procedures. This multivariate statistical method has important advantages over the univariate, or variable-by-variable, perspective more commonly followed. Because speech and writing are both produced and comprehended as a combination of interrelated language features, rather than a series of independent words, it is reasonable to believe that greater construct validity (Kerlinger, 1973) can be attained through the use of multivariate procedures. Such procedures identify weighted combinations of variables for the purpose of predicting some criterion variable—in this case, communicator gender. Although this approach has been followed in only a handful of linguistic studies, we employed it because it more accurately characterizes the way people produce and comprehend language.

We first used this method to analyze the public speeches of 30 university students (Mulac, Lundell, & Bradac, 1986). Eleven trained individuals coded 35 language features selected as potential discriminators of gender. Results of the stepwise discriminant analysis (see Table 6.3) show that a combination of 20 of these variables permitted 100% accuracy of gender prediction. This provides clear evidence of gender-linked language differences in public speaking.

Similarly, Mulac and Lundell (1986) analyzed oral descriptions of landscape photographs by 48 speakers ranging from 11 to 69 years of age. A combination of 17 variables predicted speaker gender with 87.5% accuracy. Mulac et al. (1988) applied the same approach to 71 dyadic interactions, coding 12 variables that significantly predicted interactant gender with 76% accuracy across same-sex and mixed-sex pairings.

The same method was used in another study (Mulac et al., 1990) to determine whether 16 girls and 16 boys from each of three public school groups (4th, 8th, and 12th grades) differed in their written essays. Again, significant discriminant analyses indicated that combinations of six-to-nine variables could accurately predict gender for 84% to 87% of the 32 writers from each grade level. Similar results were uncovered in a study of 40 university students' written photograph descriptions (Mulac & Lundell, 1994), where 72% accuracy of gender reclassification was established.

Additional support for gender differences was found in our analysis of 108 university students' problem solving interactions in same-sex and mixed-sex pairs (Mulac & Bradac, 1995). A combination of 12 features was able to accurately determine interactant gender for 70% of the individuals. Finally, significant gender determination was found in 140 interactions of spouses and strangers (members of 20 couples engaging in seven dyadic interactions), with an identification accuracy of 78% (Fitzpatrick & Mulac,

TABLE 6.3
Summary of Stepwise Discriminant Analysis[a] of
35 Language Variables Predicting Speaker Gender
in a Public Speaking Setting (Mulac et al., 1986)

Language Variable[b]	Gender Predicted	Canonical Coefficient[c]	F to Remove	Wilks' Lambda
Sentence-initial adverbials	Female	−170.56	13.31	.68
Oppositions	Female	−65.80	12.24	.47
Syllables per word	Male	489.74	6.67	.37
Rhetorical questions	Female	−16.56	3.86	.32
References to emotion	Female	−143.12	4.99	.27
Fillers	Female	−36.04	5.09	.22
"I" references	Male	16.45	5.45	.17
Prepositional phrases	Female	−21.58	5.94	.14
Action verbs	Female	−52.59	3.22	.12
Present tense verbs	Male	20.25	3.94	.10
Mean length sentence	Female	−16.78	7.74	.07
Vocalized pauses	Male	26.29	4.02	.05
Definite/demonst. noun phrases	Male	23.82	2.53	.05
Grammatical errors	Male	35.91	6.24	.03
Negations	Female	−35.05	2.74	.03
Active voice verbs	Male	33.75	3.86	.02
Progressive verbs	Male	12.07	7.32	.01
Judgmental adjectives	Male	11.85	1.28	.01
References to people	Male	8.96	2.17	.01
Intensive adverbs	Female	−8.17	1.23	.01

[a]Wilks' Lambda = 0.01, $F(20, 9) = 51.45$, $p < .0001$.
[b]Language features are listed in the order that they entered the discriminant function.
[c]The canonical coefficients are not standardized.

1995; Fitzpatrick, Mulac, & Dindia, 1995). In all seven studies that employed this procedure, speaker or writer gender was predicted by a weighted combination of the language features, with an accuracy substantially better than chance. In these investigations, the computer program was able to guess speaker gender on the basis of language use, with an accuracy of 70% to 100%.

The results of these investigations indicate that trained language coders, working individually in teams of 5 to 11 people, can provide linguistic data that demonstrate subtle language preferences when analyzed by sophisticated statistical procedures. Through these means, we have discovered language differences so small that they escape the notice of intelligent, untrained adults who are unable to guess communicator sex. However, the question remains: If scholars have to employ teams of trained observers and high-powered statistical programs to ferret out these discriminators, how important are these gender-linked language differences? Put another way: Do language differences *really* make a difference?

EFFECT OF LANGUAGE DIFFERENCES

The Gender-Linked Language Effect

The answer to the previous challenge is a resounding "Yes!" The reason for the declamatory nature of this answer is that women's and men's language use leads them to be judged differently on psychological dimensions that are of consequence. That is, they are judged differently because of differences in their linguistic strategies. We have called this pattern of judgments the *gender-linked language effect*. This effect is defined as the evaluative consequences of gender-differentiating language use and has been investigated in a substantial number of communication settings.

In our research, we have had women and men of different ages read the female and male transcripts and then rate each speaker or writer as a person. For this purpose, they have employed a 12-item semantic differential, the Speech Dialect Attitudinal Scale (SDAS; Mulac, 1975, 1976). Factor analyses of their ratings consistently yield the following three-factor structure: (a) *Socio-Intellectual Status* (high social status/low social status, white collar/blue collar, literate/illiterate, and rich/poor), (b) *Aesthetic Quality* (pleasant/unpleasant, beautiful/ugly, sweet/sour, nice/awful), and (c) *Dynamism* (strong/weak, active/passive, loud/soft, aggressive/unaggressive). Reliability coefficients from these investigations have shown that raters are able to use these psychological dimensions in a consistent, stable fashion.

Typical of this research was our investigation of 30 university students' first speech in a public speaking class (Mulac & Lundell, 1982). We recorded over 100 four- to five-minute extemporaneous speeches to inform or persuade on a topic of the students' choice. To ensure that the speech topics did not reveal the sex of the speakers, we asked graduate teaching assistants to guess speaker sex from the speech topics (e.g., "Euthanasia" and "How to change a flat tire"). We chose for transcription the 15 male and 15 female speeches that yielded the lowest sex-guess accuracy. From these recordings, we produced 1-minute orthographic transcripts that were read by 204 university students who, as mentioned earlier, unsuccessfully attempted to guess the sex of the speakers.

The 30 transcripts were then evaluated by two other groups of untrained raters—132 students (median age = 19 years) and 126 older nonstudents (median age = 45 years)—using the 12-item SDAS (Mulac, 1975, 1976). Results demonstrate what has become the classic pattern of the gender-linked language effect: The women were generally rated higher on *Socio-Intellectual Status* and *Aesthetic Quality*, whereas the men were evaluated higher on *Dynamism* (see Fig. 6.1). That is, the women were seen as more rich, literate, white collar, and high social status, as well as more beautiful, sweet,

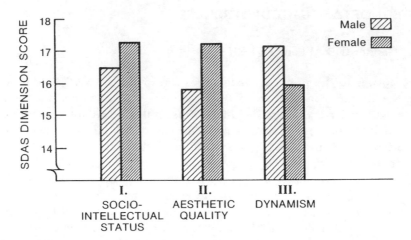

FIG. 6.1. Mean SDAS dimension scores for male and female speakers demonstrating the classic pattern of the Gender-Linked Language Effect (Mulac & Lundell, 1982).

nice, and pleasant. In contrast, the men were perceived as more active, strong, loud, and aggressive.

Although this general effect was substantial across the group of 30 speakers, it did not hold for all of them. For example, two of the top five rated speakers on *Socio-Intellectual Status* were men, although only one of the lowest five rated speakers was a women. The highest evaluated speaker on *Aesthetic Quality* was a man, although the next three were women and the bottom five were all men. Finally on *Dynamism,* although the top rated three speakers were male (including the man who was judged highest on the first two dimensions), the fourth and fifth ranking scores were received by female speakers.

Despite this within-gender variability, the overall effect—an effect that statistically took into account the within-gender variation—was striking in that it could have occurred by chance less than 1 time in 1,000. The effect sizes of these findings may be interpreted as small/medium for *Socio-Intellectual Status,* large for *Aesthetic Quality,* and medium for *Dynamism* (Cohen & Cohen, 1975).[3]

We first discovered what was to become the gender-linked language effect in a study of American dialects (Mulac & Rudd, 1977). In that investigation, we asked raters to evaluate, using the SDAS (Mulac, 1975, 1976), recordings of 12 speakers who represented three regions. In addition, we had another group of raters evaluate printed transcripts of what

[3]The percent of variance accounted for by speaker gender was as follows, given in the form of *eta*^{2}: *Sociointellectual Status* = .06, *Aesthetic Quality* = .23, and *Dynamism* = .15.

those speakers said, using the SDAS, to control statistically (through analysis of covariance [ANCOVA]) for the effect of the language used by the speakers. Analysis of reader judgments demonstrated that women's transcripts were rated higher on *Aesthetic Quality* and men's were judged higher on *Dynamism*—a partial glimpse at the pattern of effects that we would study in the ensuing program of research.

A follow-up investigation (Mulac & Lundell, 1980) sought to establish the effect with rigor and to determine whether it existed equally for different age groups: sixth graders, university freshmen and sophomores, graduate teaching assistants and lecturers, and people in their 50s and 60s. Forty-eight speakers representing the four age groups were recorded as they described landscape photographs; 45-second segments were transcribed. Results demonstrate that the female speakers were rated higher on *Socio-Intellectual Status* and *Aesthetic Quality,* and the males higher on *Dynamism.* In addition, we found that the male–female disparity was greater for the two older groups of speakers: (a) on *Aesthetic Quality,* older women were favored more in comparison with older men than were younger women compared with younger men; and (b) on *Dynamism,* older male speakers were favored more in comparison with older females than were younger males over younger females. The literature on gender stereotypes shows men are perceived as strong, active, hard, aggressive, and dominating, whereas women are thought to be charming, sensitive, and attractive (Mulac, Incontro, & James, 1985). Therefore, this finding suggests that the language effect measured for older speakers was more consistent with gender stereotypes than it was for younger speakers.

Although the prior efforts tested the effects of spoken communication, we also investigated consequences of written language. In the first of these studies (Mulac et al., 1990), we assessed the writing of three groups (32 students each) of primary and secondary school children: 4th graders, 8th graders, and 12th graders. In their English classes, they were asked to write an essay on this topic: Is it important to tell the truth? Can it ever be better to lie? Ratings of the fourth graders' transcripts favored girls on *Socio-Intellectual Status* and *Aesthetic Quality;* ratings favored boys on *Dynamism.* However, for the 8th and 12th graders, the only difference was on *Dynamism,* favoring boys. This showed the existence of the gender-linked language effect by the time students had reached the fourth grade. It also indicated the effect's modification by the 8th and 12th grades, by which time the boys had learned to write in ways that made them appear to be as literate and pleasant as the girls.

In our second study on the effects of writing, we requested that university students in a communication class write impromptu descriptions of two landscape photographs (Mulac & Lundell, 1994). Ratings of their 40 transcripts demonstrated the gender-linked language effect for *Socio-Intellec-*

tual Status, Aesthetic Quality, and *Dynamism.* In contrast to the 8th and 12th graders writing philosophical essays in English classes (Mulac et al., 1990), these university students apparently felt less bound to follow formal require-ments of essay writing. Interestingly, the judgments of their writing were virtually identical to the ones we found earlier for transcripts of university students' extemporaneous public speeches (Mulac & Lundell, 1982).

The final communication setting we analyzed was same-sex and mixed-sex dyadic interactions. In the first investigation (Mulac et al., 1988), we asked 63 male and 79 female university students to engage in a problem-solving task (e.g., The five most important ingredients of personal success are . . .) with a partner whom they did not know well. For same-sex dyads, the results show support for the gender-linked language effect on *Socio-In-tellectual Status* and *Aesthetic Quality,* but not on *Dynamism,* where no differ-ences were found. Faced with an interactive problem-solving task, in which participants were instructed that the quality of their solutions was para-mount, these university women spoke with as much strength and aggres-siveness as did the men. As hypothesized on the basis of speech accom-modation theory (Giles, Mulac, Bradac, & Johnson, 1987), the results for mixed-sex dyads demonstrate a convergence of ratings for both male and female interactants.

In our latest assessment of language use and effects in paired interac-tions, we recorded 108 university students (54 men and 54 women) in both same-sex and mixed-sex dyads (Mulac & Bradac, 1995). Their task was to cooperatively solve problems such as, What are the best ways to relieve school stress? and How will life be different in the year 2000? This design provided a direct test of potential language convergence and its effects because the same men and women were measured in both dyad settings. Analyses supported the gender-linked language effect for all three dimensions in both same-sex and mixed-sex interactions. That is, no lan-guage effect accommodation was seen. In both dyad compositions, the women were rated higher on *Socio-Intellectual Status* and *Aesthetic Quality,* and the men were rated higher on *Dynamism.*

These findings are all the more important because, in all eight investi-gations that found evidence of the gender-linked language effect, the pat-tern of judgments provided by female and male raters was identical. That is, purely on the basis of communicators' language samples, women and men both perceive female communicators to be of a higher social status and more literate, as well as nicer and more beautiful, than males. However, both rated males as stronger and more aggressive. This indicates that women and men have similar judgmental standards for gender-differenti-ating language use.

In three of these studies, we tested the possibility that older nonstudents (median age over 40 years) would render judgments that differed from university student raters (median age less than 20). These two age groups rated: (a) university students' public speeches (Mulac & Lundell, 1982), (b) landscape photograph descriptions of older teachers (Mulac, Incontro, & James, 1985), and (c) essays of 4th, 8th, and 12th graders (Mulac et al., 1990). In all three investigations, the older nonstudents and university students provided virtually identical ratings of the transcript communicators. These results demonstrate that the same effect is perceived by observers who are female and male, as well as those who are older and younger adults. These consistent findings substantiate the broad generalizibility of the consequences of gender-differentiating language.

Prediction of the Gender-Linked Language Effect From Language Features

In keeping with our final theoretical assumption, we examined the extent to which language differences are implicated in the psychological judgments that form the gender-linked language effect. For this purpose, we utilized multiple-regression analyses to predict *Socio-Intellectual Status, Aesthetic Quality,* and *Dynamism* ratings on the basis of the gender-discriminating language features such as references to emotion and elliptical sentences. As is the case with discriminant analysis, this multivariate procedure seeks to determine the weighted combination of variables that best explains the predicted, or criterion, variable. We reasoned that if the language features could predict a significant percentage of psychological judgments, these features could be seen to be implicated in these judgments. To that extent, they would be truly resulting in the demonstrated outcome. However, if that predictive link was not found, the judgments would have to be the result of some factor other than gender-linked language.

Typical of this approach was our assessment of the effects of university students' impromptu photograph description essays (Mulac & Lundell, 1994). Here we sought to determine the extent to which the nine gender-discriminating linguistic variables found in the first phase of the investigation could predict the psychological ratings rendered by readers in the second phase. Table 6.4 shows the results of one of the multiple-regression analyses predicting *Socio-Intellectual Status* ratings of the writers on the basis of their language use. The first language feature to enter the predictive equation, and therefore the best overall predictor, was sentence-initial adverbials ("Because there's new snow on the trees and on the ground, this appears to be . . ."). Speakers who employed this form tended to receive higher *Socio-Intellectual Status* ratings. References to emotion, the second most important predictor ("There's a mournful quality . . ."), also led to higher ratings of status and, like the first predictor, was used more by female writers. The next two features, in order of importance, were judg-

TABLE 6.4
Summary of Stepwise Multiple-Regression Analysis[a] of
Nine Gender-Discriminating Language Features to Predict
Socio-Intellectual Status in a Written Photograph
Description Setting (Mulac & Lundell, 1994)

MRA Step	Language Variable	Standard Regression Coefficient[b]	Adjusted[c] R^2	F to Remove	Gender[d] Predicted by DA	Consistent With GLLE?[e]
1	Sentence initial adverbials	0.38	.189	.69	Female	Yes
2	References to emotion	0.67	.222	.64	Female	Yes
3	Judgmental adjectives	−0.41	.252	.73	Male	Yes
4	Elliptical sentences	−0.18	.261	.74	Male	Yes
5	Uncertainty verbs	−0.13	.260	.75	Female	No

[a]F (5,34) = 3.75, $p < .01$; Adjusted R^2 = .26.

[b]Negative standardized regression coefficients were predictive of lower *Socio-Intellectual Status* ratings (i.e., the more the writers used that language feature, the lower they were rated on this psychological dimension).

[c]Coefficients of multiple determination (R^2) are here adjusted for the number of writers and the number of language variables included in the regression function (Theil, 1971).

[d]Gender predicted by discriminant analysis.

[e]Answers the question of whether the psychological judgment effect of the language feature was consistent with the gender-linked language effect (e.g., Did a particular female-indicating language feature—references to emotion—predict higher *Socio-Intellectual Status* ratings?).

mental adjectives ("This is fabulous!") and elliptical sentences ("Winter time."). Both features were displayed more in men's writing and both were predictive of lower *Socio-Intellectual Status* ratings. Because of their use by men and women, and due to their effect on *Socio-Intellectual Status* perceptions, these first four features are completely consistent with the gender-linked language effect. However, the fifth was not. Uncertainty verbs ("It seems to be early winter"), a female language feature, was found to be predictive of lower ratings of *Socio-Intellectual Status*, not higher. Although this was the last variable to enter the predictive equation, and was therefore the least important predictor, its effect was in conflict with the gender-linked language effect. However, use of uncertainty verbs lacked the necessary power to eliminate that effect. In terms of the second psychological dimension, *Aesthetic Quality*, substantial prediction was also evidenced for a different combination of features. However, in this study, language could not be tied to *Dynamism* scores, although earlier investigations had shown that *Dynamism* could also be predicted by gender-linked language.

In an assessment of oral descriptions of landscape photographs by sixth graders, university freshmen and sophomores, graduate teaching assistants, and people in their 50s and 60s (Mulac & Lundell, 1986), we reported that language differences predicted substantial proportions of the ratings on all three psychological dimensions. Similar results were obtained for university students' public speeches (Mulac et al., 1986), with language features again able to predict meaningful proportions of all three dimensions that distinguished speaker gender. In addition, our analysis of essays by 4th, 8th, and 12th graders showed that differences in language could meaningfully predict psychological ratings in 80% of the analyses (Mulac et al., 1990). Finally, our assessment of university students' same-sex and mixed-sex dyads also demonstrated that interactants' language use could meaningfully predict *Socio-Intellectual Status, Aesthetic Quality,* and *Dynamism* (Mulac & Bradac, 1995).

These five investigations showed that the gender-differentiating language features found in the linguistic analysis phase of the studies could predict 32% to 70% of the variance of the psychological ratings in the same studies. These results support our hypothesis that the effects found for gender differences in ratings are actually the result of the gender-linked language differences located in those same transcripts. Without this link between language and ratings, we could not properly call the phenomenon the gender-linked language effect.

Comparison of the Gender-Linked Language Effect and Gender Stereotypes

Finally, in a related experimental investigation (Mulac, Incontro, & James, 1985), we tested the correspondence of the gender-linked language effect and gender stereotypes. This comparison was prompted by our review of literature that demonstrated a startling similarity between these two effects. Therefore, we tested the extent to which judgments based on gender stereotypes and those based on effects of gender-linked language were: (a) independent of each other (i.e., could be produced separately or in combination), and (b) related to each other (having similar patterns). In this study, we experimentally manipulated the same set of 12 photograph description transcripts to produce four transcript conditions: (a) language effect only (with speaker sex not indicated and not guessable), (b) language plus stereotype (speaker sex correctly identified 100% of the time), (c) stereotype effect only (50% correct sex identification), and (d) language pitted against stereotype (0% correct identification).

The language effect was produced by transcripts of the 12 speakers, for which speaker sex was not identified and could not be accurately guessed (as indicated by our sex-guess data). The gender stereotype effect was produced by having the same 12 transcripts rated, but with 50% of the six women's transcripts identified as "A WOMAN" and the other 50% indicated as "A MAN." The same manipulation of attributed speaker sex was also accomplished for the six men's transcripts. The female stereotype scores were found by combining all six transcripts' ratings identified as "A

WOMAN," one half of which were really those of male speakers. The male stereotype scores combined all six ratings for "A MAN," one half of which were actually spoken by female speakers. In this way, the effect of the speakers' language was controlled experimentally. Analysis of ratings for the four conditions supported the independence of the two effects: Each consequence could be produced without the other being present, both could be combined congruently to double their effect and, when pitted against each other, they canceled out each other.

However, in the look-alike contest to assess their similarity, the correlation of judgments resulting from stereotypes, as compared with those from language, demonstrated an astoundingly high relationship ($r = .93$). That is, the two effects shared a remarkable 86% of the individual effect variance. Therefore, although the two effects are independent of each other, their patterns are virtually identical. This implies that the way men and women speak or write reinforces gender stereotypes. It also suggests that gender stereotypes might influence the way people learn to speak, perhaps as a manifestation of cultural expectations.

IMPLICATIONS OF THE FINDINGS

Our findings for women's and men's language use present a curious paradox: We observe, at the same time, similarity *and* difference. Far from appearing as if they come from different planets, the women and men studied appear to have come from different states in the same country. It is obvious that they grew up in different groups—groups that have subtly different styles and therefore subtly different ways of accomplishing the same communication task.

The findings that support the notion of similarities in language choice are twofold: First, when the communication of men and women, or boys and girls, is transcribed and presented to university students whose first language is American English, the students are unable to guess the sex of the communicators with an accuracy that is any better than chance. This was the consistent finding in all five of our empirical investigations that tested communicators' gender guessability. Because native speakers of American English cannot identify the sex of these individuals, the communicators must be displaying a high degree of linguistic similarity. In addition to the lack of guessability, we have observed that the summary statistics of how much male and female speakers use particular language features argue more for their similarity than for their difference.

In contrast, related findings demonstrate significant differences in men's and women's linguistic style. Our summary of over 30 empirical investigations show 16 variables that generally characterize stylistic differences. Features used more often by male communicators included: references to quantity, judgmental adjectives, elliptical sentences, directives, locatives, and "I" references. Those employed more by female speakers and writers were: intensive adverbs, references to emotions, dependent clauses, sentence-initial adverbials, uncertainty verbs, oppositions, negations, hedges, questions, and longer mean length sentences. This long list of linguistic preferences certainly weighs in heavily on the side of the difference argument. Moreover, these 16 features provide a consistent and coherent pattern in which male style can be seen as direct, succinct, personal, and instrumental. Female preferences are at the other end of these stylistic dimensions—indirect, elaborate, and affective.

We have also seen that discriminant analysis procedures can locate weighted combinations of language features coded for the transcripts and accurately determine communicator gender at a precision of 70% to 100%, although untrained readers cannot. The results of seven investigations have demonstrated the efficacy of this approach for locating clusters of linguistic features that distinguish gender.

Of greatest importance for the difference argument is that, although subtle, the language differences have judgmental consequences. That is, observers perceive the female and male speakers differently based on their language use. The pattern of these perceptions, the gender-linked language effect, consists of female communicators being rated higher on *Socio-Intellectual Status* (high social status and literate) and *Aesthetic Quality* (nice and beautiful), whereas males are rated higher on *Dynamism* (strong and aggressive). The results of eight studies support this outcome, in whole or in part. Although the magnitude of the effect appears to be of moderate size, its pervasive nature amplifies its impact in daily communication.

These investigations demonstrate the omnipresent nature of the effect because it has been found for naturally occurring language from a broad range of communication tasks and settings: (a) oral descriptions of landscape photographs, (b) written descriptions of landscape photographs, (c) public speeches, (d) written essays on practical morality, and (e) same-sex and mixed-sex problem-solving dyadic interactions. Across these contexts, the pattern of judgments has been remarkably consistent—in fact, virtually identical. In addition, the effect has been located for communicators as young as 9 to 10 years of age and as old as 50 to 60 years. What is more, it has been seen equally in the speaker ratings provided by male and female observers, as well as by younger and older ones.

In support of another theoretical assumption, we have demonstrated in five investigations that gender-based language differences are implicated in the effect. The findings show that the communicator's gender-distinguishing language use could predict 30% to 70% of their gender-differentiating psychological ratings. Thus, we can see that the consistent establishment of the gender-linked language effect answers the challenge: *So what* if men and women use language differently?

Finally, we have shown that the gender-linked language effect is independent of gender stereotypes. That is, either one can be induced experimentally without the other, they can be joined to double their effect, and they can be pitted against each other to cancel out each other. However, despite their demonstrated independence, the results also show that the pattern of judgments emerging from the two effects is overwhelmingly similar—the two manifest an 86% degree of similarity. This finding suggests that societally held norms may play a part in the learning of gender-appropriate language use and that stereotypes are reinforced by everyday speech and writing. The mechanism that causes this similarity of effects will require substantial investigation in the future.

We are left with a paradox: Our findings indicate that, along with overwhelming similarities in their use of language, women and men produce subtle differences in a wide variety of communication contexts. More important, observers are responsive to these subtle differences as they make judgments about women and men—judgments that are remarkably similar to those brought about by gender stereotypes. Moreover, these evaluations are the same whether the observer is female or male, middle-aged, or young. No matter who makes the appraisals, the subtle language differences have substantial consequences in how communicators are evaluated. The inescapable conclusion is this: The language differences *really do* make a difference.

ACKNOWLEDGMENT

The author wishes to acknowledge Sandra L. Thompson's generous and insightful comments on an earlier version of this chapter.

APPENDIX

Descriptions, examples, and citations[a] for 21 language features found in empirical studies to predict communicator gender follow.

Sentences

1. *Elliptical sentences:* ("Gorgeous!", "A beautiful snowy setting," "Day time") A unit beginning with a capital letter and ending with a period

---

[a]Citations indicate empirical studies in which the variable was found to differ for male and female communicators.

in which either the subject or predicate is understood (Mulac & Lundell, 1986, M+[b] [oral descriptions of photographs]; Mulac & Lundell, 1994, M+ [written descriptions of photographs]).

2. *Questions:* ("What is [Communication] 12?", "What do you do?") Directives in question form were not counted (Fishman, 1978, F+ [couple's conversations]; Mulac et al., 1988, F+ [dyadic interactions]).

3. *Tag questions:* ("It's early winter, isn't it?") An assertion that is followed immediately by a question asking for support (Crosby & Nyquist, 1977, F+ [dyadic interactions]; Dubois & Crouch, 1975, M+ [conference participation]; Lapadat & Seesahai, 1978, M+ [informal conversations]; Hartman, 1976, F+ [interviews]; McMillan, Clifton, McGrath, & Gale, 1977, F+ [problem-solving groups]; Mulac & Lundell, 1986, F+ [oral descriptions of photographs]).

4. *Directives:* ("Think of another," "Why don't we put that down?") Apparently telling another person what to do (Haas, 1979, M+ [interviews]; Mulac et al., 1988, M+ [dyadic interactions]).

5. *Negations:* ("You don't feel like looking . . .") A statement of what something is not (Mulac & Lundell, 1986, F+ [oral descriptions of photographs]; Mulac et al., 1986, F+ [public speeches]).

6. *Mean length sentence:* The number of words divided by the number of sentences, defined as sequences of words beginning with a capital letter and ending with a period (Hunt, 1965, F+ [written essays]; Mulac et al., 1986, F+ [public speaking]; Mulac & Lundell, 1986, F+ [oral descriptions of photographs]; Mulac & Lundell, 1994, F+ [written descriptions of photographs]; Mulac et al., 1990, M+ [fourth-grade essays]; Poole, 1979, F+ [interviews]).

Clauses and Phrases

1. *Sentence-initial adverbials:* ("Instead of being the light blue . . . , it is . . . ," "Because the trees still have snow . . . , it looks like . . .") Answers the questions: how? when? or where? regarding the main clause (Mulac et al., 1986, F+ [public speeches]; Mulac et al., 1988, F+ [dyadic interactions]; Mulac & Lundell, 1994, F+ [written descriptions of photographs]; Mulac et al., 1990, F+ [fourth-grade written essays]).

2. *Dependent clauses:* (". . . which is mostly covered . . . ;" ". . . where the shadows are," ". . . in which something . . .") A clause that serves to

---

[b]Gender distinctions, in terms of whether the variable was more indicative of male or female communicators, are as follows: M+ = Male, F+ = Female. (Note, however, that the linguistic categories were not in all cases precisely equivalent across studies.) Communication contexts in which gender differences were found are indicated in brackets.

specify or qualify the words that convey primary meaning (Beck, 1978, F+ [oral descriptions of TAT cards]; Hunt, 1965, F+ [written essays]; Mulac et al., 1990, F+ [fourth-grade impromptu essays]; Mulac & Lundell, 1994, F+ [written descriptions of photographs]; Poole, 1979, F+ [interviews]).

3. *Oppositions:* ("The snow must have fallen fairly recently, but it has been a while . . . ," " . . . very peaceful, yet full of movement . . .") Retracting a statement and posing one with an opposite meaning (Mulac & Lundell, 1986, F+ [oral descriptions of photographs]; Mulac et al., 1986, F+ [public speeches]).

4. *Judgmental adjectives:* ("distracting," "bothersome," "nice") These indicate personal evaluations rather than merely description (Mulac & Lundell, 1994, M+ [written descriptions of photographs]; Mulac et al., 1990, M+ [4th-, 8th-, and 12th-grade impromptu essays]; Sause, 1976, M+ [interviews]).

Verb Phrases

1. *Uncertainty verbs:* ("I wonder if . . . ," "seems to be . . . ," "I'm not sure . . .") Verb phrases indicating apparent lack of certainty (Hartman, 1976, F+ [interviews]; Mulac & Lundell, 1994, F+ [written descriptions of photographs]; Poole, 1979, F+ [interviews]).

2. *Progressive verbs:* ("predicting," "melting," "moving") Verbs presented in the "-ing" form (Mulac et al., 1986, M+ [public speeches]; Mulac & Lundell, 1994, F+ [written descriptions of photographs]; Mulac et al., 1990, F+ [8th- and 12th- grade impromptu essays]).

Modifiers

1. *Intensive adverbs:* ("very," "really," "quite"). (Crosby & Nyquist, 1977, F+ [dyadic interactions]; Lapadat & Seesahai, 1977, F+ [group discussions]; McMillan, Clifton, McGrath, & Gale, 1997, F+ [group discussions]; Mulac & Lundell, 1986, F+ [oral descriptions of photographs]; Mulac et al., 1986, F+ [public speeches]; Mulac et al., 1988, F+ [dyadic interactions]).

2. *Hedges:* ("sort of," "kind of," "possibly," "maybe") Modifiers that indicate lack of confidence in, or diminished assuredness of, the statement (Crosby & Nyquist, 1977, F+ [dyadic interactions]; Mulac et al., 1990, F+ [fourth-grade impromptu essays]).

3. *Justifiers:* ("It's winter because there's snow. . . ," "It's not sandstone though because . . .") A reason is given for a previous statement (Mulac & Lundell, 1986, M+ [oral descriptions of photographs]; Mulac et al., 1988, F+ [dyadic interactions]).

References

1. *References to emotion:* ("happy," "enticing," "depressing") Any mention of an emotion or feeling (Balswick & Avertt, 1977, F+ [written response to questionnaire]; Gleser, Gottschalk, & John; 1959, F+ [event descriptions]; Mulac & Lundell, 1994, F+ [written descriptions of photographs]; Mulac et al., 1986, F+ [public speeches]; Staley, 1982, F+ [oral descriptions of pictures]).

2. *References to quantity:* ("below 32° F," "most of the area," "6–8 thousand feet elevation") References to an amount or quantity (Gleser et al., 1959, M+ [event description]; Mulac & Lundell, 1986, M+ [oral descriptions of photographs]; Sause, 1976, M+ [interviews]; Warshay, 1972, M+ [event description essays]; Wood, 1966, M+ [oral descriptions of pictures]).

3. *Locatives:* ("right next to the . . . ," "in the background") Usually indicating the location or position of objects (Mulac & Lundell, 1986, M+ [oral descriptions of photographs]; Mulac & Lundell, 1994, M+ [written descriptions of photographs]).

4. *Personal pronouns:* ("I," "you," "we") Words that stand for beings (Gleser et al., 1959, F+ [event descriptions]; Haslett, 1983, F+ [written stories]; Koenigsknecht & Friedman, 1976, F+ [recounting tales and free play]; Mulac & Lundell, 1986, F+ [oral descriptions of photographs]; Mulac & Lundell, 1994, M+ [written descriptions of photographs]; Mulac et al., 1990, M+ [fourth-grade impromptu essays]; Mulac et al., 1988, F+ [dyadic interactions]; Poole, 1979, F+ [interviews]; Westmoreland, Starr, Shelton, & Pasadeos, 1977, F+ [newspaper articles]).

5. *"I" references:* ("I think we should . . . ") First person singular pronoun in the subjective case (Mulac & Lundell, 1994, M+ [written descriptions of photographs]; Mulac et al., 1990, M+ [fourth-grade impromptu essays]).

Miscellaneous

1. *Fillers:* ("you know," "like") Words or phrases used without apparent semantic intent (Hirschman, 1973, F+ [conversation]; Mulac & Lundell, 1986, M+ [oral picture description]; Mulac et al., 1986, F+ [public speeches]; Mulac et al., 1990, F+ [fourth-grade essays]; Mulac et al., 1988, M+ [dyadic interactions]).

REFERENCES

Balswick, J., & Avertt, C. P. (1977). Differences in expressiveness: Gender, interpersonal orientation, and perceived parental expressiveness as contributing factors. *Journal of Marriage and the Family, 39,* 121–127.

Beck, R. (1978). Sex differentiated speech codes. *International Journal of Women's Studies, 1,* 566–572.

Cohen, J., & Cohen, P. (1975). *Applied multiple regression/correlation analysis for the behavioral sciences.* Hillsdale, NJ: Lawrence Erlbaum Associates.

Crosby, F., & Nyquist, L. (1977). The female register: An empirical study of Lakoff's hypothesis. *Language in Society, 6,* 313–322.

Dubois, B. L., & Crouch, I. (1975). The question of tag questions in women's speech: They don't really use more of them, do they? *Language in Society, 4,* 289–294.

Fishman, P. M. (1978). Interaction: The work women do. *Social Problems, 25,* 397–406.

Fitzpatrick, M. A., & Mulac, A. (1995). Relating to spouse and stranger: Gender-preferential language use. In P. J. Kalbfleisch & M. J. Cody (Eds.), *Gender, power and communication* (pp. 213–231). *Hillsdale, NJ: Lawrence Erlbaum Associates.*

Fitzpatrick, M. A., Mulac, A., & Dindia, K. (1995). Gender-preferential language use in spouse and stranger interaction. *Journal of Language and Social Psychology, 14,* 18–39.

Giles, H., Mulac, A., Bradac, J. J., & Johnson, P. (1987). Speech accommodation theory: The first decade and beyond. In M. L. McLaughlin (Ed.), *Communication yearbook, 10* (pp. 13–48). Newbury Park, CA: Sage.

Giles, H., Scherer, K. R., & Taylor, D. M. (1979). Speech markers in social interaction. In K. R. Scherer & H. Giles (Eds.), *Social markers in speech* (pp. 343–381). Cambridge, England: Cambridge University Press.

Gleser, G. C., Gottschalk, L. A., & John, W. (1959). The relationship of sex and intelligence to choice of words: A normative study of verbal behavior. *Journal of Clinical Psychology, 15,* 182–191.

Gudykunst, W. B., & Ting-Toomey, S. (1988). *Culture and interpersonal communication.* Newbury Park, CA: Sage.

Haas, A. (1979). The acquisition of genderlect. In J. Orsanu, M. K. Slater, & L. L. Adler, (Eds.), *Language, sex and gender* (pp. 101–113). New York: New York Academy of Sciences.

Hartman, M. (1976). A descriptive study of the language of men and women born in Maine around 1900 as it reflects the Lakoff hypotheses in *Language and woman's place.* In B. L. Dubois & I. Crouch (Eds.), *The sociology of the languages of American women* (pp. 81–90). San Antonio, TX: Trinity University Press.

Haslett, B. J. (1983). Children's strategies for maintaining cohesion in their written and oral stories. *Communication Education, 32,* 91–105.

Hirschman, L. (1973, December). *Female-male differences in conversational interaction.* Paper presented at the meeting of the Linguistic Society of America, San Diego, CA.

Hunt, K. W. (1965). *Grammatical structures written at three grade levels.* Champaign, IL: National Council of Teachers of English.

Kerlinger, F. N. (1973). *Foundations of behavioral research* (2nd ed.). New York: Holt, Rinehart & Winston.

Koenigsknecht, R. A., & Friedman, P. (1976). Syntax development in boys and girls. *Child Development, 47,* 1109–1115.

Lapadat, J., & Seesahai, M. (1978). Male versus female codes in informal contexts. *Sociolinguistics Newsletter, 8,* 7–8.

Maltz, D. N., & Borker, R. A. (1982). A cultural approach to male-female miscommunication. In J. J. Gumperz (Ed.), *Language and social identity* (pp. 196–216). Cambridge, England: Cambridge University Press.

McMillan, J. R., Clifton, A. K., McGrath, D., & Gale, W. S. (1997). Women's language: Uncertainty or interpersonal sensitivity and emotionality? *Sex Roles, 3,* 545–559.

Mulac, A. (1975). Evaluation of the speech dialect attitudinal scale. *Speech Monographs, 42,* 1982–1989.

Mulac, A. (1976). Assessment and application of the revised speech dialect attitudinal scale. *Communication Monographs, 43,* 238–245.

Mulac, A., & Bradac, J. J. (1995). Women's style in problem solving interactions: Powerless, or simply feminine? In P. J. Kalbfleish & M. J. Cody (Eds.), *Gender, power and communication* (pp. 83–104). Hillsdale, NJ: Lawrence Erlbaum Associates.

Mulac, A., Bradac, J. J., & Mann, S. K. (1985). Male/female language differences and attributional consequences in children's television. *Human Communication Research, 11,* 481–506.

Mulac, A., & Gibbons, P. (1993, May). *Empirical support for the "gender as culture" hypothesis: An intercultural analysis of male/female language differences.* Paper presented at the meetings of the International Communication Association, Washington, DC.

Mulac, A., Incontro, C. R., & James, M. R. (1985). Comparison of the gender-linked language effect and sex role stereotypes. *Journal of Personality and Social Psychology, 49,* 1099–1110.

Mulac, A., & Lundell, T. L. (1980). Differences in perceptions created by syntactic-semantic productions of male and female speakers. *Communication Monographs, 47,* 111–118.

Mulac, A., & Lundell, T. L. (1982). An empirical test of the gender-linked language effect in a public speaking setting. *Language and Speech, 25,* 243–256.

Mulac, A., & Lundell, T. L. (1986). Linguistic contributors to the gender-linked language effect. *Journal of Language and Social Psychology, 5,* 81–101.

Mulac, A., & Lundell, T. L. (1994). Effects of gender-linked language differences in adults' written discourse: Multivariate tests of language effects. *Language and Communication, 14,* 299–309.

Mulac, A., Lundell, T. L., & Bradac, J. J. (1986). Male/female language differences and attributional consequences in a public speaking situation: Toward an explanation of the gender-linked language effect. *Communication Monographs, 53,* 115–129.

Mulac, A., & Rudd, M. J. (1977). Effects of selected American regional dialects upon regional audience members. *Communication Monographs, 44,* 185–195.

Mulac, A., Studley, L. B., & Blau, S. (1990). The gender-linked language effect in primary and secondary students' impromptu essays. *Sex Roles, 23,* 439–469.

Mulac, A., Wiemann, J. M., Widenmann, S. J., & Gibson, T. W. (1988). Male/female language differences and effects in same-sex and mixed-sex dyads: The gender-linked language effect. *Communication Monographs, 55,* 315–335.

Poole, M. E. (1979). Social class, sex, and linguistic coding. *Language and Speech, 22,* 49–67.

Sause, E. F. (1976). Computer content analysis of sex differences in the language of children. *Journal of Psycholinguistic Research, 5,* 311–324.

Smith, P. M. (1985). *Language, the sexes and society.* Oxford, England: Basil Blackwell.

Staley, C. M. (1982). Sex-related differences in the style of children's language. *Journal of Psycholinguistic Research, 11,* 141–158.

Tannen, D. (1994). *Gender and discourse.* New York: Oxford University Press.

Theil, H. (1971). *Principles of econometrics.* New York: John Wiley & Sons.

Warshay, D. W. (1972). Sex differences in language style. In C. Safilios-Rothchild (Ed.), *Toward a sociology of women* (pp. 3–9). Lexington, MA: Xerox College Publishers.

Westmoreland, R., Starr, D. P., Shelton, K., & Pasadeos, Y. (1977). News writing styles of male and female students. *Journalism Quarterly, 54,* 599–601.

Wood, M. M. (1966). The influence of sex and knowledge of communication effectiveness on spontaneous speech. *Word, 22,* 112–137.

Chapter 7

How Big Are Nonverbal Sex Differences? The Case of Smiling and Sensitivity to Nonverbal Cues

Judith A. Hall
Northeastern University

Any sensible perspective for judging the magnitude of research findings requires that magnitude be regarded as a relative matter.

—Eagly, 1995, p. 150

In stereotype, women smile more than men do and women are more sensitive to nonverbal cues than men are (Briton & Hall, 1995). These beliefs are consistent with the popular notion that women are warm and attuned to others. These beliefs are also accurate in that the empirical evidence shows that women do, in fact, exceed men on both smiling and sensitivity to nonverbal cues. This conclusion is based on meta-analytic reviews that reveal quite consistent differences for both of these traits (Hall, 1978, 1984; Hall & Halberstadt, 1986).

The meta-analytic summary of sex differences has greatly advanced our understanding of overall differences in men's and women's psychology as well as of variables that moderate those differences (Eagly, 1987; Eagly & Wood, 1991; Hyde & Frost, 1993; Hyde & Linn, 1986). However, although it is possible to express such differences precisely using effect size estimates such as the point-biserial correlation or Cohen's d (Cohen, 1988), the interpretation of the size of the differences remains an ambiguous, indeed contentious, task (Eagly, 1995; Hyde & Plant, 1995). Because there is no universal standard by which to appraise magnitude, it is easy to conclude either that sex differences are substantial or that they are trivial, depending on one's theoretical preference and methodological approach. Although the present chapter cannot provide a final answer, it attempts to inform the debate with a more comprehensive analysis than has been undertaken thus far. Differences between the sexes in smiling and sensitivity to non-verbal cues were picked as demonstration cases for this exercise.

One approach to understanding the magnitude of a sex difference is to treat the effect size in an absolute manner by calculating the proportion of variation accounted for by sex. A related approach emphasizes the degree of overlap between the male and female distributions. When these approaches are applied to sex effects as well as nearly all effects in social-personality psychology, they tend to yield the following conclusion: the effects are trivial because so little variation is explained (or, equivalently, because there is such a great overlap between the distributions).

Although these approaches do not lack descriptive correctness, they remain mute with respect to an understanding of the practical impact of sex and lack a contextual perspective. Rosenthal and Rubin (1982) used their binomial effect size display to argue that a relatively small correlation can make for an impressive difference when expressed in terms of population proportions. For example, a point-biserial correlation of .30 between sex and smiling would mean that only 9% of the variance in smiling is accounted for by sex. However, when smiling and sex are expressed as dichotomies with equal overall population frequencies, this correlation translates into a rate of smiling of 65% among women but only 35% among men. Expressed in this manner, the modest correlation invites new attention.

Although an awareness of the limits of the variance-accounted-for approach can help prevent the trivialization of sex differences (Eagly, 1995), a comparative approach is still needed. Three kinds of comparative questions can be posed:

1. *How do sex differences compare to effects in other domains of social-personality psychology?* It appears that many effects in other domains (many of which have been subjected to meta-analytic summary) are in the medium range according to Cohen's (1988) conventions, being roughly in the $r = .25–.30$ range (Eagly, 1995), accounting for 5% to 9% of the variance. According to Cohen, this is an expected upper limit to obtainable effects given the poor control of extraneous variation typical of studies in social-personality psychology. Although sex differences are highly variable across different variables, many have been shown to be in this range (Eagly, 1995). Thus, a tentative answer to this first question is that sex differences are probably comparable to other effects in social-personality psychology.

2. *How does one sex difference (or class of sex differences) compare to other sex differences?* Here the "how big" question is focused on comparisons among sex differences. To answer this question with respect to sex differences in

nonverbal communication, Hall (1984) compared nonverbal sex differences to sex differences for other psychological variables for which meta-analytic summaries were available. Hall concluded that "although nonverbal sex differences are not large in absolute magnitude, they are as large or larger than those found for most of the psychological variables that have been summarized so far" (1984, p. 148). At the time Hall reached this conclusion, not many other sex differences had been summarized meta-analytically, which could limit the generality of the conclusion. Currently, the situation is very different because many more meta-analyses of sex differences exist. One goal of the present chapter is to compare sex differences for smiling and nonverbal sensitivity to sex differences for a much longer list of traits and behaviors (cf. Hyde & Frost, 1993).

3. *How does the magnitude of a particular sex difference compare to the magnitudes of other correlates of that same trait or behavior?* To my knowledge, this third comparative question has not been asked with respect to any sex differences. Therefore, the second major goal of the present chapter is to compare the magnitude of sex differences in smiling and nonverbal sensitivity to the magnitude of other correlates of smiling and nonverbal sensitivity. Thus, unlike the first comparative question posed earlier, this approach examines the same psychological variables that are at issue in the sex-difference evaluations. Obviously this is a much more focused question.

SEX DIFFERENCES IN SMILING AND NONVERBAL SENSITIVITY

Results of previously published meta-analyses of sex differences in smiling and nonverbal sensitivity are shown in Table 7.1 (Hall, 1978, 1984). More recent results are mentioned later, where relevant. Only data for adolescents and adults are discussed in this chapter unless indicated otherwise.

Smiling

For smiling in social interaction, Hall (1984) concluded that, in the 15 studies for which the effect size could be calculated, the average point-biserial correlation (r) between sex (0 = male, 1 = female) and amount of smiling was .30 (Table 7.1). Over 90% of the studies showed more female than male smiling, and over 50% found this difference to be statistically significant. It was also found (Hall, 1984; Hall & Halberstadt, 1986) that the smiling difference was greatly reduced in less social situations (e.g., when people were observed alone or passing on the street).

TABLE 7.1
Sex Differences in Smiling and Nonverbal Sensitivity (Meta-Analyses)

Behavior and source	N of studies	Mean (Median) r
Smiling		
Hall (1984)	15	.30
Nonverbal sensitivity		
Rosenthal et al. (1979)	133	.20
Hall (1978)	46	.20
Hall (1984)	18	.25

Studies of social interaction located since the 1984 review also show women to smile more than men: Deutsch (1990), $r = .33$ and $r = .09$; Halberstadt, Hayes, and Pike (1988), $r = .35$; Hall, Irish, Roter, Ehrlich, and Miller (1994), $r = .35$; McAdams, Jackson, and Kirshnit (1984), $r = .38$; and Johnson (1994), $r = .04$ and $r = .15$. The average of these effects is .24, which is somewhat smaller than those in the Hall (1984) summary. (Note that unreported effects and those for which r could not be calculated are excluded here because they are in the summary shown in Table 7.1. For summary figures that include unreported effects as $r = .00$, see Hall, 1984.)

Nonverbal Sensitivity

The concern here is with people's ability to infer the meanings of nondeceptive, nondiscrepant, nonverbal cues conveyed in the face, body, and vocal channels. In one extensive analysis, Rosenthal, Hall, DiMatteo, Rogers, and Archer (1979) compared male and female scores on the Profile of Nonverbal Sensitivity (PONS) in 133 samples; participants from third grade through adulthood were included but analyses demonstrated no interaction of age and sex. The PONS consists of 220 two-second clips of silent video, content-masked speech, or combined video and content-masked speech of a young woman enacting 20 different interpersonal scenarios (for validity data, see Rosenthal et al., 1979). In these 133 samples, females scored higher 80% of the time and the median effect size (r) was .20 (see Table 7.1)—a figure close to the correlation of .23 found in a large normative sample of U.S. high school students tested with the PONS.

More extensive summaries of the published literature on sex differences in nonverbal sensitivity were also conducted (Hall, 1978, 1984). In these summaries, care was taken to include only a small number of studies based on the PONS so that a nonredundant analysis could be made. The nonverbal sensitivity tests included in Hall (1978, 1984) were conceptually similar to the PONS: They used drawings, photographs, silent video, or content-masked speech (or combinations thereof) in testing the accuracy of people's inferences about (mainly affective) nonverbal cues. For 46 studies located up through 1978, the average correlation was .20; for an additional 18 studies published between 1978 and 1984, the average correlation was .25 (Table 7.1). Again there was no interaction of age and sex. Thus, extraordinary consistency is seen in the size of the sex difference for sensitivity to nonverbal cues.

Results located subsequently also show on average that women are more accurate at judging nonverbal cues: Ambady, Hallahan, and Rosenthal (1995), $r = .28$; Costanzo and Archer (1989),[1] $r = .15$; Firth, Conger, Kuhlenschmidt, and Dorcey (1986), $r = -.08$; Heilbrun (1984), $r = .39$; Keeley-Dyreson, Burgoon, and Bailey (1991), $r = .17$; Kombos and Fournet (1985), $r = .60$; Simon, Francis, and Lombardo (1990), $r = .14$; and Wagner, MacDonald, and Manstead (1986), $r = .00$. The average of these correlations is .21—a figure virtually identical to both of the earlier summaries. (As with the smiling data, unreported effects and those for which r could not be calculated are excluded here, just as they are in the summary shown in Table 7.1.)

Although the overall sex difference is extremely reliable, there are qualifications to the tendency of women to judge nonverbal cues more accurately than men. First, women's advantage is most evident when they judge the face as opposed to other nonverbal channels (Rosenthal & DePaulo, 1979a). Second, women's advantage decreases markedly when discrepant, very brief, or deceptive cues are being judged (Rosenthal & DePaulo, 1979b; Zuckerman, DePaulo, & Rosenthal, 1981). Third, the *empathic accuracy* that has been studied by Ickes and colleagues, defined as a person's accuracy at identifying the thoughts and feelings of his or her actual conversation partner (as assessed during videotape playback), often shows no sex difference on average (Marangoni, Garcia, Ickes, & Teng, 1995). However, the empathic accuracy measure is different in several respects from standard nonverbal cue-decoding measures (e.g., it involves memory for prior events and includes informative verbal cues).

Other Sex Differences

Table 7.2 presents other psychological sex differences that have been summarized using meta-analysis. Studies are grouped for convenience into the domains of nonverbal communication, cognition, personality, small-group/organizational behavior and attitudes, and other social behaviors

---

[1]The test developed by Costanzo and Archer (1989) includes verbal and nonverbal cues. However, because the verbal cues are intentionally ambiguous, test takers must rely primarily on nonverbal information in answering test items.

TABLE 7.2
Other Sex Differences (Meta-Analyses)

Source	Behavior	N of studies	Mean r
Nonverbal communication			
Hall (1984)	Face-recognition skill	12	.17
	Expression accuracy[a]	20	.31
	Expression accuracy[a]	15	.18
	Facial expressiveness	5	.45
	Gazing	30	.32
	Distance of approach to others	17	−.27
	Restlessness of body	6	−.34
	Expansive movements	6	−.46
	Nods/forward lean	7	.16
	Gestural expressiveness	7	.28
	Self-touching	5	.22
	Speech errors	6	−.33
	Filled pauses	6	−.51
Cognitive domain			
Hyde, Fennema, & Lamon(1990)	Math performance	143	−.17
Voyer et al. (1995)	Spatial ability	212	−.20
Fleming & Malone (1983)	Science achievement	17	−.08
Hyde & Linn (1988)	Verbal ability	17	.06
Hyde (1981)	Field independence	14	−.24
Hyde, Fennema, Ryan, Frost,	Math confidence	26	−.12
& Hopp (1990)	Math anxiety	43	.08
Fleming & Malone (1983)	Positive science attitudes	15	−.06
Rosen & Maguire (1990)	Computerphobia	19	.15
Hembree (1988)	Test anxiety	39	.14
Personality			
Cohn (1991)	Ego development	63	.16
Thoma (1986)	Moral judgment	53	.10
Hattie (1979)	Self-actualization	6	.08
Feingold (1994)	Self-esteem	39	−.07
Hall (1984)	Self-esteem	10	−.06
Feingold (1994)	Internal locus of control	20	−.03
Hall (1984)	Internal locus of control	16	−.12
Feingold (1994)	Anxiety	24	.10
Hall (1984)	Anxiety	14	.16
Feingold (1994)	Anxiety	25	.14
	Assertiveness	25	−.24
	Assertiveness	22	−.09
Hall (1984)	Social poise/dominance/assertiveness	14	−.06
Feingold (1994)	Gregariousness	22	.08
Hall (1984)	Extraversion	17	.02
	Fear of success	11	.03
	Achievement motivation/values	13	−.05
	Masculinity	12	−.25
	Femininity	12	.37

(Continued)

TABLE 7.2
(Continued)

Source	Behavior	N of studies	Mean r
	Loneliness	6	−.08
	Depression	5	.08
	Neuroticism	14	.16
	Psychoticism	8	−.14
Feingold (1994)	Impulsiveness	14	−.03
	Activity	13	−.04
	Openness to ideas	12	−.02
	Trustingness	11	.12
	Tendermindedness	18	.44
	Conscientiousness	7	.06
Rosenthal & DePaulo (1979a)	Self-monitoring	10	−.11
Behavior in small groups/organizations			
Eagly et al. (1995)	Leader effectiveness	76	.01
Eagly & Karau (1991)	Emergence as a task leader	34	−.20
	Emergence as a social leader	15	.09
	Interpersonal leadership style	136	.02
	Task leadership style	139	.00
Wood (1987)	Performance in groups	19	−.19
Eagly et al. (1994)	Motivation to manage	51	−.11
Dobbins & Platz (1986)	Leadership style:		
	Initiating structure	8	.02
	Initiating consideration	8	.02
Eagly & Carli (1981)	Persuasibility	33	.08
	Conformity under group pressure	46	.16
	Conformity in other situations	11	.14
Carli (1982)	Socioemotional contributions in small groups	9	.28
	Task contribution in small groups	10	−.28
	Divides rewards equally	17	.05
	Divides rewards equitably	10	−.10
	Takes smaller rewards for self	11	.14
	Behaves cooperatively in mixed-motive games	47	−.04
Other social behaviors/attitudes			
Eagly & Crowley (1986)	Helping behavior	99	−.17
Eagly & Steffen (1986)	Aggression	50	−.15
Dindia & Allen (1992)	Self-disclosure	205	.09
Hall (1984)	Liberal sex role attitudes	6	.25
	Liking/emotional closeness with others	10	.22
Warr (1971)	Attributing positive traits to people	6	.21
Lirgg (1991)	Self-confidence in physical activities	27	−.23
Wood et al. (1989)	Subjective well-being	18	.02
Martocchio & O'Leary (1989)	Occupational stress	19	−.01

(Continued)

TABLE 7.2
(Continued)

Source	Behavior	N of studies	Mean r
Oliver & Hyde (1993)[b]	Positive attitudes toward:		
	Premarital sexual intercourse	46	−.18
	Sexual permissiveness	39	−.27
	Amount of intercourse experience	28	−.06
	Younger age at first intercourse	135	−.16
	Masturbation frequency	26	−.43
Whitley & Kite (1995)		91	.13
Frieze et al. (1982)	Attributes successful performance to:		
	Ability	13	−.10
	Effort	9	.06
	Task	9	.00
	Luck	12	.14
	Attributes unsuccessful performance to:		
	Ability	12	−.11
	Effort	9	−.11
	Task	8	−.01
	Luck	12	.18
Hall & Dornan (1990)	Satisfaction with medical care	19	−.01
Feingold (1992)	Valuing the following in a mate:		
	High socioeconomic status	15	.33
	Ambition	10	.32
	Character	13	.17
	Intelligence	15	.15
	Humor	7	.07
	Personality	5	.04
Zuckerman et al. (1981)	Ability to deceive	9	−.02
	Ability to detect deception	14	.08

Note. All variables are scaled so that the named behavior describes the high end of the scale. Effect sizes are the point-biserial correlation (r) coded so that higher values signify higher scores for women.

[a]Includes studies of children.

[b]Because Oliver and Hyde (1993) presented many variables, only those that were measured in 25 or more studies are included here.

and attitudes. The appendix provides information on inclusion criteria and other methodological decisions.

A comparison of Tables 7.1 and 7.2 allows one to ask how the sex differences for smiling and nonverbal sensitivity compare to other sex differences. The absolute values of the correlations (r) within each category are used as the indicator of magnitude (the absolute value is used because directionality of effects is not an issue here). Table 7.2 reveals that other nonverbal communication variables produced a median absolute r with sex of .32, which is comparable in magnitude to the smiling difference and somewhat larger than the nonverbal sensitivity difference. A correlation of around .30, according to Cohen (1988), is of medium magnitude and is large enough to be apparent on the basis of everyday observation.

Sex differences in the cognitive domain were smaller (Table 7.2). For ability/achievement (the first five entries in the cognitive domain), the median absolute *r* was .17; for attitudes about academic performance (the remaining entries), the median absolute *r* was .12.

For personality, the differences were smaller still (Table 7.2), with a median absolute *r* of .08. However, the range was much greater than in the cognitive domain; the effects for assertiveness, masculinity, femininity, and tendermindedness were comparable to those for smiling and nonverbal sensitivity.

Behavior and attitudes in small groups and organizations (Table 7.2) had a median absolute *r* of .10, with only two effects (task and socioemotional contributions in groups) having magnitudes comparable to the sex difference in smiling. Other social behaviors and attitudes, admittedly a heterogeneous collection, had a median absolute *r* of .14. Sex differences in sex role attitudes, sexual permissiveness, masturbation frequency, and value placed on high socioeconomic status (SES) and ambition in a mate were all within approximately the same range as the smiling sex difference.

On balance, then, one can reach the broad conclusion that sex differences in smiling and nonverbal sensitivity, like sex differences for other nonverbal communication variables, exceed most of the sex differences found in other domains of psychology. This is consistent with an earlier conclusion (Hall, 1984).

Correlates of Smiling and Nonverbal Sensitivity

The next approach to assessing the magnitude of the smiling and nonverbal sex differences is addressed in Tables 7.3 and 7.4, which present correlations of smiling and nonverbal sensitivity, respectively, with other psychological variables besides sex. The tables include only adolescent and adult Western, nonclinical samples. The table for smiling excludes physiological measures and electromyographic (EMG) studies (i.e., studies of electrical activity in the facial muscles). The table for sensitivity excludes physiological variables, comparisons across cultures, and correlations with other nonverbal sensitivity tests.

The results in the tables were located via PsycLit searches from 1974 to the present and by bibliographic searches of textbooks and articles. Although a sincere effort was made to locate results, there are undoubtedly many studies reporting correlates of smiling and nonverbal sensitivity that were not retrieved. Moreover, for a small number of studies that reported numerous results, only a subset of the results are displayed in the present

TABLE 7.3
Correlates of Smiling

Source	Correlate	r
Cognitive domain		
Mehrabian & Williams (1969)	Vocabulary	−.18
Personality		
Frances (1979)	Sociability	.51
	Wants inclusion	.43
	Affiliation	.39
	Nurturance	.34
	Deference	.37
	Abasement	.34
	Toughmindedness	−.39
LaFrance & Carmen (1980)	Femininity	.47
Rosenfeld (1966a)	Need for social approval	.29
Ruch (1994)	Extraversion	.40
Interpersonal behavior		
D'Augelli (1974)	Nodding	.20
	Interpersonal skill	.22
	Warmth	.18
Deutsch (1990)	Perception of control	−.39
	Feelings of dominance	−.26
Fairbanks et al. (1982)	When talking to a more mentally ill patient	−.29
Halberstadt et al. (1988)	Talking on happy topic (vs. sad)	.52
	While talking (vs. listening)	.25
Hill et al. (1981)	Counselor's empathy/positive regard	.31
	Satisfaction of one's counselees	.13
Kraut & Johnston (1979)	Friend as target (vs. bowling pins)	.50
	Greeting/conversing (vs. not)	.55
Lee et al. (1980)	Nonverbal sensitivity	−.20
Lee & Hallberg (1982)	Better counseling skill	.10
McAdams et al. (1984)	Speaking time	−.10
	Laughing	.56
	Eye contact	.49
	Intimacy motivation	.30
Mehrabian (1971)	Verbal facilitators	.32
	Positive verbal messages	.38
	Hand/arm gestures	.30
	Positive voice tone	.33
Rosenfeld (1966a)	When seeking approval	.40
	Nodding (2)	.46
	Self-touching	−.56
	Posture shifts	−.22
	Gesticulating	.58
Rosenfeld (1966b)	When seeking approval	.32
	Self-touching	−.53
	Positive evaluation by other	.15
Zuckerman & Driver (1985)	Act of deception (19)	−.04
Chaikin et al. (1974)	Positive expectancies for pupils	.75

(Continued)

164

TABLE 7.3
(Continued)

Source	Correlate	r
Coutts & Schneider (1976)	Friend as target (vs. stranger)	.32
	While gazing	.43
Cupchik & Leventhal (1974)	Effect of canned laughter	.31
	Effect of canned laughter	.32
Other		
Cupchik & Leventhal (1974)	Subjects' own ratings of cartoon funniness	.50
	Objective ratings of cartoon funniness	.80
Kraut & Johnston (1979)	Better weather	.12

Note. If the result is based on more than one sample or study, the number of summarized results is given in parentheses and the value in the correlation column is the mean over those results.

TABLE 7.4
Correlates of Nonverbal Sensitivity

Source	Correlate	r
Cognitive domain		
Barnes & Sternberg (1989)	Mental ability	.19
	School performance	.15
Bernieri (1991)	Amount learned from teacher	.51
Rosenthal et al. (1979)	IQ (6)	.15
	Scholastic Aptitude Test (6)	.15
	Field independence (3)	.16
	Greater cognitive complexity (2)	.28
Personality		
Funder & Harris (1986)	Empathy	.21
Barnes & Sternberg (1989)	Empathy	.18
	Self-monitoring	.14
	Social competence	.24
Costanzo & Archer (1989)	Machiavellianism	.17
	Self-monitoring	.25
DiMatteo (1979)	Self-monitoring	.07
Hall (1979)	Empathy (10)	.01
Hall et al. (1996)	Dominance (11)	.14
	Capacity for status (11)	.15
Rosenthal et al. (1979)	California Psychological Inventory:	
	Sociability (5)	.10
	Social presence (5)	.26
	Self-acceptance (5)	.31
	Well-being (5)	.24
	Responsibility (5)	.18
	Socialization (5)	.30
	Self-control (5)	.01
	Tolerance (5)	.26
	Communality (5)	.50

(Continued)

TABLE 7.4
(Continued)

Source	Correlate	r
	Achievement via conformance (5)	.27
	Achievement via independence (5)	.31
	Intellectual efficiency (5)	.32
	Psychological mindedness	.23
	Flexibility (5)	.31
	Femininity (5)	.13
	Personality Research Form:	
	Impulsivity (3)	−.03
	Change (2)	−.02
	Harm avoidance (3)	−.07
	Order (3)	.11
	Cognitive structure (2)	.12
	Achievement (3)	.07
	Endurance (3)	.05
	Play (3)	.09
	Succorance (2)	.00
	Autonomy (3)	−.10
	Understanding (3)	−.02
	Sentience (2)	−.19
	Dominance (3)	−.05
	Abasement (2)	−.16
	Affiliation (3)	.08
	Nurturance (3)	.18
	Exhibition (3)	−.07
	Social recognition (3)	.04
	Aggression (3)	−.08
	Defendence (2)	−.14
	Dogmatism (2)	−.20
	Need for social approval	.00
	Machiavellianism (4)	−.08
	Values	
	Theoretical	−.29
	Economic	−.20
	Aesthetic	−.02
	Social	.22
	Political	−.17
	Religious	.35
	Extraversion (3)	−.02
	Self-monitoring (6)	−.08
Sabatelli et al. (1983)	Internal locus of control	−.04
	Interpersonal trust	.26
Schroeder (1995)	Shyness	−.33
	Sociability	.27
	Public self-consciousness	.39
	Private self-consciousness	.01
	Social anxiety	−.23
	Self-monitoring	−.03

(Continued)

TABLE 7.4
(Continued)

Source	Correlate	r
Simon et al. (1990)	Masculinity	.14
	Machiavellianism	−.23
Hodgins & Koestner (1993)	Mother's ratings of easy childhood temperament	.32
Interpersonal behavior		
Lee & Hallberg (1982)	Better counseling skill	−.03
Lee et al. (1980)	Smiling	−.20
Rosenthal et al. (1979)	Eye contact	.31
Littlepage et al. (1983)	Skill in detecting deception	.16
Firth et al. (1986)	Ability to judge others' social competence	.27
Fingeret et al. (1985)	Behavioral anxiety	−.52
	Skill in role playing	.54
Cooper & Hazelrigg (1988)	Greater susceptibility to experimenter expectancy effect (10)	.11
Hazelrigg et al. (1991)	Greater susceptibility to experimenter expectancy effect	.12
Rosenthal et al. (1979)	Teacher's observed encouragingness to pupils (2)	.76
Interpersonal impressions		
Costanzo & Archer (1989)	Other-rated sensitivity	.48
Funder & Harris (1986)	Other-rated hostility	−.35
	Other-rated manipulativeness	−.32
	Other-rated assertiveness	−.27
	Other-rated seeks reassurance from others	.50
	Other-rated warmth	.35
	Other-rated perfectionism	.29
	Other-rated dependability	.29
Rosenthal et al. (1979)	Other-rated clinical skill (13)	.21
	Other-rated quality as a foreign service officer	.30
	Other-rated nonverbal sensitivity (22)	.16
	Other-rated popularity (2)	.20
DiMatteo (1979)	Satisfaction of one's patients (2)	.14
Other		
Hall et al. (1996)	Higher socioeconomic status (17)	.15
Blanck et al. (1980)	Sibling's nonverbal sensitivity	.09
Buller & Aune (1988)	Liking for fast speech	.18
Keeley-Dyreson et al. (1991)	Experimenter-induced stress while taking decoding test	−.08
Rosenthal et al. (1979)	Age (3rd grade through adults) (124)	.34
	Better interpersonal judgment (paper and pencil)	.26
	Self-rated interpersonal success (3)	.06
	Self-rated nonverbal sensitivity	.08
	Task orientation as a leader	.21
	Democratic attitudes as a teacher (2)	.24
Smith et al. (1991)	Self-rated accuracy on decoding test	.08
Zuckerman & Larrance (1979)	Self-rated nonverbal sensitivity	.13
Zuckerman & Przewuzman (1979)	Spouse's nonverbal sensitivity	.14
	Advantage of decoding familiar other	.40
	Better school adjustment in one's child	.25

Note. If the result is based on more than one sample or study, the number of summarized results is given in parentheses and the value in the correlation column is the mean over those results.

tables. The purpose is not to present an exhaustive compilation of corre-lates of these nonverbal variables, but rather to present a reasonably rep-resentative and extensive array of results that can provide a basis for com-parison with their respective sex differences shown in Table 7.1. Although Tables 7.3 and 7.4 were not limited to meta-analytic summaries as Tables 7.1 and 7.2 were, inspection reveals that a substantial number of the find-ings in Table 7.4 are based on multiple results. This is especially the case for findings based on the PONS (Rosenthal et al., 1979).

Smiling

Studies in Table 7.3, showing correlations of smiling with other variables, are grouped into the categories of cognition, personality, interpersonal behavior, and other. The one study in the cognitive domain showed a correlation of −.18. Studies of personality had a median absolute r of .39, and studies of social interaction had a median absolute r of .32. The category of "other" correlates had a median absolute r of .50 (based on only three studies). Thus, smiling shows many substantial correlations with other psychological and situational variables. These relations tend to be somewhat, but not greatly, larger than the sex difference in smiling.

Nonverbal Sensitivity

Table 7.4 presents correlates of sensitivity to nonverbal cues, with the correlates divided into the categories of cognition, personality, interper-sonal behavior, interpersonal impressions, and other. The median absolute r in the cognitive domain was .16. Within this category, all the correlations for cognitive abilities were closely grouped around this value but two cor-relations were larger: for cognitive complexity (a measure of cognitive style, not ability) and for amount learned during a teaching session. Be-cause the latter involved face-to-face communication, it carries a flavor of social interaction that might justify placing it in the social interaction category rather than the cognitive one.[2]

For the personality variables in Table 7.3, there was a median absolute r of .15 with nonverbal sensitivity, but this was associated with a wide range of correlations. Interpersonal behavior and impressions both had larger median absolute rs of .24 and .29, respectively. Finally, the category of

---

[2]When considering the cognitive ability variables, the distinction between convergent and discriminant validity becomes relevant. Whereas most, and possibly all, of the other variables in Tables 7.3 and 7.4 are ones for which the original investigators likely expected nonzero correlations with the nonverbal variables, the cognitive variables are different. Rosenthal et al. (1979) clearly treated cognitive ability in the context of discriminant validity, meaning specifically that no, or at least negligible, correlations with nonverbal sensitivity were predicted.

"other" correlates had a median absolute r of .15. Thus, it appears that the effect size for the sex difference in nonverbal sensitivity falls well within the range of other correlates of nonverbal sensitivity—being smaller than the two interpersonal categories but larger than the cognitive, personality, and other categories.

DISCUSSION

Based on this comparison among effect sizes, it is justified to conclude that sex differences for smiling and nonverbal sensitivity are relatively large. This conclusion is based on two kinds of evidence. First, sex differences for smiling and nonverbal sensitivity, as well as for several other nonverbal variables, are larger than most other psychological sex differences that have been subjected to meta-analysis. Of course, one cannot reach a conclusion about psychological sex differences that have not been summarized using meta-analysis. Many sex differences have been measured but not subjected to meta-analysis, and many others have never been studied at all. We can only say that, provisionally, sex differences in the nonverbal domain appear to be larger than sex differences for many other attitudes, behaviors, abilities, and traits, and they are comparable in magnitude to a number of others.

The second line of evidence supporting the conclusion that the smiling and nonverbal sensitivity sex differences are relatively large is based on comparisons between the relationships between these two variables and sex, on the one hand, and the relationships between these two variables and other psychological variables, on the other. This comparison revealed that the sex differences for smiling and nonverbal sensitivity are of comparable magnitude to other correlates of these two variables, although this is clearly a generalization because the range was very wide. The fact that the sex differences were roughly similar to other effects might indicate that psychometric factors in the measurement of smiling and nonverbal sensitivity place an upper limit on the size of effects that can be obtained, as suggested by Cohen (1988). For smiling, the sex difference is about $r = .30$, and other correlates of smiling are not too far from this approximate value. For nonverbal sensitivity, the sex difference is about $r = .20$, and other correlates are roughly in this range. Thus, smiling produces larger correlations, both with sex and other psychological variables, than does nonverbal sensitivity. The reason for this cannot be determined from the present analysis, but one possibility is differences in the reliability and validity with which these constructs are measured (cf. Rosenthal et al., 1979).

The effects for sex are roughly equivalent to other effects for smiling and nonverbal sensitivity. This means that, although sex does not account for a large amount of variation in these traits, its predictive validity is as good (on average) as that of many other personal and situational variables. Thus, we can say that these two nonverbal sex differences exceed many other sex differences and that sex is as strongly related to these two variables as other variables are. The latter finding greatly bolsters confidence that these particular sex effects are worth discussion.

Of course, documenting a sex difference is much easier than explaining it. There is no consensus on the roots of the sex differences in smiling and nonverbal sensitivity, nor for any of the other nonverbal communication variables described here, nor for any other psychological variables, for that matter (Eagly, 1987, 1995; Hall, 1984; Hall & Halberstadt, 1994; Hall, Halberstadt, & O'Brien, in press; LaFrance & Henley, 1994; Noller, 1986). Many psychological sex differences are clearly part of gender stereotypes (Briton & Hall, 1995; Swim, 1994), but this may be as much a reflection of the robust and observable nature of the actual differences as an explanation for their existence.

In a recent effort to understand possible sources of the gender differences discussed in this chapter, students at Northeastern University were asked to rate the traits and behaviors shown in Tables 7.1 and 7.2 on their centrality to their own gender identity (Hall & Carter, 1996). There was a high degree of within-sex consensus on how central the traits and behaviors were, and the male and female centrality ratings were positively, but not strongly, correlated with each other. This means that men and women did not regard the traits and behaviors as equally relevant to their gender self-concepts. When the averaged centrality ratings were correlated, within sex, with the actual sex differences from Table 7.2, it was found that, for men, the more they said the traits and behaviors were central to their gender identity, the less the actual sex difference favored women. Similarly, the more the women said the traits and behaviors were central, the more the actual sex differences favored women. The correlation between the differences between men's and women's centrality ratings and the actual sex differences was .68 ($p < .0001$), indicating that sex differences parallel, to an impressive degree, people's assessments of how important those behaviors are to their gender identity. For this sample, only the traits of liking/emotional closeness to others, femininity, masculinity, and liberal sex role attitudes showed bigger male–female differences in centrality than did smiling. This suggests that smiling is indeed very important to men's and women's basic conceptions of themselves, and it may provide some insight into the relative strength of this sex difference.

Of course, such findings could merely signify that people are aware both of the sex stereotypes and the actual differences (see, e.g., Briton & Hall, 1995; Swim, 1994; Zuckerman & Larrance, 1979), and that they structure their own gender role values to conform to these stereotypical and actual differences. If this is the case, the gender role centrality ratings may again be more a consequence than a cause of the sex differences. Because of the power of expectations to shape behavior, any such beliefs and expectations could in turn shape men's and women's actual behavior (Eccles, Jacobs, & Harold, 1990; Hall & Briton, 1993).

Moving beyond smiling and nonverbal sensitivity in particular, the present chapter reveals that the entire nonverbal domain stands out in terms of the size of sex differences. It may be that, developmentally, as gender role identity is shaped and maintained, the interpersonal realm is much more important to this process than is the more intrapsychic realm (which would include cognitive skills and attitudes, and personality traits). In the quest for gender role identity, feedback about acceptance and rejection by others is much more likely to shape behavior and self-concept than are the more intrapsychic processes. Thus, face-to-face interactions in which one can display one's gender and receive reactions from others may be crucial for gender role development. In this light, it would not be surprising if the development of a gender-consistent repertoire of interpersonal behaviors holds high priority for individuals and is related to the development of rather pronounced between-sex differences in this domain. This idea is reminiscent of Birdwhistell's (1970) conceptualization of male–female differences in nonverbal communication as tertiary sexual characteristics— sexual characteristics that are learned and social-behavioral in form, unlike primary and secondary sexual characteristics. Such tertiary sexual characteristics would likely be crucial for mating, division of labor, and maintenance of gender roles in general.

ACKNOWLEDGMENTS

Preparation of this chapter was supported by National Science Foundation grant SBR-9311544. The comments of Amy Halberstadt on this chapter are greatly appreciated.

APPENDIX

Inclusion Criteria for Studies Shown in Table 7.2

1. The table includes (a) the meta-analyses to which Hall (1984) compared nonverbal sex differences, which are identifiable by their dates (prior to 1984); (b) personality differences collected from four journals over a 9-year period by Hall (1984), referred to in the table as Hall (1984); (c) meta-analyses located via PsycLit searches using the terms *gender and meta-*

analysis and *sex and meta-analysis* (for the year 1974 to the present); and (d) other meta-analyses in the present author's files.

2. Any psychological variable (observed behavior, attitude, or self-reported trait) is included but not physiological/motor variables or IQ.

3. Results were expressed as the point-biserial correlation (*r*) or in a form that was easily transformed into that metric (e.g., a standardized two-group comparison such as Cohen's *d* or means and standard deviations; Rosenthal, 1991).

4. Mean effect sizes reported are based on summaries of known effect sizes wherever possible (i.e., summaries that included unknown effect sizes as having an effect size of *r* = 0 were avoided).

5. Mean effect sizes were based on at least five studies.

6. When possible, the mean effect size weighted by sample size is reported.

7. Only sex main effects are included, and typically only a meta-analysis's main result (i.e., secondary results and moderated effects are not always included).

8. A meta-analysis is not included if it was substantially superseded by a later meta-analysis of the same behavior. Meta-analyses of the same behavior shown in the table are based on nonoverlapping groups of studies.

9. Results for adolescents and adults only are included; to achieve this end, mean effect sizes were recalculated from data supplied in a meta-analysis when necessary.

10. Samples were nonclinical and were from Western countries (except for second entry, which included some non-Western groups).

11. The journal and issue containing the meta-analysis were available in the present author's university library.

REFERENCES

Ambady, N., Hallahan, M., & Rosenthal, R. (1995). On judging and being judged accurately in zero-acquaintance situations. *Journal of Personality and Social Psychology, 69*, 518–529.

Barnes, M. L., & Sternberg, R. J. (1989). Social intelligence and decoding of nonverbal cues. *Intelligence, 13*, 263–287.

Bernieri, F. J. (1991). Interpersonal sensitivity in teaching interactions. *Personality and Social Psychology Bulletin, 17*, 98–103.

Birdwhistell, R. L. (1970). *Kinesics and context.* Philadelphia: University of Pennsylvania Press.

Blanck, P. D., Zuckerman, M., DePaulo, B. M., & Rosenthal, R. (1980). Sibling resemblances in nonverbal skill and style. *Journal of Nonverbal Behavior, 4*, 219–226.

Briton, N. J., & Hall, J. A. (1995). Beliefs about female and male nonverbal communication. *Sex Roles, 32*, 79–90.

Buller, D. B., & Aune, R. K. (1988). The effects of vocalics and nonverbal sensitivity on compliance: A speech accommodation theory explanation. *Human Communication Research, 14*, 301–332.

Carli, L. L. (1982). *Are women more social and men more task oriented? A meta-analytic review of sex differences in group interaction, reward allocation, coalition formation, and cooperation in the Prisoner's Dilemma Game*. Unpublished manuscript, University of Massachusetts, Amherst.

Chaikin, A. L., Sigler, E., & Derlega, V. J. (1984). Nonverbal mediators of teacher expectancy effects. *Journal of Personality and Social Psychology, 30,* 144–149.

Cohen, J. (1988). *Statistical power analysis for the behavioral sciences* (2nd ed.). New York: Academic Press.

Cohn, L. D. (1991). Sex differences in the course of personality development: A meta-analysis. *Psychological Bulletin, 109,* 252–266.

Cooper, H., & Hazelrigg, P. (1988). Personality moderators of interpersonal expectancy effects: An integrating research review. *Journal of Personality and Social Psychology, 55,* 937–949.

Costanzo, M., & Archer, D. (1989). Interpreting the expressive behavior of others: The Interpersonal Perception Task. *Journal of Nonverbal Behavior, 13,* 225–245.

Coutts, L. M., & Schneider, F. W. (1976). Affiliative conflict theory: An investigation of the intimacy equilibrium and compensation hypothesis. *Journal of Personality and Social Psychology, 34,* 1135–1142.

Cupchik, G. C., & Leventhal, H. (1974). Consistency between expressive behavior and the elevation of humorous stimuli: The role of sex and self-observation. *Journal of Personality and Social Psychology, 30,* 429–442.

D'Augelli, A. R. (1974). Nonverbal behavior of helpers in initial helping interactions. *Journal of Counseling Psychology, 21,* 360–363.

Deutsch, F. M. (1990). Status, sex, and smiling: The effect of role on smiling in men and women. *Personality and Social Psychology Bulletin, 16,* 531–540.

Dindia, K., & Allen, M. (1992). Sex differences in self-disclosure: A meta-analysis. *Psychological Bulletin, 112,* 106–124.

DiMatteo, M. R. (1979). Nonverbal skill and the physician-patient relationship. In R. Rosenthal (Ed.), *Skill in nonverbal communication: Individual differences* (pp. 104–134). Cambridge, MA: Oelgeschlager, Gunn & Hain.

Dobbins, G. H., & Platz, S. J. (1986). Sex differences in leadership: How real are they? *Academy of Management Review, 11,* 118–127.

Eagly, A. H. (1987). *Sex differences in social behavior: A social-role interpretation*. Hillsdale, NJ: Lawrence Erlbaum Associates.

Eagly, A. H. (1995). The science and politics of comparing women and men. *American Psychologist, 50,* 145–158.

Eagly, A. H., & Carli, L. L. (1981). Sex researchers and sex-typed communications as determinants of sex differences in influenceability. *Psychological Bulletin, 90,* 1–20.

Eagly, A. H., & Crowley, M. (1986). Gender and helping behavior: A meta-analytic review of the social psychological literature. *Psychological Bulletin, 100,* 283–308.

Eagly, A. H., & Johnson, B. T. (1990). Gender and leadership style: A meta-analysis. *Psychological Bulletin, 108,* 233–256.

Eagly, A. H., & Karau, S. J. (1991). Gender and the emergence of leaders: A meta-analysis. *Journal of Personality and Social Psychology, 60,* 685–710.

Eagly, A. H., Karau, S. J., & Makhijani, M. G. (1995). Gender and the effectiveness of leaders: A meta-analysis. *Psychological Bulletin, 117,* 125–145.

Eagly, A. H., Karau, S. J., Miner, J. B., & Johnson, B. T. (1994). Gender and motivation to manage in hierarchic organizations: A meta-analysis. *Leadership Quarterly, 5,* 135–159.

Eagly, A. H., & Steffen, V. J. (1986). Gender and aggressive behavior: A meta-analytic review of the social psychological literature. *Psychological Bulletin, 100,* 309–330.

Eagly, A. H., & Wood, W. (1991). Explaining sex differences in social behavior: A meta-analytic perspective. *Personality and Social Psychology Bulletin, 17,* 306–315.

Eccles, J. S., Jacobs, J. E., & Harold, R. D. (1990). Gender role stereotypes, expectancy effects, and parents' socialization of gender differences. *Journal of Social Issues, 46*(2), 183–201.

Fairbanks, L. A., McGuire, M. T., & Harris, C. J. (1982). Nonverbal interaction of patients and therapists during psychiatric interviews. *Journal of Abnormal Psychology, 91*, 109–119.

Feingold, A. (1992). Gender differences in mate selection preferences: A test of the parental investment model. *Psychological Bulletin, 112*, 125–139.

Feingold, A. (1994). Gender differences in personality: A meta-analysis. *Psychological Bulletin, 116*, 429–456.

Fingeret, A. L., Monti, P. M., & Paxson, M. A. (1985). Social perception, social performance, and self-perception: A study with psychiatric and nonpsychiatric patients. *Behavior Modification, 9*, 345–356.

Firth, E. A., Conger, J. C., Kuhlenschmidt, S., & Dorcey, T. (1986). Social competence and social perceptivity. *Journal of Social and Clinical Psychology, 4*, 85–100.

Fleming, M. L., & Malone, M. R. (1983). The relationship of student characteristics and student performance in science as viewed by meta-analysis research. *Journal of Research in Science Teaching, 20*, 481–495.

Frances, S. J. (1979). Sex differences in nonverbal behavior. *Sex Roles, 5*, 519–535.

Frieze, I. H., Whitley, B. E., Hanusa, B. H., & McHugh, M. C. (1982). Assessing the theoretical models for sex differences in causal attributions for success and failure. *Sex Roles, 8*, 333–343.

Funder, D. C., & Harris, M. J. (1986). On the several facets of personality assessment: The case of social acuity. *Journal of Personality, 54*, 528–550.

Halberstadt, A. G., Hayes, C. W., & Pike, K. M. (1988). Gender and gender role differences in smiling and communication consistency. *Sex Roles, 19*, 589–604.

Hall, J. A. (1978). Gender effects in decoding nonverbal cues. *Psychological Bulletin, 85*, 845–857.

Hall, J. A. (1979). Gender, gender roles, and nonverbal communication skills. In R. Rosenthal (Ed.), *Skill in nonverbal communication: Individual differences* (pp. 32–67). Cambridge, MA: Oelgeschlager, Gunn & Hain.

Hall, J. A. (1984). *Nonverbal sex differences: Communication accuracy and expressive style.* Baltimore: The Johns Hopkins University Press.

Hall, J. A., & Briton, N. J. (1993). Gender, nonverbal behavior, and expectations. In P. D. Blanck (Ed.), *Interpersonal expectations: Theory, research, and applications* (pp. 276–295). Cambridge, England: Cambridge University Press.

Hall, J. A., & Carter, J. D. (1996). Unpublished data, Northeastern University.

Hall, J. A., & Dornan, M. C. (1990). Patient sociodemographic characteristics as predictors of satisfaction with medical care: A meta-analysis. *Social Science & Medicine, 30*, 811–818.

Hall, J. A., & Halberstadt, A. G. (1986). Smiling and gazing. In J. S. Hyde & M. C. Linn (Eds.), *The psychology of gender: Advances through meta-analysis* (pp. 136–158). Baltimore: The Johns Hopkins University Press.

Hall, J. A., & Halberstadt, A. G. (1994). "Subordination" and sensitivity to nonverbal cues: A study of married working women. *Sex Roles, 31*, 149–165.

Hall, J. A., & Halberstadt, A. G. (1996). Subordination and nonverbal sensitivity: A hypothesis in search of support. In M. R. Walsh (Ed.), *Women, men, and gender: Ongoing debates* (pp. 120–133). New Haven, CT: Yale University Press.

Hall, J. A., Halberstadt, A. G., & O'Brien, C. E. (in press). "Subordination" and nonverbal sensitivity: A study and synthesis of findings based on trait measures. *Sex Roles.*

Hall, J. A., Irish, J. T., Roter, D. L., Ehrlich, C. M., & Miller, L. H. (1994). Gender in medical encounters: An analysis of physician and patient communication in a primary care setting. *Health Psychology, 13*, 384–392.

Hattie, J. (1979). Stability of results across many studies: Sex differences on the Personal Orientation Inventory. *Journal of Personality Assessment, 43*, 627–628.

Hazelrigg, P. J., Cooper, H., & Strathman, A. J. (1991). Personality moderators of the experimenter expectancy effect: A reexamination of five hypotheses. *Personality and Social Psychology Bulletin, 17,* 569–579.

Heilbrun, A. B. (1984). Sex-based models of androgyny: A further cognitive elaboration of competence differences. *Journal of Personality and Social Psychology, 46,* 216–229.

Hembree, R. (1988). Correlates, causes, effects, and treatment of test anxiety. *Review of Educational Research, 58,* 47–77.

Hill, C. E., Siegelman, L., Gronsky, B. R., Sturniolo, F., & Fretz, B. R. (1981). Nonverbal communication and counseling outcome. *Journal of Counseling Psychology, 28,* 203–212.

Hodgins, H. S., & Koestner, R. (1993). The origins of nonverbal sensitivity. *Personality and Social Psychology Bulletin, 19,* 466–473.

Hyde, J. S. (1981). How large are cognitive gender differences? A meta-analysis using ω^2 and d. *American Psychologist, 36,* 892–901.

Hyde, J. S., Fennema, E., & Lamon, S. J. (1990). Gender differences in mathematics performance: A meta-analysis. *Psychological Bulletin, 107,* 139–155.

Hyde, J. S., Fennema, E., Ryan, M., Frost, L. A., & Hopp, C. (1990). Gender comparisons of mathematics attitudes and affect: A meta-analysis. *Psychology of Women Quarterly, 14,* 299–324.

Hyde, J. S., & Frost, L. A. (1993). Meta-analysis in the psychology of women. In F. L. Denmark & M. A. Paludi (Eds.), *Psychology of women: A handbook of issues and theories* (pp. 67–103). Westport, CT: Greenwood.

Hyde, J. S., & Linn, M. C. (Eds.). (1986). *The psychology of gender: Advances through meta-analysis.* Baltimore: The Johns Hopkins University Press.

Hyde, J. S., & Linn, M. C. (1988). Gender differences in verbal ability: A meta-analysis. *Psychological Bulletin, 104,* 53–69.

Hyde, J. S., & Plant, E. A. (1995). Magnitude of psychological gender differences: Another side to the story. *American Psychologist, 50,* 159–161.

Johnson, C. (1994). Gender, legitimate authority, and leader-subordinate conversations. *American Sociological Review, 59,* 122–135.

Keeley-Dyreson, M., Burgoon, J. K., & Bailey, W. (1991). The effects of stress and gender on nonverbal decoding accuracy in kinesic and vocalic channels. *Human Communication Research, 17,* 584–605.

Kombos, N. A., & Fournet, G. P. (1985). Effects of dominance-submissiveness and gender on recognition of nonverbal emotional cues. *Educational and Psychological Research, 5,* 19–28.

Kraut, R. E., & Johnston, R. E. (1979). Social and emotional messages of smiling: An ethological approach. *Journal of Personality and Social Psychology, 37,* 1539–1553.

LaFrance, M., & Carmen, B. (1980). The nonverbal display of psychological androgyny. *Journal of Personality and Social Psychology, 38,* 36–49.

LaFrance, M., & Henley, N. M. (1994). On oppressing hypotheses: Or differences in nonverbal sensitivity revisited. In H. L. Radtke & H. J. Stam (Eds.), *Power/gender: Social relations in theory and practice* (pp. 287–311). London: Sage.

Lee, D. Y., & Hallberg, E. T. (1982). Nonverbal behaviors of "good" and "poor" counselors. *Journal of Counseling Psychology, 29,* 414–417.

Lee, D. Y., Hallberg, E. T., Kocsis, M., & Haase, R. F. (1980). Decoding skills in nonverbal communication and perceived interviewer effectiveness. *Journal of Counseling Psychology, 27,* 89–92.

Lirgg, C. D. (1991). Gender differences in self-confidence in physical activity: A meta-analysis of recent studies. *Journal of Sport and Exercise Psychology, 13,* 294–310.

Littlepage, G. E., McKinnie, R., & Pineault, M. A. (1983). Relationship between nonverbal sensitivities and detection of deception. *Perceptual and Motor Skills, 57,* 651–657.

Marangoni, C., Garcia, S., Ickes, W., & Teng, G. (1995). Empathic accuracy in a clinical relevant situation. *Journal of Personality and Social Psychology, 68,* 854–869.

Martocchio, J. J., & O'Leary, A. M. (1989). Sex differences in occupational stress: A meta-analytic review. *Journal of Applied Psychology, 74,* 495–501.

McAdams, D. P., Jackson, R. J., & Kirshnit, C. (1984). Looking, laughing, and smiling in dyads as a function of intimacy motivation and reciprocity. *Journal of Personality, 52,* 261–273.

Mehrabian, A. (1971). Verbal and nonverbal interaction of strangers in a waiting situation. *Journal of Experimental Research in Personality, 5,* 127–138.

Mehrabian, A., & Williams, M. (1969). Nonverbal concimitants of perceived and intended persuasiveness. *Journal of Personality and Social Psychology, 13,* 37–58.

Noller, P. (1986). Sex differences in nonverbal communication: Advantage lost or supremacy regained? *Australian Journal of Psychology, 38,* 23–32.

Oliver, M. B., & Hyde, J. S. (1993). Gender differences in sexuality: A meta-analysis. *Psychological Bulletin, 114,* 29–51.

Rosen, L. D., & Maguire, P. (1990). Myths and realities of computerphobia: A meta-analysis. *Anxiety Research, 3,* 175–191.

Rosenfeld, H. M. (1966a). Instrumental affiliative functions of facial and gestural expressions. *Journal of Personality and Social Psychology, 4,* 65–72.

Rosenfeld, H. M. (1966b). Approval-inducing functions of verbal and nonverbal responses in the dyad. *Journal of Personality and Social Psychology, 4,* 597–605.

Rosenthal, R., & DePaulo, B. M. (1979a). Sex differences in accommodation in nonverbal communication. In R. Rosenthal (Ed.), *Skill in nonverbal communication: Individual differences* (pp. 68–103). Cambridge, MA: Oelgeschlager, Gunn & Hain.

Rosenthal, R., & DePaulo, B. M. (1979b). Sex differences in eavesdropping on nonverbal cues. *Journal of Personality and Social Psychology, 37,* 273–285.

Rosenthal, R., Hall, J. A., DiMatteo, M. R., Rogers, P. L., & Archer, D. (1979). *Sensitivity to nonverbal communication: The PONS test.* Baltimore: The Johns Hopkins University Press.

Rosenthal, R., & Rubin, D. B. (1982). A simple, general purpose display of magnitude of experimental effect. *Journal of Educational Psychology, 74,* 166–169.

Ruch, W. (1994). Extraversion, alcohol, and enjoyment. *Personality and Individual Differences, 16,* 89–102.

Sabatelli, R. M., Buck, R., & Dreyer, A. (1983). Locus of control, interpersonal trust, and nonverbal communication accuracy. *Journal of Personality and Social Psychology, 44,* 399–409.

Schroeder, J. E. (1995). Interpersonal perception skills: Self-concept correlates. *Perceptual and Motor Skills, 80,* 51–56.

Simon, L. J., Francis, P. L., & Lombardo, J. P. (1990). Sex, sex-role, and Machiavellianism as correlates of decoding ability. *Perceptual and Motor Skills, 71,* 243–247.

Smith, H. J., Archer, D., & Costanzo, M. (1991). "Just a hunch": Accuracy and awareness in person perception. *Journal of Nonverbal Behavior, 15,* 3–18.

Swim, J. K. (1994). Perceived versus meta-analytic effect sizes: An assessment of the accuracy of gender stereotypes. *Journal of Personality and Social Psychology, 66,* 21–36.

Thoma, S. J. (1986). Estimating gender differences in the comprehension and preference of moral issues. *Developmental Review, 6,* 165–180.

Voyer, D., Voyer, S., & Bryden, M. P. (1995). Magnitude of sex differences in spatial abilities: A meta-analysis and consideration of critical variables. *Psychological Bulletin, 117,* 250–270.

Wagner, H. L.., MacDonald, C. J., & Manstead, A. S. R. (1986). Communication of individual emotions by spontaneous facial expressions. *Journal of Personality and Social Psychology, 50,* 737–743.

Warr, P. B. (1971). Pollyanna's personal judgements. *European Journal of Social Psychology, 1,* 327–338.

Whitley, B. E., Jr., & Kite, M. E. (1995). Sex differences in attitudes toward homosexuality: A comment on Oliver and Hyde (1993). *Psychological Bulletin, 117,* 146–154.

Wood, W. (1987). Meta-analytic review of sex differences in group performance. *Psychological Bulletin, 102,* 53–71.

Wood, W., Rhodes, N., & Whelan, M. (1989). Sex differences in positive well-being: A consideration of emotional style and marital status. *Psycological Bulletin, 106,* 249–264.

Zuckerman, M., & Driver, R. E. (1985). Telling lies: Verbal and nonverbal correlates of deception. In A. W. Siegman & S. Feldstein (Eds.), *Multichannel integrations of nonverbal behavior* (pp. 129–147). Hillsdale, NJ: Lawrence Erlbaum Associates.

Zuckerman, M., & Larrance, D. T. (1979). In R. Rosenthal (Ed.), *Skill in nonverbal communication: Individual differences* (pp. 171–203). Cambridge, MA: Oelgeschlager, Gunn & Hain.

Zuckerman, M., & Przewuzman, S. J. (1979). Decoding and encoding facial expressions in preschool-age children. *Environmental Psychology and Nonverbal Behavior, 3,* 147–163.

Zuckerman, M., DePaulo, B. M., & Rosenthal, R. (1981). Verbal and nonverbal communication of deception. In L. Berkowitz (Ed.), *Advances in experimental social psychology* (Vol. 14, pp. 1–59). New York: Academic Press.

Chapter 8

Gender as a Culturally Determined Construct: Communication Styles in Japan and the United States

Vincent R. Waldron
Lesley Di Mare
Arizona State University West

Currently, a debate exists in the discipline of communication studies regarding the usefulness of continuing traditional, behaviorally based research on gender in interpersonal and organizational settings. It has been argued by a number of quantitative researchers (e.g., Canary & Hause, 1993; Harper & Hirokawa, 1988; Hirokawa, Mickey, & Miura, 1991; Wilkins & Andersen, 1991) that evidence of sex differences in communicative behavior are tiny and contradictory and that many of our views of women's communicative styles reflect stereotypes rather than empirical observations. For example, Wilkins and Andersen's (1991) *MCQ* article found only half of 1% of variance in organizational communication behaviors due to sex differences.

In contrast, a body of literature that constitutes qualitative, ethnographic, and cultural analyses of how men and women communicate indicates that there are decided differences in the overall communicative style and with the specific communication strategies employed by men and women in a variety of contexts (Bass & Avolio, 1994; Belenky, Clinchy, Goldberger, & Tarule, 1986; Darus, 1994; Eagly & Johnson, 1990; Holloway, 1995; Lee, 1994; Lipman-Blumen, 1992; Roesner, 1990; Troemel-Ploetz, 1994; Zellner, 1994). The contradiction in these two bodies of research has lead to numerous issues surrounding the study of sex differences in communication.

To further complicate the matter, we would argue, along with other scholars, that yet another issue needs to be included in the discussion surrounding communication and sex differences—specifically, how gender is manifested in other cultures (Bond & Ho, 1978; Collier, 1991). Some researchers have argued that sex as a variable has been largely neglected or overlooked in regions such as Africa, Asia, Latin America, and Mexico (Collier, 1991; Suzuki, 1991). We agree. However, we would caution researchers against imposing a Western view of sex differences on other societies. For researchers in one culture to suggest that sex is a variable that is largely neglected in other cultures may reflect a society's predisposition to particular heuristic approaches that dichotomize and emphasize gender roles as well as other dimensions of a culture (Sinha & Tripathi, 1994). That is, sex in one culture simply may not operate as an organizing principle in the development of communicative styles in the same way that it does for other cultures and thus may not be considered a variable worth studying.

If sex differences are due to gender (a culturally determined concept), sex differences as they are manifested in countries and cultures may vary due to differences in social roles, power structures, religious practices, and other cultural factors. For the purposes of this chapter we would argue that sex differences are culturally determined (Chambers, 1992). As such, they vary from culture to culture. As scholars of cross-cultural communication have long noted (e.g., Barnlund, 1975), careful examination of the communication practices of other cultures can create a heightened awareness of our own taken-for-granted behavior patterns and beliefs. We would suggest that this is also the case for sex differences and the ways in which our view of these differences may or may not affect communicative styles.

One of the purposes in this chapter is to determine whether it is sex, culture, or a combination of these things that best accounts for differences in communication in Japan and the United States. In addition, we examine Western conceptions and stereotypes regarding sex differences in Japan and determine whether the research supports these perceptions. To achieve these objectives, this chapter begins with a review of the literature that documents Western perceptions of the Japanese. It then moves to a review of the quantitative and qualitative literature that examines the relative importance of sex and culture in explaining communication styles of each group.

We believe that comparing Japan with America is useful for several reasons. First, Japan has been perceived as an extremely patriarchal and gendered society; indeed, to a far greater degree than the United States as evidenced in popular conceptions and in a number of studies conducted on Japanese culture and communicative styles (Connor, 1985; Saso, 1990). Second, research suggests that fundamental differences exist concerning assumptions and attitudes about human interaction in Japan versus the West (Wetzel, 1993). Finally, international ties between Japan and America suggest that continued analysis of communicative interaction between the two cultures is important.

WESTERN PERCEPTIONS OF GENDER IN JAPAN

The perception that Westerners maintain of Asian societies, particularly the Japanese, is that these cultures are extremely gendered, patriarchal, and masculine. For example, Hofstede's (1980) influential analysis of cultures as masculine or feminine defined the Japanese culture as high on masculinity and American culture as high on femininity. According to Hofstede, masculinity predominates in cultures where there are clearly differentiated sex roles, whereas femininity predominates in cultures where there are fluid sex roles and androgyny is the ideal. Gudykunst, Nishida, and Schmidt (1989) reinforced Hofstede's notion of Japan as a masculine society and, as such, one likely to assign particular roles to individuals based on their sex.

Saso (1990) pointed out that writers of popular literature tend to present women in Japanese society as a subordinate subculture that endures the long apprenticeship of *geisha* and handles the duties of tea pouring in Japanese executive offices. Saso pointed out that this quaint depiction of Japanese women in the Japanese culture began when Japan came to the attention of the West in the middle of the 19th century. These perceptions manifest themselves in descriptions that are often offered about the ways in which males and females communicate in Japan and the reasons for which roles are assigned to both, respectively.

Although some scholarly research indicates that Japan is a masculine society, recent research indicates that conceptions of the Japanese as a gendered society are, to some extent, stereotypical and more representative of how Westerners perceive the Japanese to behave communicatively. Although the issue of equality of the sexes in Japan appears to be an ongoing one, Tanaka (1990) noted that it is mostly those outside of Japan who maintain stereotypes of Japanese women as passive and submissive. Connor (1985) argued that the mass media and popular press in America inscribe Japan as the "last bastion of male supremacy" while depicting the Japanese woman as dependent, docile, deferent, shy, submissive, and subservient. He argued further that Americans' confusion between the concepts of *female* and *mother* in Japan allows us to perpetuate stereotypes of men and women in that culture. Schooler and Smith (1978) showed that Japanese women resist the stereotype of the Japanese wife as "a paragon of domesticity who selflessly and subserviently meets all of her husband's domestic needs" (p. 23). Instead, Japanese women see themselves as equal to their husbands because of the importance of the role of mother and person in Japanese society. Schooler and Smith's findings make sense when one considers Smith's (1992) observation that in Japan (unlike America) the "public domain is seen to include the family, to the extent that traditional notions of family as having a public, corporate character, with rigid hierarchical ranking of its members, continue to influence domestic interactions" (p. 59). Consequently, a systematic review of the quantitative and qualitative research is needed to determine the ways in which sex, gender, and cultural differences affect and create communication patterns in Japan and the United States.

A review of the quantitative literature could yield evidence supporting one or more of the following outcomes. First, this body of comparative research may indicate that sex is a significant factor influencing communication in both the United States and Japan. In statistical terms, this would constitute a main effect involving gender differences. In contrast, it may be *culture* (defined as nation status) that is the primary source of variation in communication style, without regard to gender (Barnlund & Araki, 1985). Third, some combination of culture and sex might account for differences in communication. Sex may be a consequential determinant of communication style in Japan but not in the United States or vice versa. Perhaps sex has equally potent but qualitatively different effects in the two nations. In determining which of the possible outcomes is supported, we have organized the quantitative literature around levels of analysis most prominent in the literature.

A review of the qualitative literature could find that philosophical and cultural differences rather than sex differences are more likely to explain the ways in which men and women in Japanese and American cultures communicate. For example, the qualitative studies reviewed herein on Japanese versus American communicative styles considered the ways in which divergent views of philosophical concepts and notions of power, position, role, and hierarchy in Japan and the United States affect communicative styles. A review of both quantitative and qualitative research should result in a better understanding of the ways in which sex differences and cultural differences may or may not affect communicative styles of Japanese and American men and women.

REVIEW OF COMPARATIVE QUANTITATIVE STUDIES

The literature comparing American and Japanese communication styles is enormous (see, e.g., Barnlund, 1975, 1989; Gudykunst, 1993; Gudykunst, Guzley, & Ota, 1993; Gudykunst & Nishida, 1993; Hirokawa & Miyahara, 1986; Klopf, 1991; Loveday, 1986). However, we necessarily narrowed our focus to studies of adults that had (a) been published in the last 20 years in a journal catalogued in one of the major indexes of communication-related studies in the United States and/or Japan, (b) included a measure of communication behavior or style as a dependent measure, (c) included sex or gender as an independent variable, and (d) included nationality as an independent variable. We searched six databases (Psyclit, Sociofile, ABI-Inform, Linguisitics and Language Behavior Abstracts, Philosophy Index, and Religion Index) likely to reference articles by Japanese or American scholars on the topics of gender, communication, and culture. The results of our review are presented in Table 8.1.

Studies of Communication Tactics

Several studies have examined Japanese and American sex differences at the tactical level of communication. Here we assume that strategies are general approaches to communication; tactics are more specific behaviors.

Persuasion and Social Influence Tactics. Steil and Hillman (1993) assessed the perceived value of direct and indirect influence tactics among samples of 138 American, 41 Japanese, and 44 Korean college students. The authors reasoned that cultural concerns for politeness and face saving (Hsu, 1983)

TABLE 8.1
Summary of Quantitative Studies Measuring the Effects of National
Culture and Sex on Communication Variables

Study	Communication Variable	Results*		
		Sex	Culture	Interaction
Communication tactics				
Steil & Hillman (1993)	Persuasion		X	
Cocroft & Ting-Toomey (1994)	Facework	X	X	
Barnlund (1975)	Self-disclosure		X	
	Facework		X	
Barnlund & Araki (1985)	Compliments		X	
Nonverbal speech characteristics and behaviors				
Loveday (1986)	Pitch			X
Miller et al. (1987)	Language intensity			X
Boyer et al. (1990)	Immediacy	X	X	
Barnlund (1975)	Touch			X
Elzinga (1975)	Touch			X
Patterns of meaning				
Higashiyama & Ono (1988)	Demonstratives	(no significant differences)		
Communication traits and styles				
Frymier et al. (1990)	Affect-orientation			X
Thompson et al. (1990)	Assertiveness	X	X	X
	Responsiveness	X	X	X
Harman et al. (1990)	Verbal Aggressiveness	X		

*Note. Our summary of results is complicated by the incomplete data and comparatively rudimentary statistical procedures reported in the early studies. We offer our interpretations in these cases. Where effect sizes are available, associated statistics are found in the text.

might yield a preference by Korean and Japanese students for indirect tactics. The apparent existence of stricter family hierarchies in Korea and Japan, as compared with the United States, was also offered as a rationale for cultural differences. In contrast to expectations, results indicate that direct tactics like state importance, convince, and reason were preferred by all participants regardless of sex or culture. Indirect tactics like evade, avoid, and use of a third-party advocate were ranked much lower by all groups. The Japanese showed a slight preference for some indirect strategies.

Face-Management Tactics. Cocroft and Ting-Toomey (1994) studied the relationship between culture and facework. Defining *face* as a claimed sense of self-respect in a relational situation (Ting-Toomey, 1988), these authors examined the tactics used by American and Japanese college students in a hypothetical face-threatening situation. A multivariate analysis of variance (MANOVA) indicated that both culture (50%) and sex (10%) accounted for significant amounts of variance in tactic use. In general, members of the U.S. culture used significantly more antisocial and self-presentation strategies. Similarly, men more than women were likely to threaten the other's face and protect their own face in interaction. The results of the study are confounded somewhat by a preliminary finding: Contrary to expectations, the Japanese respondents reported themselves to be more collectivist and more individualistic then their American counterparts.

In an earlier study, Barnlund (1975) found no sex differences in the communication strategies used by men and women to respond to interpersonally threatening communication. Barnlund's comparison was based on a large-scale survey that asked American and Japanese students to describe their interaction patterns. A second comparison based on the same descriptive data set found no sex difference in self-disclosure preferences.

Compliments. The nature and frequency of compliments delivered by American and Japanese males and females were the foci of two studies reported by Barnlund and Araki (1985). In a preliminary interview study of a small sample of college students, the authors apparently found evidence that members of both cultures believed that women engaged in more compliments then men. Based on scenarios derived from the interview data, Barnlund and Araki administered a questionnaire measuring preferences in complimenting behavior to a sample of 520 students; the sample was split equally between Americans and Japanese of both sexes. Men and women showed no differences in their preferences, and both cultures preferred indirect strategies. A small cultural difference in preference for type of indirect strategy was reported.

Studies of Speech Characteristics and Nonverbal Behavior

Several authors have conducted comparisons based on primarily nonsymbolic, nonstrategic aspects of communication such as speech characteristics and nonverbal behavior.

Pitch and Intonation. Loveday (1986) reported a comparative study of the pitch and intonation used by English and Japanese speakers. Japanese speakers were selected to represent the two major dialectical regions of Japan (Western and Eastern). The results suggest that Japanese- and English-speaking males used broadly similar patterns of intonation, as did English-speaking males and females. The most striking difference was found in the comparison of Japanese males and females. Japanese females adopted an extremely high pitch, particularly when expressing Japanese politeness formulae. The author suggested that in situations requiring formal politeness (in this case, an encounter with a male acquaintance) Japanese women are expected to be decorative and feminine in their speech. The use of artificially high speech emphasizes this femininity. Loveday speculated that Japanese men working in service jobs (e.g., hotel staff) use a similarly high pitch. Thus, in Japan, gender differences in speech behavior may be situational and possibly confounded with occupational role.

Language Intensity. Miller, Reynolds, and Cambra (1987) examined the effects of gender and cultural ancestry on language intensity—a message component frequently linked to persuasiveness (e.g., Bradac, Bowers, & Courtwright, 1979). They expected sex differences in language use to be more pronounced among Chinese and Japanese cultural groups due to sex-based status asymmetries observed in Japanese society by several authors (Buck, Newton, & Muramatsu, 1984; Lebra, 1984). Miller et al. compared 107 male and female students of American, Chinese, and Japanese descent using a blanked paragraph procedure in which participants completed a narrative by choosing from a list of words that varied in intensity.

The primary result of this study was a statistical interaction between sex and cultural identity. Specifically, within the Japanese and Chinese cultural groups, men chose more intense language than did women. No sex difference was evident in the statistical comparison of American men and women. These results are qualified by the fact that the participants in the Miller, Reynolds, and Cambra (1987) study were Hawaiian Islanders of Japanese, Chinese, or American descent.

Immediacy. Verbal and nonverbal messages that promote distance or closeness were the focus of one study comparing Japanese and American men and women (Boyer, Thompson, Klopf, & Ishii, 1990). The study found significant main effects for both culture and sex, with Americans reporting greater use of immediacy behaviors than the Japanese and women of both cultures reporting greater use of immediacy behavior.

Touch. Several older studies examined touching preferences in Japan and the United States. Barnlund (1975) found that touching preferences were generally similar across the two cultures, although culture and sex apparently interacted in minor ways in some relational contexts. In a related study, Elzinga (1975) compared the touching preferences of 143 Japanese women and 32 men against American norms (as derived from previous studies). The study's rudimentary statistical procedures make comparisons difficult, but generally the two cultures showed similar touch preferences. The Japanese sample appeared to initiate less body contact in certain relational contexts but not others. Moreover, Japanese females used more physical touch than Japanese males. Based on this data, Elzinga claimed that this difference is greater than that found in the United States, suggesting an interaction of sex with culture.

Studies of Meaning

Some authors have examined the role of sex differences in the meanings associated with symbols and concepts. For example, Higashiyama and Ono (1988) studied how Japanese speakers use the demonstratives of *koko, soko,* and *asoko* to divide personal space. In Japanese dictionaries, they mean "the place near the speaker," "the place near the listener," and "the place away from the two parties." These terms correspond loosely to English terms like *here* and *there.* The authors also examined English speakers' use of these terms. The authors concluded that the cultures divide personal space similarly and that the use of demonstratives is partially a function of the distance between speakers. The authors found no differences in the way American or Japanese males and females describe personal space.

Studies of Communication Traits, Tendencies, and Styles

Studies classified here examine individual differences in characteristics directly related to communication. In most cases, these differences are measured through self-report.

Affect Orientation. Affect orientation is the tendency to use emotional rather than logical appeals in persuasion (Booth-Butterfield & Booth-Butterfield, 1990). Frymier, Klopf, and Ishii (1990) studied differences among Japanese and American students in use of affect orientation. Results indicate that, in general, Japanese scored lower than Americans on the affect-orientation measure. Sex was also a factor but only among the American students. Analysis of the interaction effect indicates that American women scored significantly higher than American men on affect orientation.

Assertiveness. *Assertiveness* refers to the ability to express opinions strongly and defend oneself verbally without abusing others. Thompson, Klopf, and Ishii (1991) compared Japanese and American students on a self-report measure of social style, which included an assertiveness component. Results indicate main effects for culture, sex, and an interaction effect, accounting for 17%, 5%, and 1% of the variance, respectively. The interaction was apparently due to large differences between American men ($M = 37.85$) and Japanese men ($M = 31.5$) with American men being more assertive. Japanese women were similar in assertiveness to Japanese men ($M = 31.3$) and less assertive then American women (35.5).

Responsiveness. *Responsiveness*, the tendency to acknowledge and support the social needs of the partner, is another dimension of social style used in the Thompson et al. (1991) study. Similar to the analysis of assertiveness, the statistical analysis yielded main effects for culture (5.5% of variance), gender (1.5%), and an interaction (2%). American women were notable for their high scores on the responsiveness measure ($M = 41.26$). Japanese men ($M = 36.9$) and Japanese women ($M = 37.04$) were similar. American men scored between the Japanese and American females ($M = 38.2$).

Verbal Aggressiveness. Verbally aggressive communicators use personal attacks rather than logical arguments in their interactions with others (Infante, 1984). A comparison of the self-reported verbal aggressiveness of Japanese and American university students was reported by Harman, Klopf, and Ishii (1990). Results show differences due to sex. Men were more verbally aggressive then women. American men scored highest on the verbal aggressiveness scale ($M = 44.5$). Japanese men scored substantially lower ($M = 42.1$). Japanese women ($M - 40.5$) and American women ($M = 39.6$) scored lowest and nearly identically on the aggressiveness measure.

Summary

Given the limitations of the studies, we are cautious in drawing generalizations about the role of sex and/or gender in Japan. However, it is interesting that, of the 16 analyses reported in the studies, only 3 (18.7%) appeared to find clean main effects for sex. Women of both cultures reported higher levels of verbal and nonverbal immediacy than did men (Boyer et al., 1990), and men of both cultures reported higher levels of verbal aggressiveness (Harman et al., 1990) and face-threatening behaviors than did women (Cocroft & Ting-Toomey, 1994). In contrast, twice as many studies—six (37.5%)—reported a main effect for culture. For example, Frymier et al. (1990) found Americans to be higher in affect orientation. Boyer et al. (1990) found that Americans reported greater use of immediacy. Thompson et al. (1991) found Americans to be more assertive than Japanese. When both culture and sex main effects were found (as with Cocroft & Ting-Toomey, 1994) culture accounted for larger amounts of variance (40% vs. 10%).

Seven studies (43.7%) found evidence for statistical interactions between culture and gender. Three of these showed gender differences existing in the United States, but not Japan on the variables of *affect orientation* (Frymier et al., 1990), *assertiveness* (Thompson et al., 1991), and *responsiveness* (Thompson et al., 1991). Loveday's (1986) study of pitch and intonation found sex differences in Japan and not the United States. One study found sex differences in language intensity among participants of Japanese heritage but not among Caucasians (Miller et al., 1987). Elzinga (1975) and Barnlund (1975) found that sex differences in touch were manifested differently in the two cultures.

Thus, it appears in this comparative literature that biological sex by itself is not an important factor in determining patterns of communication in Japan or the United States. However, sex may combine with cultural factors to affect communication patterns. In some cases, Japanese men and women are significantly different, whereas American men and women are not. This seems most obvious in studies of nonstrategic and nonverbal communication. However, in about the same number of cases, gender differences found in the United States are not found in Japan. In contrast to the prevailing American view of Japan as a society in which sex differences are magnified, in these studies it appears that Japanese men and women, like American men and women, are more similar than different in most areas of communication.

REVIEW OF QUANTITATIVE STUDIES IN JAPAN

Given that studies reviewed in the previous section indicate that sex may be manifested somewhat differently in the communication of Japanese and Americans, we looked for additional evidence about the nature of sex differences in Japanese communication. Using the same search procedure described earlier, we located and reviewed both qualitative and quantitative studies that compared Japanese men and women only. In general, conflicting results and only minor sex differences were found in these studies. Some of those differences that are reported are different from those found in studies of Americans.

Nakanishi (1986) examined the effects of level of self-disclosure (high, medium, low) and sex on perceptions of social attractiveness of 192 Japanese males and females. She found that sex interacted with self-disclosure level, such that Japanese males reported being more at ease with high disclosure than did the females. In contrast, females reported themselves to be more at ease (than the males) in low-disclosure situations. The effects of sex difference might have been confounded by the sexual topic of the high-disclosure dialogues she used in her study. Nakanishi claimed that sex was a taboo topic for women in Japan, although Japanese males discussed it freely.

More recently, Oguchi (1990) studied the self-disclosure of 199 Japanese males and females to determine the effects of recipient openness on the disclosers' willingness to disclose and liking for the recipient. The recipients' willingness to convey the self-disclosure was also examined for its effects on the discloser. The only substantive gender difference found was that Japanese female disclosive behavior was more responsive to recipients' willingness to reveal the disclosure to a third party.

Wada (1989) observed nonverbal behavior of 32 acquaintances and strangers paired in same-sex dyads. After videotaping 7-minute conversations, the author measured eye contact, frequency of look, smiling behavior, and head and body orientation. In addition to the expected differences due to relationship type and interpersonal distance, the author reported sex differences on measures of frequency of look, duration of smile, body lean, and eye contact.

Gender differences in nonverbal behavior were also the focus of Bond and Ho (1978) in their study of interview behavior. Thirty-two Japanese college students, equally divided between men and women, were interviewed by male or female interviewers of high and low social status. Results indicate several sex differences, with women versus men showing longer response latencies, less body lean, shorter glances, and more smiles. According to the authors, the manner in which men and women construed the formality and social distance of the interview situation may be the underlying source of differences in nonverbal behavior. They noted that some of the sex differences (e.g., eye contact) are the exact opposite of those found in studies of Western men and women.

The rules governing Japanese conversation in various social contexts were the focus of one study (Kuwabara, Nishida, Ura, & Kayano, 1989). The authors collected descriptions of 51 conversational rules for 29 male and female undergraduates. Subsequently, 128 male and female undergraduates rated the importance of each rule in different dyadic contexts (defined by the intimacy of the relationship and sex composition of the dyad). No evidence was reported to indicate that the sexes differed in their application of the rules.

Ide, Hori, Kawasaki, Ikuta, and Haga (1986) explored sex differences in the usage of politeness forms using a survey method. Participants were 256 men and 271 women, all parents of students at the Japanese Women's University. Ages ranged from 40 to 70 years. The authors claimed that language choice in interpersonal interactions was determined in part by male–female differences in the perception of the linguistic forms. The sexes were expected to disagree on the degree to which certain kinds of utterances were inherently impolite. In addition, sex differences were expected in the way that men and women viewed social relationships. Women more than men were expected to view relationships as requiring more social distance. These factors would then determine the choice of communicative behavior in a social situation.

Ide et al. (1986) found a complex set of results. Generally, they found that sex did not directly predict the frequency of use of politeness forms. Some sex differences were found in the ratings of politeness forms and social situations. These in turn predicted (self-reported) frequency of use. This result suggests that individual interpretations of cultural norms, moderated somewhat by gender, are the most important predictors of politeness behavior in Japan.

Finally, two studies compared the linguistic patterns of women and men in Japan. Using a quantitative technique to summarize patterns in linguistic data, Ogino (1986) found that Japanese women used more polite honorifics than their male counterparts. But in a wider ranging unpublished study of sociolinguistic behavior, Hibaya (1988; cited by Chambers, 1992) found no significant correlations between linguistic variables and sex.

Summary

This limited body of studies provides only mixed support for the prominence of gender differences in Japanese communication. One study of self-disclosure found that gender differences exist but attributed them to topical taboos imposed on Japanese women in high-disclosure situations. In the more recent self-disclosure study (Oguchi, 1990), sex differences were minimal. The results of the studies correlating sex and linguistic behaviors also conflict. Ide et al. (1986) indicate that sex differences in Japan may be most obvious in the way men and women define social relationships. These perceptual differences may or may not result in observable differences in actual behavior. Only Wada's (1989) study of nonverbal behavior shows a clear pattern of sex differences. Interestingly, some of the sex differences observed here are opposite those found in the West. Perhaps Japanese cultural influences on gender relations are most obviously manifested in the realm of nonstrategic, nonverbal behavior (as was the case with the Loveday, 1986, study reviewed previously). The remainder of this chapter looks to qualitative studies, which better address the cultural milieu in which Japanese gender differences and similarities are expressed.

REVIEW OF QUALITATIVE STUDIES

The qualitative research examined in this chapter includes studies on communication and gender in the Japanese culture and on communication and gender interculturally between Japanese and Americans. These studies utilized open-ended questionnaires, observational data, discourse analysis, and theories of sociolinguistics as frameworks to guide their investigations.

The Japanese cultural concepts of *integrated independence* and *independence* are considered by Kamitani (1993), who pointed out that, although the Japanese concept of *jiritsu* denotes an independent personality, the concept is ambiguous and, as of yet, there has been no intensive study of the word. Nevertheless, Kamitani emphasized that the concept of *jiritsu* must be viewed differently than the Western concept of *independence*. This is so because the study of the ego in the West typically defines a mature ego as one that separates one from others and emphasizes individual independence. In contrast, the Japanese notion of a mature ego is one that allows the individual to maintain his or her independence while co-existing with others. (Although Kamitani's study is quantitative in methodology, we found the concept of *jiritsu* useful in framing cultural differences between Japan and the United States.)

Based on this distinction, Kamitani (1993) posited a structural concept of *jiritsu,* which is defined as follows:

> A relationship of coexistence but not dependence, of independence but not rejection; a relationship in which one does not utterly rely on another person, but trusts and pays respect to others and, putting oneself in their place, helps while maintaining a strong stand on independence in making decisions and acting on one's own judgments and responsibilities. (p. 857)

A Jiritsu scale was developed to measure the level of *jiritsu* exhibited by each of 479 female college students. Based on these results, Kamitani's findings indicate that young Japanese women exhibit both integrated independence and independence, or *jiritsu.*

Chambers (1992) explored the notion that the failure to make the distinction between gender and sex in sociolinguistic studies may disguise significant correlations of linguistic variation with gender on the one hand and sex on the other. Chambers posited that the hypothesis of sex-based variability must be added to our study of how men and women interact. Specifically, Chambers argued that sex and gender must be differentiated in studies on sociolinguistics to understand whether differences in language are culturally or biologically based. The terms *sex-based variability* and *gender-based variability* suggest differences in language due to sex (biological) or gender (social). Chambers makes this claim specifically in regard to Japanese men and women, where she refuted prior research that argues that the sociolinguistic behavior of Japanese men and women is primarily gender-specific. However, Chambers' findings indicate that, although male–female linguistic differences persist even in the absence of well-defined gender roles, sex differences are less important linguistically than gender differences.

Smith (1992) reviewed studies that drew on a general theory of politeness and culturally specific, gendered strategies for encoding politeness and authority in Japan. These studies focused on the ways in which gender has equated the speech of women with powerlessness. Smith compared the linguistic practices of Japanese men and women as they gave directions to subordinates in a variety of situations. Smith analyzed directives drawn from transcripts of videotaped television cartoons, instructional television, and 2-hour detective/police action television shows. In all of these situations, Smith found that women tend to be more polite than their male counterparts. According to Smith, this appears to be the case whether Japanese women occupy traditional or nontraditional roles.

Smith (1992) also suggested that a unified set of linguistic behaviors, directives, in Japanese interaction relates to underlying cultural notions. She indicated that Japanese women who acquire positions of authority in nontraditional domains do experience linguistic conflict. However, Smith's research, unlike a previous study that found that Japanese women in positions of authority attempted to defeminize their speech, suggests something rather different. Specifically, Smith said:

> women [Japanese] may rather attempt to resolve the conflict by empowering their own speech (by adopting the Motherese Strategy as a public-domain power strategy) and that they are creating new and powerful strategies (e.g., the Passive Power Strategy) on a female power continuum that is distinct from the male power continuum. (p. 79)

Smith (1992) explained that Japanese women in positions of authority appear to be finding ways (such as the Motherese strategy) to ameliorate the problematic of choosing power forms of verbs, pronouns, and so on over the more linguistically appropriate female speech forms, which include honorifics. According to Smith, the Motherese strategy reflects Japanese women's ability to blend politeness with authority in issuing directives.

This approach is used by Japanese mothers with their children and has been successful in gaining compliance with male subordinates when used in the public domain. In interviews with urban professional women, Smith found that Japanese women in positions of authority perceived themselves as accepted by their female and male subordinates as long as "they were *gentle, open, and considerate,* when, in their own words, they stressed solidarity over authority." This emphasis on solidarity, combined with an informal, less polite style of speech, creates what Smith identified as a special dimension in an emergent female leadership style. Smith also showed that the Japanese usage of rank terms like *shocho* (director) or *kacho* (section chief) for address may create a sex-blind hierarchy that insulates Japanese men and women from their sexual identities. This differs from the United States, where "sex identity is inseparable from each individual, male or female, precisely due to its egalitarianism and individualism, which does away with a structural insulator" (Smith, 1992, p. 63).

Wetzel (1988) examined the striking parallel claims made concerning Japanese communication strategies and female communication strategies in the West. Wetzel posited that miscommunication between Japan and the West resembles miscommunication between the sexes in the West. Wetzel particularly focused on issues of power in both the West and Japan. Referencing Maltz and Borker's (1982) anthropological framework for identifying differences between Western women's and men's rules for interaction, Wetzel compared interaction patterns of Japanese and Western women (i.e., tag questions, hedges, etc.).

Her findings indicate that parallel descriptions of communication between the two groups are not coincidental. In fact, in contrast to Hofstede's (1980) claims that the Japanese culture is a masculine one, Wetzel (1988) argued that much of Japanese communicative behavior viewed from a Western perspective is identified as feminine and therefore as powerless interaction. Wetzel pointed out that, by Western standards, power is an attribute of the individual rather than of the role, position, or status an individual occupies. However, in Japanese culture, power is less an attribute of the individual than of role and position. This perspective reflects the Japanese view of power as relational and emphasizes the importance that Japanese people place on role interaction within the power structure or hierarchy as opposed to the individual. Wetzel's subsequent work on the issue of communication, gender, and power in Japan becomes useful to researchers in the West, who argue that the three variables are inextricably linked.

Wetzel (1993) argued that although the notion of power in the West has been the subject of a great deal of debate and controversy, it has not received the same sort of attention in Japan. According to Wetzel, power in the West is tied to every conceivable dimension of society's infrastructure:

political, social, personal, psychological, and linguistic. Wetzel described this phenomenon as the West's "penchant for viewing and analyzing the world in terms of power relationships, regardless of how they chose to define the term" (p. 393). Wetzel reviewed a variety of definitions that Western scholars offered to operationalize the concept of *power*, starting with thinkers from the Renaissance and Reformation up through the work of contemporary scholars such as Foucault, Bartky, Galbraith, Collins, and others. Wetzel observed that most definitions of *power* by Western scholars tie the notion of power to the act of domination and characterize power as a locus of control residing within the individual. Wetzel emphasized that power, according to a Western perspective, is characterized by six features: (a) the individual is the locus of power, (b) power is tied to domination, (c) power creates choice and engenders individual autonomy, (d) power is unidirectional and nonreciprocal, (e) power is self-actualizing in terms of ego, and (f) power is evidenced in command and decision making.

Wetzel (1993) also observed that it is difficult to find a lexical item in Japanese that parallels our Western concept of power. In fact, Wetzel noted that in Japanese the terms *kenryoku* (power) or *shihai* (control), which might begin to be the linguistic equivalent to the English notion of power, simply do not reflect the behavior that [Western] linguists want to examine as illustrative of power. For the Japanese, the concept of *power* is not a core concept for native descriptions or analysis of behavior in Japan; this becomes most clear when one notes that "*Japanese writing about Japan in Japanese for a Japanese audience does not focus on power*" (Wetzel, 1993, p. 394; italics added). Relationships in Japan, whether male–female or superior–subordinate, rely on Confucian-influenced notions of role and vertical social structure tied to a paternalism that is almost maternalistic in nature: nurturing, benevolent, kind, and supportive. These sorts of relationships rely in great part on the Japanese concept of *amae*, which reflects a need for mutual dependency in vertical relationships in Japan. Wetzel made the point that the West's understanding of paternalism in Japan is to a great degree a Western construct—one that imposes the notions of power, authoritarianism, and domination in a way that simply does not exist in the Japanese culture.

Di Mare (1995) extended Wetzel's (1988, 1993) findings concerning parallel linguistic constructs of the Japanese culture and American women to include the following forms of communicative practices: indirect communication, nonconfrontational communication, nonargumentative communication, information sharing, and consensus reaching in the decision-making process. According to Di Mare, the philosophical concepts of *wa* and *amae*, which are important in the construction of Japanese communicative practice, are also important in the construction of communicative practices of American women. Di Mare found that the literature on communicative styles of the Japanese and American women indicated that styles representative of both groups are undergirded by notions of harmony and interdependence. Based on their studies, Wetzel (1988, 1993) and Di Mare (1995) argued that scholars need to consider how culture influences communication and gender roles.

Summary

Several conclusions can be drawn from the qualitative research concerning Japanese communication styles. First, as was the case with the quantitative literature, we were struck by the relative scarcity of studies that examined the impact of sex and gender differences on communication practices of Japanese. Of the five studies reviewed, only one examined whether the sociolinguistic behavior of Japanese men and women is influenced by sex or gender. Results indicate that although sex differences should be considered in our study of how men and women interact, gender differences are more important in affecting linguistic choices.

Two studies compared the use of specific linguistic choices—honorifics and linguistic forms of politeness—by Japanese men and women. The results of both of these studies indicate that Japanese women tend to be more polite than Japanese men. However, both studies found that the use of more polite linguistic structures by women is governed by a number of variables. These variables include role or status of the listener, the domain where the interaction takes place (employment or private), and the fact that Japanese women assess individual linguistic forms as less polite than do Japanese men.

The final three studies compared particular linguistic structures and communicative styles representative of the Japanese men and women to those of American women. They found a number of striking similarities between these linguistic structures and communicative practices. Researchers of these studies argued that similarities in the communicative structures of the two groups grow out of parallel sociocultural conditions and philosophical perspectives concerning relationships.

CONCLUSIONS

First, in reviewing both sets of literature, quantitative and qualitative, it was found that there were not major differences in communicative styles between Japanese men and women. The few differences that did emerge reflected the use of linguistic structures of politeness and honorifics. Additionally, there appear to be minor differences involving nonverbal behavior. When studies examined culture (defined as nationality, as in American or Japanese) and sex, culture was the more important variable. In the quantitative studies, the statistical effects of culture were of greater magnitude. In the qualitative studies, culture also emerged as the significant factor in establishing differences in communicative styles. As was established by Smith (1992), linguistic structures such as directives relate to underlying cultural notions and role more than sex. Wetzel (1988, 1993) and Di Mare (1995) found that both linguistic choices and communicative styles were grounded in and affected by cultural and philosophical perspectives.

Second, Western perceptions of sex and gender in Japanese communication styles are largely unconfirmed by the studies we reviewed. For example, the notion that Japanese men exhibit masculine forms of communication and that Japanese women exhibit feminine forms of communication is largely unsupported by the evidence. Another stereotype—that Japanese women are submissive—again is not supported by the evidence. For example, Steil and Hillman (1993) found that Japanese women use direct influence strategies as frequently as do Japanese men. Barnlund and Araki (1985) found no sex differences in the use of complimenting behavior. Thompson et al. (1991) reported that Japanese women and men reported similar levels of assertiveness. Smith (1992) found that Japanese women utilize more polite forms of speech. However, Smith indicated polite forms of speech reflect a power base that is established in Japan through the mothering role. This is in contrast to Western culture where the role and communicative behaviors of the mother are often denigrated and devalued.

The notion that power-based language differs cross-culturally was reinforced in Wetzel's (1988, 1993) findings. Wetzel indicated that because Japanese and Westerners have different concepts of the notion of power, what appears to be powerless speech in the West is not the case in Japan.

This leads to the third point. That is, to the extent that sex differences become manifest in Japan, they often manifest differently than in the United States. In the quantitative literature, this point has been supported by statistical interactions between culture and sex. Differences between men and women in Japan are not the same as differences found between men and women in the United States. For example, Elzinga (1975) found that both Japanese and American men and women use touch differently. However, the touch preferences of American women are not always the same as those of Japanese women. The same is true for Japanese and American men. Bond and Ho (1978) and Wada (1989) reported similar findings with other forms of nonverbal behaviors.

Fourth, the research on sex differences in Japan is limited. There are relatively few quantitative and qualitative studies that examine the impact of gender on the communication practices of Japanese and between Americans and Japanese. In contrast, studies of gender in the United States are extremely common, as are studies that compare the citizens of the two nations on psychological, sociological, and business-related variables. In our review, only 16 comparative studies (Japanese and American communication practices) and 10 intracultural studies (Japanese communication practices) that examined sex or gender were found. This contrast leads us to wonder in what ways gender is prioritized (if at all) in Japan and how that compares to the way in which it is prioritized in the United States. We would also suggest that role, unrelated to sex or gender, may be more of a governing variable in Japan than it is in the United States.

Fifth, methodological problems in the research lead us to be cautious in interpreting the studies. In the quantitative studies, particularly in earlier studies, statistical procedures were often unsophisticated or incomplete. A separate criticism is that much of the research only examined sex not gender. Often these terms were used interchangeably. Similarly, we are concerned that in most studies culture is equated with nationality, thus overlooking the social, political, and historical factors that shape and diversify a culture.

In addition, nearly every study reported here used samples comprised solely of college students. The communication practices and preferences of college students in the United States, typically are not considered representative of the larger population. Moreover, among college students, who arguably are sheltered from the role requirements and status hierarchies experienced in larger society, gender differences might be masked or latent. Clearly, quantitative comparative researchers need to extend their studies to other segments of Japanese and American society.

Another severe limitation of the research is that nearly all of the communication variables were operationalized through self-report procedures of some type (but see Loveday, 1986). Although efficient, self-reports measure perceived, rather than actual, communication practices. This difference is most clear in the article by Barnlund and Araki (1985), who, based on preliminary data, reported that Japanese and Americans believed that women offered more compliments then did men. However, when they asked men and women to describe their behavior in specific scenarios, no sex differences were found. Most of the measures used in these studies required participants to summarize their behaviors across contexts, which creates the possibility that contexts in which gender and cultural differences are strong are canceled out by contexts in which they are weak. Studies that examined specific relational contexts (e.g., Steil & Hillman, 1993) found that gender differences were manifested in some contexts but not in others.

Finally, most of the studies reviewed were conducted by American or Japanese researchers who utilized Western methodologies. Suzuki (1991) indicated that the study of gender (sex role attitudes of Japanese men and women) began in Japan in the 1970s by some social scientists and government offices. Areas that were investigated included attitudes toward women's issues and findings of demographic variables related to different sex role attitudes.

Because there was no original scale developed to measure Japanese sex role attitudes, American scales were used (Suzuki, 1991). Thus, research on gender and/or the measurement of sex role attitudes of Japanese males and females may be distorted by Western research models that cannot adequately represent cross-cultural viewpoints.

In view of the preceding discussion, future research in the area of sex, gender, and communication needs to be more sensitive to the cultural and contextual factors that can distort gender differences. In the quantitative studies of communication and sex, the separation of the act of communication from the context of a society's culture was common. Although qualitative research is still circumscribed by its own cultural context, it is reflexive and more attentive to communication processes in their actual cultural milieu (e.g., Winch, 1964). Although the qualitative studies considered the cultural milieu out of which communication styles emerged, such research often did not offer descriptions of actual communication behaviors. Based on our study, it appears that our research has yet to capture either the cultural or contextual complexities of sex or gender and how those complexities shape and reinforce communication styles. We would hope that this chapter encourages researchers in the field to consider alternative approaches to the study of gender and communication that better capture such complexities.

ACKNOWLEDGMENTS

The authors would like to thank the following Japanese officials and representatives for their contributions to this study: Nick Kitamura, Senior Trade Advisor to Arizona; Hiro Kanda, JETRO Tokyo; Ichiro Sone, JETRO Los Angeles.

REFERENCES

Barnlund, D. C. (1975). *Public and private self in Japan and the United States.* Tokyo: Simul Press.

Barnlund, D. C. (1989). *Communicative styles of Japanese and Americans: Images and realities.* Belmont, CA: Wadsworth.

Barnlund, D. C., & Araki, S. (1985). Intercultural encounters: The management of compliments by Japanese and Americans. *Journal of Cross-Cultural Psychology, 16,* 9–26.

Bass, B. M., & Avolio, B. J. (1994). Shatter the glass-ceiling: Women may make better managers. *Human Resource Management, 33*(4), 549–560.

Belenky, M. F., Clinchy, B. M., Goldberger, N. R., & Tarule, J. M. (1986). *Women's ways of knowing*. New York: Basic Books.

Bond, M. H., & Ho, H. Y. (1978). The effect of relative status and the sex composition of a dyad on cognitive responses and nonverbal behavior of Japanese interviewees. *Psychologia, 21*, 128–136.

Booth-Butterfield, M., & Booth-Butterfield, S. (1990). Conceptualizing affect as information in communication production. *Human Communication Research, 16*, 451–476.

Boyer, L. M., Thompson, C. A., Klopf, D. W., & Ishii, S. (1990). An intercultural comparison of immediacy among Japanese and Americans. *Perceptual and Motor Skills, 71*, 65–66.

Bradac, J. J., Bowers, J. W., & Courtwright, J. A. (1979). Three language variables in communication research: Intensity, immediacy and diversity. *Human Communication Research, 5*, 257–269.

Buck, E. B., Newton, B. J., & Muramatsu, Y. (1984). Independence and obedience in the United States and Japan. *International Journal of Intercultural Relations, 8*, 279–300.

Canary, D., & Hause, K. (1993). Is there any reason to research sex differences in communication? *Communication Quarterly, 41*, 129–144.

Chambers, J. K. (1992). Linguistic correlates of gender and sex. *English World-Wide, 13*, 173–218.

Cocroft, B. K., & Ting-Toomey, S. (1994). Facework in Japan and the United States. *International Journal of Intercultural Relations, 18*, 469–506.

Collier, M. J. (1991). Conflict competence within African, Mexican and Anglo American friendships. In S. Ting-Toomey & F. Korzenny (Eds.), *Cross-cultural interpersonal communication* (pp. 132–154). Newbury Park, CA: Sage.

Connor, J. W. (1985). Differential socialization and role stereotypes in Japanese females introduction. *Journal of Psychoanalytic Anthropology, 8*, 29–45.

Darus, H. J. (1994). Argumentativeness in the workplace: A trait by situation study. *Communication Research Reports, 11*(1), 90–100.

Di Mare, L. (1995, July). *Japanese communication practices and communication styles*. Paper presented at the bi-annual World Communication Conference, Vancouver, Canada.

Eagly, A. H., & Johnson, B. T. (1990). Gender and leadership style: A meta analysis. *Psychological Bulletin, 100*(2), 233–250.

Elzinga, R. H. (1975). Nonverbal communication: Body accessibility among the Japanese. *Psychologia, 18*, 205–211.

Frymier, A. B., Klopf, D. W., & Ishii, S. (1990). Japanese and Americans compared on the affect orientation construct. *Psychological Reports, 66*, 985–986.

Gudykunst, W. B. (Ed.). (1993). *Communication in Japan and the United States*. Albany, NY: State University of New York Press.

Gudykunst, W. B., Guzley, R. M., & Ota, H. (1993). Issues for future research on communication in Japan and the United States. In W. B. Gudykunst (Ed.), *Communication in Japan and the United States* (pp. 291–322). Albany, NY: State University of New York Press.

Gudykunst, W. B., & Nishida, T. (1993). Interpersonal and intergroup communication in Japan and the United States. In W. B. Gudykunst (Ed.), *Communication in Japan and the United States* (pp. 149–214). Albany, NY: State University of New York Press.

Gudykunst, W. B., Nishida, T., & Schmidt, K. L. (1989). The influence of cultural, relational, and personality factors on uncertainty reduction processes. *Western Journal of Speech Communication, 53*, 13–29.

Harman, C. M., Klopf, D. W., & Ishii, S. (1990). Verbal aggression among Japanese and American students. *Perceptual and Motor Skills, 70*, 1130.

Harper, N. L., & Hirokawa, R. Y. (1988). A comparison of persuasive strategies used by female and male managers: I. An examination of downward influence. *Communication Quarterly, 36*, 157–168.

Hibaya, J. (1988). *A quantitative study of Tokyo Japanese.* Unpublished doctoral dissertation, University of Pennsylvania.

Higashiyama, A., & Ono, H. (1988). "Koko," "soko," and "asoko" ("here" and "there") as verbal dividers of space. *Japanese Psychological Research, 30*, 18–24.

Hirokawa, R. Y., Mickey, J., & Miura, S. (1991). Effects of request legitimacy on the compliance-gaining tactics of male and female managers. *Communication Monographs, 58*, 421–436.

Hirokawa, R. Y., & Miyahara, A. (1986). A comparison of influence strategies utilized by managers in American and Japanese organizations. *Communication Quarterly, 34*, 250–265.

Hofstede, G. (1980). *Culture's consequences: International differences in work-related values.* Beverly Hills, CA: Sage.

Holloway, J. S. (1995). It's time to recognize that both management styles can be effective. *Small Business Forum, 13*(1), 79–80.

Hsu, J. (1983). Asian family interaction patterns and their therapeutic implications. *International Journal of Family Psychiatry, 4*, 307–320.

Ide, S., Hori, M., Kawasaki, A., Ikuta, S., & Haga, H. (1986). Sex differences and politeness in Japanese. *International Journal of the Sociology of Language, 58*, 25–36.

Infante, D. A. (1984). Aggressiveness. In J. C. McCroskey & J. A. Daly (Eds.), *Personality and interpersonal communication* (pp. 157–192). Beverly Hills, CA: Sage.

Kamitani, Y. (1993). The structure of jiritsu (socially sensitive independence) in young Japanese women. *Psychological Reports, 72,* 855–866.

Klopf, D. W. (1991). Japanese communication practices: Recent comparative research. *Communication Quarterly, 39*, 130–143.

Kuwabara, T., Nishida, K., Ura, M., & Kayano, J. (1989). A examination of conversation process in social context. *Japanese Journal of Psychology, 60*, 163–169.

Lebra, T. S. (1984). *Japanese women.* Honolulu, HI: University of Hawaii Press.

Lee, C. (1994). The feminization of management. *Training, 31*(11), 25–31.

Lipman-Blumen, J. (1992). Connective leadership: Female leadership styles in the 21st century workplace. *Sociological Perspectives, 35*(1), 103–203.

Loveday, L. (1986). *Explorations in Japanese sociolinguistics.* Philadelphia: John Benjamins.

Maltz, D. N., & Borker, R. A. (1982). A cultural approach to male-female miscommunication. In J. J. Gumperz (Ed.), *Language and social identity* (pp. 196–216). Cambridge, England: Cambridge University Press.

Miller, M. D., Reynolds, R. A., & Cambra, R. E. (1987). The influence on gender and culture on language intensity. *Communication Monographs, 54*, 101–105.

Nakanishi, M. (1986). Perceptions of self-disclosure in initial interaction: A Japanese sample. *Human Communication Research, 13*, 167–190.

Ogino, T. (1986). Quantification of politeness based on the usage patterns of honorific expressions. *International Journal of the Sociology of Language, 58*, 37–58.

Oguchi, T. (1990). The effects of a recipient's openness and conveyance to a third party of the self-disclosure on change in the discloser's liking and self-disclosure. *Japanese Journal of Psychology, 61*, 147–154.

Roesner, J. B. (1990, November–December). Ways women lead. *Harvard Business Review*, pp. 119–125.

Saso, M. (1990). *Women in the Japanese workplace.* London: Hilary Shipman.

Schooler, C., & Smith, K. C. (1978). ". . . and a Japanese wife." Social structural antecedents of women's role values in Japan. *Sex Roles, 4*, 23–41.

Sinha, D., & Tripathi, R. C. (1994). Individualism in a collectivist culture: A case of coexistence of opposites. In U. Kim, H. C. Triandis, Ç. Kâgitbâsi, S. Choi, & G. Yoon (Eds.),

Individualism and collectivism: Theory method and applications (pp. 123–136). Thousand Oaks, CA: Sage.

Smith, J. S. (1992). Women in charge: Politeness and directives in the speech of Japanese women. *Language in Society, 21*, 59–82.

Steil, J. M., & Hillman, J. L. (1993). The perceived value of direct and indirect influence strategies: A cross-cultural comparison. *Psychology of Women Quarterly, 17*, 457–462.

Suzuki, A. (1991). Egalitarian sex role attitudes: Scale development and comparison of American and Japanese women. *Sex Roles, 24*, 245–259.

Tanaka, Y. (1990). Women's growing role in contemporary Japan. *International Journal of Psychology, 25*, 751–765.

Thompson, C. A., Klopf, D. W., & Ishii, S. (1990). Japanese and Americans compared on assertiveness/responsiveness. *Psychological Reports, 66*, 829–830.

Thompson, C. A., Klopf, D. W., & Ishii, S. (1991). A comparison of social style between Japanese and Americans. *Communication Research Reports, 8*, 165–172.

Ting-Toomey, S. (1988). Intercultural conflict styles: A face negotiation theory. In Y. Kim & W. B. Gudykunst (Eds.), *Theories in intercultural communication* (pp. 213–238). Newbury Park, CA: Sage.

Troemel-Ploetz, S. (1994). "Let me put it this way, John": Conversational strategies of women in leadership positions. *Journal of Pragmatics, 22*, 199–209.

Wada, M. (1989). Effects of interpersonal relationship, interpersonal distance and gender on nonverbal behavior in dyads of strangers and acquaintances. *Japanese Journal of Psychology, 60*, 31–37.

Wetzel, P. J. (1988). Are "powerless" communication strategies the Japanese norm? *Language in Society, 17*, 555–564.

Wetzel, P. (1993). The language of vertical relationships and linguistic analysis. *Multilingua, 12*, 387–406.

Wilkins, B. M., & Andersen, P. A. (1991). Gender similarities and differences in management communication: A meta-analysis. *Management Communication Quarterly, 5*, 6–35.

Winch, P. (1964). Understanding a primitive society. *American Philosophical Quarterly, 1*, 307–324.

Zellner, W. (1994). Women entrepreneurs. *Business Week*, pp. 104–110.

Chapter 9

Gender Differences in Intimacy and Related Behaviors: Context and Process

Harry T. Reis
University of Rochester

Arguably, no behavioral science topic has sustained as much lasting popular interest as have sex differences in intimacy and related behaviors. Treatises on the nature of men's and women's behavior in close relationships precede the advent of empirical behavioral science as far back in recorded history as Greek philosophy and mythology and early Judeo-Christian writing. This interest continues unabated. Lillian Rubin's (1983) *Intimate Strangers: Men and Women Together,* Deborah Tannen's (1990) *You Just Don't Understand,* and John Gray's (1992) *Men Are From Mars, Women Are From Venus* are recent best sellers. Differences in men's and women's relationships also provide an ever-present theme for modern fiction and film— witness critical comparisons of the female protagonists' friendship in *Thelma and Louise* and *Fried Green Tomatoes* with those of male buddies in *Wayne's World* and *Lethal Weapon.* Of course empiricists have also taken their turn on this issue, beginning in earnest with the 1958 publication of Jourard and Lasakow's self-disclosure research. Sex differences seemed to them a natural topic to study, and many researchers have followed their lead. Literally hundreds of studies have been published, leading to both qualitative and meta-analytic summaries (e.g., Cozby, 1973; Dindia & Allen, 1992). In other words, there has been no lack of interest in this question within either the lay or scientific communities.

Despite all this attention, no clear consensus has yet emerged. To be sure, most reviews conclude that women tend to self-disclose somewhat more than men do, which is consistent with the folk wisdom that women's friendships are more open and intimate than are men's friendships. Nevertheless, the scope, validity, and proper interpretation of this conclusion are often challenged. Crosby, for example, stated that there is little scientific evidence to support the stereotypic preconception that women "care more about and are better at intimate relations than are men" (p. 130). In their exhaustive review of sex differences, Maccoby and Jacklin (1974) concluded that the belief that girls are more social than boys is unfounded.[1] Others have acknowledged the possibility of sex differences, but claimed that they reflect not true differences but rather divergences in the manner by which intimacy is defined or created. For example, Tiger (1969) suggested that, in contrast to women, men bond together emotionally through shared activities such as work, sports, politics, and secret societies. Others have argued that men's and women's friendships differ not in the experience of intimacy and closeness, but rather in the type of interaction that defines and engenders these feelings (Duck & Wright, 1993; Markman & Kraft, 1989; J. Wood & Inman, 1993). The strength of claims and counterclaims regarding these sex differences is such that not long ago, Wright (1988) felt compelled to assert, in an article evocatively subtitled "A case for moderation and a plea for caution," that "the ubiquity and 'importance' of the modal pattern is often exaggerated, sometimes greatly so" (p. 368), and, "While not a complete myth, the phenomenon of male inexpressiveness seems to be at least a near myth" (p. 369).

The goal of this chapter is to selectively consider evidence concerning the role that gender plays in the realization and expression of intimacy within social interaction. First, it describes a theoretical model of the intimacy process that informs studies of sex differences and similarities. Next, it reviews several lines of research on the nature and prevalence of sex differences in social interaction intimacy. Because several excellent reviews and meta-analyses are available (e.g., Dindia & Allen, 1992), there is no need here for a comprehensive literature summary. Instead, the present review is selective, focusing on research that speaks directly to intimacy and related emotions. The final section discusses several potential explanations for the sex differences observed. Two kinds of accounts are covered: Those that seek to minimize the relevance of these data to social life and those that propose causal mechanisms. The overarching aim here is to provide a coherent framework for integrating research—one that permits the thoughtful consideration that Wright called for while acknowledging the extensive body of empirical findings that compellingly points to an important difference between men and women.

---

[1]This category encompassed, among various characteristics, self-disclosure and empathy. They noted the need for additional research as well as the positive finding that boys tend to socialize in larger groups than girls do.

THE INTERPERSONAL CONTEXT OF INTIMACY

The interpersonal process model first proposed by Reis and Shaver (1988) and later extended by Reis and Patrick (1996) suggests that the perception of intimacy is closely linked to certain characteristics of social interaction. A modified version of this model appears in Fig. 9.1. To conserve space, description of the model is limited to those features most relevant to the present chapter.

The intimacy process begins when one person, whom I call Judy, expresses personally relevant thoughts and feelings to another person, whom I name Elise. These expressions may occur verbally or nonverbally, intentionally or unintentionally, and explicitly or implicitly; what is critical is that some important aspect of Judy's self is communicated to Elise. Traditional models of self-disclosure emphasize the normative privacy of revealed facts, whereas our model focuses on the expression of emotionally central material—(i.e., the desires, anxieties, beliefs, and other conceptions that comprise the "inner self"). The essential self is often theorized to have an affective core consisting of self-evaluations and self-perceptions—in other words, hopes, goals, fears, and motives (e.g., Andersen & Ross, 1984; Emde, 1983; Markus & Nurius, 1986). The intimacy process requires that this innermost core be made at least partly accessible to the other. Con-

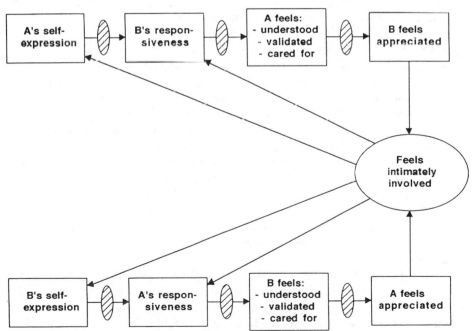

FIG. 9.1. The intimacy process model.

sistent with this proposition, a diary study by Lin (1992) demonstrated that disclosure of personal thoughts and feelings predicted relationship intimacy better than disclosure of personal facts did.

Because intimacy is an interactional process, it depends not only on one partner's self-expression but also on the other's response. Our model therefore incorporates Elise's response to Judy's self-expression. Responses perceived to be uncomprehending, disinterested, unsupportive, or otherwise inappropriate are likely to deter the process, if not halt it altogether, whereas thoughtful, empathic reactions that communicate appreciation and respect are likely to facilitate intimacy (Davis, 1982; Miller & Berg, 1984). Responsiveness is communicated through words as well as nonverbal channels such as facial expressions, eye contact, body posture, gestures, and the timing, tone, and sequencing of speech (e.g., Hatfield, Cacioppo, & Rapson, 1994; Patterson, 1994; Stern, 1986; Warner, 1988). Because nonverbal messages may differ from the words they accompany and because they are less controllable than verbal content (Zuckerman, DePaulo, & Rosenthal, 1981), intimacy development is often regulated more by unintentional nonverbal cues than by deliberately constructed messages.

For interaction to be perceived as intimate, we theorize that Judy must experience three characteristics in Elise's response: understanding, validation, and caring. *Understanding* refers to Judy's belief that Elise has accurately comprehended Judy's self-conception, including qualities that Judy is aware of expressing and other qualities that Elise may have discerned on her own. Understanding is central to intimacy for two reasons. First, and obviously, if the goal of self- disclosure is to reveal the self to another (Miller & Read, 1987), perceived misunderstanding signifies failed communication (Chelune, Robison, & Kommor, 1984). Second, validation and caring are unlikely to emerge if the other is perceived to possess discrepant views of oneself. That is, if Judy feels misunderstood by Elise, Elise's responses—no matter how well intentioned or seemingly sympathetic—are likely to be experienced as irrelevant, misinformed, or perhaps even hostile. Thus, the importance of understanding rests primarily in providing a context, in the form of shared views of oneself (and the relationship), for expression and receipt of validation and caring. Achieving such understanding does not require partners to agree with one's self-conceptions, but rather that they recognize and acknowledge these views. This sort of understanding involves metaperspectives (Kenny, 1994; Monsour, Betty, & Kurzweil, 1993).

Validation refers to the sense that the other values and respects one's attributes and world view, or what Sullivan (1953) called confirmation of "all components of personal worth" (p. 246). Thus, Judy would experience her interaction with Elise as validating and hence intimate if, in reaction to Elise's response, she feels valued and esteemed. Validation is a key component of intimacy because it represents one partner's acknowledgment of the other's innermost, affective self. Far from being a by-product of self-disclosure, anticipated validation is a prime motive for self-disclosure (as it was in Jourard's, 1964, seminal theorizing). Much research documents the role of validation in the choice of friends and lovers—*ceteris paribus,* people generally choose to interact with others who seem likely to affirm their views of themselves—and in affective experience within relationships (e.g., Gottman, 1994; Reis & Patrick, 1996; Wheeler, 1974).

The third and final component of Judy's reaction to Elise's response is *caring.* Abundant evidence attests that feeling liked is fundamental to interpersonal attraction and relationship development (Berscheid & Reis, in press). Aside from its inherent desirability, there are several reasons why caring is particularly pertinent to intimacy. For one, people are unlikely to express their innermost thoughts and feelings if they anticipate rejection, scorn, or criticism (Altman & Taylor, 1973), precluding understanding and validation. Second, caring and security are central features in lay prototypes of intimacy (Helgeson, Shaver, & Dyer, 1987; Waring, Tillman, Frelick, Russell, & Weisz, 1980). Third, feelings of security, safety, and acceptance provide some of the most potent bonds between partners in close relationships, as adult attachment research shows (Shaver & Hazan, 1993). Bowlby (1969) proposed that human infants have been primed through natural selection to feel positive emotions (e.g., joy and security) when in close proximity with caregivers and negative emotions (e.g., anxiety, sadness, and anger) when unwillingly separated from them. In adults, these tendencies are often manifested in predispositions to seek or avoid intimate relations (Bartholomew, 1990; Bowlby, 1988).

The intimacy process is intrinsically interdependent and does not terminate with Judy's experience of Elise's response. If and when Judy begins to feel understood, validated, and cared for, her verbal and nonverbal reactions are likely to set off a complementary affective reaction in Elise. If Elise realizes that Judy feels understood and appreciated, she in turn may experience a similar sense of intimate involvement accompanied by feelings of closeness and personal satisfaction. These feelings arise from two sources: Elise's vicarious experience of Judy's emotions, a process that Hatfield et al. (1994) referred to as *emotional contagion,* and Elise's personal feelings about the impact she has had on Judy. People often feel positive emotions such as joy and pride when they have been supportive, empathic, or helpful to another (Notarius & Herrick, 1988; Williamson & Clark, 1989). Furthermore, observing one's positive impact on a partner provides some of the most potent rewards of a close relationship (Kelley, 1984). The present model is unique in describing intimacy as a truly interdependent process: Not only does Elise's response affect Judy's experience, as most theories propose, but Judy's reaction also affects Elise's experience.

I have not commented on the interpretative filters that appear in Fig. 9.1. These filters refer to the motives, goals, needs, and expectations that influence interpretations of situations and people, as well as behavioral reactions to others. Space does not permit discussion of these filters, but the considerable impact of individual predispositions (e.g., personality traits, inner working models of self and others; see summaries in Reis & Patrick, 1996; Shaver, Collins, & Clark, 1996), situationally based goals and expectations (Miller & Read, 1987), and cognitive and motivational processes (Fiske & Taylor, 1991) is well documented. Judy and Elise's reactions to each other are determined not only by objective characteristics of their behavior, but also by idiosyncratic interpretations of those behaviors.

EVIDENCE FOR SEX DIFFERENCES IN INTERACTION INTIMACY

This section provides a selective review of empirical evidence concerning sex differences in intimacy. It begins with studies that use diary methods to examine ongoing interaction, most of which were conducted in our lab. It then ties this research to reviews of sex differences in closely related areas. The aim here is to take a relatively broad perspective on sex differences in intimacy and intimacy-related behavior, capturing both the robustness with which sex differences have been demonstrated and the variety of distinct yet related phenomena that support similar conclusions.

Studies of Ongoing Social Interaction: The Event-Sampling Approach

Because self-reports are almost always retrospective, and often substantially so, they are commonly criticized for providing biased data. That is, the act of recalling and aggregating activities as diverse and numerous as social interaction may influence to varying degrees the data that are obtained (Reis & Wheeler, 1991; Ross, 1989; Schwarz & Sudman, 1996). Event-sampling methods, in which data are collected as interactions occur, are intended not only to compensate for the vicissitudes of retrospection, but also to provide insight into that process (Wheeler & Reis, 1991). With these methods, participants provide data immediately after an event occurs, thereby minimizing distortion due to memory loss and other cognitive processes. The obtained data provide detailed, contemporaneous accounts of whatever activities or feelings are under investigation. Event sampling represents more than a methodological fix; daily activity, embedded as it is in the ebb and flow of everyday life, affords a different perspective on social life than do traditional methods, which tend to focus on salient, memorable, or experimenter-specified events (Reis, 1994, in press).

One such tool is the Rochester Interaction Record (RIR; Reis & Wheeler, 1991; Wheeler & Nezlek, 1977). Participants complete a standardized record for any social interaction lasting 10 minutes or longer. The record is flexible, allowing researchers to assess whatever dimensions are of interest. Because data are provided immediately, or soon after the event, and are selected and aggregated in a digitized database, rather than participants' memory, distortions attributable to cognitive and affective processes are minimized. Furthermore, and perhaps more important, the RIR focuses attention on the details of everyday social life. Especially in the domain of intimacy, the cumulative impact of these events may be substantial.

A major advantage of studying intimacy via the RIR is that retrospective or global evaluations of intimacy are often based on a respondent's general sense that intimacy exists, absent of a clear definition or a specific recollection—a judgment that seems particularly amenable to retrospective distortion. In contrast, by providing contemporaneous reports of actual social events, RIR data have allowed us to compare men's and women's experience of intimacy as it occurs naturally.

Data are presented from eight separate studies. In each study, participants completed one record after every social interaction lasting 10 minutes or longer. One item asked participants to rate the degree of intimacy in that interaction, using a 7-point scale from *superficial* (1) to *meaningful* (7). No explicit definition of intimacy was provided except to note that it referred to the personal meaningfulness of an interaction, as subjects felt during the interaction and not necessarily sexuality. Nothing in the RIR protocol restricted record keeping or ratings to conversation—any social event in which participants responded to one another or adjusted their behavior in response to another person was to be recorded.

Subjects in the first study (Wheeler & Nezlek, 1977) were first-year students at the University of Rochester who kept the RIR for 2 weeks in October and 2 weeks in April. Nezlek (1978) also studied first-year students, but his participants filled out the RIR four times during their first year each time for 10 days. Participants in Wheeler, Reis, and Nezlek (1983) were seniors at the University of Rochester who completed records for 2 weeks. Introductory Psychology students kept the RIR for 1 week in three studies: Reis, Senchak, and Solomon (1985); Reis, McAdam, and Rosen (1986); and Hodgins and Zuckerman (1990). Tidwell, Reis, and Shaver's (1996) participants were Introductory Psychology students at the State University of New York–Buffalo. Their data were collected for 1 week in October of their first college year. Finally, subjects in Reis, Lin, Bennett, and Nezlek (1993) were adults between the ages of 27 and 32 years who completed the RIR for 2 weeks. Although all were graduates of the University of Rochester, their residences were dispersed across the United States and several other nations. Thus, the samples were somewhat diverse, including college students and adults in varying locales and contexts; some were adjusting to a new environment and others were established within that environment.

Estimates obtained from diary records tend to be highly reliable because mean levels for a single participant typically aggregate across many events—in a typical 2-week study, an average participant completes about 85 records. We computed mean intimacy ratings for each participant for all interactions falling into various composition categories, two of which are pertinent to the present chapter—interactions involving same-sex others and interactions involving opposite-sex others. Tables 9.1 and 9.2 provide meta-analytic summaries of sex differences obtained in these eight studies. The result is unambiguous: Men's same-sex interaction is substantially less intimate than is women's same-sex interaction (see Table 9.1), whereas opposite-sex interaction yields no consistent trend (see Table 9.2). The magnitude of these effects is particularly noteworthy. In same-sex interaction, the average effect size, d, was .85 ($p < .001$). Cohen (1988) described ds of .80 or greater as large effects, exemplifying ds of this magnitude with the mean height difference of 13- and 18-year-old girls. By way of further contrast, Hyde and Plant (1995) reported effect sizes for 171 variables included in published meta-analyses of sex differences. Eighty-three per-

TABLE 9.1
Sex Differences in Same-Sex Interaction Intimacy:
A Meta-Analysis of Eight Studies

Researchers	Male Mean	Female Mean	p	Effect Size[a]
Wheeler & Nezlek (1977)				
56 first-year students	3.03	3.32	<.13	.32
Nezlek (1978)				
69 first-year students	3.37	3.70	<.08	.35
Wheeler, Reis, & Nezlek (1983)				
94 college seniors	3.35	4.33	<.001	1.04
Reis, Senchak, & Solomon (1985)				
49 college students	3.10	4.43	<.001	1.54
Reis, McAdam, & Rosen (1986)				
101 college students	3.40	4.36	<.001	1.04
Reis, Lin, Bennett, & Nezlek (1993)				
113 28- to 32-year-olds	3.78	4.23	<.005	.52
Tidwell, Reis, & Shaver (1996)				
122 first-year students	3.09	4.47	<.001	.95
Hodgins & Zuckerman (1990)				
51 second- to fourth-year students	3.89	4.32	<.02	.61

Note. Overall $z = 9.68$, $p < .00000001$. Overall effect size $d = .85$.
[a]The measure of effect size is Cohen's d.

TABLE 9.2
Sex Differences in Opposite-Sex Interaction Intimacy:
A Meta-Analysis of Eight Studies

Researchers	Male Mean	Female Mean	p	Effect Size[a]
Wheeler & Nezlek (1977)				
56 first-year students	4.09	3.46	<.02	−.61
Nezlek (1978)				
69 first-year students	4.07	3.92	<.32	−.12
Wheeler, Reis, & Nezlek (1983)				
94 college seniors	4.17	4.30	<.26	.14
Reis, Senchak, & Solomon (1985)				
49 college students	3.93	4.68	<.02	.65
Reis, McAdam, & Rosen (1986)				
101 college students	4.10	4.48	<.05	.35
Reis, Lin, Bennett, & Nezlek (1993)				
113 28- to 32-year-olds	4.36	4.34	<.45	−.02
Tidwell, Reis, & Shaver (1996)				
122 first-year students	4.35	4.61	<.13	.22
Hodgins & Zuckerman (1991)				
51 second- to fourth-year students	4.51	4.40	<.25	−.20

Note. Overall $z = 1.20$, $p < .12$.
[a]The measure of effect size is Cohen's *d*. Negative effect sizes indicate that the male mean is higher than the female mean.

cent of these effects had *d*s smaller than .66, whereas only 3% of *d*s were greater than 1. Thus, the male–female difference in same-sex interaction intimacy found in our research is reliable and substantial, and it is also among the largest sex differences reported in the literature.

Reviewers of this work have sometimes suggested that this result may be a by-product of selective interaction; perhaps men are simply more selective in choosing partners with whom to socialize intimately, restricting intimacy to one or two best friends (in Sullivan's, 1953, word, *chums*). Our data do not support this contention. Each of the eight tabled studies allowed us to isolate interactions involving only same-sex best friends. In some studies, a behavioral criterion was used—participants' most frequent same-sex partner. In others, participants nominated a best friend from among their social contacts. Although interaction with same-sex best friends was of course more intimate than interaction with same-sex others for both men and women, the sex differences shown in Table 9.1 remained intact with essentially similar magnitude.

This effect is best understood not as a main effect of sex, but rather as a sex-by-context interaction. When interacting with the opposite sex, mean ratings by male and female participants did not differ significantly—the trend across studies was neither reliable nor consistent in direction. The presence of at least one woman in a social encounter is thus associated with no sex difference in reports of intimacy. We do not yet know what mechanism underlies this pattern. One possibility is that women, perhaps because of better communication skills (discussed shortly), elicit intimacy from more reticent men. A related alternative is that men deliberately avoid intimacy with other men, instead seeking female companionship for such qualities. In contrast, women may not differentiate targets for intimacy on the basis of sex. A third possibility is that men behave similarly irrespective of their partner's gender; intimacy stems largely from women's contribution to an interaction. Regardless of which interpretation is ultimately borne out, interpreting this finding in sex-by-context terms has important theoretical implications (which are discussed in the third major section of this chapter). As Eagly (1995) asserted, "All theories of sex differences have the task of explaining not just overall differences in various behaviors but also the patterning of these differences across studies and therefore across social settings" (p. 149).

Evidence From Research on Related Phenomena

Gender differences in intimacy and intimacy-related behaviors have been the subject of innumerable studies and many reviews. Intimacy is not a singular phenomenon, and relevant evidence can bolster the generality and pervasiveness of the findings just discussed. Focus on an array of related yet conceptually distinct phenomena also illustrates how understanding of sex differences in intimacy can help answer broader questions about affective interdependence in close relationships. In other words, identifying consistent differences between men and women may highlight the central role of intimacy processes in interpersonal relations.

Self-Disclosure. Sex differences in self-disclosure have been studied often since Jourard's (1964) seminal research. Dindia and Allen (1992) reviewed 205 such studies with 23,702 participants. Some of these studies found greater self-disclosure by women, others (but fewer) revealed greater self-disclosure by men, and still others obtained no sex difference. Although this inconsistency appears to trouble some commentators, especially because moderating variables have not been confirmed, it would be shortsighted to infer that the literature fails to support a clear conclusion.

In fact, given the diversity of operational definitions, empirical methods, subject samples, and contextual variations within this literature, it would be surprising not to obtain a complex pattern of findings. In some studies, self-disclosure is assessed via checklists on which subjects indicate their willingness to discuss with a stranger topics of predetermined privateness. Other investigations rely on independent ratings of the degree of emotional depth in spousal conversations about marital problems or on global self-ratings of typical behavior with friends and acquaintances. These methods differ along dimensions known to influence self-disclosure, such as the nature and depth of the respondent–target relationship; the sex of the target; whether the interaction is actual, hypothetical, or reminisced; whether disclosure is evaluated normatively, according to conceptually defined criteria or by participants' personal standards; and whether the disclosure task is framed instrumentally or is embedded in an ongoing relationship. Any of these variables may moderate the degree to which men's and women's self-disclosure differs.

Dindia and Allen's (1992) meta-analysis shows that there is indeed a discernible forest among these trees. Their review identified a reliable tendency for women to self-disclose more than men do. Moreover, women were more often the targets of self-disclosure than were men, corroborating our RIR finding that sex differences were greater in same-sex interaction than in opposite-sex interaction. One further conclusion by Dindia and Allen is noteworthy: Self-disclosure was greater within existing relationships (including friends, spouses, and parents with their children) than between strangers. In summary, then, despite some inconsistency and notwithstanding the need to identify moderator variables and underlying explanatory mechanisms, the weight of evidence indicates overwhelmingly that women are generally more self-disclosing than are men, especially with same-sex partners (but see also Aries, chap. 3, this volume; Wood & Dindia, chap. 1, this volume).

Nonverbal Communication. Many of the most important cues for establishing and regulating intimacy are communicated nonverbally. Nonverbal displays may provide information about deception or affect that modifies the meaning of verbal content (e.g., admission of a painful secret means something different when accompanied by eye contact and a sad expression than by averted gaze and a broad smile). Nonverbal factors influence intimacy beyond their semantic meaning, however. Nonverbal cues help people regulate the experience of immediacy versus distance—an important component of intimacy (Patterson, 1994). Also, responsive caring and concern are usually signaled nonverbally, such as by facial expressions, touch, tone of voice, and eye contact.

An extensive literature summarized in Hall's (1984) sweeping meta-analytic review demonstrates that, in comparison to men, women are more nonverbally open and expressive and are more skilled at deliberate nonverbal communication. Hall concluded that women generally express more facial affect, both positive and negative, than men do. Although negative affect differences might reflect men's greater tendency to avoid conflict (Gottman & Levenson, 1987), the parallel finding for positive affect suggests the operation of some other mechanism. Beyond the age of 12, for example, women smile more (Hall & Halberstadt, 1986)—a tendency that includes "Duchenne" smiles, a particular type of smile that denotes enjoyment and is difficult to control voluntarily (Ekman, Davidson, & Friesen, 1990; von Salisch, 1992). Hall also concluded that women gaze at interaction partners more, are gazed at more often, and express heightened involvement on dimensions such as touch and body movement (Hall, 1984; Stier & Hall, 1984). Nonverbal immediacy also tends to be greater between women than between men, as indicated by studies of physical distance (Patterson & Schaefer, 1977) and the frequency of laughter, smiles, and eye contact (McAdams, Jackson, & Kirshnit, 1984).

Women also tend to be more accurate than men in decoding visual and auditory nonverbal channels (Hall, 1978). The ability to successfully decode nonverbal expressions of emotion facilitates development of intimacy because, as discussed earlier, the full meaning of self-disclosure is often revealed best by nonverbal cues. A recent review of studies of empathic accuracy suggests that women's decoding advantage may be confined to the special case of nondeceptive facial expressions (Graham & Ickes, 1997). However, most of these studies involved strangers. Graham and Ickes' review noted that women's relative advantage may be more pervasive in close relationships.

These strands of evidence imply that, all other factors being equal, women should be more effective listeners in intimate interaction than are men. Women are more frequently the target of self-disclosure than are men (Dindia & Allen, 1992), and both sexes are more likely to rely on a woman than a man as a confidant (Belle, 1987). The intimacy process depends not only on an active discloser, but also on a responsive, encouraging listener. To the extent that responsiveness is facilitated by better skills at decoding a partner's expressions and at encoding one's own sympathetic reaction, women should be better able to foster intimate relations once the process has begun. Furthermore, empathic responses depend not only on accurate comprehension of the other's message but also on genuine sympathy and support (a distinction reflected in mixed usages of the term *empathy*; Wispé, 1986). In this regard, women also tend to feel and express more sympathy and support than do men (Eisenberg & Lennon, 1983).

Giving and Receiving Social Support. One of the best established findings in the health psychology literature is that perceived social support is positively associated with mental and physical health. Reviews of this literature indicate that women generally give and receive support more than men do (e.g., Hobfoll & Stokes, 1988; Vaux, 1988). Nevertheless, because social support is a diverse, multidimensional construct, qualifications of this general pattern are informative.

Researchers commonly differentiate between structural and functional support (Cohen & Wills, 1985). Structural measures assess relatively objective features of social activity and ties, such as frequency of social contact or network size. A recent review by Berscheid and Reis (in press) concluded that structural support and well-being tend to be more highly correlated among men than among women (e.g., in coping with divorce and bereavement). However, significant correlations are evident for both sexes (see also House, Landis, & Umberson, 1988; Shumaker & Hill, 1991; Wood, Rhodes, & Whelan, 1989).

Functional support refers to satisfaction of psychological needs and goals in relationships and falls into four general categories: tangible assistance, appraisal (i.e., advice and guidance), group belonging, and emotional support (i.e., feeling loved, valued, and cared for). The most consistent and strongest sex differences have been shown for emotional support, which is of course conceptually linked to qualities such as interpersonal warmth, perceived responsiveness, and intimacy. Smaller sex differences have been found for tangible support, which typically involves helpful actions and material or physical assistance. In an extensive meta-analysis of the helping literature, Eagly and Crowley (1988) suggested that men may be more helpful than women in heroic and chivalrous settings (i.e., tasks that involve danger, physical risk or stress, or stereotypic courtesy), which seem comparable to tangible support. However, Eagly and Crowley also proposed that women are likely to be more helpful in contexts requiring nurturance or caring, which seem more consonant with emotional support. Perhaps this distinction underlies Gottlieb and Wagner's (1991) observation that marital conflict in coping with a child's serious illness may arise from the different coping styles that fathers and mothers enact. Fathers tend to prefer task-focused coping, whereas mothers tend to favor emotional support.

In summary, although a one-unit increment in social support may have somewhat greater health-promoting value for men than for women, emotional support is more prevalent among women.[2] Perceived support, especially emotional support, is closely linked with intimacy through such subprocesses as responsiveness and feeling cared for. Thus, gender differences in social support provide further foundation for establishing the generality of sex differences in intimacy.

Loneliness. Although *loneliness* is defined as the absence of desired levels of social contact (Russell, Peplau, & Cutrona, 1980), some types of social deficits seem likely to produce stronger emotional reactions than others do. To determine which particular relational shortcomings most closely

---

[2]The divergence may arise for precisely this reason. If support is a relatively more scarce commodity for men than for women, a given dose of support may be expected to be more distinctive and hence useful.

accompany feelings of loneliness, Wheeler et al. (1983) had subjects complete the UCLA Loneliness Scale immediately following 2 weeks of RIR record keeping. These data identified two correlates of loneliness: amount of interaction with women and mean intimacy level across all interactions. Interactions involving at least one woman tended to be higher in intimacy than interactions involving men only, consistent with the trend noted earlier, leading Wheeler et al. to conclude that low intimacy was the *sine qua non* of loneliness.

If so, one might expect men to report feeling lonelier than women do. Although published findings are mixed, Borys and Perlman's (1985) meta-analysis of 20 studies supported this inference. Furthermore, loneliness tends to correlate significantly and negatively with sex role femininity (e.g., Wheeler et al., 1983; Wittenberg & Reis, 1986). Other evidence also implies that, all other things being equal, men tend to be lonelier than women. For example, men have more difficulty coping with bereavement than women do and remarry sooner (Stroebe & Stroebe, 1983). Although this tendency might be attributable to the greater availability of marriage-eligible women in older samples, it also fits with our contention that men attain intimacy primarily when interacting with women. Therefore, men may experience greater loneliness following bereavement than do women. Epidemiological studies of divorce similarly show that divorce has more negative effects on men's mental and physical well-being than on women's (Bloom, Asher, & White, 1978). Thus, disruption of intimate relationships appears to be more detrimental for men than for women, suggesting that, in comparison with women, men are less likely to obtain intimacy from relationships other than marriage.

Friendship Style. The question of whether and how friendship differs as a function of sex has been enduring and controversial (see Wright, chap. 2, this volume). Many researchers describe men's same-sex friendships in terms of joint activities, whereas women's friendships are characterized in terms of shared thoughts and feelings (e.g., Caldwell & Peplau, 1982; Deaux, 1976). Diverse manifestations of this distinction have been investigated using various labels (e.g., agentic vs. communal; status-asserting vs. status-neutralizing; instrumental vs. expressive). In a general sense, however, there is reasonable consensus that, compared with men, on average interaction among female friends tends to be more socioemotionally expressive (Aries, 1996, provides a recent summary; see also, Clark, chap. 13, this volume; Wright, chap. 2, this volume).[3] Of course, emotion-centered interaction is more likely to generate intimacy as depicted in Fig. 9.1.

---

[3]This distinction refers to mean differences, of course, not absolutes. Many individual difference factors moderate the degree of expressiveness present in a particular man and woman's friendships.

Nevertheless, this conclusion does not imply that activity-centered interaction cannot engender intimacy. Expressing a notion that has become popular, Tiger (1969) proposed that male bonding in activity-centered groups may foster feelings of closeness and affection. For example, in discussing what has become known as the "two cultures" hypothesis, Wood and Inman (1993) suggested that shared instrumental activity may create intimacy and closeness among men. Their proposal is consistent with our theoretical model in two respects: (a) the intimacy process explicitly encompasses any and all behavior that reveals the innermost self to others—a process that may occur during personally meaningful activities; and (b) the model specifies that any interaction leading one to believe that a partner understands, validates, and cares will be experienced as intimate. Cooperative task-oriented activity may engender such perceptions.

Reed (1994) tested Tiger's hypothesis by developing a self-report measure of bonding using items that mapped onto dimensions described by Tiger (e.g., feeling connected and close, trust, sense of identity). This measure was then administered to male and female members of four athletic teams at the University of Rochester (basketball, swimming, soccer, and tennis) as well as to a nonathlete control group.[4] The results did not support Tiger's hypothesis. Female soccer players expressed significantly more bonding than did male soccer players; among swimmers, tennis players, and the control group, there was a nonsignificant tendency for women to report higher bonding scores than men. Male athletes reported higher levels of bonding than female athletes in only one instance (basketball), and this difference was slight and not significant. Reed's findings indicate that, even in settings presumed to facilitate men's involvement with same-sex peers, women still reported greater closeness.

Developmental research indicates that sex-differentiated preferences for intimacy emerge during adolescence. Buhrmester and Furman (1987) found that second-grade boys and girls did not differ in their preference for intimate friendship (defined in terms of sharing secrets and private feelings), but fifth- and eighth-grade girls cited intimacy increasingly, whereas boys showed little change. Similar trends have been found in studies of middle to late adolescents using various definitions of *intimacy* (e.g., Sharabany, Gershoni, & Hofman, 1981; see review by Berndt & Hanna, 1995). Girls' friendships tend to be based on intimate ties with a few close friends, whereas boys' friendships tend to emphasize activities and larger groups (Waldrop & Halverson, 1975). As in adult samples, children's interaction with partners other than same-sex peers (e.g., op-

---

[4]Athletic teams were studied because they are often described as prototypes of the sort of activity-focused groups that may engender feelings of closeness and connection among men.

posite-sex peers, adult family members; Blyth & Foster-Clark, 1987; Buhrmester & Furman, 1987) is less likely to show sex differences.

HOW SHOULD THESE FINDINGS BE INTERPRETED?

The evidence reviewed herein, spanning hundreds of studies with thousands of participants in dozens of research areas, indicates that men tend
to interact less intimately than do women. Confidence in this conclusion
is bolstered by the breadth and scope of evidence. Indeed, it seems somewhat remarkable that several meta-analyses, each covering a substantial,
conceptually distinct literature, would reach similar conclusions. Given the
pervasiveness, robustness, and consistency of these findings, the most parsimonious and straightforward interpretation would seem to be the obvious
one—that men do in fact socialize less intimately than do women, particularly with same-sex partners. Nevertheless, several objections and qualifications have been offered, all intended to support a different or less
sweeping account. These alternatives vary greatly: Some aim to discount
the basic finding by citing artifacts, whereas others substitute interpretations more limited in scope or generality. The next section addresses some
of these alternatives.

Sex Differences in How Intimacy Is Defined

Some critics have suggested that men and women define *intimacy* differently. For example, Rubin (1983) proposed that for women intimacy refers
to communication, whereas for men intimacy concerns proximity. Others
have argued that for men intimacy is based on shared activity in same-sex
interaction and sexuality in opposite-sex interaction, but female intimacy
derives from talking and affection regardless of partners (e.g., Duck &
Wright, 1993; Markman & Kraft, 1989; Wood & Inman, 1993). These proposals imply that sex differences in intimacy may reflect different criteria
for determining what is intimate, rather than actual behavioral and affective
differences.

But do men and women define *intimacy* differently? One of the most
comprehensive studies of this question was conducted by Helgeson, Shaver,
and Dyer (1987), who asked subjects to describe in detail two intimate
and two distant past experiences, one each with a male and female partner.
Overall, men's and women's prototypes were very similar, although there
were a few differences: (a) Women mentioned talk more than men did,
especially in same-sex interaction; (b) men cited joint activity more than
women did, but only in same-sex interaction (in opposite-sex interaction,
women were more likely to mention shared activity); (c) physical contact,

including sexuality, was more central in men's descriptions of opposite-sex intimacy than women's; and (d) in same-sex interaction, men were more likely to cite appreciation for their partner, whereas in opposite-sex interaction, appreciation was mentioned more often by women.

Helgeson et al. noted that similarities were far more common than differences; both sexes listed appreciation, warmth, disclosure of personal feelings, and shared activity as central components of intimacy. Other studies have found similar results. For example, Waring et al. (1980) detected no substantial differences in spouses' replies to the question, "What does intimacy mean to you?" (affection and expression were mentioned most frequently by both spouses). Spontaneous descriptions by men and women of the meaning of intimacy produced similar rank orderings; both ranked self-disclosure number one (Monsour, 1992; see also Jones, 1991). Reis (1990) found no sex differences beyond chance in college students' ratings of the personal importance of various friendship goals. Burleson, Kunkel, Samter, and Werking (1996) asked men and women to evaluate the importance of eight social skills in friendship and romance. They found few sex differences (both men and women rated affective skills as considerably more important than instrumental skills). Finally, men's and women's standards for romantic relationships were essentially the same in another study (Vangelisti & Daly, in press).

This evidence suggests that slight differences notwithstanding, men and women clearly define intimacy and closeness in much the same way. Moreover, the slight differences do not signify that interaction differences should be ascribed to sex-differentiated criteria. Helgeson et al.'s (1987) respondents were asked to describe actual interaction experiences, past or present. Sex-differentiated reports might reflect disparities in actual interaction experiences. For example, if women in reality talk to each other about personal thoughts and feelings more than men do, one would expect women's spontaneous descriptions to cite emotional communication more prominently. Men might still experience emotional communication as highly intimate, if and when it occurs, but would be less likely to mention it spontaneously due to its lesser salience.

More direct evidence that sex differences in reports of intimacy are not due to diverging definitions was provided by Reis et al. (1985). Their research examined three plausible alternative explanations, all of which might implicate judgmental factors rather than behavior differences. The first alternative, the differing criteria hypothesis, proposed that men and women may look for different cues when evaluating an interaction as intimate. Ten same-sex dyads—five male and five female—were videotaped in a 3-minute conversation about topics preselected to include low (e.g., hobbies), medium (e.g., career plans), and high (e.g., likes and dislikes in romantic partners, actions you have regretted) levels of intimacy. Other than being randomly assigned a topic, conversants were encouraged to speak freely. Perceived intimacy levels of these conversations were then judged by 28 female and 26 male raters whose RIR interaction data had previously shown the typical same-sex difference. Raters were instructed to use their own personal standard for defining intimacy. As expected, the rated intimacy level of topics differed greatly, but men's and women's ratings did not differ significantly. In fact, men rated the conversations as slightly more intimate than did women. Thus, there was no evidence that men and women use different criteria to define intimacy.

Another alternative is that men and women may differ in their willingness to label interactions as intimate because same-sex intimacy connotes femininity and possibly homosexuality in American culture (Lewis, 1978)—images that men may wish to avoid. We examined this hypothesis by asking participants to come to our laboratory with their best same-sex friend. After arriving, both persons provided independent written narratives of their conversation on the way to the laboratory and their last meaningful conversation with each other. Instructions explicitly avoided the terms *intimacy* and *self-disclosure*. After identifying information had been deleted, intimacy levels were rated by judges once again relying on their personal standard. Narratives written by women were seen as significantly more intimate than narratives written by men. Thus, even when the label *intimacy* was avoided, men and women still differed. Similar attempts to trace women's reports of more intense emotions to labeling and other measurement biases also have failed (Fujita, Diener, & Sandvik, 1991).

Finally, it is possible that women's conversations are judged more intimate because intimacy is stereotypically associated with women. If so, regardless of content, any interaction involving at least one woman might be seen as more intimate—in much the manner that any stereotype may influence social perception (Taylor & Fiske, 1991). To test this hypothesis, the 10 videotapes described earlier were transcribed verbatim in one of three forms: involving two men, two women, or one man and one woman. Only names, pronouns, and sex-linked references (e.g., policeman) were altered. These transcripts were rated by a new sample of judges. Once again, male raters perceived slightly higher levels of intimacy than did female judges. More to the point, the sex pairing of conversants had no effect on intimacy ratings.

Thus, when asked to assess the intimacy level of existing conversations, men and women show no signs of relying on different criteria. Respondent methods, in which judges evaluate preselected material, have several advantages over operant methods, in which spontaneous descriptions are collected; primarily, they do not require explicit awareness by participants of the factors contributing to their judgments. Also, articulateness and thoroughness are less important. To the extent that intimacy is a complex or fuzzy phenomenon, as Prager (1995) argued that it is, lay persons are likely to find holistic impressions of an existing conversation considerably easier to provide than precise, complete self-generated definitions.

In short, although men and women may differ subtly in spontaneous definitions of intimacy, these divergences play a minor, inconsequential role in shaping the observed and powerful behavior differences described earlier. (Kunkel & Burleson, chap. 5, this volume, discuss this issue more extensively and reach a similar conclusion.)

That Conversations Differ, But Interactions Do Not

Several theorists (e.g., Duck & Wright, 1993; Wood & Inman, 1993) have argued that men's and women's friendships differ primarily with regard to spoken exchanges. Women achieve intimacy through verbal disclosure of personal information, whereas men do so through shared activity. In their view, men's and women's friendships are more or less equivalent in terms of intimacy, but prior research has obtained differences by focusing on conversation.

The literature emphasizes conversation and verbal content, and the conversational behavior of men and women does differ in certain respects (Aries, 1996; Tannen, 1990). Nevertheless, intimacy research is not invariably limited to discourse. For example, RIR studies include all interactions and not just conversations.[5] Reportable events in RIR studies are defined as any and all interactions lasting 10 minutes or longer in which participants mutually responded to one another. It is expressly stated that interaction may or may not involve conversation, and supporting examples are usually provided. Of course, the vast majority of interactions do involve talk; only rarely in real life does silence engender intimacy. In our studies, intimacy always correlates highly with self- and other-disclosure in both sexes.

Furthermore, as reviewed earlier, studies of nonverbal communication demonstrate that women interact with each other more intimately than do men. Compared with men, women are more facially expressive, smile more often, touch and look at each other more frequently, interact at closer distance, and use more involved, expressive body movements (Aries, 1996; Hall, 1984; Stier & Hall, 1984). These nonverbal behaviors generally indicate positive interpersonal affect—an important component of intimacy. It is difficult to imagine how men would develop intimacy through channels other than verbal exchange, as the "lesser-reliance-on-conversation" position requires, while expressing less positive nonverbal affect than do women. Thus, there is little evidence to support the contention that

---

[5]In fact, because conversation and interaction differ, Duck, Rutt, Hurst, and Strejc (1991) developed the Iowa Communication Record—an event-sampling procedure that focuses on conversation rather than interaction.

overreliance on conversational measures has masked a fundamental equivalence between men and women in the experience of social interaction intimacy.

Biological Priming or Social Contexts?

A provocative and highly cited article by Gottman and Levenson (1987) proposed that men withdraw from interactions involving negative affect more readily than women because men experience conflict as more stressful and aversive. Drawing on human and animal studies, Gottman and Levenson traced this tendency to physiological differences between the sexes in stress reactivity—notably autonomic and endocrine arousal fostered by selective evolutionary pressures. An implication of their position is that men may tend to avoid intimate interaction, which often includes negative affect, because they have been primed by evolution to feel greater stress and arousal in such situations than women do.

Because not all intimate interaction involves negative affect, Gottman and Levenson may not have intended their hypothesis to apply to intimacy. Nevertheless, open communication about negative affect is widely regarded as an essential feature of long-term intimate relationships and is usually perceived as highly intimate (Morton, 1978). Moreover, marriage researchers often conceptualize problems of communicating about conflictual issues in terms of intimacy processes (i.e., emotional self-disclosure, responsiveness, and validation; Gottman, 1994; Notarius & Markman, 1993). Thus, men's greater reluctance to engage in intimate dialogue is sometimes attributed to biological differences in stress reactivity (e.g., Markman & Kraft, 1989).

There is reason to doubt whether sex differences in stress reactivity apply to intimate relations, however. Several rigorous experiments by Kiecolt-Glaser, Malarkey, Cacioppo, and Glaser (1994) showed that women's physiological reactions to marital conflict may be stronger and more persistent than men's reactions. Furthermore, although sex differences in intimacy-related behaviors are larger in same-sex than in opposite-sex interaction, the potential for negative affect is likely to be considerably greater in romantic relationships, which are highly and emotionally interdependent (Berscheid, 1983) and usually heterosexual. Also, men tend to rely on women, particularly romantic partners, for intimacy, which seems a poor strategy to minimize biologically heightened sensitivity to stress and negative affect.

Men's relative tendency to avoid same-sex intimacy may instead be linked to socialization practices and the social context of interaction (Huston & Ashmore, 1986). Relevant evidence is provided by four replications of our RIR studies in cultures characterized by different beliefs about the propriety and desirability of same- and opposite-sex socializing.[6] We reasoned that contemporary American beliefs encourage men to view women as supportive and nurturant, and therefore as desirable partners for intimacy and confiding, whereas emotional openness and expressions of affection with other men are discouraged (Lewis, 1978). In cultures without such prohibitions, or in which heterosexual friendship is considered inappropriate, the same-sex intimacy difference found in American samples should disappear. If so, evolutionary or physiological explanations would seem less likely.

RIR data are available from two Western and two non-Western countries: Germany (Schumacher, 1992), the Netherlands (Reis, Delespaul, & deVries, 1991), Hong Kong (Wheeler, Reis, & Bond, 1989), and Jordan (Reis, Haddad, & Lin, 1992). In the first two countries, prohibitions against same-sex intimacy seem weaker than in the United States; in Hong Kong and Jordan, extrafamilial opposite-sex intimacy is discouraged and same-sex bonds, especially among men, are valued. RIR data were collected from representative samples of college students in each culture.[7] These data are presented in Figs. 9.2A and 9.2B along with similar data from a matched comparison group (similar age, residential status, and school standing) of American students.

As expected, there was a significant culture $\times$ sex interaction for same-sex intimacy—such that the male–female difference varied from culture to culture. The difference was largest in the United States ($d = .95$) and Germany ($d = .70$), nonsignificant but in the same direction in the Netherlands ($d = .39$) and Hong Kong ($d = .34$), and in the opposite direction (nonsignificantly) in Jordan ($d = -.12$). Furthermore, in the three Western cultures, men reported significantly higher intimacy with male than with female partners, whereas in Jordan and Hong Kong, on average, men showed no differences as a function of partner sex. Finally, there was no sex $\times$ country interaction for intimacy in opposite-sex interaction.[8] These data support the hypothesis that sex differences in intimacy are influenced by cultural norms.

One further bit of evidence suggesting that intimacy sex differences may be more a matter of preference than innate capacity was furnished by Reis et al. (1985). In this study, we reasoned that contextual pressures can lead men to inhibit self-disclosure and intimacy. Therefore, we created a context in which intimate dialogue was not only sanctioned but instrumental. Subjects and their same-sex best friends were instructed to have

---

[6]Such data are critical because, as with biologically based theories, socialization-based explanations should not be accepted until supported by empirical evidence.

[7]As a group, one would expect college students to have adopted some Western norms working against the possibility of finding cross-cultural differences.

[8]Thus, the obtained same-sex difference cannot be attributed to differences in how individuals in different cultures use these ratings scales.

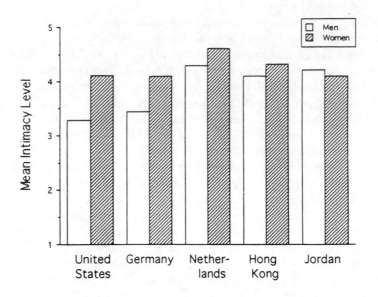

FIG. 9.2A. Intimacy in five cultures: same-sex interaction.

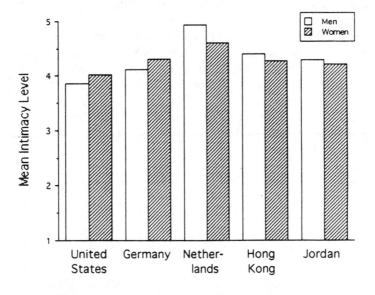

FIG. 9.2B. Intimacy in five cultures: opposite-sex interaction.

a meaningful conversation for the purpose of gathering videotapes to be used in training clinical psychologists. To further enhance the perceived desirability of intimacy for our male subjects, the experimenter was an attractive woman.

These conversations were then rated for intimacy twice: by the conversants and by seven female graduate students unacquainted with our research. In neither set of ratings were there any significant sex differences or trends. Real-world RIR data for these same dyads, which recount their spontaneous, everyday interaction, revealed the standard sex difference. Thus, an experimentally created context mandating intimacy eliminated a sex difference that was evident in everyday life.

In summary, social learning plays an important role in shaping men's reluctance to engage in intimate interaction with one another. This conclusion does not contradict the potential importance of physiological correlates of intimate expression and repression. However, it does indicate that differences between men and women depend less on these correlates and other innate factors than on the social context and what people learn about it.

CONCLUDING COMMENTS

Not long ago, I overheard a conversation at a local health club. One man approached another, and asked how he was doing.

"Terrible," he answered, "I lost my job today, my marriage is falling apart, and the kids are a mess."

"That's too bad," the first man replied, with visible sympathy. "But you know, it can be good to talk about your feelings and get them off your chest. So if you've got one or two minutes, come talk to me." And then he ran off to play tennis. It is not easy to imagine this same interaction occurring between two women.

This chapter began by asking whether men and women differ in their approach to intimate interaction. It then reviewed abundant evidence suggesting that, with regard to intimacy and intimacy-related variables, they indeed do: Men socialize less intimately with one another than women do. These differences are both stronger and more consistent in same-sex than in opposite-sex relationships, denoting that the nature of male–male relationships, rather than anything intrinsic to the character of men, underlies this observation.

This chapter also indicates that intimacy differences between men and women reflect real behaviors and not artifacts of measurement, definition, or interpretation. Of course, this phenomenon reflects a mean difference and not an absolute standard; many men have intimate friendships with each other and many women do not. In general, however, the breadth of findings across different research areas, paradigms, and methods, as well as the impressive magnitude of obtained differences, establishes that men's friendships are substantially less intimate than those of women.

The evidence discussed in this chapter does not support the two cultures hypothesis (i.e., that men define friendship differently than women do, and that if researchers took these differences into account, sex differences would be minimal; e.g., Wood & Inman, 1993). In fact, consistent with Kunkel and Burleson's chapter, this chapter indicates that men and women define intimacy and closeness in largely the same way and aspire to essentially the same relationship qualities.

The most significant implication of rejecting the two cultures hypothesis is to focus attention on the existence of a real difference with real implications. Because intimacy and its absence have well-established associations with health and well-being across a diverse and impressive range of physical, psychological, and interpersonal outcomes (McAdams, 1989; Reis, 1990; Reis & Franks, 1994), the sex differences reviewed in this chapter imply a shortfall with important consequences. Thus, it is time for researchers to move beyond arguments about whether men and women really differ to questions about causes, consequences, and moderators. We need to better understand the contextual, relational, and developmental variables that inhibit or facilitate intimacy; the personality and temperamental factors that characterize people who interact more or less intimately; the socialization practices that foster or constrain cognitive and social skills needed for interacting intimately; and how intimacy research can be applied to individual and relational therapy. Insight into these questions is not only germane to understanding sex differences; it is also likely to provide important clues for the next generation of theorizing about the role of relationships in the human condition.

REFERENCES

Altman, I., & Taylor, D. A. (1973). *Social penetration: The development of interpersonal relationships.* New York: Holt, Rinehart & Winston.

Andersen, S. M., & Ross, L. (1984). Self-knowledge and social inference: I. The impact of cognitive/affective and behavioral data. *Journal of Personality and Social Psychology, 46,* 280–293.

Aries, E. (1996). *Men and women in interaction.* New York: Oxford University Press.

Bartholomew, K. (1990). Avoidance of intimacy: An attachment perspective. *Journal of Social and Personal Relationships, 7,* 147–178.

Belle, D. (1987). Gender differences in the social moderators of stress. In R. C. Barnett, L. Biener, & G. K. Baruch (Eds.), *Gender and stress* (pp. 257–277). New York: The Free Press.

Berndt, T. J., & Hanna, N. A. (1995). Intimacy and self- disclosure in friendships. In K. J. Rotenberg (Ed.), *Disclosure processes in children and adolescents* (pp. 57–77). New York: Cambridge University Press.

Berscheid, E. (1983). Emotion. In H. H. Kelley, E. Berscheid, A. Christensen, J. H. Harvey, T. L. Huston, G. Levinger, E. McClintock, L. A. Peplau, & D. R. Peterson *Close relationships* (pp. 110–168). New York: Freeman.

Berscheid, E., & Reis, H. T. (in press). Interpersonal attraction and close relationships. In S. Fiske, D. Gilbert, G. Lindzey, & E. Aronson (Eds.), *Handbook of social psychology* (4th ed.). New York: Random House.

Bloom, B. L., Asher, S. J., & White, S. W. (1978). Marital disruption as a stressor: A review and analysis. *Psychological Bulletin, 85*, 867–894.

Blyth, D. A., & Foster-Clark, F. S. (1987). Gender differences in perceived intimacy with different members of adolescents' social networks. *Sex Roles, 17*, 689–718.

Borys, S., & Perlman, D. (1985). Gender differences in loneliness. *Personality and Social Psychology Bulletin, 11*, 63–74.

Bowlby, J. (1988). *A secure base.* New York: Basic Books.

Buhrmester, D., & Furman, W. (1987). The development of companionship and intimacy. *Child Development, 58*, 1101–1113.

Burleson, B. R., Kunkel, A. W., Samter, W., & Werking, K. J. (1996). Men's and women's evaluations of communication skills in personal relationships: When sex differences make a difference—and when they don't. *Journal of Social and Personal Relationships, 13*, 201–224.

Caldwell, M. A., & Peplau, L. A. (1982). Sex differences in same-sex friendship. *Sex Roles, 8*, 721–732.

Chelune, G. J., Robison, J. T., & Kommor, M. J. (1984). A cognitive interactional model of intimate relationships. In V. J. Derlega (Ed.), *Communication, intimacy and close relationships* (pp. 11–40). New York: Academic Press.

Cohen, J. (1988). *Statistical power analysis for the behavioral sciences* (2nd ed.). Hillsdale, NJ: Lawrence Erlbaum Associates.

Cohen, S., & Wills, T. A. (1985). Stress, social support, and the buffering hypothesis. *Psychological Bulletin, 98*, 310–357.

Cozby, P. C. (1973). Self-disclosure: A literature review. *Psychological Bulletin, 79*, 73–91.

Crosby, F. J. (1991). *Juggling: The unexpected advantages of balancing career and home for women and their families.* New York: The Free Press.

Davis, D. (1982). Determinants of responsiveness in dyadic interaction. In W. I. Ickes & E. S. Knowles (Eds.), *Personality, roles, and social behaviors* (pp. 85–139). New York: Springer-Verlag.

Deaux, K. (1976). *The behavior of women and men.* Monterey, CA: Brooks/Cole.

Dindia, K., & Allen, M. (1992). Sex differences in self-disclosure: A meta-analysis. *Psychological Bulletin, 112*, 106–124.

Duck, S., Rutt, D. J., Hurst, M. H., & Strejc, H. (1991). Some evident truths about conversations in everyday relationships: All communications are not created equal. *Human Communication Research, 18*, 228–267.

Duck, S. W., & Wright, P. H. (1993). Reexamining gender differences in same-gender friendships: A close look at two kinds of data. *Sex Roles, 28*, 709–727.

Eagly, A. H. (1995). The science and politics of comparing women and men. *American Psychologist, 50*, 145–158.

Eagly, A. H., & Crowley, M. (1988). Gender and helping behavior: A meta-analytic review of the social psychological literature. *Psychological Bulletin, 100*, 283–308.

Eisenberg, N., & Lennon, R. (1983). Sex differences in empathy and related capacities. *Psychological Bulletin, 94*, 100–131.

Ekman, P., Davidson, R. J., & Friesen, W. V. (1990). The Duchenne smile: Emotional expression and brain physiology: II. *Journal of Personality and Social Psychology, 58*, 342–353.

Emde, R. (1983). The prerepresentational self and its affective core. *Psychoanalytic Study of the Child, 38*, 165–192.

Fiske, S. T., & Taylor, S. E. (1991). *Social cognition* (2nd ed.). New York: McGraw-Hill.

Fujita, F., Diener, E., & Sandvik, E. (1991). Gender differences in negative affect and well-being: The case for emotional intensity. *Journal of Personality and Social Psychology, 61,* 427–434.

Gottlieb, B. H., & Wagner, F. (1991). Stress and support processes in close relationships. In J. Eckenrode (Ed.), *The social context of coping* (pp. 165–188). New York: Plenum.

Gottman, J. (1994). *What predicts divorce?* Hillsdale, NJ: Lawrence Erlbaum Associates.

Gottman, J., & Levenson, R. (1987). The social psychophysiology of marriage. In M. A. Fitzpatrick & P. Noller (Eds.), *Perspectives on marital interaction* (pp. 182–200). Clevedon, England: Multilingual Matters Ltd.

Graham, T., & Ickes, W. (1997). When women's intuition isn't greater than men's. In W. Ickes (Ed.), *Empathic accuracy* (pp. 117–143). New York: Guilford.

Gray, J. (1992). *Men are from Mars, women are from Venus: A practical guide for improving communication and getting what you want from in your relationships.* New York: HarperCollins.

Hall, J. A. (1978). Gender effects in decoding nonverbal cues. *Psychological Bulletin, 85,* 845–875.

Hall, J. A. (1984). *Nonverbal sex differences: Communication accuracy and expressive style.* Baltimore: Johns Hopkins University Press.

Hall, J. A., & Halberstadt, A. G. (1986). Smiling and gazing. In J. S. Hyde & M. C. Linn (Eds.), *The psychology of gender: Advances through meta-analysis* (pp. 136–158). Baltimore: Johns Hopkins University Press.

Hatfield, E., Cacioppo, J. T., & Rapson, R. L. (1994). *Emotional contagion.* New York: Cambridge University Press.

Helgeson, V. S., Shaver, P., & Dyer, M. (1987). Prototypes of intimacy and distance in same-sex and opposite-sex relationships. *Journal of Social and Personal Relationships, 4,* 195–233.

Hobfoll, S. E., & Stokes, J. P. (1988). The processes and mechanics of social support. In S. Duck (Ed.), *Handbook of personal relationships: Theory, research and interventions* (pp. 497–518). New York: Wiley.

Hodgins, H. S., & Zuckerman, M. (1990). The effect of nonverbal sensitivity on social interaction. *Journal of Nonverbal Behavior, 14,* 155–170.

House, J. S., Landis, K. R., & Umberson, D. (1988). Social relationships and health. *Science, 241,* 540–545.

Huston, T. L., & Ashmore, R. D. (1986). Women and men in personal relationships. In R. D. Ashmore & F. K. Del Boca (Eds.), *The social psychology of female-male relations* (pp. 167–210). Orlando, FL: Academic Press.

Hyde, J. S., & Plant, E. A. (1995). Magnitude of psychological gender differences: Another side to the story. *American Psychologist, 50,* 159–161.

Jones, D. C. (1991). Friendship satisfaction and gender: An examination of sex differences in contributors to friendship satisfaction. *Journal of Social and Personal Relationships, 8,* 167–185.

Jourard, S. M. (1964). *The transparent self.* New York: Van Nostrand.

Jourard, S. M., & Lasakow, P. (1958). Some factors in self-disclosure. *Journal of Abnormal and Social Psychology, 56,* 91–98.

Kelley, H. H. (1984). Affect in interpersonal relations. In P. R. Shaver (Ed.), *Review of personality and social psychology* (Vol. 5, pp. 89–115). Beverly Hills, CA: Sage.

Kenny, D. A. (1994). *Interpersonal perception.* New York: Guilford.

Kiecolt-Glaser, J. K., Malarkey, W. B., Cacioppo, J. T., & Glaser, R. (1994). Stressful personal relationships: Immune and endocrine function. In R. Glaser & J. K. Kiecolt- Glaser (Eds.), *Handbook of human stress and immunity* (pp. 321–339). San Diego: Academic Press.

Lewis, R. A. (1978). Emotional intimacy among men. *Journal of Social Issues, 34,* 108–121.

Lin, Y. C. (1992). *The construction of the sense of intimacy from everyday social interaction.* Unpublished doctoral dissertation, University of Rochester.

Maccoby, E. E., & Jacklin, C. N. (1974). *The psychology of sex differences.* Stanford, CA: Stanford University Press.

Markman, H. J., & Kraft, S. A. (1989). Men and women in marriage: Dealing with gender differences in marital therapy. *The Behavior Therapist, 12,* 51–56.

Markus, H. J., & Nurius, P. S. (1986). Possible selves. *American Psychologist, 41,* 954–969.

McAdams, D. P. (1989). *Intimacy: The need to be close.* New York: Doubleday.

McAdams, D. P., Jackson, R. J., & Kirshnit, C. (1984). Looking, laughing, and smiling in dyads as a function of intimacy motivation and reciprocity. *Journal of Personality, 52,* 261–273.

Miller, L. C., & Berg, J. H. (1984). Selectivity and urgency in interpersonal exchange. In V. J. Derlega (Ed.), *Communication, intimacy, and close relationships* (pp. 161–205). New York: Academic Press.

Miller, L. C., & Read, S. J. (1987). Why am I telling you this? Self-disclosure in a goal based model of personality. In V. Derlega & J. Berg (Eds.), *Self-disclosure: Theory research and therapy* (pp. 101–130). New York: Plenum.

Monsour, M. (1992). Meanings of intimacy in cross- and same-sex friendships. *Journal of Social and Personal Relationships, 9,* 277–296.

Monsour, M., Betty, S., & Kurzweil, N. (1993). Levels of perspectives and the perception of intimacy in cross-sex friendships: A balance theory explanation of shared perceptual reality. *Journal of Social and Personal Relationships, 10,* 529–550.

Morton, T. L. (1978). Intimacy and reciprocity of exchange: A comparison of spouses and strangers. *Journal of Personality and Social Psychology, 36,* 72–81.

Nezlek, J. B. (1978). *The social behavior of first year college students: General patterns, sex differences, and relationship to socialization history.* Unpublished doctoral dissertation, University of Rochester.

Notarius, C., & Herrick, L. R. (1988). Listener response strategies to a distressed other. *Journal of Social and Personal Relationships, 5,* 97–108.

Notarius, C., & Markman, H. (1993). *We can work it out: Making sense of marital conflict.* New York: Putnam.

Patterson, M. L. (1994). Strategic functions of nonverbal exchange. In J. A. Daly & J. M. Wiemann (Eds.), *Strategic interpersonal communication* (pp. 273–293). Hillsdale, NJ: Lawrence Erlbaum Associates.

Patterson, M. L., & Schaefer, R. E. (1977). Effects of size and sex composition on interaction distance, participation, and satisfaction in small groups. *Small Group Behavior, 8,* 433–442.

Prager, K. J. (1995). *The psychology of intimacy.* New York: Guilford.

Reed, C. E. (1994). *Gender differences in same-sex interaction in intimacy: The role of male bonding.* Unpublished master's thesis, University of Rochester.

Reis, H. T. (1990). The role of intimacy in interpersonal relations. *Journal of Social and Clinical Psychology, 9,* 15–30.

Reis, H. T. (1994). Domains of experience: Investigating relationship processes from three perspectives. In R. Erber & R. Gilmour (Eds.), *Theoretical frameworks for personal relationships* (pp. 87–110). Hillsdale, NJ: Lawrence Erlbaum Associates.

Reis, H. T. (in press). Methods of assessing daily life experiences. In H. T. Reis & C. Judd (Eds.), *Handbook of research methods in social psychology.* New York: Cambridge University Press.

Reis, H. T., Delespaul, P. A. E. G., & deVries, M. (1991). Social interaction among Dutch students. Unpublished manuscript, University of Rochester.

Reis, H. T., & Franks, P. (1994). The role of intimacy and social support in health outcomes: Two processes or one? *Personal Relationships, 1,* 185–197.

Reis, H. T., Haddad, Y., & Lin, Y. C. (1992). *Social interaction in three cultures.* Unpublished data, University of Rochester.

Reis, H. T., Lin, Y. C., Bennett, E. S., & Nezlek, J. (1993). Change and consistency in social participation during early adulthood. *Developmental Psychology, 29*, 633–645.

Reis, H. T., McAdam, A., & Rosen, E. (1986). *Social interaction and stress.* Unpublished data, University of Rochester.

Reis, H. T., & Patrick, B. C. (1996). Attachment and intimacy: Component processes. In A. Kruglanski & E. T. Higgins (Eds.), *Social psychology: Handbook of basic principles* (pp. 523–563). New York: Guilford.

Reis, H. T., Senchak, M., & Solomon, B. (1985). Sex differences in the intimacy of social interaction: Further examination of potential explanations. *Journal of Personality and Social Psychology, 48*, 1204–1217.

Reis, H. T., & Shaver, P. (1988). Intimacy as an interpersonal process. In S. Duck (Ed.), *Handbook of personal relationships* (pp. 367–389). Chichester, England: Wiley.

Reis, H. T., & Wheeler, L. (1991). Studying social interaction with the Rochester Interaction Record. In M. P. Zanna (Ed.), *Advances in experimental social psychology* (Vol. 24, pp. 270–318). San Diego: Academic Press.

Ross, M. (1989). Relation of implicit theories to the construction of personal histories. *Psychological Review, 96*, 341–357.

Rubin, L. B. (1983). *Intimate strangers: Men and women together.* New York: Harper & Row.

Russell, D., Peplau, L. A., & Cutrona, C. E. (1980). The revised UCLA loneliness scale: Concurrent and discriminant validity evidence. *Journal of Personality and Social Psychology, 39*, 472–480.

Schumacher, A. (1992). Eine deutsche fassung des Rochester- Interaktionsfragebogens: Anwendbarkeit und erste ergebnisse [A German version of the Rochester Interaction Record: Practicality and first results]. *Zeitschrift für Sozialpsychologie, 23*, 140–149.

Schwarz, N., & Sudman, S. (1996). *Thinking about answers: The application of cognitive processes to survey methodology.* San Francisco: Jossey-Bass.

Sharabany, R., Gershoni, R., & Hoffman, J. E. (1981). Girlfriend, boyfriend: Age and sex differences in intimate friendship. *Developmental Psychology, 17*, 800–808.

Shaver, P. R., Collins, N., & Clark, C. L. (1996). Attachment styles and internal working models of self and relationship partners. In G. Fletcher & J. Fitness (Eds.), *Knowledge structures and interaction in close relationships: A social psychological approach* (pp. 25–61). Hillsdale, NJ: Lawrence Erlbaum Associates.

Shaver, P. R., & Hazan, C. (1993). Adult romantic attachment: Theory and evidence. In D. Perlman & W. Jones (Eds.), *Advances in personal relationships* (Vol. 4, pp. 29–70). London: Jessica Kingsley.

Shumaker, S. A., & Hill, D. R. (1991). Gender differences in social support and physical health. *Health Psychology, 10*, 102–111.

Stern, D. N. (1986). *The interpersonal world of the infant.* New York: Basic Books.

Stier, D. S., & Hall, J. A. (1984). Gender differences in touch: An empirical and theoretical review. *Journal of Personality and Social Psychology, 47*, 440–459.

Stroebe, M. S., & Stroebe, W. (1983). Who suffers more? Sex differences in health risks of the widowed. *Psychological Bulletin, 93*, 279–301.

Sullivan, H. S. (1953). *The interpersonal theory of psychiatry.* New York: Norton.

Tannen, D. (1990). *You just don't understand: Women and men in conversation.* New York: William Morrow.

Taylor, S. E., & Fiske, S. T. (1991). *Social cognition* (2nd ed.). New York: McGraw-Hill.

Tidwell, M., Reis, H. T., & Shaver, P. R. (1996). Attachment, attractiveness, and daily social interactions: A diary study. *Journal of Personality and Social Psychology, 71*, 729–745.

Tiger, L. (1969). *Men in groups.* New York: Random House.

Vanglelisti, A. L., & Daly, J. A. (in press). Gender differences in standards for romantic relationships. *Personal Relationships.*

Vaux, A. (1988). *Social support: Theory, research, and intervention.* New York: Praeger.

von Salisch, M. (1992). Zwischen offenheit und rucksichtnahme: Madchen und jungen im konfliktmit freundinnen und freunden [Between openness and consideration: Boys and girls in conflict with same-sex friends]. *Zeitschrift für Sozialpsychologie, 23*, 54–63.

Waldrop, M. F., & Halverson, C. F., Jr. (1975). Intensive and extensive peer behavior: Longitudinal and cross-sectional analyses. *Child Development, 46*, 19–26.

Waring, E. M., Tillman, M. P., Frelick, L., Russell, L., & Weisz, G. (1980). Concepts of intimacy in the general population. *Journal of Nervous and Mental Disease, 168*, 471–474.

Warner, R. M. (1988). Rhythm in social interaction. In J. E. McGrath (Ed.), *The social psychology of time: New perspectives* (pp. 63–88). Beverly Hills, CA: Sage.

Wheeler, L. (1974). Selective affiliation for purposes of social comparison. In T. Huston (Ed.), *Perspectives on interpersonal attraction* (pp. 309–329). New York: Academic Press.

Wheeler, L., & Nezlek, J. (1977). Sex differences in social participation. *Journal of Personality and Social Psychology, 35*, 742–754.

Wheeler, L., & Reis, H. T. (1991). Self-recording of events in everyday life. *Journal of Personality, 59*, 339–354.

Wheeler, L., Reis, H. T., & Bond, M. H. (1989). Collectivism-individualism in everyday social life: The middle kingdom and the melting pot. *Journal of Personality and Social Psychology, 57*, 79–96.

Wheeler, L., Reis, H., & Nezlek, J. (1983). Loneliness, social interaction, and sex roles. *Journal of Personality and Social Psychology, 45*, 943–953.

Williamson, G. M., & Clark, M. S. (1989). Providing help and desired relationship type as determinants of changes in moods and self-evaluations. *Journal of Personality and Social Psychology, 56*, 722–734.

Wispé, L. (1986). The distinction between sympathy and empathy: To call forth a concept, a word is needed. *Journal of Personality and Social Psychology, 50*, 314–321.

Wittenberg, M., & Reis, H. T. (1986). Loneliness, social skills, and social perception. *Personality and Social Psychology Bulletin, 12*, 121–130.

Wood, J. T., & Inman, C. C. (1993). In a different mode: Masculine styles of communicating closeness. *Journal of Applied Communication Research, 21*, 279–295.

Wood, W., Rhodes, N., & Whelan, M. (1989). Sex differences in positive well-being: A consideration of emotional style and marital status. *Psychological Bulletin, 106*, 249–264.

Wright, P. H. (1988). Interpreting research on gender differences in friendship: A case for moderation and a plea for caution. *Journal of Social and Personal Relationships, 5*, 367–374.

Zuckerman, M., DePaulo, B. M., & Rosenthal, R. (1981). The verbal and nonverbal communication of deception. In L. Berkowitz (Ed.), *Advances in experimental social psychology* (Vol. 14, pp. 2–59). New York: Academic Press.

Chapter 10

An Evolutionary View on Understanding Sex Effects in Communicating Attraction

Melanie R. Trost
Jess K. Alberts
Arizona State University

As interpersonal communication researchers, we both examine interpersonal processes because we are fascinated by the basic questions about how people meet and form romantic relationships. For example, "Why do males so often take the initiative in locating and courting mates, and why do females so often reject their suitors?" "Why do males so often fight with one another over females?" "Why do females so often seem to prefer males that have bizarre ornaments and strange behavioral displays?" Bizarre ornaments and strange behavioral displays? Actually, these questions are not ours; they were written by Alcock (1993, p. 394), an ethologist who studies animal behavior. He is referring more to peacock plumes and strutting chimpanzees than to human behavior. But the same questions have been asked about flirting and rejecting in our own species; quite frankly, we have always been a bit mystified by the appeal of puka beads in the 1970s or the ornamental eyebrow piercing on our students today.

Interest in these relational issues, not only within our own species, but across species as well, may be a function of their importance for the proliferation of life. That is, finding a partner and developing an intimate interpersonal bond are critically important tasks for us. Even if our ancestors had been superb at other survival-related tasks, such as foraging and hunting for food, fending off predators and enemies, or building impressive structures to keep out the elements, had they not been able to attract partners and propagate we would not be here to talk about it. This process of procreation begins with meeting an appropriate partner—a task that often involves some amount of flirtation. Eibl-Eibesfeldt (1975) filmed women's reactions to flirtation in both industrialized cultures and hunter–gatherer cultures (including Samoa, Papua, France, Japan, and several different tribes in South America and Africa) and found a common sequence of motor actions that can easily be observed at the local book store or nightclub. The sequence begins with a quick smile and "eyebrow flash" (eyes opened wide, accompanied by raising the eyebrows), followed by dropping and turning the head and then a sidelong glance. It is not so difficult to understand why a behavior that is as elemental as initiating a relationship might have evolved to show cross-cultural similarities in form and expression, given that successfully reproducing and raising offspring was vital for our ancestors' evolution. The roles of women and men differ in the mating process, however. The goal of this chapter is to describe how an evolutionary perspective can provide insight into and explanations about sex differences and similarities in courting behaviors and about flirtation in particular.

This chapter specifically addresses sex differences (i.e., variations in communication that may be traced to differences in biological sex not social roles). Canary and Hause's (1993) indictment against using sex as a variable in communication research aptly argued against looking for sex differences, or differences between women and men, in communication processes when there is no theoretical reason to expect any. Even the theories they suggested as hopeful candidates for examining sex differences offered no essential explanation for why sex differences may exist. Among others, Kramare's (1981) muted groups theory explains sex differences in speech and interaction styles as due to men's dominant social position. Deaux and Major's (1987) causal process model attributes sex differences to variations in the gender-relevant schemata of communicators. These proximate mechanisms of social dominance and cognitive processes beg the question of the ultimate explanations underlying why men are the dominant social group or what these arbitrary gender schemata are based on (Alcock, 1993; Kenrick & Trost, 1997). In fact, in closing, Canary and Hause lamented, "Without theory the task of clarifying further the relationship(s) between sex and communication is impossible" (p. 141). They went on to say, "We believe there are sex differences in communication, but they are eluding us. Perhaps a definitive answer to the question of sex differences in communication will arrive within the next fifty years" (p. 141). We propose that one overlooked explanation for sex differences in communicative behavior has already been available for over 100 years—ever since Darwin first advanced a theory of human evolution in 1859.

AN EVOLUTIONARY FRAMEWORK

Darwin's (1859) theory of natural selection is based on the processes of random variation and selective retention. Due to limited resources in any environment, all animals compete for access to food, shelter, and mating partners—the essential elements for survival. Genetic characteristics that benefit an individual's acquisition of resources allow the individual to live longer, reproduce for a longer period of time, and enjoy more success in mating. Random variation in genetic characteristics that enhance adaptation, survival, and reproduction are therefore more likely to be passed on to subsequent generations. In this way, nature selects certain adaptive characteristics over others. This force is analogous to the artificial selection exercised by animal breeders, whose predilections for particular traits have led to hairless cats and aggressive pit bull dogs. In his book on the expression of emotion, Darwin (1872) noted that this process of natural selection can also have implications for behavior. Snarling communicates an intention to attack, and animals who recognize the signal and avoid a snarling opponent save themselves from potentially deadly encounters. This results in the selection of natural abilities to both transmit and receive emotional communications.

What do hairless cats and snarling dogs have to do with human relationship formation? Some abilities, such as accurately reading emotional expression, are universally adaptive for all humans, regardless of sex, age, or environmental conditions. Ekman and his colleagues have found that basic emotional states, such as anger and joy, show cross-cultural consistency in expression and recognition (Ekman, 1992; Ekman & Friesen, 1971; Ekman et al., 1987). However, Darwin (1859) was equally intrigued by the recognition that some animal behaviors seemed adaptive for attracting mates but maladaptive to individual survival. For instance, during mating season in Australia, the male satin bowerbird builds an elaborate lair for the single purpose of luring mates (Borgia, 1986). The male constructs an intricate bower of interconnected twigs, then proceeds to decorate it with eye-catching debris such as colorful parrot feathers, flower petals, rubberbands, and so on (Alcock, 1993). He woos the females with his attractive boudoir as well as a loud and varied musical serenade. The females shop around, inspecting a number of bowers before entering the one they find the most tempting and then mating with the owner. Even after the female has mated and left, the male will continue to upgrade his abode, leaving the invitation open for more females to hop in (Borgia, 1985). One male was observed to mate with 33 different females in his bower, whereas other males did not mate at all. Hence, constructing a marvelous bower is a highly adaptive characteristic that will be selected by the females who choose to mate with the master builders, ensuring that their genes will be passed on to the next generation. However, this flashy mating behavior may be costly from a survival viewpoint. The male bowerbirds engage in an energetic, noisy, and exposed process, making them not only highly noticeable to interested females, but to interested predators—definitely not a survival-related advantage.

Evolution Via Reproductive Fitness

The process by which characteristics evolve because of their reproductive benefits rather than their survival benefits is known as *sexual selection* (Darwin, 1859). Sexual selection operates through two key processes: intersexual choice, in which a trait gains an advantage because (like the bowerbird's bower or the flashy tail feathers of a male peacock) it is attractive to the opposite sex; and intrasexual competition, in which a trait gains an advantage because (like horns on a male bighorn sheep) it helps an individual compete with same-sex rivals for access to opposite-sex partners. Building on this notion of selection based on reproductive fitness, Trivers (1972) developed the theory of differential parental investment. According to this theory, the sex with the initially higher investment in the offspring becomes a resource for which the opposite sex competes.

One implication of differential parental investment in offspring is that the sex that has more to lose from a poor mating choice will also demand more before agreeing to mate. Among mammals, the biological reality of internal gestation means that females have a much higher initial investment than males in their offspring. Therefore, females should be more selective about choosing mates because they must give their bodies for the gestation and nurturing of the progeny. Most male mammals can reproduce with little cost, and, frequently, the male's direct input into procreation does not extend beyond copulation. For example, male bighorn sheep butt horns during mating season to show dominance because the females in the group prefer to mate with only a few rams—those who prove themselves to be the most powerful (i.e., most genetically fit) through this competition. In such species, males tend to be nonselective about their mates, whereas females tend to be extremely demanding. In the few species in which the male has a larger initial investment, the mating behaviors follow the parental investment model. For example, seahorses and pipefishes reproduce through internal gestation in the male (Daly & Wilson, 1983); accordingly, the females are more brightly colored and aggressive in courtship.

Female internal gestation gives rise to a second important concern for males—certainty of paternity. That is, a male in natural circumstances can never be certain that the young are his, making him more susceptible to the danger of wasting his resources on another male's genetic legacy (Daly & Wilson, 1983). Avoiding cuckoldry (so named after the cuckoo bird, who lays her eggs for incubating and hatching in the nest of "foster" parents) is of paramount importance for males, who lose genetic fitness by investing their precious resources in offspring whom are not their own. For this reason, males tend to be careful about guarding access to their partners and ensuring the fidelity of their mating activities. For instance, a male langur who takes over a new troop of females may kill the infants left by his predecessor (Hrdy, 1981). The infanticide ensures that his protection and resources are not wasted on another male's offspring. For most species, then, the biological facts of disproportionate maternal investment and paternal uncertainty lead to different strategies and sensitivities in the two sexes' mating-related behaviors.

A Qualified Differential Parental Investment Model for Humans

Like other mammals, humans reproduce via internal gestation—women conceive and carry the child inside their bodies and men do not. Unlike most other mammals, however, humans tend to be a pair-bonding species, forming long-term, intimate relationships that help ensure the survival of the fragile offspring until self-sufficiency is achieved (Benshoof & Thornhill, 1979; Daly & Wilson, 1983; Kenrick & Trost, 1987; Mellen, 1981). In this pattern of monogamous pairs within larger social groups, we are unique among mammals (Benshoof & Thornhill, 1979). All human societies have some form of marriage (Daly & Wilson, 1983), and anthropological evidence indicates that romantic love is present across a wide variety of cultures and mating strategies (Jankowiak & Fischer, 1992). The universality of marriage may, at first blush, appear to interfere with reproductive fitness, especially for men who are required to invest little physical effort into parenting. The adaptive logic of love is relatively straightforward, however, if not particularly romantic.

Evolution occurs at the level of the "selfish gene" (Dawkins, 1976); that is, if a genetic predisposition toward the behaviors of monogamy and fidelity enhances the ability of any single individual's genes to be replicated in offspring and survive to produce future offspring, those behaviors will be selected (Williams, 1966). Therefore, to be selected, pair bonding (whether it be monogamous, polygamous, or polyandrous) has to provide advantages in reproductive fitness for both women and men. For instance, among birds pair bonding is common in those species that incubate the young for long periods of time or that have helpless infants who require extensive parental care (Alcock, 1993). For humans, several factors favor relational bonding beyond simply ensuring paternity (Benshoof & Thornhill, 1979). One factor is the already mentioned vulnerability of the offspring. Human infants, at birth and for many months after, are totally dependent on older humans for survival. They can neither nourish nor defend themselves. There has been speculation that the relatively immature state of human infants may be a response to the competing pressures of the bipedal stance, which favored a more narrow pelvis, and the increasing size of the brain, which would favor a wider birth canal. Regardless of the genesis, helpless infants require constant supervision, making requisite food gathering difficult for any single parent. For most of our evolutionary history, an infant left unattended while its mother (the higher investment parent) foraged for food would be an easy target for predators. A second, related factor is the evolution of hunting, which enabled a man to contribute substantially to the health and development of the offspring by providing a source of high-energy protein with relatively little effort. Finally, the gradual evolution of a large brain with the capacity for and dependence on cultural transmission of knowledge likely favored infants who received teachings from two parents rather than one. Hence, the benefits from significant paternal investment in offspring increased to rival those of the mother, and our hearts were selected to bond with the person who sets it aflutter.

Given that men typically invest a great number of valuable resources in their offspring, including time, money, and emotional support, human mating should follow a somewhat modified parental investment model (Kenrick, Groth, Trost, & Sadalla, 1993; Kenrick, Sadalla, Groth, & Trost, 1990; Kenrick & Trost, 1989). In particular, men's level of selectivity in choosing a long-term, committed partner should approach the selectivity of women. However, the resources that men and women contribute to any offspring from the union differ. Therefore, they should both take care to choose partners who maximize their reproductive fitness by selecting a mate who exhibits the resources most needed by their sex. Women contribute their physical bodies, so men would be expected to value indications of health, such as body and facial symmetry or a clear, smooth complexion (Ford & Beach, 1951; Langlois & Roggman, 1990; Symons, 1979; Thornhill & Gangestad, 1994), and fertility, such as a waist–hip ratio that indicates sexual maturity (Singh, 1993). In contrast, men contribute their genes and indirect resources, such as money and shelter. Therefore, women would also be expected to look for indicators of health (e.g., body and facial symmetry or a clear complexion) and physical dominance (e.g., a V-shaped physique—broad shoulders, a well-developed chest, and a narrow waist; Lavrakas, 1975), as well as indirect indicators of the ability to produce resources (e.g., social status, ambition, and acquired wealth; Buss, 1989; Buss & Barnes, 1986; Kenrick et al., 1990, 1993). Pair bonding also requires cooperation between the father and mother in raising the offspring. Therefore, in addition to these different relational goals, men and women should also both desire qualities that reflect stability and commitment (Buss, 1994; Kenrick & Trost, 1997).

Research findings on human mate preferences reflect the predictions of a differential parental investment model that recognizes that both sexes invest heavily in a committed relationship, but have disparate investments in uncommitted liaisons. Based on such a model, neither sex should be particularly choosy at low levels of commitment, such as a single date. At high levels of commitment, such as steady dating or marriage, both sexes should be more demanding, but equally so, given that both women and men will contribute significant resources to the relationship. Sex differences in selectivity should be most pronounced for people engaged in uncommitted sexual relationships: Women run the relatively greater risk of impregnation (and subsequent single motherhood) by a man who has the opportunity to proliferate his genes with relatively little risk of having to commit time, energy, or resources.

In three separate studies, Kenrick and his colleagues (Kenrick et al., 1990, 1993) asked women and men to rate 24 characteristics of potential partners at different relationship stages to see if the level of relationship involvement affected their selectivity on characteristics such as physical attractiveness, dominance, agreeableness, stability, and so on. For example, respondents rated the minimal amount of intelligence acceptable in a partner at four relationship levels: a date, sexual relations, dating steadily, or marriage. The results are consistent with a qualified differential parental investment model. First, as expected, women were generally more selective at all relationship levels when aggregating across all characteristics (Kenrick et al., 1990, 1993). Second, the only characteristic that men rated consistently higher than women was physical attractiveness (Kenrick et al., 1990) and an attractiveness composite (including physically attractive, sexy, and healthy; Kenrick et al., 1993). Even so, women did value physical attractiveness just slightly less than did men—the sex differences were significant only at the levels of marriage (Kenrick et al., 1990, 1993, Study 2) and a single date (Kenrick et al., 1993, Study 2). Third, women were significantly more selective than men on traits reflecting dominance and status across all three studies (such as good earning capacity and college education). These sex-differentiated values were also found in a large, cross-cultural study of mate preferences, with men valuing youth and physical attractiveness more highly than did women and women valuing characteristics associated with resource acquisition more highly than did men (Buss, 1989). A meta-analysis of mate preference studies also found that women were more attentive to characteristics related to resource acquisition than were men (Feingold, 1992).

Kenrick and his colleagues (1990, 1993) also found a relatively consistent pattern that emphasizes the importance of pair bonding to both men and women while highlighting the differential costs involved in casual sexual liaisons. This pattern is illustrated in the intelligence results presented in Fig. 10.1. Generally, men and women were equally choosy when thinking of partners to date steadily and marry, as would be expected given the implied

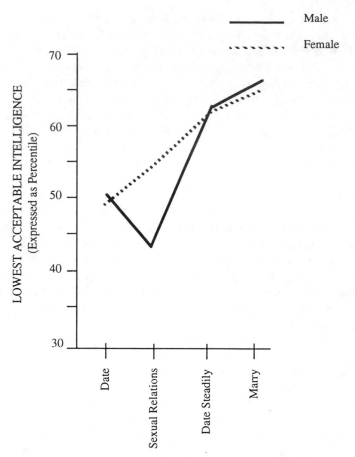

FIG. 10.1. Minimal amount of intelligence required in a partner at increasingly committed relationship levels, by sex. Figure illustrates data reported in Kenrick et al. (1990).

relational commitment. However, when thinking of partners for sexual relations, men were often willing to have sex with someone who would not meet most of their minimum criteria for a date. This sex difference was exaggerated when respondents were asked to describe the desirable characteristics of a partner for a one-night stand—a situation that maximizes the costs for women, who could be impregnated by a man they will never see again, and maximizes the benefits for men, who have a low-cost opportunity to spread their genes (Kenrick et al., 1993). Under these particularly risky circumstances, women's selectivity approached that of committed relationships (even their physical attractiveness requirements exceeded those of men), whereas men's standards dropped to their lowest point on every characteristic except physical attractiveness (the drop was significantly large

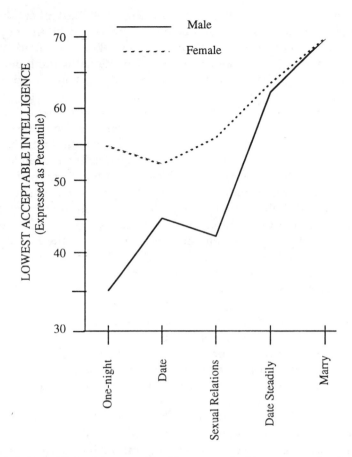

FIG 10.2. Minimal amount of intelligence required in a partner at various relationship levels, including a casual sexual opportunity, by sex. Figure illustrates data reported in Kenrick et al. (1993).

for 11 of 17 comparisons). Comparable results for the intelligence ratings are presented in Fig. 10.2. Again, these patterns are suggestive of the two sexes' differential costs associated with mating. They also illustrate that both sexes are capable of enacting both short- and long-term mating strategies (for corroborating evidence, see Buss & Schmitt, 1993).

Implications of Differential Parental Investment for Developing Relationships

Men's universal preoccupation with women's physical characteristics and fidelity and women's universal preoccupation with men's status and dominance should also be reflected in different mate-seeking behaviors (Buss,

1989, 1995; Daly & Wilson, 1983; Kenrick & Trost, 1997). Women interested in a long-term relationship should be most concerned with finding a partner who will commit to that relationship. Accordingly, women are more likely than men to engage in secret tests of relational commitment, such as piquing men's jealousy (Baxter & Wilmot, 1984), and to report more distress over imagined threats to the strength of the relational bond than to their partner's imagined sexual infidelity, as long as the sexual infidelity does not include a relational attachment to the other woman (Buss, Larsen, Westen, Semmelroth, 1992). In contrast, men want to find a faithful mate to avoid cuckoldry. The effects of paternal uncertainty are reflected in a variety of ways: Men universally value chastity more so than do women (Buss, 1989); men report more distress over their partner's imagined sexual infidelity than to their partner's romantic bond to another man (Buss et al., 1992); and men throughout the world jealously guard access to their partners through seclusion—adultery laws that support the harsh punishment of wives' infidelity (including death) but lenient treatment of husbands' infidelity—and practices such as clitoridectomy and infibulation, which are clearly designed to control female sexuality (Daly & Wilson, 1983).

One final consideration that is an important implication of the differential parental investment model is that men—who have little to lose and a great deal to gain from promiscuous mating opportunities—should be more unrestricted in their sexual desires and behaviors—a supposition borne out across a wide variety of research studies and contexts. Men not only want to have sex with more partners during their lifetimes (Buss & Schmitt, 1993), but on average they actually do. Although men prefer to marry women who are low in sexual permissiveness, they prefer to date women who are high in permissiveness, even though they do not see these women as marriage material (Oliver & Sedikides, 1992). They want to have sex sooner in relationships (Buss & Schmitt, 1993), have more extramarital affairs (Daly & Wilson, 1983), are more interested in erotica (Kenrick, Stringfield, Wagenhals, Dahl, & Ransdell, 1980), and are more likely to have sex with animals and inanimate objects (Daly & Wilson, 1983).

Evidence of this differential interest in promiscuous sex is nicely illustrated in research by Clark and Hatfield (1989), who asked confederates to approach members of the opposite sex and make one of three invitations: go out tonight, come over to my apartment, or go to bed with me. About half of the women said yes to a date, only 3% would go to the man's apartment, and not one woman would agree to go to bed with the man. Similarly, about half of the men said yes to a date, but the two sexes diverge at that point: Approximately 70% of the men were willing to either go to the woman's apartment or go to the bed with the female stranger. In other words, men want sex and women control access to it (Symons, 1979). This is not to say that women will not engage in casual sex. In fact, women do exercise short-term mating strategies for predictable and reproductively adaptive reasons (Buss, 1994). For instance, when seeking casual sexual partners, women prefer men who are physically attractive (Kenrick et al., 1993) and willing to generously spend money on them (Buss & Schmitt, 1993). Women in Great Britain were most likely to have short-term extra-marital affairs with men whose status exceeded their husbands' and to do so at the point of peak fertility during their monthly cycle (Baker & Bellis, 1994). Under circumstances that make short-term mating advantageous, women are willing to do so but are less likely to do so than men.

The combined pressures of determining the level of relational interest in a potential partner (and hence their level of potential investment), as well as screening for commitment and faithfulness (among other characteristics), makes relationship initiation a particularly challenging endeavor. The next section examines a particularly important aspect of relationship initiation—flirting—within an evolutionary context.

EVOLUTIONARY THEORY AND COURTSHIP INTERACTION

Because men and women face disparate reproductive realities, they should behave differently during courtship interactions (Grammar, 1990; Moore, 1995). The remainder of this chapter considers how these differential reproductive pressures might affect flirting behavior and presents evidence that is consistent with an evolutionary perspective. This review reorganizes findings from the current flirtation literature within an evolutionary framework, even though the research may not have been specifically designed to test evolutionary hypotheses. The intent here is to show the adaptive nature of flirtation as well as how our knowledge of interpersonal processes can enrich our understanding of evolutionary processes in humans. Herein is a review of research on both evolutionary theory and interpersonal relationships indicating that, during courtship, women are generally more discerning than men, find high-status men more attractive and desirable, and control the mating process through signaling their proceptivity to appropriate men. This research also reveals that, during courtship, men generally attempt to gain intersexual advantage by overtly displaying their status and dominance, are sensitive to and engage in intrasexual competition, and are more likely to approach women who have selectively signaled proceptivity. As these topics indicate, courtship is a reciprocal process, and the concerns of one sex mirror the concerns of the other. However, how women and men address these concerns differs during the initial stages of courtship—that is, during flirtation.

Predictions From Evolutionary Theory
for Women's Courtship Behavior

As noted earlier, the balance between the ultimate costs and benefits of romantic heterosexual involvement predicts differences in men's and women's goals at the initial flirtation stage. For instance, because women have more to lose from a botched pair bond, they should be more discerning about how and with whom they flirt. Thus, contrary to the notion that women are pawns who are played by more socially dominant men, women are generally the more discriminating sex and control the flirting process (Kenrick, Trost, & Sheets, 1996; Moore, 1985; Perper, 1985). The female's ultimate control over the mating process is dramatically illustrated in the Barbary macaques (Small, 1992). A female in estrus is obvious: The pink tissues around her hind end swell, indicating to the male that she is ready to mate. However, *she* selects her partner by approaching the desired male and swinging her hind end into his face. As noted by Small (1992), "if the male is also interested, which he generally is, the two monkeys mate" (p. 149). Human courtship rituals, by nature of our physiology and bonding patterns, may be less sensational but nonetheless interesting in the intricacies of their execution.

The mating process presents different dilemmas for each sex (Grammar, 1990), which influence how men and women flirt. Specifically, women must be capable of signaling their proceptivity clearly, but with a subtlety that borders on ambiguity (Givens, 1978; Moore, 1995). Because men are sensitive to the threat of intrasexual competition (Buss, 1988), a man may only respond to signals he believes are directed at him to minimize rejection. Therefore, a woman must be clearly proceptive to the desired man, but not to others. One of the legacies of paternal uncertainty is that a man who is interested in more than a fleeting relationship must also be sensitive to signs that a woman is promiscuous or unfaithful—a potential cuckold. Consequently, a woman needs to be able to direct her attentions to avoid appearing as if she is signaling to any and every man in the environment. These pressures both argue for a woman to isolate a desirable man and signal her attractions loudly and clearly. However, a woman also faces the humiliating possibility of rejection. Thus, subtle signals can both minimize the possibility of suffering rejection as well as ensure the targeted man of her exclusivity and fidelity. Moreover, while managing this complex and subtle projection of availability and interest, a woman must simultaneously screen the desired man for cues of status, interest, and stability, especially if she is interested in a long-term relationship. As noted by Moore (1995), "The use of direct signaling early in the relationship may not provide an opportunity for a woman to discover whether the man she has expressed an interest in is truly available and of high quality" (p. 321). Finally, a woman must be able to clearly but subtly reject undesirable suitors in the environment who might interfere with her ability to attract an appropriate mate while still protecting the face of the unwanted suitor so as to avoid provoking a violent or abusive retaliation (Trost & Engstrom, 1994).

Based on evolutionary principles and the dilemmas that women face in the courtship process outlined earlier, one can predict that during flirting interactions women will (a) be more skillful at encoding and decoding nonverbal behaviors, (b) possess a larger repertoire of flirting/proceptivity behaviors to signal the men they wish to attract, (c) possess a larger repertoire of rejection strategies, and (d) be approached by men when they exhibit behaviors that are interpreted as flirtatious.

Research on Women's Courtship Behavior

Research on flirting and mating behavior supports each of these predictions. First, women would be expected to exhibit more skill at encoding and decoding nonverbal behavior to clearly but subtly display proceptivity, as well as to discern male signals of status, interest, and stability. In fact, we know from nonverbal researchers that women are more accurate than men at both encoding and decoding nonverbal communication (Buck, 1984; Hall, 1978, 1979, 1985, see also Hall, chap. 7, this volume; Noller, 1986); even when the differences are not significant, they favor women (Noller, 1986). According to meta-analyses of expression accuracy (Hall, 1984), women are better at expressing their emotions and feelings, with effect sizes ranging from $r = .12$ to $r = .31$. Hall (chap. 7, this volume) has conducted several meta-analytic reviews of sex differences in nonverbal sensitivity, or ability to decode nonverbal cues, and found that the size of the effect favoring women is very consistent, ranging from $r = .20$ to $r = .25$. Given that flirting is typically initiated through visual contact, it is also relevant that women's ability to encode and decode nonverbal signals is typically greater for the visual channel (Drag & Shaw, 1967), particularly the face (Rosenthal & DePaulo, 1979), than the vocal (Hall, 1979; Noller, 1985). Perhaps most significantly, women's superiority at nonverbal coding and decoding is most pronounced when the target is a stranger. That is, men approach women's facility at encoding and decoding the nonverbal signals of people whom they know, but women are equally competent with both known and unknown targets (Noller, 1986). Thus, women are likely to be more skillful than men at delivering and detecting nonverbal cues in the flirting context where the target typically is a stranger or an acquaintance.

The second prediction suggests that women should possess a large repertoire of flirtation or proceptivity strategies to signal their interest in men. Once again, research results support such a claim. A number of studies

have established that women possess a broad range of strategies for signaling their interest. For example, Muehlenhard, Koralewski, Andrews,
and Burdick (1986) delineated 21 verbal and 15 nonverbal cues that women
use to convey interest, whereas Perper and Weiss' (1987) subjects identified
22 strategies they used to attract men. In a comprehensive and naturalistic
study of female flirtation behaviors, Moore (1985) conducted observations
in singles bars and identified 52 different nonverbal flirtation behaviors
exhibited by women. Out of 12 coded behaviors, McCormick and Jones
(1989) found that women exhibited a wider variety of and more frequent
flirtation gestures than did men, especially early in the flirtation episode.

Studies reveal that women not only possess a broad range of flirtation
strategies but that they are active participants in, and even initiators of,
the flirtation. Based on observations of 70 couples, McCormick and Jones
determined that women were more active in escalating the flirting sequence
and more nonverbally active in initiating flirtation than were men. In over
900 hours of observation in bars, Perper (1985) also observed that women's
signals were most likely to initiate the flirting episode. Both studies indicate
that women are actively involved in attracting a partner during the early
stages of flirting interactions.

The third prediction arising out of evolutionary theory proposes that
women will have a larger repertoire of rejection strategies than will men.
As noted earlier, the advantages of capitalizing on opportunistic mating
possibilities are greater for men than for women, implying that men may
have been evolutionarily selected for their "salesmanship" and women for
their "sales resistance" (Barash, 1977). Therefore, women need to be able
to reject unsuitable men who approach them. Although less research has
been conducted on rejection strategies than on proceptive strategies, existing literature supports the claim that women have a more varied repertoire of rejection strategies than do men. Of course, rejection can simply
be the absence of flirtation, but rejection becomes more than the absence
of flirtation when an overt approach by an interested party must be acknowledged and, in some manner, deflated. Consequently, women, who
are more likely to be approached than men, should have a wider array of
strategies from which to choose. As expected, women do report rejecting
men more frequently than vice versa (Trost, 1996), and women report
using significantly more rejection strategies that span a broader range of
categories than do men (Trost & Engstrom, 1994).

The fourth and final prediction concerning women's flirtation behavior
suggests that women who exhibit flirtatious behaviors will be approached
more by men than women who do not. To argue that a behavior has an
adaptive function in attracting men indicates that it should be present in
those situations in which flirting is possible and absent in those situations in
which flirting is unlikely to occur. In a direct test of the contextual nature of

flirtation, Moore (1985) found that women were more likely to exhibit effective flirting behaviors in environments that included a large proportion of men, such as a bar, than in an environment with few men, such as a women's meeting. Research also demonstrates that the use of flirtation strategies influences the likelihood that a woman will actually be approached by a man. For example, Walsh and Hewitt (1985) found that repeated signaling of more than one type of flirtation gesture significantly influenced a woman's probability of being approached by a man. Moore (1985) found that women who emitted a higher number of nonverbal flirtation displays (in this case, 35 or more per hour) received more than 4 approaches per hour. However, women who displayed low levels of nonverbal flirtation behaviors elicited fewer than .48 approaches per hour. Also, women who used a broader range of categories (more than 10) were more likely to be approached by a male. In fact, the correlation between the number of women's proceptivity signals and the number of male approaches across three contexts (bar, library, snack bar) was .89. Although approaches were most frequent in a bar, where displays were most frequent, those women who signaled often were those most often approached, regardless of context. Later research also indicated that women's courtship signaling was far more instrumental than other factors, including the woman's physical attractiveness, in eliciting male advances (Moore & Butler, 1989).

In sum, a woman who is interested in connecting with a man faces a daunting task that requires a high degree of skill and sensitivity. She must simultaneously transmit availability to the desired man, avoid rejection by him, express fidelity, reject unwanted suitors, and deduce his characteristics and intentions—a process that is fraught with the potential for dangerous miscommunication. On the other hand, the process of connecting is fraught with no little amount of danger for men.

Predictions From Evolutionary Theory for Men's Courtship Behavior

The mating dilemmas for men, although equally difficult, are somewhat different from those faced by women. To be successful as targets of women's proceptive behavior, men need to attract a woman's attention by signaling status and competing successfully with other men in the vicinity. These two tasks are intertwined. That is, the first dilemma for men is to advertise their desirability as mates so as to elicit female attention and proceptive behavior. Unfortunately for men, although status is valuable, it is a difficult commodity to signal nonverbally. Second, in most species, intrasexual competition is greater within the sex that makes a lower initial investment into the offspring—that is, the male (Trivers, 1972). As examples, bull elephant seals bite their competition with sharp teeth until one of them retreats, and bighorn sheep run at each other and ram foreheads with a force that would scare most defensive linemen. Because humans do engage in pair bonding, men and women should both attend to and attempt to minimize their competition to a certain extent. Even so, women are the gatekeepers to relationships, and men will still vie with each other for entree to the women they most desire. Consequently, men should tend toward overt advertisement of the qualities most desired by women—not only to attract women but to hopefully silence the competition (Barash, 1977; Buss, 1988). Grammar (1990) proposed that men can deal with these dilemmas by enacting one of two possible strategies: (a) approach only females who signal interest, which reduces the likelihood of rejection and losing face in front of the competition; or (b) take immediate and fast action to beat the competition to a valuable woman.

Thus, an evolutionary perspective can assist one in making predictions about men's flirting behaviors as well. According to this perspective, men will: (a) attempt to signal status and dominance, (b) approach women who signal interest, and (c) take immediate and fast action once signaled. Although research does exist to support these predictions, considerably less research has been conducted on men's flirtation behavior than on women's behavior.

Research on Men's Courtship Behavior

In one examination of the prediction that men will attempt to display status and dominance, Buss (1988) asked both men and women to describe behaviors that they use to make themselves attractive to the opposite sex. Some of the behaviors were similar for both men and women, including showing a sense of humor or being sympathetic, well mannered, and well groomed—all characteristics that are related to long-term relational stability. In keeping with the expectation that men want to signal status and dominance, however, men reported being significantly more likely to display resources, such as flashing money (an act that has the double advantage of impressing a potential partner and intimidating the competition). Men were also more likely to exaggerate their display of dominance or resources (e.g., by wearing expensive label clothing that was actually beyond their means), brag about their superior intelligence, or exaggerate their level of sexual activity and sexual popularity (Tooke & Camire, 1991). In other words, men's awareness of the need to display dominance and undermine the competition extends not only to accurate reporting of their resources, but may lead to some slight embellishments as well. In keeping with the view that the pair-bonded nature of our species elicits similar attention to competition among women, it is important to note that women also reported elaborating on their mating potential by exaggerating the characteristics most valued by men—namely, enhancing their bodily appearance through behaviors such as dieting, wearing perfume, suntanning, and walking with a greater swing than normal when around men (Tooke & Camire, 1991). Individual differences can also affect women's display behaviors. For example, women who do not expect to find men who are willing to invest in their offspring are more likely to wear sexy clothing and engage in sex than women who expect to find high-investment males (Cashdan, 1993).

The second prediction—that men are more likely to approach women who signal their interest—is supported by Moore's (1985) work cited earlier; that is, men are eight times more likely to approach a woman who uses a high number of flirtation signals and are more likely to approach women who use multiple nonverbal channels (Moore, 1985; Walsh & Hewitt, 1985). In addition, studies that have asked men about their likelihood of approaching women reveal that men are unlikely to ask a woman for a date unless she provides cues of interest (Muehlenhard & McFall, 1981; Muehlenhard & Miller, 1988).

The final prediction—that men will take immediate and fast action in mating contexts—has not been tested directly. However, this issue has been addressed indirectly in research examining men's motivations for flirting and their interpretations of women's behaviors as friendly versus flirtatious. Grammar (1990) argued that men outmaneuver the competition by responding quickly to a woman's signals of interest. Although men and women do not appear to differ in their perceptions of what constitutes flirtatious communication, men tend to rate those behaviors as more inviting than do women (Abrahams, 1994). Related research indicates that men are more likely than women to interpret women's nonverbal behavior as flirtatious or sexual than friendly (Abbey, 1982, 1987; Abbey & Melby, 1986; Montgomery, 1987; Saal, Johnson, & Weber, 1989; Shotland & Craig, 1988) perhaps because the flirtation of young men, in particular, appears to be motivated by sexual intentions (Montgomery, 1987). Overall, men impute more sexual meaning to heterosexual interaction (Abbey, 1982) and show more interest in returning flirtation (Downey & Vitulli, 1987). Thus, one response to competition and the need to establish dominance is for men to interpret women's nonverbal and conversational cues in a romantic framework (Rytting, 1976).

In sum, a framework of evolutionary pressures and adaptations can be useful in predicting how the process of flirtation differs for women and men. In particular, rather than viewing women as passive recipients of men's amorous advances, an evolutionary perspective underscores the importance of female choice in courtship and reproduction (Darwin, 1859). The parental investment model allows one to predict that women, as the more selective sex, should initiate a flirtatious episode by nonverbally signaling their proceptivity, be approached by the targeted man, and then continue escalation of the interaction (if desired) or reject the pursuit (if not). As we have implied throughout, research indicates that women do initiate the flirting process through their nonverbal behavior (McCormick & Jones, 1989; Perper, 1985), men are more likely to physically approach women than vice versa (Trost & Engstrom, 1994), and women use more and more varied rejection strategies (Perper & Weiss, 1987; Trost & Engstrom, 1994). Although this chapter has addressed the communication demands on men and women separately, it is important to note that neither sex totally commands a successful flirtation episode (Moore, 1995; Perper & Weiss, 1987). Continued escalation of the encounter requires a reciprocated sequence of approach behaviors from both parties involved in the interaction. Although the phases that describe a flirtation episode may appear to be relatively fixed (Givens, 1978; Perper, 1985), the exact combination of behaviors exhibited in the exchange can differ dramatically, enhancing the aura of magic that pervades the experience. Moreover, our description has been limited to flirtation that is intended to ultimately result in an intimate relationship, although such intimacy is not always the intended outcome of flirtation (Montgomery, 1987). Certainly other motivations for flirting can be adaptive as well; however, the evolutionary perspective is particularly relevant to predicting reproductive behaviors.

CONCLUSIONS

Our response to Canary and Hause's (1993) suggestion that the exploration of sex differences is confusing in the absence of theory is that, in fact, an evolutionary framework can be useful in predicting and explaining sex differences in behavior. One caveat when taking this perspective is that evolutionary constraints on behavior will only apply to those tasks for which men and women face different selection pressures, such as finding an appropriate mate. At an ultimate level of analysis, women stand to lose the most from an ill-fated match and will benefit by being particularly selective in looking for stable men who can provide the resources necessary to raise their offspring. Therefore, women should reflect a high preference for men who are able to establish dominance, exhibit adequate resources, and show an ability to commit. In contrast, men have less personal physical investment in their offspring, and, as their initial investment is lower, they should compete with other males for access to desirable women. As indicated, cross-cultural evidence indicates that there are universals in mate preferences that are consistent with the differential parental investment model (Buss, 1989; Kenrick & Keefe, 1992). Moreover, aspects of women's flirtatious behavior appear to be universal as well (Eibl-Eibesfeldt, 1975). Cross-cultural evidence is only one way to test hypotheses based on evolutionary principles (for a fuller discussion, see Buss, 1995; Capella, 1991; Kenrick & Trost, 1987, 1997). Continued examination of how evolutionary adaptiveness may interact with cultural pressures and individual personality will hopefully provide a more complete picture of the role of sex differences in behavior.

This chapter specifically examined how women's and men's search behaviors may differ based on their different goals in finding a partner. Taking an evolutionary perspective has led to observations that, in fact, women control the flirtation process (Moore, 1985), although the behaviors need not always be conscious (Silver & Spitzberg, 1992). The myth of the passive female who patiently waits to be swept away by her Prince Charming has, indeed, been relegated to the status of a fairy tale (Hrdy, 1981; Small, 1992). As noted by Daly and Wilson (1983),

> Men usually appear to be running the show, but it can be argued with some justice that they are peripheral hangers-on whose posturing and prancing is largely irrelevant to the essential business of human life and procreation. But even if men are not necessarily the prime movers of society, they certainly make themselves conspicuous! Men are everywhere the more political sex. They wheel and deal, bluster and bluff, compete overtly for valuable commodities and for mere symbols. Ultimately, these male machinations reflect a struggle for access to female reproductive capacity. (p. 288)

As people who observe behavior for a living, interpersonal researchers are particularly attuned to the nuances of expressive behavior; it is a topic in which we are naturally interested. But, as biological organisms, we should all be naturally interested in discriminating those who are interested in us from those who are not. For if we fail to successfully negotiate the intricate steps of meeting and mating, we will cease to exist.

ACKNOWLEDGMENTS

We appreciate the helpful comments of Daniel Canary, Kathryn Dindia, and Douglas Kenrick on an earlier version of this manuscript. Parts of this chapter were presented at the Western States Communication Association Convention, Pasadena, CA, February 1996; and the International Communication Association Convention, Chicago, IL, May 1996.

REFERENCES

Abbey, A. (1982). Sex differences in attributions for friendly behavior: Do males misperceive females' friendliness? *Journal of Personality and Social Psychology, 42*, 830–838.

Abbey, A. (1987). Misperceptions of friendly behavior as sexual interest: A survey of naturally occurring incidents. *Psychology of Women Quarterly, 11*, 173–194.

Abbey, A., & Melby, C. (1986). The effects of nonverbal cues on gender differences in perceptions of sexual intent. *Sex Roles, 15*, 283–298.

Abrahams, M. F. (1994). Perceiving flirtatious communication: An exploration of the perceptual dimensions underlying judgments of flirtatiousness. *Journal of Sex Research, 31*, 283–292.

Alcock, J. (1993). *Animal behavior: An evolutionary approach* (5th ed.). Sunderland, MA: Sinauer Associates.

Baker, R. R., & Bellis, M. A. (1994). *Human sperm competition: Copulation, masturbation, and infidelity.* London: Chapman & Hall.

Barash, D. P. (1977). *Sociobiology and behavior.* New York: Elsevier.

Baxter, L. A., & Wilmot, W. W. (1984). "Secret tests": Social strategies for acquiring information about the state of the relationship. *Human Communication Research, 11*, 171–201.

Benshoof, L., & Thornhill, R. (1979). The evolution of monogamy and concealed ovulation in humans. *Journal of Social and Biological Structures, 2*, 95–106.

Borgia, G. (1985). Bower destruction and sexual competition in the satin bowerbird. *Behavioral Ecology and Sociobiology, 18*, 91–100.

Borgia, G. (1986). Sexual selection in bowerbirds. *Scientific American, 254*, 92–100.

Buck, R. (1984). *The communication of emotion.* New York: Guilford.

Buss, D. M. (1988). The evolution of intrasexual competition: Tactics of mate attraction. *Journal of Personality and Social Psychology, 54*, 616–628.

Buss, D. M. (1989). Sex differences in human mate preferences: Evolutionary hypotheses tested in 37 cultures. *Behavioral and Brain Sciences, 12*, 1–49.

Buss, D. M. (1994). *The evolution of desire: Strategies of human mating.* New York: HarperCollins.

Buss, D. M. (1995). Evolutionary psychology: A new paradigm for psychological science. *Psychological Inquiry, 6*, 1–30.

Buss, D. M., & Barnes, M. F. (1986). Preferences in human mate selection. *Journal of Personality and Social Psychology, 50*, 559–570.

Buss, D. M., Larsen, R., Westen, D., & Semmelroth, J. (1992). Sex differences in jealousy: Evolution, physiology, and psychology. *Psychological Science, 3*, 251–255.

Buss, D. M., & Schmitt, D. P. (1993). Sexual strategies theory: An evolutionary perspective on human mating. *Psychological Review, 100*, 204–232.

Canary, D. J., & Hause, K. S. (1993). Is there any reason to research sex differences in communication? *Communication Quarterly, 41*, 129–144.

Capella, J. N. (1991). The biological origins of automated patterns of human interaction. *Communication Theory, 1*, 4–35.

Cashdan, E. (1993). Attracting mates: Effects of parental investment on mate attraction strategies. *Ethology and Sociobiology, 14*, 1–23.

Clark, R. D., & Hatfield, E. (1989). Gender differences in receptivity to sexual offers. *Journal of Psychology and Human Sexuality, 2*, 39–55.

Daly, M., & Wilson, M. (1983). *Sex, evolution, and behavior* (2nd ed.). Belmont, CA: Wadsworth.

Darwin, C. (1859). *The origin of species.* London: Murray.

Darwin, C. (1872). *The expression of emotions in man and animals.* London: Murray.

Dawkins, R. (1976). *The selfish gene.* Oxford: Oxford University Press.

Deaux, K., & Major, B. (1987). Putting gender into context: An interactive model of gender-related behavior. *Psychological Bulletin, 94*, 369–389.

Downey, J. L., & Vitulli, W. F. (1987). Self-report measures of behavioral attributions related to interpersonal flirtation situations. *Psychological Reports, 61*, 899–904.

Drag, R. M., & Shaw, M. E. (1967). Factors influencing the communication of emotional intent by facial expressions. *Psychonomic Science, 8*, 137–138.

Eibl-Eibesfeldt, I. (1975). *Ethology: The biology of behavior* (2nd ed.). New York: Holt, Rinehart & Winston.

Ekman, P. (1992). An argument for basic emotions. *Cognition and Emotion, 6*, 169–200.

Ekman, P., & Friesen, W. V. (1971). Constants across cultures in the face and emotion. *Journal of Personality and Social Psychology, 17*, 124–129.

Ekman, P., Friesen, W. V., O'Sullivan, M., Chan, A., Diacoyanni-Tarlatzis, I., Heider, K., Krause, R., LeCompte, W. A., Pitcairn, T., Ricci-Bitti, P. E., Scherer, K., Tomita, M., & Tzavaras, A. (1987). Universals and cultural differences in the judgments of facial expressions of emotion. *Journal of Personality and Social Psychology, 53*, 712–717.

Feingold, A. (1992). Gender differences in mate selection preferences: A test of the parental investment model. *Psychological Bulletin, 112*, 125–139.

Ford, C. S., & Beach, F. A. (1951). *Patterns of sexual behavior.* New York: Harper & Row.

Givens, D. B. (1978). The nonverbal basis of attraction: Flirtation, courtship, and seduction. *Psychiatry, 41*, 346–359.

Grammar, K. (1990). Strangers meet: Laughter and nonverbal signs of interest in opposite-sex encounters. *Journal of Nonverbal Behavior, 14*, 209–236.

Hall, J. A. (1978). Gender effects in decoding nonverbal cues. *Psychological Bulletin, 85*, 845–857.

Hall, J. A. (1979). Gender, gender roles, and nonverbal skills. In R. Rosenthal (Ed.), *Skill in nonverbal communication: Individual differences* (pp. 177–200). Cambridge MA: Oelgeschlager, Gunn & Hain.

Hall, J. A. (1984). *Nonverbal sex differences.* Baltimore: Johns Hopkins University Press.

Hall, J. A. (1985). Male and female nonverbal behavior. In A. W. Siegman & S. Feldstein (Eds.), *Multichannel integrations of nonverbal behavior* (pp. 195–225). Hillsdale, NJ: Lawrence Erlbaum Associates.

Hrdy, S. B. (1981). *The woman that never evolved.* Cambridge, MA: Harvard University Press.

Jankowiak, W. R., & Fischer, E. F. (1992). A cross-cultural perspective on romantic love. *Ethnology, 31*, 149–155.

Kenrick, D. T., Groth, G., Trost, M. R., & Sadalla, E. K. (1993). Integrating evolutionary and social exchange perspectives on relationships: Effects of gender, self-appraisal, and involvement level on mate selection. *Journal of Personality and Social Psychology, 64*, 951–969.

Kenrick, D. T., & Keefe, R. C. (1992). Age preferences in mates reflect sex differences in reproductive strategies. *Behavioral and Brain Sciences, 15*, 75–133.

Kenrick, D. T., Sadalla, E. K., Groth, G., & Trost, M. R. (1990). Evolution, traits, and the stages of human courtship: Qualifying the parental investment model. *Journal of Personality, 58*, 97–116.

Kenrick, D. T., Stringfield, D. O., Wagenhals, W. L., Dahl, R. H., & Ransdell, H. J. (1980). Sex differences, androgyny, and approach responses to erotica: A new variation on the old volunteer problem. *Journal of Personality and Social Psychology, 38*, 517–524.

Kenrick, D. T., & Trost, M. R. (1987). A biosocial model of relationship formation. In K. Kelley (Ed.), *Females, males, and sexuality: Theories and research* (pp. 58–100). Albany, NY: SUNY Press.

Kenrick, D. T., & Trost, M. R. (1989). A reproductive exchange model of heterosexual relationships: Putting proximate economics in ultimate perspective. In C. Hendrick (Ed.), *Review of personality and social psychology: Close relationships* (Vol. 10, pp. 92–118). Newbury Park, CA: Sage.

Kenrick, D. T., & Trost, M. R. (1997). Evolutionary approaches to relationships. In S. Duck (Ed.), *Handbook of personal relationships* (2nd ed., pp. 151–177). London: Wiley.

Kenrick, D. T., Trost, M. R., & Sheets, V. L. (1996). Power, harassment, and trophy mates: The feminist advantages of an evolutionary perspective. In D. M. Buss & N. M. Malamuth (Eds.), *Sex, power, conflict: Evolutionary and feminist perspectives* (pp. 29–53). New York: Oxford University Press.

Kramare, C. (1981). *Women and men speaking.* Rowley, MA: Newbury House.

Langlois, J. H., & Roggman, L. A. (1990). Attractive faces are only average. *Psychological Science, 1*, 115–121.

Lavrakas, P. J. (1975). Female preferences for male physiques. *Journal of Research in Personality*, *9*, 324–334.

McCormick, N. B., & Jones, A. J. (1989). Gender differences in nonverbal flirtation. *Journal of Sex Education and Therapy*, *15*, 271–282.

Mellen, S. L. W. (1981). *The evolution of love*. San Francisco: Freeman.

Montgomery, B. M. (1987, May). *Sociable vs. sensual flirting: The influence of gender*. Paper presented at the annual meeting of the International Communication Association, Montreal, Canada.

Moore, M. M. (1985). Nonverbal courtship patterns in women: Context and consequences. *Ethology and Sociobiology*, *6*, 237–247.

Moore, M. M. (1995). Courtship signaling and adolescents: "Girls just wanna have fun"? *Journal of Sex Research*, *32*, 319–328.

Moore, M. M., & Butler, D. L. (1989). Predictive aspects of nonverbal courtship behavior in women. *Semiotica*, *3*, 205–215.

Muehlenhard, C. L., Koralewski, M. A., Andrews, S. L., & Burdick, C. A. (1986). Verbal and nonverbal cues that convey interest in dating: Two studies. *Behavior Therapy*, *17*, 404–419.

Muehlenhard, C. L., & McFall, R. M. (1981). Dating initiation from a woman's perspective. *Behavior Therapy*, *12*, 682–691.

Muehlenhard, C. L., & Miller, E. N. (1988). Traditional and nontraditional men's responses to women's dating initiation. *Behavior Therapy*, *12*, 682–691.

Noller, P. (1985). The video primacy effect: A further look. *Journal of Nonverbal Behavior*, *9*, 28–47.

Noller, P. (1986). Sex differences in nonverbal communication: Advantage lost or supremacy regained? *Australian Journal of Psychology*, *38*, 23–32.

Oliver, M. B., & Sedikides, C. (1992). Effects of sexual permissiveness on desirability of partner as a function of low and high commitment to relationship. *Social Psychology Quarterly*, *55*, 321–333.

Perper, T. (1985). *Sex signals: The biology of love*. Philadelphia: ISI Press.

Perper, T., & Weiss, D. L. (1987). Proceptive and rejective strategies of U.S. and Canadian college women. *Journal of Sex Research*, *23*, 455–480.

Rosenthal, R., & DePaulo, B. M. (1979). Sex differences in accommodation in nonverbal communication. In R. Rosenthal (Ed.), *Skill in nonverbal communication: Individual differences* (pp. 68–103). Cambridge, MA: Oelgeschlager, Gunn & Hain.

Rytting, M. B. (1976, May). *Sex or intimacy: Male and female versions of heterosexual relationships*. Paper presented at the annual meeting of the Midwestern Psychological Association, Chicago, IL.

Saal, F. E., Johnson, C. B., & Weber, N. (1989). Friendly or sexy?: It may depend upon whom you ask. *Psychology of Women Quarterly*, *13*, 263–276.

Shotland, R. L., & Craig, J.M. (1988). Can men and women differentiate between friendly and sexually interested behavior? *Social Psychology Quarterly*, *51*, 66–73.

Silver, C. A., & Spitzberg, B. H. (1992, July). *Flirtation as social intercourse: Developing a measure of flirtatious behavior*. Paper presented at the 6th International Conference on Personal Relationships, Orono, Maine.

Singh, D. (1993). Adaptive significance of female physical attractiveness: Role of waist-to-hip ratio. *Journal of Personality and Social Psychology*, *65*, 293–307.

Small, M. F. (1992). Female choice in mating. *American Scientist*, *80*, 142–151.

Symons, D. (1979). *The evolution of human sexuality*. New York: Oxford University Press.

Thornhill, R., & Gangestad, S. W. (1994). Human fluctuating asymmetry and sexual behavior. *Psychological Science*, *5*, 297–302.

Tooke, W., & Camire, L. (1991). Patterns of deception in intersexual and intrasexual mating strategies. *Ethology and Sociobiology*, *12*, 345–364.

Trivers, R. L. (1972). Parental investment and sexual selection. In B. Campbell (Ed.), *Sexual selection and the descent of man 1871–1971* (pp. 136–179). Chicago: Aldine.

Trost, M. R. (1996, August). *"Let's stay friends" and other strategies for rejecting romance.* Paper presented at the meeting of the American Psychological Association, Toronto, Ontario, Canada.

Trost, M. R., & Engstrom, C. (1994, February). *"Hit the Road, Jack": Strategies for rejecting flirtatious advances.* Paper presented at the Western States Communication Association Convention, San Jose, CA.

Walsh, D. G., & Hewitt, J. (1985). Giving men the come-on: Effect of eye contact and smiling in a bar environment. *Perceptual and Motor Skills, 61,* 873–874.

Williams, G. C. (1966). *Adaptation and natural selection.* Princeton, NJ: Princeton University Press.

Chapter 11

Gender Differences in Being Influential and/or Influenced: A Challenge to Prior Explanations

Michael Burgoon
University of Arizona

Renee S. Klingle
University of Hawaii, Manoa

Research activity in given areas follows a pendulumlike motion: Areas of research become popular and voluminous only to be followed by a period of quiescence in which there is little or no activity (M. Burgoon & Milller, 1990). This start and stop kind of activity has many different causes. Sometimes the intellectual efforts sufficiently answer the questions of import and there is little left about which to be curious. In other instances, the findings are so obvious as to need no further inquiry or explanation. At other times, results are politically unpopular and questions about such data are left unposed or explained away with *a posteriori* reasoning that makes the research results more palatable to the scholarly community and/or reading public. Such explanations, offered with minimal support and without sound reasoning, can encourage a premature reification of inaccurate speculations as valid explanations. Given the general feeling that little is left to be learned, lines of inquiry often cease.

Because of the acceptance of past research, post hoc explanations, and inaccurate conclusions brought forth in the allied disciplines of social psychology and communication, questions about social influence and gender are no longer of great interest to the research community (certainly in comparison with issues raised in other chapters in this volume). In fact, researchers have come to accept as truisms certain statements about sex differences or similarities in the ability to influence or the influenceability of men and women with little vigorous intellectual debate. For example, if one were to trace the history of research on sex differences in social influence research from the halcyon days of 30 years ago, when social psychologists were routinely publishing articles on persuasion and persuasibility, through the years when communication researchers became interested in the same kinds of issues, similar explanations would reign. Textbooks and compilations merely provide narratives on the state of presumed knowledge in the area of gender and social influence. A similar pattern emerges of repetitive reporting of empirical data with few confounding results, followed by speculations as to why gender differences occur in the ability of men and women to influence others and the differential receptivity of women and men to persuasive arguments.

A careful reading of the extant data would lead one to a rather unequivocal conclusion that, at least in this culture, men are generally more persuasive than women across topics, situations, and time, whereas women are generally more persuasible than men in a variety of situations. Although not all would unabashedly embrace this interpretation of the results, the more predominant response by scholars has been to accept sex differences and offer a variety of speculations about why the empirical results obtain with such regularity. The bulk of this explanatory activity has centered on the female persuasibility findings, rather than on why men seem to be generally more influential than women in this culture. In fact, a great deal of space has been devoted to political explanations, social commentaries, and post hoc speculations about why women seem to be more susceptible to influence attempts than men.

In addition, much of the research on sex differences in social influence has been atheoretical. No a priori explanations, or predictions with much theoretical weight, guide this rather voluminous research area. In fact, sex differences appear to be discovered as an afterthought in many studies. Different scholars have simply accepted the notion that such differences occur and have utilized inductive reasoning to explain the differences. However, few have attempted to build theoretical models specifying why sex differences should occur, much less incorporated gender as a central feature of their theoretical explications.

Thus, we have a mountain of empirical data on sex differences in social influence that has been unguided by theoretical positions. For example, Eagly and Carli (1981) and Becker (1986) offered comprehensive reviews of the literature on female persuasibility. Their conclusions and speculations—inductively created—have been repeated, with little alteration, in specialized books on persuasion in the allied social science disciplines as explanations of female persuasibility ever since (cf. Brewer & Crano, 1994; Eagly & Chaiken; 1993; Littlejohn & Jabusch, 1987; O'Keefe, 1990; Petty & Cacioppo, 1986). These same explanations have further found their way into most of the introductory textbooks in both psychology and communication. Thus, if one looks at the diffusion of knowledge about gender and social influence, there seems to be a truth by consensus about how men and women fare in persuasive attempts and how they differ in their persuasibility. Unfortunately, it appears that this consensus may be based on little more than the repeated offerings of the same early speculations about underlying causes that are inaccurate, ill informed, and open to attack by research from divergent perspectives. This chapter carefully examines the extant research evidence and the proffered explanations for gender differences, and provides evidence from a distinctly separate and almost totally ignored research program that challenges past explanations.

THE ISSUE OF GENDER DIFFERENCES IN ABILITY TO INFLUENCE

As previously eluded to earlier, the primary focus of concern has not been on whether or why men seem to be generally more persuasive than women in varied transactions. Rather, the topic of most concern has been the questions surrounding female persuasibility. The space allocation in this chapter devoted to gender persuasiveness versus persuasibility will not necessarily reflect that general interest. There are questions about gender differences in the ability to influence that warrant detailed scrutiny and theoretical explanation.

It is not our intention to take issue with the research evidence that clearly suggests that men in this culture—across a number of contexts, topics, and time—appear to be more influential than women. Both men and women are more susceptible to persuasive messages encoded by men. It may even be that women are more persuaded by men and significantly more resistant to persuasion by equally qualified women (M. Burgoon & Stewart, 1974). However, a research effort that offers a theoretical umbrella under which to explain sex differences in the ability to influence has not been incorporated in the social influence literature by a number of writers.

In recent years, this program of research has led to two relatively formalized theories about message strategies and compliance gaining, attitude-behavior change, and social influence. It is beyond the scope of this chapter to fully articulate the complete theoretical formulations. Instead, a synopsis of the propositional frameworks and a summary of some of the important hypothesized relationships and empirical findings that are most germane to researchers interested in gender and communication are offered.

Language Expectancy Theory

The General Expectancy Model. To illuminate how this theory developed over the past 25 years, a brief summary of the basic tenets of the theory is in order. M. Burgoon and Miller (1985) summarized their theoretical position on the relationship between language and persuasion with the following introduction:

Our language affects our lives powerfully. Others make attributions about social and professional status, background and education, and even the intent of communication by evaluating our language choices. Those intrigued with social influence whether classical scholars or media image-makers, have long pondered the influence of such language choices on the success or failure of persuasive attempts. The decision to appeal to people's logic or emotional side is manifest in the language used in persuasive messages: Persuaders try to mollify, justify, terrify or crucify by altering the language in their appeals. (p. 199; italics added)

The original logic underlying language expectancy theory (M. Burgoon, 1989; M. Burgoon, Jones, & Stewart, 1975; M. Burgoon & Miller, 1985) begins with the assumptions that language is a rule-governed system and that people develop macrosociological expectations and preferences concerning the messages employed by others in persuasive attempts. These expectations are primarily a function of cultural and sociological norms. Preferences are usually a function of cultural values and societal standards or ideals for what is competent communication performance, and those differ for men and women. It is important to develop this model in a volume devoted to gender, sex, and communication because the entire propositional framework leads to an explanation of why women tend to be generally less persuasive and offers firm support for the kinds of messages that are most effective for men and women. Moreover, the theory clearly informs women about the kinds of messages that are most and least likely to succeed in persuasive attempts.

M. Burgoon and Miller (1985) provided a detailed propositional logic outlining the formative explanatory calculus of language expectancy theory. M. Burgoon (1989, 1990) later presented a major refinement of the model and discussed the effects of both positive and negative violations of expectations in persuasive attempts. For the purposes of a brief summary, Fig. 11.1 graphically presents the basic tenets of language expectancy theory.

Briefly, change in the direction desired by a source occurs when positive violations of expectations occur. Positive violations obtain in two ways: (a) when the source's enacted behavior is better or more preferred than that which was expected in the situation, or (b) when negatively evaluated sources conform more closely than expected to cultural values, societal norms, or situational exigencies. Change occurs in the first case because enacted behavior is outside the normative band width in a positive direction and such behavior prompts attitude and/or behavioral changes. In the second condition, a person who is expected to behave incompetently or inappropriately conforms to cultural norms and/or expected social roles that result in an overly positive evaluation of the source and, subsequently, change advocated by that actor occurs. Negative violations of expectations result from language choices or the selection of message strategies that lie

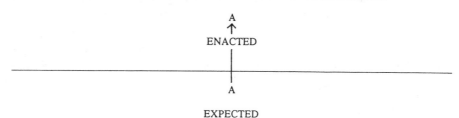

AREA OF POSITIVE VIOLATIONS OF COMMUNICATION NORMS

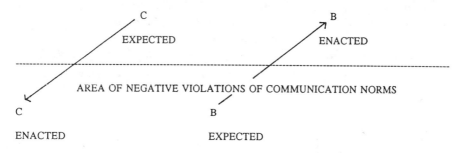

FIG. 11.1. Language expectancy theory predictions about message strategies and attitude/behavior change

CASE A: Positive violation of expectations by performing unexpected, positively valued behaviors. Enacted behavior outside the expected, normative band width in positive direction. Attitude/behavior change in the direction advocated by the source.

CASE B: Positive violation of expectations by negatively evaluated source conforming more closely to norms of communication behavior. Enacted behavior within the expected normative band width. Attitude/behavior change predicted in direction advocated by the source because of overly positive evaluation of source behavior.

CASE C: Negative violation of expectations by performing unexpected, negatively valued behaviors. Enacted behavior outside the expected, normative band width in negative direction. No attitude/behavior change or actual changes in opposite direction advocated by the source.

outside the band width of socially acceptable behavior in a negative direction. The result is no attitude and/or behavioral changes or changes in the opposite direction intended by the persuader.

The Fundamental Propositions (Modified). The first proposition in the formal articulation of the theory merely laid out the fundamental assumptions of the theoretical model. This higher order proposition, from which all else follows, approaches being axiomatic in content and structure:

Proposition 1: People develop cultural and sociological expectations about language behaviors that subsequently affect their acceptance or rejection of persuasive messages.

Two corollary propositions, of obvious origin given the previous discussion, are required as a beginning point for developing a more complete theoretical synthesis of the relationship between language effects and persuasion:

Proposition 2: Use of language that negatively violates societal expectations about appropriate persuasive communication behavior inhibits persuasion and results either in no attitude change or changes in position opposite to that advocated by the communicator.

Proposition 3: Use of language that positively violates societal expectations about appropriate persuasive communication behavior facilitates persuasive effectiveness.

The propositions with considerable nomothetic force and a wealth of empirical support are as follows:[1]

Proposition 4: People in this society have normative expectations about the level of fear arousing appeals, opinionated language, language intensity, sequential message techniques, and compliance-gaining attempts varying in instrumental verbal aggression appropriate to persuasive discourse.

Proposition 5: Highly credible communicators have the freedom (wide band width) to select varied language strategies and compliance-gaining techniques in developing persuasive messages, whereas low-credible communicators must conform to more limited language options and compliance-gaining messages if they wish to be effective.

---

[1]A complete review of the voluminous research literature encompassed under the umbrella of the following propositions, as previously stated, is beyond the scope of the present chapter. However, detailed reviews of the fear appeal literature, research on opinionatedness, and language intensity are readily available in the M. Burgoon and Miller (1985) initial review. M. Burgoon (1989) extended that review to include a number of microlevel message variables as special cases of what has been called a type of instrumental verbal aggression. In an article published shortly after that review and extension of language expectancy theory, M. Burgoon (1990) explained the results of more macrolevel persuasion strategies (e.g., sequential message strategies such as foot-in-the-door; Dillard, Hunter, & Burgoon, 1984; and door-in-the-face; Cann, Sherman, & Elkes, 1975) and techniques, as well as the compliance-gaining message strategy research (cf. Marwell & Schmitt, 1967a, 1967b; Miller, Boster, Roloff, & Seibold, 1977, 1987) from an expectancy theory perspective.

Proposition 6: Because of normative impacts of source credibility, high-credible sources can use low-intensity appeals and more aggressive compliance-gaining messages and be more persuasive than low-credible communicators using either strong, mild language, or more prosocial compliance-gaining strategies.

Proposition 7: Communicators perceived as low in credibility or those unsure of their perceived credibility will usually be more persuasive if they employ appeals low in instrumental verbal aggression or elect to use more prosocial compliance-gaining message strategies.

Proposition 8: People in this society have normative expectations about appropriate persuasive communication behavior that are gender specific, such that (a) men are usually more persuasive using highly intense persuasive appeals and aggressive compliance-gaining message attempts, whereas (b) women are usually more persuasive using low-intensity appeals and unaggressive compliance-gaining messages.

Research in Gender and Persuasion From an Expectancy Theory Perspective.
Early research (M. Burgoon, Jones, & Stewart, 1975; M. Burgoon & Miller, 1985) providing the foundations for language expectancy theory clearly demonstrated that women have a much narrower band width of socially acceptable behavior than do men in this society. In other words, women are limited in their choice of stategies if they wish to avoid negatively violating expectations and being ineffective in compliance-gaining attempts. In fact, it is difficult for women to positively violate expectations. Yet it is quite likely that any deviations—even relatively trivial changes—from the expected roles of women will result in negative violations of expectations and increase the probability of noncompliance.

Although a host of other researchers have suggested that communicator credibility on either a macro- or microlevel was the explanatory mechanism for understanding why men are generally more persuasive than women, most of these comments are simply speculations, anecdotal in nature, or dismissive—in that the easiest way to explain the differences was to simply say that in this society women are generally seen as less credible regardless of actual competence or character. However, the psychology and communication literature is replete with research that allows credibility differences between men and women to exist in the same study with men relatively high and women only moderately credible. Thus, it is not a surprise that the dominant and repeated findings from the cumulative research is that higher speaker credibility leads to attitude change (or, said another way, men are more persuasive than women).

A more satisfactory approach to examining the credibility effect in gender research would obviously be to use highly credible sources of both sexes as actors attempting to affect change. With such a control, it could be determined if men and women do have different band widths of acceptable behaviors and if such expectations account for men having more linguistic and strategic latitude in constructing effective persuasive messages than women.

Reasoning that physicians of both sexes should have relatively high credibility in this society, M. Burgoon, Birk, and Hall (1991) chose clinical physicians as communicators to test sex differences in influence attempts. However, even in the high-prestige profession of medicine, it was found highly problematic, if not impossible, to completely equalize the credibility of men and women with the same professional standing.

Although there has been little research on the effects of sex differences in the medical context, a wealth of research suggests that, in general, women are more nurturant, less verbally aggressive, more likely to express caring and concern, and more empathic in their enacted communication behaviors (M. Burgoon, Dillard, & Doran, 1984; Eakins & Eakins, 1978; Infante & Wigley, 1986). To the extent that such behaviors are products of early sex role socialization, they are most resistant to change (Scanzoni, 1975). Therefore, it is unlikely that professional socialization would completely counteract sex role differences among physicians. This is supported by the finding that female physicians have been found to use more affiliative behaviors than their male counterparts (Maheux, Dufort, & Beland, 1988; Maheux, Dufort, Beland, Jacques, & Levesque, 1990; Weisman & Teitelbaum, 1985, 1989). Rosenberg (1979) offered further support when finding that female medical students tend to recognize more psychosocial issues for patients, whereas male medical students tend to see themselves in control of communication with patients. In summary, if female physicians have been socialized to the traditional female sex role, they should be more nurturant and expressive and have stronger interpersonal orientations than male physicians.

Another line of reasoning, based on notions of credibility, would suggest that female physicians have a high probability of negatively violating expectations if they use verbally aggressive or neutral message strategies in compliance-gaining attempts. M. Burgoon et al. (1975) illustrated how women, in general, are considered as less credible communicators than men by both men and women in this culture. According to language expectancy theory, less credible communicators have a restricted band width and the use of aggressive message strategies is non-normative and clearly a negative violation of expectations.

Although both male and female physicians enjoy relatively high normative status in this society, differences remain in the perceptions of credibility of men and women in the health care professions. For example, Engleman (1974) found that a majority of both men (84%) and women (75%) preferred a male doctor as their regular physician. In a more recent study,

Klingle (1994) had patients rate one of two transcripts of a physician–patient interaction, varied only by physician sex. Klingle found that patients perceived male physicians as more rewarding and socially attractive than female physicians. A limited amount of research attests to the fact that, although female physicians are held in somewhat high esteem by most people in this society, they are still seen as less credible than their male counterparts and, therefore, should have less freedom to use aggressive strategies. This credibility differential, coupled with socialization processes, results in the enactment of unaggressive strategies by females because part of the female role suggests that any deviation from such verbally unaggressive compliance-gaining strategies will increase noncompliance.

It is clear that male physicians have a great deal of freedom to select compliance-gaining strategies. First, they have high normative status, and the socialization process provides them with an extremely wide band width of acceptable behaviors. Second, research suggests that socialization makes aggressive behavior not only acceptable but preferred for highly credible male communicators in this society (M. Burgoon & Miller, 1985). The enacted (and thus expected) communication behaviors for male physicians, however, include strategies that are neutral in emotional tone, such as direction giving and negative expertise (M. Burgoon & J. Burgoon, 1990). All of these strategies fall near the center of the instrumental verbal aggression continuum. Evidence suggests that high levels of verbal aggression on the part of male physicians is often perceived by patients as an expression of personal concern and considered a positive violation of expectations, increasing levels of compliance (M. Burgoon et al., 1991).

Moreover, because male physicians are expected to be affectively neutral in both treatment and prevention situations, affiliative strategies such as the expression of caring and concern can also be a positive violation of expectations for male physicians. Such personalization in the clinical visit is preferred by most people, but rarely experienced in a visit to a male physician. Thus, the only strategies that seem to be ineffective for male physicians are the ones most often used: a combination of simple direction giving and expertise. All of this taken together allowed M. Burgoon et al. (1991) to offer the following hypotheses:

Hypothesis 1: There are perceived differences in expected communication behaviors such that male physicians are expected to use more aggressive verbal strategies, whereas female physicians are expected to utilize less aggressive verbal strategies.

Hypothesis 2: There will be an interaction between the source of a persuasive message and message strategy such that: (a) among male physicians, a deviation from moderately aggressive language either in the direction of more instrumentally verbally aggressive or less aggressive strategies will result in increased levels of reported compliance; and (b) among female physicians, there will be an inverse linear relationship between level of verbal aggression and reported compliance.

In this study (M. Burgoon et al., 1991), manipulation checks were completed to verify significant differences in expected communication behaviors between male and female physicians. Using adult patients as subjects, strong support for the prior hypotheses (derived directly from language expectancy theory) was found. Moreover, there was no decrease in satisfaction when male physicians used either unexpectedly aggressive or unaggressive strategies.

Reinforcement Expectancy Theory

Based on the notion that noncompliance in the medical setting is often related to patient difficulties in adhering to long-term lifestyle management, Klingle (1993, in press) developed reinforcement expectancy theory (RET) to address how male and female physicians can communicatively motivate patients to adhere to medical recommendations over time—a generally ignored subject in compliance-gaining research. The theoretical framework incorporates the basic tenants of language expectancy theory and extends it in several important ways. Similar to language expectancy theory, the framework is grounded in the notion that socially appropriate communication is a necessary condition for success in persuading others. *Appropriate communication* is defined as communication that is either expected or more preferred than that which is expected for a given communicator, whereas *inappropriate communication* is defined as communication that is unexpected in a negative direction. Because cultural and sociological norms influence language expectancies, judgments of communication appropriateness are moderated by communicator sex with men having the ability to use more aversive communication than women. RET extends language expectancy theory by applying well-accepted reinforcement principles, in conjunction with language expectancy claims, to predict the most effective use of communication to improve *both* inital compliance and long-term medical adherence.

Compliance-Gaining Strategies in Initial Influence Attempts. RET is based on the central premise that influence messages used by physicians shape patients' communication reinforcement expectations and, in turn, motivate and guide patients' present and future actions. According to the framework, strategy effectiveness is based on a two-appraisal process in which receivers first judge the appropriateness of the persuasion attempt and then assess the motivational value of the communication. If the message is viewed as inappropriate, patients immediately reject the message; the motivational value of the message is not ascertained. Evaluating the message as socially appropriate triggers the second appraisal process. Here receivers ascertain the reward value of the message. Messages having reward value (e.g., messages we want to keep or remove in the future) are stored in working memory called reinforcement expectations and guide human behavior.

Based on findings from a series of studies testing language expectancy theory (for review, see M. Burgoon, 1995), RET argues that sociological norms allow men considerable flexibility in their language choices, whereas women are limited to using nonaggressive communication behaviors. In summary, men are expected and allowed to use fairly aggressive behaviors, whereas women are not. Although acceptable communication is a necessary condition for success at persuading others, RET acknowledges that it is not a sufficient condition for increasing adherence rates for people who need motivation. Messages that are viewed as socially appropriate are next judged in terms of their reward value.

Grounded in basic reinforcement principles, Klingle (1993) argued that human behavior is driven by the need to gain rewarding communication and eliminate aversive communication. Thus, reinforcement expectations motivate patients to comply with physicians' requests. This assumption also coincides with most mutual influence models (e.g., Andersen, 1984; J. Burgoon & Hale, 1988; Cappella & Green, 1982) that assume receivers adjust their behavior to maintain pleasant communication exchanges or avoid unpleasant ones.

Based on the notion that humans have a strong need for approval and respect from others (Harre, 1980), messages used in RET framework are broadly characterized by the degree to which they relationally signal positive, negative, or neutral regard for patients and/or patients' actions. *Positive regard strategies* are defined as influence choices that signal approval or affect for others and/or their actions (e.g., nonverbal immediacy and verbal strategies that show support, stress goal commonality, or validate the patient's feelings/actions). *Negative regard strategies* are defined as influence attempts that indicate disapproval or lack of affect for others and/or their actions (e.g., nonverbal nonimmediacy, nonsupportive verbal requests, threats, or messages that invalidate the patient's feelings or actions). *Neutral regard strategies* refer to influence attempts that, when used in isolation, neither validate or invalidate the patient (e.g., simple directives or justifications for action).

Conceptualizing messages based on their reward value allows the framework to apply reinforcement principles and to determine what influence attempts are appropriate for men and women. Because this conceptualization scheme is consistent with the instrumental verbal aggression continuum (negative regard equated with aggressive language, neutral regard falling in the center of the continuum, and positive regard equated with nonaggressive language), RET argues that receivers judge negative regard strategies as inappropriate communication action when used by women as opposed to men. Consequently, negative regard messages used by women are rejected by receivers (e.g., ineffective influence attempts). All other regard strategies are viewed as appropriate, but only positive and negative regard strategies have reinforcement properties and, thus, have the characteristics necessary to guide human behavior.

In summary, for initial influence attempts, physicians can motivate patients by using influence attempts that signal either approval (positive regard strategies) or disapproval (negative regard strategies). However, the strategy used must also be viewed by patients as socially appropriate. In short, because of sociological norms and the motivational properties of various communication messages, male physicians can motivate patients in inital encounters by using either negative or positive regard strategies, whereas female physicians must use messages of approval to motivate patients during initial influence attempts. These predictions for initial encounters are consistent with language expectancy but are based on a reinforcement explanatory framework rather than an expectancy violations model. Figure 11.2 summarizes the basic predictions for male and female persuaders in initial influence attempts.

Sequential Compliance-Gaining Attempts. Patients who visit physicians on a more regular basis have the opportunity to continually observe the reinforcement behavior of the physician and formulate reinforcement expectations. Although the frequent use of rewarding communication by the physician would seem to establish the strongest reinforcement expectancy, RET argues that the occasional use of nonreinforcing exchanges is needed to develop motivating reinforcement expectations. The theory indicates that repetitive communication patterns used by physicians (e.g., all rewarding communication, all aversive communication, or all neutral communication) cause patients to believe that their behavior does not and cannot influence the physician's behavior. Thus, nonmotivating reinforcement expectations develop because patients, in these situations, expect reinforcement regardless of their behavioral adjustment. Physicians who vary their strategy usage (e.g., use both positive and negative regard messages) help patients to develop motivating reinforcement expectations, or expectations that the physician's behavior is linked to their health-related actions.

RET proposed that strategy combinations would only be effective if they involve appropriate language choices. Thus, although all strategy combinations (e.g., positive and negative, positive and neutral, or negative and neutral) were predicted to be motivating for male physicians, female phy-

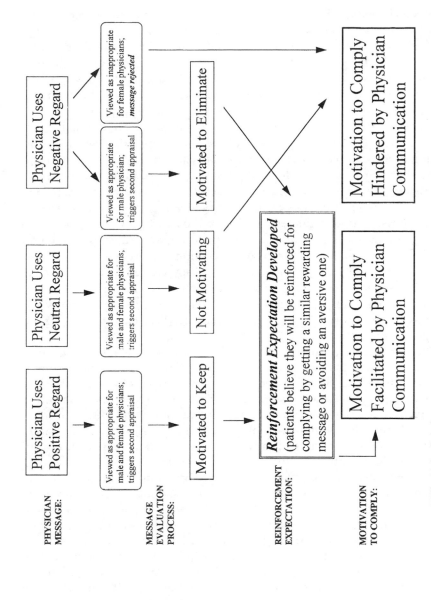

FIG. 11.2. Reinforcement expectancy theory predictions about message strategies and attitude/behavior change.

sicians were presumed to be limited to the use of combinations including only positive and neutral regard strategies.

Research Testing RET. Utilizing reinforcement expectancy theory, a two-part study was undertaken to assess the effectiveness of communication strategies designed to improve initial and long-term medical adherence (Klingle & M. Burgoon, 1995). The first study analyzed patients' evaluations of communication regard strategies and the effectiveness of these strategies in initial encounters. It was predicted that physician sex would play a major role in patients' perceptions regarding language appropriateness, whereas message reward value was presumed to determine which acceptable messages would be motivating or persuasive. As predicted, negative regard strategies were perceived as more appropriate when used by male physicians than when used by female physicians. In addition, physician sex interacted with strategy effectiveness such that male physicians were persuasive if they used either positive or negative regard strategies, whereas female physicians were limited to using only positive regard strategies. The results also indicate that the use of negative regard strategies by men did not hinder satisfaction or physician perceptions, whereas the use of negative regard strategies by women was negatively related to these outcome measures. This latter finding provides a relatively complete replication of the earlier research conducted from a language expectancy theory perspective that obviously dealt with one-time medical encounters (e.g., M. Burgoon et al., 1991).

The second study analyzed the consequences of strategy combinations used over time by male and female physicians. Ongoing influence attempts, involving the same physician and patient, were created by combining four manipulated consultation sessions from Study 1 to create six conceptually different strategy combinations. Klingle and M. Burgoon (1995) confirmed the prediction that communication patterns involving occasional nonreinforcement produced more motivating reinforcement expectations and greater patient motivation than repetitive communication patterns (e.g., all positive, all negative, or all neutral combinations). The predicted interaction for physician sex, however, was not significant. In addition, no significant differences were found between male and female physicians on any of the dependent variables. In summary, although Study 1 confirmed predicted sex differences in language appropriateness perceptions for each of the episodes used to create strategy combinations in Study 2, these differences seemed to disappear when the single episodes were combined to create the appearance of an ongoing relationship with the physician. We concluded that communication expectations for established relationships have the potential to override sex role stereotypes.

Several researchers have claimed that getting to know a person causes sex role stereotypes to play a less significant role (Crocker, Fiske, & Taylor, 1984;

Deaux & Lewis, 1984) and that communication expectations are different for initial versus established relationships (Derlega, Winstead, Wong, & Greenspan, 1987; Roloff, 1987). According to Roloff (1987), dissatisfying communication exchanges are expected and tolerated more as relational familiarity increases. Given that Study 2 used the same episodes that were tested in Study 1 (and that were found to be evaluated differentially based on physician sex), the results of Study 2 seem to suggest that expectations for ongoing relationships may diminish sex role stereotypes.

In summary, neither of these studies do violence to the proposition, or the accumulated research evidence in psychology and communication, that men are generally more persuasive than women in a number of situations. The medical encounter was simply used to provide a clear context in which the credibility of male and female sources could be as equal as possible. It is important to note that not much has changed in the past 30 years to diminish the relative advantage of male persuaders compared with female persuaders in our culture, especially for one-shot influence attempts. However, the theoretical positions here suggest that communicator sex must be considered along with the kind of persuasive message being used if valid predictions about persuasive success are to be accurate.

These two theoretical formulations, along with supporting data, provide insight on when men and women are advised to develop message strategies to be optimally effective change agents. Moreover, it is clear that men do have a great latitude to select among available means of persuasion; women do not enjoy that same freedom and must carefully select message strategies or risk being ineffective in persuasive attempts. Although this research is certainly not offered as the final word on sex differences in the ability to influence, it at least offers some theoretical insights and prescriptive advice for how to tailor messages that goes considerably beyond just dismissing differences as due to perhaps an intractable difference in credibility of men and women in our society.

THE ISSUE OF GENDER DIFFERENCES
IN SUSCEPTIBILITY TO INFLUENCE ATTEMPTS

Existing Research Findings and Explanations

For many decades, it has been generally accepted that women were more susceptible to social influence than were men. The early social psychology literature simply accepted this susceptibility as an empirical regularity that required little scrutiny and/or explanation (Allen & Crutchfield, 1963; Reitan & Shaw, 1964; Whittaker, 1963). However, that tradition of acceptance gave way to a program of research by Alice Eagly and her associates

(Eagly, 1978; 1983; Eagly & Carli, 1981; Eagly, Wood, & Fishbaugh, 1981), which provided a close look at the accumulated data on female persuasibility. An objective reading of these data reaffirms that there is a consistent and predictable sex difference in persuasibility with women being generally more susceptible to influence attempts. Eagly and Carli (1981) reported an average effect size of .16, indicating that women are more influenceable than men. However, there are a variety of qualifications and speculations that seem to attempt to explain away these differences (as opposed to the usual way scientists attempt the process of explanation). In summary, they seem to indicate that they do not believe their own data. One could infer from the way they interpret the data that Eagly and Carli are implying that "Although we are women, we are never influenced; therefore, male scientists are wrong (especially Michael Burgoon)."

As stated earlier, researchers and writers have repeated these qualifications and speculations in the disciplines of communication and social psychology. One interpretation of this corpus of repetitive explanations is that the focus was on women and all scholars attempted to posit some sort of deficit model to discuss the phenomenon of the supposed susceptibility of women to persuasive messages. As is usual in the social sciences, the first proposed deficit was in the experimental methods used in the laboratory work being published. For example, O'Keefe (1990) provided a summary of the claimed methodological deficits in the persuasion research that have abounded in print since the work of Eagly and her associates was published.

The most often cited criticism is that the consistent patterns of differences in female susceptibility to influence is due to the fact that experimenters almost always used male topics in their research (i.e., topics on which males would have more knowledge and/or interest). Although this became a commonplace explanation in the literature, such a claim does not stand up under empirical scrutiny. Even the work of Eagly and Carli (1981) found that male topics were not overrepresented in the literature. In fact, some claim that this particular analysis found that persuasion topics used in research tended to be slightly more interesting to women than men (O'Keefe, 1990). The data did not deter this deficit hypothesis of topic contamination from remaining alive in the literature even though it is clearly not supportable by any research.

A second methodological deficit suggested that the underlying observed gender difference manifested as female susceptibility to influence was related to the sex of the investigator. Eagly and Carli (1981) claimed that female investigators find no sex differences in persuasibility, whereas male experimenters regularly find women to be more persuasible than men. Unfortunately, Eagly and Carli were unable to include very many women investigators in their study because most of the persuasion research of the time was being conducted by men. In a much more methodologically sound study, Becker (1986) provided no support for the thesis put forth by Eagly and Carli. Although there were other forays criticizing research methods, it has become clear that none is especially accurate and/or satisfactory.

Besides the account of female susceptibility to influence as a methodological artifact, we find another genre of deficit explanation: the socialization hypothesis, which suggests that women, from the time of birth, are taught to be nurturant, submissive, and accepting and to strive for social harmony. In contrast, men are taught to be critical, analytical, and independent thinkers. According to O'Keefe (1990) and many others, this cultural training and socialization are responsible for "creating conditions that foster the *appearance* of sex differences in persuasibility" (p. 177; italics added). This is still a deficit-type explanation in that all of the writers seem to believe that the persuasibility of women is some sort of a problem that needs to be explained away by some quasipolitically correct discourse. However, the conclusions of O'Keefe and others who have touted this explanation have the *appearance* of an extremely sexist interpretation; moreover, there is absolutely no way that the socialization/acculturation hypothesis can be falsified by scientific research. It is a political observation without a shred of evidence to suggest that any such early learning is related to gender differences in susceptibility to influence.

Likewise, Petty and Cacioppo (1986) claimed that women engage in more peripheral rather than central processing of arguments—a cognitive interpretation not unlike the so-called socialization hypotheses suggesting that men are more analytical in information processing (analogous certainly to the so-called central processing schema in the elaboration likelihood model [ELM]). Again, the evidence to support such an information-processing difference is not compelling because falsification of route usage is near impossible. Moreover, ELM apears to provide another deficit explanation focused on women.

An alternative explanation is to simply dismiss the findings as small (O'Keefe, 1990)—a claim that is completely inaccurate and not isomorphic with the published research. By making such a claim, O'Keefe can therefore imply that such differences are of little import. The differences, however, are not small. If one converts the published data to binomial standardized effect sizes, one could conclude that 20% to 25% of women tend to be more persuasible than is the population of men. That is clearly neither a small nor trivial difference.

If one wanted to keep the focus on women to account for these differences, female superiority explanations could be advanced that actually negate the claim that the data suggest some sort of negatively laden term like *female gullibility* as the root cause of these differences or that suceptibility to influence is a problem of and for females. More flattering explanations are no less speculative nor necessarily more correct than the deficit models discussed earlier, but they are certainly less discussed in the literature.

For instance, one might suggest that the phenomenon of female persuasibility is biologically determined in that women have a superior ability to act on larger amounts of information and, thus, are changed when they receive new information. There is as much evidence to support this kind of speculation as there is to accept the socialization/acculturation claims. It might also be suggested that, because most of the data have been collected in scientific experiments in which we would expect people to use rational arguments and evidence to elicit change, the *desired* and *appropriate* response in most experiments is to change, not to be resistant to change. In this light, women being more persuasible could be viewed not as a deficit but as socially appropriate responses in the situations studied. Again, these explanations are no less reasonable than those that are much more popular in the literature. However, unlike our contemporaries, we suggest that there are little data to buttress our contentions. They are merely offered as illustrative of how a problem could as easily be viewed as a virtue. In addition, other ways of viewing gender differences in persuasibility, supported by a wealth of data overlooked by researchers in their discussion, appear to be a more productive path.

An Alternative Analysis of Gender Differences in Persuasibility

Clearly, although we accept that there are differences in how persuadable men and women are and do not quarrel with the claims that such regularity exists in the research literature, we are not enamored with the explanations offered for this empirical phenomenon. It appears that a major part of the confusion results from a focus on female susceptibility to influence, with its various deficit-type account models. It might be more fruitful to carefully examine the nonchange of males in attitude/persuasion research, although changes might be the socially appropriate response, as noted previously.

However, it is crucial that this attitudinal rigidity on the part of at least some men should not be confused by labeling men as *resistant to persuasion*, if that phrase is to retain the meaning it has had in the social science literature (M. Burgoon, Cohen, Miller, & Montgomery, 1978; McGuire, 1964; Miller & M. Burgoon, 1973). The resistance to persuasion paradigm is characterized by induced counterarguing, rational argumentation, and specific message strategies in which not changing is the appropriate response in the experimental situation. It is not claimed that men are more resistant to persuasive attempts because of an advantage over women in their ability to complete any of the aforementioned cognitive responses. Rather, we contend that a relatively large percentage of men are unwilling to change their attitudes and/or behaviors regardless of the situation, which is the cause of the regular main effect for gender and persuasibility that appears in the corpus of experimental research literature.

If one considers our earlier claim that the statistical data, when converted to binomial standardized effects, indicates that 20% to 25% of females are *more* willing to change their attitudes across situations, the corollary must be that it is logically (and empirically) just as likely that 20% to 25% of the male population is simply *less* willing. Although people have been so focused on the explanation of female susceptibility to change attempts, few have ventured to closely examine males' intractability across topics, situations, and time. However, data exist from a number of sources to suggest that such a focus on men would provide a more parsimonious explanation of gender differences than has been advanced to date. There are four lines of inquiry that provide intriguing data to buttress our claim that such a group of males indeed is responsible for the myriad of findings discussed in the gender and persuasion literature.

Sex Roles Versus Gender. Nearly 20 years ago, arguments were advanced that there was a conceptual obfuscation in the literature due to the focus on persuasibility rather than on an examination of actual attitude change or nonchange (Montgomery & M. Burgoon, 1978). Arguments about the inadequacy of explanations of gender differences were articulated in that early article, although there was insufficient evidence then to dismiss all of the socialization/acculturation claims and a host of other explanations that abounded at the time.

Montgomery and Burgoon (1978) found Bem's (1975) then recent research on sex roles and the concept of *androgyny* to be intriguing. Bem (1975) claimed that at least 35% of the population did not "march to a sex-typed drummer" (p. 8). According to this account, Bem had developed a measurement instrument to identify feminine females (traditional sex roles), androgynous males and females (nontraditional sex roles), and masculine males (traditional). Attempting to further examine the socialization/acculturation explanation, Montgomery and Burgoon reasoned that sex role socialization might explain sex differences in the persuasion research. Thus, we predicted an interaction between androgyny and sex such that traditional women would change more than traditionally sex typed men *and* that this difference would be greater than the difference between androgynous men and women. Had such a hypothesis received support, there would be empirical evidence to bolster socialization accounts of male–female differences in persuasibility. However, the results ran counter to their expectations. Specifically, traditional females, androgynous females, and androgynous males all demonstrated significant attitude change. Moreover, *no* differences in attitude change scores among these three groups were found. However, the group of masculine males (traditional sex roles), comprising 22% of their sample, demonstrated zero attitude change in the direction advocated by the messages. A comparison of the three change groups to the no-change group (traditional male) yielded a very large effect size ($\eta^2 > .40$).

Using a language expectancy theory perspective, Montgomery and M. Burgoon (1980) replicated these results with a different sample and selection of experimental topics. Simply stated, traditionally sex typed males, which was almost 25% of the second sample, again showed no attitude change toward the positions advocated in the multiple experimental messages. The other three groups changed attitudes as predicted in the different experimental conditions. Although Montgomery and Burgoon warned about basing predictions concerning attitude change or persuasibility on biological sex alone, their message did not penetrate the research world of either communication or psychology. It was their contention that persuasion researchers were likely to encounter a large portion (20%–25%) of any total sample population that would demonstrate little, if any, attitude change regardless of context, situation, or time.

Although androgyny as a factor in socialization was intended to bolster the socialization explanation offered by so many other investigators, it turned out, even if serendipitous, that the research of Montgomery and M. Burgoon (1978, 1980) was among the first to discount the efficacy of a socialization and female persuasibility explanation of gender differences in attitude change research.

Misanthropy (Cynical Hostility) and Gender Differences in Attitude Change. Some years later, a program of field research in health communication and compliance was completed by the first author; it shed further light on gender differences in social influence research (Alvaro & Burgoon, 1995). In a series of three studies, a variety of hypotheses about source evaluation, susceptibility to influence, effects of the mass media, and intent to change lifestyles and/or comply with physicians' prescriptions and suggestions were tested. The database for these studies consisted of a random sample of 1,310 adults between the ages of 18 and 82, with a mean age in the mid-40s—a representative sample of the population at large. Based on a cognitive-processing model, Alvaro and Burgoon (1995) developed a theoretical rationale that suggested how such people would derogate the sources of persuasive messages, inaccurately process and recall arguments, ascribe negative intent to change agents, and be generally resistant to prosocial persuasive attempts in the health care arena. Specifically, it was posited that any negative message cue directed at misanthropic individuals would result in a defensive heuristic processing of persuasive messages and a discounting of those persuasive messages so they would remain immune to influence.

The results were consistent with the predictions advanced by the theoretical rationale for how cynically hostile or misanthropic individuals would both process messages and evaluate sources. Although not primarily concerned with sex as a variable of theoretical interest, Alvaro and Burgoon's series of investigations provided some striking results for researchers interested in sex and persuasion. First, the population of cynically hostile/misanthropic individuals in the adult sample was relatively large (approximately 25%); moreover, more than 80% classified as cynically hostile were men (about 20% of the total sample). It was further demonstrated that these men who were cynically hostile had more stress-induced diseases, possessed more health risks than any other group in the studies, had a greater vested interest in complying with the prosocial health messages, and should have been highly involved in the message topics. However, this group was the most resistant to persuasion, most likely to discount messages, most likely to attribute negative motivations to message sources, and demonstrated almost no attitude or intent to behave differently.

Had Alvaro and Burgoon not segregated what turned out to be approximately 20% of their large sample into this predominantly male group they called *cynically hostile people*, they would have found a main effect for source credibility and attitude change/compliance with women being *more* positive and susceptible to influence, with about the same effect size as has been reported in the sex and persuasion literature for three decades. However, 80% of the sample (men and women) were almost identical in their responses, and the reporting of a main effect for sex would have been misleading at best. Again, what the data suggest is that about 20% of subjects (almost all men), whether in laboratory experiments or naturalistic environments, are not likely to show much if any attitude change regardless of topic, vested interest, or personal situation.

Reactance and Gender Differences in Response to Persuasive Messages. There are two notions of reactance from the literature of psychology that bear on the discussion of sex and persuasibility. First, the psychophysical reactivity model posits that hostility and aggression contribute to cardiovascular and other diseases through an association with physiological mechanisms such as heightened cardiovascular and neuroendocrine reactivity. This physiological reactance is predominantly a male phenomenon in our society and may be related to disease as well as general psychological states of distrust, cynicism, and inaction. Although a physiological explanation for males' resistance to persuasive attempts is tenuous at best, it is interesting that the people who were most likely to be candidates for physiological reactance fit the profile of the men in the Alvaro and Burgoon (1995) study, who demonstrated no changed attitudes or behaviors in health matters for which they were at high risk.

Another form of reactance—psychological reactance—is much more familiar to social scientists interested in influence processes. Although Brehm's (1966) theory of psychological reactance (Brehm & Brehm, 1981) has not generated much research in recent years, and in fact is considered to be a moribund theoretical artifact by many, there is a renewed interest in some quarters in this theoretical model. Briefly, psychological reactance is motivated by the individual's basic need for self-determination and in effecting his or her own environment. This need for effectance and autonomy is predicated on the basic assumption that, in regard to certain limited and specifiable areas of behavior, people have a distinct and strong preference to perceive themselves as masters of their own fate. The theory predicts that when an individual's perceived freedom is threatened by a proscribed attitude or behavior (many kinds of direct influence attempts), the individual will experience a motivating pressure toward reestablishing the threatened behavior (Heilman & Toffler, 1976). One way to restore freedom is to engage in the forbidden behavior or embrace the attitude threatened by the proscription (Brehm, 1966; Brehm & Brehm, 1981). Research supporting this type of restoration has demonstrated a phenomenon known as the *boomerang effect*—a condition producing the opposite effect than that desired—in response to persuasive messages.

This model of reactance could be of import to communication researchers investigating why people respond negatively to disease prevention and control messages that are prosocial in nature and meant to persuade people to lead a healthier life and avoid diseases. Questions about why subgroups of people behave in the opposite direction of persuasive messages advocating changes that are in their vested interests remain unexplained (Alvaro & Burgoon; 1995; M. Burgoon, 1996). It is interesting to note that psychological reactance, which is concerned with such boomerang effects, is more predominant among men than women and that adolescent and young men are highly reactive and most likely to engage in forbidden activities like substance abuse, the initiation of using tobacco products, and consumption of excessive amounts of alcohol (cf. Lee, Gilpin, & Pierce, 1993). Considerable evidence exists to suggest that young men are relatively immune to change attempts in the health arena as well as other campaigns stressing basically prosocial themes. That is another way of restating that there are a large number of men who are resistant to change on many topics. Because the experimental research that has spawned most of the discussion of sex differences in persuasion was completed on young college students, it is plausible to suggest that these young men, whether experiencing psychological reactance or not, are unlikely to change attitudes and behaviors in the situations studied. Thus, again there is reason to believe that the supposed female susceptibility to influence previously reported in a wealth of empirical research efforts is perhaps more a statistical artifact and an interpretation error that could be attributed to the behavior of a relatively sizable group of men who are immune to persuasive messages of various types and forms.

Incentives to Change Attitudes and Gender Differences in Persuasion. Much of the prior attitude change research that was reviewed and analyzed by people interested in female susceptibility to influence included a number of experiments that provided incentives for changing attitudes and/or behaviors (Becker, 1986; Eagly, 1978, 1983; Eagly & Carli, 1981; Eagly et al., 1981). Much of the early psychological research on persuasion was completed by researchers with some interest in learning models and the effects of various incentives on the change process. Sex differences might occur in reactions to incentives offered for changed behavior, which merit examination.

Deci (1971, 1975; Deci & Ryan, 1985) proposed cognitive evaluation theory, which has not been discovered by most communication scholars, to explicate the psychological need for effectance, competence, and self-determination that underlies intrinsically motivated behaviors and encourages internalization (as opposed to externally monitored compliance) in learning and attitude formation. Deci (1971) began his investigations by looking at the effects of externally mediated rewards on intrinsic motivation. This and other research resulted in robust findings demonstrating the deleterious effects of the controlling aspects of extrinsic rewards on intrinsically motivated activities in both children and adults. Lepper, Green, and Nisbett (1973) termed this undermining of intrinsic interest overjustification and warned against the ignorance of the net effects of certain reward systems on subsequent behavior. Of central theoretical importance is the notion that extrinsic incentives are considered nonself-determined (and what behaviorists would refer to as nonreinforcing) to the extent that they are coerced or pressured by an external contingency such as a promised reward. Such contingent rewards represent a threat to autonomy and thus can be expected to encourage psychological reactance, as discussed earlier.

In addition to Deci's cognitive evaluation theory, several other theoretical frameworks have attempted to explain the overjustification effect. In an attempt to integrate the various findings and theoretical perspectives, Crano and his colleagues (Crano, Gorenflo, & Shackelford, 1988; Crano & Sivacek, 1984) proposed an incentive-aroused ambivalence hypothesis. It predicts that the inducement of an attitude through the use of unnecessary extrinsic incentives can stimulate a mixed reaction on the part of the receiver, sensitizing him or her to the possibility that a change of opinion toward the attitude object might be appropriate. Such an ambivalent state in the mind of receivers prompts the question, What's the catch? or, more literally, What gives? and provides a reluctance to modify the underlying induced attitude.

The incentive-aroused ambivalence hypothesis predicts that extrinsic incentives will diminish internalization of an advocated attitudinal position if the receiver discovers (or invents) information that confirms the presence of a *catch*. Crano and associates' formulation of the overjustification effect can predict either a simple reinforcement effect or a reverse-incentive effect as a result of the confirmation or disconfirmation of the apprehension generated as a result of extrinsic inducements. Confirmation results in the belief that there is indeed a catch. Thus, confirmation represents a price to be paid to an external controlling agent. More important, it represents a threat to one's autonomy, freedom, and self-determination and produces reactance.

Not surprisingly, it has been demonstrated that men are significantly more likely than women to look for the catch, respond negatively to a variety of incentives, be suspicious of and derogate the incentive giver, and not change attitudes and/or behaviors in the presence of incentives (Alvaro & Burgoon, 1995). In fact, the group of cynically hostile/misanthropic men were more likely to change their attitudes in the opposite direction of the position advocated even in the presence of minimal, externally offered incentives to comply.

All of the explanations offered (sex roles, cynical hostility/misanthropy, reactance theory, and the overjustification effect) for the intractability of a relatively large group of men likely result from related cognitive-processing styles (or perhaps even the same style with different names applied) in the presence of influence attempts. However, each explanation is theoretically grounded. The consistent pattern of empirical data suggesting that a large group of male nonchangers is present in persuasion research presents a different focus for understanding sex differences in persuasion than has been offered previously in the literature.

CONCLUSION AND DISCUSSION

Although it is evident that we have been concerned with gender differences and persuasion for some time, we should mention that research programs in disease prevention and control reinvigorated our interest in sex/gender as a variable both from the point of view of differences in the influence abilities of male and female physicians and the effects of health messages designed to gain compliance in situations ranging from clinical encounters to mass media public health campaigns (M. Burgoon, 1996; M. Burgoon et al., 1991; Klingle, 1993, in press; Klingle & M. Burgoon, 1995). The discussion presented in this chapter details our views, supported by data, about gender differences in the ability to influence. Our intention was to provide information on how both women and men can tailor their persuasive messages to be more effective while recognizing that women have a restricted range of choices on how they select persuasive messages compared with their male counterparts in this society. This analysis merely extends other research literatures documenting credibility and influence ability differences that are gender related and occur with regularity.

Our experience with the clinical practice of medicine rekindled our interest in a closer examination of sex differences in susceptibility to influence attempts, specifically compliance-gaining message strategies. We are not in agreement with others who claim support for large differences in male–female patient interactions with their physicians. It is a bit of a stretch to make much out of the extant differences and many treatises on gender differences in physician–patient interaction that are often political editorials rather than good science. There is a wealth of data to suggest that gender is not a predictor of patient compliance or persuasiveness in either clinical encounters or responses to public health campaigns (see M. Burgoon, 1995, 1996; M. Burgoon & J. Burgoon, 1990, for extensive reviews).

Such similarities in the susceptibility of men and women to health-related messages appear to be quite at odds with a voluminous amount of research suggesting that differences exist. The explanation for the similarities is not overly complex. All medical research, whether social scientific or clinical in nature, suffers from including only patients as part of the subject pool. Nonpatients are rarely, if ever, discussed in the disease prevention and control literature. Alvaro and Burgoon (1995) provided a summary of the evidence that research teams led by the first author had been presenting for about 10 years. Simply stated, samples of patients underestimate the numbers of men between the ages of 45–64 who are at risk for cancer and cardiovascular disease, but who are committed health care avoiders; they simply avoid physicians and other health professionals. Given that this group of men resists persuasion and change, it is quite possible that their unintentional exclusion from many research efforts may be the best explanation for the nonsignificant differences in male and female susceptibility to influence attempts in patient populations. Were this group to be included, it is highly likely that data collected in this socially important, naturalistic environment would mirror that regularly found in laboratory research efforts.

It is obvious that our focus on men as an explanation for gender differences in susceptibility to influence is somewhat unique; the usual concern has been on explaining why women are more persuasible. Not only is our focus different from others who have examined this area but, more important, the explanations offered here are grounded in theory-based research and supported by empirical data; they make absolutely no attempt to suggest that *all* men can be discussed as either susceptible or resistant to persuasion. Rather, we have specified the characteristics of 20% to 25%

of the population that might be responsible for misdirecting the attention of others interested in gender differences to only examine deficits in women as usually unverifiable explanations/speculations. Some may claim that we have just substituted a male deficit model for the more typical female deficit model. Although we might not appreciate our work being labeled a male-deficit model, we would concede that one could view the resistance of a part of the male population as some sort of deficit explanation. However, that is quite different from talking about all males or all females in any one explanatory attempt.

Our conclusions about gender differences and similarities in social influence attempts could have a major influence on how researchers treat sex and gender differences in future discussions. Whether such an attempt will have much impact on those satisfied with either politically expedient arguments or base speculations on innate or socialized differences is yet to be seen.

ACKNOWLEDGMENTS

This research was supported, in part, by funds from the National Cancer Institute, National Institutes of Health, #RO1CA62968 and #RO1CA 59726, and by an award from the National Institutes of Child Health/Human Development, National Institutes of Health, #1RO1HD31360, from the Gannett Foundation of Arlington, VA, and from the Office of the Provost of the University of Arizona to the first author. The opinions and interpretations are those of the authors and not the named funding agencies.

REFERENCES

Allen, V. L., & Crutchfield, R. S. (1963). Generalizations of experimentally reinforced conformity. *Journal of Abnormal and Social Psychology, 67,* 326–333.

Alvaro, E. M., & Burgoon, M. (1995). Individual differences in responses to social influence attempts: Theory and research on the effects of misanthropy. *Communication Research, 22,* 347–384.

Andersen, P. A. (1984, April). *An arousal-valence model of immediacy exchange.* Paper presented at the Central States Speech Association Convention, Chicago.

Becker, B. J. (1986). Influence again: An examination of reviews and studies of gender differences in social influence. In J. S. Hyde & M. C. Lynn (Eds.), *The psychology of gender: Advances through meta-analysis* (pp. 178–209). Baltimore, MD: Johns Hopkins University Press.

Bem, S. L. (1975, September). Androgyny versus the tight little lives of fluffy women and chesty men. *Psychology Today, 9,* p. 58.

Brehm, J. W. (1966). *A theory of psychological reactance.* New York: Academic Press.

Brehm, S. S., & Brehm, J. W. (1981). *Psychological reactance: A theory of freedom and control.* San Diego: Academic Press.

Brewer, M. B., & Crano, W. S. (1994). *Social psychology.* St. Paul, MN: West.

Burgoon, J. K., & Hale, J. L. (1988). Nonverbal expectancy violations: Model elaboration and application to immediacy behaviors. *Communication Monographs, 55,* 58–79.

Burgoon, M. (1989). The effects of message variables on opinion and attitude change. In J. Bradac (Ed.), *Messages in communication sciences: Contemporary approaches to the study of effects* (pp. 129–164). Newbury Park, CA: Sage.

Burgoon, M. (1990). Social psychological concepts and language: Social influence. In H. Giles & P. Robinson (Eds.), *Handbook of social psychology and language* (pp. 51–72). London: Wiley.

Burgoon, M. (1995). Communication between physicians and patients: Methods for gaining compliance. In L. Fuller & L.M. Shilling (Eds.), *Communicating about communicable diseases* (pp. 225–242) Amherst, MA: HRD Press.

Burgoon, M. (1996). (Non)compliance with disease prevention and control messages: Communication correlates and psychological predictors. *Journal of Health Psychology, 1,* 279–296.

Burgoon, M., Birk, T., & Hall, J. (1991). Compliance and satisfaction with physician-patient communication: An expectancy theory interpretation of gender differences. *Human Communication Research, 18,* 177–208.

Burgoon, M., & Burgoon, J. (1990). Compliance-gaining and health care. In J.P. Dillard (Ed.), *Seeking compliance: The production of interpersonal influence messages* (pp. 161–188). Phoenix, AZ: Gorsuch Scarisbrick.

Burgoon, M., Cohen, M. M., Miller, M. D., & Montgomery, C. L. (1978). An empirical test of a model of resistance to persuasion. *Human Communication Research, 5,* 27–39.

Burgoon, M., Dillard, J. P., & Doran, N. (1984). Friendly or unfriendly persuasion: The effects of violations of expectations by males and females. *Human Communication Research, 10,* 283–294.

Burgoon, M., Jones, S. B., & Stewart, D. (1975). Toward a message-centered theory of persuasion: Three empirical investigations of language intensity. *Human Communication Research, 1,* 240–256.

Burgoon, M., & Miller, G. R. (1985). An expectancy interpretation of language and persuasion. In H. Giles & R. St. Clair (Eds.), *Recent advances in language, communication, and social psychology* (pp. 199–229). London: Lawrence Erlbaum Associates.

Burgoon, M., & Miller, G. R. (1990). PATHS. *Communication Monographs, 57,* 152–160.

Burgoon, M., & Stewart, D. L. (1974). Toward a message-centered theory of persuasion: Empirical investigations of language intensity: I. The effects of sex of source, receiver, and language intensity on attitude change. *Human Communication Research, 1,* 241–248.

Cann, A., Sherman, S. J., & Elkes, R. (1975). Effects of initial request size and timing of the second request on compliance: The foot-in-the-door and the door-in-the-face. *Journal of Personality and Social Psychology, 32,* 774–782.

Cappella, J. N., & Green, J. O. (1982). A discrepancy-arousal explanation of mutual influence in expressive behavior for adult and infant-adult interaction. *Communication Monographs, 49,* 89–114.

Crano, W. D., Gorenflo, D. W., & Shackelford, S. L. (1988). Overjustification, assumed consensus and attitude change: Further investigation of the incentive-aroused ambivalence hypothesis. *Journal of Personality and Social Psychology, 55,* 12–22.

Crano, W. D., & Sivacek, J. (1984). The influence of incentive-aroused ambivalence on overjustification effects in attitude change. *Journal of Experimental Social Psychology, 20,* 137–158.

Crocker, J., Fiske, S. T., & Taylor, S. E. (1984). Schematic bases of belief change. In J. R. Eiser (Ed.), *Attitudinal judgment* (pp. 197–226). New York: Springer-Verlag.

Deci, E. L. (1971). Effects of externally mediated rewards on intrinsic motivation. *Journal of Personality and Social Psychology, 18,* 105–115.

Deci, E. L. (1975). *Intrinsic motivation.* New York: Plenum.

Deci, E. L., & Ryan, R. M. (1985). *Intrinsic motivation and self-determination in human behavior.* New York: Plenum.

Deaux, K., & Lewis, L. L. (1984). The structure of gender stereotypes: Interrelationships among components and gender label. *Journal of Personality and Social Psychology, 46,* 991–1004.

Derlega, V. J., Winstead, B. A., Wong, P. T., & Greenspan, M. (1987). Self-disclosure and relationship development: An attributional analysis. In M. E. Roloff & G. R. Miller (Eds.), *Interpersonal processes: New directions in communication research* (pp. 172–187). Beverly Hills, CA: Sage.

Dillard, J. P., Hunter, J. E., & Burgoon, M. (1984). A meta-analysis of two sequential request strategies for gaining compliance: Foot-in-the-door and door-in-the-face. *Human Communication Research, 10,* 461–488.

Eagly, A. H. (1978). Sex differences in influenceability. *Psychological Bulletin, 85,* 86–116.

Eagly, A. H. (1983). Gender and social influence: A social psychological analysis. *American Psychologist, 38,* 971–981.

Eagly A. H., & Carli, L. L. (1981). Sex of researchers and sex-typed communication as determinants of sex differences in influencability. *Psychological Bulletin, 90,* 1–20.

Eagly, A. H., & Chaiken, S. (1993). *The psychology of attitudes.* Ft. Worth, TX: Harcourt Brace.

Eagly, A. H., Wood, W. W., & Fishbaugh, L. (1981). Sex differences in conformity: Surveillance by the group as a determinant of male nonconformity. *Journal of Personality and Social Psychology, 40,* 384–394.

Eakins, B. W., & Eakins, R. G. (1978). *Sex differences in human communication.* Boston: Houghton-Mifflin.

Engleman, E. G. (1974). Attitudes toward women physicians: A study of 500 clinic patients. *Western Journal of Medicine, 120,* 95.

Harre, R. (1980). *Social being.* Totowa, NJ: Adams.

Heilman, M. E., & Toffler, B. L. (1976). Reacting to reactance: An interpersonal interpretation of the need for freedom. *Journal of Experimental Psychology, 12,* 519–529.

Infante, D. A., & Wigley, C. J. (1986). Verbal aggressiveness: An interpersonal model and measure. *Communication Monographs, 53,* 61–69.

Klingle, R. S. (1993). Bringing time into physician compliance gaining research: Toward a Reinforcement Expectancy Theory of strategy effectiveness. *Health Communication, 5,* 283–308.

Klingle, R. S. (1994). *Patient compliance and satisfaction with physician influence attempts: A reinforcement expectancy approach to compliance-gaining over time.* Unpublished doctoral dissertation, University of Arizona.

Klingle, R. S., & Burgoon, M. (1995). Patient compliance and satisfaction with physician influence attempts: A reinforcement expectancy approach to compliance gaining over time. *Communication Research, 22,* 148–187.

Klingle, R. S. (in press). Physician communication as a motivational tool for long-term compliance: Reinforcement Expectancy Theory. *Communication Studies.*

Lee, L., Gilpin, E. A., & Pierce, J. P. (1993). Changes in the patterns of initiation of cigarette smoking in the United States: 1950, 1965 and 1980. *Cancer Epidemiology Biomarkers Prevention, 2,* 593–597.

Lepper, M. R., Greene, D., & Nisbett, R. E. (1973). Undermining children's intrinsic interest with extrinsic reward: A test of the "overjustification" hypothesis. *Journal of Personality and Social Psychology, 28,* 129–137.

Littlejohn, S. W., & Jabusch, D. M. (1987). *Persuasive transactions.* Glenview, IL: Scott, Foresman.

Maheux, B., Dufort, R., & Beland, F. (1988). Professional sociopolitical attitudes of medical students: Gender references reconsidered. *Journal of American Medical Women, 43,* 7376–7379.

Maheux, B., Dufort, F., Beland, F., Jacques, A., & Levesque, A. (1990). Female medical practitioners: More preventive and patient oriented? *Medical Care, 28,* 87–92.

Marwell, G., & Schmitt, D. R. (1967a). Compliance-gaining behavior: A synthesis and model. *Sociological Quarterly, 8,* 317–328.

Marwell, G., & Schmitt, D. R. (1967b). Dimensions of compliance-gaining behavior: An empirical analysis. *Sociometry, 30,* 350–364.

McGuire, W. J. (1964). Inducing resistance to persuasion: Some contemporary approaches. In L. Berkowitz (Ed.), *Advances in experimental social psychology* (Vol. 1, pp. 191–229). San Diego, CA: Academic Press.

Miller, G. R., Boster, F., Roloff, M., & Seibold, D. (1977). Compliance-gaining message strategies: A typology and some findings concerning effects of situational differences. *Communication Monographs, 44,* 37–51.

Miller, G. R., Boster, F., Roloff, M., & Seibold, D. (1987). MBRS rekindled: Some thoughts on compliance gaining in interpersonal settings. In M. E. Roloff & G. R. Miller (Eds.), *Interpersonal processes: New directions in communication research* (pp. 89–116). Newbury Park, CA: Sage.

Miller, G. R., & Burgoon, M. (1973). *New techniques of persuasion.* New York: Harper & Row.

Montgomery, C. L., & Burgoon, M. (1978). An experimental study of the interactive effects of sex and androgyny on attitude change. *Communication Monographs, 44,* 130–135.

Montgomery, C. L., & Burgoon, M. (1980). The effects of androgyny and message expectations on resistance to persuasive communication. *Communication Monographs, 47,* 56–67.

O'Keefe, D. (1990). *Persuasion: Theory and research.* Newbury Park, CA: Sage.

Petty, R. E., & Cacioppo, J. T. (1886). The elaboration likelihood model of persuasion. In L. Berkowitz (Ed.), *Advances in experimental social psychology* (Vol. 19, pp. 123–205). Orlando, FL: Academic Press.

Reitan, H. T., & Shaw, M. E. (1964). Group membership, sex-composition of the group and conformity behavior. *Journal of Social Psychology, 64,* 45–51.

Roloff, M. E. (1987). Communication and reciprocity within intimate relationships. In M. E. Roloff & G. R. Miller (Eds.), *Interpersonal processes: New directions in communication research* (pp. 11–38). Beverly Hills, CA: Sage.

Rosenberg, P. R. (1979). Catch-22-The medical model. In E. C. Shapiro & L. M. Lowenstein (Eds.), *Becoming a physician: Development of values and attitudes in medicine* (pp. 81–92). Cambridge, MA: Ballinger.

Scanzoni, J. H. (1975). *Sex roles, life styles, and childbearing.* New York: The Free Press.

Whittaker, J. (1963). Opinion change as a function of communication-attitude discrepancy. *Psychological Reports, 13,* 763–772.

Weisman, C. S., & Teitelbaum, M. A. (1985). Physician gender and the physician-patient relationship: Recent evidence and relevant questions. *Social Science and Medicine, 20,* 1119–1127.

Weisman, C. S., & Teitelbaum, M. A. (1989). Women and health care communication. *Patient Education and Counseling, 13,* 183–199.

Chapter 12

Theoretical Approaches to Understanding Sex Differences and Similarities in Conflict Behavior

Lynda M. Sagrestano
Southern Illinois University at Carbondale

Christopher L. Heavey
University of Nevada at Las Vegas

Andrew Christensen
University of California at Los Angeles

If a trip to the psychology section at your local bookstore were any indicator, a creature visiting from another place and time would be compelled to believe that men and women are two inherently different beings. Popular psychology and the media have grabbed on to the notion that the sexes differ and have built a multimillion dollar industry out of telling us why we are different and how we can learn to live with each other (e.g., Gray, 1992). But does the evidence from research support this notion? Do women speak one language and men another or are men and women basically the same?

In this chapter, we outline two schools of thought that have developed in the psychological literature to address the question of whether men and women are similar or different. The first approach is an *individual differences approach,* in which characteristics of the individual, such as biological sex, are examined to understand group differences in behavior. The second approach is a *social structural approach,* in which characteristics of the social context, both at the situational level and at the broader social-cultural level, are examined to understand the behavior of individuals in situations. An individual differences approach focuses on between-group variability while neglecting within-group variability, which is often much greater (Feingold, 1995; Hare-Mustin & Marecek, 1988, 1990; Unger, 1979), whereas a social structural approach focuses on within-group variability but may neglect between-group differences. This chapter first presents the theoretical underpinnings for each of these approaches. Second, it provides empirical evidence for and against these approaches from research in the area of conflict in marriage and the use of social influence techniques in peer and marital relationships. The chapter concludes with a discussion of the importance of identifying gender differences and similarities, and, when there are differences, understanding the underlying mechanisms that lead to these differences.

INDIVIDUAL DIFFERENCES APPROACHES

One individual differences approach is a biological or physiological approach. From this perspective, men and women are biologically or physiologically different. As a result, they respond differently to certain types of stimuli, thus resulting in behavioral differences. These differences are presented as innate to men and women, residing within the individual. For example, men have been found to react more physiologically to stress (Gottman & Levenson, 1986, 1988). This difference in physiology has been used to explain behavioral differences between men and women. Specifically, researchers have suggested that, as a result of their physiological reactivity, men withdraw more from conflict with their spouses than do women, in an attempt to avoid discomfort (Gottman & Levenson, 1988; Levenson, Carstensen, & Gottman, 1994). However, these assertions have not been empirically tested.

A second individual differences approach is a socialization approach, growing out of psychodynamic theory. It suggests that men and women grow up in different social worlds, develop different identities, pursue different goals, and, as a result, behave differently. Miller (1976) posited that women develop a sense of self that is organized around forming and maintaining relationships, in contrast to men, who develop a sense of self that is organized around separation from others. Building on the work of Miller (1976), Chodorow (1978) and Rubin (1983) posited that the differences between women and men derive from the traditional family structure, wherein women assume responsibility for early child care (Chodorow, 1978; Rubin, 1983). Boys and girls grow up in different social environments. Although both boys and girls experience the same developmental imperatives, the tasks they must perform are different, and these differences lead to profound sex differences in personality, which are formed at an early age, deep rooted, and hard to change (Rubin, 1983).

Gilligan (1982) hypothesized that these differences in personality have far reaching effects on the behavior of women and men. She argued that women and men have different ways of imagining the human condition and different values. These differences in perspective lead to differences in their ways of relating to each other, with women approaching issues from an ethic of responsibility and caring for others, and men approaching issues from an ethic of fairness and justice. Gilligan suggested that women's development follows a different trajectory from men's development, noting the importance of valuing women's voices. This notion has led to further theorizing on women's ways of knowing (Belenky, Clinchy, Goldberger, & Tarule, 1986), with a focus on connected knowing or relational development (Jordan, Kaplan, Miller, Stiver, & Surrey, 1991). These theorists posited that women's ways of thinking and relating grow out of their experiences in families and schools that devalue them and their ideas, thus compelling women to work in collaboration with others in a connected community where they learn through sharing and listening to others and women's ideas are valued. Ultimately, women have a predisposition for connection with others, which affects their communication behavior (Belenky et al., 1986; Jordan et al., 1991).

Much research has focused on the notion of men and women communicating in different ways based on their different orientations. Lakoff (1975) began the focus on sex differences in communication styles by asserting that women's speech is overly polite, hesitant, deferential, and as a result, ineffective. Her analysis sparked the assertiveness training movement, designed to cure women of their poor communication styles (see Crawford, 1995, for a full discussion of the assertiveness training movement). More recently, Tannen (1990) has received substantial attention in both the academic literature and the popular media for her work on sex differences in communication. According to Tannen, boys and girls grow up in different environments that require them to use language for different purposes. Girls use language to seek confirmation and reinforce intimacy, usually in dyadic or small group situations. In contrast, boys interact in larger groups and use language to protect their independence and negotiate status in the group. These patterns of communication are learned in childhood and become a part of women's and men's interaction styles in adulthood. Similar to the analyses of Chodorow and Rubin, Tannen posited that women's language centers on connection and intimacy. Women use language to negotiate friendship networks, minimize differences among network members, and avoid status hierarchies. In contrast, men's language centers on maintaining independence as a means of establishing their place in the status hierarchy. As a result, Tannen argued that men and women not only use language differently, but they also interpret conversations differently. What is offensive from one perspective is completely logical from the other, thus leading to conflict. Tannen proposed that the solution requires men and women to understand the underlying differences that motivate their divergent conversational styles and accept these differences as fundamental and nonchangeable.

SOCIAL STRUCTURAL APPROACHES

The individual differences approach to understanding sex differences and similarities in behavior met with much criticism from many psychologists who felt that sex differences were being exaggerated and politicized (Crawford, 1989). Specifically, empirical psychologists argued that the consideration of sex as a biological category does not recognize social structural differences (i.e., situational and sociocultural differences in contextual factors) in the experiences of women and men. Researchers were focusing on person-based causes of differences instead of examining the social, historical, and cultural forces that underlie these apparent differences, such as the uneven balance of power between women and men, which may be more predictive of behavior (Crawford, 1989, 1995; Hare-Mustin & Marecek, 1988, 1990; Yoder & Kahn, 1992). Including social structural factors allows researchers to find possible underlying mechanisms of emerging individual differences (Fine & Gordon, 1989; Hare-Mustin & Marecek, 1988, 1990).

The social structural approach emerged to encompass sociocultural variables into theories designed to explain sex differences and similarities in behavior. Unger (1979) proposed that we use the term *sex* to refer to biological mechanisms and physiological differences between women and men, but the term *gender* to refer to the "nonphysiological components of sex that are culturally regarded as appropriate to males or to females" (p. 1086). However, this terminology does not solve the problem of determining which differences are due to sex and which are due to gender. At the core of this confusion is the difficulty in determining causality, as the mechanisms underlying most behaviors likely have both biological and sociocultural components (Deaux, 1993; Unger & Crawford, 1993).

Within the literature on social structural approaches to studying sex and gender, power and social roles have emerged as variables of particular interest (Eagly, 1983, 1987; Henley, 1977; Sagrestano, 1992a, 1992b; Sherif, 1982; Unger, 1978; Wallston, 1987; Yoder & Kahn, 1992). One major theory that exemplifies the social structural approach is the social role model (Eagly, 1983, 1987; Eagly & Steffen, 1984; Eagly & Wood, 1982). According to the social role model, men and women are differentially distributed into social roles, with men tending to occupy higher status roles than women. High status has been found to be associated with expectations of high competence, and men are perceived to be more competent than women (Wood & Karten, 1986). As a result of the unequal distribution of men and women into social roles, individuals perceive women as more easily influenced than men because lower status individuals are seen as more easily influenced (Eagly & Wood, 1982). In addition, Eagly suggested that the distribution of women and men into social roles underlies current gender stereotypes. For example, people in homemaker roles (usually women) are regarded as more communal, whereas people in employee occupations are perceived as more agentic (Eagly & Steffen, 1984). This hierarchical distribution leads to social norms that then legitimize the unequal status of women and men. This may lead to a type of self-fulfilling prophesy in which expectancies about men and women are played out in interactions that confirm expectations and therefore maintain them (Eagly, 1983, 1987). The social role model suggests that as men's and women's roles change, gender differences will also change, such that as women gain status in society, gender differences will decrease (Eagly, 1983).

The exploration of the effects of social structural variables on communication was sparked by Henley's (1977) book *Body Politics*, in which she outlined how those with power use language to maintain the social hierarchy. For example, those with power or authority often touch their subordinates but subordinates rarely touch their supervisors. As men tend to hold higher status positions, they tend to touch others more often. When the balance of power is more evenly distributed, sex differences are reduced. Although Henley's original analysis pertained to nonverbal communication, her argument is equally relevant to verbal forms of communication (Crawford, 1995; Thorne, Kramarae, & Henley, 1983). Crawford and Henley argued that little evidence exists to support the notion that women and men use language differently (Crawford, 1995; Henley & Kramarae, 1991). Instead, differences can be explained as *transactional.* In other words, observed differences between men and women are not a function of sex, but a function of situations and interactions that encourage certain types of behaviors while suppressing other types. For example, situations in which men routinely have more power than women may encourage men to touch women more often than women touch men. As such, these types of gender differences are not rooted in early socialization, as is argued in an individual differences approach, but rather in social power and how it shapes our verbal and nonverbal language. By focusing on sex rather than other social structural variables such as power relationships, social structural variables become invisible (Crawford, 1995).

It is possible to conduct research in which these approaches are compared and contrasted. Two such programs of research in the area of communication and conflict interaction that have addressed such issues are presented in the following sections.

THE DEMAND–WITHDRAW INTERACTION PATTERN AND MARITAL CONFLICT

One of the earliest empirical studies of marriage (Terman, Buttenwieser, Ferguson, Johnson, & Wilson, 1938) found wives often complained that their husbands were emotionally or physically withdrawn, whereas husbands complained about feeling pressured and nagged by their wives. More recent studies have indicated that women tend to be more conflict engaging and coercive, whereas men are more pacifying and withdrawing (see review by Gottman & Levenson, 1988). In our own studies of the demand–withdraw interaction pattern (a pattern in which one partner tries to discuss problems, criticizes and blames the partner for the problems, and requests or demands change while the other partner tries to avoid discussion of the problems, defends self against the criticisms, and withdraws from the discussion), we have consistently found that women are more likely to be demanding and men withdrawing whether they are assessed with self-report measures (Christensen, 1987; Christensen & Shenk, 1991) or observational measures (Christensen & Heavey, 1990; Heavey, Layne, & Christensen, 1993; Heavey, Christensen, & Malamuth, 1995).

What leads to this asymmetry in interaction and its association with gender? Why does one partner demand and the other withdraw, and why is the former usually the woman and the latter the man? To answer this question, we must first make an important distinction between the structure and the process of conflict (Christensen & Heavey, 1993). The *structure* of conflict means the conflict of interest between people (Peterson, 1983), that is, the differences between them that create a problem or dilemma for them. The *process* of conflict means the overt conflictual interaction that takes place between them. For example, a couple may have a structural conflict about how much time they should spend with the wife's family of origin. She wants to spend a lot of time; he wants to spend little time. The process of their conflict refers to how they solve this problem through their interaction. For example, one could regularly give in to the other but pout about it, they could mutually criticize each other for their positions, either one could try to gently persuade the other, and so forth.

A frequent structural conflict in marriage concerns the amount of closeness or intimacy spouses desire in their relationship (Christensen, 1987; Jacobson, 1989). We reasoned that this conflict might lead to a conflict process of demand–withdraw interaction. The spouse wanting greater closeness might engage in demanding behaviors because these behaviors could bring about closeness—trying to talk to the other about the problem, criticizing the other for his or her distance, and requesting or demanding greater closeness. However, the partner wanting greater distance might naturally engage in withdrawing behaviors to achieve distance—avoiding conversation, defending one's position regarding distance, and withdrawing from any conversation about distance. Based on the work of Miller (1976), Chodorow (1978), and Rubin (1983) described earlier, we also reasoned that women would be more likely than men to want greater closeness and intimacy. Therefore, women would more likely demand because of women's greater interest in closeness and intimacy.

To test this idea, we developed a measure of conflict over closeness and intimacy (Christensen, 1987). In three studies, we have shown that the amount of structural conflict regarding closeness is positively correlated with the total amount of demand–withdraw interaction (Christensen, 1987; Christensen & Shenk, 1991; Walczynski, Schmidt, Christensen, & Sweeney, 1991). That is, couples who reported discrepancies in their desired closeness (more time together, more sharing of feelings) and independence (more time alone, more privacy) were more likely to report engaging in the demand–withdraw interaction pattern. We also found that women want greater closeness, and (in spouses, but not dating couples) those who want greater closeness more likely occupy the demanding role (Christensen, 1987; Walczynski et al., 1991).

Despite its importance, conflict over closeness is hardly the only conflict that troubles couples. Other conflicts also likely lead to the demand–withdraw interaction pattern. We reasoned that conflicts of interest, including the conflict over closeness in which there was an asymmetry in dependence on the partner for resolution of the conflict, would lead to demand–withdraw interaction. Asymmetry of dependence means that one person can achieve resolution of the conflict only with the partner's cooperation, but the other can achieve resolution of the conflict without the partner's cooperation. For example, in the conflict over closeness, the partner wanting greater closeness can only achieve that goal with the partner's cooperation. However, the partner wanting greater distance can achieve that unilaterally. Conflicts of interest with asymmetry of dependence can be distinguished from conflicts of interest with symmetrical dependence. For example, if Marge wants to spend the Christmas holidays with her family and Joe wants to spend them with his family and they both want to be together for these holidays, there is a conflict with symmetrical dependence. Both Marge and Joe are dependent on the other for the successful resolution of the conflict. Neither can unilaterally achieve his or her goal.

We reasoned that in a conflict with asymmetrical dependence, the partner who needed the other's cooperation for resolution of the conflict would likely engage in demanding behavior. However, the partner who can achieve satisfaction without the other would likely engage in withdrawing behavior. To test these ideas we conducted three studies where we compared spouse's interaction under two conditions: one in which they discussed an issue identified by the wife and one in which they discussed an issue identified by the husband. We solicited issues in which the husband or wife wanted change in the other because these kind of issues represent unequal dependence. If the wife selects an issue in which she wants change in her husband, she is dependent on him to make the change. He is not dependent on her to make a change in himself and is presumably more likely to favor the status quo of no change or is at least less invested in change than is his wife.

Two competing hypotheses were tested. From a social structural approach, we would expect to find that each partner was more likely to demand on their own issue and withdraw on their partner's issue. However, if the conflict interaction process operates independently from the structure of the conflict but is instead tied directly to the sex or personality of the participants, we would expect to find each partner having a similar, stable level of demand and withdraw across the two interactions. Thus, our study directly tested a social structural versus individual differences approach.

In the first study, Christensen and Heavey (1990) examined data from 31 couples who had boys ages 7 to 12 in a summer camp program. Because the study was conducted as part of this summer camp program, the focus was on changes in parenting. Parents were asked to rate how much change they would like in five areas of childrearing by their partner (e.g., being more positive with son, being more strict or consistent with son, etc.). They were then asked to discuss the area in which they had made the most extreme rating (i.e., they wanted the most change from their partner in this area). Results on both the self-report and observational measures indicated that the nature of the interaction shifted dramatically depending on what issue was discussed. Overall, a main effect emerged such that husbands and wives were more demanding on their own issues and more withdrawing on their partner's issues. However, an interaction effect emerged in which on wives' issues, wife demand–husband withdraw was much more likely than the reverse, whereas on husbands' issues, there were no differences between wife demand–husband withdraw and the reverse.

This study was limited by an exclusive focus on childrearing issues. Because childrearing has often been the primary province of the wife, perhaps wives have a greater investment in change on these issues. This disparity in the investment in these issues may have resulted in greater polarization on wives' issues than on husbands' issues. To correct this problem we conducted a study on 29 couples, each with a preschool age child (Heavey et al., 1993), but we asked husbands and wives to rate the amount of change they each wanted on 20 common areas of change in marriage that were not limited to childrearing issues (e.g., more affection, more time together). We selected issues for discussion that had high ratings of change and equivalent ratings of change (e.g., the husband's issue and the wife's issue had the same rating of change). In this way we hoped to ensure equal investment in change by both husband and wife. Despite this improvement in methodology, the results were essentially the same as in the first study on both self-report and observational measures. Spouses changed their interaction when they discussed different issues. They showed polarization in demand–withdraw on the wife's issues but not as much on the husbands' issues.

In a dissertation by Heavey (1991), we moved from a strict focus on change in partner because when we asked partners to talk about a specific change they wanted in the other we may have prompted them to be demanding. Instead, couples rated their dissatisfaction with a number of content areas such as finances and physical affection. The husband's issue was identified as the area in which he rated the most dissatisfaction; the wife's issue was the area in which she rated the most dissatisfaction. When the experimenters gave instructions to the couple, they asked them to discuss these content areas, not specific changes in them. Despite this different methodology (and a somewhat different observational coding system), the results were similar to those of the previous studies.

These three studies have consistently demonstrated an effect of conflict structure on demand–withdraw interaction. When partners discuss their own issue, they more likely demand, but when discussing their partner's issue they more likely withdraw. However, we found a greater polarization of demand–withdraw interaction when partners focused on women's issues than on men's issues.

We can now explain our finding that, overall, women are more likely to be demanding and men withdrawing in conflict (Christensen, 1987; Christensen & Heavey, 1990; Christensen & Shenk, 1991; Heavey et al., 1993; Heavey et al., 1995). Earlier we described data suggesting that women want more closeness in marriage than do men. Considerable data also demonstrate that women do the burden of housework and child care even when both spouses are employed full time outside the home (Biernat & Wortman, 1991). Therefore, it is not surprising that women in general (versus men) want more changes in marriage (Margolin, Talovic, & Weinstein, 1983). Often the kinds of changes they seek are that husbands have a closer relationship with them and be more involved in child care and housework. These changes can only be achieved with the husband's cooperation. However, if the husband does not want a closer relationship or greater involvement in housework or child care, he can simply not engage in the requisite behaviors. This conflict structure is precisely the kind that our studies suggest would elicit demands by the partner wanting change and withdrawing behavior by the partner not wanting change.

The problem remains of explaining the greater polarization that occurs in demand–withdraw interaction on women's issues versus men's issues. Our current inclination is to examine the history of the relationship to determine the possible reasons. Given that men tend to have greater resources in the marital relationship, and thus may be able to structure the relationship as they want, couples may have been more successful in resolving men's issues and accommodating men's needs. If women have deferred to men's wishes more often than men have deferred to women's wishes, a greater degree of polarization could be expected to develop as a pattern over time with women's issues. This explanation is consistent with a social structural view, that is, men's greater power in the social structure leads to different reactions to men's versus women's needs and desires for change.

Similarly, if women have simply had more desires for change than have men, couples are more likely to have had discussions around wives' desired changes than around husbands' desired changes. The greater frequency of discussion around these issues may lead to greater polarization in the stands that husbands and wives take. Thus, over time one might expect more conflict and greater polarization over women's issues. This explanation is more consistent with an individual differences approach, suggesting that women in general want more from relationships than men, which leads to differences in behavior. However, the underlying reason for women wanting more change and men wanting less change in the relationship may be socially determined rather than inherent to women. Thus, these explanations are not mutually exclusive; it is possible that both may find some support. Future empirical work is needed to shed light on these questions.

SOCIAL INFLUENCE TECHNIQUES

Much of the research on the use of social influence techniques has focused on individual differences and, in particular, sex differences (Falbo & Peplau, 1980; Kelley, Cunningham, Grisham, Lefebvre, Sink, & Yalom, 1978; Witteman & Fitzpatrick, 1986). For example, Falbo and Peplau found that, in a study of dating couples, men used more direct and bilateral techniques, whereas women used more indirect and unilateral techniques to influence their partners. From a social structural perspective, researchers have focused on power and social roles (Howard, Blumstein, & Schwartz, 1986; Kipnis, Schmidt, & Wilkinson, 1980), and have typically concluded that social roles play an important part in the choice of influence techniques. However, few studies have simultaneously examined sex, social roles, and the use of social influence techniques. Therefore, we conducted a series of studies to examine gender, social roles, and social influence in peer and marital relationships. These studies were designed to compare hypotheses derived from social structural and individual differences perspectives.

In the first study (Sagrestano, 1992a), college students responded to a series of scenarios in which social power was manipulated via expertise, which has been shown to be related to persuasiveness in previous research (French & Raven, 1959; Maddux & Rogers, 1980). Men and women responded to three scenarios in which they interacted with an imagined partner in situations in which they had different levels of interpersonal power: more power than their partner (expert), less power (novice), and the same amount of power (equivalent). The dyads were either same-sex or mixed-sex. No sex differences in the use of influence were found, and both men and women chose the same five techniques most often: persuasion, reasoning, discussing, asking, and persistence. However, direct techniques were used more often when participants had expert power over their partners, whereas bilateral techniques were the first choice of participants in the equivalent condition.

This study provided preliminary support for a social structural interpretation of the use of social influence techniques in nonintimate relationships. However, the self-report data and hypothetical nature limit the extent to which conclusions can be drawn about actual behavior. As such, we next designed a laboratory simulation in which we examined gender, social roles, and the use of influence using mixed-sex and same-sex dyads. In this study (Sagrestano, 1995), participants completed pretest questionnaires to determine their attitudes on a set of controversial issues. They were then matched into same-sex and mixed-sex dyads such that they disagreed on the topic of discussion, and were scheduled for the laboratory portion of the study. Social roles were manipulated through expertise, such that one participant was trained to be more expert on the topic than the other. Participants spent 10 minutes discussing the topic and trying to persuade their partners to agree with them; the interactions were coded for the use of influence techniques. Results indicate that expertise, but not gender, predicted the use of influence techniques. Furthermore, men and women in positions of high and low expertise power used techniques in similar sequences (e.g., persuasion, reasoning, discussing, asking, persistence).

Although this study provided additional support for a social structural interpretation of influence technique use in nonintimate relationships, both of the studies described earlier examined influence in settings depicting clear power differences. Furthermore, participants in the observational study met in the laboratory and did not have expectations for their relationship continuing beyond the experiment. Therefore, we designed the third study to examine the use of influence in ongoing marital relationships in which the balance of power was not externally delineated.

The third study (Sagrestano, Christensen, & Heavey, in press) used data from two existing studies (Christensen & Heavey, 1990; Heavey et al., 1993) to examine how social roles affect the use of social influence. We believe that social roles are conceptually linked to the power structure of the relationship. More specifically, we would argue that power in close relationships operates on at least two levels: the overarching balance of power, and domain-specific power that is manifested at the situational level (see Sagrestano et al., in press, for a more in-depth discussion of this issue). Given that power and social roles are not clearly defined in most close relationships, we chose to focus on a situational manipulation of social roles. However, we recognize that this approach does not allow for an examination of the effects of the overarching balance of power.

As described earlier, spouses spent time discussing two issues in their marriage: one in which the wife wanted change in the husband and one in which the husband wanted change in the wife. This created two alternate roles for the partners. In each discussion, one person enacted the role of seeking change, whereas the partner enacted the role of being asked to change and perhaps trying to avoid being influenced. Results replicating across both data sets support a social structural perspective. Social roles, operationalized as who was seeking change during a particular interaction, was related to the use of influence techniques, whereas sex was not (e.g., partners seeking change engaged in more explaining of behavior, defending behavior, and suggesting change; partners resisting change engaged in more questioning to clarify problems and use of self-attributions). These results suggest that men and women do not differ in their choice of influence techniques, but rather that when men and women occupy similar social roles they behave in similar fashion.

One limitation of our research on social influence in marriage is that no self-report measures of power were included. Instead, the balance of power was manipulated situationally through asymmetrical dependence. We are currently examining how the role of perceptions of the overall balance of power in the relationship affect behavior in asymmetrical dependence situations, allowing us to better disentangle the role of power in the use of social influence.

CONCLUSION

Research on the demand–withdraw interaction pattern supports both the individual differences approach and the social structural approach with regard to sex differences in communication. Specifically, in asymmetrical dependence situations, when partners discuss their own topics they are more likely to demand, whereas when discussing their partner's issues they are more likely to withdraw. This supports a social structural perspective in which the context of the goals of the interaction predicts demand–withdraw behavior.

The demand–withdraw interaction pattern, however, is more polarized on the women's issues than on the men's issues. That is, men and women are more likely to conform to rigid demand–withdraw patterns when the woman is requesting the man to change than when the man is requesting the woman to change. From a social structural perspective, this may reflect a pattern that has developed over time as a result of general asymmetry in the relationship. From an individual differences perspective, this may reflect a sex difference in relationship expectations resulting in women desiring more change. However, these two interpretations are confounded in that women's greater need for change may be the result of general power asymmetry in the relationship as well. Unfortunately, participants in marital research cannot be randomly assigned to be in the traditionally higher or lower power position (i.e., husband or wife). Therefore, neither a social structural nor an individual differences explanation can ever be ruled out. However, further research with same-sex intimate couples may help to further disentangle these effects.

The research on social influence can partially address the problem of random assignment in that two of the studies were conducted in peer relationships. By examining both same-sex and mixed-sex dyads, the role of broader asymmetry in the balance of power between women and men could be examined. The overwhelming lack of sex differences across individuals and dyads provides support for a social structural interpretation. This was further augmented by our marital studies of social influence in which sex differences again did not emerge.

These findings point out the importance of considering both individual difference and social structural variables when conducting research. An individual differences perspective tends to neglect within-group variability, whereas a social structural perspective tends to neglect between-group variability. Inclusion of both types of variables allows researchers to avoid both exaggerating and minimizing sex differences by examining the effects of each simultaneously. In doing so, we would be better able to understand the emerging pattern of sex differences and similarities.

ACKNOWLEDGMENTS

This research was supported, in part, by National Institute of Mental Health Training Grants (T32 MH15750 and T32 MH19933) to the first author.

REFERENCES

Belenky, M. F., Clinchy, B. M., Goldberger, N. R., & Tarule, J. M. (1986). *Women's ways of knowing: The development of self, voice, and mind.* New York: Basic Books.

Biernat, M., & Wortman, C. B. (1991). Sharing of home responsibilities between professionally employed women and their husbands. *Journal of Personality and Social Psychology, 60,* 844–860.

Chodorow, N. (1978). *The reproduction of motherhood: Psychoanalysis and the sociology of gender.* Berkeley: University of California Press.

Christensen, A. (1987). Detection of conflict patterns in couples. In K. Halweg & M. J. Goldstein (Eds.), *Understanding major mental disorders: The contribution of family interaction research* (pp. 250–265). New York: Family Process Press.

Christensen, A., & Heavey, C. L. (1990). Gender and social structure in the demand/withdraw pattern of marital conflict. *Journal of Personality and Social Psychology, 59*, 73–81.

Christensen, A., & Heavey, C. L. (1993). Gender differences in marital conflict: The demand–withdraw interaction pattern. In S. Oskamp & M. Costanzo (Eds.), *Gender issues in contemporary society*. Newbury Park, CA: Sage.

Christensen, A., & Shenk, J. L. (1991). Communication, conflict, and psychological distance in nondistressed, clinic, and divorcing couples. *Journal of Consulting and Clinical Psychology, 59*, 458–463.

Crawford, M. (1989). Agreeing to differ: Feminist epistemologies and women's ways of knowing. In M. Crawford & M. Gentry (Eds.), *Gender and thought: Psychological perspectives* (pp. 128–145). New York: Springer-Verlag.

Crawford, M. (1995). *Talking difference: On gender and language*. Thousand Oaks, CA: Sage.

Deaux, K. (1984). From individual differences to social categories: Analysis of a decade's research on gender. *American Psychologist, 39*, 105–116.

Deaux, K. (1993). Commentary: Sorry, wrong number–a reply to Gentile's call. *Psychological Science, 4*, 125–126.

Eagly, A. H. (1983). Gender and social influence: A social psychological analysis. *American Psychologist, 38*, 971–981.

Eagly, A. H. (1987). *Sex differences in social behavior: A social role interpretation*. Hillsdale, NJ: Lawrence Erlbaum Associates.

Eagly, A. H., & Steffen, V. J. (1984). Gender stereotypes stem from the distribution of men and women into social roles. *Journal of Personality and Social Psychology, 46*, 735–754.

Eagly, A. H., & Wood, W. (1982). Inferred sex differences in status as a determinant of gender stereotypes about social influence. *Journal of Personality and Social Psychology, 43*, 915–928.

Falbo, T., & Peplau, L. A. (1980). Power strategies in intimate relationships. *Journal of Personality and Social Psychology, 38*, 618–628.

Feingold, A. (1995). The additive effects of differences in central tendency and variability are important in comparisons between groups. *American Psychologist, 50*, 5–13.

Fine, M., & Gordon, S. M. (1989). Feminist transformations of/despite psychology. In M. Crawford & M. Gentry (Eds.), *Gender and thought: Psychological perspectives* (pp. 146–174). New York: Springer-Verlag.

French, J. R. P., Jr., & Raven, B. H. (1959). The bases of social power. In D. Cartwright (Ed.), *Studies in social power* (pp. 150–167). Ann Arbor: University of Michigan Press.

Gilligan, C. (1982). *In a different voice: Psychological theory and women's development*. Cambridge, MA: Harvard University Press.

Gottman, J., & Levenson, R. W. (1986). Assessing the role of emotion in marriage. *Behavioral Assessment, 8*, 31–48.

Gottman, J. M., & Levenson, R. W. (1988). The social psychophysiology of marriage. In P. Noller & M. Fitzpatrick (Eds.), *Perspectives on marital interaction* (pp. 182–200). Philadelphia: Multilingual Matters Ltd.

Gray, J. (1992). *Men are from Mars, women are from Venus: A practical guide to improving communication and getting what you want in your relationships*. New York: HarperCollins.

Hare-Mustin, R. T., & Marecek, J. (1988). The meaning of difference: Gender theory, postmodernism, and psychology. *American Psychologist, 43*, 455–464.

Hare-Mustin, R. T., & Marecek, J. (Eds.). (1990). *Making a difference: Psychology and the construction of gender*. New Haven, CT: Yale University Press.

Heavey, C. L. (1991). *Causes and consequences of destructive conflicts in romantic relationships: Cognitive, affective, and behavioral predictors of course and outcome*. Unpublished doctoral dissertation, University of California, Los Angeles.

Heavey, C. L., Layne, C., & Christensen, A. (1993). Gender and conflict structure in marital interaction: A replication and extension. *Journal of Consulting and Clinical Psychology, 61*, 16–27.

Heavey, C. L., Christensen, A., & Malamuth, N. M. (1995). The longitudinal impact of demand and withdrawal during marital conflict. *Journal of Consulting and Clinical Psychology, 63,* 797–801.

Henley, N. M. (1977). *Body politics: Power, sex, and nonverbal communication.* Englewood Cliffs, NJ: Prentice-Hall.

Henley, N. M., & Kramarae, C. (1991). Gender, power, and miscommunication. In N. Coupland, H. Giles, & J. M. Wiemann (Eds.), *"Miscommunication" and problematic talk* (pp. 18–43). Newbury Park, CA: Sage.

Howard, J. A., Blumstein, P., & Schwartz, P. (1986). Sex, power, and influence tactics in intimate relationships. *Journal of Personality and Social Psychology, 51,* 102–109.

Jacobson, N. (1989). The maintenance of treatment gains following social learning-based marital therapy. *Behavior Therapy, 20,* 325–336.

Jordan, J. V., Kaplan, A. G., Miller, J. B., Stiver, I. P., & Surrey, J. L. (1991). *Women's growth in connection: Writings from the Stone Center.* New York: Guilford.

Kelley, H. H., Cunningham, J. D., Grisham, J. A., Lefebvre, L. M., Sink, C. R., & Yalom, G. (1978). Sex differences in comments made during conflict within close heterosexual pairs. *Sex Roles, 4,* 473–492.

Kipnis, D., Schmidt, S. M., & Wilkinson, I. (1980). Intraorganizational influence tactics: Explorations in getting one's way. *Journal of Applied Psychology, 65,* 440–452.

Lakoff, R. (1975). *Language and woman's place.* New York: Harper & Row.

Levenson, R. W., Carstensen, L. L., & Gottman, J. M. (1994). The influence of age and gender on affect, physiology, and their intercorrelations: A study of long-term marriages. *Journal of Personality and Social Psychology, 67,* 56–68.

Maddux, J. E., & Rogers, R. W. (1980). Effects of source expertness, physical attractiveness, and supporting arguments on persuasion: A case of brains over beauty. *Journal of Personality and Social Psychology, 39,* 235–244.

Margolin, G., Talovic, S., & Weinstein, C. D. (1983). Areas of change questionnaire: A practical approach to marital assessment. *Journal of Consulting and Clinical Psychology, 51,* 920–931.

Miller, J. B (1976). *Toward a new psychology of women.* Boston: Beacon.

Peterson, D. R. (1983). Conflict. In H. H. Kelley, E. Berscheid, A. Christensen, J. H. Harvey, T. L. Huston, G. Levinger, E. McClintock, L. A. Peplau, & D. R. Peterson (Eds.), *Close relationships* (pp. 360–396). New York: Freeman.

Rubin, L. B. (1983). *Intimate strangers: Men and women together.* New York: Harper & Row.

Sagrestano, L. M. (1992a). Power strategies in interpersonal relationships: Effects of expertise and gender. *Psychology of Women Quarterly, 16,* 481–496.

Sagrestano, L. M. (1992b). The use of power and influence in a gendered world. *Psychology of Women Quarterly, 16,* 439–448.

Sagrestano, L. M. (1995). *The effects of gender and power on the use of influence techniques in peer relationships.* Manuscript submitted for publication.

Sagrestano, L. M., Christensen, A., & Heavey, C. L. (in press). Social influence techniques during marital conflict. *Personal Relationships.*

Sherif, C. W. (1982). Needed concepts in the study of gender identity. *Psychology of Women Quarterly, 6,* 375–398.

Tannen, D. (1990). *You just don't understand: Women and men in conversation.* New York: William Morrow.

Terman, L. M., Buttenwieser, P., Ferguson, L. W., Johnson, W. B., & Wilson, D. P. (1938). *Psychological factors in marital happiness.* New York: McGraw-Hill.

Thorne, B., Kramarae, C., & Henley, N. M. (1983). *Language, gender, and society.* Rowley, MA: Newbury House.

Unger, R. K. (1978). The politics of gender: A review of relevant literature. In J. A. Sherman & F. L. Denmark (Eds.), *The psychology of women: Future directions in research* (pp. 461–518). New York: Psychological Dimensions.

Unger, R. K. (1979). Toward a redefinition of sex and gender. *American Psychologist, 34,* 1085–1094.

Unger, R. K., & Crawford, M. (1993). Commentary: Sex and gender: The troubled relationship between terms and concepts. *Psychological Science, 4,* 122–124.

Walczynski, P. T., Schmidt, G. W., Christensen, A., & Sweeney, L. (1991, August). *Demand/withdraw interaction in dating couples.* Paper presented at the meeting of the American Psychological Association, San Francisco.

Wallston, B. S. (1987). Social psychology of women and gender. *Journal of Applied Social Psychology, 17,* 1025–1050.

Witteman, H., & Fitzpatrick, M. A. (1986). Compliance-gaining in marital interaction: Power bases, processes, and outcomes. *Communication Monographs, 53,* 130–143.

Wood, W., & Karten, S. J. (1986). Sex differences in interaction style as a product of perceived sex differences in competence. *Journal of Personality and Social Psychology, 50,* 341–347.

Yoder, J. D., & Kahn, A. S. (1992). Toward a feminist understanding of women and power. *Psychology of Women Quarterly, 16,* 381–388.

Chapter 13

A Comparison of Topics and Objectives in a Cross Section of Young Men's and Women's Everyday Conversations

Ruth Anne Clark
University of Illinois

Casual observers as well as scholars recognize that children across the globe spend several years of their lives in play that is largely segregated by sex (LaFreniere, Strayer, & Gauthier, 1984; Maccoby, 1988, 1990). This period of development, which can be observed as early as age 3 (Wasserman & Stern, 1978), is quite obvious by age 6 (Maccoby, 1988), extends until early adolescence (Maccoby, 1988), and creates an environment that makes it possible for each sex to establish unique interactional patterns.

In fact, a number of scholars have concluded that boys and girls do display differences in their interactional styles. Maltz and Borker (1983) summarized some of these differences. All-boy groups (compared with all-girl groups) exhibit more of the following kinds of behavior: heckling, storytelling, joke and suspenseful storytelling, interruptions, use of commands, refusal to comply with commands, threats, boasting, and giving information. In contrast to all-boy groups, all-girl groups display other kinds of behavior more frequently: acknowledging what the other has said, giving the other an opportunity to speak, and expressing agreement with what the other has said.

By early adolescence, the barrier to talking with members of the opposite sex begins to crumble, but many researchers believe that some important differences in interactional style remain. One difference frequently cited concerns the topics discussed. Bischoping (1993) reviewed the major studies of topic within each sex, beginning with the 1922 study by Henry T. Moore, and then attempted to replicate Moore's initial study. She concluded that, although differences in topic between all-female and all-male conversations are not as large today as they were three quarters of a century ago, differences in topics discussed by women and men still exist. Bischoping reported that women remain more likely to discuss members of the opposite sex and appearances, whereas men talk more about work and leisure activities. Phrased somewhat differently, but consistent with Bischoping's results, Samter, Burleson, Kunkel, and Werking (1994) concluded that in conversations of same-sex friends, "men typically discuss topical issues such as sports, careers, and politics whereas women focus on the discussion of feelings, motivations, relationships, and personal problems" (p. 4).

These differences in topics, particularly the tendency for women to talk about people and relationships, closely relate to the most commonly cited variations in the function that interaction serves for men and women. Women's self-disclosure about their feelings, relationships, and problems is interpreted as a means of creating a greater sense of closeness and intimacy than exists in men's relationships (Reis, Senchak, & Solomon, 1985). Based on a review of the literature on the intimacy of women's friendships compared with men's, Elkins and Peterson (1993) concluded that "women regard their same-gender friendships as closer and more satisfying than do men" (p. 498). By contrast, men report that their friendships are based more in the pursuit of activities (Elkins & Peterson, 1993).

Recent research on sex-linked styles in communication has focused to a greater degree on the underlying motivations, values, and objectives that may account for the behavioral differences that have been observed. Maccoby (1988) argued that during the period of sex-segregated interaction, boys and girls develop different underlying organizational principles. Girls tend to form close friendships with one or two other girls, whereas boys interact in larger groups that display dominance hierarchies and well-defined roles that lead to competitiveness and power assertion.

Some scholars believe that these motivations persist into adulthood and, in fact, view the male communicative pattern as designed to assert and maintain power, particularly in cross-sex interaction (Henley & Kramarae, 1991; West & Zimmerman, 1977; Zimmerman & West, 1975). However, other scholars have argued that men and women do not differ in their fundamental motivations and values in communication, but have been socialized to use different behaviors to attain similar objectives (Tannen, 1986, 1990; Wood & Inman, 1993).

This latter position has led to a different stream of research that shifts the focus from sex differences in behavioral patterns to an attempt to assess underlying values and objectives of men and women in conversation. Researchers are beginning to ask individuals about their objectives and values rather than simply imputing motivations from behavior. In a large-scale analysis of diary reports, Duck and Wright (1993) found that men and women hold similar objectives, with the most common objective being talk for talk's sake followed by talk to accomplish some task and then talk to facilitate the relationship. Focusing on the value attached to specific communicative skills, Samter, Burleson, Kunkel, and Werking (1994) reported that both men and women place higher value on affective than instrumental skills.

The present study extends the effort to identify the objectives individuals pursue in their everyday conversations. The particular design of the present study was guided by a number of considerations. The first was a desire to refine our understanding of what objectives are considered significant by participants in talk for talk's sake. Thus, a more elaborated set of objectives than that used by Duck and Wright (1993) was employed in the present study.

A second consideration was a desire to obtain a cross section of everyday conversations. This seems critical because some of the most commonly mentioned differences in conversations of men and women may occur in only a small portion of conversations. For instance, self-disclosure seems to occur much less frequently in ordinary conversations than we have previously thought (Dindia, Fitzpatrick, & Kenny, 1989; Duck, Rutt, Hurst, & Strejc, 1991). Thus, in the present study, participants were asked to report on their most recent conversation (in some cases with a good friend and in other cases with a casual acquaintance) as a means to obtain a cross-section of ordinary conversations.

A third consideration was the desire to secure information on the topics discussed because topics and objectives appear intertwined in some respects. The summary of sex comparisons provided by Bischoping, as well as her recent work (Bischoping, 1993), has one major limitation: The conversations analyzed primarily were ones overheard in public contexts. If it is true that women discuss more intimate topics and feelings than do men, this difference might be more evident in conversations that may occur outside the public arena. Thus, a cross section of ordinary conversations not constrained by context seemed to provide a better opportunity to compare conversational topics of men and women.

Finally, the present study investigated conversations of both good friends and casual acquaintances. The importance of close relationships to individuals' health and happiness is well established. Recently, Milardo and Wellman (1992) called for expanding research beyond intimate relationships to include study of acquaintanceships. As they observed, individuals have far more acquaintances than close relationships and these acquaintances "lend familiarity and a sense of community to daily routines" (Milardo & Wellman, 1992, p. 340). Therefore, it seemed useful to compare the interactions of men and women with casual acquaintances as well as with good friends.

Thus, two broad questions guided the current project:

R1: Do men and women differ in the topics they discuss in a cross section of everyday conversations held either with a good friend or a casual acquaintance?

R2: Do men and women differ in their objectives in a cross section of everyday conversations held either with a good friend or a casual acquaintance?

METHOD

Participants

Three hundred and seventy-two undergraduates who were enrolled in sections of a beginning public speaking course at the University of Illinois participated in the study. Of these, 153 were men and 219 were women. Two thirds of the participants were first-year students.

Task

To obtain ecologically valid information, students were asked to report on a recent interaction.

Instructions. Participants were asked to think of the most recent time they talked for at least 3 minutes with someone of the same sex. Approximately half the participants were asked to recall a conversation with a good friend and the other half were asked to think about their most recent conversation with a casual acquaintance. Anonymity was guaranteed.

Basic Description of Conversation. On the first page of the instrument, participants indicated their sex, year in school, how long ago the conversation transpired, how long they had known their conversational partner, the estimated length of the conversation, and the estimated percentage of the time they talked. To encourage participants to mentally reconstruct the conversation before responding to more structured questions, they were asked to list all the topics discussed, note anything that made them feel good about the conversation, and identify anything that bothered them about the conversation. Next, participants indicated how satisfying they had found the conversation on a 5-point scale (from *not at all* to *very much*)

Topics. Following their description of the conversation, participants identified the topics discussed from a list of 11 options. Of these categories of topics, 10 were the subtopics used by Bischoping (1993) in her summary analysis. The categories appear in Table 13.1. The 11th category, *immediate*

TABLE 13.1
All Topics Discussed

Topic	Good Friend		Casual Acquaintance	
	Men (76)	Women (106)	Men (77)	Women (113)
Persons of same sex	57	79	47	63
	75.0%	74.5%	61.0%	55.8%
Persons of opposite sex	65	94	51	81
	85.1%	88.7%	66.2%	71.7%*
Academic	46	65	45	82
	60.5%	61.3%	58.4%	72.6%
Career plans	21	28	24	28
	27.6%	26.4%	31.2%	24.8%
Jobs	34	44	24	37
	44.7%	41.5%	31.2%	32.7%
Money	32	44	34	37
	42.1%	41.5%	44.2%	32.7%
Sports	41	20	39	21
	53.9%	18.9%***	50.6%	18.6%***
Other leisure activities	48	66	44	67
	63.2%	62.3%	57.1%	59.3%
Personal appearance and clothing	13	38	14	41
	17.1%	35.8%	18.2%	36.3%**
Social and political issues	12	16	14	10
	15.8%	15.1%	18.2%	8.8%
Immediate surroundings or activities	51	80	41	72
	67.1%	75.5%	36.3%	63.7%

*$p \leq .05$. **$p \leq .01$. ***$p \leq .001$.

surroundings and activities, was included because the conversations were potentially brief and half of them occurred between casual acquaintances, thereby making immediate surroundings and activities a possible topic choice. Illustrations were provided for each category. Thus, for the category of *money*, the examples were *borrowing, earning, spending*. Participants were instructed to place an "X" by all topics discussed and to place an "XXX" by the topic discussed most. Responses of participants who marked more than one dominant topic were excluded from the analysis of dominant topic.

Objectives. Twenty-two objectives were presented next. All items began with the stem *tried to. . . .* Eight items corresponded to the eight skills assessed by Burleson and Samter (1990). Also incorporated were items that reflected reported sex differences (e.g., *tried to be humorous*, and *tried to reveal a recent success*). Because most research in interpersonal interactions has focused on intimate relationships, some additional objectives thought to be relevant to conversations with casual acquaintances, such as *tried to get to know more about the other*, and *tried to be friendly*, were included.

Participants were asked to indicate all of their personal objectives by placing a "Y" for "you" beside the objective. Once they had completed that task, they were asked to identify the dominant objective in the conversation by placing "XXX" beside it. If participants indicated more than one dominant objective, their response was omitted from the analysis of dominant objectives.

Administration of the Instrument.   The instrument was completed during regularly scheduled classes. The alternative forms—*good friend* and *casual acquaintance*—were randomly assigned to intact classes. Participants took approximately 12 to 15 minutes to complete the task.

RESULTS

The length of time that had elapsed since the recalled conversation was not significantly different for men and women conversing with casual acquaintances or good friends. Eighty-four percent of women had talked with a good friend during the past 2 days, whereas 67% of men had. Although women reported knowing good friends a shorter period of time than did men, this difference was not significant.

The length of the conversation did not vary significantly between men and women talking with good friends (M = 24.95 minutes; W = 29.51 minutes), although it did for casual acquaintances (F = 7.01, df = 1, $p <$ .01), with men talking longer than women (M = 24.00 minutes; W = 17.50 minutes). Both men and women reported having talked just under 50% of the time with both good friends and casual acquaintances.

No significant differences were reported for satisfaction with either good friends (M = 4.01; W = 4.04) or casual acquaintances (M = 3.83; W = 3.76). In general, participants found their conversations with both good friends and casual acquaintances quite satisfying, with ratings of approximately 4 on a 5-point scale.

Topics

When considering all the topics that were introduced in the conversation with a good friend (Table 13.1), there is striking similarity in the most commonly discussed topics of men and women. *Persons of the opposite sex* was the most frequently listed topic, followed by *persons of the same sex, immediate surroundings, other leisure activities,* and *academics.* The one significant difference (F = 24.59, df = 1, $p <$ .001) found was for *sports;* almost 54% of men reported having discussed *sports* compared with 19% of women.

Regarding the dominant topic in conversations with good friends, however, the differences between men and women seem more marked (Table 13.2) if one takes into account similar categories ($F = 30.88$, $df = 10$, $p <$ .001). Although *persons of the opposite sex* comprised the dominant topic for both men and women, almost half the women (48.8%) listed it as dominant, compared with just over one third of men (34.5%). In fact, for women the dominant topic was other people: 64% of women's conversations were dominated by *persons of the opposite sex* or *persons of the same sex.* For men, *sports* (18.2%) and *other leisure activities* (18.2%) followed *persons of the opposite sex* as dominant topics, accounting for over 70% of the dominant topics in the conversations of males with their good friends.

In conversations with casual acquaintances (Table 13.1), many of the topics frequently discussed with good friends again emerged as commonly discussed: *persons of the opposite sex, persons of the same sex, academics,* and *other leisure activities.* The percentage of conversations that involved discussion of other people, either of the same sex or opposite sex, however, was between 15% and 20% lower in conversations with casual acquaintances than with good friends. Differences between men and women emerged

TABLE 13.2
Dominant Topic

Topic	Good Friend		Casual Acquaintance	
	Men (55)	Women (86)	Men (54)	Women (83)
Persons of same sex	3	13	3	3
	5.5%	15.1%	5.6%	3.6%
Persons of opposite sex	19	42	11	28
	34.5%	48.8%	20.4%	33.7%
Academic	3	6	8	13
	5.5%	7.0%	14.8%	15.7%
Career plans	1	3	2	3
	1.8%	3.5%	3.7%	3.6%
Jobs	1	0	1	5
	1.8%	0%	1.9%	6.0%
Money	1	0	3	2
	1.8%	0%	5.6%	2.4%
Sports	10	0	9	0
	18.2%	0%	16.7%	0%
Other leisure activities	10	10	8	15
	18.2%	11.6%	14.8%	18.1%
Personal appearance and clothing	0	1	3	4
	0%	1.2%	5.6%	4.8%
Social and political issues	2	1	2	1
	3.6%	1.2%	3.7%	1.2%
Immediate surroundings or activities	5	10	4	9
	9.1%	11.6%	7.4%	10.8%

for four topics: men discussed *sports* ($F = 21.75$, $df = 1$, $p < .001$) and *social and political issues* ($F = 3.54$, $df = 1$, $p < .05$) more frequently than did women, whereas women talked about *academics* ($F = 4.09$, $df = 1$, $p < .05$) and *personal appearance* ($F = 7.58$, $df = 1$, $p < .01$) more than did men.

Analysis of the topic that dominated the conversation with a casual acquaintance (Table 13.2) yielded a significant difference ($F = 23.09$, $df = 10$, $p < .01$). More conversations of women than of men were dominated by talk about *persons of the opposite sex* ($W = 33.7\%$; $M = 20.4\%$), although the percentage of conversations dominated by *persons of the opposite sex* was substantially lower than it had been for good friends for both sexes. Conversations of males compared with females were more frequently dominated by *sports* ($M = 16.7\%$; $W = 0\%$).

Objectives

When considering all the objectives that participants indicated that they pursued, four objectives were identified by at least three quarters of the participants, by both men and women and regardless of whether the conversation was with a good friend or a casual acquaintance (Table 13.3). The objectives that permeated most conversations were *show interest in what the other says, be friendly, talk about topics of interest to the other,* and *make the conversation enjoyable.* For casual acquaintances, one additional objective was also listed by at least three quarters of the participants: *keep the conversation going smoothly.*

In conversations with good friends, the proportion of men and women pursuing some objectives (Table 13.3) differed significantly. A higher percentage of women than men reported the objectives of "offering helpful advice" ($W = 63.2\%$; $M = 48.7\%$; $F = 3.81$, $df = 1$, $p < .01$), *comforting the other* ($W = 49.1\%$; $M = 22.4\%$; $F = 13.86$, $df = 1$, $p < .001$), *helping the other feel good about himself/herself* ($W = 51.9\%$; $M = 25.0\%$; $F = 13.64$, $df = 1$, $p < .001$), *avoid offending the other* ($W = 54.7\%$; $M = 35.5\%$; $F = 6.61$, $df = 1$, $p < .01$), and *letting the other know you care about him/her,* ($W = 69.8\%$; $M = 28.9\%$; $F = 30.46$, $df = 1$, $p < .001$). A higher percentage of men than women identified the objectives of *being humorous* ($M = 85.5\%$; $W = 67.9\%$; $F = 7.72$, $df = 1$, $p < .01$) and *influencing the other* ($M = 28.9\%$; $W = 15.1\%$; $F = 5.08$, $df = 1$, $p < .05$). Approaching significance was *tease the other in a good humored way* ($M = 73.7\%$; $W = 60.4\%$; $F = 3.54$, $df = 1$, $p < .06$).

When individuals identified their dominant objective in conversations with good friends (Table 13.4), the results were statistically significant ($F = 38.58$, $df = 19$, $p < .01$). However, with responses divided among 22 alternatives, the percentage of individuals reporting any one objective was not large. For men, the most commonly mentioned objective was *being humorous* (23.5%). For women, the two most frequently identified objectives

TABLE 13.3
All Objectives Identified

Objective	Good Friend		Casual Acquaintance	
	Men (76)	Women (106)	Men (77)	Women (113)
Be friendly	62	94	68	105
	81.6%	88.7%	88.3%	92.9%
Show interest in	70	101	74	109
what other says	92.1%	95.3%	96.1%	96.5%
Get to know each other	36	66	51	77
	47.4%	62.3%	66.2%	68.1%
Keep conversation	52	81	62	86
going smoothly	68.4%	76.4%	80.5%	76.1%
Talk about topics of	60	82	60	89
interest to other	78.9%	77.4%	77.9%	78.8%
Avoid upsetting topics	25	49	43	49
	32.9%	46.2%	55.8%	43.4%
Be humorous	65	72	61	77
	85.5%	67.9%**	79.2%	68.1%
Tease other in	56	64	45	43
good-humored way	73.7%	60.4%	58.4%	38.1%**
Reveal a success	25	29	23	25
	32.9%	27.4%	29.9%	22.1%
Tell an interesting story	51	72	52	54
	67.1%	67.9%	67.5%	47.8%
Offer useful information	38	64	42	57
	50.0%	60.0%	54.5%	50.4%
Offer helpful advice	37	67	32	50
	48.7%	63.2%*	41.6%	44.2%
Comfort other	17	52	9	37
	22.4%	49.1%***	11.7%	32.7%***
Help other feel better	19	55	12	35
about self	25.0%	51.9%***	15.6%	31.0%***
Avoid offending	27	58	33	52
	35.5%	54.7%**	42.9%	46.0%
Let other know you	22	74	9	40
care about him/her	28.9%	69.8%***	11.7%	35.4%***
Present favorable	23	39	27	44
self-image	30.3%	36.8%	35.1%	38.9%
Help resolve conflict	23	36	15	15
	30.3%	34.0%	19.5%	13.3%
Explain something	50	74	57	68
	65.8%	69.8%	74.0%	60.2%*
Influence other	22	16	14	11
	28.9%	15.1%*	18.2%	9.7%
Tell other what he/she	17	26	13	11
is doing wrong	22.4%	24.5%	16.9%	9.7%
Make conversation	60	86	69	94
enjoyable	78.9%	81.1%	89.6%	83.2%

*$p \leq .05$. **$p \leq .01$. ***$p < .001$.

TABLE 13.4
Dominant Objective

Objective	Good Friend		Casual Acquaintance	
	Men (68)	Women (95)	Men (71)	Women (104)
Be friendly	2	1	5	14
	2.9%	1.1%	7.0%	13.5%
Show interest in	5	12	5	8
what other says	7.4%	12.6%	7.0%	7.7%
Get to know each other	4	8	8	7
	5.9%	8.4%	11.3%	6.7%
Keep conversation	0	2	5	2
going smoothly	0%	2.1%	7.0%	1.9%
Talk about topics of	2	3	3	6
interest to other	2.9%	3.2%	4.2%	5.8%
Avoid upsetting topics	1	0	0	1
	1.5%	0%	0%	1.0%
Be humorous	16	3	6	6
	23.5%	3.2%	8.5%	5.8%
Tease other in	2	3	1	1
good-humored way	2.9%	3.2%	1.4%	1.0%
Reveal a success	0	0	1	0
	0%	0%	1.4%	0%
Tell an interesting story	4	4	4	7
	5.9%	4.2%	5.6%	6.7%
Offer useful information	1	6	5	7
	1.5%	6.3%	7.0%	6.7%
Offer helpful advice	5	9	1	10
	7.4%	9.5%	1.4%	9.6%
Comfort other	1	6	1	5
	1.5%	6.3%	1.4%	4.8%
Help other feel better	2	9	3	4
about self	2.9%	9.5%	4.2%	3.8%
Avoid offending	0	0	0	1
	0%	0%	0%	1.0%
Let other know you	3	12	0	5
care about him/her	4.4%	12.6%	0%	4.8%
Present favorable	1	1	0	1
self-image	1.5%	1.1%	0%	1.0%
Help resolve conflict	4	5	2	4
	5.9%	5.3%	2.8%	3.8%
Explain something	8	2	6	3
	11.8%	2.1%	8.5%	2.9%
Influence other	1	2	0	0
	1.5%	2.1%	0%	0%
Tell other what he/she	1	1	2	0
is doing wrong	1.5%	1.1%	2.8%	0%
Make conversation	5	6	13	12
enjoyable	7.4%	6.3%	18.3%	11.5%

were *show interest in what the other says* (12.6%) and *let the other know you care about him/her* (12.6%), followed closely by *offer helpful advice* (9.5%) and *help the other feel better about himself/herself* (9.5%).

Fewer sex differences were observed in objectives with casual acquaintances than with good friends (Table 13.3). With casual acquaintances, a higher percentage of women than men identified the objectives of *comforting the other* (W = 32.7%; M = 11.7%; F = 11.87, df = 1, $p <$ .001), *helping the other feel better about himself/herself* (W = 31.0%; M = 15.6%; F = 6.07, df = 1, $p <$ .01), and *letting the other know you care about him/her* (W = 35.4%; M = 11.7%; F = 14.50, df = 1, $p <$ .001). A higher proportion of men than women reported the objective of *explaining something* (M = 74.0%; W = 60.2%; F = 3.97, df = 1, $p <$ .05) and *teasing the other in a good humored way* (M = 58.4%; W = 38.1%; F = 7.69, df = 1, $p <$ .01).

The dominant objective identified in conversations with casual acquaintances (Table 13.4) differed significantly for men and women (F = 31.04, df = 20, $p <$ .05), but responses were scattered across many different objectives. For men, the most commonly mentioned objective was *make the conversation enjoyable* (18.3%). For women, the most frequently identified objectives were *be friendly* (13.5%) and *make the conversation enjoyable* (11.5%).

DISCUSSION

In interpreting the results of the present study, it is important to emphasize that the conversations analyzed represent a cross section of everyday conversations of young adult college students. They may not manifest the full range of communicative objectives pursued by adults in all circumstances. The findings hopefully reflect typical topics and objectives of ordinary conversations among same-sex college students.

In general, there were striking similarities in both the topics discussed and the objectives guiding the conversations of the young men and women involved in this study. The conversations of both sexes commonly ranged across the topics of individuals of the opposite sex and same sex, leisure activities, and academics. For both men and women, their primary objectives centered on showing interest and positive affect toward the other interactant and making the conversation enjoyable. As is evident in the details of the findings that follow, the differences found between the men and women were primarily in the frequency with which some topics and objectives emerged and in the nuances with which they were developed.

Topics

On the whole, the findings regarding topics discussed seem consistent with earlier work. It is clear that with good friends, young women's conversations ranged across a variety of topics but tended to focus heavily on other individuals, particularly persons of the opposite sex, which was the dominant topic in almost half the conversations of women with their good friends. The dominant topic in young men's conversations with their good friends was divided between two major categories: Approximately one third focused on persons of the opposite sex and another third focused on sports and other leisure activities.

From the open-ended listings of topics, as well as from comments regarding what made participants feel good about the conversation, young men and women appear to have a slightly different focus when discussing other people, particularly members of the opposite sex. Women appeared to be talking through problems and decisions more frequently than men, whereas men less commonly mentioned the terms *relationship* and *problems* when indicating that they had discussed other people. One response that was typical of several from women was that the topics discussed included "my boyfriend and the problem we're having, the money problems my family is having, the conversation with my boyfriend about our problems, and her studying for her chemistry test." The aspect of the conversation that made the participant feel good about it was that "she (the partner) helped me feel better about my problem."

By contrast, a typical response from a young man who had also discussed persons of the opposite sex with a good friend identified the topics discussed as "NCAA basketball tournament, school, parties, and girls." The feature of the conversation that most made him feel good was that "we joke around and make fun of different things and people." The coding scheme developed by Bischoping is not designed to capture the nature of the discussion of other people. However, certainly the phrasing of the topics and comments regarding what made the participant feel good reinforces the observations of other researchers—that women are more likely than men to discuss feelings, relationships, and personal problems with good friends (Samter et al., 1994).

Although young women talked about persons of the opposite sex more than they did any other single topic with casual acquaintances, they did so considerably less frequently than when interacting with good friends. Academics and other leisure activities were more likely to dominate the conversations of women with casual acquaintances than with good friends, although these topics were still less common than persons of the opposite sex. For young men, when conversing with casual acquaintances, sports and other leisure activities were the most common dominant topics, with persons of the opposite sex and academics also quite common.

In summary, when considering the array of topics mentioned as well as the dominant ones, support emerged for Bischoping's (1993) conclusion that women talk more about persons of the opposite sex and appearances than do men and that men talk more about sports than do women. In fact, the young people in this study talked about persons of the opposite sex in a much higher percentage of conversations than those analyzed by Bischoping. In contrast to Bischoping's findings, men did not talk significantly more about jobs and money than did women. In interpreting these findings, however, one should keep in mind that most participants were at the beginning of their college studies rather than actively engaged in careers and were at an age characterized by a high degree of interest in the opposite sex.

Objectives

Results of the present study provide grounds for three kinds of general observations about individuals' objectives in everyday conversations. First, some fundamental objectives pervade almost all ordinary conversations. These include being friendly, showing interest in what the other says, talking about topics of interest to the other, and making the conversation enjoyable. These might be collapsed into two even more fundamental objectives: (a) showing interest and positive affect toward the other, and (b) doing your part to make the conversation pleasurable (with one way being sure to select topics of interest to the other). As noted earlier, these objectives were identified as ones that three fourths of all participants indicated that they had pursued, regardless of sex and regardless of whether the partner was a casual acquaintance or a good friend. Thus, talk for talk's sake (Duck & Wright, 1993) appears to have key attributes that most individuals consider essential to satisfying talk for talk's sake.

A second and quite striking generalization emerging from the study was the enormous value placed on the entertainment function of the conversation, particularly by men but by women as well. In addition to the pervasive objectives discussed earlier of making the conversation enjoyable and talking about topics of interest to others, additional objectives that seemed directed toward the pleasure value of the conversation were pursued in a large percentage of the conversations. Being humorous was an objective of 85% of men and 68% of women with good friends and of 80% of men and 68% of women with casual acquaintances. Telling an interesting story was an objective of more than two thirds of the men with both good friends and casual acquaintances and was equally common with women when talking with good friends, although somewhat less so when conversing with casual acquaintances.

The entertainment value of the conversation was mentioned frequently in the comments regarding what made the participant feel good about the conversation, particularly by the men. Comments such as "we were having a good time," "we laughed a lot," "we had a few laughs," and "it was fun" were typical. Baxter's (1992) recent work on playfulness identified a number of functions that playfulness can serve in interpersonal relationships. The comments of participants just cited suggest that playfulness itself frequently represents a valued end.

The importance of pleasure as a function of everyday conversation has been observed in other research. Rubin, Perse, and Barbato (1998) found pleasure to be one of the primary motivations for interpersonal conversations. In fact, if we reexamine the results reported by Samter et al. (1994), we discover that, although both men and women value a cluster of affectively oriented skills more than a cluster of task-oriented ones, the single skill most valued by males in their same-sex friends (reported in the first study) is what the authors labeled *conversational skill.* Conversation skill embodies the ability to make the conversation easy and fun (Burleson & Samter, 1990). In summary, results of the present study are consistent with other indications that entertainment itself constitutes an end in a large number of ordinary conversations.

The third cluster of observations concerns similarities and differences between men's and women's objectives in ordinary conversations. A great number of similarities emerged and, in fact, more similarities than differences. As already noted, most men and women consider it critical to display positive affect toward the other, make the conversation pleasant for the other, and go beyond just being pleasant to make the conversation entertaining.

Despite the high degree of overlap in the objectives of men and women, a cluster of feeling-centered objectives played a larger role in women's conversations than in men's. With good friends, women were more likely to comfort the other (as well as offer helpful advice), help the other feel better about herself, let the other know she cared about her, and avoid offending her. Approximately 50% to 60% of women identified these objectives in their conversations with good friends. These results are not surprising if one recalls the topics women discussed. They frequently talked about their relationships and problems with other persons—topics for which affectively oriented objectives seem appropriate.

In examining what the participants indicated made them feel good about the conversation, typical comments by women about their conversations with good friends were "she confided in me," "she helped me feel better about my problem," and "she reassured me that things will work out and that I am a good, smart person." One important point to be made about these affectively oriented objectives was that the sense of closeness or intimacy seemed valued in its own right, regardless of whether the conversation was problem-centered. Characteristic of responses reflecting this orientation were "my friend cared about what was going on" and "I shared a piece of myself with somebody and I also received their perspective." Even with good friends, almost two thirds of women, compared with just over one third of men, cited getting to know more about the other person as an objective.

Despite the real emphasis that women placed on letting their partners know that they cared about them, helping their partners feel better about themselves, and providing advice and comforting if needed, it is important to emphasize that women did *not* pursue these affectively oriented objectives more frequently than they did the pure pleasure or entertainment objectives. For women as well as men, the pleasure and entertainment objectives were at least as common in these ordinary conversations as were the affectively oriented ones.

Before discussing the objectives that men pursued more frequently than did women, we might note that two potential differences between men and women observed in earlier research did not emerge. Because males have been thought to do more bragging than females (Maltz & Borker, 1983) and because establishing status has been considered a key motivation in men's communicative behavior (Maccoby, 1988), it seemed possible that men would be more likely than women to reveal a recent success or attempt to present a favorable image of themselves. Yet no differences between sexes were found for these objectives and were cited as objectives in only approximately one third of the conversations by either men or women. It may be that men reflect these behaviors more commonly in groups than in dyadic interaction, that these motivations are ones imputed by researchers but not ascribed by men to themselves, or that these motivations simply do not exist in young adult college men.

One type of objective that men did pursue to a greater extent than did women involved having fun. Although entertainment was a high priority for both men and women, it received even more emphasis from men. When talking with good friends, significantly more men than women reported an attempt to be humorous and to tease the other in a good-natured way. When asked to isolate their dominant objective, men cited being humorous more frequently than any other in conversations with good friends. Humor played only a slightly less significant role in men's conversations with casual acquaintances, where they attenuated teasing.

Because some research has indicated that men find their friendships less satisfying than do women (Elkins & Peterson, 1993), it is important to note that men found their everyday conversations just as satisfying as did women. The present study suggests that it is no accident that men's conversations focus on having fun more than on dealing with feelings. To a large extent, young men apparently intend to engage in conversation to have fun and are quite satisfied with the way they do it. Moreover, members of both sexes acknowledge that men are good at communication for the sake of entertainment. In a study of the choice of conversational partners of 4th through 10th graders (Clark, 1994), a majority of both boys and girls selected a boy as their conversational partner when they wanted to be entertained with jokes and stories, even during the period of sex-segregated interaction. As children mature and come to play less and talk more (Berndt, 1982), talk itself is constructed as a form of entertainment, with this entertainment function being valued by members of both sexes but by men to an even greater extent than by women.

Certainly results of the present study should not be interpreted as indicating that only women pursue affective ends and only men use communication for entertainment. It is clear that both men and women have affective and entertainment objectives, but that the frequency with which they pursue these ends varies somewhat. Although the present study analyzed only same-sex conversations, it is tempting to speculate about the motivations individuals have for turning to conversational partners of the opposite sex. There is some evidence that men find women more satisfying interactional partners for functions such as ego support, declarations of liking, and self-affirmation (Elkins & Peterson, 1993). It seems quite possible that at times women turn to men as conversational partners when they wish to talk simply to have fun.

In summary, the present study revealed substantial similarity in the objectives pursued by both young men and young women—in particular showing interest in and positive affect toward the other participant as well as making the conversation pleasurable. At the same time, results indicate that women place more emphasis on feeling-centered objectives than do men and that men accord the entertainment function of conversation even more significance than do women. As already noted, both men and women expressed satisfaction with the quality of their conversations. Rather than characterizing sex differences as reflecting deficits, as some scholars have, perhaps we should view each sex as having developed communicative specialties.

REFERENCES

Baxter, L. A. (1992). Forms and functions of intimate play in personal relationships. *Human Communication Research, 18,* 336–363.

Berndt, T. J. (1982). The features and effects of friendship in early adolescence. *Child Development, 53,* 1447–1460.

Bischoping, K. (1993). Gender differences in conversation topic, 1922–1990. *Sex Roles, 28,* 1–18.

Burleson, B. R., & Samter, W. (1990). Effects of cognitive complexity on the perceived importance of communication skills in friends. *Communication Research, 17,* 165–182.

Clark, R. A. (1994). Children's and adolescents' gender preferences for conversational partners for specific objectives. *Journal of Social and Personal Relationships, 11,* 313–319.

Dindia, K., Fitzpatrick, M. A., & Kenny, D. A. (1989, May). *Self disclosure in spouse and stranger interactions: A social relations analysis.* Paper presented at the annual meetings of the International Communication Association, New Orleans.

Duck, S., Rutt, D. J., Hurst, M. H., & Strejc, H. (1991). Some evident truths about everyday conversation: All communication is not created equal. *Human Communication Research, 18,* 228–267.

Duck, S., & Wright, P. H. (1993). Reexamining gender differences in same-gender friendships: A close look at two kinds of data. *Sex Roles, 28,* 709–727.

Elkins, L. E., & Peterson, C. (1993). Gender differences in best friendships. *Sex Roles, 29,* 497–508.

Henley, N., & Kramarae, C. (1991). Gender, power and miscommunication. In N. Coupland, H. Giles, & J. M. Wiemann (Eds.), *"Miscommunication" and problematic talk* (pp. 18–43). Newbury Park, CA: Sage.

LaFreniere, P., Strayer, F. F., & Gauthier, R. (1984). The emergence of same-sex preferences among preschool peers: A developmental ethological perspective. *Child Development, 55,* 1958–1965.

Maccoby, E. E. (1988). Gender as a social category. *Developmental Psychology, 24,* 755–765.

Maccoby, E. E. (1990). Gender and relationships: A developmental account. *American Psychologist, 45,* 513–520.

Maltz, D. N., & Borker, R. A. (1983). A cultural approach to male-female miscommunication. In J. A. Gumperz (Ed.), *Language and social identity* (pp. 195–216). New York: Cambridge University Press.

Milardo, R. M., & Wellman, B. (1992). The personal is social. *Journal of Social and Personal Relationships, 9,* 339–342.

Moore H. T. (1922). Further data concerning sex differences. *Journal of Abnormal Psychology, 17,* 210–214.

Reis, H. T., Senchak, M., & Solomon, B. (1985). Sex differences in the intimacy of social interaction: Further examination of potential explanations. *Journal of Personality and Social Psychology, 48,* 1204–1217.

Rubin, R. B., Perse, E. M., & Barbato, C. A. (1988). Conceptualization and measurement of interpersonal communication motives. *Human Communication Research, 14,* 602–628.

Samter, W., Burleson, B. R., Kunkel, A. W., & Werking, K. J. (1994, July). *Gender and beliefs about communication in intimate relationships: Moderating effects of type of communication and type of relationship (or, when gender differences make a difference—and when they don't).* Paper presented at the annual meetings of the International Communication Association, Sydney, Australia.

Tannen, D. (1986). *That's not what I meant: How conversational style makes or breaks relationships.* New York: Ballantine.

Tannen, D. (1990). *You just don't understand: Women and men in conversation.* New York: William Morrow.

Wasserman, G. A., & Stern, D. (1978). An early manifestation of differential behavior toward children of the same and opposite sex. *Journal of Genetic Psychology, 133,* 129–137.

West, C., & Zimmerman, D. H. (1977). Women's place in everyday talk: Reflections on parent-child interaction. *Social Problems, 24,* 521–529.

Wood, J. T., & Inman, C. C. (1993). In a different mode: Masculine styles of communicating closeness. *Journal of Applied Communication Research, 21,* 279–295.

Zimmerman, D. H., & West, C. (1975). Sex roles, interruptions and silences in conversation. In B. Thorne & N. Henley (Eds.), *Language and sex: Difference and dominance* (pp. 105–129). Rowley, MA: Newbury House.

Chapter 14

Expressing Emotion: Sex Differences in Social Skills and Communicative Responses to Anger, Sadness, and Jealousy

Laura K. Guerrero
Arizona State University

Rencé L. Reiter
Pennsylvania State University

We have all heard the sayings and catchy phrases: "Big boys don't cry!" "It's women's intuition!" Although encoding and decoding emotional information are far more complex processes than such sayings imply, research has provided some empirical support for these adages. Research indicates that men and women possess different skills related to the sending and receiving of emotion. In general, women are more emotionally expressive (e.g., Lewis, 1976; Miller, 1976), whereas men are better able to conceal or control their emotional displays (e.g., Buck, Miller, & Caul, 1974; Riggio, 1993). In addition to their encoding ability, women appear to have a general advantage decoding emotional expressions (Hall, 1978, chap. 7, this volume). Women tend to express emotion through facial expression and interpersonal communication, whereas men generally express emotion through actions such as engaging in aggressive, dangerous, or distracting behavior (Brody, 1993; Strayer, 1986).

Given these findings, it is not surprising that research has uncovered subtle differences in how men and women respond to a number of discrete emotions, including anger, sadness, and jealousy. Social skills related to encoding and decoding emotion likely contribute to these sex differences. For example, if women encode emotions spontaneously and accurately, they may be apt to discuss emotions readily with friends and loved ones. This chapter examines these issues by: (a) reviewing literature on the bases of sex differences in social skills and emotional communication, and (b) offering new data that extend past research by investigating sex differences (and similarities) in a variety of social skills and communicative responses to anger, sadness, and jealousy. *Social skill* refers to individual differences in people's general skill in encoding and decoding verbal and nonverbal messages (Riggio, 1993). In contrast, communicative responses to emotion are the specific types of messages that people use to communicate (or avoid communicating) their emotional states to others. Available evidence suggests that men and women may differ both in their general social skills and their specific communicative responses to emotion. For example, Burleson and associates have proposed a social skill explanation for sex differences and similarities in communication (see Kunkel & Burleson, chap. 5, this volume). According to this view, men and women learn different social skills and these skills translate into different patterns of interpersonal communication, including the communication of comfort, support, and emotion.

PERSPECTIVES ON SEX DIFFERENCES IN SOCIAL SKILLS AND EMOTIONAL COMMUNICATION

Research on sex differences in emotion is often guided by theory focusing on biological, evolutionary explanations and/or socialization processes. In their perspective on emotional communication, Andersen and Guerrero (1998) presented six propositions relevant to emotional communication. Among these, two propositions focus on evolution and socialization: (a) socially adaptive emotional communication is positively selected in the evolution process, and (b) socialization processes provide guidelines for the management and communication of emotion. Brody (1985) argued that, "Males and females may differ in the ways in which emotions become activated, either because of innate differences in emotional functioning, learned differences, or because of the interaction between the two" (p. 137). Similarly, Buck (1983) argued that encoding and decoding abilities may be based on "biologically based systems of 'temperament,' which in turn may be influenced by social learning" (p. 211). This chapter now turns to a more detailed discussion of the biological and social forces that contribute to sex differences in social skills and emotional communication.

Biological and Evolutionary Explanations

Research on the biological bases for sex differences in emotional communication has focused on three main lines of thought: (a) selection processes and evolution, (b) hormones and temperament, and (c) cerebral hemispheric processing. In line with the "selection process" explanation, Buck (1983) argued that the ability to encode and decode emotional states has adaptive value. He explained that individuals who express emotion accurately signal their needs and intentions to other social group members. Similarly, individuals who are skilled at responding to the emotional states of others are likely to be highly valued members of families and communities. Hall (1978) forwarded a similar argument when she stated that women may be

> "wired" from birth to be especially sensitive to nonverbal cues or to be especially quick learners of such cues. This would make evolutionary sense, because nonverbal sensitivity on a mother's part might enable her to detect distress in her youngsters or threatening signals from other adults, thus enhancing the survival chances of her offspring. (p. 854)

In contrast, men may be wired to control certain emotions. For example, controlling fear displays had adaptive value when men were hunting or evading predators. Men may also have an innate tendency toward encoding aggressive, hostile expressions in competitive situations.

According to the biological perspective, evolution and natural selection processes, along with genetic heritage, contribute to sex differences in hormones and temperament (see also Andersen, chap. 4, this volume). These hormonal and temperamental differences lead to sex differences in social behavior, including social skills and emotional communication. Susman et al. (1987) investigated the influence of hormones on negative affect in adolescents. They determined that pubertal hormones (e.g., testosterone-estradiol ratios, androstenedione levels) were related to sad and anxious affect in adolescent boys. Similarly, Brooks-Gunn and Warren (1989) concluded that rising hormonal levels were associated with negative affect in adolescent girls. However, their findings indicate that only 4% of the variance in negative affect was accounted for by hormones while a larger portion of variance was explained by social factors. Thus, Brody (1993) concluded, hormones likely contribute to the development of emotional expressiveness, although less significantly than do social influences.

Sex differences in temperament have also been hypothesized to influence emotional expressiveness. For example, some theorists have suggested that infant boys, due to differences in temperament and extroversion, express emotion with more intensity than do infant girls (e.g., Malatesta & Haviland, 1982). Thus, parents tend to discourage boys from engaging in emotional expressiveness if their affect level is already overly intense (Brody, 1985). This difference in parental behavior, which may have been based initially on temperament differences between sons and daughters, likely contributes to later sex differences in emotional expressiveness.

Finally, some researchers have proposed that neurological differences between the sexes influence how men and women encode and decode emotion (e.g., Buck, 1982). One common hypothesis is that sex differences in cerebral lateralization contribute to sex differences in emotional functioning. Specifically, the right cerebral hemisphere supposedly regulates facial recognition (Ekman & Oster, 1979) along with the more spontaneous aspects of emotional functioning, whereas the left hemisphere has been theorized to direct the more cognitive, analytic aspects of emotional functioning (Buck, 1982). Some neuropsychologists have suggested that men process emotional information using the more analytic left-hemispheric strategies to a greater extent than do women. In contrast, women purportedly use more intuitive right-hemispheric strategies for emotional processing (Buck, 1982). Researchers (e.g., Brody, 1993; Witelson, 1976) have also suggested that women tend to use both cerebral hemispheres more symmetrically, whereas men tend to process emotional information using more pronounced cerebral lateralization (i.e., dependence on one hemisphere over the other). Furthermore, men's brains appear to work harder than women's brains when decoding emotion, particularly when the person emitting emotion is a woman. Despite these interesting findings, many researchers have cautioned against accepting these conclusions as fact until more research is conducted (e.g., Bleier, 1991; Bryden, 1982). Nonetheless, it seems likely that sex differences in cerebral processing have some effect on emotional functioning.

Socialization Explanations

Although innate, biological forces likely set the stage for sex differences in emotional functioning, socialization reinforces and solidifies these differences. Brody (1993) contended that differential socialization of boys and girls leads to sex differences in emotional expressiveness. Maccoby (1988) argued that, as a result of socialization, "Most individuals emerge from childhood into adulthood equipped with the sex-typed characteristics that their societies deem appropriate" (p. 755).

Research shows that parents play an important role in this differential socialization process. For example, numerous findings indicate that parents more often discuss emotions with girls than boys (except anger, disgust, contempt, and other outwardly negative emotions) and tend to exhibit more facial expressions to girls than to boys, starting at very young ages (Brody, 1993). Greif, Alvarez, and Ulman (1981) demonstrated that when parents told stories to their children out of a wordless storybook, they developed different stories for their preschool sons versus daughters. Fathers used significantly more emotion words (e.g., *happy, sad, love*) and mothers significantly less anger words (e.g., *mad, hate*) with the girls. Dunn, Bretherton, and Munn (1987) demonstrated that mothers talk more about emotions with their 18- to 24-month-old daughters and by 2 years old, girls (relative to boys) produce more emotion words. Similarly, Fivush (1989) found that mothers generally focused more on the emotion state with daughters and, conversely, on the cause and consequence of the emotion state with sons. For example, if a girl falls down and skins her knee, the mother may ask "how much it hurts." But if a boy is hurt, she may focus on the action rather than the emotion (e.g., "Did you fall down and go boom?"). Fivush concluded that parents teach their sons control over emotions while teaching daughters to be more sensitive to emotion.

Assigning certain attributes to male versus female behavior appears to influence how adults communicate with children as early as infancy. In a study by Condry and Condry (1976), supposed knowledge of an infant's sex determined how adult observers interpreted the infant's emotional state. Half of the adult observers were told that they were watching a female infant and the other half were told they were watching a male infant. Negative displays of emotion were more likely labeled *anger* when the infant was perceived to be a boy but *fear* when the infant was perceived to be a girl (Condry & Condry, 1976). Stewart, Stewart, Friedley and Cooper (1990) contended that this sex typed emotional-labeling process subsequently impacts parental behavior, in that the infant perceived to be an angry male will be treated differently than the infant perceived to be a fearful female. A frightened infant will most likely be soothed and comforted by parents, whereas an angry infant may be scolded or ignored. Thus, parents may unwittingly reinforce emotional expressiveness in daughters while discouraging the same expressiveness in boys. A study by Fuchs and Thelen (1988) illustrated how this reinforcement works. In their study on elementary school children, girls expected their mothers to act negatively toward them if they displayed anger but positively if they displayed sadness. In contrast, boys expected their parents to react negatively if they expressed sadness. In a review of the anger literature, Lemerise and Dodge (1993) drew a similar conclusion: "Boys' anger is more likely to elicit some form of maternal attention, and boys are more likely to be rewarded for anger. Girls' angry behavior, on the other hand, is more likely to elicit ignoring or a command to stop" (p. 541).

Parents also tend to display a wider range of emotional facial expressions to girls than to boys and to encourage girls to be socially oriented. For example, two studies have shown that mothers express more positive affect to their infant and toddler daughters than to their same-age sons (Malatesta, Culver, Tesman, & Shepard, 1989; Parnell, 1992). Beckwith (1972) contended that, as a result of this differential treatment, female infants tend to be more socially oriented during infancy than males. For example, Klein and Durfee (1978) determined that by the time children reach their first birthday, girls direct more positive communicative behaviors to their mothers than do boys. Cherry and Lewis (1976) showed that as children grow older, mothers engage in increasingly active verbal inter-action with their daughters, but encourage their sons to seek physical independence and handle problems on their own.

It appears, then, that boys are raised to be independent and emotionally guarded, whereas girls are raised to seek and give emotional support. Block (1979) found that parents encourage boys more than girls to control af-fective expression, be independent, and assume personal responsibility. Similar findings by Barry, Bacon, and Child (1957) show that girls receive more pressure to be nurturing and obedient, whereas boys are pressured to achieve and be self-reliant. Block (1973) demonstrated that parents encourage daughters to be emotional and nonaggressive. Conversely, par-ents encourage sons to be aggressive, but unemotional. Thus, parents tend to act in more instrumental, task-oriented, mastery-emphasizing ways with sons and in more expressive, less achievement-oriented, dependency-rein-forcing ways with daughters (Block, 1973). This differentiation then con-tributes to later sex differences in emotional expressiveness and control (Greif et al., 1981; Malatesta & Haviland, 1982).

Brody (1985; Brody & Hall, 1993) summarized the implications of prior literature on socialization processes. She argued that boys learn to inhibit the expression of emotions through words or facial expressions, with the possible exception of outwardly directed negative emotions such as anger and contempt. In contrast, girls are encouraged to express all their emo-tions through words and facial expressions, with the exception of socially unacceptable emotions such as anger, which they learn to inhibit. Various studies have demonstrated that for boys the level of expressiveness for all emotions decreases with age, whereas for girls only their expression of negative affect decreases (Buck, 1977; Saarni, 1982). Brody (1985) inter-preted these findings as evidence that boys are generally socialized to inhibit emotional displays, whereas girls are socialized to express all but the most socially unacceptable emotions.

THE PRESENT STUDIES

Research on the biological and social bases for sex differences in emotion suggest that men and women differ in terms of social skills and emotional functioning. Differential skills and social norms likely translate to differ-ences in the communication of discrete emotions. This is particularly likely because research suggests that sex differences in emotional communication are more pronounced than are sex differences in the subjective experience of emotion (Fabes & Martin, 1991; Johnson & Shulman, 1988).

The two studies presented in this chapter focus on these issues by ex-amining sex differences in social skills and communicative responses to anger, sadness, and jealousy. The data reported here were collected from two undergraduate populations. The first of these consisted of 237 students (female $n = 148$; male $n = 88$; average age = 19.5 years) enrolled in a multisectioned introductory psychology course at a large northeastern university. These individuals completed questionnaires relevant to social skills and responses to anger and sadness. The second population, which was limited to individuals involved in serious romantic relationships, consisted of 410 students (female $n = 239$; male $n = 171$; average age = 21.3 years) enrolled in a variety of upper division communication courses at two southwestern universities. This second sample completed questionnaires on communicative responses to jealousy.

Anger, sadness, and jealousy were selected for several reasons. First, researchers have found that negative emotions are more intense, enduring, and memorable than positive emotions (Frijda, 1988; Thomas & Diener, 1990). Second, people regulate negative emotions more closely than positive emotions, making social and emotional control relevant social skills (Aune, Buller, & Aune, 1996; Friedman & Riggio, 1981). Third, people often share negative emotions with others in an effort to gain social support (Rimé, Mesquita, Phillippot, & Boca, 1991). Social skills in encoding and decoding negative emotions are crucial to the success of social support seeking and giving. Fourth, these three emotions function in different ways. Anger constitutes a form of outwardly directed negative affect that usually focuses on external causes such as other people (Brody & Hall, 1993). Sadness, in contrast, represents an intropunitive emotion that is often internalized and self-directed (Brody & Hall, 1993). Jealousy involves a threat to the quality or existence of one's romantic relationship (White & Mullen, 1989). Thus, these three emotions represent negative emotions that are directed at others, the self, and the relationship. Before discussing data related to the expression of these three specific emotions, we focus on sex differences in general social skills.

Sex Differences in Social Skills

Background. Social skill in encoding and decoding is widely recognized as a critical component in interpersonal interaction (Buck, 1983), and men and women appear to possess different abilities in terms of these critical skills. Numerous research findings attest to the empirical generalization that women (as opposed to men) tend to be better encoders and decoders of emotional information (e.g., Buck et al., 1974; Sabatelli, Buck, & Dreyer, 1980; Wagner, MacDonald, & Manstead, 1986). Hall (1978) summarized the results of 75 studies that measured the reported accuracy of females and males at decoding nonverbal communication. She concluded that females are significantly better able to discern nonverbal emotional cues than are males. Hall further suggested that nonverbal sensitivity is particularly socially adaptive for females. Other research shows women to be superior at encoding emotion but men to be superior at controlling emotional displays (Buck, 1979; Buck et al., 1974; Riggio, 1993). Two studies, however, have illustrated that sex differences in encoding and decoding ability may be moderated by the type of emotion being judged. Both of these studies (Rotter & Rotter, 1988; Wagner et al., 1986) found men to decode anger more accurately than women. One of the studies (Wagner et al., 1986) found women to outperform men overall, but their decoding superiority was most pronounced when judging surprise or indifference. Men were better at encoding sadness.

Nonetheless, the evidence on sex differences in social skills relevant to emotion is quite consistent: Men appear to have an advantage when it comes to controlling emotion, whereas women appear to have an advantage when it comes to encoding and decoding most emotions. This led us to extend past research on general encoding and decoding skills by hypothesizing that young men and women differ in social skill at six different levels: social expressivity, emotional expressivity, social sensitivity, emotional sensitivity, social control, and emotional control.

These six skills are incorporated into Riggio's (1986, 1993) model of social skills, which focuses on self-perceptions of both nonverbal and verbal abilities. We felt it was important to investigate both nonverbal and verbal skills because emotions are often communicated with both words and behaviors (Rimé et al., 1991). On the nonverbal side, *emotional expressivity* refers to the ability to express emotion spontaneously and accurately. *Emotional control*, in contrast, refers to nonverbal skill in regulating affect. Those skilled in emotional control can hide an inappropriate emotion by appearing unaffected or masking it with a more appropriate emotion. *Emotional sensitivity* refers to skill in recognizing, responding to, and empathizing with the emotional states of others. On the verbal side, *social expressivity* refers to skill in verbal speaking and engaging others in social conversation. In contrast, *social control* refers to the regulation of verbal performance, including careful impression management and the ability to play various social roles and assume leadership positions. Finally, *social sensitivity* refers to skill in determining how others feel and think toward oneself and toward social situations.

Current Findings. Based on Riggio's system and the available literature on socialization processes, we expected women to rate themselves as more emotionally expressive, socially expressive, emotionally sensitive, and socially sensitive than men. In contrast, we expected men to rate themselves as higher in emotional and social control. Our data were generally consistent with these predictions. Respondents rated their skills using abbreviated versions (i.e., 8 rather than 15 items) of each of Riggio's (1986) six social skill inventory measures. Interitem reliabilities for these scales ranged from .71 to .87. The t tests showed that, as expected, women rated themselves higher in terms of expressivity and sensitivity (see Table 14.1). Men, in contrast, rated themselves higher on emotional control. There were no sex differences on social control.

Commentary. Differential socialization processes may contribute to these sex differences in self-perceptions of social skills. As discussed previously, various studies have demonstrated that parents verbally discuss emotions more with girls than boys (e.g., Dunn, Bretherton, & Munn, 1987) and that parents teach daughters to be more sensitive to their emotional states (Fivush, 1989). These findings are consistent with the current evidence that women view themselves as more emotionally expressive (i.e., able to express emotions spontaneously and accurately) and emotionally sensitive (i.e., able to recognize and respond to others' emotional states) than do men. The current findings also demonstrate that women perceive themselves as more socially expressive (i.e., skilled in verbal speaking and engaging others in social interaction) and socially sensitive (i.e., skilled in identifying and interpreting verbal messages accurately) than do men. Taken together, these studies suggest that women—who are socialized to interact with others and be socially oriented from a young age—should be adept at a wide variety of social skills, including both verbal and nonverbal encoding and decoding.

The data, however, do not paint a completely rosy picture for women, nor do they paint a completely bleak picture for men. For example, high levels of emotional expressivity can actually be detrimental under certain circumstances. Work on cultural display rules (Ekman, 1978) demonstrates

TABLE 14.1
Means and Standard Deviations Associated With Significant t tests
Comparing Men and Women on Self-Perceived Social Skill

Skill	*Men*	*Women*	$t(235)$	η^2
Emotional Expressivity	4.21 (.97)	4.95 (.94)	5.78*	.13
Emotional Sensitivity	4.43 (.84)	4.90 (.77)	4.28*	.08
Social Expressivity	4.34 (1.03)	4.92 (1.12)	3.94*	.06
Social Sensitivity	4.30 (1.05)	4.69 (1.15)	2.55*	.03
Emotional Control	4.70 (.92)	4.22 (1.02)	3.61*	.05
Social Control	4.35 (.72)	4.46 (.97)	.92	.00

Note. Standard deviations are in parentheses. Means are on 1–7 scales, with 7 representing the highest level of social skill.
*$p < .001$.

that there are times when people should inhibit, de-intensify, or mask their emotions. Similarly, Andersen and Guerrero (1998) discussed a process called *channelling*, which involves the selective display of certain emotions in particular contexts but not others (see also Carmas, 1985). For example, when people are denied promotions, it might be in their best interest to inhibit their sadness and/or anger until they get home. Females who are highly expressive (i.e., they express emotions spontaneously and accurately) may be at a disadvantage in such situations compared to their less emotionally expressive male counterparts. Indeed, the present study's data suggest that men have a general advantage when it comes to inhibiting or managing emotional displays (see also Burgoon, Buller, Grandpre, & Kalbfleisch, chap. 15, this volume).

High levels of social sensitivity can also be detrimental under certain circumstances. The items that measure this skill include the following: "I am often concerned with what others are thinking of me," "I am very sensitive of criticism," and "Sometimes I think that I take things that other people say to me too personally." Statements such as these reflect an overreliance on other people's opinions. Moreover, Guerrero (1996) found that skill in social sensitivity (as measured by Riggio's scale) associated positively with insecurity and the need for external validation. Moderate levels of social sensitivity probably relate to a healthy awareness of and sensitivity to others' thoughts and opinions. Furthermore, individuals who are moderately socially sensitive are probably good listeners and accurate decoders of information. In contrast, individuals with high levels of social sensitivity are likely to be oversensitive and preoccupied with what others think of them.

Taken together, these findings demonstrate that women are not uniformly more socially skilled than men, as is sometimes implied in the literature. Rather, men and women possess similar skills, but women have a slight edge when it comes to encoding and decoding nonverbal and verbal communication, whereas men have a slight edge when it comes to controlling or managing the nonverbal expression of emotion. In general, women may also have more problems with oversensitivity than men.

An intriguing avenue for future research is investigating how interaction patterns influence and are influenced by sex differences in social skills. Sex differences in social skills are probably promoted in children's same-sex play groups. Girls may reciprocate one another's verbal and nonverbal expressivity and they may expect other girls to be responsive and sensitive to their thoughts and feelings. Boys likely feel pressure to inhibit certain emotional displays in their play groups. As a case in point, boys may learn to act cool and unaffected when punished or tough when in pain. As children grow older and opposite-sex interaction becomes more frequent, sex differences in social skills probably play off one another. For example, women may need to be highly expressive if their male partners are relatively unsensitive to their nonverbal and verbal cues. In some situations, it may be functional for men to inhibit emotional expression, especially if their female partners would be overly sensitive to their emotional cues. By the same token, there may be times when it is functional for women to be extra sensitive to their male partner's cues especially when they are inhibiting emotions that could be shared constructively. Future research should examine these possibilities further.

Sex Differences in Communicative Responses to Anger

Background. Research has produced inconsistent findings regarding sex differences in the experience and communication of anger. Shields (1984) found that men and women did not differ in the degree to which they felt anger, but women reported feeling more physiological symptoms of anger. Similarly, Buck (1979) argued that in aggressive situations the general trend on internalizing/externalizing is reversed, with women more likely to internalize their anger (and therefore feel more internalized arousal) and men more likely to externalize it. In contrast, Burrowes and Halberstadt (1987) failed to find sex differences in anger experience or expression despite analyzing self-reports and reports from family and friends. Thomas (1989) examined both the suppression and expression of anger and found no evidence for sex differences in suppression. However, women reported being more likely to disclose anger than men did. Still other research indicates that, although people overwhelmingly view females as the more emotional sex, people expect men to express anger more than women (Shields, 1987).

Studies on sex differences among children and adolescents tend to be more consistent, showing boys to be more outwardly angry and aggressive than girls. For example, Harris and Howard (1987) found adolescent boys to report more intense anger experiences than adolescent girls. Researchers have also found boys to use more retaliation and aggression in response to anger (Fabes & Eisenberg, 1991). Whitesell, Robinson, and Harter (1991) found that angry boys tend to hit and use other expressive strategies, whereas angry girls are more likely to employ both approach and avoidant strategies. It may be that adult men learn to control their angry outbursts better than young boys or adolescent males do.

The relatively inconsistent findings on sex differences in the way that anger is communicated point to the need for more research. In particular, research could benefit from examining finer-tuned modes of anger expression. For example, some research does not consider whether anger is communicated in an assertive or an aggressive manner, or an indirect or direct manner. Thus, the present research examines four types of communicative responses to anger proposed by Guerrero (1994). These four communicative responses are characterized by differences on dimensions of directness and threat. *Assertive* responses to anger involve direct and nonthreatening communication, such as calmly discussing angry thoughts and feelings with others. *Aggressive* responses involve communicating anger in a direct and threatening manner, such as arguing with the partner and slamming doors. When angry individuals communicate in a *passive–aggressive* manner, they use strategies that are indirect but threatening, such as giving cold or dirty looks and ignoring others. Finally, individuals can engage in *nonassertive denial* when experiencing anger. These individuals use indirect, nonthreatening communication, such as becoming quiet and avoiding anger-provoking situations.

The research on sex differences in the communication of anger suggests that men may be more likely to report using aggression than women. However, Guerrero (1994) found that men and women did not differ in their self-reports of angry aggression. Instead, Guerrero found that women perceived themselves to use less aggression than their partners perceived them to use. Sex differences did emerge for passive aggression and nonassertive denial, with data indicating that women use more of these strategies than do men. However, the sex difference for passive aggression was found for partner reports (rather than for self-reports). These findings suggest that individuals and their partners may perceive the same behavior differently.

Current Findings. Data from the present study's sample revealed a pattern that was somewhat inconsistent with Guerrero's (1994) results despite using identical scales. In the present study, interitem reliabilities ranged from .71 to .87 on the four scales. Results from t tests demonstrated that women reported significantly more passive aggression than men, whereas men reported more nonassertive denial than women (see Table 14.2). There were no differences for assertive or aggressive responses to anger.

Commentary. It is particularly interesting that men did not report using more angry aggression given that past studies have found boys to engage in more aggressive, violent behavior than girls. It may be that sex differences in aggression are more likely when comparing young boys and girls than when comparing young men and women. Presumably, young adults have learned rules of social appropriateness and will strive to avoid aggressive communication. Indeed, mean scores (see Table 14.2) suggest that angry people report using aggressive communication less often than assertive communication, which validates the contention that anger does not necessarily lead to or even reliably predict aggression (Canary, Spitzberg, & Semic, 1998; Guerrero, 1994). Of course, both men and women may

TABLE 14.2
Means and Standard Deviations Associated With Significant
t tests Comparing Men and Women on Self-Reports
of Communicative Responses to Anger

Communicative Responses	Men	Women	t(235)	η^2
Assertion	5.15 (.96)	5.01 (1.07)	1.01	.00
Aggression	3.21 (1.04)	3.16 (.99)	.39	.00
Passive Aggression	3.55 (1.12)	3.99 (1.39)	2.52*	.03
Nonassertive Denial	4.14 (1.38)	3.65 (1.54)	2.54*	.03

Note. Standard deviations are in parentheses. Means are on 1–7 scales, with 7 representing that a response was perceived to be used frequently.
*$p < .05$.

underreport their use of aggressive, angry displays to make their behavior appear more socially desirable.

The finding that women reported using passive aggression more than men is consistent with Guerrero's (1994) findings. In the case of an intense, negative emotion such as anger, women may find it somewhat difficult to control or hide their feelings. Yet women have been taught to refrain from expressing outwardly directed negative emotion. Hence, women may learn to channel their aggression through indirect channels, such as angrily leaving the scene or ignoring the partner. However, more research should be conducted before firm conclusions can be drawn regarding sex differences in expressing anger in a passive–aggressive manner. This is particularly true given the small effect size ($\eta^2 = .03$) connected to this finding.

Similarly, more research needs to be conducted on sex differences in nonassertive denial. The present study found that men reported using nonassertive denial in response to anger more than women. However, Guerrero's (1994) study found the exact opposite. Given that men have been found to be better at controlling their emotions than women, it makes intuitive sense that they would be able to deny or hide their angry feelings. However, Buck (1979) argued that when it comes to the expression of anger the externalizing/internalizing trend is reversed, with women more likely to internalize their anger and men more likely to externalize it. Thus, the jury is still out on which sex (if either) uses nonassertive denial more often as a means of coping with anger.

One possible explanation for the contradictory findings on nonassertive denial lies in the samples used in the present study and in Guerrero's (1994) study. In the present study, respondents were asked to reference the last few times they felt angry and to report how they generally respond to anger. Therefore, these respondents probably referenced a variety of targets for their anger, including friends, loved ones, acquaintances, coworkers, and even strangers. In contrast, the respondents in Guerrero's (1994) study were dyadic partners who were involved in dating or marital relationships. These respondents were asked to report on the way that anger was communicated in their romantic relationships. Hence, it is possible that sex differences in nonassertive denial are contingent on the type of relationship in which anger occurs. In general, men may use more nonassertive denial, presumably as a function of their ability to inhibit emotional displays. In their romantic relationships, however, men may feel emotion more intensely and therefore may externalize their emotions. This interpretation is consistent with research showing that men report being more emotionally expressive and self-disclosive in opposite-sex interactions as opposed to same-sex interactions (e.g., Afifi, Guerrero, & Egland, 1994; Aukett, Ritchie, & Mill, 1988; Burhke & Fuqua, 1987).

Sex Differences in Communicative Responses to Sadness

Background. Research has uncovered fairly reliable sex differences in the experience and expression of sadness and depression. Considerable evidence shows that women are more likely than men to be sad and depressed (e.g., Harris & Howard, 1987; Nolen-Hoeksema, 1987 Stapley & Haviland, 1989). Furthermore, emerging evidence suggests that depressed men tend to engage in activities designed to distract themselves from their depressed mood (e.g., engaging in sports) and to withdraw socially (Hammen & Peters, 1977; Oliver & Toner, 1990). In contrast, depressed women tend to be less active and engage in more rumination about the possible causes of their mood as well as the implications of their depression (Nolen-Hoeksema, 1987), and to engage in more interpersonal communication about their problems (e.g., Snell, Miller, Belk, Garcia-Falconi, & Hernandez-Sanchez, 1989; Wallbott, Ricci-Bitti, & Banninger-Huber, 1986). Similarly, Blier and Blier-Wilson (1989) found that college-age women (vs. college-age men) rate themselves as better at expressing sadness to others.

Research has also uncovered sex differences in the specific tactics chosen to cope with sadness and depression. Nolen-Hoeksema (1987) found men to report using the following tactics more often: "I avoid thinking of reasons why I'm depressed," "I do something physical," "I play a sport," and "I take drugs." Similarly, Kleinke, Staneski, and Mason (1982) found that depressed male college students were likely to cope with their sadness by thinking about unrelated items, ignoring their problem, or taking part in a physical activity. These types of responses likely distract men from their current depressive mood (Nolen-Hoeksema, 1987). Women have reported engaging in the following responses more often than men: "I try to determine why I'm depressed,' "I cry to relieve the tension," and "I talk to other people about my feelings" (Nolen-Hoeksema, 1987). Women also reported decreasing responsibilities and activities, confronting their feelings, and blaming themselves for their depressive state more often than did men (Kleinke et al., 1982). According to Nolen-Hoeksema, these responses incline women to focus and maintain attention on their depressive mood.

Similar sex differences in the communication of sadness and depression have been reported for children. Nolen-Hoeksema, Girgus, and Seligman (1986) found that depressed boys are more likely than depressed girls to endorse misbehavior (i.e., "I never do what I am told" and "I do bad things"). In contrast, depressed girls are more likely to endorse items indicative of negative self-evaluation and loneliness, such as "I feel alone," "I hate myself," and "I'll never be as good as other kids" (Nolen-Hoeksema et al., 1986). Nolen-Hoeksema (1987) concluded that among elementary school children, depressed boys tend to be more active and outer-directed, whereas depressed girls tend to be more contemplative and self-focused. Other studies have come to analogous conclusions, showing that girls tend to appear anxious, internalize their emotions, and seek comfort when dealing with sadness or depression, whereas boys tend to be aggressive, engage in distracting activities, or misbehave (Anderson, Williams, McGee, & Silva, 1989; Edelbrock, 1984; Ruble, Greulich, Pomerantz, & Gochberg, 1993).

These findings for sadness and depression resemble much of the general literature on emotion. For example, Brody and Hall (1993) noted a tendency for boys to act on their emotions (often aggressively) or avoid their feelings rather than talk about them with others. Girls, in contrast, show a tendency to internalize intropunitive emotions and reach out to others for comfort and support. Given these tendencies, we expected women (as compared with men) to respond to sadness by seeking social support and withdrawing from normal activity. We also expected men to exceed women in their use of activity as a distraction device. Thus, women should report greater reliance on interpersonal communication and relaxing or escaping from their normal routine as ways to cope with sadness. In contrast, men should report more frequent use of distracting behaviors, such as taking on new challenges or engaging in risky behavior.

Current Findings. Before testing our predictions, we developed scales for measuring communicative responses to sadness. In past research, the majority of scales measuring responses to sadness or depression have focused on cognitive responses, such as dwelling on one's problems or trying to think positively. Scales including behavioral responses have tended to focus on social withdrawal, distraction behaviors, and social support seeking (see Rohde, Tilson, Lewinsohn, & Seeley, 1990). However, we felt that there was a more diverse assortment of responses to sadness than was represented by these three categories. Thus, we culled 36 tactics from the literature and converted them to 7-point Likert-type scales. About half of these tactics were modeled after those reported in Rohde et al. (1990). All 36 tactics focused on communicative behavior or avoidance or had implications for how sadness would be communicated to others.

Principal components analysis with orthogonal rotation was utilized to test the factor structure of these 36 items. One item, spending quality time with others, was dropped from the analysis because it failed to load above .50 on any factor. The remaining 35 items produced a nine-factor solution that accounted for nearly 72% of the variance. Items were considered to be associated with a factor if the primary loading exceeded .50 and the secondary loading was at least .15 less than the primary loading. The nine scales derived from this analysis, and their interitem reliabilities, are shown in Table 14.3. *Activity* refers to attempts to keep oneself busy with usual or new activities. *Social support seeking* refers to efforts to spend time with and seek comfort and advice from one's social network. *Solitude* comprises spending time alone and avoiding others. *Positivity and distractions* focus on attempts to maintain a positive attitude and manage impressions. *Dependent behavior* comprises active and passive attempts to get others to help. *Dangerous behavior* refers to engaging in daring or reckless actions as a form of distraction. When people use *immobilization* tactics they deviate from their normal routine by staying in bed, moping around the house, and/or skipping school or work. *Cognitive control* refers to thinking things through before expressing one's feelings to others. Finally, *escapism* comprises efforts to indulge oneself by getting away from it all or spoiling oneself. Because of its low reliability, the scale representing escapism is not included in subsequent analyses.

Results from *t* tests reveal sex differences for two out of eight responses to sadness (see Table 14.4). As expected, women reported seeking more social support and men reported engaging in more dangerous behavior. Contrary to our predictions, sex differences did not emerge for activity, positivity and distractions, or immobilization.

Commentary.   Although sex differences only surfaced for two of the eight responses to sadness, the two that did emerge were generally consistent with past work on differential socialization and social skills. For example, in response to sadness, women reported seeking more social support than men. This finding makes sense in light of findings showing that women are skilled in emotional and social expressivity. Moreover, because women are sensitive to others' emotions, they may feel that others will reciprocate by listening and being empathic to their problems and concerns. In contrast, men perceived themselves to engage in more dangerous behavior in response to sadness. This finding comports with past work showing that young boys learn to seek physical and psychological independence from others and to handle problems on their own (Block, 1979, 1983; Cherry

TABLE 14.3
Interitem Reliabilities and Primary Factor Loadings
Associated With the Communicative Responses to Sadness Scales

Scales	Primary Loadings
ACTIVITY (α = .83)	
1. I try to keep myself busy with things that I like to do	.64
2. I take on a new and/or challenging activity	.75
3. I do something enjoyable	.56
4. I do something to restore my pride	.54
5. I busy myself in my ususal work	.72
6. I get involved in a new project or activity	.78
SOCIAL SUPPORT SEEKING (α = .85)	
1. I seek comfort from my social circle	.68
2. I spend time with friends or family	.55
3. I ask others for support and/or advice	.74
4. I talk over my problems with someone close to me	.51
5. I avoid talking about my problem with others (recoded)	.65
SOLITUDE (α = .82)	
1. I keep away from people	.80
2. I avoid other people	.67
3. I spend time alone	.67
POSITIVITY AND DISTRACTIONS (α = .81)	
1. I try to act cheerful so my mood will change	.55
2. I try to forget about my problems and act happy	.71
3. I do something to try and distract myself from my problems	.82
4. I do something to get my mind off the situation	.73
5. I try to act positive to keep my spirits up	.57
DEPENDENT BEHAVIOR (α = .75)	
1. I wait for someone to help me	.74
2. I try to get the attention of others	.66
3. I depend on others for help	.61
4. I rely on people who are close to me to see me through my problems	.53
DANGEROUS BEHAVIOR (α = .85)	
1. I do something rather dangerous or daring	.87
2. I do something reckless (like driving a car fast)	.90
IMMOBLIZATION (α = .65)	
1. I stay in bed	.75
2. I mope around the house	.51
3. I do nothing in particular	.66
4. I skip school or work	.53
5. I relax and take things easy for a while	.56
COGNITIVE CONTROL (α = .69)	
1. I tell myself to "stop and think" before doing anything impulsive	.73
2. I consider my actions very carefully before expressing myself	.83
ESCAPISM (α = .49)	
1. I plan to spend some time away	.69
2. I "spoil" myself	.51
3. I get away and do something pleasant	.75

TABLE 14.4
Means and Standard Deviations Associated With Significant t tests
Comparing Men and Women on Self-Reports of Communicative
Responses to Sadness

Communicative Responses	Men	Women	$t(235)$	η^2
Activity	4.22 (1.02)	4.37 (1.11)	1.07	.01
Social Support Seeking	4.32 (1.22)	5.07 (1.33)	4.34*	.07
Solitude	4.28 (1.33)	4.26 (1.45)	.14	.00
Positivity and Distractions	4.54 (.98)	4.64 (1.18)	.63	.00
Dependent Behavior	3.56 (1.23)	3.54 (1.23)	.12	.00
Dangerous Behavior	3.41 (1.64)	2.23 (1.44)	5.82*	.13
Immobilization	4.03 (1.00)	4.10 (1.07)	.50	.00
Cognitive Control	4.27 (1.31)	4.33 (1.35)	.33	.00

Note. Standard deviations are in parentheses. Means are on 1–7 scales, with 7 representing
that a response was perceived to be used frequently.
   *$p < .001$.

& Lewis, 1976). Hence, men may sometimes avoid seeking social support
when experiencing negative emotions and instead may engage in dangerous behavior that allows for the private release of emotional tension.

   These findings also replicate past research on sex differences in the
expression of sadness and depression. Previous research has shown that sad
or depressed women (vs. men) use interpersonal communication to try to
solve their problems and seek comfort from others (Nolen-Hoeksema, 1987;
Snell et al., 1989; Wallbott et al., 1986). Previous research also suggests that
men are more likely to respond to sadness by engaging in dangerous actions,
misbehavior, and aggression (Nolen-Hoeksema, 1987; Nolen-Hoeksema et
al., 1986). Thus, sad men may be more likely than sad women to engage in
behaviors such as getting drunk, picking a fight, driving a car fast, or bungee
jumping. Interestingly, however, there were no sex differences in general
activity (e.g., keeping busy, taking on new challenges) or positivity/distrac-
tions (e.g., keeping one's mind off the problem by thinking positively). This
suggests that men and women may not differ in their use of distraction as a
general response to sadness. Instead, men may exceed women in their use
of one specific type of distraction—dangerous behavior.

   Sex differences also failed to surface for immobilization. Given that
researchers (e.g., Kleinke et al., 1982; Nolen-Hoeksema, 1987) have reported that women are more likely to dwell on their sadness and decrease
their participation in responsibilities and activities, we predicted that
women would report more immobilization. Instead, women reported seeking the support of friends and loved ones. Thus, an interesting new research
direction is to determine what types of social support seeking and giving
are successful in alleviating sadness. As Nolen-Hoeksema (1987) argued,
excessive mulling about sadness leads women to focus on their negative
emotional state. In some situations, talking about problems with others

may actually keep sad people focused on their problems. In other cases, discussing problems with friends may lead to emotional catharsis and cognitive re-appraisal. As Burleson and Goldsmith (1998) argued, comforting messages are only effective when they lead a distressed person to re-appraise her or his situation as more positive (or less negative). Thus, the association between different forms of social support seeking, social support giving, cognitive mulling, and appraisal processes represents a rich area for future study. Given that men report engaging in more dangerous behavior, researchers may also wish to consider how dangerous behavior associates with cognitive mulling and re-appraisal processes.

Sex Differences in Communicative Responses to Jealousy

Background. Research focusing on sex differences in the experience and expression of jealousy has yielded some consistent patterns but also some mixed results. One fairly consistent difference in jealousy experience involves the nature of the jealous threat. Research has shown that situations involving the perception that one's partner has been sexually unfaithful lead to the most intense jealousy, followed by situations in which there is a perceived strong emotional bond between the partner and a rival (Buunk & Hupka, 1987; Hansen, 1985). Of course, situations involving both sexual infidelity and strong emotional connection to the rival are viewed as the most threatening and lead to the strongest feelings of jealousy, betrayal, and loss. When both sexuality and emotionality are threatened, research suggests that men may focus more on the sexual infidelity, whereas women may focus more on the emotional connection between the partner and rival (White & Mullen, 1989). This sex difference in focus may lead men and women to cope with jealousy in different ways.

Other research suggests that women internalize their jealousy through the experience of intropunitive emotions such as anxiety, sadness, and confusion while also directing anger toward their partners and feeling betrayed (Bryson, 1976). Guerrero, Eloy, Jorgensen, and Andersen (1993) found women to experience more envy, anxiety, discomfort, and upset than men when feeling jealous. Presumably, jealous women feel sad and anxious because they are worried about losing their relationships, and they feel anger and upset because they they perceive that their partners have betrayed them (White & Mullen, 1989). Men, in contrast, have been found to get angry at themselves (Bryson, 1976), deny jealous feelings (Buunk, 1982; White, 1981), and focus on threats to self-esteem (Buunk, 1982). Thus, men appear to focus more on individual concerns, whereas women appear to focus more on relational concerns.

Sex differences in coping strategies reflect women's relational concerns. White and Mullen (1989) concluded that jealous women are "more oriented toward solving relationship problems or directly expressing their emotions" (p. 129). Research has found jealous women to use several coping strategies more than men. These include: (a) inducing counter-jealousy in the partner; (b) trying to get even with the partner; (c) improving one's physical appearance; (d) seeking support from others; (e) trying to improve the relationship; (f) demanding commitment; and (g) using direct, relatively positive forms of communication (Amstutz, 1982; Bryson, 1976; Buss, 1988; Buunk, 1981; Guerrero et al., 1993; Parker, 1994; White, 1981). Although many of these strategies focus on solving relationship problems and directly expressing emotions, others such as getting even with the partner focus on retaliation. Such responses may stem from the intense feelings of betrayal that women report feeling.

Jealous men appear to engage in more dangerous, sexually aggressive, and possessive behavior and to interfere more with the rival relationship (Buss, 1988; White & Mullen, 1989; but see Parker, 1994, for an exception). Men have reported using the following strategies more than women: (a) getting drunk, confronting the rival, (b) keeping the partner away from potential rivals, (c) derogating the partner in front of potential rivals, (d) becoming sexually aggressive or promiscuous with others, (e) getting a friend to talk to the partner about the situation, (f) developing alternatives, and (g) breaking off the relationship (Amstutz, 1982; Bryson, 1976; Buss, 1988; Mathes, 1992; Weghorst, 1980; White & Mullen, 1989). In addition, Buss (1988) found jealous men to display resources (e.g., spend money on or buy gifts for the partner), use sexual inducements (e.g., give in to sexual requests), and debase themselves (e.g., say he'll change for her and let her have her way) more than jealous women. Taken together, these findings suggest that men engage in behavior designed to guard the primary relationship (Buss, 1988). If this behavior is unsuccessful, males may either try to preserve their relationship through resource displays, sexual inducements, or debasement, or they may seek new alternatives and terminate the relationship.

There are at least two jealous behaviors for which the evidence on sex differences is mixed: avoidance and verbal aggression. Some studies have found men to report using avoidance and denial more than women (e..g, Parker, 1994; White, 1981). Buunk (1986) also found a stronger relationship between jealousy and denial for men as compared to women. However, another study by Buunk (1982) indicated that women were more likely than men to avoid jealous situations, and Guerrero et al. (1993) found women to report more avoidance when recalling their jealous behavior. When verbal aggression is considered, findings are also contradictory. Some research indicates that men are more aggressive and derogate their partners more (e.g., Amstutz, 1982), although other research indicates that women engage in more distributive communication, such as arguing, making accusations, and yelling (e.g., Guerrero et al., 1993), and more derogation of the partner (Parker, 1994).

Current Findings. Given the prior evidence, women were expected to report using the following communicative responses to jealousy more than men: integrative communication, negative affect expression, counterjealousy inductions, revenge strategies, and appearance enhancement. In contrast, men were expected to report contacting the rival, restricting the partner's access to the rival, buying gifts for or spending money on the partner, and terminating the relationship more than women. In addition, we were interested in investigating potential sex differences in avoidance/denial and distributive communication because past findings for these two responses have been inconsistent.

To test these predictions, respondents completed several subscales from Guerrero, Andersen, Jorgensen, Spitzberg, and Eloy's (1995) Communicative Responses to Jealousy scale. The *integrative communication* scale measures an individual's tendency to use direct, nonaggressive forms of communication, such as actively discussing relational feelings. *Negative affect expression* comprises nonverbal expressions of jealousy-related affect, including acting nervous or appearing hurt. *Rival contacts* refers to communicating directly with the rival about the jealousy situation, including confronting the rival. *Avoidance/denial* measures the tendency to avoid communicating about jealousy and to deny jealous feelings. *Distributive communication* refers to direct, aggressive forms of communication, such as being sarcastic or rude and yelling at the partner. Interitem reliabilities for these five scales ranged from .75 to .84.

Several other tactics relevant to our predictions were measured using single-item scales. These items read as follows: (a) I try to make my partner feel jealous too; (b) I try to get "revenge" or "get back at" my partner; (c) I try to be more attractive and/or appealing than the rival; (d) I buy gifts for or spend money on my partner; (e) I restrict my partner's access to potential rivals; and (f) I de-escalate or terminate the relationship.

Results demonstrate that, as predicted, women reported using integrative communication, expressing negative affect, and enhancing their appearance more than men (see Table 14.5). Also consistent with expectations, men reported contacting the rival, restricting the partner's access to potential rivals, and giving gifts/spending money more than women. Contrary to our predictions, there were no sex differences for counterjealousy inductions, revenge strategies, relationship termination, avoidance/denial, or distributive communication.

Commentary. Overall, the significant results are consistent with past findings. The finding that women report more integrative communication corresponds with past research showing jealous women to engage in more

TABLE 14.5
Means and Standard Deviations Associated With Significant
t tests Comparing Men and Women on Self-Reports
of Communicative Responses to Jealousy

Communicative Responses	Men	Women	t(408)	η²
Integrative Communication	4.35 (1.39)	4.72 (1.43)	2.67*	.02
Negative Affect Expression	3.28 (1.21)	3.74 (1.42)	3.45**	.03
Counterjealousy Inductions	3.79 (1.78)	3.89 (2.01)	.39	.00
Revenge Strategies	2.41 (1.69)	2.26 (1.95)	−.62	.00
Attractiveness Enhancement	3.65 (1.70)	4.82 (1.61)	6.14**	.08
Rival Contact	2.51 (1.42)	1.98 (1.18)	4.09**	.05
Access Restriction	2.45 (1.71)	1.89 (1.52)	3.77**	.03
Giving Gifts/Spending Money	3.92 (1.88)	3.47 (1.73)	2.52*	.02
Relationship Termination	2.07 (1.62)	2.08 (1.71)	−.04	.00
Avoidance/Denial	3.90 (1.29)	3.90 (1.33)	.04	.00
Distributive Communication	2.96 (1.31)	2.96 (1.53)	.06	.00

Note. Standard deviations are in parentheses. Means are on 1–7 scales, with 7 representing that a response was perceived to be used frequently.
*p < .01; **p < .001.

positive, direct communication with their partners (Guerrero et al., 1993), question their partners more (Salovey & Rodin, 1985), and see communication as a more effective means of coping with jealousy (Buunk, 1981) than do men. It was also not surprising that women reported expressing jealous emotion more than men, given that women rated themselves as more emotionally expressive in the first study. Other research (e.g., Guerrero et al., 1993) also suggests that women experience and express more jealous emotion than men. Our finding that jealous women attempt to enhance their physical attractiveness corresponds with research by Buss (1988), which suggests that jealous women engage in a number of appearance–enhancing strategies, such as wearing the latest fashions and fixing one's hair, to a greater extent than jealous men (see also Salovey & Rodin, 1985).

The profiles for men are also consistent with past research. Our finding that men reported more contact with the rival is similar to Weghorst's (1980) field study findings. Weghorst found that jealous men were likely to look at the rival, whereas jealous women were unlikely to look at or speak to the rival. Similarly, our finding that men reported restricting their partners' access to rivals replicates Buss' (1988) research. Buss found men to engage in a variety of strategies designed to conceal their mates, such as refusing to introduce the partner to his friends and leading her away from potential rivals. Taken together, these results suggest that men and women differ in the ways they cope with the rival: Men are more likely to *interfere* with the rival relationship by contacting the rival or trying to restrict the partner's access to the rival, whereas women are more likely to *compete* with the rival by presenting themselves as more attractive and appealing than the rival. Our finding that jealous men (as compared with jealous women) reported giving more gifts and spending more money also mirrors Buss' (1988) findings. Thus, when jealous individuals try to maintain their relationships, men are more likely than women to buy gifts and spend money on their partners. In contrast, women are more likely than men to enhance their appearance and use integrative communication.

The null findings are also worth mentioning here. Based on past research, we hypothesized that women would report inducing counterjealousy and seeking revenge more than men. We also predicted that men would report terminating the relationship more often. These predictions were not supported. It is noteworthy that all of these strategies probably have negative connotations and could therefore be underreported. Therefore, more research using a variety of methods (other than self-report) is needed before these potential sex differences are dismissed. We also failed to find significant sex differences for avoidance/denial and distributive communication. Past research has been inconsistent on these measures, with some studies showing no sex differences, others showing females to favor these strategies, and still others showing males to favor these strategies (e.g., Amstutz, 1982; Buunk, 1982; Guerrero et al., 1993; Parker, 1994; White, 1981). Thus, it would be fruitful in the future to determine if there are relational or situational factors that moderate sex differences in avoidance/denial and distributive communication. For example, Parker (1994) demonstrated that factors such as the type of jealous threat (e.g., sexual vs. emotional), the attractiveness of the rival, and the relationship between the jealous person and the rival can all influence how jealousy is experienced and communicated.

CONCLUSIONS

Before proposing conclusions, it is important to note two limitations to the present studies. First, self-report measures can be problematic in several respects. Social desirability biases, inaccurate recall, and reliance on gender stereotypes can all influence how men and women report their skills and communication strategies. Therefore, more research is necessary to determine how social skills are reflected in actual interpersonal interaction between men and women. Similarly, it is important to examine how emotions are communicated in interactive situations. Second, the samples used in the present studies consisted of undergraduate students, most of whom were unmarried. Maccoby (1988) claimed that young adults are an ideal population for testing sex differences because they have recently developed individual identities but are still not far removed from the socialization processes of their youth. Nonetheless, the sex differences found in the present studies may not generalize to older and/or married individuals.

Although these limitations should be kept in mind, the present studies' findings are largely consistent with past research, which has utilized a variety of different methods and samples. Therefore, when findings from the present study are integrated with past literature on sex differences in social skills and emotional communication, several general conclusions can be drawn. This final section discusses these conclusions and explains them in light of biological and socialization explanations for sex differences in social skills and emotional communication.

The first two conclusions juxtapose findings related to general social skills against findings related to specific communicative responses to emotion. First, men and women differ in their self-perceptions of social skills: Women view themselves as superior at expressing and decoding emotion, whereas men view themselves as superior at controlling their emotional displays. This conclusion is consistent with past work showing sex differences in the encoding, decoding, and control of emotional expression (e.g., Buck et al., 1974; Burgoon et al., chap. 15, this volume; Hall, 1978; Riggio, 1993). Second, despite social skill differences, men and women report more similarity than difference in their communicative responses to anger, sadness, and jealousy. This is evidenced by the fact that only 10 out of 23 responses to these emotions produced sex differences. Moreover, in the present study and others, the effects sizes connected to significant sex differences in communicative responses to emotion are relatively small. In the present study, sex accounted for between 2% and 13% of the variance, with the majority of significant findings accounting for 5% or less. Thus, when differences do emerge, they appear to be subtle.

However, some sex differences do appear to be relatively consistent when comparing the present studies' results with past research. In fact, at least four more conclusions, all based on sex differences in the communication of discrete emotions, can be drawn:

1. In response to sadness, women report seeking more social support than men.
2. In response to sadness, men report engaging in more dangerous behavior than women.
3. In response to jealousy, women are more likely than men to report discussing their thoughts and feelings, expressing emotion nonverbally, and enhancing their physical appearance.
4. In response to jealousy, men are more likely than women to report focusing on the rival (either by confronting the rival or restricting the partner's access to potential rivals) and buying gifts or spending money on the partner.

From both evolutionary and social learning perspectives, these conclusions make theoretical sense. Natural selection processes are likely to favor an overall profile of emotional communication that generalizes somewhat to both sexes. For example, it is adaptive for both men and women to know how to comfort others, to be able to express pain or sadness when they need help, and to be able to hide fear or anxiety in certain situations. Socialization processes refine this adaptation process even more by helping to establish particular cultural rules for displaying and responding to emotion. In North American culture, for instance, people learn that it is appropriate to appear sad and subdued at a funeral, but that it is inappropriate to appear sad or disappointed if one receives a disliked gift. Thus, many of the same types of emotional communication are adaptive and socially sanctioned for both men and women within the same culture.

Some subtle sex differences, however, do emerge. Presumably these differences arise due to the specialized adaptive value that certain types of emotional communication have for each sex, as well as the sex role stereotypes that are valued within a culture. For example, evolutionary theory suggests that women more than men are valued for their physical attractiveness, whereas men are valued for their resources (e.g., Kenrick & Trost, 1989). If this is true, it is not surprising that jealous women strive to make themselves more physically attractive than potential rivals, whereas jealous men shower more gifts and money on their partners. Similarly, the social learning perspective suggests that women are taught to seek the support of others when feeling distress. Thus, it makes sense that women report seeking more support when sad and engaging in more integrative communication when jealous. Put simply, men and women who share a common genetic and cultural history are likely to express emotions similarly overall, despite some specialized sex differences in social skill and emotional communication.

REFERENCES

Afifi, W. A., Guerrero, L. K., & Egland, K. L. (1994, June). *Maintenance behaviors in same- and opposite-sex friendships: Connections to gender, relational closeness, and equity issues.* Paper presented at the annual meeting of the International Network on Personal Relationships, Iowa City, IA.

Amstutz, D. (1982). *Androgyny and jealousy.* Unpublished doctoral dissertation, Northern Illinois University.

Andersen, P. A., & Guerrero, L. K. (1998). Principles of communication and emotion in social interaction. In P. A. Andersen & L. K. Guerrero (Eds.), *Handbook of communication and emotion: Research, theory, applications, and contexts* (pp. 49–96). San Diego, CA: Academic Press.

Anderson, J., Williams, S., McGee, R., & Silva, P. (1989). Cognitive and social correlates of DSM-III disorders in preadolescent children. *Journal of American Academy of Child Adolescent Psychiatry, 28,* 842–846.

Aukett, R., Ritchie, J., & Mill, K. (1988). Gender differences in friendship patterns. *Sex Roles,* *19,* 57–66.

Aune, K. S., Buller, D. B., & Aune, R. K. (1996). Display rule development in romantic relationships: Emotion management and perceived appropriateness of emotions across relationship stages. *Human Communication Research, 23,* 115–143.

Barry, H., Bacon, M. K., & Child, I. L. (1957). A cross cultural survey of some sex differences in socialization. *Journal of Abnormal and Social Psychology, 55,* 327–332.

Beckwith, L. (1972). Relationships between infants' social behavior and their mothers' behavior. *Child Development, 43,* 397–411.

Bleier, R. (1991). Gender ideology and the brain: Sex differences research. In M. Notman & C. Nadelson (Eds.), *Women and men: New perspectives on gender differences* (pp. 63–73). Washington, DC: American Psychiatric Press.

Blier, M. J., & Blier-Wilson, L. A. (1989). Gender differences in self-rated emotional expressiveness. *Sex Roles, 21,* 287–295.

Block, J. H. (1973). Conceptions of sex role: Some cross-cultural and longitudinal perspectives. *American Psychologist, 28,* 512–526.

Block, J. H. (1979). Another look at sex differentiation in the socialization behavior of mothers and fathers. In J. Sherman & F. L. Denmark (Eds.), *Psychology of women: Future directions of research* (pp. 71–101). New York: Psychological Dimensions.

Block, J. H. (1983). Differential premises arising from differential socialization of the sexes: Some conjectures. *Child Development, 54,* 1335–1354.

Brody, L. R. (1985). Gender differences in emotional development: A review of theories and research. *Journal of Personality, 53*(2), 102–149.

Brody, L. R. (1993). On understanding gender differences in the expression of emotion: Gender roles, socialization, and language. In S. L. Ablon, D. Brown, E. J. Khantzian, & J. E. Mack (Eds.), *Human feelings: Explorations in affect development and meaning* (pp. 87–121). Hillsdale, NJ: Analytic Press.

Brody, L. R., & Hall, J. A. (1993). Gender and emotion. In M. Lewis & J. M. Haviland (Eds.), *Handbook of emotions* (pp. 447–460). New York: Guilford.

Brooks-Gunn, J., & Warren, M. P. (1989). Biological and social contributions to negative affect in young adolescent girls. *Child Development, 60,* 40–55.

Bryden, M. P. (1982). *Laterality: Functional asymmetry in the intact brain.* New York: Academic Press.

Bryson, J. B. (1976, September). *The nature of sexual jealousy: An exploratory paper.* Paper presented at the annual meeting of the American Psychological Association, Washington, DC.

Buck, R. (1977). Nonverbal communication of affect in preschool children: Relationships with personality and skin conductance. *Journal of Personality and Social Psychology, 35,* 225–236.

Buck, R. (1979). Individual differences in nonverbal sending accuracy and electrodermal responding: The externalizing-internalizing dimension. In R. Rosenthal (Ed.), *Skill in nonverbal communication: Individual differences* (pp. 140–170). Cambridge, MA: Oelgeschlager, Gunn & Hain.

Buck, R. (1982). Spontaneous and symbolic nonverbal behavior and the ontogeny of communication. In R. S. Feldman (Ed.), *Development of nonverbal behavior in children* (pp. 29–62). New York: Springer-Verlag.

Buck, R. (1983). Nonverbal receiving ability. In J. M. Wiemann & R. P. Harrison (Eds.), *Nonverbal interaction* (pp. 209–242). Beverly Hills, CA: Sage.

Buck, R., Miller, R. E., & Caul, W. F. (1974). Sex, personality, and physiological variables in the communication of affect via facial expression. *Journal of Personality and Social Psychology, 30,* 587–596.

Burhke, R. A., & Fuqua, D. R. (1987). Sex differences in same- and cross-sex friendships. *Sex Roles, 17*, 339–352.

Burleson, B. R., & Goldsmith, D. J. (1998). How the comforting process works: Alleviating emotional distress through conversationally induced reappraisals. In P. A. Andersen & L. K. Guerrero (Eds.), *Handbook of communication and emotion: Research, theory, applications, and contexts* (pp. 245–280). San Diego, CA: Academic Press.

Burrowes, B. D., & Halberstadt, A. G. (1987). Self- and family-expressiveness styles in the experience and expression of anger. *Journal of Nonverbal Behavior, 11*, 254–268.

Buss, D. M. (1988). From vigilance to violence: Tactics of mate retention in American undergraduates. *Ethology and Sociobiology, 9*, 291–317.

Buunk, B. (1981). Jealousy in sexually open marriages. *Alternative Lifestyles, 4*, 357–372.

Buunk, B. (1982). Strategies of jealousy: Styles of coping with extramarital involvement of the spouse. *Family Relations, 31*, 13–18.

Buunk, B. (1986). Husband's jealousy. In R. A. Lewis & R. E. Salt (Eds.), *Men in families* (pp. 97–114). Beverly Hills, CA: Sage.

Buunk, B., & Hupka, R. B. (1987). Cross-cultural differences in the elicitation of sexual jealousy. *Journal of Sex Research, 23*, 12–22.

Canary, D. J., Spitzberg, B. H., & Semic, B. A. (1998). The experience and expression of anger in social interaction. In P. A. Andersen & L. K. Guerrero (Eds.), *Handbook of communication and emotion: Research, theory, applications, and contexts* (pp. 189–213). San Diego, CA: Academic Press.

Carmas, L. A. (1985). Socialization of affect communication. In M. Lewis & C. Saarni (Eds.), *The socialization of emotion* (pp. 141–160). New York: Plenum.

Cherry, L., & Lewis, M. (1976). Mothers and two-year-olds: A study of sex differential aspects of verbal interaction. *Developmental Psychology, 12*, 278–282.

Condry, J., & Condry, S. (1976). Sex differences: A study of the eye of the beholder. *Child Development, 47*, 812–819.

Dunn, J., Bretherton, I., & Munn, P. (1987). Conversations about feeling states between mothers and their children. *Developmental Psychology, 23*, 132–139.

Edelbrock, C. (1984). Developmental considerations. In T. Ollendick & M. Herson (Eds.), *Child behavioral assessment* (pp. 20–37). New York: Pergamon.

Ekman, P. (1978). Facial expression. In A. W. Siegman & S. Feldstein (Eds.), *Nonverbal behavior and communication* (pp. 97–116). Hillsdale, NJ: Lawrence Erlbaum Associates.

Ekman, P., & Oster, H. (1979). Facial expressions of emotion. *Annual Review of Psychology, 30*, 527–554.

Fabes, R. A., & Eisenberg, N. (1991, April). *Children's coping with interpersonal anger: Individual and situational correlates.* Paper presented at the biennial meeting of the Society for Research in Child Development, Seattle, WA.

Fabes, R. A., & Martin, C. J. (1991). Gender and age stereotypes of emotionality. *Personality and Social Psychology Bulletin, 17*, 532–540.

Fivush, R. (1989). Exploring sex differences in the emotional content of mother–child conversations about the past. *Sex Roles, 20*, 675–691.

Friedman, H. S., & Riggio, R. E. (1981). Effects of individual differences in nonverbal expressiveness on transmission of emotion. *Journal of Nonverbal Behavior, 6*, 96–103.

Frijda, N. (1988). The laws of emotion. *American Psychologist, 43*, 349–358.

Fuchs, D., & Thelen, M. (1988). Children's expected interpersonal consequences of communicating their affective state and reported likelihood of expression. *Child Development, 59* 1314–1322.

Greif, E., Alvarez, M., & Ulman, K. (1981, April). *Recognizing emotions in other people: Sex differences in socialization.* Paper presented at the biennial meeting of the Society for Research in Child Development, Boston, MA.

Guerrero, L. K. (1994). "I'm so mad I could scream": The effects of anger expression on relational satisfaction and communication competence. *The Southern Communication Journal, 59,* 125–141.

Guerrero, L. K. (1996, November). *Attachment-style differences in communication skills and the expression of anger and sadness.* Paper presented at the annual meeting of the Speech Communication Association, San Diego, CA.

Guerrero, L. K., Andersen, P. A., Jorgensen, P. F., Spitzberg, B. H., & Eloy, S. V. (1995). Coping with the green-eyed monster: Conceptualizing and measuring communicative responses to romantic jealousy. *Western Journal of Communication, 59,* 270–304.

Guerrero, L. K., Eloy, S. V., Jorgensen, P. F., & Andersen, P. A. (1993). Hers or his? The experience and communication of jealousy in close relationships. In P. J. Kalbfleisch (Ed.), *Interpersonal communication: Evolving interpersonal relationships* (pp. 109–132). Hillsdale, NJ: Lawrence Erlbaum Associates.

Hall, J. A. (1978). Gender effects in decoding nonverbal cues. *Psychological Bulletin, 85,* 845–857.

Hammen, C. L., & Peters, S. D. (1977). Differential responses to male and female depressive reactions. *Journal of Consulting and Clinical Psychology, 45,* 994–1001.

Hansen, G. L. (1985). Dating jealousy among college students. *Sex Roles, 12,* 713–721.

Harris, I. D., & Howard, K. I. (1987). Correlates of depression and anger in adolescence. *Journal of Child and Adolescent Psychotherapy, 4,* 199–203.

Johnson, J. T., & Shulman, G. A. (1988). More alike than meets the eye: Perceived gender differences in subjective experience and its display. *Sex Roles, 19,* 67–79.

Kenrick, D. T., & Trost, M. R. (1989). A reproductive exchange model of heterosexual relationships: Putting proximate economics in ultimate perspective. In C. Hendrick (Ed.), *Close relationships* (pp. 92–118). Newbury Park, CA: Sage.

Klein, R. P., & Durfee, J. T. (1978). Effects of sex and birth order on infant social behavior. *Infant Behavior and Development, 1,* 106–117.

Kleinke, C. L., Staneski, R. A., & Mason, J. K. (1982). Sex differences in coping with depression. *Sex Roles, 8,* 877–889.

Lemerise, E. A., & Dodge, K. A. (1993). The development of anger and hostile interactions. In M. Lewis & J. M. Haviland (Eds.), *Handbook of emotions* (pp. 537–546). New York: Guilford.

Lewis, H. B. (1976). *Psychic war in men and women.* New York: New York University Press.

Maccoby, E. E. (1988). Gender as a social category. *Developmental Psychology, 24,* 755–765.

Malatesta, C. Z., Culver, C., Tesman, J., & Shepard, B. (1989). The development of emotion expression during the first two years of life. *Monographs of the Society for Research in Child Development, 50* (1–2, Serial No. 219).

Malatesta, C. Z., & Haviland, J. M. (1982). Learning display rules: The socialization of emotion expression in infancy. *Child Development, 53,* 991–1003.

Mathes, E. W. (1992). *Jealousy: The psychological data.* Lanham, MD: University Press of America.

Miller, J. B. (1976). *Toward a new psychology of women.* Boston: Beacon.

Nolen-Hoeksema, S. (1987). Sex differences in unipolar depression: Evidence and theory. *Psychological Bulletin, 101,* 259–282.

Nolen-Hoeksema, S., Girgus, J. S., & Seligman, M. E. P. (1986). *Sex differences in depressive symptoms in children.* Unpublished manuscript, University of Pennsylvania, Philadelphia, PA.

Oliver, S. J., & Toner, B. B. (1990). The influence of gender role typing on the expression of depressive symptoms. *Sex Roles, 22,* 775–790.

Parker, R. G. (1994, November). *An examination of the influence of situational determinants upon strategies for coping with romantic jealousy.* Paper presented at the annual meeting of the Speech Communication Association, New Orleans, LA.

Parnell, K. (1992). Toddler interaction in relation to mother and peers. (Doctoral dissertation, Boston University, 1992). *Dissertation Abstracts International, 53*(6-B), 3183.

Riggio, R. E. (1986). Assessment of basic social skills. *Journal of Personality and Social Psychology, 51,* 649–660.

Riggio, R. E. (1993). Social interaction skills and nonverbal behavior. In R. S. Feldman (Ed.), *Applications of nonverbal behavioral theories and research* (pp. 3–30). Hillsdale, NJ: Lawrence Erlbaum Associates.

Rimé, B., Mesquita, B., Phillippot, P., & Boca, S. (1991). Six studies on the sharing of emotion. *Cognition and Emotion, 5,* 435–465.

Rohde, P., Tilson, M., Lewinsohn, P. M., & Seeley, J. R. (1990). Dimensionality of coping and its relation to depression. *Journal of Personality and Social Psychology, 58,* 499–511.

Rotter, N. G., & Rotter, G. S. (1988). Sex differences in the encoding and decoding of negative facial emotions. *Journal of Nonverbal Behavior, 12,* 139–148.

Ruble, D. N., Greulich, F., Pomerantz, E. M., & Gochberg, B. (1993). The role of gender-related processes in the development of sex differences in self-evaluation and depression. *Journal of Affective Disorders, 29,* 97–128.

Saarni, C. (1982). Social and affective functions of nonverbal behavior: Developmental concerns. In R. S. Feldman (Ed.), *Development of nonverbal behavior in children* (pp. 123–147). New York: Springer-Verlag.

Sabatelli, R., Buck, R., & Dreyer, A. (1980). Communication via facial cues in intimate dyads. *Personality and Social Psychology Bulletin, 6,* 242–247.

Salovey, P., & Rodin, J. (1985). The heart of jealousy. *Psychology Today, 19*(9), 22–25, 28–29.

Shields, S. A. (1984). Reports of bodily change in anxiety, sadness, and anger. *Motivation and Emotion, 8,* 1–21.

Shields, S. A. (1987). Women, men, and the dilemma of emotion. In P. Shaver & C. Hendrick (Eds.), *Sex and gender* (pp. 229–250). Newbury Park, CA: Sage.

Snell, W. E., Miller, R. S., Belk, S. S., Garcia-Falconi, R., & Hernandez-Sanchez, J. E. (1989). Men's and women's emotional disclosures: The impact of disclosure recipient, culture, and the masculine role. *Sex Roles, 21,* 467–485.

Stapley, J. C., & Haviland, J. M. (1989). Beyond depression: Gender differences in normal adolescents' emotional experiences. *Sex Roles, 20,* 295–308.

Stewart, L. P., Stewart, A. D., Friedley, S. A., & Cooper, P. J. (1990). *Communication between the sexes: Sex differences and sex-role stereotypes.* Scottsdale, AZ: Gorsuch-Scarisbrick.

Strayer, J. (1986). Children's attributions regarding the situational determinants of emotion in self and others. *Developmental Psychology, 22,* 649–654.

Susman, E., Inoff-Germain, G., Nottelmann, E. D., Loriaux, D. L., Cutler, G. B., & Chrousos, G. (1987). Hormones, emotional dispositions, and aggressive attributes in young adolescents. *Child Development, 58,* 1114–1134.

Thomas, D. L., & Diener, E. (1990). Memory accuracy in the recall of emotions. *Journal of Personality and Social Psychology, 18,* 199–206.

Wagner, H. L., MacDonald, C. J., & Manstead, A. S. R. (1986). Communication of individual emotions by spontaneous facial expressions. *Journal of Personality and Social Psychology, 50,* 737–743.

Wallbott, H. G., Ricci-Bitti, P., & Banninger-Huber, E. (1986). Non-verbal reactions to emotional experiences. In K. R. Scherer, H. G. Wallbott, & A. B. Summerfield (Eds.), *Experiencing emotion: A cross-cultural study* (pp. 98–116). Cambridge, England: Cambridge University Press.

Weghorst, S. J. (1980, June). *Behavioral correlates of self-reported jealousy in a field experiment.* Paper presented at a meeting of the Animal Behavior Society, Ft. Collins, CO.

White, G. L. (1981). Jealousy and partner's perceived motives for attraction to a rival. *Social Psychology Quarterly, 44,* 24–30.

White, G. L., & Mullen, P. E. (1989). *Jealousy: Theory, research, and clinical strategies.* New York: Guilford.

Whitesell, N. R., Robinson, N. S., & Harter, S. E. (1991, April). *Anger in early adolescence: Prototypical causes and gender differences in coping strategies.* Paper presented at the biennial meeting of the Society for Research in Child Development, Seattle, WA.

Witelson, S. (1976). Sex and the single hemisphere: Right hemisphere specialization for spatial processing. *Science, 193,* 425–427.

Chapter 15

Sex Differences in Presenting and Detecting Deceptive Messages

Judee K. Burgoon
David B. Buller
Joseph R. Grandpre
University of Arizona

Pamela Kalbfleisch
University of Wyoming

By all historical accounts, dissembling, equivocating, misdirection, and exaggeration have been a part of the male and female condition for millennia. But does that mean that men's deceptive communication is inevitably and inescapably different from women's deceptive communication? Or might men and women, as members of the same genotypic family inhabiting the same earth and subject to the same life-molding experiences, and like their primate relatives, having recognized the significant gains to be had from deceit, have honed similar strategies for duping others? Having been subjected throughout history to others' duplicity, might men and women have become equally adept or inept at recognizing deceit?

The answer offered here is a qualified yes. We review literature and report data suggestive of the conclusion that, at least in the domain of encoding and decoding deception, men and women have largely achieved parity. We begin by summarizing the extant literature on sex differences in nonverbal and verbal deception displays, followed by a presentation of results from three experiments that we have reanalyzed to tease out any differences between male and female deceivers and truthtellers. We then consider the literature on deception detection, again looking for evidence of sex differences. We conclude with some speculations on why men and women might be similar or different.

COMMUNICATOR SEX AND THE ENCODING
OF DECEPTION

Two meta-analyses (Kalbfleisch, 1985; Zuckerman, DePaulo, & Rosenthal, 1981) have shown that female deception tends to be less successful (more readily detected) than male deception. However, a perusal of the wealth of deception research quickly reveals that, for the most part, the primary focus has been on uncovering behavioral profiles (verbal and nonverbal) that might allow men and women to detect deception in others, rather than on differences between men and women in those deception displays (e.g., Buller & Aune, 1987; Buller, Burgoon, Buslig, & Roiger, 1996; Buller, Comstock, Aune, & Strzyzewski, 1989; Buller, Strzyzewski, & Comstock, 1991; Burgoon & Buller, 1994; DePaulo & Rosenthal, 1979; DePaulo, Rosenthal, Rosenkrantz, & Green, 1982; deTurck & Miller, 1985; Ekman & Friesen, 1969, 1974; Hocking, Bauchner, Kaminski, & Miller, 1979; Kraut, 1978; Kraut & Poe, 1980; Littlepage & Pineault, 1978; Riggio & Friedman, 1983; Zuckerman, Koestner, & Alton, 1984; Zuckerman, Koestner, & Colella, 1985).

The results of such studies and several meta-analyses and summaries (e.g., DePaulo, Stone, & Lassiter, 1985; Zuckerman, DePaulo, & Rosenthal, 1981; Zuckerman & Driver, 1985) suggest that any analysis of sex differences in encoding may benefit from a strategic–nonstrategic distinction (Buller & Burgoon, 1994, 1996). Strategic cues are those that deceivers attempt to control deliberately during deception. They consist of (a) efforts to manage a message's information, (b) efforts to manage accompanying nonverbal behaviors, and (c) image- and relationship-protecting behavior. Such strategic cues include fewer factual assertions, fewer self-references, more leveling terms, shorter turns at talk, longer response latencies and pauses, smiling and nodding, and other behaviors. Although individuals may be able to control certain aspects of their behavior to appear more truthful, it is doubtful they can control all of these aspects at once; thus, some nonstrategic leakage is bound to occur. Nonstrategic classes of cues are those that arise unbidden and often involuntarily, including (a) revealing arousal and nervousness, (b) revealing negative affect, and (c) incompetent communication performances. Examples include, but are not limited to, more blinking, more self-adaptors, higher pitch, vocal nervousness, more speech errors, less gesturing, longer response latencies, stiffness, restricted trunk and limb movement, more leg/foot movement, more postural shifts, less nodding or smiling, less gaze, and more speech errors. This leakage and/or the sender's inability to properly control other cues may lead the receiver to believe that deception is taking place.

Of course, several preinteraction variables may moderate the appearance of strategic and nonstrategic cues. For example, communicators with strong social skills, such as the ability to adapt to different situations, are more successful at deception (Brandt, Miller, & Hocking, 1980; Burgoon, Buller, Guerrero, & Feldman, 1994; Miller, deTurck, & Kalbfleisch, 1983). However, none of these factors has been systematically linked to sex, and two experiments failed to show that men and women differ in demeanor bias (i.e., one sex does not look more suspicious than another; Duncan & Kalbfleisch, 1995; Riggio, Tucker, & Throckmorton, 1987). Moreover, no theoretical account of deceptive communication emphasizes sex as an important feature.

Indeed, sex differences have been mixed and inconclusive in studies of deception. For example, Cody and O'Hair (1983) reported that only leg/foot movements and hand gestures differentiated men from women. In general, male liars engaged in more leg/foot movements than did female liars. As the interaction progressed, male liars and female truthtellers engaged in more leg/foot movement, possibly indicating increased comfort over time regardless of deceptiveness. However, when male liars had time to prepare their answers, they tended to suppress these leg/foot movements as well as their gestures. These suppression effects were attributed to men better controlling leakage during prepared lies—a common behavior management strategy (Buller & Burgoon, 1996).

By contrast, Donaghy, Grandpre, and Davies (1994) found that women who had not rehearsed their lies had the most foot/leg movement, whereas unrehearsed men had the least movement. Men and women giving rehearsed lies had approximately equivalent amounts of leg/foot movement. Donaghy et al. also found that women had longer response latencies and more head movement when lying than when telling the truth, whereas men showed just the opposite behaviors (longer response latencies and more head movement when telling the truth). Previously, deTurck and Miller (1985) found no differences for men and women on leg/foot movement, response latencies, or head movement. These limited and contradictory findings do little to warrant definitive conclusions about kinesic differences between male and female liars.

In research on the vocal channel, O'Hair and Cody (1987) showed that women had more vocal stress than men when lying, particularly when telling prepared lies, whereas men showed the same level of vocal stress for truthful and deceptive responses. The authors speculated that women may release or leak their internal arousal through an increase in vocal stress. Likewise, DePaulo (1992) contended that women may have more difficulty concealing their deceit because they are more spontaneously expressive, which might be evident in women's vocal stress during deception.

Do these meager findings indicate minimal differences between men and women in their deceptive displays? Not necessarily. The voluminous nonverbal and verbal literature tells us that men and women's nonverbal expressions differ in many ways (see e.g., Burgoon, Buller, & Woodall,

1996; Hall, 1984; Tannen, 1994, for summaries). For example, women tend to smile and gaze more than men. Women also have less relaxed and more closed off body positions and, in general, are more approachable and expressive. Conceivably, these could result in different forms of deception displays. Their pleasant, immediate style may help women strategically create a favorable image when deceiving. Their lack of relaxation and greater expressiveness may result in more nonstrategic leakage of nervousness and negative affect. However, numerous other studies (e.g., Burgoon, 1991; Burgoon, Le Poire, & Rosenthal, 1995; deTurck, 1991; Miller et al., 1981; Riggio & Friedman, 1983) have failed to find sex differences in nonverbal cue displays during deception, leading Burgoon et al. (1996) to conclude that the extent of sex differences may be overstated.

To address the issue of sex differences and encoding directly, we revisited three of our recent deception experiments to determine whether men and women might differ systematically in the ways they produce deception. These investigations were all undertaken as part of a program of research testing Interpersonal Deception Theory (IDT; Buller & Burgoon, 1996) and so included multiple verbal and nonverbal measures designed to assess strategic and nonstrategic activity during interpersonal interactions. Although it would have been ideal to consider sex of sender, sex of receiver, and the resultant sex composition of each dyad, an imbalance in the numbers of male–male, male–female, and female–male dyads precluded doing so. Thus, the focus here is strictly on sex differences in deceptive versus truthful encoding.

THREE DECEPTION EXPERIMENTS

Deceptive Versus Truthful Presentations During Interviews

The first experiment (Burgoon & Buller, 1994) employed an interview format during which participants who were randomly assigned to an interviewee (EE) role truthfully or deceptively answered a series of preset interview questions. Other participants randomly assigned to an interviewer (ER) role were or were not induced to be suspicious. (The suspicion induction is not relevant here; those results are reported in Burgoon, Buller, Dillman, & Walther, 1995).

Sample. A sample of 240 undergraduate students participated in 120 dyadic interactions. Half of these dyads were strangers and the other half friends (but not best friends or romantic partners). The current analysis focused on the senders in these dyads (i.e., the interviewees [EEs]), 48 of whom were male and 74 female.

Method. An interview situation was selected to facilitate the type of dynamic interaction one would expect from a normal interview while maintaining some experimental control over topics and interviewer (ER) behavior. After consenting to being videotaped and completing a true–false survey related to socially desirable, undesirable, or misanthropic attitudes, one half of the EEs were told that "some people, when answering these kinds of questions in actual conversation, tend to misrepresent their true feelings and actions. We want to determine if conversational partners can detect such lies." These EEs were instructed to answer the first five questions truthfully but to lie on the subsequent questions. The remaining EEs, assigned to the truthful condition, were simply told that we wanted to determine if their partner could detect truthful answers, so they needed to answer each question truthfully. Meanwhile, ERs also completed consent forms, reviewed the same items (recast in question form to be the basis for the interview), and received the suspicion induction.

Interviews were conducted in a living room-style laboratory complete with a one-way mirror through which interviews could be videotaped with minimal intrusiveness. The interviews were allowed to progress for 5 minutes past when deception commenced or until all questions were completed. EEs and ERs then separated, completed questionnaires regarding their own and the other participant's behavior during the interview, and were debriefed.

Subsequently, teams of trained coders rated a large number of EE nonverbal and verbal behaviors that were reduced to 18 composite and individual measures designed to measure multiple strategies and tactics for behavior, image, and information management. The nonverbal measures chosen to capture behavior management were three dimensions related to nonverbal involvement: (a) nonverbal immediacy (body lean, closeness, facing, eye gaze), (b) social anxiety (vocal and kinesic relaxation, object adaptors, self-adaptors, random movement, rocking and twisting), and (c) conversational management (smoothness of turn exchanges and fluency). Measuring image management were three scales related to pleasantness (vocal and kinesic pleasantness and nodding). Finally, reflecting information management were the verbal measures of talk time (brevity of turns) and verbal nonimmediacy (modifiers, levelers, self-references, and group-references).

Results. Each dependent measure was analyzed in a 2 (truth/deception) × 2 (sex of sender) × 2 (time periods following onset of deception) mixed model analysis of variance (ANOVA), with time as a repeated factor. Results produced many sex differences but few related specifically to deception.

First considering sex effects regardless of truthfulness, nearly all of the immediacy behaviors were implicated. The combined nonverbal immediacy score showed that women ($M = .11$) were more immediate than men ($M = -.20$), $F(1,76) = 4.37$, $p = .010$, $\eta^2 = .083$. Women also became less immediate over time ($M_{t1} = 0.13$, $M_{t2} = 0.09$), whereas men became somewhat more immediate ($M_{t1} = -0.22$, $M_{t2} = -0.17$), $F(1,76) = 4.06$, $p = .047$, $\eta^2 = .05$. A main effect for closeness, $F(1,76) = 6.60$, $p = .012$, $\eta^2 = .08$, indicated that female EEs sat closer to ERs ($M = 3.47$) than did male EEs ($M = 2.65$). A similar main effect for body lean, $F(1,76) = 4.89$, $p = .030$, $\eta^2 = .06$, revealed that female EEs leaned toward the ER ($M = 2.27$) more than did male EEs ($M = 1.74$). Sex also interacted with time on gaze, $F(1,76) = 7.08$, $p = .01$, $\eta^2 = .08$. Male EEs increased gaze toward the interviewer over time ($M_{t1} = 5.16$, $M_{t2} = 5.54$), whereas female EEs were more consistent in their gaze patterns over time ($M_{t1} = 5.55$, $M_{t2} = 5.57$).

For nonverbal behaviors involving deception differences, four variables showed systematic relationships. A sex × deception interaction for rocking, $F(1,76) = 6.54$, $p = .013$, $\eta^2 = .08$, indicated that deceptive women ($M = 4.11$) and truthful men ($M = 4.10$) rocked more than deceptive men ($M = 3.51$) and truthful women ($M = 2.88$). A sex × deception × time interaction emerged for nods, $F(1,76) = 5.67$, $p = .020$, $\eta^2 = .07$. Truthful men increased their number of nods over time ($M_{t1} = 2.92$, $M_{t2} = 3.37$), whereas deceptive men decreased them ($M_{t1} = 3.08$, $M_{t2} = 2.61$); women showed very little change over time or between truth and deception (truthful $M_{t1} = 3.25$, $M_{t2} = 3.19$; deceptive $M_{t1} = 3.59$, $M_{t2} = 3.58$) and their amount of nodding during deception exceeded men's. Another sex × deception × time interaction emerged on number of self-adaptors, $F(1,76) = 4.31$, $p = .041$, $\eta^2 = .054$. Truthful men increased their number of self-adaptors from Time 1 to Time 2 ($M_{t1} = 2.37$, $M_{t2} = 2.74$), whereas truthful women decreased them slightly from Time 1 to Time 2 ($M_{t1} = 3.31$, $M_{t2} = 3.00$). Deceptive males exhibited fewer self-adaptors and maintained their low number from Time 1 to Time 2 ($M_{t1} = 2.30$, $M_{t2} = 2.21$). By contrast, deceptive women increased them over time ($M_{t1} = 2.36$, $M_{t2} = 2.81$) although not to the same level as truthful women. Overall, deceptive men were less active physically and more inclined to decrease activity over time relative to truthful men, whereas women tended to show an increase in activity under deception.

Examination of turn exchanges showed that deception was more disruptive for women than for men. When deceiving, men increasingly shortened their response latencies over time ($M_{t1} = 4.34$, $M_{t2} = 5.27$, where $7 = $ *very short*), whereas women's latencies became longer (less short) over time ($M_{t1} = 4.61$, $M_{t2} = 4.05$). When telling the truth, both men and women showed little change in their response latencies (men $M_{t1} = 4.87$, $M_{t2} = 4.90$; women $M_{t1} = 4.82$, $M_{t2} = 5.25$), sex × deception × time, $F(1,76) = 5.96$, $p = .017$, $\eta^2 = .07$. Overall, women had more smooth transitions (M

= 4.81) than did men ($M = 4.57$), F(1,76) = 5.59, $p = .021$, $\eta^2 = .07$, but this difference did not change with deceptiveness.

Verbally, a significant sex × deception interaction effect emerged for brevity, $F(1,95) = 6.37$, $p = .013$, $\eta^2 = .06$. Deceptive women enacted notably longer turns ($M = 6.29$) than deceptive men ($M = 4.46$). Moreover, turn length for deceptive men was similar to that for truthful men ($M = 4.31$) and women ($M = 4.27$). Sex, however, had no effect on the verbal nonimmediacy cues of modifiers, levelers, self-references, and group references (all $p > .05$).

Discussion. Sex had a limited effect on verbal and nonverbal performance in these deceptive conversations. Women exhibited higher nonverbal immediacy, consistent with past research on sex differences in conversation (Burgoon et al., 1996; Hall, 1984), although men increased some of these cues as the conversations progressed. However, the majority of nonverbal and verbal behaviors tested from this experiment showed no interaction between sender sex and sender deceptiveness. The few behaviors manifesting sex differences are suggestive of men strategically restricting their behavior to avoid arousal cues: They displayed less rocking and fewer self-adaptors than women when deceiving as compared with when they told the truth. Curtailed activity by deceptive men was also seen by Cody and O'Hair (1983), especially when men had the opportunity to plan their lies. However, this reduction in activity may have unwittingly eroded men's credibility by making them look overly restrained, stiff, and uninvolved. For example, the reduction in head nodding, which is a common show of attentiveness and interest, might be viewed as an inadvertent by-product of an overall suppression of activity. By comparison, women remained active, in line with DePaulo's (1992) contention that women may do less well controlling their expressivity. This tendency also might account for why women, compared with men, became more talkative when deceiving.

In other respects, men were more successful at managing turn-related behavior than women: Their response latencies while deceiving decreased over time, whereas women's response latencies increased. It is noteworthy that this sex difference bolsters recent findings by Donaghy et al. (1994) that women used longer response latencies.

Although these sex differences are tantalizing, they must be viewed within the context of the large number of cues that did not distinguish men from women during deceptive performances. Comparatively, fewer behaviors showed differences than did not. The effect sizes (5%–8% of variance) likewise failed to lend much credence to a claim of substantial differences between male and female deceivers. Thus, this investigation is more consistent with a sex similarity than a sex differences position.

Types of Deception During Interviews

A second experiment (Buller, Burgoon, White, & Ebesu, 1994) was similar to that of the first experiment: Participants were assigned to an interview situation as either an interviewee (EE) or interviewer (ER) where the ER would ask the EE a series of questions. However, in this case, EEs engaged in one of three different types of deception: fabrication (i.e., completely untrue statement), equivocation (i.e., vague, unclear, indirect, or ambiguous statement), or concealment (i.e., statement that withholds or omits relevant truthful information).

Sample. Participants were adults recruited from the local community (N = 72) and instructors and other post personnel from a U.S. army intelligence school ($N = 60$). Once again, analyses were conducted only on senders in the experimental dyads. There were 41 men and 25 women. Half of the senders were paired with a stranger and the other half with a friend.

Method. Initial procedures paralleled those of the preceding investigation. During the separation of EEs and ERs, EEs were again told that it is not always in one's best interest to tell the whole truth. To practice their skills at adapting to such situations, they were asked to answer the first three questions truthfully, but then to answer all subsequent questions deceptively. Some were told to give completely untrue answers (fabrication; $n = 23$); others were instructed to give vague, unclear, indirect, or ambiguous answers (equivocation; $n = 21$); the remainder were asked to withhold or omit relevant information from their answers (concealment; $n = 22$). EEs had an opportunity to review samples of the assigned deception type and practice answering potential questions. Meantime, one half of the ERs received a suspicion induction (see Burgoon, Buller, Ebesu, Rockwell, & White, 1996) and reviewed the interview questions.

Once EEs and ERs were reunited, the interviews were allowed to proceed for 15 minutes or until all the questions had been answered. Participants were again separated, debriefed, and asked to complete several posttest measures. Trained coders working in pairs assessed EEs' involvement, pleasantness, dominance, formality, vocal and kinesic expressiveness, vocal and kinesic tension, rate, pitch, loudness, articulation, filled pauses, unfilled pauses, repetitions, and stuttering. The last four variables were combined into a single measure of fluency. Finally, verbal nonimmediacy (levelers, modifiers, self- and group references, past- and present-tense verbs) and humor (sarcasm and statements that make light of a topic) were measured.

Results. Analyses of these data were conducted with mixed-model multivariate analysis of variance (MANOVA) procedures. Sex of sender and type of deception (falsification, equivocation, and concealment) were between-subjects factors and truth/deception was a within-subjects factor. Generally speaking, women ($M = 7.14$) encoded a more pleasant demeanor than did men ($M = 6.46$), $F(1,55) = 15.30$, $p < .001$, $\eta^2 = .22$. Vocally, men ($M = 4.22$) spoke slower than did women ($M = 4.63$), $F(1,54) = 4.43$, $p = .040$, partial $\eta^2 = .08$; this difference persisted regardless of truthfulness ($p > .05$) or type of deception ($p > .05$). As would be expected, women ($M = 4.73$) spoke in a higher pitch than did men ($M = 3.95$). Verbally, women ($M = 2.40$) had a higher rate of group references than did men ($M = 1.1$), $F(1,54) = 5.67$, $p = .02$, $\eta^2 = .09$.[1] However, these latter two differences did not differ across deception type and truthfulness.

Regarding pitch, men decreased their pitch in the equivocation condition (fabrication $M = 4.18$, equivocation $M = 3.60$, concealment $M = 4.06$), when compared with fabrication and concealment conditions, sex × type of deception $F(2,54) = 4.15$, $p = .021$, partial $\eta^2 = .13$. By contrast, women increased their pitch in the equivocation condition (fabrication $M = 4.45$, equivocation $M = 5.10$, concealment $M = 4.63$). Additionally, sex moderated vocal expressivity under deception, sex × type of deception × truth $F(2,56) = 3.20$, $p = .048$, $\eta^2 = .103$. Men were especially less vocally expressive when equivocating ($M = 5.76$) as compared with when they fabricated ($M = 6.61$) and concealed ($M = 6.19$), whereas women remained vocally expressive in all types of deception (fabrication $M = 6.78$, equivocation $M = 6.78$, concealment $M = 6.74$). When telling the truth, women were somewhat more vocally expressive (fabrication $M = 6.91$, equivocation $M = 6.53$, concealment $M = 6.73$) than were men (fabrication $M = 6.41$, equivocation $M = 6.29$, concealment $M = 6.19$).

Regarding rate of group references, the rate generally increased when both sexes deceived, but women (vs. men) increased their use of group references far more when deceiving (female truth $M = .04$, deception $M = 4.5$; male truth $M = 0.2$, deception $M = 2.0$), $F(1,54) = 5.40$, $p = .02$, $\eta^2 = .09$. Finally, women ($M = 6.06$) were much more formal than men were ($M = 5.15$) when telling the truth, but when deceiving women became much less formal ($M = 5.28$) and more similar to men ($M = 4.89$), $F(1,55) = 5.88$, $p = .019$, $\eta^2 = .10$. Sex did not affect any other verbal or nonverbal behaviors enacted by deceivers and truthtellers.

Discussion. Once again, the most prominent finding was that sex had little influence on behavior when senders dissembled, although the few sex differences that did emerge were larger in size (7%–22% of variance) than those witnessed in the first experiment. Women were more pleasant, more expressive on average, used a higher pitch, spoke faster, and used more group references than men regardless of deceptiveness. These be-

---

[1]Measures of verbal behaviors were expressed as rates per second to remove the effect of loquacity on frequency of verbal behavior. Mean rates per second were extremely low. Thus, the mean rates were multiplied by 100 to aid interpretation.

havioral patterns are consistent with prototypical communication profiles of women being generally more expressive and pleasant than men (e.g., LaFrance, Hecht, & Noyes, 1994).

However, sex had limited moderating impact on deception displays. Tests on global measures of involvement, pleasantness, dominance, kinesic expressiveness, vocal tension, and kinesic tension revealed no interactions between sender sex and sender deceptiveness. Neither did specific measures of loudness, articulation, fluency, leveling terms, modifiers, self-references, past- and present-tense verbs, and humor. In the few instances where sex did alter deception displays, the differences might be seen as reflecting alternate strategic efforts by men and women when deceiving. Men decreased vocal expressivity and lowered their pitch when equivocating, perhaps as part of the general behavior management strategy of reducing activity and expressiveness to avoid displaying arousal cues. As noted earlier, Cody and O'Hair (1983) and Donaghy et al. (1994) reported evidence for a similar strategy by men.

Comparatively, women remained more expressive. Although this might be interpreted as support for the contention that women experience greater difficulty in controlling such cues during deception (DePaulo, 1992), an alternative interpretation is that maintaining expressivity reflects the twin behavior and image management strategies of projecting a normal-appearing demeanor during deception and engagement in the conversation.

Two other behavioral changes in line with viewing female displays as strategic are women's increased informality and use of group references when deceiving, relative to telling the truth; comparatively, men did not make such adjustments. Informality may have been an image management strategy by women to appear more positive to the receiver. Originally, the tactic of using more group references was conceived as part of a larger information management strategy of verbal nonimmediacy and disassociation designed to reduce responsibility for one's utterances. The fact that women (vs. men) also used more group references during truthtelling implies that it is not a linguistic move associated exclusively with deception. Although it may signal lack of autonomy (or, more pejoratively, dependence and powerlessness), thereby weakening one's individual responsibility for what is said, it may also signal inclusiveness, solidarity, and affiliation. This affiliative function would have the effect of capitalizing on partner sympathies and creating a positive image of oneself as friendly and trustworthy. Given that many linguistic and nonverbal choices are polysemous and can satisfy dual functions simultaneously (Tannen, 1994), use of more group references may have been designed to accomplish both image and information management. Absent independent corroboration of senders' motivations, either interpretation is tenable. This argues for closer attention to senders' objectives vis-à-vis their actual performance. As before, the number of sex differences during deception is so small that we are reluctant to make a strong case for the role of sex in deceptive performances.

Deceptive and Truthful Presentations
During Dyadic Discussions

The third investigation (Burgoon, Buller, Floyd, & Grandpre, 1996) was undertaken partly as a test of the extent to which deceivers share common strategies when attempting to deceive and partly as a pilot test of procedures for a larger investigation of interactive and noninteractive deception. Included in the latter objective was an assessment of the correspondence among sender, receiver, and observer perceptions of sender verbal and nonverbal behavior. Therefore, the investigation afforded a comparison between senders' intended strategies and their realization in the eyes of coparticipants or third parties.

Sample. Participants ($N = 46$) were students from upper division business courses who received extra course credit for engaging in a study of how people discuss personal topics and how such discussions differ among strangers and friends. Students in the friends condition were invited to bring a same-sex friend to the study. A coin toss determined one's assignment to the condition of sender (Person A), receiver (Person B), or observer (Person C) roles. Eighteen interacting dyads were formed (13 strangers, 5 friends; 10 same-sex, 8 mixed-sex), 10 of which had observers. Because of the small sample size and imbalance between friend and stranger dyads, only deception and sex effects are reported.

Method. Participants reported to the research laboratory where they were told that they would be discussing various topics taken from a game designed to encourage open communication. They were shown examples of the game cards on which topics were written. All participants were then separated, ostensibly to prevent discussion before being videotaped and to complete a brief preinteraction questionnaire on demographics (and, for friends, on the state of their relationship). During this separation, participants and observers received their respective experimental instructions.

The deception induction given to Persons A (senders) consisted of telling them that "sometimes situations arise when it is not in one's best interest to tell the truth, the whole truth, and nothing but the truth—for instance, to present your best image, to protect another's feelings, to avoid unpleasant circumstances. A certain level of communication skill is necessary to be able to adapt to these situations." The assistant proceeded to ask them to practice their skills in the upcoming discussion by being totally truthful on some questions but *not* telling the truth on others. Their cue to tell or not tell the truth would be a red or blue number printed at the top of the card. They were encouraged to use a variety of options to deceive (e.g., giving clear but completely untrue answers; being vague, indirect, unclear, and ambiguous; withholding, omitting, or avoiding discussing relevant information) and rely on their "own communication techniques and style to give answers which fall short of being the truth, the whole truth, and nothing but the truth." As an incentive, they were informed that they would receive a prize at the end of the interaction if they were successful.

Persons B (receivers) were told that their main objective was to keep the interaction flowing smoothly, for which they could receive a small prize as an incentive if performed successfully. (They were blind to the deception manipulation.) Persons C (observers) observed the discussion through a one-way mirror and were cued to complete ratings of Person A (discussed later) after the first deceptive topic. Discussions took place in the same interaction room as the two previous experiments and continued until participants had discussed three topics: one baseline truthful, one additional truthful, and one deceptive. Order of the truthful and deceptive questions was rotated so that no two dyads would answer the same truthful and deceptive questions in the same order.

Persons A and B were again separated to complete postmeasures. Person A was initially interviewed by a research assistant about what happened during the truthful and deceptive topics and specifically what they attempted to do verbally and nonverbally while deceiving. To produce cued recall, they then watched the videotape of their second and third topics and, after each, completed a series of Likert format items rating their verbal and nonverbal behaviors. Persons B watched the same videotaped topics and completed the same ratings on Person A's behavior. The rating forms consisted of 28 items designed to measure four composite dimensions of information management (veridicality, information completeness, directness/relevance, and clarity/personalism) and an additional 32 items measuring five dimensions of nonverbal involvement (immediacy, expressivity, altercentrism, conversation management, and social anxiety), nonverbal pleasantness, dominance, surveillance, and general desirability of Person A's performance.

Results. Person A's self-ratings on the information management dimensions produced some main effects for deception but no sex main effects or deception by sex interactions. The same was true for Person B and observer reports. Thus, no sex differences either related or unrelated to deception emerged on verbal behavior.

For the nonverbal involvement dimensions, a mixed model MANOVA produced a sex x deception interaction on senders' self ratings, $F(1,12) = 11.26$, $p = .006$, with significant effects in the univariate analyses for immediacy, $F(1,12) = 5.03$, $p = .045$, $\eta^2 = .30$, and altercentrism, $F(1,12) =$

11.26, $p = .006$, $\eta^2 = .48$. Men saw themselves as less immediate while deceiving ($M = 4.25$) than when telling the truth ($M = 5.25$). Men (vs. women) also reported being less immediate ($M = 6.33$) when deceiving (female truth $M = 4.71$). Men similarly reported being less altercentered while under deception ($M = 3.75$) than under truthful conditions ($M = 6.00$). Women, by contrast, reported being more altercentered than men and remaining altercentered from deception ($M = 6.22$) to truth ($M = 6.54$).

For nonverbal dominance, ANOVA yielded a deception × sex × question interaction on senders' self ratings, $F(1,7) = 10.06$, $p = .016$, $\eta^2 = .590$. Men saw themselves as becoming more dominant when deceiving ($M = 5.00$) than when telling the truth ($M = 3.00$), whereas women saw themselves as becoming less dominant when deceiving ($M = 2.38$) than when telling the truth ($M = 3.71$). This meant that men also saw themselves as much more dominant than women did when deceiving. Interestingly, observers did not share male senders' perceptions. They saw both men and women as less dominant under deception and women as especially submissive.

Discussion. Once again, sex produced a few main effects and a few interactions with deception but the number of nonsignificant relationships outnumbered the significant ones by a large margin. However, the ones that did emerge again implicated involvement and dominance as key sites for diverging male and female nonverbal patterns.

Conclusions About the Sex Effects in Encoding of Deception

A reexamination of all three experiments showed that sex was not very influential on the verbal and nonverbal demeanor of deceivers in interpersonal exchanges, and the differences that emerged were usually small (often accounting for less than 10% of variance). Although there was some variability in the cues examined in each experiment, where the same measures appeared at least twice, sex failed consistently to alter the same nonverbal and verbal deception displays across those studies. Moreover, in any given study, the number of nonsignificant sex × deception interactions far exceeded the number of significant ones. Given this, we believe that any claims for a pervasive effect of sex in deceptive performances is wildly overstated. At best, sex differences appear to play a small role in deceptive conversations.

Nevertheless, there are a few provocative patterns that emerge from our three experiments and from previous work by Donaghy et al. (1994) and Cody and O'Hair (1983). These imply that sex modestly alters strategic behavior, image, and information management, as well as nonstrategic leakage and performance decrements (Buller & Burgoon, 1994, 1996).

Men may opt to enact behavior management strategies that restrict non-verbal activity, with resultant decrements in expressivity. If this is a strategic ploy for controlling leakage by restraining physical activity, it may be an unwise choice (especially when coupled with a tendency to withdraw from the interaction) because the combined tactics run the risk of appearing abnormal and suspicious if overdone.

A pattern of greater female involvement is the most recurrent sex difference across the three experiments. Women may leak more arousal when deceiving as compared with their male counterparts, but may also create more of an appearance of expressivity, immediacy, and engagement by their talking more than men do when deceiving. As a strategy, involvement also may be more efficacious in light of previous findings that higher involvement and the appearance of normalcy while deceiving are most likely to earn high credibility ratings and evade detection (Burgoon, Buller, Guerrero, & Feldman, 1994). However, the greater activation associated with appearing involved risks conveying nervousness. It is also possible that men attempt to become more conversationally dominant than women when deceiving, but their self-assessments are not borne out by observers' perceptions so this may be more perceived than real.

Women and men also were inconsistent in their use of image management strategies that projected a positive front. In one experiment, men nodded less than women when deceiving—a behavior that typically occurs in the backchannel as a sign of agreement or attentiveness. In another experiment, women adopted a less formal conversational style when deceiving as opposed to telling the truth and, if our interpretation of group references is correct, created a greater sense of inclusiveness and solidarity. It is therefore possible that women and men use different image management strategies, but we are hesitant to make such a claim on the basis of the limited evidence across these three investigations.

Overall, the evidence is not compelling that men and women differ substantially in their deception profiles. Consequently, we suggest that researchers focus on other variables in the conversational context. We continue to believe, as stated in IDT (Buller & Burgoon, 1996), that the behaviors enacted by conversational partners and their conjoint behavioral patterns exert a greater influence on the exact nature of deceptive displays than do participants' personal characteristics and other preinteraction factors.

COMMUNICATOR SEX AND THE DECODING OF DECEPTION

If the literature on the production of deception displays does little to support sex differences, the decoding literature is equally anemic. There are few sex differences reported despite that in the last 56 years over 100 studies have examined humans' abilities to detect deceit (see Fay & Middleton, 1941; Marston, 1920, for the earliest work; see Burgoon, Buller, Guerrero, Afifi, & Feldman, 1996; Buller, Burgoon, White, & Ebesu, 1994; Feeley & deTurck, 1995; Feeley, deTurck, & Young, 1995; Robinson, 1996, for recent studies). Although the paucity of sex differences in the literature on detection might stem from the fact that few studies have examined sex differences, the lack of profound sex differences in those studies argues against devoting a lot of energy to searching for them.

Sex Differences in Overall Accuracy

Two meta-analyses of the research on deception detection ability suggest that women (vs. men) detect deception better. Kalbfleisch (1985, 1990) reported that women were better able to detect the deception of both men and other women. However, accuracy was extremely variable and depended on the combination of receiver and sender sex and channel access; average effects ranged from 50% accuracy for men observing other men to 80% accuracy for female observers examining transcripts. Zuckerman, DePaulo, and Rosenthal (1981) reported a comparable finding in their meta-analysis: Women were slightly better at detecting deception than men.[2]

This small detection advantage enjoyed by women is consistent with women's general superiority at judging nonverbal behavior and women's greater social sensitivity (see also Hall, chap. 7, this volume). However, it is far from pervasive, and other studies suggest that women's social style may actually cause them to overlook deception. Rosenthal and DePaulo (1979a, 1979b) argued that women are more accommodating in their interpretations of messages from conversational partners in that they are more likely to attribute intended meanings and assign positive interpretations to messages than are men. Consequently, they may misinterpret deception cues because deception is an unfavorable meaning that can have undesirable social consequences. Recently, DePaulo, Epstein, and Wyer (1993) confirmed that women were more positive and accommodating in their perceptions of others than were men; female observers judged deceptive communicators to be more genuine in their praise of a painting than did male observers. In other words, women in this study were more likely than men to accept the communicators' expressions of positivity at

---

[2]The two meta-analyses differed in terms of which studies were included (only four studies were reviewed in common), what dependent variable was analyzed (Kalbfleisch's analysis only focused on mean accuracy scores calculated as a proportion of correct honesty judgments), and what summary statistic was reported (Zuckerman et al. reported d statistics that Kalbfleisch argued were incorrectly calculated and provided overinflated results of relationships between variables). Given these differences, we did not provide a direct comparison of summary statistics from each meta-analysis in this chapter. The reader should consult Kalbfleisch (1985, 1990) for a complete discussion of the differences between the two meta-analyses, a decision logic for including studies in meta-analysis, and issues regarding the proper summary statistic.

face value. Hence, women were less accurate than men in their judgments of sender veracity.

However, several recent experiments have failed to turn up sex differences in deception detection (Feeley, deTurck, & Young, 1995; Millar & Millar, 1995; Vrij & Semin, 1996). Research over the last decade has also demonstrated that two preinteractional features—sex composition of the communication dyad and training in detection skills—modify or eliminate female superiority. Therefore, it is dangerous to claim that women are more capable deception detectors than men in all circumstances.

Sex Composition of the Sender–Receiver Dyad

Both meta-analyses alluded to earlier (Kalbfleisch, 1985; Zuckerman et al., 1981) implicate the sex composition of the sender–receiver dyads as an important mediator of sex differences in detection ability, but they disagree as to the exact nature of this mediation. Both studies found that female deceivers are more detectable than male deceivers to both female and male receivers. However, in Kalbfleisch's analysis, men had difficulty judging the deception perpetrated by other men, but women were somewhat accurate detecting deception by men. By contrast, Zuckerman et al. found greater accuracy in same-sex than opposite-sex dyads. Kalbfleisch attributed the conflicting findings in part to the fact that the two meta-analyses only summarized four studies in common (Footnote 2).

Recent studies of dyadic sex composition have only added to this confusion. DePaulo and associates (DePaulo, Stone, & Lassiter, 1985; DePaulo & Tang, 1994) found that deceptions by opposite-sex senders were more easily detected than those by same-sex senders (consistent with Kalbfleisch's findings for male deceivers but opposite Zuckerman et al.) and that lies told by women were more often detected than those told by men (consistent with the findings from both meta-analyses). Complicating matters further, however, is Feeley and deTurck's (1995) report that both male and female observers were more accurate when judging the veracity of male communicators' deceptive messages than when they evaluated male communicators' truthful messages. In addition, DePaulo and Tang (1994) found that men low in social anxiety were more accurate at detecting the lies of female communicators than the lies of male communicators. High-anxiety men and low- and high-anxiety women shared similar detection success.

One reason that sex composition of the dyad alters detection abilities may be that men and women judge the behavior of other men and women differently. O'Hair, Cody, Goss, and Krayer (1988) found that men evaluated male communicators as being more honest when they exhibited high levels of attentiveness and female communicators as being more honest when they exhibited high levels of friendliness. However, female observers primarily relied on perceptions of attentiveness when judging the honesty of both male and female communicators; perceptions of friendliness were secondary predictors of these honesty judgments. However, the confusing effects of sex composition suggest that differences in interpretation may not be as simple and neat as implied by O'Hair et al. (1988). The safest conclusion at this point is that the sex composition of the dyad affects deception detection. We cannot predict exactly how because prior research paints a blurred portrait of the effect of sex composition on detection accuracy.

Training in Detection Skills

Men seem to benefit more than women from training in detection skills. DeTurck, Harszlak, Bodhorn, and Texter (1990) found that training significantly improved male observers' decoding of deceptive and truthful performances, although a replication using the same stimuli did not show detection gains by men (Grandpre & Donaghy, 1994). However, both studies were unable to show that female observers benefited from training in deception detection skills.

Reactions to Detected Deception

The only other tangentially related literature concerns how men and women differ in their responses to deception. Women (vs. men) consider deception to be less permissible and more reprehensible (Camden, Motley, & Wilson, 1984; Robinson, 1996), which fits with women's (vs. men's) tendency to be more accommodating (Rosenthal & DePaulo, 1979a, 1979b). Because women choose to believe what others say to them, they may consider deception to be a more serious violation of the conversational expectation or maxim for honesty. This may be why women said that they would more vigorously pursue serious lies when they suspected they are being duped than did men (DePaulo et al., 1993). Their pursuit supposedly would include scrutinizing behavior, looking for additional evidence, and expressing their suspicions to others. Further, women reported being angry and upset by serious lies to a much greater degree and for a longer period of time than did men. These intense reactions to deception might account for the slight detection advantage that women might enjoy. That they do not translate into far greater sensitivity and decoding accuracy may be attributable to the mix of factors noted earlier, including a proclivity to favor senders' intended signals and overlook unintended ones.

CONCLUSION AND SUMMARY

This review of the research on sex differences and similarities reported in the deception and detection literature is relatively sparse considering the magnitude of research available on encoding and decoding deceptive and truthful messages. It appears either that few researchers looking at deception have considered sex differences or they have failed to find such differences and their nonsignificant findings have been relegated to the file drawer.

Although sex produces some reliable differences in nonverbal and verbal conversational behavior, it does not appear to have a consistent or powerful effect on deceptive performances. The emerging hints of differences are not consistent. Sex differences that do emerge may reflect subtle variations in tactics rather than massive departures from overall deception strategies. That is, both men and women probably attempt to control physical activity and convey a normal level of conversational involvement, but men may be more inclined to emphasize the former and women to accentuate the latter. In this vein, men (vs. women) may opt for (a) reduced nonverbal immediacy and greater physical restraint (resulting in less apparent alter-centrism); (b) shorter response latencies, to manage the conversation and counteract other noninvolvement cues; and (c) briefer turns, which may provide greater information control. Women (vs. men) may opt for maintaining a normal appearance through greater immediacy and expressivity (with concomitant leakage of arousal) and minimizing personal responsibility for their discourse by shows of informality and solidarity. These depictions, of course, are tentative and deserve further investigation as to why these alternative strategies might be selected.

At this stage, we can only offer as a first-pass speculation that men and women may each be playing to their long suit, featuring those aspects of their communication style that are overlearned and most familiar. Thus, men may adopt the strong, silent routine, whereas women take on a more feminine, affiliative demeanor. It might also be worthwhile to investigate whether the sex composition of the dyad affects deceptive encoding inasmuch as it influences detection accuracy. In many other respects, men and women appear to behave similarly, especially in terms of appearing pleasant and involved in a global sense. We believe this reflects the overriding importance of conversational demands and the internalization, by men and women, of standard interaction routines that enable deception success despite feelings of arousal and negative affect. Such routines allow deceivers to overcome temporary decrements in performance and to mask their true intents.

The three original investigations reported here did not permit examining effects of sex composition of the dyad on deception displays because of the imbalances in same-sex and opposite-sex dyads. In light of the effects of sex composition on deception detection, this sex-linked factor warrants further attention. It is possible that stereotypic masculine and feminine demeanors will be more prevalent in mixed-sex than same-sex pairs. Therefore, we consider it prudent to continue to include sex as a factor in deception research and work more assiduously to obtain samples balanced on sex composition in the future. Still, we are less than optimistic that such investments will produce a large yield in terms of sizable sex-linked effects. Rather, we suspect that such investments will enable greater confidence in claims that deception displays transcend the boundaries of biological sex.

Regarding sex and decoding of deception, the claim of an overall superiority for women is debatable in view of women's accommodating style of interpreting messages, the small differences found, and the moderating impact of the sex composition of the sender–receiver dyad. Here again, any sex differences appear to be slight or highly susceptible to interactional influences. We would welcome serious attempts to sort out these conflicting findings and urge the prudent approach of testing sex effects in future detection research. Again, we are convinced that pursuing sex—a preinteractional feature of conversations—will yield a meager harvest. Interaction features such as type of deception, receiver suspicion, and sender–receiver behavior are likely to be more theoretically informative.

REFERENCES

Brandt, D. R., Miller, G. R., & Hocking, J. E. (1980). The truth-deception attribution: Effects of familiarity on the ability of observers to detect deception. *Human Communication Research, 6*, 99–110.

Buller, D. B., & Aune, R. K. (1987). Nonverbal cues to deception among intimates, friends, and strangers. *Journal of Nonverbal Behavior, 11*, 269–290.

Buller, D. B., & Burgoon, J. K. (1994). Deception: Strategic and nonstrategic communication. In J. A. Daly & J. M. Wiemann (Eds.), *Strategic interpersonal communication* (pp. 191–223). Hillsdale, NJ: Lawrence Erlbaum Associates.

Buller, D. B., & Burgoon, J. K. (in press). Interpersonal deception theory. *Communication Theory, 6*, 203–242.

Buller, D. B., Burgoon, J. K., Buslig, A., & Roiger, J. (1996). Testing interpersonal deception: The language of interpersonal deception. *Communication Theory, 6*, 268–288.

Buller, D. B., Burgoon, J. K., White, C., & Ebesu, A. (1994). Interpersonal deception: VII. Behavioral profiles of falsification, concealment, and equivocation. *Journal of Language and Social Psychology, 13*, 396–417.

Buller, D. B., Comstock, J., Aune, R. K., & Strzyzewski, K. D. (1989). The effect of probing on deceivers and truthtellers. *Journal of Nonverbal Behavior, 13*, 155–170.

Buller, D. B., Strzyzewski, K. D., & Comstock, J. (1991). Interpersonal deception: I. Deceivers' reactions to receivers' suspicions and probing. *Communication Monographs, 58*, 1–24.

Burgoon, J. K. (1991). Relational messages interpretation of touch, conversational distance, and posture. *Journal of Nonverbal Behavior, 15*, 233–260.

Burgoon, J. K., & Buller, D. B. (1994). Interpersonal deception: III. Effects of deceit on perceived communication and nonverbal behavior dynamics. *Journal of Nonverbal Behavior, 18*, 155–184.

Burgoon, J. K., Buller, D. B., Dillman, L., & Walther, J. B. (1995). Interpersonal deception: IV. Effects of suspicion on perceived communication and nonverbal behavior dynamics. *Human Communication Research, 22*, 163–196.

Burgoon, J. K., Buller, D. B., Ebesu, A., Rockwell, P., & White, C. (1996). Testing interpersonal deception theory: Effects of suspicion on nonverbal behavior and relational messages. *Communication Theory, 6*, 243–267.

Burgoon, J. K., Buller, D. B., Floyd, K., & Grandpre, J. (1996). Deceptive realities: Sender, receiver, and observer perspectives in deceptive conversations. *Communication Research, 23*, 724–748.

Burgoon, J. K., Buller, D. B., Guerrero, L. K., Afiffi, W. A., & Feldman, C. M. (1996). Interpersonal deception: XII. Information management dimensions underlying deceptive and truthful messages. *Communication Monographs, 63*, 50–69.

Burgoon, J. K., Buller, D. B., Guerrero, L. K., & Feldman, C. M. (1994). Interpersonal deception: VI. Viewing deception success from deceiver and observer perspectives: Effects of preinteractional and interactional factors. *Communication Studies, 45*, 263–280.

Burgoon, J. K., Buller, D. B., & Woodall, G. (1996). *Nonverbal communication: The unspoken dialogue* (2nd ed.). New York: McGraw-Hill.

Burgoon, J. K., Le Poire, B. A., & Rosenthal, R. (1995). Effects of preinteraction expectancies and target communication on reciprocity and compensation in dyadic interaction. *Journal of Experimental Social Psychology, 31*, 287–321.

Camden, C., Motley, M. T., & Wilson, A. (1984). White lies in interpersonal communication: A taxonomy and preliminary investigations of social motivations. *Western Journal of Speech Communication 48*, 309–325.

Cody, M. J., & O'Hair, H. D. (1983). Nonverbal communication and deception: Differences in deception cues due to gender and communicator dominance. *Communication Monographs, 50*, 175–192.

DePaulo, B. M. (1992). Nonverbal behavior and self-presentation. *Psychological Bulletin, 111*, 203–243.

DePaulo, B. M., Epstein, J. A., & Wyer, M. M. (1993). Sex differences in lying: How women and men deal with the dilemma of deceit. In M. Lewis & C. Saarni (Eds.), *Lying and deception in everyday life* (pp. 126–147). New York: Guilford.

DePaulo, B. M., & Rosenthal, R. (1979). Telling lies. *Journal of Personality and Social Psychology, 37*, 1713–1722.

DePaulo, B. M., Rosenthal, R., Rosenkrantz, J., & Green, C. R. (1982). Actual and perceived cues to deception: A closer look at speech. *Basic and Applied Psychology, 3*, 291–312.

DePaulo, B. M., Stone, J. I., & Lassiter, G. D. (1985). Deceiving and detecting deceit. In B. R. Schlenker (Ed.), *The self and social life* (pp. 323–370). New York: McGraw-Hill.

DePaulo, B. M., & Tang, J. (1994). Social anxiety and social judgment: The example of detecting deception. *Journal of Research in Personality, 28*, 142–153.

deTurck, M. A. (1991). Training observers to detect spontaneous deception: Effects of gender. *Communication Reports, 4*, 81–88.

deTurck, M. A., Harszlak, J. J., Bodhorn, D. J., & Texter, L. A. (1990). The effects of training social perceivers to detect deception from behavioral cues. *Communication Quarterly, 38*, 189–199.

deTurck, M. A., & Miller, G. R. (1985). Deception and arousal: Isolating the behavioral correlates of deception. *Human Communication Research, 12*, 181–201.

Donaghy, W. C., Grandpre, J. R., & Davies, L. (1994, February). *Validating deception detection stimuli: Grouped data vs. subject-to-subject approaches.* Paper presented to the annual meeting of the Western Speech Communication Association, San Jose, CA.

Duncan, V. J., & Kalbfleisch, P. J. (1995, May). *Race, gender, and perceptions of deceptiveness.* Paper presented at the annual convention of the International Communication Association, Albuquerque, NM.

Ekman, P., & Friesen W. V. (1969). Nonverbal leakage and clues to deception. *Psychiatry, 32,* 88–105.

Ekman, P., & Friesen W. V. (1974). Detecting deception from the body or face. *Journal of Personality and Social Psychology, 29* 188–198.

Fay, P. J., & Middleton, W. C. (1941). The ability to judge truth-telling, or lying, from the voice as transmitted over a public address system. *Journal of General Psychology, 24,* 211–215.

Feeley, T. H., & deTurck, M. A. (1995). Global cue usage in behavioral lie detection. *Communication Quarterly, 43,* 420–430.

Feeley, T. H., deTurck, M. A., & Young, M. J. (1995). Baseline familiarity in lie detection. *Communication Research Reports, 12,* 160–169.

Grandpre, J. R., & Donaghy, W. C. (1994, February). *To catch a lie: An examination of the behavioral cues associated with deception detection.* Paper presented to the annual meeting of the Western States Communication Association, San Jose, CA.

Hall, J. A. (1984). *Nonverbal sex differences: Communication accuracy and expressive style.* Baltimore, MD: Johns Hopkins University Press.

Hocking, J. E., Bauchner, J., Kaminski, E. P., & Miller, G. R. (1979). Detecting deceptive communication from verbal, visual, and paralinguistic cues. *Human Communication Research, 6,* 33–46.

Kalbfleisch, P. J. (1985). Accuracy in deception detection: A quantitative review (Doctoral dissertation, Michigan State University, 1986). *Dissertation Abstracts International, 46,* 4453B.

Kalbfleisch, P. J. (1990). Listening for deception: The effects of medium on accuracy of detection. In R. N. Bostrom (Ed.), *Listening behavior: Measurement and application* (pp. 155–176). New York: Guilford.

Kraut, R. E. (1978). Verbal and nonverbal cues in the perception of lying. *Journal of Personality and Social Psychology, 36,* 380–391.

Kraut, R. E., & Poe, D. (1980). Behavioral roots to person perceptions: The deception judgments of customs inspectors and laymen. *Journal of Personality and Social Psychology, 39,* 784–798.

LaFrance, M., Hecht, M. A., & Noyes, A. (1994, October). *Who is smiling now? A meta-analysis of sex differences in smiling.* Paper presented at the annual meeting of the Society of Experimental Social Psychology, Lake Tahoe, NV.

Littlepage, G., & Pineault, T. (1978). Verbal, facial, and paralinguistic cues to the detection of truth and lying. *Personality and Social Psychology Bulletin, 4,* 461–464.

Marston, W. M. (1920). Reaction-time symptoms of deception. *Journal of Experimental Psychology, 3,* 72–87.

Millar, M., & Millar, K. (1995). Detection of deception in familiar and unfamiliar persons: The effects of information restriction. *Journal of Nonverbal Behavior, 19,* 69–84.

Miller, G. R., Bauchner, J. E., Hocking, J. E., Fontes, N. E., Kaminski, E. P., & Brandt, D. R. (1981). ". . . And nothing but the truth": How well can observers detect deceptive testimony? In B. D. Sales (Ed.), *The trial process* (pp. 145–179). New York: Plenum.

Miller, G. R., deTurck, M. A., & Kalbfleisch, P. J. (1983). Self-monitoring, rehearsal, and deceptive communication. *Human Communication Research, 10,* 97–117.

O'Hair, H. D., & Cody, M. J. (1987). Gender and vocal stress differences during truthful and deceptive information sequences. *Human Relations, 40,* 1–14.

O'Hair, H. D., Cody, M. J., Goss, B., & Krayer, K. J. (1988). The effect of gender, deceit orientation and communicator style on macro-assessments of honesty. *Communication Quarterly, 36,* 77–93.

Riggio, R. E., & Friedman, H. S. (1983). Individual differences and cues to deception. *Journal of Personality and Social Psychology, 45,* 899–915.

Riggio, R. E., Tucker, J., & Throckmorton, B. (1987). Social skills and deception ability. *Personality and Social Psychology Bulletin, 13,* 568–577.

Robinson, W. P. (1996). *Deceit, delusion, and detection.* Thousand Oaks, CA: Sage.

Rosenthal, R., & DePaulo, B. M. (1979a). Sex differences in accommodation in nonverbal communication. In R. Rosenthal (Ed.), *Skill in nonverbal communication* (pp. 68–103). Cambridge, MA: Oelgeschlanger, Gunn & Hain.

Rosenthal, R., & DePaulo, B. M. (1979b). Sex differences in eavesdropping on nonverbal cues. *Journal of Personality and Social Psychology, 37,* 273–285.

Tannen, D. (1994). *Gender and discourse.* New York: Oxford University Press.

Vrij, A., & Semin, G. R. (1996). Lie experts' beliefs about nonverbal indicators of deception. *Journal of Nonverbal Behavior, 20,* 65–80.

Zuckerman, M., DePaulo, B. M., & Rosenthal, R. (1981). Verbal and nonverbal communication of deception. In L. Berkowitz (Ed.), *Advances in experimental psychology* (pp. 2–51). New York: Academic Press.

Zuckerman, M., & Driver, R. E. (1985). Telling lies: Verbal and nonverbal correlates of deception. In A. W. Siegman & S. Feldstein (Eds.), *Multichannel integrations of nonverbal behavior* (pp. 129–148). Hillsdale, NJ: Lawrence Erlbaum Associates.

Zuckerman, M., Koestner, R., & Alton, A. O. (1984). Learning to detect deception. *Journal of Personality and Social Psychology, 46,* 519–528.

Zuckerman, M., Koestner, R., & Colella, M. J. (1985). Learning to detect deception from three communication channels. *Journal of Nonverbal Behavior, 9,* 188–194.

Chapter 16

Conversational Maintenance Behaviors of Husbands and Wives: An Observational Analysis

Elizabeth B. Robey
Washington University in St. Louis

Daniel J. Canary
Pennsylvania State University

Cynthia S. Burggraf
College of Wooster

Research has recently yielded much information about the macroscopic strategies people use to maintain their relationships (e.g., Ayres, 1983; Dindia & Baxter, 1987). These strategies most often reference proactive and constructive approaches such as showing an active interest in the partner's activities, being open, assuring the partner, being positive, and so on (e.g., Stafford & Canary, 1991). Although such approaches present a general image of behaviors that couples enact, they cannot depict with much precision molecular communication behaviors that couples use to maintain their dyadic systems. Research on the microlevel of conversation can provide additional insights into how women and men attempt to maintain their relationships through the communication they enact. As Bradac (1983) suggested, "language is both constitutive of the relationship and an important influence upon it" (p. 152).

Maintaining a relationship is seen as the attempt to sustain the relationship as the partners want it to be (Ayres, 1983; Dindia & Baxter, 1987). Likewise, maintaining conversation refers to the energy exerted to keep conversation at a comfortable level—where at least one person provides attention to the partner (Fishman, 1978). Conversations require work to maintain them. However, whether women or men do more of the work is unclear.

BACKGROUND RESEARCH IN CONVERSATIONAL
MAINTENANCE

To our knowledge, research that has examined the conversational maintenance behaviors of couples is limited to three studies: Fishman's (1978)
initial analysis of couple conversations, a replication by DeFrancisco (1990,
1991),[1] and an observational study of maintenance behaviors used in discussions concerning conflict topics (Kollack, Blumstein, & Schwartz, 1985).
The underlying assumption of these studies is that women (vs. men) consistently work harder to keep conversations going. Thus, women are the
primary maintainers of conversation.

Fishman (1978) examined three conjugal heterosexual couples. All but
one couple included a graduate student at the time of the study; two
couples were married, and the other couple was living together. The data
consisted of tape-recorded conversations between the couples in their
apartments, which the couples could censor. Fifty-two hours of conversation
were obtained, but only 5 hours were content analyzed for amount of talk
time, back channels, question asking, attention beginnings, minimal responses, and topic choice.

Using a dominance/power theoretical framework, Fishman reported
that, in conversation, men exerted power in a number of ways; men tended
to talk more, dominating the floor and having their topic choice be the
focus of conversation. Fishman also reported that women asked more
questions about topics that were important to men, whereas men did not
show as much effort in asking questions and choosing topics that might
interest women. Fishman also examined back channels (i.e., verbal utterances that promote continuance of the partner's turn, such as *Oh yes, I
see, uh-huh*, or *hmm*) as indicators of conversational involvement. She found
that women offered more back channels in conversation than did men.

In a follow-up study examining seven couples, DeFrancisco (1990) also
held that women invest more energy to maintain conversations. DeFrancisco examined an average of 12 hours of interaction per couple and, in
addition to interruptions, looked at the same variables as did Fishman.
DeFrancisco found different results in terms of talk time, question asking,
and back channels. Contrary to Fishman, she found that women talked
more. DeFrancisco argued that women talked to fill in dead air until they
hit on a topic that interested their husbands, and thus fulfilled the burden
of conversational maintenance. DeFrancisco also reported that men (relative to women) in some conversations asked more questions, but these

---

[1]DeFrancisco's (1991) article is a variation of her 1990 paper. Some of the findings from
the 1980 study were omitted. We report results and interpretation from both studies to be
inclusive.

questions were more critical than women's questions. Finally, DeFrancisco found (unlike Fishman) that neither sex engaged in many back channels.

Kollack et al. (1985) observed 35 dyads who were same-sex and cross-sex roommates engaged in discussions of conflict issues. Kollack et al. hypothesized that the perceived power balance of the relationship (equal vs. unequal) would predict conversational maintenance behaviors regardless of sex. Like DeFrancisco, Kollack et al. found more similarities than differences between sexes in terms of their conversational maintenance behaviors. The authors reported that men and women interrupted their partners equally. Additionally, in all dyads, the more powerful person attempted and succeeded at interruptions. Kollack et al. also found that male and female roommates engaged in equal amounts of talk (although men tended to speak a bit longer) and engaged in an equal number of back channels (as DeFrancisco reported). Unlike Fishman, Kollack et al. found that male roommates asked significantly more questions than did their female roommates.

These alternative findings indicate that researchers have little basis to infer that women (vs. men) consistently and more actively maintain conversations. First, the sample sizes in both the Fishman and DeFrancisco studies were quite small (Fishman studied three couples, DeFrancisco observed seven). Accordingly, one cannot make the following, widely cited inference with much confidence: "The active maintenance of a female gender requires women to be available to do what needs to be done in interaction, to do the shitwork and not complain" (Fishman, 1978, p. 404). Rather than generalize to all men and women pairs, both Fishman's and DeFrancisco's research should instead be viewed as conversational analyses that illuminate how men and women in those particular samples enacted various interaction behaviors.

Second, in the Fishman and DeFrancisco studies, the hypotheses were nonfalsifiable to the extent that opposite results regarding talk time and the like appear to confirm the same expectation (i.e., that women more actively maintain the conversation). Although the results of these two studies are different in important respects, both researchers arrived at the conclusion that women invest more energy during conversation. For example, Fishman found that men talked more in everyday conversations and dominated the floor, whereas women displayed more maintenance behaviors such as back channel cues (to keep men talking). On the contrary, DeFrancisco reported that, although women did more of the talking, men still dominated the conversation (claiming that women were likely to keep talking until they hit on a subject that interested their husband). Despite such differences in talk time between the two studies, the same interpretation (i.e., that women primarily sustain marital interaction) was supported.

As indicated earlier, Kollack et al. found little support for strong effects due to sex when examining roommate conflict interactions. Rather, these authors found that the more powerful person (as measured on a scale regarding eight decision issues, such as when to eat) tended to enact more dominant behaviors. These authors concluded that, although men and women are clearly different, understanding conversational behavior must go beyond sex differences and look to alternative structural differences (e.g., power imbalance).

The purpose of this study is to add to this research regarding whether men or women engage in more conversational maintenance behaviors. Our target population consists of married couples engaged in small talk, in concordance with Fishman and DeFrancisco. However, unlike those studies, we do not presume that women more actively maintain the conversation. Instead, we view the issue as open for discussion. First, we review the dominance model approach driving both of these studies. Next, we briefly review the conversational maintenance activities pursued in this chapter. Finally, we report a study that utilizes observations of married couples' small talk.

THE DOMINANCE MODEL REVISITED

Fishman and DeFrancisco both relied on the dominance model, which asserts that men remain dominant in our culture. This is exemplified in a number of ways: Terminology is predominantly male centered, women are excluded when the generic use of *he* and *man* is used, and social pressure on women to adopt the man's last name at marriage reflects an exclusionary practice. Although women have more lables to describe themselves, such terms are often negative. Moreover, language indicates the status of a relationship and power imbalances (Bradac, 1983), which explains why words such as *whore, bitch,* and *old maid* have far more negative connotations than do male terms such as *stud, bastard,* and *bachelor.* Women are also referenced in food-linked terms that are demeaning, such as *cupcake* and *sugar pie.*

By using a dominance model as a conceptualizing framework, one can explain gender inequality in conversation (see, e.g., Thorne & Henley, 1975). In their study of cross-sex conversations, for example, West and Zimmerman (1977) argued that women are often spoken to as children and restricted in their rights to speak. This is illustrated in a study by Woods (1988), who found gender-based dominance within mixed sex groups regardless of status differences. In Woods' study, men dominated in each group in terms of interruptions and talk time regardless of whether they were in a superior or subordinate position. Men also received far more minimal responses than did women, indicating that men, being the dominant group, are encouraged more than women to continue talking. Both Fishman (1978) and DeFrancisco (1990) argued that a clear power structure underlies marital relationships, and everyday interaction illustrates instances of male dominance over women. Fishman argued power is a "human accomplishment" (p. 397); by analyzing conversation, one can witness the accomplishment of power in interaction. However, Kollack et al. (1985) indicated that this point of view was interesting although not empirically verified through extensive research.

Although one might assume that men dominate women, it is important to consider the contexts in which dominance emerges. Deaux and Major (1987) argued that, "the enactment of gender primarily takes place within the context of social interaction" (p. 370). They stressed the importance of examining gender as an interactive, episode-specific factor that occurs within the context of relational development and knowledge of particular partners. Deaux and Major hypothesized that, "perceivers [will] form expectancies more on the basis of individuated information about the target to the extent that it is available" (p. 373). Similarly, in their analysis of marital communication research, Burggraf and Sillars (1987) found that studies do not support sex stereotyped behaviors that have been found within other samples. Instead, they argued that within a marriage context, ". . . the intimacy and temporal permanence of family relationships allow spouses to abandon culturally determined standards for behaviors and replace them with personally negotiated norms" (p. 278). Accordingly, for most close couples most of the time, individually negotiated rules underlying their relationships indicate appropriate and effective interaction behaviors. The manner of negotiation may be implicit, however, as people adhere to different schemes regarding what marriage entails (Fitzpatrick, 1988). In this vein, examples of dominance might not be as apparent within married couples as opposed to unmarried couples.

According to cultural stereotypes of men and women, women are often dominated by assertive men. Yet research has also indicated that it is not men who dominate in close involvements (for reviews, see Aries, 1996; Canary, Emmers-Sommer, & Faulkner, 1997). Instead, conversational roles affect people's behavior more than gender does (Dumas, 1976). For example, Fisher (1983) found that cooperative versus competitive role orientations swamped any effects due to sex differences on five dimensions of interaction (i.e., relational control, information source, time reference orientations, evolution of information, and reducing equivocality). Likewise, in one of the few interactional studies on interruption behavior, Dindia (1987) found that men and women interrupted each other in equal amounts with similar intensity and the frequency of partners' interruptions was highly associated. Even in organizational contexts, where one would anticipate women are dominated, women and men engage in similar conversational behaviors (Wilkins & Andersen, 1991). Wilkins and Andersen found one half of 1% variation in interaction behavior due to sex differences.

A less restrictive and more interactive approach to viewing gender, communication, and dominance must be adopted. If one adheres to a dominance model that reflects sex stereotypes, one expects examples of dominance to occur in conversation when none or little may actually exist. Although there are cases in which men dominate, we should expect less stereotypic behaviors in close relationships. Overreliance on sex stereotypes to guide behavior polarizes the sexes and obscures subtle differences between them (Aries, 1996; Bem, 1993; Canary & Hause, 1993; Ragan, 1989). More precisely, intimate couples (such as married couples) form expectations of each other based on knowledge of each other and their interdependent patterns; they probably do not rely on sex stereotypic beliefs. A closer look at the communication behaviors we reference would be helpful.

CONVERSATIONAL MAINTENANCE BEHAVIORS

At this point, we briefly review variables relevant to conversational maintenance: talk time, back channels, interruptions, and question asking. We do not question issues of inclusiveness or appropriateness at this juncture. Instead, we adopt these behaviors as measures of conversational maintenance to extend information comparable to previous studies. More extensive examinations of these conversation variables separately are provided elsewhere (e.g., Aries, 1996; Dindia, 1987; Fitzpatrick & Dindia, 1986; Tannen, 1990).

Talk Time

Talk time is necessary to the study of conversational maintenance. According to Fishman (1978), talk time reveals how much work or energy someone puts into a conversation to maintain it at a comfortable level. A common assumption prevalent in society is that women do most of the talking (Kollack et al., 1985). When Kramer (1977) investigated perceptions of women and their language, responses were quite negative. Many thought that women engaged in too much talking and that the type of talk they engaged in was unimportant or trivial. Although women are perceived as talking more than men, results of sex differences in talk time have been mixed. Although some studies suggest that men talk more than women (e.g., Argyle, Mansur, & Cook, 1968; Doherty, 1974; Eakins & Eakins, 1978; Fishman, 1978; Marlett, 1970), other studies report that there are no clear gender differences (Martin & Craig, 1982; McMillan, Clifton, McGrath, & Gale, 1977) or that women talk more than men (DeFrancisco, 1990). In addition, Kollack et al. (1985) found that talk time was shared equally between roommates who reported equal power, whereas in power imbalanced situations the more powerful roommate talked longer. To examine the issue of talk time in conversation, the following research question is proposed:

RQ 1: Within married couple conversation, do women or men engage in more talk?

Back Channels

Kennedy and Camden (1982) observed that back channels serve "a facilitating function in topic development" (p. 49). They can be utterances such as *um-hmm uh-huh,* and *yeah,* or they can take the form of quasiquestions (West, 1984) such as *really?, oh?,* and *ya know?* Fishman (1978) suggested that women use back channels to encourage men to speak, thus maintaining conversations. Tannen (1990) stated that, although this active listening is a typically female behavior, men listen in less verbal ways: Men may not demonstrate as many active listening skills as women, but this is not necessarily an indication of ignoring the speaker; men simply have different approaches to listening. Contrary to both Fishman and Tannen, DeFrancisco (1990) found that back channels were not used predominately by one sex or the other: Both men and women engaged in them equally. However, DeFrancisco asserted that men used back channels as a way to fake attention. Kollack et al. (1985) found no main effects due to sex. Rather, the less powerful person engaged in back channels. Given these different findings and interpretations, the second research question is posed:

RQ 2: Within married couple conversations, do women or men use more back channels?

Interruptions

Different explanations exist regarding why interruptions occur. A long withstanding view suggests that interruptions reflect the intent to dominate conversation. Many studies that found that men interrupt more than women sought to explain the results through the dominance perspective (e.g., DeFrancisco, 1990; Kramer, 1977; West & Zimmerman, 1983; Zimmerman & West, 1975). For example, Zimmerman and West (1975) concluded that, "men deny equal status to women as conversational partners with respect to rights to full utilization of their turns and support for the development of their topics" (p. 125). Other studies have found that interruptions can be a way to encourage conversation and/or show involve-

ment and therefore be conceptualized as a maintenance behavior. Based
on her extensive review of the literature, Aries (1996) concluded that,

> A critical reevaluation of the literature on interruptions, however, suggests
> that there may be more studies that report no gender differences in inter-
> ruptions than there are studies that find such differences, and that inter-
> ruptions may be used for many functions in conversation other than to
> convey dominance. (p. 80)

Interruptions play an important role in the analysis of conversational
maintenance. To interrupt, one has to be involved in conversation. Flow
of conversation can depend on the type of interruption. Kennedy and
Camden (1982) used Watzlawick, Beavin, and Jackson's (1967) categories
of interruptions—confirmation, rejection, and disconfirmation—to examine different interruption functions. They found that nearly half of the
interruptions "appeared to function as healthy functional communicative
acts" (p. 35). Kennedy and Camden, however, did not examine sex differences in type of interruptions used. Tannen (1990) argued that women
are more likely than men to use interruptions as a way to establish and
maintain connection to what the other person is saying; men view interruptions as an attempt to compete for talk time and dominate the floor.
The research findings in conversational maintenance studies regarding
interruptions are mixed and gloss over the distinctions among confirmation, rejection, and disconfirmation. Accordingly, the following research
questions are offered.

RQ 3: Within married couple conversations, do women or men engage
in more confirming interruptions?

RQ 4: Within married couple conversations, do women or men engage
in more rejecting interruptions?

RQ 5: Within married couple conversations, do women or men engage
in more disconfirming interruptions?

Question Asking

Question asking shows involvement in conversation because it applies a
pressure to respond (Sacks, Schegloff, & Jefferson, 1974). Questions ensure
at least minimal interaction and generate involvement in conversation.
They are clearly a significant contributor to conversational maintenance.

As with the previous conversational variables, studies are equivocal with
regard to sex differences about question asking. Reflecting a dominance
point of view, Eakins and Eakins (1978) suggested that question asking
involves a superior–subordinate relationship, where those in superior positions asked more questions and those in subordinate roles replied more.

Kollack et al. (1985) and Rosenfeld (1966) found that men asked more questions, but Fishman (1978) found that women asked more questions. DeFrancisco (1990) reported that within some of the married couples men asked more questions, but they were often critical in nature. The variation in findings regarding question asking leads us to explore two research questions—one concerned with nonhostile and one concerned with hostile questions:

RQ 6: Within married couple conversations, do women or men ask more nonhostile questions?

RQ 7: Within married couple conversations, are men's questions more critical than women's?

METHODS

Sample

Married couples were recruited through use of local organizations, as well as from students in introductory communication courses at a midwestern university. The average age of the participants was 33 years, and the couples had been married 8.5 years on average. All participants had completed at least high school. Although 23 couples took part in the study, only 20 couples could be used for analysis due to technical difficulties with the audio tapes. These couples generated over 1,250 conversational speaking turns for analysis—a figure that comports with other observational research (Burggraf & Sillars, 1987).

Procedures

A researcher met with each couple at the communication lab or at the organization from which they were recruited. At this time, a researcher greeted the couples and explained the nature of the project. The researcher informed each couple that they could withdraw from the study at any time for any reason. Following this procedure, the researcher told the couples to "talk about anything they would like" for approximately 7 minutes while being tape recorded. The researcher started the audio recorder and then left the room closed for the participants to talk.

Operationalizations

The lead author formalized a coding scheme for the behaviors under investigation and trained two graduate student assistant coders. The coders worked independently and unaware of the research purpose. Each coder

TABLE 16.1
Frequencies for Conversational Maintenance Behaviors

Conversational Behavior	Sum	M	SD
Wives' behavior			
Back channels	66	3.20	2.98
Confirming interruptions	49	2.45	2.33
Disconfirming interruptions	2	0.10	0.31
Rejecting interruptions	16	0.80	1.01
Hostile questions	5	0.25	0.72
Nonhostile questions	241	12.05	9.86
Talk time	3,965	198.26	85.69
Husband's behavior			
Back channels	100	5.00	4.18
Confirming interruptions	59	2.95	2.87
Disconfirming interruptions	3	0.15	0.37
Rejecting interruptions	10	0.50	0.76
Hostile questions	2	0.10	0.45
Nonhostile questions	157	7.85	7.41
Talk time	3,453	172.63	100.14

Note. Talk time is in seconds.

made four passes through the tape. Talk time was calibrated on the first pass. Back channels were coded on the second pass. The three types of interruptions were coded on the third pass. Finally, the coders counted instances of the various types of question asking. Thus, 1,294 turns were coded. For reliability purposes, three tapes involving 366 turns were randomly selected and coded. Table 16.1 summarizes the descriptive statistics for each of the variables.

Talk Time. Talk time was measured by a hand-held stopwatch that recorded to the 10th of a second that the speaker maintained the floor. Clocking began with the speaker's first utterance and ended with the last utterance of the particular turn being timed. Because this is a ratio-level measure, a Pearson correlation was conducted. The correlation between the two coders approached unity ($r = .99$). The range for talk time was 0 to 102.1 seconds. The average turn was 5.7 seconds, with a standard deviation of 9.6 seconds.

Back Channels. Back channels were counted as they occurred in the process of conversation. They were carefully differentiated from what might have been interpreted as interruptions. Percent of agreement between coders was .84.

Question Asking. Sacks, Schegloff, and Jefferson (1973) defined questions as a two-part sequence, where if one person asks a question the other feels a greater responsibility to reply than if not asked a question. Consistent with Sacks et al., question asking did not include such utterances as *oh?* or *really?*. Such questions constitute quasiquestions (West, 1984), which were coded as back channels because they encourage conversation by commenting on what was just said. They do not advance the conversation by asking for a reply (Sacks et al., 1973).

To identify underlying criticism, we used Sillars' (1986) distinction between hostile and nonhostile questions. Sillars defined *hostile questions* as "directive or leading questions that fault the partner" (p. 14). Hostile questions can also be recognized through the tone of a speaker's voice. *Nonhostile questions*, according to Sillars, occurs when Person A solicits disclosure from Person B without implying criticism. Percent of agreement between coders for hostile and nonhostile questions was high at .98. One reason for the high agreement was lack of hostile questions.

Interruptions. Watzlawick et al. (1967) distinguished three types of interruptions. *Confirming interruptions* were identified as expressions of approval or understanding of another's position. *Rejections* referenced disagreement or disapproval of what the partner said. Finally, *disconfirming interruptions* were coded in instances when one did not even acknowledge another's comment. Disconfirming interruptions were enacted through a variety of mechanisms (e.g., subject change, tangential reply, etc.). Again, the level of agreement between coders was very high: .87 for confirming, .96 for rejection, and .99 for disconfirmation.

We distinguished between interruptions and overlaps. *Overlaps*, as defined by Pearson, Turner, and Todd-Mancillas (1991), occur "when the individual who is listening makes a statement before the other person has finished speaking, but at about the same time as the speaker's last word is uttered, or a word which could be perceived as his or her last word" (p. 147). Overlaps were not analyzed in the present study.

Analyses

We undertook two sets of analyses to examine sex differences in married couples' conversations. First, we used the couple as the unit of analysis, where the sum of the behaviors within a given conversation operationalized the dependent variables. Second, we used the turn as the unit of analysis, based in part on the assumption that conversational behaviors as enacted reflect sex differences. For each set of analyses, paired *t* tests between wives and their husbands were computed to assess behavioral differences.

RESULTS

Talk Time

The first research question concerned who talks more. There was no significant difference between husbands and wives regarding talk time. Although the average sum for women was higher than it was for men (198.3 vs.172.6 seconds, respectively), paired t tests revealed no significant difference, t (19) = 0.73, p = .47. At the turn level, similar results were obtained, as within each turn wives talked slightly longer than did their husbands (M = 6.1 for wives, M = 5.3 for husbands). Again, however, this differences was not significant, t (638) = 1.60, p = 11.

Back Channels

The second research question regarded use of back channels. Dyadic level of analysis revealed that husbands offered more back channels than did wives (M = 3.3 for wives, M = 5.0 for husbands), although the difference was not significant, t (19) = 1.45, p = .16. However, turn-level analysis indicated that males engaged in more back channels per turn than did females (M = 0.15 for males, M = 0.10 for females), which was statistically significant, t (638) = 2.33, p < .05. In short, support was found for differential use of back channels, with husbands enacting more than their wives.

Types of Interruptions

The third through fifth research questions concerned three types of interruptions—confirming, rejection, and disconfirming. As Table 16.1 indicates, no substantive differences were obtained regarding differences in interruption behavior. At the dyadic level of analysis, wives and husbands equally engaged in confirming interruptions (M = 2.45 for wives, M = 2.95 for husbands), t = 0.98, p = .34; in rejecting interruptions (M = .80 for wives, M = .50 for husbands), t = 1.06, p = .30; and in disconfirming interruptions (M = .10 for wives, M = .15 for husbands), t = 0.44, p = .66. At the turn level of analysis, husbands had an average of .09 confirming interruptions and wives' average of confirming interruptions was .08, t (638) = 0.96, p = .34. For rejection interruptions, women and men had similar means (M = .03 for wives, M = .02 for husbands), t (638) = 1.23, p = .22. Finally, for disconfirming interruptions, husbands' average proportion was .005 and wives' average was .003, t (638) = 0 .45, p = .66.

Question Asking

The sixth and seventh research questions concerned two types of question asking—nonhostile and hostile (critical). At the dyadic level of analysis, wives (relative to their husbands) tended to ask more nonhostile questions

($M = 12.05$ for wives, $M = 7.85$ for husbands), although the difference was not significant, $t = 1.52$, $p = .15$. At the turn level of analysis, however, wives engaged in significantly more nonhostile questions ($M = .38$ for wives, $M = .24$ for husbands), t (638) $= 4.12$, $p < .001$.

We found no statistically significant difference between husbands and wives regarding their use of hostile questions. Although women engaged in more hostile questions ($M = .25$ for wives, $M = .10$ for husbands), these means were not significantly different, t (19) $= 0.9$, $p = .38$. Similarly, at the turn level, the husbands' average was .003 and the wives' average was .007, which were not significantly different, t (638) $= 0.83$, $p = .41$.

In summary, and based on most of the analyses conducted, husbands and wives enacted conversational maintenance behaviors to a similar extent. Overall, husbands (vs. wives) tended to enact more maintenance behaviors, although the statistical comparisons tended not to be significant. However, husbands did engage in significantly more back channels and wives enaged in significantly more nonhostile questions. The following section discusses these findings.

DISCUSSION

The purpose of this study was to replicate and extend previous work in the area of conversational maintenance. Thus, we wanted to examine the same variables examined in previous research (i.e., those cited in DeFrancisco, 1990, 1991; Fishman, 1978; Kollack et al., 1985).

Findings

The most interesting results of the present study were not the differences between women and men, but rather the similarities between them. In most cases, the results contradict expectations based on stereotypes of men and women interacting. More precisely, the findings in this study were as follows:

1. Women and men did not differ significantly in terms of their talk time. Contrary to Fishman (1978), men did not dominate the conversation by talking more. Contrary to DeFrancisco (1990), women did not engage in significantly more discussion to maintain conversation.

2. Women and men took roughly an equal number of turns talking for similar amounts of time. This particular result might imply that women and men both understand the need to balance conversation so both people meet the burden of maintaining it. Within an equitable system of turn taking and talk time, neither men nor women dominate conversation or feel the need to fill dead air when conversation seems strained. Both

women and men appear to bear the burden of talking by talking for equal amounts of time.

3. Contrary to stereotypic beliefs, husbands engaged in significantly more back channels than did wives. Had women talked significantly more than men, one might see an artifactual reason for men's greater amount of back channels. In this study, however, men and women engaged in similar amounts of talk time so the greater amount of back channels exhibited by men appears to represent more male (vs. female) conversational maintenance effort. These findings contradict Fishman's (1978) as well as DeFrancisco's (1990) findings, where the women in both studies offered more back channels. The assumption that women are more likely to display affirming verbal back channels is not necessarily true.

4. Wives (vs. their husbands) asked significantly more nonhostile questions. Asking questions enables the other person to talk and accordingly comprises one way to maintain conversation. In both Fishman (1978) and DeFrancisco (1990), women asked more questions than did men. However, in the Kollack et al. (1985) study, male roommates asked more questions than did their female counterparts, including those couples wherein the male was reported as being more powerful than the female.

5. Neither husbands nor wives engaged in significantly more hostile question asking. In fact, there were few hostile questions. Among all couple conversations, the topics that were generally pursued appeared to be nonthreatening. This might have been the reason for so few hostile questions. Had the research been focused on couples discussing areas of tension in their relationship, then more hostile questioning might have appeared. In these particular conversations, hostile question asking was rare. The clear implication is that neither men nor women dominate small talk conversation by asking hostile questions.

6. Neither sex engaged in significantly more of any of the three types of interruptions—confirming, rejection, or disconfirming. Although previous research suggests that women might engage in more assuring interruptions and men in more challenging ones (e.g., Tannen, 1990), the results of this study suggest that husbands and wives engage in equal amounts of interruptions, with confirming being the most frequently displayed type.

This last result is of particular interest because previous research on conversational maintenance has not accounted for different interruption types. It has been assumed that interruption represents a means of dominating conversation. By delineating interruptions into three areas, the present study was able to explore in more detail the types of interruptions displayed in married couples' conversations. As a result, interruptions on the whole were quite healthy acts that displayed involvement by encouraging conversation and letting the other know that attention was being paid to them. Both women and men engaged in these behaviors equally.

The findings reflect an alternative view of conceptualizing gender and communication than that offered by the dominance model—one that is based more on egalitarian and/or idiosyncratic rule cultures and partner knowledge. Whereas the results of nonhostile question asking are consistent with stereotypic views of women and previous research in conversational maintenance, other variables examined show no indication of gender differences. Moreover, at least one finding contradicts what is normally perceived as stereotypic female and male behaviors (i.e., husbands used more back channel cues).

The findings strongly suggest that gender represents a flexible, interaction-based construct. That is, gender is created and re-created in interaction (Deaux & Major, 1987; Rakow, 1986). In our view, gender derives from the enactment of social actions and activities, and men and women alike share in such activities (Canary et al., 1997). Accordingly, men and women appear to share similar patterns of communication behavior in the maintenance of conversational behavior.

Flexibility at defining one's gender role identity can be more apparent in married couples, where, after a period of time, sex roles lose their rigidity and women and men become more alike in their behaviors (Aries, 1987). Contrary to traditional sex role expectations, the literature suggests that husbands (vs. wives) converge more to their partner's conversational style (Fitzpatrick & Mulac, 1995). In this study, where married couples were asked to talk about anything they wanted, participants were able to carry a conversation involving a balance of maintenance work for women and men.

An alternative interpretation of similar findings for husbands and wives derives from the dual cultures approach (e.g., Henley & Kramarae, 1991; Maltz & Borker, 1982). The central tenet of this approach holds that girls' and boys' experiences are so varied that the two groups' experiences are tantamount to being socialized in different cultures; girls learn to emphasize closeness and boys learn to emphasize achievements other than their relationships. Along these lines, women would use conversation as a means to establish and maintain relationships, whereas men would see conversation as a mechanism to control the situation (Maltz & Borker, 1982). In this manner, women would perceive back channel cues as signals of involvement, whereas men would perceive back channels as indicators of deference or agreement. To illustrate the point further, questions could be used to achieve an instrumental definition of reality that has little to do with maintaining the conversation. Accordingly, although women and men would engage in the same behavior, they would hold alternative expectations and explanations for such behavior. In this light, sex differences do not pertain to actual behavior but rather to the meanings the parties lend them.

The two cultures perspective gives rise to the question of whether one can operationally define maintenance behavior similarly for men and women; whether one defines any communicative behavior as an act of dominance or maintenance may depend on the point of view from which one approaches the conversation. Whether this interpretation is correct cannot be tested with the data we have at the present. At a minimum, however, this interpretation provides one way that one can see large sex differences operating within identical behavior.

The domain of interaction known as *conversational maintenance* would appear to lend itself to an unambiguous examination of different roles of men and women in close relationships as they invest energy in their communicative activities. That this domain of research began within a dominance orientation (i.e., with the view than men control women through conversation) underscores the expectation that certain behaviors should serve a relationally promoting function (DeFrancisco, 1990, 1991; Fishman, 1978). The dual cultures interpretation would permit us to second guess our tests, view the hypotheses as nonfalsifiable, and argue that future research should explore potential meanings that particular behaviors have for men and women before we conclude that men and women engage in similar kinds of conversational maintenance behaviors (see also Kunkel & Burleson, chap. 5, this volume). Although it is possible that men and women engage in the same behaviors within different interpretive frames, our data do not permit an examination of this claim. Accordingly and based on the presumptions underlying the conversational maintenance literature, we must conclude that, at present, no clear data exist that show women, more than their male partners, maintain conversations.

Conclusion

Men and women in close relationships engage in similar kinds and amounts of conversational maintenance behaviors. The similarities in conversational maintenance behaviors used by husbands and wives clearly outweigh the differences and defy a dominance model of interaction. The question now is whether an alternative, more circumspect theory can indicate how dynamics of conversational behaviors might be related to gender as a social acitivity. One possibility is to define *gender* as the cluster of activities that men and women enact, allowing for the possibility that men and women have overlapping gender roles that are defined according to dimensions that transcend the traditional communal versus agenic poles (Canary et al., 1997). Future research should focus on how gender roles are constructed in the daily activities of men and women, and how differences in power are reflected in conversation in addition to or even regardless of one's biological sex.

The limitations of the present study also indicate springboards from which future research can be directed. One problem concerns the laboratory setting in which the study took place, which may have limited negative interaction behaviors. A second limitation was the short amount of time each couple had to talk. Seven minutes represent only a slice of these married couples' lives and one of thousands of conversations they experience. Still, these conversations permitted us to explore maintenance work with a larger sample than previous work had. We were able to examine three times as many cross-sex couples as Fishman and DeFrancisco did and more than Kollack et al. observed. A third drawback concerns a lack of variance in some behaviors. For example, couples rarely displayed hostile question asking, rejection, or disconfirming interruptions. Allowing a longer period for couples to talk—perhaps in their homes—may have permitted more negative behaviors. Yet it should not alarm anyone that couples, especially men, may not display these dominant behaviors in small talk episodes. In most of the conversations, couples tend to talk about routine, nonvolatile topics. When in conversation, there is no reason to display hostile behaviors if the topic at hand is not controversial or emotional. Indeed one strength of this study may concern how the conversational task (i.e., discuss any issue the participants wish) would require at least one partner to engage in the chore of maintaining a conversation of small talk.[2]

Although the variables examined in the present study represent several conversational maintenance behaviors, they are not necessarily exhaustive. Other conversational maintenance behaviors likely include different nonverbal behaviors such as head nods, smiling, eye contact, and body lean. Such behaviors may represent alternative ways to show how someone invests energy into conversation. Moreover, we did not explore how partners might silence each other (e.g., by offering truncated responses; DeFrancisco, 1991). Furthermore, relational satisfaction should be considered when studying gender and conversational maintenance behaviors. Gottman (1994) reported that unsatisfied partners—husbands especially—are more likely to withdraw from conversation and display more hostility than would partners in satisfied couples. By indicating whether couples are satisfied with their marriage, certain conversational maintenance behaviors such as back channels and question asking may differ in number and quality.

Finally, theory and research suggest that different couple types have alternative forms of marriage and engage in different kinds of conversations (Fitzpatrick, 1988). Likewise, blue- versus white-collar families show emo-

---

[2]Kathryn Dindia provided this insight.

tion differently during conversation (e.g., Komarovsky, 1967; Krokoff, Gottman, & Roy, 1988). Whether traditional or working class couples enact behaviors differently than egalitarian and white-collar couples, such as those in this study, needs investigation. Perhaps women do the *shitwork* in relationships that adopt a conventional ideology regarding sex roles. Such a proposition also comports with research on the unfair division of household labor that is most evident in traditional marriages (Hochschild, 1989). Regardless, being a woman did not necessitate *shitwork*, at least not for the women who participated in this investigation.

ACKNOWLEDGMENTS

The authors wish to thank Kathryn Dindia and Walter Zakahi for their helpful comments. We are also indebted to Laurel Ranson and Anne Wenner for their assistance in coding conversations.

REFERENCES

Argyle, M., Mansur, L., & Cook, M. (1968). The effects of visibility on interaction in a dyad. *Human Relations, 21*, 3–17.

Aries, E. (1987). Gender and communication. In P. Shaver & C. Hendrick (Eds.), *Sex and gender* (pp. 149–176). Newbury Park, CA: Sage.

Aries, E. (1996). *Men and women in interaction: Reconsidering the differences.* New York: Oxford University Press.

Ayres, J. (1983). Strategies to maintain relationships: Their identification and perceived usage. *Communication Quarterly, 31*, 62–67.

Bem, S. L. (1993). *The lenses of gender.* New Haven, CT: Yale University Press.

Bradac, J. J. (1983). The language of lovers, flowers, and friends: Communicating in social and personal relationships. *Journal of Language and Social Psychology, 2*, 141–161.

Burggraf, C. S., & Sillars, A. L. (1987). A critical examination of sex differences in marital communication. *Communication Monographs, 54*, 276–294.

Canary, D. J., Emmers-Sommer, T. M., & Faulkner, S. (1997). *Sex differences in personal relationships: Toward an activity-based model of gender.* New York: Guilford.

Canary, D. J., & Hause, K. S. (1993). Is there any reason to research sex differences in communication? *Communication Quarterly, 41*, 129–144.

Deaux, K., & Major, B. (1987). Putting gender into context: An interactive model of gender-related behavior. *Psychological Review, 94*, 369–389.

DeFrancisco, V. L. (1990, November). *Response to Pamela Fishman: A qualitative study of on-going interactions in heterosexual couples' homes.* Paper presented at the Speech Communication Association Convention, Chicago, IL.

DeFrancisco, V. L. (1991). The sounds of silence: How men silence women in marital relations. *Discourse and Society, 2*, 413–423.

Dindia, K. (1987). The effects of sex of subject and sex of partner on interruptions. *Human Communication Research, 13*, 345–371.

Dindia, K., & Baxter, L. (1987). Strategies in maintaining and repairing marital relationships. *Journal of Social and Personal Relationships, 4*, 159–177.

Doherty, E. G. (1974). Therapeutic community meetings: A study of communication patterns, sex, status, and staff attendance. *Small Group Behavior, 5,* 244–256.

Dumas, B. (1976). Male-female conversational interaction cues: Using data from dialect surveys. In B. Dubois & I. Crouch (Eds.), *The sociology of the language of American women.* San Antonio, TX: Trinity University Press.

Eakins, B. W., & Eakins, R. G. (1978). *Sex differences in communication.* Boston: Houghton-Mifflin.

Fisher, B. A. (1983). Differential effects of sexual composition and interactional context on interaction patterns in dyads. *Human Communication Research, 9,* 225–238.

Fishman, P. (1978). Interaction: The work women do. *Social Problems, 25,* 397–406.

Fitzpatrick, M. A. (1988). *Between husbands and wives: Communication in marriage.* Newbury Park, CA: Sage.

Fitzpatrick, M. A., & Dindia, K. (1986). Couples and other strangers: Talktime in spouse-stranger interaction. *Communication Research, 13,* 625–652.

Fitzpatrick, M. A., & Mulac, A. (1995). Relating to spouse and stranger: Gender-preferential language use. In P. J. Kalbfleisch & M. J. Cody (Eds.), *Gender, power, and communication in human relationships* (pp. 213–231). Hillsdale, NJ: Lawrence Erlbaum Associates.

Gottman, J. M. (1994). *What predicts divorce? The relationship between marital processes and marital outcomes.* Hillsdale, NJ: Lawrence Erlbaum Associates.

Henley, N. M., & Kramarae, C. (1991). Gender, power, and miscommunication. In N. Coupland, H. Giles, & J. Wiemann (Eds.), *Miscommunication and problematic talk* (pp. 18–43). Newbury Park, CA: Sage.

Hochschild, A., with Machung, A. (1989). *The second shift: Working parents and the revolution at home.* New York: Viking Press.

Kennedy, C. W., & Camden, C. T. (1982). A new look at interruptions. *The Western Journal of Speech Communication, 47,* 45–58.

Kollack, P., Blumstein, P., & Schwartz, P. (1985). Sex and power in interaction: Conversational privileges and duties. *American Sociological Review, 50,* 34–60.

Komarovsky, M. (1967). *Blue collar marriage.* New York: Vintage Press.

Kramer, C. (1977). Perceptions of female and male speech. *Language and Speech, 20,* 151–161.

Kramarae, C. (1981). *Women and men speaking.* Rowley, MA: Newbury House.

Krokoff, L. J, Gottman, J. M., & Roy, A. K. (1988). Blue-collar and white-collar marital interaction and communication orientation. *Journal of Social and Personal Relationships, 5,* 201–221.

Maltz, D. N., & Borker, R. A. (1982). A cultural approach to male-female miscommunication. In J. J. Gumpertz (Ed.), *Language and social identity* (pp. 196–216). New York: Cambridge University Press.

Marlett, G. A. (1970). A comparison of vicarious and direct reinforcement control of verbal behavior in an interview setting. *Journal of Personality and Social Psychology, 16,* 695–703.

Martin, J. N., & Craig, R. T. (1982). Selected linguistic sex differences during initial social interactions of same-sex and mixed-sex student dyads. *The Western Journal of Speech Communication, 47,* 16–28.

McMillan, J. R., Clifton, A. K., McGrath, D., & Gale, W. S. (1977). Women's language: Uncertainty or interpersonal sensitivity and emotionality? *Sex Roles, 3,* 545–559.

Pearson, J. C., Turner, L., & Todd-Mancillas, W. (1991). *Gender and communication.* Dubuque, IA: Brown.

Ragan, S. L. (1989). Communication between the sexes: A consideration of sex differences in adult communication. In J. F. Nussbaum (Ed.), *Life-span communication: Normative processes* (pp. 179–193). Hillsdale, NJ: Lawrence Erlbaum Associates.

Rakow, L. (1986). Rethinking gender research in communication. *Journal of Communication, 36,* 11–26.

Rosenfeld, H. M. (1966). Approval-seeking and approval-inducing functions of verbal and nonverbal responses in the dyad. *Journal of Personality and Social Psychology, 4,* 597–605.

Sacks, H., Schegloff, E., & Jefferson, G. (1974). A simplist systematics for the organization of turn-taking of conversation. *Language, 50,* 696–735.

Sillars, A. L. (1986, April). *Procedures for coding interpersonal conflict.* Unpublished manuscript, Department of Interpersonal Communication, University of Montana, Missoula.

Stafford, L., & Canary, D. J. (1991). Maintenance strategies and romantic relationship type, gender, and relational characteristics. *Journal of Social and Personal Relationships, 8,* 217–242.

Tannen, D. (1990). *You just don't understand: Women and men in conversation.* New York: William Morrow.

Thorne, B., & Henley, N. (1975). Difference and dominance: An overview of language, gender and society. In B. Thorne & N. Henley (Eds.), *Language and sex: Difference and dominance* (pp. 5–42). Rowley, MA: Newbury House.

Watzlawick, P., Beavin, J. H., & Jackson, D. D. (1967). *Pragmatics of human communication: A study of interactional patterns, pathologies, and paradoxes.* New York: W. W. Norton.

West, C. (1984). When the doctor is a lady. *Symbolic Interaction, 7,* 87–106.

West, C., & Zimmerman, D. H. (1977). Women's place in everyday talk: Reflections on parent-child interaction. *Social Problems, 24,* 521–529.

West, C., & Zimmerman, D. H. (1983). Small insults: A study of interruptions in cross-sex conversations between unacquainted persons. In B. Thorne, C. Kramarae, & N. Henley (Eds.), *Language, gender, and society* (pp. 103–107). Rowley, MA: Newbury House.

Wilkins, B. M., & Andersen, P. A. (1991). Gender differences and similarities in management communication: A meta-analysis. *Management Communication Quarterly, 5,* 6–35.

Woods, N. (1988). Talking shop: Sex and status as determinants of floor apportionment in a work setting. In J. Coates & D. Cameron (Eds.), *Women in their speech communities* (pp. 141–157). Essex, England: Longman.

Zimmerman, D. H., & West, C. (1975). Sex roles, interruptions and silences in conversation. In B. Thorne & N. Henley (Eds.), *Language and sex: Difference and dominance* (pp. 105–129). Rowley, MA: Newbury House.

Chapter 17

Perceptions of Men and Women Departing From Conversational Sex Role Stereotypes During Initial Interaction

A. Elizabeth Lindsey
Walter R. Zakahi
New Mexico State University

Recently Stephanie Glazer filed a $1 million gender bias suit against the New York Rangers hockey franchise. The suit is based on her claim that she was "removed from the [hockey] arena for using 'unfeminine' language" ("Female Hockey Fan," 1995, p. C2). Even as she was being removed, however, Glazer charges that male hockey fans were yelling obscenities "in an effort to bait the usher," but Glazer quotes a security guard who winked and smiled as saying, "Guys, no bad language." Glazer's suit presents an extreme example of what might happen when people violate sex role norms. We are all familiar with the feminine stereotype that women should behave like ladies. An important part of this stereotype, apparently even at some hockey games, is that ladies do not use vulgar language. By contrast, one stereotype of men is that they more commonly use vulgar and obscene language (De Klerk, 1991).

The consequences of sex role violations are not usually as extreme as Ms. Glazer claims to have suffered. It is more likely that the sanctions for sex role violations are more implicit. Such subtle sanctions, however, remain common in the context of day-to-day interaction. Nonverbal behaviors such as dirty looks or verbal sanctions such as a request for behavior change are not uncommon. For example, the male author of this chapter recalls being only rarely sanctioned for his use of vulgar language in public, whereas the female author has used the same type of language and received negative comments.

Barring overt verbal and nonverbal sanctions, violations of sex role norms may influence our behavior in more subtle and insidious ways. We may select mating partners and friends, hire, elect club members, and just generally favor some individuals over others based on whether they conform to or violate sex role norms. Underlying all these behaviors are the negative perceptions and evaluations we may have of people who violate any norm, including sex role norms. This chapter reviews the literature on sex role stereotypes and violations and describes two experiments designed to examine perceptions and evaluations of sex role norm violations, with an emphasis on the violation of conversational behaviors in initial interaction.

In recent years, researchers have questioned the value of positing differences between the sexes (e.g., Canary & Hause, 1993; Shibley Hyde & Plant, 1995), arguing that research on sex differences has failed to reveal meaningful differences between men and women (but see Eagly, 1987; Shibley Hyde & Frost, 1993). The population of the United States, however, seems to be blissfully unaware that sex differences are supposed to be only minimal and may continue to operate under the assumptions of sex role stereotypes.

SEX ROLE STEREOTYPES

Scholars have described the use of sex role stereotypes as extensive (Eagly, 1987; Ruble, 1983; Smith & Midlarsky, 1985) or even pervasive (Broverman, Vogel, Broverman, Clarkson, & Rosenkrantz, 1972; Deaux & Major, 1987; Williams & Best, 1982). For example, Broverman et al. measured the extent to which more than 900 people (varying widely in age, education, socioeconomic status, religion, marital status, and sex) agreed on conceptions of male and female stereotypical characteristics. Based on the percentage of agreement, Broverman et al. concluded: "The finding that sex-role stereotypes continue to be held by large and relatively varied samples of the population and furthermore are incorporated into the self-concepts of both men and women indicates how deeply ingrained these attitudes are in our society" (p. 76). Several researchers have argued that sex roles are not only widespread but persistent (Ruble, 1983; Werner & LaRussa, 1985). Werner and LaRussa replicated research conducted by Sherriffs and McKee in 1957 to find little change in sex role stereotypes over time. Borisoff and Merrill (1992) argued that male and female stereotypes "have been with us for centuries" (p. 16).

At a broad level, the content of sex role stereotypes ascribes an agentic quality to men and a communal quality to women (Deaux & Kite, 1993; Eagly, 1987; Smith, 1985). Described more specifically, the agentic stereotype of men includes qualities such as "self assertion (e.g., aggressive ambitious, dominant forceful acts as a leader) and independence from other people (e.g., independent, self-reliant, self-sufficient, individualistic)" (Eagly, 1987, p. 16). The communal stereotype describes women as nurturing, affectionate, helpful, and emotionally expressive. Generally, women are portrayed as being "concerned for the welfare of other people" (Deaux & Kite, 1993, p. 113).

The agentic and communal stereotypes of men and women are typified by several communication behaviors. Women tend to be more inclusive and encouraging of others during conversation. For example, women are more likely than men to invite and encourage the participation of others in conversation (Fishman, 1978; McMillan, Clifton, McGrath, & Gale, 1977; Wood, 1996). Women smile, provide more attentiveness signals, and make more eye contact than do men (Basow, 1986; Duncan & Fiske, 1977). The agentic and controlling stereotype of men may manifest in communication behaviors such as talking for longer periods of time than women, particularly during opposite-sex interactions (Borisoff & Merrill, 1992). Nonverbally, men tend to be less facially expressive, use a loud voice, and invade space (Ortega Murphy & Zorn, 1996). Two theoretical approaches, one developed by Eagly (1987) and one developed by Deaux and Major (1987), provide a framework for understanding how agentic and communal stereotypical behaviors become manifest during interaction.

INTERACTION-BASED MODEL OF SEX ROLES

Deaux and Major (1987) provided an explanation for sex role behavior at the level of the conversation. In their model, gender-related behavior is a product of a dynamic process in which each participant's gender belief system (including sex role stereotypes) influences his or her partner's behavior as well as his or her own behavior. Deaux and Major argued that gender behavior is a product of negotiations that occur during interaction. This negotiation process is a product of two competing forces. First, a person's sex role stereotypes can influence his or her partner's behavior through the expectancies that he or she communicates. Sex role stereotypes operate as expectations for the appropriate behavior of men and women in interaction. Sex role stereotypes, like other behavioral expectations, tend to be confirmed. Deaux and Major (1987) highlighted the substantial evidence on expectancy confirmation in general and on sex role expectations in particular. While acknowledging the powerful influence of expectations to influence behavior, Deaux and Major recognized that expectations do not operate independently of the target's own self-concept and self-expectancies.

The second contributor to this process is the target's self-concept. The target's sex role stereotype will tend to influence his or her own behavior so as to construct a particular self-presentation (Deaux & Major, 1990). The target holds a self-schema that includes a gender identity; this identity is partially a product of the actor's own sex role stereotypes.

Activation of sex role schema constitutes a significant part of the Deaux and Major (1987) model. Sex role schema only matter if they have been raised to an awareness level for the actors in a conversation. Deaux and Major did not assume that all interaction results in the activation of sex role schema. Certain situations more likely activate schema than do others. For example, a target's personal attributes may activate schema. Conversing with a petite woman or a rugged looking man may stimulate sex role schema. The situation also activates sex role schema. A school-sponsored dance may make sex role beliefs more salient or conversing with the only man or women working for your company may activate sex role schema.

Of particular interest to our work is the uncertainty of an initial interaction between men and women and how it is likely to activate sex role schema. According to Bierhoff (1989), schemas and stereotypes in general are likely to be employed during initial social encounters because they allow perceivers to quickly and simply reduce uncertainty. It is noteworthy that such activation can occur below the perceiver's level of awareness. Schneider, Hastorf, and Ellsworth (1979) noted that people can be responsive to the behavior of others even when they are not consciously aware of the other person's behavior.

SOCIAL ROLE INTERPRETATIONS OF STEREOTYPES

Eagly (1987) offered social roles as an alternative to socialization and biology as explanations for sex differences. Eagly borrowed the concepts of structural and cultural approaches from House (1981) to explain her approach. Cultural approaches explain group differences as an outgrowth of socialization. Children learn cultural beliefs and values that later help to account for their behavior as adults. By contrast, structural explanations, such as Eagly's role theory, argue that group differences occur because "members of social groups experience common situational constraints because they tend to have the same or similar social positions within organizations and other structures such as families" (Eagly, 1987, p. 9). Sex role stereotypes are an important part of Eagly's explanation of sex differences. Sex roles and sex role stereotypes are a product of the social roles generally held by men or women. For Eagly, social roles explain the communal stereotype of women and the agentic stereotype of men explained earlier.

For Eagly (1987), social roles can be a product of sex role stereotypes. We hold stereotypes of men and women that become expectations. Because these expectations are shared by the community, they form social norms.

Because members of the community consistently hold expectations for men and women, they are especially potent. Like Deaux and Major (1987), Eagly noted that evidence strongly supports the idea that expectations result in behavioral confirmation. Eagly contended that some of the strongest evidence for behavioral confirmation of stereotypes resides in research dealing with sex stereotypes.

If sex role stereotypes contain the power to create expectations for the behavior of others, it should be no surprise that these stereotypes are also internalized and have an influence on the target independent of the expectations of a particular perceiver. Eagly's (1987) argument appears similar to Deaux and Major's (1987) position: Sex role stereotypes have the power to shape the behavior of a target both externally (other expectancies) and internally (self-expectancies).

SEX ROLE VIOLATIONS

If a target's behavior deviates from the perceiver's sex role expectations, different perceptions of the target will be produced than those derived from behavior that supports sex role expectations. Violations or deviations from norms offer more information than does behavior conforming to norms (Berger & Bradac, 1982; Jones & McGillis, 1976); they also require explanation, whereas conforming behavior usually does not (Fiske & Taylor, 1991). Goffman (1963) proposed that people who deviate from the norm are perceived negatively and denied the respect accorded to people who conform to societal expectations. Theoretical models examining the violation of expectations for verbal and nonverbal behavior also suggest that perceptions may be negative or less than positive (e.g., J. Burgoon & Hale, 1988; M. Burgoon & Miller, 1985; Cappella & Greene, 1982). According to these models, evaluations of the violation and the violator are determined by characteristics of the target, characteristics of the perceiver, and/or characteristics of the relationship between target and perceiver.

Biological sex, as argued here, is a characteristic of the target affecting an interactant's perception. Previous research suggests that violations of target expectancies based on sex are likely to be evaluated negatively. Three studies by Costrich, Feinstein, Kidder, Marecek, and Pascale (1975) demonstrated that popularity ratings of men and women were adversely affected when women acted aggressively and men passively. Sadalla, Kenrick, and Vershure (1987) found in three studies that men engaging in less dominant behaviors were rated as less attractive than men acting in a dominant manner. Research by M. Burgoon, Birk, and Hall (1991) indicated that female physicians communicating in an aggressive manner were rated less positively than female physicians who were affiliative in their style of communication.

A characteristic of the perceiver relevant to perceptions of gender norm-violating behavior is the degree to which the perceiver is gender schematic (Deaux & Major, 1987). Gender-schematic individuals tend to adhere to traditional conceptions of male and female behavior (Deaux & Major, 1987; Martin, 1987) and may be more sensitive to and less tolerant of the violation of gender norms than are gender aschematics, who tend to hold fewer if any sex role expectations for individuals. According to Deaux and Major (1987), gender-schematic individuals hold descriptive and prescriptive beliefs about men and women: Gender schematics believe that traits such as instrumentality, dominance, and assertiveness are and should be associated with men, whereas affiliation, warmth, and concern are and should be associated with women. Martin (1987) proposed that these beliefs are founded on actual characteristics of men and women, although gender schematics tend to exaggerate the differences in characteristics between men and women. Accurate or not, the beliefs provide consistent and, more important, specific expectations for gender-appropriate behavior (Deaux & Major, 1987).

Not only do schematics tend to hold specific expectations for male and female behavior, but their schema are easily triggered by situations potentially eliciting the use of stereotyping (Deaux & Major, 1987; Martin, 1987; McKenzie-Mohr & Zanna, 1990). Initial interactions, situations where biological sex is observable, and situations that are sex linked (especially interactions with heterosexual overtones) trigger the use of sex role stereotyping but are particularly likely to do so for schematics (Deaux & Major, 1987). As a result, schematics tend to stereotype others (Martin, 1987)—particularly members of the opposite sex (e.g., Anderson & Bem, 1981; Park & Hahn, 1988).

A last factor to affect the evaluations of behavior departing from gender norms concerns the level of intimacy in the relationship—a characteristic of the relationship between the target and the perceiver. Generally, people show less tolerance for deviations from expectations during initial interaction than in developed relationships (Cappella & Greene, 1982). This suggests that the violation of sex role norms will be perceived less positively during initial interaction than in the context of a developed relationship.

TWO SEX ROLE NORMS FOR BEHAVIOR
DURING INITIAL INTERACTION

Given that initial interaction represents a context wherein the violation of sex role norms may be particularly influential on evaluations of individuals, we conducted two studies examining the violation of norms for conversational behavior that typically occur during initial interaction: question asking and talking about the self. Both behaviors constitute methods for reduction of uncertainty in interaction (Berger, 1979; Berger & Bradac, 1982; Douglas, 1990) but are not equally characteristics of men and women.

We maintain that part of the communal stereotype for women is that they typically ask questions during initial interaction, whereas men are more likely to talk about themselves as a form of control. There are two types of evidence to support these assertions. The first is that question asking and talking about the self are behaviors frequently demonstrated by women and men and as such, are indicative of sex role stereotypes. Both Deaux and Major (1987) and Eagly (1987) suggested that regularly performed behaviors may be evidence of the influence of a sex role stereotype held by the self and/or others during interaction.

Question asking is widely viewed as a behavior characteristic of women rather than men (e.g., Deaux, 1977; Harding, 1975; Lakoff, 1975; Spender, 1980; but see McKinney & Donaghy, 1993). For example, Fishman (1978) examined male and female dyads, noting that women in the dyads asked two and a half times more questions than did men. McCloskey (1987) later replicated these results in a study of third-grade girls and boys. The results of her study show that girls in both mixed- and same-sex interactions asked two times more questions than boys in both mixed- and same-sex interactions. Question asking may be especially pronounced when women are interacting with men. Brouwer, Gerritsen, and Dehaan (1979) reported that women asked more questions than men when purchasing a train ticket and that this pattern was most evident when the person selling the ticket was male. McMillan et al. (1977) found the same pattern in mixed- and same-sex problem-solving groups. Deaux (1977) suggested that question asking serves as a self-presentational strategy aimed toward bonding or affiliation in interaction. A second function is to facilitate conversation (Fishman, 1978; McCloskey, 1987; Spender, 1980). The behavior of asking questions is consistent with the communal stereotype of women. That is, question asking serves to help people feel included in or part of a social activity, and Coates (1986) argued directly that asking questions reflects societal expectations for women.

Societal expectations for the agentic behavior of men are reflected more in talking about the self. Research demonstrates that men talk about themselves more than do women during interactions with strangers or acquaintances (Davis, 1978; Derlega, Winstead, Wong, & Hunter, 1985; Lockheed & Hall, 1976; Stokes, Childs, & Fuehrer, 1981; Stokes, Fuehrer, & Childs, 1980) and the talk may serve one or both of two purposes. The first, as suggested by Davis (1978), is to control the intimacy level of a conversation during initial interaction. Derlega et al. argued that this strategy allows men to take advantage of reciprocity norms, so that "a man can select relatively intimate topics to disclose to a woman in order to get the woman to disclose more intimately about herself in return" (p. 27). A second function of talking about the self is to present oneself favorably. Derlega, Metts, Petronio, and Margulis (1993) noted that men are selective when talking about themselves and, more specifically, may withhold information about their vulnerabilities; men tend to talk more often about their successes (Aries, 1987). Both functions appear consistent with the male stereotype of control and assertiveness.

A second form of evidence is a survey we conducted to test the idea that question asking and talking about oneself are sex role stereotypical behaviors. We presented 211 undergraduate students at our university with the following scenario:

> Person A and Person B are two people of about the same age who meet for the first time at a party. They carry on a conversation that lasts about 10 minutes. During the conversation, Person A talks a lot about his or her accomplishments, interests, and hobbies and mostly reveals strengths rather than weaknesses. Person A appears to be trying to impress Person B and to control the conversation. By contrast Person B takes on the burden of keeping the conversation going by asking Person A lots of questions about him or herself.

Approximately half ($n = 106$) of the participants were asked to identify the sex of Person A. The remaining participants ($n = 105$) were asked to identify the sex of Person B. All of the participants were asked if this was a same-sex or opposite-sex interaction. Participants were significantly more likely [$\chi^2(1) = 18.26$, $p < .001$] to identify Person A as a male (79%) and Person B as a female (67%) [$\chi^2(1) = 11.67$, $p < .01$]. We purposely did not identify this as a cross-sex conversation to avoid the possibility that participants used the process of elimination to identify the sex of either person. When asked, however, if it was a same- or cross-sex conversation, 85% of the participants identified it as a cross-sex conversation [$\chi^2(1) = 110.14$, $p < .001$]. The results of the survey indicate that question asking and talking about oneself are behaviors stereotypically assigned to women and men, respectively.

STUDY 1

Our first investigation of responses to sex role norm violations utilized opposite-sex dyads in actual interaction. Based on our initial rationale, we hypothesized that behavior violating sex role norms would be received less positively by perceivers than would behavior following sex role norms. However, we also proposed that those responses would be mediated by the extent to which perceivers had the tendency to use sex role stereotypes or to be gender schematic. We expected gender schematics to be more sensitive to norm violations than gender aschematics and that this difference would be evident in two ways. First, we expected gender-schematic individuals to respond less positively to sex role norm-violating behavior than to behavior following norms; we did not expect a similar difference in response from gender-aschematic individuals. Second, we expected gender schematics to have less positive responses to norm-violating behavior than would gender aschematics.

To conduct the study, we paired 39 male and 39 female *perceivers* with opposite-sex strangers who were designated as *targets*.[1] All participants completed Martin's (1987) ratio measure of sex stereotyping before arriving to the study. On arrival to the study, both perceivers and targets were told they were going to interact with an opposite-sex stranger for 5 minutes. Prior to interacting with the perceivers, however, targets were randomly assigned to either the *ask* or *tell* conditions in the study and each received one of two sets of instructions.

Targets in the ask condition were told to ask as much as they could about their partner during the interaction regardless of what the partner did. Targets assigned to the tell condition were instructed to tell as much about themselves as they could to their partner regardless of their partner's behavior during the interaction. To check the manipulation and ensure that targets followed instructions, we later examined videotapes of the interactions recorded with participants' knowledge and counted the number of questions actually asked by the targets. A one-tailed t test, $t(68) = 6.27$, $p < .01$, indicated that targets in the ask condition ($M = 12.51$) asked almost twice as many questions as did the tell targets ($M = 6.38$).[2]

The dependent variables in this study were the degree to which perceivers felt positively during the interaction and perceptions of the targets' social attractiveness.[3] We conducted two separate 2 (sex of target) × 2 (ask vs. tell) × 2 (high vs. low gender schematicity) analyses of covariance (AN-

---

[1]Three of the dyads were excluded from the study prior to data analysis. One target did not follow instructions and a second target was sightless. The perceiver partner in the third dyad was dropped because he did not complete the measures.

[2]Poor quality of videotaping prevented us from being able to count questions for five of the videotaped dyads.

[3]The procedure for calculating participants' scores on the index of sex stereotyping are detailed in both Martin (1987) and Lindsey and Zakahi (1996). High ($M = 1.206$, $SD = .681$) and low ($M = .312$, $SD = .187$) gender-schematic groups were created by use of a median split (median = .591, $M = .765$, $SD = .672$) on scores for the total index of sex stereotyping. Social attractiveness was assessed via items from a revised version of McCroskey and McCain's (1974) Interpersonal Attraction Scale (McCroskey & Richmond, 1979). The 10 positive items from Watson, Clark, and Tellegen's (1988) Positive and Negative Affect Schedule were used to assess ratings of positive affect. Alpha reliabilities were .87 and .83 for the Attraction and Positive Affect scales, consecutively.

COVA)—one for each dependent variable. Because our targets had been instructed to either ask or tell regardless of the partner's behavior during the interaction, we anticipated that all targets might be perceived as manipulative and controlling regardless of ask or tell conditions, and thus we included a measure of perceived manipulativeness to control for these possible negative perceptions.[4] Each ANCOVA produced a significant main effect for perceived manipulativeness and a three-way interaction for the effects of ask versus tell, target sex, and gender schemacity of perceiver.

The significant three-way interaction effect on perceivers' positive affect $[F(1,68) = 9.28, p = .003, \eta^2 = .14]$ demonstrated that gender-schematic male perceivers felt significantly less positive during their interactions with women in the tell condition than they did with women who asked questions. Gender-aschematic male perceivers, however, did not experience a similar difference in positive affect between the tell and ask conditions. Neither the gender-schematic nor gender-aschematic female perceivers reported differences in the positive affect they experienced between the male tell and ask conditions. In comparison with gender-aschematic women, however, gender-schematic women experienced significantly less positive affect when men asked questions. These results provide evidence that male schematic perceivers experienced less interest and pleasurable engagement (positive affect) during initial interaction when encountering female behavior contrary to sex role norms. Both male and female gender schematics were also more likely than gender aschematics to be bothered by norm-violating behavior. The means for each condition are reported in Table 17.1.

Although the results for positive affect were consistent with our hypotheses, almost opposite results were produced in the analysis of targets' social attractiveness. A significant three-way interaction $[F = 5.38, p = .02, \eta^2 = .08]$ indicated that female targets engaging in the sex role norm-violating behavior of tell were perceived as much less socially attractive than female targets asking questions. However, the differences in perception occurred for male aschematic perceivers rather than male schematic perceivers (see Table 17.2). Male perceivers with a tendency to gender stereotype made no significant distinction in their social attraction toward women who asked versus women who talked about themselves, nor did they find their female partners who told to be any less socially attractive than did their aschematic counterparts. When it came to female perceivers, gender schematics had different perceptions of men who asked versus men who talked, but they perceived the male norm-violating behavior of asking questions to be sig-

---

[4]Eight 7-point Likert-type items were used to assess perceived manipulativeness (see Lindsey & Zakahi, 1996). Cronbach's alpha for the eight items was .75. Perceived manipulativeness was a significant covariate in the analyses of ratings for both social attraction, $t(73) = 4.57, p < .01$, and positive affect, $t(73) = -5.23, p < .01$. There were no interactions between the covariate and any of the independent variables in the analyses.

TABLE 17.1
Means, Standard Deviations for Positive Affect,
Sex × Task × Schemacity Interaction (Study 1)

Ask Condition	N	Adjusted Mean	SD	
Aschematic perceivers of males	8	3.67	.72	A
Schematic perceivers of males	10	3.03	.48	B
Aschematic perceivers of females	10	2.93	1.03	B
Schematic perceivers of females	9	3.64	.69	A
Tell Condition				
Aschematic perceivers of males	9	3.10	.57	
Schematic perceivers of males	10	3.25	.54	
Aschematic perceivers of females	10	3.29	.79	
Schematic perceivers of females	9	3.00	.99	B

Note. Categories with different letters are significantly different using the Duncan procedure. From Lindsey and Zakahi (1996). Reprinted with permission.

nificantly more (rather than less) socially attractive than they did the male norm behavior of tell. Further, gender-schematic women found the male target asking questions to be more socially attractive than did gender-aschematic women.

Despite the results obtained for positive affect, the results from the analysis of social attractiveness indicate that not all perceptions of norm violators are less than positive and in fact may be more positive. In addition, gender schematics are not neccessarily likely to be put off by behavior

TABLE 17.2
Cell Means, Standard Deviations for Social Attraction,
Sex × Task × Schematicity Interaction (Study 1)

Ask Condition	N	Adjusted Mean	SD	
Aschematic perceivers of males	8	5.28	.44	B
Schematic perceivers of males	10	5.99	.61	A
Aschematic perceivers of females	10	5.93	.50	A
Schematic perceivers of females	9	5.69	.73	
Tell Condition				
Aschematic perceivers of males	9	5.15	.99	B
Schematic perceivers of males	10	5.19	.74	B
Aschematic perceivers of females	10	5.30	.99	B
Schematic perceivers of females	9	5.73	.44	

Note. Categories with different letters are significantly different using the Duncan procedure. From Lindsey and Zakahi (1996). Reprinted with permission.

departing from sex role expectations, although overall they had stronger responses to the non-normative targets than did gender aschematics. These results are contrary to our hypotheses and, further, are almost opposite to those we found for positive affect. Why would female schematics find men who ask questions to be more socially attractive while feeling less positively during those interactions? Why would male schematics indicate no preference between female ask and tell when it came to social attractiveness while reporting less positive affect when they interacted with the female tell? One explanation is that gender schematics experienced less positive affect as result of not knowing how to interact with norm violators. Although they may like the other individual, they may experience less pleasure due to uncertainty. Another explanation may lie in a difference between the two dependent variables. Social attraction and positive affect correlate significantly, but not highly ($r = .42$, $p < .05$); whereas social attraction is an evaluation of the partner, positive affect is a more global evaluation. The degree of positive affect experienced during the interaction may include the partner, the interaction as a whole, and, more important, the self.

The pattern of results produced for positive affect, in comparison with that for social attractiveness, may reflect a difference in how the participants felt about themselves and how they felt about the target. Perceptions of norm violators were positive, but perceptions of the self may have been less so. We suggest, as do Smith-Lovin and Robinson (1992) and Deaux and Major (1987), that behavior departing from sex role norms was as disconfirming of the perceiver's gender identity as it was of the target's— and perhaps more so. Although the perceivers may not have felt that the norm-violating behavior reflected negatively on the norm violator, it may have reflected negatively on the self. Thus, a gender-schematic woman may find men asking questions to be attractive while also feeling as if she's not fulfilling her gender role obligations. A gender-schematic man may not care whether a woman acts like a traditional woman beyond how it makes him feel about his own traditional role.

STUDY 2

Our second study on the violation of sex role normative communication varied from the first in a number of ways. In the second study, perceivers viewed a videotape of an opposite-sex interaction, rather than actually participating in the interaction. We utilized videotapes to maintain more consistency in the appearance and behavior of targets than was afforded in our first study. In the videotapes, we maintained more control over the targets' level of physical attractiveness and age. We were also able to control for the topics of conversation. The second study also investigated opposite- and same-sex perceptions of norm violations during initial interaction. Last, we included an additional dependent variable in the study: perceived communicative competence.

Perceived competence was examined for two reasons. First, we wanted to test Tannen's (1995) claim that women should consider using gender-opposite communication if they want to be perceived as more competent by males. Second, we intended to compare patterns of results for competency to those for social attraction. A study by Bradley (1981) found that ratings of social attractiveness did not vary significantly according to whether women engaged in behavior violating sex role norms for communication. However, Bradley did find variations in ratings of perceived competence. Women who engaged in communicative behavior counter to a feminine stereotype were perceived as more competent than women who engaged in sex role normative behavior; they were also perceived as more competent than men engaging in either gender-normative or gender-opposite behaviors. Bradley (1981) concluded that, although women violating sex role norms may "succeed in being influential or are credited with intelligence and knowledge, their interpersonal relationships may yet not flourish" (p. 89). Bradley examined the use of tag questions and disclaimers as a female sex role communicative behavior. We were interested in extending her observations to the asking of questions and talking about the self.

Seventy-two men and 56 women participated in our second study. Participants were randomly assigned to one of four experimental conditions. Participants viewed a videotape of a woman asking a man questions during an initial interaction (female ask), a woman talking about herself to a man during an initial interaction (female tell), a man asking questions of a woman during an initial interaction (male ask), or a man talking about himself to a woman during initial interaction (male tell). Male and female *ask* targets asked similar questions of their partner (e.g., "How many classes did you have today?" "What are you studying?" "Do you have any free time?" "Do you get to go out much?") and male and female *tell* targets provided similar answers (e.g., both had five classes that day, were taking 18 credit hours, were electrical engineering majors, seniors with little free time who mostly studied and played golf when given the opportunity). In addition to similarity in verbal content, male and female ask targets responded to the answers of their partners with smiling, head nodding, and back channel responses (nonverbal indicants of affiliativeness). When talking about the self, tell targets avoided direct gaze and were generally nonresponsive to their partner (nonverbal indicants of control). The same man and woman were conversing in each videotape and were similar in level of age and physical attractiveness. Only the target for each condition

TABLE 17.3
Cell Means, Standard Deviations for Social Attractiveness,
Target Sex × Task Interaction (Study 2)

Condition	N	Adjusted Mean	SD	
Male tell	33	3.79	1.09	A
Male ask	33	4.58	0.85	B
Female ask	31	4.90	0.84	B
Female tell	31	5.09	0.75	B

Note. Categories with different letters are significantly different using the Scheffé procedure.

could be seen in the videotape. The conversational partner was off-screen but could be heard by participants.

The two dependent variables investigated in this study were *perceived communication competence* and, as in the previous study, *social attraction*. Ratings for each were tested in separate 2 (sex of target) × 2 (ask vs. tell) × 2 (sex of perceiver) ANCOVAs. We included gender schematicity as a covariate due to its previously determined influence on perception in Study 1. We also included the age of the perceiver as a covariate because age has been determined to produce differences in perceptions of male and female behavior (Eagly, 1987).[5] Interestingly and despite the results of our previous study, gender schematicity was not related to perceptions of either social attraction or perceived communication competence in this study, hence it was excluded from any further analyses. Age was related only to perceptions of competence. The older the perceiver, the lower the rating of perceived communicative competence [$t(126)$ = -2.20, p = .03].

Results produced by our analysis of social attraction reveal that the sex of the perceiver had no effect on how the target was perceived. We did find, however, a significant two-way interaction indicating that the male and female targets were perceived differently according to whether they asked or told [F = 3.88, p = .05, η^2 = .03]. Perceivers rated the female target asking questions, the female target talking about herself, and the male target asking questions as being similarly socially attractive, but the male target talking about himself was rated as significantly less socially attractive than all other targets (see Table 17.3). These results are consistent with those found for the gender-schematic perceivers in the first study, showing that men engaging in the gender-opposite behavior were perceived as more socially attractive than men engaging in the sex role norm behavior.

---

[5]Gender schematicity and social attraction were assessed with measures identical to those in Study 1. Communication competence was measured using a 10-item semantic differential measure developed by Gonzales, White, and Spitzberg (1995). The reliability of the competence measure was .83.

There were also no differences in social attraction due to the female target's behavior, and these results were consistent with both our own and Bradley's (1981) findings of no differences in the perceived social attractiveness of women who followed sex role norms versus women who engaged in gender-opposite behaviors.

The analysis of communicative competence produced two significant two-way interactions. The first interaction indicated that perceptions of the male and female targets varied according to the sex of the perceiver [$F = 3.78$, $p = .05$, $\eta^2 = .03$]. There was no difference in how female perceivers rated the competency of the male and female targets. However, male perceivers found the female target to be more competent than the male, despite the fact that the male and female targets engaged in the same communication behaviors (see Table 17.4). The absence of a three-way interaction indicates that these differences occurred regardless of whether the targets asked questions or talked about themselves and, consequently, regardless of whether the behavior was normative or norm violating.

The second two-way interaction indicated that perceptions of the male and female targets' competence differed according to whether they engaged in asking or telling [$F = 12.54$, $p = .001$, $\eta^2 = .11$]. The female target was perceived as more communicatively competent when she engaged in the gender-opposite, tell behavior than when she asked questions (Table 17.5).

TABLE 17.4
Means, Standard Deviations for Competence,
Target Sex × Perceiver Sex (Study 2)

Perceiver Sex	Target Sex	N	Adjusted Mean	SD
Male	Male	36	3.52	0.76 A
Female	Male	30	3.88	0.67 A B
Female	Female	26	4.40	0.79 C B
Male	Female	36	4.58	0.85 C

Note. Categories with different letters are significantly different using the Scheffé procedure.

TABLE 17.5
Cell Means, Standard Deviations for Competence,
Target Sex × Task Interaction (Study 2)

Condition	N	Adjusted Mean	SD
Male tell	33	3.52	0.75 A
Male ask	33	3.86	0.76 A B
Female ask	31	4.23	0.77 B
Female tell	31	4.83	0.77 C

Note. Categories with different letters are significantly different using the Scheffé procedure.

She was also judged as more competent when talking about herself than was the male target in either the ask or tell conditions. There were no significant differences in ratings of competence between male ask and tell. The results for communicative competence are similar to those of Bradley (1980, 1981) in that the female communicative behavior violating sex role norms was found to be most competent. Bradley (1980) explained these results as a product of a positive violation of expectations for lower competence. The results also lend credence to Tannen's (1995) suggestion that women attempt to adopt gender-opposite communication behaviors if they wish to be perceived as more competent.

A combination of the results for both social attraction and communication competence enabled us to conclude, as did Bradley (1980, 1981), that women who take on gender-opposite behaviors will be perceived as more competent, but not necessarily as more socially attractive, than women who engage in behaviors more typical of traditional sex role norms. For men, gender-opposite behaviors may increase perceived social attractiveness but make little difference in terms of perceived competence. These perceptions occur regardless of the perceivers' own sex and, of particular note given the results of Study 1, perceivers' level of gender schematicity.

Differences due to the level of gender schematicity were not a factor governing perceptions of social attractiveness and communication competence in the second study, as evidenced by the fact that it was not a significant covariate in our analyses. Rather, all individuals in the second study tended to display patterns of perception demonstrated by gender schematics in the first study. Rather than suggesting that the effects of gender schematicity are inconsistent, however, we propose that the different results between the two studies are a consequence of the different procedures. It could be that, with the addition of sex-stereotypical affiliative and agentic nonverbal behaviors, we reinforced or strengthened the targets' sex role stereotypical or atypical image to the point that the targets would be perceived as such regardless of the perceivers' level of gender schematicity. That is, in situations where sex role characteristics are highly salient, gender schemas may be activated for all perceivers, not just perceivers with a dispositional tendency toward use of gender schemas (Deaux & Major, 1987).

CONCLUSION

We created both norm-following and norm-violating conditions where men and women either asked questions or talked about themselves in both an actual interaction (Study 1) and on videotape (Study 2). In our first study, we examined the extent to which perceivers felt positively and were socially attracted to both norm-violating and norm-following targets. In our second study, we again investigated the social attractiveness of targets as well as perceptions of their communication competence.

Results from both studies indicate that responses to persons departing from sex role norms are in many cases different from responses to individuals who conform to those norms and that gender schematicity influences those responses. However, the responses to norm violations are both more and less positive depending on the dimension of evaluation. For example, results from the first study indicate that men who ask questions are regarded as more socially attractive but elicit less positive affect in gender-schematic women. A combination of both studies suggests that women who talk about themselves are seen as more competent but may engender less positive affect in schematic males. On some dimensions, there were no significant differences in perceptions; both studies indicate that women who talk are not significantly more or less socially attractive than women who ask questions. Because perceivers' responses to persons departing from sex role norms for conversation varied, we cannot make the broad statement that violations are necessarily perceived negatively. Rather, we need to conduct further research to determine why some departures are regarded more positively on some dimensions and less positively on others. For example, we would like to test the explanations we have offered for the differences in the results between social attractiveness and positive affect (Study 1).

We also cannot make broad statements about departures from all sex role conversational norms until we investigate other types. To this point, we have focused on only one set of complementary behaviors: women asking questions, men talking about themselves, in initial interaction and their converse. In addition to being only one set of several potentially gender-linked conversational behaviors, these behaviors are fairly subtle. Less subtle departures, such as might be illustrated by the opening example of Stephanie Glazer, could produce more extreme and possibly negative responses.

Although currently we are reluctant to make any sweeping conclusions about perceptions of men and women who depart from conversational sex role stereotypical norms pending further research, we believe that for everyday social interaction it may be better to selectively depart from sex role stereotypes. Results from both studies suggest that men may form more positive social impressions by asking questions rather than talking about themselves. Conversely, women may be perceived as more competent when they talk about themselves rather than asking questions.

ACKNOWLEDGMENT

The authors would like to acknowledge the comments and contributions of the editors during the preparation of this chapter.

REFERENCES

Anderson, S. M., & Bem, S. L. (1981). Sex typing and androgyny in dyadic interaction: Individual differences in response to physical attractiveness. *Journal of Personality and Social Psychology, 41,* 74–86.

Aries, E. (1987). Gender and communication. In P. Shaver & C. Hendrick (Eds.), *Sex and gender* (pp. 124–148). Newbury Park CA: Sage.

Basow, S. (1986). *Gender stereotypes: Traditions and alternatives* (2nd ed.). Pacific Grove, CA: Brooks/Cole.

Berger, C. R. (1979). Beyond initial interaction: Uncertainty, understanding, and the development of interpersonal relationships. In H. Giles & R. St. Clair (Eds.), *Language and social psychology* (pp. 122–144). Oxford, England: Blackwell.

Berger, C. R., & Bradac, J. J. (1982). *Language and social knowledge: Uncertainty reduction in interpersonal relations.* London: Edward Arnold.

Bierhoff, H. W. (1989). *Person perception and attribution.* Berlin: Springer-Verlag.

Borisoff, D., & Merrill, L. (1992). *The power to communicate: Gender differences as barriers.* Prospect Heights, IL: Waveland Press.

Bradley, P. (1980). Sex, competence and opinion deviation: An expectation states approach. *Communication Monographs, 47,* 101–110.

Bradley, P. (1981). The folk-linguistics of women's speech: An empirical examination. *Communication Monographs, 48,* 73–90.

Brouwer, D., Gerritsen, M. M., & Dehaan, D. (1979). Speech differences between women and men: On the wrong track? *Language in Society, 8,* 33–50.

Broverman, I. K., Vogel, S. R., Broverman, D. M., Clarkson, F. E., & Rosenkrantz, P. S. (1972). Sex-role stereotypes: A current appraisal. *Journal of Social Issues, 28,* 59–78.

Burgoon, J. K., & Hale, J. L. (1988). Nonverbal expectancy violations theory: Model elaboration and application to immediacy behaviors. *Communication Monographs, 55,* 58–79.

Burgoon, M., Birk, T., & Hall, J. R. (1991). Compliance and satisfaction with physician-patient communication: An expectancy theory interpretation of gender differences. *Human Communication Research, 18,* 177–208.

Burgoon, M., & Miller, G. R. (1985). An expectancy interpretation of language and persuasion. In H. Giles & R. St. Clair (Eds.), *Recent advanced in language, communication and social psychology* (pp. 199–229). London: Lawrence Erlbaum Associates.

Canary, D. J., & Hause, K. S. (1993). Is there any reason to research sex differences in communication? *Communication Quarterly, 41,* 129–144.

Cappella, J., & Greene, J. (1982). A discrepancy-arousal explanation of mutual influence in expressive behavior for adult and infant-adult interaction. *Communication Monographs, 49,* 89–114.

Coates, J. (1986). *Women, men and language.* New York: Longman.

Costrich, N., Feinstein, J., Kidder, L., Marecek, J., & Pascale, L. (1975). When stereotypes hurt: Three studies of penalties for sex-role reversals. *Journal of Experimental Social Psychology, 11,* 520–530.

Davis, J. D. (1978). When boy meets girl: Sex roles and the negotiation of intimacy in an acquaintance exercise. *Journal of Personality and Social Psychology, 36,* 684–692.

Deaux, K. (1977). Sex differences. In T. Blass (Ed.), *Personality variances in social behavior* (pp. 357–377). Hillsdale, NJ: Lawrence Erlbaum Associates.

Deaux, K., & Kite, M. (1993). Gender stereotypes. In F. L. Denmark & M. A. Paludi (Eds.), *Psychology of women: A handbook of issues and theories* (pp. 107–139). Westport, CT: Greenwood.

Deaux, K., & Major, B. (1987). Putting gender into context: An interactive model of gender-related behavior. *Psychological Review, 94,* 369–389.

Deaux, K., & Major, B. (1990). A social-psychological model of gender. In D. L. Rhode (Ed.), *Theoretical perspectives on sexual difference* (pp. 89–99). New Haven, CT: Yale University Press.

De Klerk, V. (1991). Expletives: Men only? *Communication Monographs, 58,* 156–169.

Derlega, V., Metts, S., Petronio, S., & Margulis, S. T. (1993). *Self disclosure.* Newbury Park, CA: Sage.

Derlega, V., Winstead, B., Wong, P., & Hunter, S. (1985). Gender effects in an initial encounter: A case where men exceeded women in disclosure. *Journal of Social and Personal Relationships, 2,* 25–44.

Douglas, W. (1990). Uncertainty, information-seeking, and liking during initial interaction. *Western Journal of Speech Communication, 54,* 66–81.

Duncan, S., & Fiske, D. W. (1977). *Face-to-face interaction: Research, methods and theory.* Hillsdale, NJ: Lawrence Erlbaum Associates.

Eagly, A. H. (1987). *Sex differences in social behavior: A social role interpretation.* Hillsdale, NJ: Lawrence Erlbaum Associates.

Female hockey fan files suit for equal right to swear a blue streak. (September 18, 1995). *The San Diego Union-Tribune,* p. C2.

Fishman, P. M. (1978). Interaction: The work women do. *Social Problems, 25,* 397–406.

Fiske, S. T., & Taylor, S. E. (1991). *Social cognition* (2nd ed.). New York: McGraw-Hill.

Goffman, E. (1963). *Stigma.* Englewood Cliffs, NJ: Prentice-Hall.

Gonzales, J., White, C., & Spitzberg, B. H. (1995, February). *Is humor all that funny? The functions of humor in interpersonal relationships.* Paper presented at the WSCA conference, Portland, OR.

Harding, S. (1975). Women and words in a Spanish village. In R. Reiter (Ed.), *Toward an anthropology of women* (pp. 294–368). New York: Monthly Review Press.

House, J. (1981). Social structure and personality. In M. Rosenberg & R. Turner (Eds.), *Social psychology: Sociological perspectives* (pp. 525–561). New York: Basic Books.

Jones, E., & McGillis, D. (1976). Correspondent inferences and the attribution cube: A comparative reappraisal. In J. H. Harvey, W. J. Ickes, & R. F. Kidd (Eds.), *New directions in attribution research* (Vol. 1, pp. 389–420). Hillsdale, NJ: Lawrence Erlbaum Associates.

Lakoff, R. (1975). *Language and women's place.* New York: Harper & Row.

Lindsey, A. E., & Zakahi, W. R. (1996). Women who tell and men who ask: Perceptions of men and women departing from gender stereotypes during initial interaction. *Sex Roles, 34,* 767–786.

Lockheed, M. E., & Hall, K. P. (1976). Conceptualizing sex as a status characteristic: Applications to leadership training strategies. *Journal of Social Issues, 32,* 111–124.

Martin, C. L. (1987). A ratio measure of sex stereotyping. *Journal of Personality and Social Psychology, 52,* 489–499.

McCloskey, L. A. (1987). Gender and conversation: Mixing and matching styles. In D. B. Carter (Ed.), *Current conceptions of sex roles and sex typing: Theory and research* (pp. 139–153). New York: Praeger.

McCroskey, J. C., & McCain, T. A. (1974). The measurement of interpersonal attraction. *Speech Monographs, 41,* 216–266.

McCroskey, J. C., & Richmond, V. P. (1979, May). *The reliability and validity of scales for the measurement of interpersonal attraction and homophily.* Paper presented at the Eastern Communication Association convention, Philadelphia, PA.

McKenzie-Mohr, D., & Zanna, M. (1990). Treating women as sexual objects: Look to the (gender-schematic) male who has viewed pornography. *Personality and Social Psychology Bulletin, 16,* 296–308.

McKinney, D. H., & Donaghy, W. C. (1993). Dyad gender structure, uncertainty reduction, and self-disclosure during initial interaction. In P. J. Kalbfleisch (Ed.), *Interpersonal communication: Evolving interpersonal relationships* (pp. 33–50). Hillsdale, NJ: Lawrence Erlbaum Associates.

McMillan, J. R., Clifton, A. K., McGrath, D., & Gale, W. S. (1977). Uncertainty or interpersonal sensitivity and emotionality? *Sex Roles, 3,* 545–559.

Ortega Murphy, B., & Zorn, T. (1996). Gendered interaction in professional relationships. In J. Wood (Ed.), *Gendered relationships* (pp. 233–252). Mountainview, CA: Mayfield.

Park, B., & Hahn, S. (1988). Sex-role identity and the perception of others. *Social Cognition, 6,* 61–87.

Ruble, T. L. (1983). Sex stereotypes: Issues of change in the 1970s. *Sex Roles, 9,* 397–402.

Sadalla, E. K., Kenrick, D. T., & Vershure, B. (1987). Dominance and heterosexual attraction. *Journal of Personality and Social Psychology, 52,* 730–738.

Schneider, D. J., Hastorf, A. H., & Ellsworth, P. C. (1979). *Person perception* (2nd ed.). Reading, MA: Addison-Wesley.

Sherriffs, A. C., & McKee, J.P. (1957). Qualitative aspects of beliefs about men and women. *Journal of Personality, 25,* 451–464.

Shibley Hyde, J., & Frost, L. A. (1993). In F. L. Denmark & M. A. Paludi (Eds.), *Psychology of women: A handbook of issues and theories* (pp. 67–103). Westport, CT: Greenwood.

Shibley Hyde, J. S., & Plant, E. A. (1995). Magnitude of psychological gender differences: Another side to the story. *American Psychologist, 50,* 159–161.

Smith, P. A., & Midlarsky, E. (1985). Empirically derived conceptions of femaleness and maleness: A current view. *Sex Roles, 12,* 313–328.

Smith, P. M. (1985). *Language, the sexes and society.* Oxford, England: Basil Blackwell.

Smith-Lovin, L., & Robinson, D. T. (1992). Gender and conversational dynamics. In C. L. Ridgeway (Ed.), *Gender, interaction, and inequality* (pp. 122–156). New York: Springer-Verlag.

Spender, D. (1980). *Man made language.* London: Routledge & Kegan Paul.

Stokes, J., Childs, L., & Fuehrer (1981). Gender and sex roles as predictors of self-disclosure. *Journal of Counseling Psychology, 28,* 510–514.

Stokes, J., Fuehrer, A., & Childs, L. (1980). Gender differences in self-disclosure to various target persons. *Journal of Counseling Psychology, 27,* 192–198.

Tannen, D. (1995). *Communicating from 9 to 5.* New York: Morrow.

Watson, D., Clark, L. A., & Tellegen, A. (1988). Development and validation of brief measures of positive and negative affect: The PANAS scale. *Journal of Personality and Social Psychology, 54,* 1063–1070.

Werner, P. D., & LaRussa, G. W. (1985). Persistence and change in sex-role stereotypes. *Sex Roles, 12,* 1089–1100.

Williams, J. E., & Best, D. L. (1982). *Measuring sex stereotypes: A thirty-nation study.* Beverly Hills, CA: Sage.

Wood, J. T. (1996). Gender, relationships, and communication. In J. T. Wood (Ed.), *Gendered relationships* (pp. 3–19). Mountainview, CA: Mayfield.

Chapter 18

First Date Initiation and Enactment: An Expectancy Violation Approach

Paul A. Mongeau
Miami University

Colleen M. Carey
Northwestern University

Mary Lynn M. Williams
University of Wisconsin–Madison

Courtship is an ancient process that has taken on many forms depending on a wide array of cultural and historical factors (Cate & Lloyd, 1992). Dating is a 20th-century, Western form of courtship. Although no longer the exclusive pathway to marriage, dating is a "ubiquitous and distinct part of modern culture" (Harris, 1993, p. 360; see also Bailey, 1988). Date initiation has traditionally been in the male's domain. The practice and acceptability of female initiation of first dates have varied across the past 75 years, following various cultural and societal norms. Female initiation of a first date has become increasingly common, particularly in the past quarter century (Bailey, 1988; Cate & Lloyd, 1992). However, it is not without its detractors (e.g., Post, 1984). Critics claim that men might interpret the initiation as a sexual invitation and the female initiator as sexually aggressive.

As with other romantic relationships, one important component of dating relationships is sexual intimacy. "Intimate relations and sexual relations are so closely connected that it is impossible to peel them apart without some particles of the one coming off on the analysis of the other" (Davis, 1983, p. xviii). As a consequence, dates are likely sexually charged events. For example, Abbey (1987) asserted that asking for a first date was a fairly explicit way to express sexual interest. Accordingly, our primary goal in this chapter is to discuss sex differences and similarities in sexual expectations for, and sexual behaviors performed on, cross-sex first dates.

First dates are important because they represent a turning point in a dating relationship's development (Baxter & Bullis, 1986). It is assumed that first dates, as a turning point, help mark a relationship's transition from platonic to romantic. This shift is likely to create uncertainty concerning both the date partner and the nature of the relationship (Baxter, 1988; Berger & Calabrese, 1975). For example, Abbey (1987) reported that around 20% of her participants had been in a situation where the partners disagreed as to whether the event was a date. Despite both personal and relational uncertainties, direct talk about the nature of the relationship (i.e., meta-relational talk) is unlikely because the relationship is likely a taboo topic on a first date (Baxter & Wilmot, 1985). Given the uncertainty and lack of meta-relational talk, sexual expectations for, and involvement on, first dates are likely a function of nonsexual behaviors or factors. A critical communicative feature that may influence partners' first date sexual expectations that has come under recent scrutiny is the form of the date initiation.

As a consequence, this chapter focuses on three major issues. First, it focuses on sex differences in sexual evaluations, particularly those created by date initiation. *Sexual evaluation* refers to perceptions of the target's desired level of sexual activity as well as the target's interest in sexual intimacy on the date. This section considers sex differences in attitudes toward casual sex, sexual evaluations following date initiation, and the enactment of intimacy on first dates. Second, this chapter attempts to place these data within a broader explanatory framework—specifically, Burgoon's (1993) expectancy violation theory. Third, this chapter considers the issue of sex differences and/or similarities and suggests several directions for future research.

SEX DIFFERENCES IN FIRST DATE SEXUAL EXPECTATIONS

Abbey (1987) argued that, "men tend to perceive other people and relationships in a more sexualized manner than women do" (p. 173). Oliver and Hyde's (1993) meta-analysis of studies investigating sex differences on a wide variety of sexual attitudes and behaviors provides the best source for research relevant to Abbey's claim. Oliver and Hyde reported that men were more sexually permissive than women (the average d statistic across studies was 0.53). They found a particularly large sex difference in attitudes toward sexual intercourse in casual relationships (i.e., where there is no emotional commitment between partners; average $d = 0.81$). Oliver and Hyde reported smaller sex differences in attitudes toward sexual intercourse in committed dating and engaged relationships (average ds are 0.49 and 0.43, respectively).

Men also report more liberal attitudes toward a variety of other, less intimate, sexual behaviors (e.g., kissing or petting). These sex differences are also largest in the least intimate relationships (such as first dates; e.g., Roche, 1986). The size of the sex differences declines as relationships grow more committed.

Although these studies rely primarily on questionnaire self-report measures, an ingenious series of studies indicated that men are more likely than women to agree to engage in casual sex (e.g., Clark, 1990; Clark & Hatfield, 1989). Clark (1990; Clark & Hatfield, 1989) had confederates approach opposite-sex strangers on a university campus. The confederate would either ask the stranger out on a date or to go to bed with him or her. In all studies, men and women were equally likely to accept a date initiation from a stranger. In contrast, nearly two thirds of men and less than 1% of women accepted an invitation to engage in casual sex.

In summary, men and women differ in attitudes toward sexual behavior that occurs early in the course of relational development. Men, but not women, are generally eager for sexual activity outside the bounds of a relationship characterized by love or commitment (Buss, 1994; Clark, 1990; Oliver & Hyde, 1993; Roche, 1986). First dates are unlikely to involve intimacy and commitment. As a consequence, sex differences in attitudes toward sexual behavior in casual encounters are likely to be a particularly important factor in sexual expectations and involvement on first dates.

First Date Initiation and Sexual Evaluations

Over the past decade, several investigators focused on the social and sexual evaluations generated by date initiation. This research has followed one of two methods. First, research using hypothetical scenarios focused on evaluations of either or both individuals involved in date initiation interactions (e.g., Bostwick & DeLucia, 1992; Mongeau & Carey, 1996; Mongeau, Hale, Johnson, & Hillis, 1993; Muehlenhard & Scardino, 1985). The second line of research focused on the enactment of intimacy by asking participants to report on their actual first date behaviors and impressions (e.g., Mongeau & Johnson, 1995; Mongeau, Yeazell, & Hale, 1994).

In the first study on evaluations following date initiation, Muehlenhard and Scardino (1985) showed male undergraduates a videotape of an interaction between a man and woman. In the videotape, the woman either did or did not ask the man on a date. Participants then evaluated the woman on a number of characteristics. These ratings indicate that men evaluated the initiating woman (when compared with the noninitiator) as more of a casual dater and more sexually active.

Mongeau et al. (1993) followed up on this research by including other forms of date initiation. In four written scenarios, the man asked, the man asked following the woman's hint, the woman asked following the man's hint, or the woman asked (without a hint from the man). Mongeau et al.

found that sexual evaluations of the woman differed depending on initiation type. Participants evaluated the woman as more of a casual dater and more sexually active when she either hinted or asked without a preceding hint, compared with when she waited and asked following his hint.

The two forms of initiation reported in Mongeau et al. (1993) that were associated with heightened evaluations of sexual activity (hinting and asking without a hint) are alike in that they both represent instances where the woman is the first person to indicate some kind of personal (potentially romantic) interest. The forms of initiation associated with lower sexual evaluations (waiting and asking following the man's hint) are alike in that in both cases the man is the first person to express personal or romantic interest in the date. In other words, women were perceived as more sexually interested when they took the lead rather than following the man's initiative.

Other scenario-based research investigated evaluations of both men and women in the same date initiation context (e.g., Bostwick & DeLucia, 1992; Mongeau & Carey, 1996). Bostwick and DeLucia (1992) found that participants evaluated date initiators (either the man or woman) as being more interested in sexual intercourse than noninitiators. Bostwick and DeLucia varied *who asked* and *who paid* in written scenarios where a couple went to a concert and then to the man's apartment to talk. They found that male and female date initiations generated similar sexual evaluations.

Mongeau and Carey (1996) reported data consistent with the assumption that men tend to evaluate an uninvited date initiation as a sexual invitation. We asked participants to read a date initiation scenario where the man asked, the woman hinted (and the man asked), or the woman asked. Scenarios described the individuals as having talked several times in class but never having outside social contact. Across all initiation type conditions, participants evaluated the male target as being more sexually interested than the female target. Sexual evaluations also depended on a combination of the sex of the initiator, the sex of the evaluator, and initiation type. Male participants evaluated the male target as expecting considerably more sexual activity on the female-initiated first date than in any of the study's other conditions. In summary, we concluded that men may enter female-initiated first dates with exceedingly optimistic sexual expectations.

Finally, in a series of studies, Muehlenhard (1988; Muehlenhard, Friedman, & Thomas, 1985) investigated the extent to which female initiation of a first date influenced perceptions of the acceptability of date rape. In this research, men tended to evaluate date rape as more justifiable on female-initiated as compared with male-initiated first dates (Muehlenhard, 1988). However, Muehlenhard argued that date rape was not seen as justifiable but significantly less unjustifiable. For example, rape justifiability ratings did not exceed 1.6 on a 1 to 7 scale (where 1 is *extremely unjustifiable*) in the Muehlenhard et al. (1985) investigation.

Together, these data indicate that men, to a greater extent than women, tend to evaluate a woman's date initiation as a sexual invitation. Direct and uninvited expressions of romantic interest by the woman (e.g., asking without a preceding hint from the male) appear to sexually charge men's evaluations. The size of these effects are small, generally explaining less than 5% of the variance in sexual evaluations. However, these data do not speak to what happens on actual first dates. As a consequence, a second line of research investigated the effect of the initiator's sex on two forms of intimacy (i.e., communicative and sexual) on first dates.

Date Initiation and First Date Intimacy

Compared with the date initiation literature, fewer studies focused on actual male- and female-initiated first dates (Mongeau et al., 1994) and only one study directly investigated sexual evaluations and involvement on these dates (Mongeau & Johnson, 1995). In the initial study, Mongeau et al. (1994) focused on the amount of intimacy partners were perceived as communicating on the date, where undergraduate students reported on their most recent male- or female-initiated first date. A variety of studies on various topics (e.g., Abbey, 1982) led us to predict that men (as compared with women) would interpret their date's behavior as communicating more intimacy (i.e., as more inviting). Moreover, we expected this pattern to be particularly strong on female-initiated first dates. Results regarding male-initiated first dates indicate no sex differences in perceptions of communicative intimacy. Results from female-initiated first dates, however, are opposite of expectations; that is, participants perceived the woman as communicating less intimacy than did the man.

In the second study on actual first dates, Mongeau and Johnson (1995) investigated the role of sex of participant and sex of the date initiator on sexual expectations and involvement. Again, we predicted that men (as compared with women) would report expecting and engaging in more intimate sexual behavior particularly on female-initiated first dates. Results indicate that, as expected, men (as compared with women) reported having more intimate sexual expectations and engaging in more intimate sexual behavior on first dates. Counter to expectations, however, Mongeau and Johnson found that participants reported less sexual involvement on female-initiated (as compared with male-initiated) first dates.

SEXUAL EXPECTANCY VIOLATIONS ON FIRST DATES

When viewed together, the data reviewed herein depict an interesting pattern. On the one hand, men (as compared with women) tend to view the social world in more sexual ways (e.g., Abbey, 1982) and to have more liberal attitudes toward sexual involvement in uncommitted relationships (i.e., events like first dates; Oliver & Hyde, 1993). Data from scenario-based date initiation studies indicate that men evaluate women who initiate dates as more sexually interested than women who do not initiate; thus, men may enter first dates initiated by women with heightened sexual expectations (Mongeau et al., 1993; Mongeau & Carey, 1996; Muehlenhard & Scardino, 1985). On the other hand, data from actual first dates indicate that participants evaluate women as communicating less intimacy than do men (Mongeau et al., 1993) and that less sexual intimacy occurs on female-initiated (as opposed to male-initiated) first dates (Mongeau & Johnson, 1995). As a consequence, Mongeau and Carey (1996) asserted that Burgoon's (1993) expectancy violation theory (EVT) provides an interesting theoretical perspective from which to view the first date initiation and enactment process.

Expectancy Violation Theory

Since our original work on actual first dates, EVT has emerged as an increasingly useful theoretical perspective. This theory provides several interesting explanations for first date phenomena and suggests several potentially profitable directions for future research. The primary goal of this section, then, is to briefly review EVT and show the relevance this theory has for first dates.

According to Burgoon (1993), expectancies represent sets of anticipated behaviors in social situations. Expectancies can be general, as in social norms (e.g., standing during the playing of the national anthem), or specific, as in behavioral expectancies for a particular partner and event (e.g., the amount and type of touch on a first date). Please recall that research from the first date studies suggests that men may enter first dates (particularly those initiated by women) with exceedingly high sexual expectations that are not met on the date itself. Theoretically, expectancies arise from three categories of characteristics: communicator, relationship, and contextual.

Subsequent behavior can either meet or violate expectancies. On recognition of an expectancy violation, partners attempt to interpret and evaluate the violation. One variable that is important to both the interpretation and evaluation of expectancy violations is communicator reward valence (CRV; Burgoon, 1993), or "whether a target co-interactant holds the prospect, on balance, of making the interaction a rewarding, pleasurable one or not" (Burgoon, 1993, p. 34).

CRV influences the interpretation of unexpected behaviors. Burgoon (1993) contended that expectancies serve as framing devices that filter the interpretation of incoming behavior. Thus, ambiguous behaviors are likely interpreted as being consistent with the initial expectation particularly when one's partner has high CRV. High-CRV partners are frequently given the benefit of the doubt after potentially violating expectations. For example, a series of aloof behaviors might be interpreted as being shy when enacted by a high-CRV partner but interpreted as rude of enacted by a low-CRV partner.

In addition, CRV can influence the evaluation of behavior. High-CRV individuals (as compared with low-CRV individuals) generally have a wider range of acceptable behaviors (Burgoon, 1993). Behavior generated by a high-reward partner must fall further from the norm (must fall far short or far exceed expectations) to be identified as a violation.

Once identified and interpreted, expectancy violations influence interaction outcomes. Generally speaking, the evaluation of the violation (i.e., whether it is positively or negatively valenced) determines the nature of the outcome(s). As compared with expectancy confirmation, positive violations generate desired outcomes, whereas negative violations generate undesirable outcomes (Burgoon, 1993).

Expectancy Violations and First Dates

With even such a cursory review of EVT, several links to first dates are evident. One such link deals with the creation of expectancies. First date expectancies are likely a function of relational, communicator, and contextual factors. However, a first date can be a couple's first meeting (as in a blind date), can occur after a single or small number of interactions, or can occur after an extensive interaction history and the establishment of a strong friendship. The extent to which first date expectancies are based on relational (e.g., familiarity, liking, and attraction) and communicator (e.g., communicator style) characteristics are likely a function of the frequency, duration, and outcomes of previous interactions between partners (Burgoon, 1993; Harris, 1993).

Contextual characteristics that create expectancies in other settings (e.g., formality, task orientation, and task structure) are generally low or absent on first dates (Harris, 1993). Although these contextual characteristics are typically absent on dates, a date's context is relevant to expectancies. Harris (1993) claimed that a date consisting of French food and the opera creates a different set of expectancies than an evening of fast food and bowling. The date initiation research indicates that the form of the initiation is also an important contextual factor that creates sexual expectancies for a first date.

The better the members of a couple know one another, personal and relational factors will likely have a stronger influence on expectancies relative to contextual factors. If partners are relative strangers, however, the contextual setting for the date (e.g., who initiated it, where the couple is to go, and what they are to do) is likely to be the primary determinant of sexual expectancies. In such cases, partners are likely to have little personal or relational information on which to base expectancies.

It is assumed that the nature of the date initiation is important in creating first date sexual expectancies, particularly when the partners do not know one another well. Men tend to equate a woman's date initiation (particularly when it represents the initial romantic move) with a sexual invitation (Mongeau et al., 1993; Mongeau & Carey, 1996). Men may then expect sexually intimate behavior from their partner on the date. In contrast, women are less likely to equate their date initiation with a sexual invitation. In other words, men's sexual expectancies for the date are likely to be negatively violated on the date.

The negative expectancy violation helps to clarify the differences between date initiation scenario research and actual first date research. That less sex occurs on female-initiated first dates is evidence that sexual expectancy violations occur. One of the outcomes of the negative violation of the man's sexual expectancies may be the reduction in the amount of intimacy that the woman is perceived as communicating (Mongeau et al., 1994).

Evaluating First Date Expectancy Violations.   The interpretation and evaluation of a first date expectancy violation may be a difficult task. First dates represent an ambiguous relational context, where sexual expectancies are implicitly communicated through interaction behavior (Abbey, 1987). Not only are sexual expectations ambiguous on first dates, but the interaction behavior that indirectly communicates them exhibits polyseny; that is, behaviors can be interpreted as having several meanings. Nonverbal behaviors used to communicate sexual attraction may be some of the same behaviors used to communicate less intimate relational meanings (Abbey, 1987; Burgoon, 1993; Harris, 1993).

Thus, on a female-initiated first date, the man may receive a series of behaviors with ambiguous and potentially inconsistent relational meanings: She asked him out on a date, which he is likely to interpret as a sign of sexual interest. Her behavior on the date is likely to be relatively immediate and friendly, however, not clearly indicative of sexual interest. The male's task, then, is to interpret and evaluate the nature of the woman's behavior.

CRV will likely play an important role in the interpretation and evaluation of such behaviors. The nature of a date as a social event, men's (exceedingly high) sexual expectations, and women's role as the sexual gatekeeper (Sprecher & McKinney, 1993) all point toward the conclusion—from the male's perspective—that his date (initially at least) is a high reward value communicator. The particular woman's CRV might also depend on her physical and social attractiveness (Burgoon, 1993).

The woman's role as a high-CRV partner has important implications for the man's evaluation of her first date behavior. For example, if the high-CRV female's behavior falls near but does not quite reach the man's sexual expectations for the date, he is unlikely to interpret her behavior as a violation. The same behavior from a less highly valued partner (assuming the same expectations) is much more likely to be identified as a violation.

Outcomes of Sexual Expectancy Violations. The date initiation research performed to date appears to fit an expectancy violation perspective. However, it also appears that these violations (if indeed they occur) are relatively minor and do not seriously harm the relationship. Mongeau et al. (1993) reported that relationships started with a male-initiated first date produced significantly more dates than did relationships begun with a female-initiated first date. Although the difference is significant, female-initiated first dates generated an average of 13 dates. As a consequence, it seems unlikely that female-initiated first dates generated many negative expectancy violations so major as to seriously harm the future relationship.

There are multiple reasons that negative expectancy violations might not harm the relationship. First, CRV is likely to directly influence the interpretation and evaluation of ambiguous behavior. The higher the CRV, the more likely the partner's ambiguous behavior is given the most positive possible spin. Second, the present review of EVT limits the interpretation and evaluation of sexually related behaviors. Contrary to this limited view, the man might positively evaluate other behaviors (besides sexual intimacy) that balance out the ambiguous sexual interest cues.

Third, first dates are not isolated events, but rather potentially important transitional points in relational development. As such, Burgoon's (1993) definition of CRV requires expansion in dating contexts. Although Burgoon focused on a particular interaction, the nature of a first date indicates that CRV should also include the extent to which a partner has the potential to make a rewarding dating relationship. Given this expansion of CRV, although a man might consider his partner's first date behavior an expectancy violation, he might perceive the future relationship as being closer to his expectancies. As a consequence, the man may forego some intimacy on the first date if he expects increased intimacy (or other rewarding outcomes) on future dates. As such, Sunnafrank's (1986) concept of *predicted outcome value* seems relevant. Predicted outcome value is the extent to which an individual feels that his or her partner has the potential to provide future relational rewards. Negative violations of first date expectancies may not have a strong deleterious impact on the relationship if future interactions are expected to be rewarding.

Finally, a man might need more than a single date to confidently identify an expectancy violation. That is to say, a male might be willing to chalk a single negative date experience to outside factors particularly if his partner is high CRV. In such a case, he may be careful to give up on the relationship too soon.

SEX DIFFERENCES OR SIMILARITIES?

Given this book's focus, it seems appropriate to consider the extent to which the preceding review is indicative of similarities or differences between men and women. Some scholars argue that the effect sizes associated with sex differences in communication are quite small (e.g., Canary & Hause, 1993). Consistent with this review, several of the date initiation studies reviewed herein contain relatively small effects sizes. For example, Mongeau and Carey (1996) reported a three-way (i.e., sex of participant × sex of target × initiation type) interaction on perceptions of sexual expectations. Specifically, they found that male participants reported more advanced sexual expectations than females—particularly for the man in the scenario on the female-initiated first date. Although consistent with EVT, the size of this effect is small (explaining only 2% of the variance in evaluations).

In addition to small effect size, Mongeau and Carey (1996) reported evidence of heterogeneity of variance in their sexual evaluation measure. Heterogeneity of variance may imply a subject × treatment interaction where people do not respond to the independent variables in the same way. In other words, variations in sexual expectations and involvement may be a result of personality rather than sex differences. One personality factor potentially relevant to sexual expectations and involvement on first dates is sociosexuality.

Sociosexuality is the extent to which an individual is willing to engage in intimate sexual behavior outside the boundaries of a committed relationship (Simpson & Gangestad, 1991). Individuals with restricted sociosexual orientation "typically insist on commitment and closeness in a relationship prior to engaging in sex with a romantic partner" (Simpson & Gangestad, 1991, p. 870). However, individuals with unrestricted sociosexual orientation "tend to feel relatively comfortable engaging in sex without commitment or closeness" (Simpson & Gangestad, 1991, p. 870). All other things being equal, individuals with unrestricted sociosexual orientation (be it a man or woman) will likely expect more intimate sexual involvement on first dates.

Sex or Gender Differences?

Another important and unanswered question concerns the genesis of these similarities and differences. Specifically, are the differences between men and women in this chapter a function of sex or gender? Buss' (1994) sexual strategies theory suggests that variations in sexual expectations and involvement are due to sex differences. Across millennia, evolutionary forces created different mating strategies for men and women. Greater parental investment lead women toward long-term mating considerations (Buss, 1994). As a consequence, women are likely to look for sexual partners who exhibit relational commitment and will contribute to raising children. In contrast, men have considerably lower minimum parental investment. As a consequence, they are likely to follow short-term mating considerations and mate with multiple partners. Therefore, men will be more positively attuned to short-term mating events (e.g., one-night stands; Buss, 1994).

From a gender-based perspective, the differences discussed in this chapter reflect cultural expectations of what it means to be *masculine* and *feminine*. "Nowhere else are cultural expectations of masculinity and femininity so salient as in romantic relationships" (Wood, 1994, p. 191). Gender differences arise because men and women are evaluated inequitably for engaging in the same behavior. From this perspective, the difference between men and women in attitudes toward casual sex is potentially due to the sexual double standard—where it is more acceptable for men (as compared with women) to engage in intercourse outside a close, committed relationship (Sprecher & McKinney, 1993).

Canary and Hause (1993) asserted that sex differences should only be investigated when there is a theoretical reason to do so. Both the sociobiological (e.g., Buss, 1994) and gender-based (e.g., Wood, 1994) perspectives provide strong rationales for studying sex/gender differences in sexual evaluations and enactments on first dates. Although the effect sizes associated with sex differences in first date research are small, the factors that produce these differences (e.g., attitudes toward casual sex, sociosexuality) exhibit stronger sex differences. From a causal perspective, these factors may be the starting point of a series of personal and relational factors that result in the first date phenomena covered in this chapter (see also Trost & Alberts, chap. 10, this volume).

DIRECTIONS FOR FUTURE RESEARCH

This chapter suggests several profitable avenues for future research. First, the EVT appears to be a productive perspective for investigating first date initiation and enactment. However, few studies have directly used EVT in investigating sexual expectancies and involvement on first dates. What influences first date sexual expectancies; how partners identify, evaluate, and interpret expectancy violations; and what impact positive and negative expectancy violations have on the future of the relationship are theoretically interesting and untested notions.

Research should investigate how partners negotiate a mutually accept-able level of sexual intimacy in their relationship. More specifically, re-search is needed on how relationships make the transition between platonic friendships and romantic entanglements. We assume that first dates play an important role in this transition. However, there are few data to support that claim. Relationships can make the transition before or after the first date. The role of the first date in the development of a romantic relation-ship is an important question to consider.

Research also needs to consider more carefully the sexual expectancies that men and women bring to first dates. One way to examine these expectations is to look at scripts individuals have for first dates. Although some research on first date scripts exists (e.g., Rose & Frieze, 1993), the script concept provides three specific future directions for this research. First, first date script research should focus specifically on sexual behaviors. Second, research should investigate the extent to which scripts differ in male- and female-initiated first dates. Third, research should investigate date initiation scripts (Anderson, 1995). In addition, research on the meaning and nego-tiation of date initiation needs to be performed. How date initiation occurs and what implications these initiation tactics have for sexual expectations for the date are important questions for future investigation.

SUMMARY

This chapter may have depicted first dates as a sexual battlefield pitting two combatants with mutually exclusive sexual goals. There are two reasons to consider *sexual warfare* to be an inadequate metaphor. First, it is difficult to understand how intimate, romantic relationships could begin under such circumstances. Second, the *battlefield* metaphor depicts males and females as more different than they likely are. In contrast, we prefer Wil-mot's (1995) metaphor of *relationships as dance.* One person initiates but the dyad must coordinate their movements to have a mutually enjoyable time. If partners are doing different dances altogether, they will likely end up stepping on each other's toes.

REFERENCES

Abbey, A. (1982). Sex differences in attributions for friendly behavior: Do males misperceive females' friendliness? *Journal of Personality and Social Psychology, 42,* 830–838.

Abbey, A. (1987). Misperceptions of friendly behavior as sexual interest: A survey of naturally occurring incidents. *Psychology of Women Quarterly, 11,* 173–194.

Anderson, J. C. (1995, February). *Female date initiation: A tricky business.* Paper presented to the Western States Communication Association, Portland, OR.

Bailey, B. L. (1988). *From front porch to back seat: Courtship in twentieth-century America.* Baltimore: Johns Hopkins University Press.

Baxter, L. A. (1988). A dialectical perspective on communication strategies in relationship development. In S. W. Duck (Ed.), *Handbook of personal relationships* (pp. 257–273). New York: Wiley.

Baxter, L. A., & Bullis, C. (1986). Turning points in developing romantic relationships. *Human Communication Research, 12,* 469–494.

Baxter, L. A., & Wilmot, W. W. (1985). Taboo topics in romantic relationships. *Journal of Social and Personal Relationships, 2,* 253–269.

Berger, C. R., & Calabrese, R. J. (1975). Some explorations in initial interaction and beyond: Toward a developmental theory of interpersonal communication. *Human Communication Research, 1,* 99–112.

Bostwick, T. D., & DeLucia, J. L. (1992). Effects of gender and specific dating behaviors on perceptions of sex willingness and date rape. *Journal of Social and Clinical Psychology, 11,* 14–25.

Burgoon, J. K. (1993). Interpersonal expectancies, expectancy violations, and emotional communication. *Journal of Language and Social Psychology, 12,* 30–48.

Buss, D. M. (1994). *The evolution of desire: Strategies of human mating.* New York: Basic Books.

Canary, D. J., & Hause, K. S. (1993). Is there any reason to research sex differences in communication? *Communication Quarterly, 41,* 129–144.

Cate, R. M., & Lloyd, S. A. (1992). *Courtship.* Newbury Park, CA: Sage.

Clark, R. D. (1990). The impact of AIDS on gender differences in willingness to engage in casual sex. *Journal of Applied Social Psychology, 20,* 771–782.

Clark, R. D., & Hatfield, E. (1989). Gender differences in receptivity to sexual offers. *Journal of Psychology and Human Sexuality, 2,* 39–55.

Davis, M. S. (1983). *Smut: Erotic reality/obscene ideology.* Chicago: University of Chicago Press.

Harris, M. J. (1993). Issues in studying the mediation of expectancy effects: A taxonomy of expectancy effects. In P. D. Blanck (Ed.), *Interpersonal expectancies: Theory, research, and applications* (pp. 350–378). New York: Cambridge University Press.

Mongeau, P. A., & Carey, C. M. (1996). Who's wooing whom: II. An experimental investigation of date-initiation and expectancy violation. *Western Journal of Communication, 60,* 195–213.

Mongeau, P. A., Hale, J. L., Johnson, K. L., & Hillis, J. D. (1993). Who's wooing whom? An investigation of female initiated dating. In P. J. Kalbfleisch (Ed.), *Interpersonal communication: Evolving interpersonal relationships* (pp. 51–68). Hillsdale, NJ: Lawrence Erlbaum Associates.

Mongeau, P. A., & Johnson, K. L. (1995). Predicting cross-sex first date sexual expectations and involvement: Contextual and individual difference factors. *Personal Relationships, 2,* 301–312.

Mongeau, P. A., Yeazell, M., & Hale, J. L. (1994). Sex differences in relational message interpretations on male- and female-initiated first dates: A research note. *Journal of Social Behavior and Personality, 9,* 731–742.

Muehlenhard, C. L. (1988). Misinterpreted dating behaviors and the risk of date rape. *Journal of Social and Clinical Psychology, 6,* 20–37.

Muehlenhard, C. L., Friedman, D. E., & Thomas, C. M. (1985). Is date rape justifiable?: The effects of date activity, who initiated, who paid, and men's attitudes toward women. *Psychology of Women Quarterly, 9,* 297–310.

Muehlenhard, C. L., & Scardino, T. J. (1985). What will he think? Men's impressions of women to initiate dates and achieve academically. *Journal of Counseling Psychology, 32,* 560–569.

Oliver, M. B., & Hyde, J. S. (1993). Gender differences in sexuality: A meta-analysis. *Psychological Bulletin, 114,* 29–51.

Post, E. L. (1984). *Emily Post's etiquette* (14th ed.). New York: Harper & Row.

Roche, J. P. (1986). Premarital sex: Attitudes and behavior by dating stage. *Adolescence, 21,* 107–121.

Rose, S., & Frieze, I. (1993). Young singles' contemporary dating scripts. *Sex Roles, 28,* 1–10.

Simpson, J. A., & Gangestad, S. W. (1991). Individual differences in sociosexuality: Evidence for convergent and discriminant validity. *Journal of Personality and Social Psychology, 60,* 870–883.

Sprecher, S., & McKinney, K. (1993). *Sexuality.* Newbury Park, CA: Sage.

Sunnafrank, M. (1986). Predicted outcome value during initial interactions: A reformulation of uncertainty reduction theory. *Human Communication Research, 13,* 3–33.

Wilmot, W. W. (1995). *Relational communication.* New York: McGraw-Hill.

Wood, J. T. (1994). *Gendered lives: Communication, gender, and culture.* Belmont, CA: Wadsworth.

Chapter 19

Methodological Considerations When Examining a Gendered World

Mike Allen
University of Wisconsin-Milwaukee

Probably no issue in the social sciences receives more attention than the difference between men and women. Whether the difference stems from biological, psychological, sociological, or some other cause continues to create attention and discussion. The politics and tone of the discussion reflect, at least for a topic in the social sciences, an issue of importance. This chapter considers some of the methodological issues involved in describing gender differences. It is divided into two parts: (a) a consideration of the measurement of sex differences, and (b) an examination of how outcomes of investigations indicate differences between men and women. The first topic deals with defining and measuring sex differences, and the second topic explores the interpretation of the statistical outcomes of investigations.

Methodological applications are viewed as germinating from prior theoretical decisions, presuming that theoretical positions should justify methodological choices. Moreover, clear theoretical explication permits an evaluation of the methodological choices of the investigator. What follows, therefore, is not an evaluative comparison of methodological choices but rather an analysis of the implications and commitments of theoretical decisions. Scientists must make such choices constantly, understanding that their decisions entail accountability and permit interpretation of data.

The central decision surrounding a conceptual definition of gender is whether gender indicates nature or nurture: Is the distinction between men and women biological, related to physiological distinctions stemming from genetic codes, or is gender nurture, the result of socialization differences that boys and girls experience growing up that becomes part of their adult world? The semantic distinction used by many academic organizations, journal editors, and the editors of the present anthology requires authors to use the term *sex differences* to indicate biological designations and *gender* to indicate psychological or sociological orientations. Such an effort is desirable only if it improves thinking and clarifies methodological choices (discussed in the next section). This chapter inconsistently uses such designations for a variety of reasons. The goal of the methodological and statistical discussion provides, whenever possible, common issues facing researchers regardless of the assumptions made about the basis of sex differences. When there is a distinction between physiological/biological sex versus psychological/sociological gender the particular designation is indicated.

A physiological definition makes gender considerations a prisoner of DNA. However, if gender constitutes a social construction, then gender represents a product created by society (although the means of this production, reproduction, and transmission, involve much discussion). The basis of the definition forms the first methodological controversy surrounding gender. When scientists argue about differences, do they mean biological/physiological differences or psychological/sociological/developmental/political/philosophical/economical/(insert the appropriate social science term here) differences?

This chapter first considers the nature of measuring the distinction: whether the scientific study considers nature (genetic) or nurture (socialization) approaches to gender. The next section considers the impact of the selection process for the participants in social scientific studies and how that process may impact on the results. The third section examines the data on gender and the lack of promising results to date. The fourth section considers a reexamination of how the previous results, generally considered disappointing, may in fact turn out to provide some important implications, but only if you consider the normal curve. The chapter concludes with the necessity of a connection between measurement of gender and the theories about the differences that may exist.

MEASURING NATURE OR NURTURE

This section considers how most scientists measure gender/sex. The impact that people's assumptions have about measurement play an important role in assessing the state of the literature. For example, many social scientists during the course of the coming year will ask thousands of participants in investigations: "Please indicate your sex (gender): Male __ Female __." The measurement issue relies on what the participants indicate when providing an answer to a simple self-report instrument. Self-reports assume that the person filling out the scale comprehends the designations available and understands how to respond appropriately. The usual controversy existing about the accuracy of self-reports (Benoit & Benoit, 1988, 1990; Ericsson & Simon, 1980; Kim & Hunter, 1993a, 1993b; Nisbett & Wilson, 1977) fails to apply to this measurement scale. No need for awareness of mental processes exists for this scale, no indication of future behavioral actions is indicated by an answer, and little confusion exists over definitions of the answers. In this case, good reasons support the belief that self-reporting one's sex is both possible and sufficient. What does this item really measure? The issue is whether the investigator shares the understanding of the question in the same manner as the person answering the question. If a participant uses biological sex as a basis for answering the item, does the participant share the same framework as the person asking the question? Often the nature of the theoretical assumptions about *gender* differences remains undefined. Theoretical assumptions that the investigator makes when asking the question are probably not a problem for the respondent (implicitly everyone knows what the question asks). The problem with a lack of explicit theorizing about gender comes when utilizing the answer.

If I saw the prior question, I would indicate my biological sex. Probably most participants in any investigation would consider the question as one directed at eliciting biological sex as well. However, this supposedly simple and direct question carries with it a number of potential implications that the investigator may or may not explicitly consider. By extension, the potential implications can affect one's interpretation of results. The judgment any consumer of scientific research should make is whether the test for gender differences relates (as directly as possible) to the particular hypothesis or research question under examination.

The biological basis of the answers that people provide may or may not reflect the true variable of interest to the researcher. Does the researcher really believe that any difference found between men and women stems from a biological/physiological cause? If I answer the question on a biological basis, then the application of the answer involves a biological assumption. The investigator, consciously or not, has, by asking the question in that manner, linked biological assumptions to the results.

Social scientists seldom formulate questions or hypotheses on the basis of biological issues. Few social scientists posit theoretical issues regarding gender in terms of genetics or biological differences (e.g., arguing that levels of testosterone or estrogen are the source of differences in behavior; however, see Andersen, chap. 4; Trost & Alberts, chap. 10, this volume). A social scientist could argue for a DNA-based causality for human behavior. However, the identification of the particular biological mechanism or genetic code linked to social behavior so far appears disappointing. In the future, such evidence may exist, but current proofs appear incomplete. When social scientists use biological indicators of gender, most are not primarily theorizing or concerned with issues of biology or genetics.

Social scientists often treat self-reported biological sex as a measure of gender or socialization differences. Thus, the single measurement item functions as a marker variable. A marker variable represents the measurement of some indicator that provides information about a variable believed to exist but which cannot be directly measured. Social scientists use a lot of marker variables (age, race, income, etc.) relating to demographic features of interest. The real difference between sexes (or most demographic variables) becomes the social construction of the variable, or what constitutes male and female. A belief in a difference between the feminine and masculine experience based on biological designations justifies the use of biological indicators.

Scholars assume that some sociological and psychological differences that exist between men and women are associated with biological sex. Basically, persons (society, family, friends, institutions) respond to or treat men and women differently. Feminist scholars (e.g., Gallagher, 1989; Rakow, 1986) have argued that the differences between men and women reflect socially structured relationships or power and economic relations sanctioned by society. Indicating your sex simply indicates the marker of those differences when comparing groups. Seldom do the scientists assuming those differences formally collect information and test those differences within investigations; instead investigations assume such differences. That is, many investigators seldom attempt to explicitly measure the processes contributing to the observance of sex differences.

Consider the investigator who finds a difference between men and women on a dependent variable. This finding may be important; unfortunately, it provides little, if any, information regarding why the two groups differ. Because the investigator may not have any measurement relating to the source of social experiences or status that differentiates men and women, the basis of the difference receives no examination. Gender research only shows when men and women differ—an empty point many would concede. The discussion and exploration of why such differences exist deserves attention by those conducting investigations.

More often, investigations conclude that no or minimal difference exists between the sexes. Considering that the measurement of gender often is indirect, this should not be surprising. The use of marker variables should diminish the size of the true relationship between the conceptual variables. The impact of attenuated measurement, restriction in range, and dichotomization of both independent and dependent variables all function to reduce the observed effect (Hunter & Schmidt, 1990). The marker variable approach substantially reduces the impact of gender differences. The real amazement is not that so few sex differences of a large magnitude exist, but rather that social science finds any differences. If and when social scientists use direct measurements of variables, these problems should fade.

WHERE MALE AND FEMALE PARTICIPANTS REALLY COME FROM

Most studies obtain male and female participants from college populations. If one considers the potential differences between these populations, does the pool of men and women found on university campuses represent other persons not in that sample? Studies utilizing college-age students to estimate the differences between the sexes might find differences not generalizable to other groups of men and women—a point made about many social scientific studies. However, the general issue of sex difference appears especially vulnerable to this point of criticism.

One could argue that the genetic pool of persons differs between college and noncollege students. At least one writing on the topic of education and intelligence (Herrnstein & Murray, 1994) indicates this possibility. One would reasonably expect that college students, on average, have more superior intellectual performance than noncollege students. However, unless one argues that the genetic pool is different for college students, biological theories would generalize to noncollege students. The key is whether the underlying causal feature—biological sex—is different for both populations (college and noncollege). This writer is not about to propose or identify the differences between the groups, but the potential for such an explanation exists.

The other dominant perspective argues for some type of difference based on social positioning that differentially affects men and women. The argument considers whether the processes of socialization, power, economics, and the like differ for college men and women when compared with noncollege men and women. Differences impacting on the dependent variable of interest create results that may not generalize to noncollege samples.

Again, the expression of the problems of generalization stem not from anything inherent in men or women, but rather are directly related to the theoretical assumptions of the investigator. The burden of theory is to specify why differences exist on the basis of gender.

DOES GENDER PRODUCE PROMISING RESULTS?

This section considers the decades of research accumulated considering the impact of gender/sex. Results regarding sex differences are disappointing in the social sciences. The old norm for literature summaries, still practiced in some quarters, is to provide a qualitative synthesis of available quantitative literature to reach a conclusion. An example of this is a qualitative review of the literature, provided by Sadker, Sadker, and Klein (1992), arguing that men and women are treated differently by the educational system. Their conclusion is that sexism in the classroom contributes to a reinforcement of sexual bias and diminished achievement for women. Unfortunately, current meta-analyses do not support the claim of consistent and large differences in achievement (Baenninger & Newcombe, 1989; Friedman, 1989; Hyde, 1981; Hyde & Linn, 1988; Linn & Peterson, 1989). The need exists for the eventual accumulation of quantitative evidence on the issues and some systematic summary of the literature.

If one goes to the various meta-analyses on sex differences, the size of the effects by and large is small (when contextualized by most theoretical arguments). Canary and Hause (1993) indicated by a review of meta-analyses relevant to communication that the differences between sexes, although existent, are rather small ($r^2 = .01$). Such small effects can appear even smaller when compared with various theoretical positions that argue for important and large-scale differences. Eagly (1995a, 1995b) argued that there are probably differences but they are not universal and do not point to some simple representation. Hyde and Plant (1995) compared the results of 171 meta-analyses (taken from Ashmore, 1990; Hyde & Frost, 1993) considering sex differences and found no consistent pattern. Although the meta-analyses of sex differences on average show small effects, the effects vary based on issues and context.

A central issue in communication research when comparing men and women has been the general lack of large differences between the groups (Canary & Hause, 1993). The Canary and Hause article takes the results of several meta-analyses and analyzes the observed differences between men and women and concludes two things: (a) the literature demonstrates few differences between sexes; and (b) the use of simple biological sex as a variable probably masks important differences that exist and impoverishes theoretical development. Many meta-analyses have examined gender differences in communication and routinely found some differences, but those are usually small in magnitude (Canary & Hause, 1993; see also Allen & D'Alessio, 1991, 1993; Allen, D'Alessio, & Brezgel, 1995; Burrell & Allen, 1995; Burrell & Koper, 1994; Dallinger & Hample, 1994; Dindia & Allen, 1992; Emmers & Allen, 1995a, 1995b, 1995c; Gayle, Preiss, & Allen, 1994; Grob & Allen, 1996; Krone, Allen, & Ludlum, 1994; Sahlstein & Allen, 1996; Wilkins & Andersen, 1992). The ability to find a generalized set of large differences between men and women on a variable has not been borne out by research (but see Reis, chap. 9, this volume).

The entire issue of whether gender differences exist is rife with political and ideological implications and arguments. Eagly (1995a, 1995b) argued that, depending on the agenda, a scholar might want to find no difference between the sexes (men and women are equal). However, other persons might want to find distinctions between the sexes within the findings (men and women have different learning styles, television representations are discriminatory, etc.). Clearly, any characterization of findings by a scientist unfortunately becomes the basis for some ideological battle. Eventually, a scientific theory of gender will emerge capable of handling the available data. The current crisis comes from a lack of scientific theory, not from a lack of scientific findings.

Many scholars presuppose that sex differences are large. The meta-analytic findings should point to large differences between men and women. Meta-analytic findings of large sex differences would support those arguing for the importance of gender as a variable worthy of consideration. Assuming the measurement issues are satisfactorily resolved, there might exist in the future some ability to synthesize the existing findings—not quantitatively using meta-analysis, but rather theoretically, taking the body of findings and generating an appropriate theory. This new argument might take the current findings and provide a context for their importance.

The issue of difference should be compared to theoretical expectations regarding the issue. If a theory expects only a 1% contribution to the variance due to gender, then finding a small effect would be consistent with that thinking. However, it could be argued that the lack of large differences observed on the basis of sex or gender undermines the general theoretical approaches to this issue. That is, the underlying theoretical arguments receive little support from existing empirical data.

Gender differences might occur in some domains and not in others. Depending on one's theoretical assumptions, differences between men and women may occur under particular circumstances. Most theories of gender fail to specify the conditions when differences should occur. The next section considers the interpretation of finding sex differences and focuses on the question of how to interpret the impact of gender differences found by an investigation or a meta-analysis. The problem with social scientific data to date is the inconsistency in the findings. Inconsistency combined with no general theoretical approach to contextualize the findings creates a lack of substantive interpretation.

NORMAL CURVE ASSUMPTIONS

Social scientists operate on a central assumption about the distribution of values for a variable: The distribution forms a normal, bell-shaped curve. The normal curve represents one of the central statistical assumptions that social scientists make to analyze data. The normal or bell-shaped curve

illustrates a defined distribution (for a formula and some of the implications, see Glass, McGaw, & Smith, 1981). Although the assumption of
normality permits the use of certain statistics, even violations of assumptions
regarding normality do not necessarily alter most parameter estimates—a
quality called *robustness* (Andersen, 1951; Boneau, 1960; Box, 1955; Welch,
1947).

This section considers the statistical issues when examining sex/gender
differences. When one considers the differences between the sexes (in the
first subsection), the trivial results of most investigations may have substantive and important implications. This is highlighted in the next section,
which discusses the implications of such findings for extreme values on
the curve. The long-term implication is found in the next to last subsection
dealing with sexual stereotypes. The impact of small effects may be in the
generation of sexual stereotypes. This stereotypic view of the world may
not be irrational but have a basis in scientific fact. The last section considers
the implication of the prior statement. The impact of stereotypes is that
individuals receive treatment based on a statistical fallacy where differences
at the extreme values are applied as if relevant to the average person.

Social science scholarship often examines differences between groups.
The basis of many of the experimental and nonexperimental designs analyzing data requires or expects that researchers classify persons on the
basis of some type of common feature. Whenever differences exist between
groups that can be replicated and verified as consistent and important
distinctions between groups, the generation of some statement about that
comparison is possible.

The normal curve is symmetric and the values tend to pile up in the
center and diminish as the values become more extreme, as measured
from the mean. These extreme values and the interpretation of them
represent a possible explanation for stereotypes. The curve defines the
existence of extreme values as occurring infrequently. Stereotypes typically
represent some extreme value on some dimension attributed to all members of the group. This section explores how, using the normal curve and
established empirical results, sexual stereotypes may have a basis in fact.
The problem is that the application of sexual stereotypes to individual
persons remains incorrect.

A central issue in the social sciences involves the comparison of distributions of experimental or natural groups. The assumption of such tests
is that each group (commonly referred to as a *cell* in a between-group
ANOVA design) possesses a normal distribution. The statistical treatments
compare the normal curves for each group often using some type of variance testing (ANOVA, *t* test, etc.). The statistical tests basically try to determine if the two (or more) normal curves for each condition come from
the same general distribution or whether any of the curves represent dif-

ferent distributions. A significant result usually indicates that the two (or n) distributions represent distinct curves. A nonsignificant result indicates that the means do not necessarily come from different distributions.

Over time the accumulation of results generates a large number of investigations on a topic or related series of topics that permit synthesis. Meta-analysis represents an attempt to statistically synthesize through organizing and unifying various investigations to reduce sampling error and solve for other potential artifacts. Meta-analysis usually accomplishes a reduction of Type II error (false positives; Allen & Preiss, 1993). Often the use of relatively small samples by individual investigations permits the possibility that a lack of significant differences between groups stems from a lack of statistical power.

Meta-analysis increases power by combining samples to produce an overall estimate based on the combined samples. The net effect increases the sample size used for the comparison. The elimination of Type II error (typically around 50% for social science investigations) means that differences found to exist probably do exist and a lack of difference indicates that no sex difference exists. The critical feature involves the explanation of what those differences indicate about the impact of sex on a particular feature.

DIFFERENCES BETWEEN THE SEXES

The existence of differences between groups constitutes a fundamental source of investigation and theorizing for social scientists. A general approach to the study of human behavior hypothesizes that some variable divides the population into groups or along a continuum. This section considers the issue of sex as a basis for group assignment.

Sex differences exist as generally small and disappointing meta-analytic findings. The results create the impression that gender differences probably play little importance in formulating theoretical arguments. Therefore, a scientist might conclude that gender should not play a major role as a theoretical variable. The conclusion simply extends the thinking that variables with small impact deserve little attention.

The question revolves around the importance of the differences that exist between men and women, not the size of the difference. Because the differences are not large, the tendency is to dismiss the differences as unimportant and trivial. This should not always be the case (Abelson, 1985; Rosenthal, 1985). The technique known as binomial effect size display (BESD) demonstrates that an effect size of one fifth a standard deviation difference ($d = .20$, the same as a correlation of $r = .10$) indicates an almost 20% increase in the number of persons past the mean when comparing two distributions of equal size (like sex).

When comparing group means or general tendencies, the use of an effect size provides evidence for little difference between the groups. If one states that the average man is not different from the average woman, this is accurate. The average woman, when comparing a man and woman with a difference between groups of $d = .20$, is not that dissimilar from her counterpart. The difference is slight because the average value of each distribution is similar. However, average values do not consider the possibility of disproportionate numbers at extreme values for the variables.

Extreme values represent considerable importance in a variety of circumstances. Suppose it is an extreme person along some dimension who becomes a mass murderer; a small initial mean difference between two groups makes an inordinate disproportionate difference at the extreme values. Although comparing the average person of each group provides little difference, small effect creates a huge disproportionate ratio within the critical group at an extreme value. The next section discusses more fully the implications of small mean differences for certain theoretical issues.

EXTREME VALUES IN COMPARING SEX DIFFERENCES

One alternative to comparing mean values is to compare the percentage of scores past a particular threshold point. Using the normal curve, this section examines the impact of what some consider to be small differences on various points of the curve. Although the average may show no difference, the extreme value may indicate enormous effect.

Suppose we have a difference between men and women and the difference is small ($d = .20$). This value happens to be the value in the Gayle, Preiss, and Allen (1994) meta-analysis comparing the use of self-reported competitiveness strategies by men and women to solve conflicts. The correlation indicates that men favor using this strategy slightly more than women (one issue unresolved in this analysis is whether reports or observations of behavior would generate different results; see Burggraf & Sillars, 1987; Cupach & Canary, 1995). Most scholars would probably square the correlation of .10, get .01, and conclude that a 1% variance accounted for is irrelevant. Rosenthal (1985) pointed out that this conclusion is often inaccurate—a point echoed in analyses by Eagly (1995a) and Abelson (1985). This section demonstrates that what most scholars would consider small effects can have important implications for the social sciences.

Consider how a comparison of normal curves operates using the typical z tables found in most textbooks on statistics or quantitative research methodology. The z table provides the percentage of the normal curve between the mean and that particular score (as represented in terms of z, or the standardized score). The standard normal curve provides for a representation of what percentage scores should be greater or less than any particular score on the curve.

At the level of curves, consider the following. Suppose men score a mean score of 100 with a standard deviation of 10 and women score a mean score of 98 with a standard deviation of 10 on some measure of competitiveness conflict strategy use. The difference between the male and female mean would be $d = .20$ ($r = .10$). A cutoff score divides the curve of scores into a percentage of area on each side of the curve (the percent reflects the number of scores on each side of the cutoff value). Fifty percent of men score above the mean for men, whereas 42.07% of women score above the mean for men. This is based on a z score of 0.00 for men and 0.20 for women. The ratio of men to women over this particular score is 50:42; for every woman scoring greater than that score there are 1.19 men scoring above that score. To put it another way, the Gayle et al. (1994) meta-analysis suggested that 19% more men score past the self-reported mean competitiveness strategy score than women at that particular cutoff point. That difference indicates that men will be more competitive than women. Table 19.1 indicates what the ratio is for the z score given a particular d score.

However, suppose we consider higher levels of competitiveness strategy use and examine the ratio at one standard deviation over the male mean (a score of 110). At this point, 15.87% of the men will score greater than the cutoff score. At this cutoff score, only 11.51% of the women score that high or higher on the aggressive scale. The ratio of men to women at this score is 15.87:11.51 or 1.38. This value indicates that for every woman above that point there is 1.38 men or an increase of 38%. Thirty-eight percent more men would endorse mildly competitive strategies to resolve conflict than women. This difference starts to become large.

TABLE 19.1
Binomial Effect Size Display for Interpreting Results

Cutoff score	Percentage of persons past the cutoff score		Ratio of Men to Women	Percentage Increase
	Men	Women		
Greater than the mean, above average	50.00	42.07	1.19:1	19
Greater than one standard deviation, mildly competitive	15.87	11.51	1.38:1	38
Greater than two standard deviations, very competitive	2.28	1.39	1.64:1	64
Greater than three standard deviations, extremely competitive	0.13	0.06	2.16:1	116

Note. The table assumes that $r = .10$ and a scale with a mean = 100, standard deviation = 10, and that each group is equal in number.

Suppose we use a cutoff score of 120 or 2 standard deviations above the mean. At this point, approximately 2.28% of the men will score greater than this value (this is a z score of 2.00). For the women ($z = 2.2$), the percentage of persons past a score of 120 is 1.39%. This is a ratio of 2.28:1.39 or 1.64, indicating a 64% increase in the number of men over women past that particular point in the curve. This cutoff score begins to represent a real difference in percentages between men and women.

Finally, suppose we use a cutoff score of 130 for the scale or 3 standard deviations above the mean. At this point, approximately .13% of the values are greater than that score for males (a z score of 3.00). At a z score of 2.8, there is .06% of the women past this score. The ratio now is .13:.06 or a 116% increase in the number of men scoring past this point. The ratio indicates more than twice as many men than women are likely to use extremely competitive strategies.

The farther the distance from the mean, the more extreme the score and the greater the ratio. The larger the cutoff score, the greater the number of men to women in the particular sample scoring greater than that value. Moreover, the relative ratio may indicate some practical implications of various selection procedures. If we are selecting persons on the basis of the overall average, the distinction between sexes is small. However, as we go to a higher and higher cutoff score, the difference in the ratio of sex selected becomes greater.

One implication of such a finding concerns whether a valid measurement device has an impact on the selection criteria creating a differential outcome for the ratio of men to women of the qualified persons. By *valid* I mean the device can be shown to measure what it intends to measure. It should be noted that the curves for both sexes are symmetric and therefore the ratio reverses itself as one considers the scores at the lower end. In other words, the ratio reverses in the case of considering the at-risk group based on some selection criteria. In the example, twice as many women would be likely to use extremely low levels of competitiveness strategy selection than men.

GENERATING SEXUAL STEREOTYPES

Stereotypes come from a combination of prototypes and extreme values. Existing stereotypes provide a sense of applying extreme values to the average situation. The assertion runs the following course: All of X possess the quality Y. The assertion usually designates an undesirable characteristic (Y) that the group (X's) possess. This section considers how social science contributes to the formation and promulgation of stereotypes. conflict style

Gayle, Preiss, and Allen's (1994) meta-analysis of self-report conflict data indicated that there are probably more than twice as many extremely competitive men than women (i.e., at three standard deviations above the mean). The argument that men are more competitive about conflict than women is probably based on the exposure to these extremely competitive persons. Accordingly, the stereotype has a basis in fact (and perhaps experience) but it also has an unwarranted application to the typical or average person.

The generation of a stereotype probably comes from the examination or experience of persons with extreme values. The issue of racism, sexism, or ageism can be regarded as the assignment of extreme values on some type of identifiable group membership to all members of that group. The result is that identifying some type of group membership potentially becomes tantamount to the invocation of a stereotype by the person. If a person starts stating that "men are more competitive" or "women are more nurturing then men," then these conclusions are unwarranted.

An extreme value indicates that the person possesses an abundance or complete absence of the personality characteristic. The stereotype indicates that the extreme value of the variable becomes generalized to the entire group. As you can tell by the percentages in the tables, the percentage of people at the extreme is minuscule. To infer from extreme data in any type of application to something other than the extreme must be done cautiously, if at all.

The assumption that the particular stereotype applies to the individual represents a statistical fallacy. Stereotypes usually represent negative representations of individuals. The mathematics of the normal curve indicate that all groups contain members with extreme values. The possibility exists for supporting any generalized claim about a group on the basis of one observed value. Under these conditions, the individual making the assignment uses a filtering mechanism to selectively interpret and represent the available data. The question is not whether one group has persons with X characteristic at an extreme value; instead, the question is the percentage or ratio of men or women at that level.

However, suppose that the dependent variable is extremely rare and easily identifiable. Take the example of serial killers, almost all of whom are men. That does not mean that all men are serial killers or that all women are not serial killers. The class *serial killers* represents an extreme value on some type of continuum. There will be female serial killers; however, the ratio of male to female serial killers might be 50 or 60:1. If we could magically create a scale to identify these individuals, the scores would probably be out 50 or so standard deviations from the mean. A small standard difference score between male and female respondents (d = .20) might be enough to produce that kind of ratio in serial killers between men and women. Hence, the identification of particular types of extreme persons could contribute to the development of stereotypes that might be considered valid. Such valid examples are exceedingly rare and probably useful only in clinical applications rather than as a basis for general social scientific theories.

Do disproportionate outcomes permit or validate the use of stereotyping? The question is thorny and tricky. No one likes to create and maintain the notion of stereotypes because this violates the concept of each person as an individual. At the same time, some stereotypes exist as a matter of accepted truth. If one says that all mass murderers are men, that constitutes a stereotype. However, the stereotype is not about men—it is about mass murderers. The statement does not say that all men are mass murderers, only that almost all mass murderers are men. The use of the stereotype should help us understand mass murderers, not issues relating to gender.

DIFFERENCES AND INDIVIDUALS

This section considers the problem of recognizing the lack of difference between average individuals while accepting the potential accuracy of stereotypes. The problem of using gender to predict individuals stems from the general lack of large differences between people on the basis of gender. The research summaries support small differences (although this can vary in some contexts). The existence of any differences does not indicate any causality or explanation of why such differences exist. The existence of any differences, whatever the genesis and despite the size, could generate the social stereotypes that permeate the belief systems of individuals. The problem with meta-analytic findings is that the comparisons of men and women require characterization in terms of theoretical importance, not simply a statement verifying the existence of such differences.

The problem of interpreting the available data on gender differences becomes one of generating an explanatory theory. If a theory says that men are more competitive than women, does such a theory promote stereotypes? The findings of the meta-analysis of self-reported conflict strategies are consistent with this stereotype. However, although the difference is statistically significant ($d = .20$), the statement that the average man and average woman are different probably violates what most people believe such a statement implies.

This chapter proposes no solution to the problems of providing a theory to handle the issues raised in this section. Initially, one must recognize the problem of both theoretical formulations and statistical conclusions that seem to promote sexual stereotypes when the data as far as mean differences are not encouraging for those arguing for the existence of generalized gender differences. At the same time, the same statistical differences may be important in identifying why the proportion of persons at the extreme values are so radically different. Perhaps one should specify where one is at on the normal curve when claiming differences do or do not exist between men and women, instead of presuming mean differences.

Although members of a particular group may exhibit slightly more of a characteristic, it is unfair to reason that all members of the group have extreme levels of that characteristic. At the same time, if there exists a basis in fact for the separation of the two groups, then the experience of the individual with extreme values will be consonant with the data.

THE NEED FOR MEASUREMENT AND THEORIES OF GENDER DIFFERENCES

The problem with the assessment of gender differences as an issue may stem from the failure of current scientific thinking and theorizing. This section points out that the problem, although linked to measurement issues, ultimately requires a theoretical solution. Sandra Harding (1986, 1991), a feminist philosopher of science, argued that until there develops an alternative set of theoretical approaches the ability for alternative conceptualizations to emerge will be difficult. Despite numerous calls for re-thinking and conceptualizing these issues (Putnam, 1982; Rakow, 1986; West & Zimmerman, 1987), a dearth of alternatives exist within the social scientific community. These alternatives require both theoretical formulations and methodological tools to permit the collection and analysis of scientific data.

The criteria for an alternative is not simply the development of an epistemology and perspective for research. The scientific requirement includes the development of operationalized devices to measure the basis of the difference between sexes. In addition, for acceptance, the measures must receive validation psychometrically as well as generate results consistent with the theoretical predictions. The controversy is likely to continue and grow as scientists and academic organizations seek to handle the issue.

The problem that Harding (1986, 1991) identified is that without the availability of an alternative conceptualization to challenge the existing thinking change will not be forthcoming. If the current scientific approaches are not up to the task, then new approaches and theories must be developed. Whether successful development of an empirical theory will come from feminist, biological, or traditional approaches remains to be seen. Even once an acceptable approach emerges, that theory eventually will be replaced by a more comprehensive and empirically accurate theory.

The generation of scientific theoretical positions fully articulated and testable eventually resolves the problem. One problem that negatively affects the scientific study of gender is the existence of polemic attitudes toward the issues. In her book, *Who Stole Feminism?*, Sommer (1994) provided a catalogue of examples with the problems that exist when scientific evidence is disregarded or distorted in the effort to advance propositions. Any scientific theory should provide the means for its own demise (part of the requirement of testable assumptions). A good scientific theory permits evaluation by commitment to statements about an empirical reality. The problem with scientific gender theories comes when political statements become entangled with factual tests. Eagly (1995a, 1995b) pointed out this problem: She indicated that one set of feminists would like to find an absence of gender distinctions as a basis for promoting equity, whereas another set of feminists would like to emphasize differences between men and women as a basis for justifying equitable practices. Eagly was right that the discussion is fraught with political peril. However, as scientists we must eventually be bound by the results of our investigations and the theories that guide us rather than by what we would like to find.

Examining sex/gender effects is not a simple case of saying men and women are similar or that men and women are different. Certainly there are differences in physiology, psychology, and sociology. One cannot simply say men and women are different. Men and women do share an astoundingly large number of physiological, psychological, and sociological characteristics. The challenge is to create, articulate, and then test a scientific theory differentiating the basis of those similarities and differences. In the long term, relying on a simple single-item measure that reflects no explicit theoretical premise is doomed to produce useless and meaningless scientific data. This chapter articulates only some of the measurement and statistical issues encountered when considering gender differences. These issues should be addressed in any ongoing program of research on sex/gender differences.

REFERENCES

Abelson, R. (1985). A variance explanation paradox: When a little is a lot. *Psychological Bulletin, 97,* 129–133.

Allen, M., & D'Alessio, D. (1991). *Meta-analysis comparing physiological effects of pornography on males and females.* Paper presented at the Organization for the Study of Communication, Language, and Gender Convention, Milwaukee, WI.

Allen, M., & D'Alessio, D. (1993). Comparing the physiological responses of males and females to pornography: A preliminary meta-analysis. *Women and Language, 15,* 50.

Allen, M., D'Alessio, D., & Brezgel, K. (1995). Summarizing the effects of pornography using meta-analysis: II. Aggression after exposure. *Human Communication Research, 22,* 258–283.

Allen, M., & Preiss, R. (1993). Replication and meta-analysis: A necessary connection. *Journal of Social Behavior and Personality, 8,* 9–20.

Anderson, N. (1951). Scales and statistics: Parametric and nonparametric. *Psychological Bulletin, 58,* 305–316.

Ashmore, R. (1990). Sex, gender, and the individual. In L. Pervin (Ed.), *Handbook of personality: Theory and research* (pp. 486–526). New York: Guilford.

Baenninger, M., & Newcombe, N. (1989). The role of experience in spatial test performance: A meta-analysis. *Sex Roles, 20,* 327–344.

Benoit, P., & Benoit, W. (1988). Consciousness: The mindless/mindfulness and verbal report controversies. *Western Journal of Speech Communication, 50,* 41–63.

Benoit, W., & Benoit, P. (1990). Memory for conversational behavior. *Southern Communication Journal, 56,* 24–34.

Boneau, C. (1960). The effects of violation of assumptions underlying the t tests. *Psychological Bulletin, 57,* 49–64.

Box, G. (1955). Non-normality and the tests on variances. *Biometrika, 42,* 318–335.

Burggraf, C., & Sillars, A. (1987). A critical examination of sex differences in marital communication. *Communication Monographs, 54,* 276–294.

Burrell, N., & Allen, M. (1995, June). *The relationship between divorcing parents, children, and social support: A meta-analysis.* Paper presented at the International Network on Personal Relationships Conference, Williamsburg, VA.

Burrell, N., & Koper, R. (1994). The efficacy of powerful/powerless language on persuasiveness/credibility: A meta-analytic review. In M. Allen & R. Preiss (Eds.), *Prospects and precautions in the use of meta-analysis* (pp. 333–354). Dubuque, IA: Brown.

Canary, D., & Hause, K. (1993). Is there any reason to research sex differences in communication? *Communication Quarterly, 41,* 129–144.

Cupach, W., & Canary, D. (1995). Managing conflict and anger: Investigating the sex stereotype hypothesis. In P. J. Kalbfleisch & M. J. Cody (Eds.), *Gender, power, and communication in human relationships* (pp. 233–252). Hillsdale, NJ: Lawrence Erlbaum Associates.

Dallinger, J., & Hample, D. (1994). The effects of gender on compliance gaining strategy endorsement and suppression. *Communication Reports, 7,* 43–49.

Dindia, K., & Allen, M. (1992). Sex differences in self-disclosure: A meta-analysis. *Psychological Bulletin, 112,* 106–124.

Eagly, A. (1995a). The sciences and politics of comparing women and men. *American Psychologist, 50,* 145–158.

Eagly, A. (1995b). Reflections of the commenters' views. *American Psychologist, 50,* 169–171.

Emmers, T., & Allen, M. (1995a, November). *Factors contributing to sexually coercive behaviors: A meta-analysis.* Paper presented to Speech Communication Association, San Antonio, TX.

Emmers, T., & Allen, M. (1995b, May). *A meta-analysis of condom usage behavior.* Paper presented at the International Communication Association Convention, Albuquerque, NM.

Emmers, T., & Allen, M. (1995c, February). *Relationship of gender to choice of sexual resistance strategies: A meta-analysis.* Paper presented at the Western Communication Association Convention, Portland, OR.

Ericsson, K., & Simon, H. (1980). Verbal reports as data. *Psychological Review, 87,* 215–261.

Friedman, L. (1989). Mathematics and the gender gap: A meta-analysis of recent studies on sex differences in mathematical tasks. *Review of Educational Research, 59,* 185–213.

Gallagher, M. (1989). A feminist paradigm for communication research. In B. Dervin, L. Grossberg, B. O'Keefe, & E. Wartella (Eds.), *Rethinking communication* (Vol. 2, pp. 75–87). Newbury Park, CA: Sage.

Gayle, B., Preiss, R., & Allen, M. (1994). Gender differences and the use of conflict strategies. In L. Turner & H. Sterk (Eds.), *Differences that make a difference: Examining the assumptions in gender research* (pp. 13–26). Westport, CT: Bergin & Garvey.

Glass, G., McGaw, B., & Smith, M. (1981). *Meta-analysis in social research.* Beverly Hills, CA: Sage.

Grob, L., & Allen, M. (1996, April). *Sex differences in powerful/powerless language use: A meta-analytic review.* Paper presented at the Central States Communication Association Convention, Minneapolis, MN.

Harding, S. (1986). *The science question in feminism.* Ithaca, NY: Cornell University Press.

Harding, S. (1991). *Whose science? Whose knowledge? Thinking from women's lives.* Ithaca, NY: Cornell University Press.

Herrnstein, R., & Murray, C. (1994). *The bell curve: Intelligence and class structure in American life.* New York: The Free Press.

Hunter, J., & Schmidt, F. (1990). *Methods of meta-analysis: Correcting error and bias in research findings.* Newbury Park, CA: Sage.

Hyde, J. (1981). How large are cognitive gender differences? A meta-analysis using omega squared and d. *American Psychologist, 36,* 892–901.

Hyde, J., & Frost, L. (1993). Meta-analysis in the psychology of women. In F. Denmark & M. Paludi (Eds.), *Psychology of women: A handbook of issues and theories* (pp. 185–207). Westport, CT: Greenwood.

Hyde, J., & Linn, M. (1988). Gender difference on verbal ability: A meta-analysis. *Psychological Bulletin, 104,* 53–69.

Hyde, J., & Plant, E. (1995). Magnitude of psychological gender differences: Another side to the story. *American Psychologist, 50,* 159–161.

Kim, M., & Hunter, J. (1993a). Attitude-behavior relations: A meta-analysis of attitudinal relevance and topic. *Journal of Communication, 43,* 101–142.

Kim, M., & Hunter, J. (1993b). Relationships among attitudes, behavioral intentions, and behavior. *Communication Research, 20,* 331–364.

Krone, K., Allen, M., & Ludlum, J. (1994). A meta-analysis of gender research in managerial influence. In L. Turner & H. Sterk (Eds.), *Differences that make a difference: Examining the assumptions in gender research* (pp. 73–84). Westport, CT: Bergin & Garvey.

Linn, M., & Peterson, J. (1989). Gender, mathematics, and science. *Educational Researcher, 18,* 17–19, 22–27.

Nisbett, R., & Wilson, T. (1977). Telling more than we can know: Verbal reports on mental processes. *Psychological Review, 84,* 231–259.

Putnam, L. (1982). In search of gender: A critique of communication and sex roles research. *Women's Studies in Communication, 5,* 1–9.

Rakow, L. (1986). Rethinking gender research in communication. *Journal of Communication, 76*(4), 11–26.

Rosenthal, R. (1985). *Meta-analysis procedures for social researchers.* Newbury Park, CA: Sage.

Sadker, M., Sadker, D., & Klein, S. (1992). The issue of gender in elementary and secondary education. *Review of Research in Education, 17,* 269–334.

Sahlstein, E., & Allen, M. (1996, April). *Gender differences in self-esteem: A meta-analytic assessment.* Paper presented at the Central States Communication Association Convention, Minneapolis, MN.

Sommer, C. (1994). *Who stole feminism? How women have betrayed women.* New York: Simon & Schuster.

Welch, B. (1947). The generalization of "students" problem when several different population variances are involved. *Biometrika, 34,* 28–35.

West, C., & Zimmerman, D. (1987). Doing gender. *Gender & Society, 1,* 125–151.

Wilkins, B., & Andersen, P. (1992). Gender differences and similarities in management communication: A meta-analysis. *Management Communication Quarterly, 5,* 3–35.

Author Index

A

Abbey, A., 249, *251*, *252*, 414, 417, 420, *424*
Abelson, R., 435, 436, *442*
Abrahams, M. F., 249, *252*
Acitelli, L., 20, *36*
Adams, R. G., 57, *61*
Adler, M. J., 26, *36*
Afifi, W. A., 334, *345*, 365, *370*
Albrecht, T. L., 107, 114, 117, 120, *121*
Alcock, J., 233, 234, 235, 237, *252*
Allen, M., 51, *61*, 68, 70, 71, *78*, 161, *173*, 203, 211, 212, 214, *227*, 432, 435, 436, 437, 438, *442*, *443*, *444*
Allen, V. L., 271, *282*
Altman, I., 207, *226*
Alton, A. O., 352, *372*
Alvarez, M., 324, 326, *347*
Alvaro, E. M., 276, 277, 278, 280, 281, *282*
Ambady, N., 159, *172*
Amstutz, D., 340, 343, *345*
Andersen, J. F., 89, 92, *99*, *100*
Andersen, P. A., 84, 85, 89, 92, *99*, 179, *201*, 322, 330, 339, 340, 341, 342, 343, *345*, *348*, 378, *392*, 432, *444*
Andersen, S. M., 205, *226*
Anderson, J., 335, *345*, 424, *424*
Anderson, L. R., 67, *78*
Anderson, N., 434, *442*
Anderson, S. M., 398, *410*
Andrews, S. L., 246, *254*
Antill, J. K., 115, *121*
Applegate, J. L., 119, 120, *121*, *122*
Applegate, J. S., 22, *38*
Araki, S., 182, 183, 184, 196, 197, *198*
Archer, D., 87, 89, 98, *100*, 158, 159, 165, 167, 168, 169, *172*, *173*, *176*

Archer, J., 93, *99*
Argyle, M., 378, *390*
Aries, E., 6, 7, *17*, 25, 29, 32, 50, *61*, *62*, 65, 70, 71, 73, 74, 76, *78*, 101, 106, 120, *121*, 216, 221, *226*, 400, *410*, 377, 378, 380, 387, *390*
Armelagos, G. J., 96, 97, *100*
Arnkoff, D. B., 74, *80*
Asher, S. J., 216, *227*
Ashmore, R. D., 24, *36*, 222, *228*, 432, *443*
Ashton, N. L., 48, *61*
Ashton, W. A., 101, 106, 107, *121*
Atkins, B., 73, *80*
Aukett, R., 47, *61*, 112, *121*, 334, *346*
Aune, K. S., 327, *346*
Aune, R. K., 87, *99*, 167, *172*, 327, *346*, 352, *369*
Avertt, C. P., 151, *151*
Avolio, B. J., 179, *199*
Ayres, J., 373, *390*

B

Backlund, P., 86, *99*
Bacon, M. K., 326, *346*
Baenninger, M., 432, *443*
Bailey, B. L., 413, *425*
Bailey, W., 159, 167, *175*
Bakan, D., 26, *36*, 43, *61*
Baker, R. R., 243, *252*
Balswick, J., 101, *121*, 151, *151*
Banninger-Huber, E., 334, 338, *349*
Barash, D. P., 246, 248, *252*
Barbato, C. A., 316, *319*
Barbee, A. P., 101, 107, 112, 119, *121*, *122*
Barnes, M. F., 238, *252*
Barnes, M. L., 165, *172*

Barnlund, D. C., 180, 182, 183, 184,
    186, 188, 196, 197, *198*
Barry, H., 326, *346*
Barth, R. J., 43, 51, 53, *61*
Bartholomew, K. , 207, *226*
Basow, S., 395, *410*
Bass, B. M., 179, *199*
Bauchner, J. E., 352, 354, *371*
Baxter, L., 22, *36*, 73, *78*, 242, *252*, 315,
    318, 373, *390*, 413, 414, *425*
Beach, F. A., 238, *253*
Beall, A. E., 4, *17*
Beavin, J. H., 380, 383, *392*
Beck, R., 150, *152*
Becker, B. J., 258, 273, 279, *282*
Beckwith, L., 325, *346*
Begley, S., 85, *99*
Beland, F., 264, *284, 285*
Belenky, M. F., 179, *199*, 289, *299*
Belk, S. S., 334, 338, *349*
Bell, R. R., 42, *61*
Belle, D., 214, *226*
Bellis, M. A., 243, *252*
Bem, S. L., 30, *36*, 275, *282*, 378, *390*,
    398, *410*
Bender, L. R., 76, *80*
Bennet, E. S., 209, 210, 211, *230*
Benoit, P., 429, *443*
Benoit, W., 429, *443*
Benshoof, L. , 237, *252*
Berg, J. H., 206, *229*
Bergen, K. J., 73, *78*
Berger, C. R., 397, 399, *410*, 414, *425*
Berger, J., 75, *78*
Berger, P. L., 117, *121*
Berman, J. J., 47, *61*
Berndt, T. J., 216, *226*, 318, *318*
Bernieri, F. J., 165, *172*
Berscheid, E., 215, 222, *227*
Best, D. L., 394, *412*
Bettelheim, B., 21, *36*
Betty, S., 206, *229*
Bierhoff, H. W., 396, *410*
Biernat, M., 295, *299*
Bingham, S., 20, *36*
Binion, V. J., 66, 74, *78*
Birdwhistell, R. L., 85, *99*, 171, *172*
Birk, T., 264, 265, 266, 270, 280, *283*,
    397, *410*
Bischoping, K., 303, 305, 306, 314, 315,
    318
Blair, C., 22, *36*
Blanchard, P. N., 67, *78*
Blanck, P. D., 167, *172*
Blau, S., 130, 137, 141, 142, 143, 145,
    149, 150, 151, *153*
Bleir, R., 19, *36*, 324, *346*
Blier, M. J., 334, *346*

Blier-Wilson, L. A., 334, *346*
Blieszner, R., 57, *61*
Block, J. D., 43, *61*
Block, J. H., 326, 336, *346*
Bloom, B. L., 216, *227*
Blumstein, P., 72, *79*, 296, *301*, 374, 375,
    376, 377, 378, 379, 381, 385, 386,
    389, *391*
Blyth, D. A., 218, *227*
Boca, S., 327, 328, *349*
Bodhorn, D. J., 367, *370*
Bohan, J. S., 77, *78*
Bond, M. H., 47, *63*, 180, 189, 196, *199*,
    434, *443*
Booth, A., 42, *61*
Booth-Butterfield, M., 186, *199*
Booth-Butterfield, S., 186, *199*
Borden, A. W., 101, *121*
Borgia, G., 235, *252*
Borisoff, D., 103, *121*, 394, 395, *410*
Borker, R. A., 29, *38*, 102, 103, 105, 106,
    118, 119, 120, *123*, 136, *152*, 193,
    200, 303, 317, *319*, 387, *391*
Borys, S., 216, *227*
Boster, F., 262, *285*
Bostwick, T. D., 415, 416, *425*
Bowers, J. W., 185, *199*
Bowlby, J., 207, *227*
Box, G., 434, *443*
Boyer, L. M., 183, 185, 187, 188, *199*
Bradac, J. J., 131, 137, 138, 142, 145,
    149, 150, 151, *152, 153*, 185, *199*,
    373, 376, *390*, 397, 399, *410*
Bradley, P., 74, *78*, 405, 407, 408, *410*
Brandt, D. R, 353, 354, *369, 371*
Brehm, J. W., 278, *282*
Brehm, S. S., 44, *61*, 278, *282*
Bretherton, I., 324, 329, *347*
Brewer, M. B., 258, *283*
Brezgel, K., 432, *442*
Briton, N. J., 155, 170, 171, *172, 174*
Brody, L. R., 321, 322, 323, 324, 326,
    327, 335, *346*
Brooks-Gunn, J., 323, *346*
Brouwer, D., 399, *410*
Broverman, D. M., 73, *78*, 394, *410*
Broverman, I. K., 73, *78*, 394, *410*
Brown, J., 22, *36*
Bruess, C. J. S., 103, 105, *121*
Bryden, M. P., 160, *176*, 324, *346*
Bryson, J. B., 339, 340, *346*
Buck, E. B., 185, *199*
Buck, R., 166, *176*, 245, *252*, 321, 322,
    324, 326, 327, 328, 331, 333, 344,
    346, 349
Buffery, A. W. H., 90, 91, 92, 93, *99*
Buhrke, R. A., 112, *121*
Buhrmester, D., 216, 217, 218, *227*

Buller, D. B., 87, *99*, 167, *172*, 327, *346*, 352, 353, 354, 357, 358, 361, 363, 364, 365, *369, 370*
Bullis, C., 413, *425*
Burda, P. C., 112, *121*
Burdick, C. A., 246, *254*
Burggraf, C. S., 377, 381, *390*, 436, *443*
Burgoon, J. K., 159, 167, *175*, 265, 267, 281, *283*, 352, 353, 354, 357, 358, 361, 363, 364, 365, *369, 370*, 397, *410*, 414, 418, 419, 420, 421, *425*
Burgoon, M., 257, *259*, 260, 262, 263, 264, 265, 266, 267, 270, 274, 275, 276, 277, 278, 280, 281, *282, 283, 284, 285*, 397, *410*
Burhke, R. A., 334, *347*
Burke, J. A., 120, *122*
Burleson, B. R., 101, 107, 110, 111, 113, 114, 115, 117, 119, 120, *121, 122, 123, 124*, 219, 226, *227*, 304, 305, 307, 314, 316, *318, 319*, 339, *347*
Burrell, N., 432, *443*
Burrowes, B. D., 331, *347*
Buslig, A., 352, *369*
Buss, D. M., 96, 97, *99*, 238, 239, 241, 242, 243, 244, 248, 250, 251, *252*, 340, 342, 343, *347*, 415, 422, 423, *425*
Butler, D. L., 247, *254*
Buttenwieser, P., 291, *301*
Buunk, B., 7, *17*, 339, 340, 342, 343, *347*

C

Cacioppo, J. T., 206, 207, 222, *228*, 258, 273, *285*
Calabrese, R. J., 414, *425*
Caldwell, M. A., 48, 49, *61*, 106, *122*, 216, *227*
Cambra, R. E., 183, 185, 188, *200*
Camden, C. T., 367, *370*, 379, 380, *391*
Camire, L., 248, 249, *254*
Canary, D. J., 6, 8, *17*, 23, 24, 26, *36*, 67, 69, *78*, 84, *99*, 120, *122*, 179, *199*, 234, 250, *252*, 332, *347*, 373, 377, 378, 387, 388, *390, 392*, 394, *410*, 422, 423, *425*, 432, 436, *443*
Cancian, F., 29, *36*, 103, 108, *122*
Candy-Gibbs, S. E., 53, *61*
Cann, A., 262, *283*
Capella, J. N., 251, *252*, 267, *283*, 397, 398, *410*
Carbonell, J. L., 71, *78*
Carey, C. M., 415, 416, 418, 420, 422, *425*
Carli, L. L., 71, *78*, 161, *173*, 258, 272, 279, *284*

Carmas, L. A., 330, *347*
Carmen, B., 164, *175*
Carrere, S., 20, *37*
Carstensen, L. L., 288, *301*
Carter, J. D., 170, *174*
Cashdan, E., 249, *252*
Cate, R. M., 413, *425*
Caul, W. F., 321, 328, 344, *346*
Chaiken, S., 258, *284*
Chaikin, A. L., 164, *173*
Chambers, J. K., 180, 190, 191, 192, *199*
Chan, A., 235, *253*
Chelune, G. J., 206, *227*
Cherry, L., 325, 336, 337, 338, *347*
Childs, L., 326, *346*, 399, *412*
Chodorow, N., 28, *36*, 288, 289, 292, *299*
Christensen, A., 292, 293, 294, 295, 297, *299, 300, 301, 302*
Chrousos, G., 323, *349*
Clark, C. L., 208, *230*
Clark, L. A., 401, *412*
Clark, M. S., 207, *231*
Clark, R. A., 101, 112, 120, *122*, 317, *318*
Clark, R. D., 242, *252*, 415, *425*
Clarke, E., 33, *36*
Clarke, S., 69, *79*
Clarkson, F. E., 73, *78*, 394, *410*
Clifton, A. K., 71, *79*, 149, 150, *152*, 378, *391*, 395, 399, *412*
Clinchy, B. M., 179, *199*, 288, *299*
Coates, J., 399, *410*
Cocroft, B. K., 183, 188, *199*
Cody, M. J., 353, 357, 360, 363, 366, 367, *370, 371*
Cohen, B. P., 75, *78*
Cohen, J., 24, 25, 27, *36*, 68, *78*, 140, *152*, 155, 156, 163, 169, *173*, 210, *227*
Cohen, M. M., 274, *283*
Cohen, P., 140, *152*
Cohen, S., 215, *227*
Cohn, L. D., 160, *173*
Colella, M. J., 352, *372*
Collaer, M. L., 86, 90, 91, 93, *99*
Collier, M. J., 180, *199*
Collins, N., 208, *230*
Collins, R. L., 101, 107, *124*
Comstock, J., 352, *369*
Condry, J., 325, *347*
Condry, S., 325, *347*
Conger, J. C., 159, 167, *174*
Connor, J. W., 180, 181, *199*
Cook, M., 378 *390*
Cooper, H., 167, *173, 175*
Cooper, P. J., 90, *100*, 103, *122*, 325, *349*
Costanzo, M., 159, 165, 167, *173, 176*
Costrich, N., 397, *410*
Courtwright, J. A., 185, *199*

Coutts, L. M. , 165, *173*
Cozby, P. C., 203, *227*
Craig, J. M., 249, *254*
Craig, R. T., 378, *391*
Crano, W. D., 279, *283*
Crano, W. S., 258, 279, *283*
Crawford, M., 2, 6, *17*, 26, 31, 32, *37*,
	103, 106, *122*, 289, 290, 291, *300*,
	302
Crocker, J., 270, *283*
Crosby, F., 149, 150, *152*, 204, *227*
Crouch, I., 149, *152*
Crowley, M., 161, *173*, 215, *227*
Crutchfield, R. S., 271, *282*
Culver, C., 325, *348*
Cunningham, J. D., 296, *301*
Cunningham, M. R., 101, 107, 112, 119,
	121
Cupach, W., 436, *443*
Cupchik, G. C., 165, *173*
Cutler, G. B., 323, *349*
Cutrona, C. E., 101, 107, *122*, 215, *230*

D

Dahl, R. H., 242, *253*
D'Alessio, D., 432, *442*
Dallinger, J., 432, *443*
Daly, J. A., 219, *230*
Daly, M., 236, 237, 242, 251, *252*
Darus, H. J., 179, *199*
Darwin, C., 235, 236, 249, *252*
D'Augelli, A. R., 164, *173*
Davidson, R.J., 214, *227*
Davies, L., 353, 357, 360, 363, *370*
Davis, B. M., 71, *78*
Davis, D., 206, *227*
Davis, J. D., 399, *410*
Davis, M. S., 413, *425*
Dawkins, R., 237, *252*
Deaux, K., 4, 6, *17*, 69, 71, *78*, 102, *122*,
	216, *227*, 234, *252*, 271, *284*, 290,
	300, 377, 387, *390*, 394, 395, 396,
	397, 398, 399, 404, 408, *410*, *411*
Deci, E. L., 279, *283*, *284*
DeFrancisco, V. L., 374, 375, 376, 377,
	379, 381, 385, 386, 388, 389, *390*
Dehaan, D., 399, *410*
De Klerk, V., 393, *411*
DeLeon, B., 66, 74, *78*
Delespaul, P. A. E. G., 223, *229*
Delia, J. G., 120, *122*
DeLucia, J. L., 415, 416, *425*
DePaulo, B. M., 87, *100*, 159, 161, 162,
	167, *172*, *176*, *177*, 206, *231*, 245,
	254, 352, 353, 357, 360, 365, 366,
	367, *370*, *372*

Derlega, V. J., 164, *173*, 271, *284*, 101,
	106, 107, 112, 119, *121*, *122*, 399,
	400, *411*
Desaulniers, J., 72, *80*
deTurck, M. A., 352, 353, 354, 365, 366,
	367, *370*, *371*
Deutsch, F. M., 158, 164, *173*
deVries, B., 48, *62*
deVries, M., 223, *229*
Diacoyanni-Tarlatzis, I., 235, *253*
Diener, E., 220, *228*, 327, *349*
Dillard, J. P., 262, 264, *283*, *284*
Dillman, L., 354, *370*
Di Mare, L., 194, 195, 196, *199*
DiMateo, M. R., 87, 89, *100*, 158, 165,
	167, 168, 169, *172*, *173*, *176*
Dindia, K., 32, *37*, 51, 56, *61*, 68, 70, 71,
	78, 138, *152*, 161, *173*, 203, 204,
	211, 212, 214, *227*, 305, *318*, 373,
	377, 378, *390*, *391*, 432, *443*
Dobbins, G. H., 161, *173*
Dodge, K. A., 325, *348*
Doherty, E. G., 378, *391*
Donaghy, W. C., 353, 357, 360, 363, 367,
	370, *371*, 399, *411*
Doran, N., 264, *283*
Dorcey, T., 159, 167, *174*
Dornan, M. C., 162, *174*
Douglas, W., 399, *411*
Downey, J. L., 249, *252*
Drag, R. M., 245, *252*
Drakich, J., 69, *79*
Dreyer, A., 166, *176*, 327, *349*
Driver, R. E., 164, *177*, 352, *372*
Druen, P. B., 101, 107, 112, 119, *121*
Dubois, B. L., 149, *152*
Duck, S., 20, *37*, 45, 48, 50, 53, 56, *61*,
	120, *122*, 204, 218, 221, *227*, 305,
	315, *319*
Dufort, R., 264, *284*, *285*
Dumas, B., 377, *391*
Duncan, S., 395, *411*
Duncan, V. J., 353, *370*
Dunn, J., 324, 329, *347*
Durfee, J. T., 325, *348*
Dyer, M., 207, 218, 219, *228*

E

Eagly, A. H., 3, 6, 12, *17*, 25, 27, *37*, 67,
	68, 70, 72, 75, *78*, 89, *99*, 155,
	156, 161, 170, *173*, 179, *199*, 211,
	215, *227*, 258, 272, 279, *284*, 290,
	291, *300*, 394, 395, 396, 397, 399,
	406, *411*, 432, 436, 442, *443*
Eakins, B. W., 72, *79*, 264, *284*, 378, 380,
	391

Eakins, R. G., 72, *79*, 264, *284*, 378, 380, *391*
Ebesu, A., 357, 358, 365, 369, *370*
Eccles, J. S., 171, *174*
Edelbrock, C., 335, *347*
Egland, K. L., 334, *345*
Ehrlich, C. M., 158, *174*
Eibl-Eibesfeldt, I., 234, 250, *252*
Eisenberg, N., 214, 227, 331, *347*
Ekman, P., 214, *227*, 235, *252*, *253*, *255*, 324, 329, *347*, 352, *371*
Elkes, R., 262, *283*
Elkins, L. E., 304, 317, 318, *319*
Ellis, D. G., 71, *79*
Ellsworth, P. C., 396, *412*
Eloy, S. V., 339, 340, 341, 342, 343, *348*
Elzinga, R. H., 183, 186, 188, 196, *199*
Embree, J. M., 101, 107, *124*
Emde, R., 205, *227*
Emmers, T. M., 432, *443*
Emmers-Sommer, T. M., 8, *17*, 377, 387, 388, *390*
Engleman, E. G., 264, *284*
Engstrom, C., 245, 246, 250, *255*
Entin, E., 67, *80*
Epstein, C. F., 21, 22, 30, 31, *37*
Epstein, J. A., 365, 367, *370*
Ericsson, K., 429, *443*
Eskilson, A., 75, *81*

F

Fabes, R. A., 326, 331, *347*
Fairbanks, L. A., 164, *174*
Falbo, T., 296, *300*
Faulkner, S., 8, *17*, 377, 387, 388, *390*
Fausto-Sterling, A., 102, *122*
Fay, P. J., 364, *371*
Feeley, T. H. , 365, 366, *371*
Fehr, B. A., 43, 44, 50, 51, *62*
Feingold, A., 160, 161, 162, *174*, 239, *253*, 287, *300*
Feinstein, J., 397, *410*
Feldman, C. M., 353, 364, 365, *370*
Fennema, E., 160, *175*
Ferguson, K. E., 120, *122*
Ferguson, L. W., 291, *301*
Fine, M., 290, *300*
Fingeret, A. L., 167, *174*
Firth, E. A., 159, 167, *174*
Fischer, C. S., 47, 48, 51, *62*
Fischer, E. F., 237, *253*
Fisek, M. H., 75, *78*
Fishbaugh, L., 272, 279, *284*
Fisher, B. A., 377, *391*
Fishman, P., 149, *152*, 373, 374, 375, 376, 377, 378, 379, 381, 385, 386, 388, 389, 395, *391*, 399, *411*

Fiske, D. W., 395, *411*
Fiske, S. T., 208, 220, *227*, *230*, 270, *283*, 397, *411*
Fitzpatrick, M. A., 56, *61*, 137, 138, *152*, 296, *302*, 305, *318*, 377, 378, 387, 389, *391*
Fivush, R., 118, *122*, 325, 329, *347*
Flaherty, J., 112, *122*
Fleming, M. L., 160, *174*
Floyd, K., 361, *370*
Fontes, N. E., 354, *371*
Ford, C. S., 238, *253*
Foster-Clark, F. S., 218, *227*
Fournet, G. P., 159, *175*
Fox-Genovese, E., 30, *37*
Frances, S. J., 164, *174*
Francis, P. L., 159, 167, *176*
Franks, P., 226, *229*
Frelick, L., 207, 219, 231
French, J. R. P., Jr., 296, *300*
Fretz, B. R., 164, *175*
Freud, S., 21, *37*
Friedley, S. A., 90, *100*, 325, *349*
Friedman, D. E., 416, *425*
Friedman, H. S., 327, *347*, 352, 354, *371*
Friedman, L., 432, *443*
Friedman, P., 151, *152*
Friesen, W. V., 214, *227*, 235, *253*, 352, *371*
Frieze, I., 424, *426*, 162, *174*
Frijda, N., 327, *347*
Frost, L. A., 24, 25, 27, 33, *37*, 155, 157, 160, *175*, 394, *412*, 432, *444*
Frymier, A. B., 183, 186, 188, *199*
Fuchs, D., 325, *347*
Fuehrer, A., 101, 106, 107, *121*, 399, *412*, 399, *412*
Fujita, F., 220, *228*
Funder, D. C., 165, 167, *174*
Fuqua, D. R., 112, *121*, 334, *347*
Furman, L. G., 54, *62*
Furman, W., 216, 217, 218, *227*

G

Gale, W. S., 71, *79*, 149, 150, *152*, 378, *391*, 395, 399, *412*
Gallagher, M., 430, *443*
Galvin, K. , 103, *122*
Gangestad, S. W., 238, *254*, 422, *426*
Garcia, S., 159, *175*
Garcia-Falconi, R., 334, 338, *349*
Garrison, J. P., 89, 92, *99*
Gaulin, S. J. C., 90, 91, 92, 93, 94, 95, 96, *99*
Gauthier, R., 303, *319*
Gayle, B., 432, 436, 437, 438, *443*
Geertz, C., 107, *122*

Gerritsen, M. M., 399, *410*
Gershoni, R., 216, *230*
Gerson, J. M., 102, *122*
Gibbons, P., 133, 134, 136, *153*
Gibson, T. W., 131, 132, 142, 150, 151, *153*
Gilbert, L. A., 71, *78*
Giles, H. , 134, 142, *152*
Gilligan, C., 29, *37*, 101, *122*, 288, *300*
Gilpin, E. A., 278, *284*
Girgus, J. S., 335, 338, *348*
Givens, D. B., 244, 250, *253*
Glaser, R., 222, *228*
Glass, G., 434, *443*
Gleser, G. C., 151, *152*
Gochberg, B., 335, *349*
Goffman, E., 397, *411*
Goldberger, N. R., 179, *199*, 289, *299*
Goldsmith, D., 107, 113, 114, 117, 120, *121*, 339, *347*
Goldsmith, T. H., 89, 94, *99*
Golombok, S., 118, *122*
Gonzales, J. , 406, *411*
Gordon, S. M., 290, *300*
Gorenflo, D. W., 279, *283*
Goss, B., 366, 367, *371*
Gottlieb, B. H., 215, *228*
Gottman, J. M., 20, *37*, 207, 212, 222, *228*, 288, 292, *300*, *301*, 389, 390, *391*, *391*
Gottschalk, L. A., 151, *152*
Gouldner, H., 54, *62*
Graham, T., 214, *228*
Grammar, K., 243, 244, 248, 249, *253*
Grandpre, J., 353, 357, 360, 361, 363, 367, *370*, *371*
Gray, J., 27, 28, 32, 34, *37*, 76, *79*, 83, *99*, 102, *122*, *123*, 203, *228*, 287, *300*
Gray, J. A., 90, 91, 92, 93, *99*
Gray, J. P., 96, *99*
Green, C. R., 352, *370*
Green, J. O., 267, *283*
Greene, D., 279, *284*
Greene, J., 397, 398, *410*
Greenspan, M., 271, *284*
Greif, E., 72, *79*, 324, 326, *347*
Greulich, F., 335, *349*
Griffiths, K., 113, *123*
Grisham, J. A., 296, *301*
Grob, L., 432, *444*
Gronsky, B. R., 164, *175*
Groth, G., 238, 239, 240, 243, *253*
Gudykunst, W. B., 136, *152*, 181, 182, *199*
Guerrero, L. K., 85, *99*, 322, 330, 332, 333, 334, 339, 340, 341, 342, 343, *345*, *348*, 353, 364, 365, *370*

Gulley, M. R., 101, 107, 112, 119, *121*
Gumperz, J. J., 105, *123*
Guzley, R. M., 182, *199*

H

Haas, A., 149, *152*
Haase, R. F., 164, 167, *175*
Hacker, H. M., 51, *62*
Haddad, Y., 223, *229*
Haga, H., 190, *200*
Hahn, D., 103, *121*
Hahn, S., 398, *412*
Halberstadt, A. G., 155, 157, 158, 164, 170, *174*, 213, *228*, 331, *347*
Hale, J. L., 267, *283*, 397, *410*, 415, 416, 417, 418, 420, 421, *425*
Hall, D., 29, *37*
Hall, J., 264, 265, 266, 270, 280, *283*, 397, *410*
Hall, J. A., *17*, 20, 23, 25, *37*, *38*, 84, 85, 86, 87, 88, 89, *99*, *100*, 212, 213, 214, 221, *228*, *230*, 245, *253*, 321, 323, 326, 327, 328, 335, 344, *346*, *348*, 354, 357, *371*, 155, 157, 158, 160, 161, 162, 163, 165, 167, 168, 169, 170, 171, *172*, *174*, *176*
Hall, K. P., 399, *411*
Hallahan, M., 159, *172*
Hallberg, E. T., 164, 167, *175*
Halpern, D. F., 85, 86, 89, 90, 91, 92, 93, 98, *99*
Halverson, C. F., Jr., 216, *231*
Hammen, C. L., 334, *348*
Hample, D., 432, *443*
Hanna, N. A., 216, *226*
Hansen, G.L., 339, *348*
Hanusa, B. H., 162, *174*
Haraway, D., 22, 29, *37*
Harding, S., 29, *37*, 399, *411*, 441, *444*
Hare-Mustin, R. T., 2, *17*, 287, 290, *300*
Harman, C. M., 183, 187, *199*
Harold, R. D., 171, *174*
Harper, N. L., 179, *200*
Harre, R., 267, *284*
Harris, A. C., 66, *79*
Harris, C. J., 164, *174*
Harris, I. D., 331, 334, *348*
Harris, M. J., 165, 167, *174*, 413, 419, 420, *425*
Harszlak, J. J., 367, *370*
Harter, S. E., 331, *350*
Hartman, M., 149, *152*
Haslett, B. J., 151, *152*
Hastorf, A.H., 396, *412*
Hatfield, E., 115, *124*, 206, 207, *228*, 242, *252*, 415, *425*

Hattie, J., 160, *174*
Hause, K. S., 6, *17*, 23, 24, 26, *36*, 67, 69, *78*, 84, *99*, 120, *122*, 179, *199*, 234, 250, *252*, 378, *390*, 394, *410*, 423, *425*, 432, *443*
Haven, C., 112, *123*
Haviland, J. M., 323, 326, 334, *348, 349*
Hawkins, K., 74, *79*
Hayes, C. W., 158, 164, *174*
Hays, R. B., 46, 52, 53, 56, *62*, 112, *123*
Hazan, C., 207, *230*
Hazelrigg, P. J., 167, *173, 175*
Healy, S., 51, *62*
Heavey, C. L., 7, 8, 292, 294, 295, 297, *300, 301*
Hecht, M. A., 360, *371*
Heider, K., 235, 249, *253*
Heilbrun, A. B., 159, *175*
Heilman, M. E., 278, *284*
Helgeson, V. S., 101, *123*, 207, 218, 219, *228*
Hembree, R., 160, *175*
Henley, N. M., 21, *37*, 72, 73, *79, 81*, 103, 105, 106, *123*, 170, *175*, 290, 291, *301*, 304, *319*, 376, 387, *391*, 392
Hernandez-Sanchez, J. E., 334, 338, *349*
Hernstein, R., 431, *444*
Herrick, L. R., 207, *229*
Hess, B. B., 58, *62*
Hewitt, J., 247, *255*
Hibaya, J., 190, *200*
Higashiyama, A., 183, 186, *200*
Hill, C. E., 164, *175*
Hill, C. T., 70, *79*
Hill, D. R., 215, *230*
Hill, J. P., 8, *17*
Hillis, J. D., 415, 416, 418, 420, 421, *425*
Hillman, J. L., 73, *80*, 183, 196, 197, *201*
Hines, M., 86, 90, 91, 93, *99*
Hirokawa, R. Y., 179, 182, *200*
Hirschman, L., 151, *152*
Hu, H. Y., 180, 189, 196, *199*
Hobfoll, S. E., 214, *228*
Hochschild, A., 390, *391*
Hocking, J. E., 352, 353, 354, *369, 371*
Hodgins, H. S., 167, *175*, 209, 210, 211, *228*
Hoffman, J. E., 216, *230*
Hoffman, M. L., 101, 102, *123*
Hofstede, G., 181, *200*
Holloway, J. S., 179, *200*
Hopp, C., 160, *175*
Hopper, R., 74, *79*
Hori, M., 190, *200*
House, J. S., 215, *228*, 396, *411*
Howard, J. A., 296, *301*
Howard, K. I., 331, 334, *348*

Hrdy, S. B., 237, 251, *253*
Hsu, J., 183, *200*
Huckabee, C. B., 107, *124*
Hunt, K. W., 149, 150, *152*
Hunter, J., 27, *37*, 262, *284*, 429, 430, *444*
Hunter, S., 399, *411*
Hupka, R. B., 339, *347*
Hurst, M. H., 56, *61*, 221, 227, 305, *319*
Huston, T. L., 222, *228*
Hyde, J. S., 3, *17*, 24, 25, 26, 27, 33, 34, *37*, 67, *79*, 90, 90, 91, *99*, 155, 157, 160, 162, *175, 176*, 210, *228*, 414, 415, 418, *425*, 432, *444*

I

Ickes, W., 115, *123*, 159, *175*, 214, *228*
Ide, S., 190, *200*
Ikuta, S., 190, *200*
Incontro, C. R., 74, *80*, 130, 141, 143, 145, *153*
Infante, D. A., 187, *200*, 264, *284*
Inman, C. C., 20, *37, 39*, 46, 52, *63*, 109, 119, *125*, 204, 216, 218, 221, 226, *231*, 304, *319*
Inoff-Germain, G., 323, *349*
Irish, J. T., 158, *174*
Ishii, S., 183, 185, 186, 187, 188, 196, *199, 201*
Ivy, P. K., 86, *99*

J

Jacklin, C. N., 204, *229*
Jackson, D. D., 380, 383, *392*
Jackson, R. J., 158, 164, *176*, 214, *229*
Jacobs, J. E., 171, *174*
Jacobson, N., 292, *301*
Jacquard, A., 93, 96, 97, *100*
Jacques, A., 264, *285*
Jaffe, J., 67, *80*
James, D., 69, *79, 80*
James, M. R., 74, *80*, 130, 141, 143, 145, *153*
Janeway, E., 21, *37*
Jankowiak, W. R., 237, *253*
Jaubusch, D. M., 258, *284*
Jefferson, G., 380, 383, *392*
Jennings, W. S., 21, *37*
John, W., 151, *152*
Johnson, B. T., 68, *78*, 161, *173*, 179, *199*
Johnson, C., 73, *79*, 158, *175*
Johnson, C. B., 249, *254*
Johnson, F. L., 20, 29, *37, 38*, 50, *61*, 105, 106, 107, 108, *121, 123*

Johnson, J. T., 326, *348*
Johnson, K. L., 415, 416, 417, 418, 420, 421, *425*
Johnson, P., 72, 73, *79*, 142, *152*
Johnson, W. B., 291, *301*
Johnston, R. E., 164, 165, *175*
Jones, A. J., 246, 250, *254*
Jones, D. C., 219, *228*
Jones, E., 397, *411*
Jones, S. B., 260, 263, *283*
Jones, S. M., 111, 123
Jordan, J. V., 289, *301*
Jorgensen, P. F., 339, 340, 341, 342, 343, *348*
Jourard, S. M., 203, 207, *228*
Jung Suh, E., 72, *80*

K

Kahn, A. S., 8, *17*, 27, 32, *38*, 290, *302*
Kalbfleisch, P. J., 352, 353, 365, 366, *370*, *371*
Kaminski, E.P., 352, 354, *371*
Kamitani, Y., 191, *200*
Kaplan, A. G., 289, *301*
Karau, S. J., 68, 70, *78*, 161, *173*
Karten, S. J., 75, *81*, 290, *302*
Kawasaki, A., 190, *200*
Kayano, J., 189, *200*
Kaye, L. W., 22, *38*
Keefe, R. C., 96, *100*, 250, *253*
Keeley-Dyreson, M., 159, 167, *175*
Kelley, H. H., 207, *228*, 296, *301*
Kennedy, C. W., 379, 380, *391*
Kenney, D. A., 56, *61*, 206, *228*
Kenny, D. A., 305, *318*
Kenrick, D. T., 96, *100*, 234, 237, 238, 239, 240, 242, 243, 244, 250, 251, *253*, 345, *348*, 397, *412*
Kerber, L. K., 29, *38*
Kerkstra, A., 7, *17*
Kerlinger, F. N., 137, *152*
Kidder, L., 397, *410*
Kiecolt-Glaser, J. K., 222, *228*
Kilkenny, R., 21, *37*
Kim, M., 429, *444*
Kinder, B. N., 43, 51, 53, *61*
Kipnis, D., 296, *301*
Kirshnit, C., 158, 164, *176*, 214, *229*
Kite, M., 162, *176*, 394, 395, *410*
Klein, R. P., 325, *348*
Klein, S., 432, *444*
Kleinke, C. L., 334, 335, 338, *348*
Kline, S. L., 120, *122*
Klingle, R. S., 265, 266, 267, 270, 280, *284*

Klonsky, B. G., 75, *78*
Klopf, D. W., 182, 183, 185, 186, 187, 188, 196, *199*, *200*, *201*
Kluckholm, C., 107, *123*
Knapp, M. L., 86, *100*
Kocsis, M., 164, 167, *175*
Koenigsknecht, R. A., 151, *152*
Koestner, R., 167, *175*, 352, *372*
Kohlberg, L., 21, *37*
Kollack, P., 374, 375, 376, 377, 378, 379, 381, 385, 386, 389, *391*
Kollock, P., 72, *79*
Komarovsky, M., 390, *391*
Kombos, N. A., 159, *175*
Kommor, M. J., 206, *227*
Koper, R., 432, *443*
Koralewski, M. A., 246, *254*
Kraft, S. A., 204, 218, 222, *229*
Kramarae, C., 66, 72, 73, *79*, 103, 105, 106, *123*, 234, *253*, 291, *301*, 304, *319*, 387, *391*
Kramer, C., 73, *79*, 378, 379, *391*
Kraus, S., 51, *62*
Krause, R., 235, *253*
Kraut, R. E., 164, 165, *175*, 352, *371*
Krayer, K. J., 366, 367, *371*
Krokoff, L. J., 390, *391*
Krone, K., 432, *444*
Kronenfeld, J. J., 94, 96, *100*
Kuhlenschmidt, S., 159, 167, *174*
Kunkel, A. W., 101, 110, 111, 112, 113, 114, 117, *122*, *123*, 219, 226, 227, 304, 305, 314, 316, *319*
Kurzweil, N., 206, *229*
Kuwabara, T., 189, *200*

L

LaFrance, M., 164, 170, *175*, 360, *371*
LaFreniere, P., 303, *319*
Lakoff, R., 105, 106, *123*, 289, *301*, 399, *411*
Lamke, L., 115, *123*
Lamon, S. J., 160, *175*
Landis, K. R., 215, *228*
Langellier, K., 29, *37*
Langlois, J. H., 238, *253*
Lapadat, J., 149, 150, *152*
Larrance, D. T., 167, 170, *177*
Larsen, R., 242, *252*
LaRussa, G. W., 73, *81*, 394, *412*
Lasakow, P., 203, *228*
Lassiter, G. D., 352, 366, *370*
Lavrakas, P. J., 238, *254*
Lawrence, S. G., 74, *79*
Layne, C., 292, 294, 295, *300*

Lea, M., 53, *62*
Lebra, T. S., 185, *200*
LeCompte, W. A., 235, *253*
Lee, C., 179, *200*
Lee, D. Y. , 164, 167, *175*
Lee, L., 278, *284*
Lefebvre, L. M., 296, *301*
Lemerise, E. A., 325, *348*
Lennon, R., 214, *227*
LePoire, B. A., 354, *370*
Lepper, M. R., 279, *284*
Levenson, R. W., 212, 222, *228*, 288, 292, *300, 301*
Leventhal, H., 165, *173*
Lever, J., 106, *123*
Levesque, A., 264, *285*
Levine, L. E. , 102, *123*
Lewinsohn, P. M., 335, 336, *349*
Lewis, C. S., 41, 61, *62*
Lewis, D., 95, *100*
Lewis, H. B., 321, *348*
Lewis, L. L., 271, *284*
Lewis, M., 325, 336-338, *347*
Lewis, R. A., 220, 223, *228*
Lin, Y. C., 206, 209, 210, 211, 223, *228, 229, 230*
Lindsey, A. E., 401, 402, 403, *411*
Linn, M. C., 67, *79*, 160, *175*, 432, *444*
Linn, M. D., 90, 91, 92, *100*
Lipman-Blumen, J., 179, *200*
Lirgg, C. D., 161, *175*
Littlejohn, S. W., 258, *284*
Littlepage, G. E., 167, *175*, 352, *371*
Lloyd, S. A., 413, *425*
Lockheed, M. E., 69, *79*, 399, *411*
Lombardo, J. P., 159, 167, *176*
Loriaux, D. L., 323, *349*
Loveday, L., 182, 183, 185, 188, 191, 197, *200*
Lowenthal, M. F., 42, 43, 53, *63*, 112, *123*
Luckmann, T., 117, *121*
Ludlum, J., 432, *444*
Lundell, T. L., 130, 137, 138, 139, 140, 141, 142, 143, 144, 145, 149, 150, 151, *153*

M

Maccoby, E. E., 20, 31, *38*, 105, *123*, 204, *229*, 303, 304, 317, *319*, 343, *348*
MacDonald, C. J., 159, *176*, 327, 328, *349*
Maddux, J. E., 296, *301*
Maguire, P., 160, *176*
Maheux, B., 264, *284, 285*
Major, B., 6, *17*, 69, 71, *78*, 102, *122*, 234, *252*, 377, 387, *390*, 394, 395, 396, 397, 398, 399, 404, 408, *410, 411*
Makhigani, M. G., 75, *78*, 161, *173*
Malamuth, N. M., 292, 295, *301*
Malarkey, W. B., 222, *228*
Malatesta, C. Z., 323, 325, 326, *348*
Malone, M. R., 160, *174*
Maltz, D. N., 29, *38*, 102, 103, 105, 106, 118, 119, 120, *123*, 136, *152*, 193, *200*, 303, 317, *319*, 387, *391*
Manderscheid, R. W., 71, *79*
Mann, S. K., 131, *153*
Manstead, A. S. R., 159, *176*, 327, 328, *349*
Mansur, L., 378, *390*
Maragoni, C., 159, *175*
Marecek, J., 2, *17*, 287, 290, *300*, 397, *410*
Margolin, G. , 295, *301*
Margulis, S. T., 106, *122*, 400, *411*
Markman, H. J., 204, 218, 222, *229*
Markus, H. J., 205, *229*
Marlett, G. A., 378, *391*
Marston, W. M., 365, *371*
Martin, C. J., 326, *347*, 398, 401, *411*
Martin, J. N. , 378, *391*
Martin, R. R., 48, *63*
Martocchio, J. J., 161, *176*
Marwell, G., 262, *285*
Mason, J. K., 334, 335, 338, *348*
Mathes, J. W., 340, *348*
Mazur, E., 106, *123*
McAdam, A., 210, 211, 226, *230*
McAdams, D. P., 51, *62*, 158, 164, *176*, 209, 214, *229, 230*
McCain, T. A., 401, *411*
McCarrick, A. K., 71, *79*
McCloskey, L. A., 399, *411*
McCormick, N. B., 246, 250, *254*
McCroskey, J. C., 401, *411*
McFall, R. M., 249, *254*
McGaw, B., 434, *443*
McGee, R., 335, *345*
McGillis, D., 397, *411*
McGrath, D., 71, *79*, 149, 150, *152*, 378, *391*, 395, 399, *412*
McGuire, M. T., 164, *174*
McGuire, W. J., 274, *285*
McHugh, M. C., 162, *174*
McKee, J. P., 394, *412*
McKenzie-Mohr, D., 398, *411*
McKinney, D. H., 399, *411*
McKinney, K., 420, 423, *426*
McKinnie, R., 167, *175*
McLachlan, A., 72, *79*
McMillan, J. R., 71, *79*, 149, 150, *152*, 378, *391*, 395, 399, *412*
Megargee, E. I., 71, *80*

Mehrabian, A., 164, *176*
Melby, C., 249, *252*
Mellen, S. L. W., 237, *254*
Merrill, L., 394, 395, *410*
Mesquita, B., 327, 328, *349*
Metts, S., 106, 115, *122, 124,* 400, *411*
Mickelson, K. D., 101, *123*
Mickey, J., 179, *200*
Middleton, W. C., 364, 365, *371*
Midlarsky, E., 394, *412*
Milardo, R. M., 305, *319*
Mill, K., 47, *61,* 112, *121,* 334, *346*
Millar, K., 366, *371*
Millar, M., 366, *371*
Miller, E. N., 249, *254*
Miller, G. R., 257, 259, 260, 262, 263,
    265, 274, *283, 285,* 352, 353, 354,
    369, 370, 371, 397, *410*
Miller, J. B., 71, *80,* 289, 292, *301,* 321,
    348
Miller, L. C., 206, 208, *229*
Miller, L. H., 158, *174*
Miller, M. D., 183, 185, 188, *200,* 274,
    283
Miller, R. E., 321, 328, 344, *346*
Miller, R. S., 334, 338, *349*
Miner, J. B., 161, *173*
Miura, S., 179, *200*
Miyahara, A., 182, *200*
Mongeau, P. A., 415, 416, 417, 420, 421,
    422, *425*
Monsour, M., 48, *62,* 206, 219, *229*
Montgomery, B. M., 249, 250, *254*
Montgomery, C. L., 274, 275, 276, *283,
    285*
Monti, P. M. , 167, *174*
Moore, H. T., 303, 304, *319*
Moore, M. M., 243, 244, 246, 247, 249,
    251, *254*
Morch, H., 107, *124*
Mortenson, S. R., 110, 111, *124*
Morton, T. L, 222, *229*
Moskowitz, D. S., 72, *80*
Motley, M. T., 367, *370*
Muehlenhard, C. L., 246, 249, *254,* 415,
    416, 418, *425*
Mulac, A., 74, *80,* 129, 130, 131, 133,
    134, 136, 137, 138, 139, 140, 141,
    142, 143, 144, 145, 149, 150, 151,
    152, 153, 387, *391*
Mullen, P. E., 327, 339, 340, *350*
Munn, P., 324, 329, *347*
Muramatsu, Y., 185, *199*
Murphy, B. O., 20, *38*
Murphy, L. B., 110, *124*
Murphy-Berman, V., 47, *61*
Murray, C., 431, *444*

N

Nakanishi, M., 189, *200*
Narus, L. R., 51, *62*
Natale, M., 67, *80*
Newcombe, N., 74, *80,* 432, *443*
Newton, B. J., 185, *199*
Nezlek, J., 112, 115, *124,* 209, 210, 211,
    216, *229, 230, 231*
Nisbett, R. E., 279, *284,* 429, *444*
Nishida, K., 181, 189, *199, 200*
Nishida, T., 182, *199*
Noddings, N., 29, *38*
Nolen-Hoeksema, S., 334, 335, 338, *348*
Noller, P., 102, 106, *123,* 170, *176,* 245,
    254
Norman, R. Z., 75, *78*
Notarius, C., 207, 222, *229*
Nottelmann, E. D., 323, *349*
Noyes, A., 360, *371*
Nurius, P. S., 205, *229*
Nyquist, L., 71, *80,* 149, 150, *152*

O

O'Barr, W., 73, *80*
O'Brien, C. E., 170, *174*
Ogino, T., 190, *200*
Oguchi, T., 189, 190, *200*
O'Hair, H. D., 353, 357, 360, 363, 366,
    367, *370, 371*
O'Keefe, D., 258, 272, 273, *285*
Okin, S. M., 20, 35, *38*
O'Leary, A. M., 161, *176*
Oliker, S. J., 47, 48, *62*
Oliver, M. B., 162, *176,* 242, *254,* 414,
    415, 418, *425*
Oliver, S. J., 334, *348*
Olver, R. R., 106, *123*
Ono, H., 183, 186, *200*
Ortega Murphy, B., 395, *412*
Oster, H., 324, *347*
O'Sullivan, M., 235, *253*
Ota, H., 182, *199*
Oxley, D., 112, *123*

P

Pachauri, A., 47, *61*
Paine, R., 57, *62*
Paradise, L. V., 48, *63*
Park, B., 398, *412*
Parker, S., 48, *62*
Parker, R. G., 340, 341, 343, *349*
Parnell, K., 325, *349*

Pasadeos, Y., 151, *153*
Pascale, L., 397, *410*
Patrick, B. C., 207, 208, *230*
Patterson, M. L., 206, 212, 214, *229*
Paxson, M. A., 167, *174*
Pearson, J. C., 86, *100*, 103, 105, *121, 391*
Peiss, K., 102, *122*
Peplau, L. A., 48, 49, *61*, 106, *122*, 215,
    216, *227, 230*, 296, *300*
Perlman, D., 216, *227*
Perper, T., 244, 246, 250, *254*
Perse, E. M., 316, *319*
Peters, S. D., 334, *348*
Petersen, A. C., 90, 91, 92, *100*
Peterson, C., 304, 317, 318, *319*
Peterson, D. R., 292, *301*
Peterson, J., 432, *444*
Petronio, S., 106, *122*, 400, *411*
Petty, R. E., 258, 273, *285*
Phillippot, P., 327, 328, *349*
Pickert, S., 48, *63*
Pierce, J. P., 278, *284*
Pike, K. M., 164, *174*
Pineault, M. A., 167, *175*
Pineault, T., 352, *371*, 235, *253*
Plant, E. A., 3, *17*, 24, 25, 26, 27, *37*,
    155, *175*, 210, *228*, 394, *412*, 432,
    444
Platz, S. J., 161, *173*
Poe, D., 352, *371*
Pomerantz, E. M., 335, *349*
Poole, M. E., 149, 150, 151, *153*
Post, E. L., 413, *425*
Prager, K. J., 221, *229*
Preiss, R., 432, 435, 436, 437, 438, *442,
    443*
Przewuzman, S. J., 167, *177*
Pugh, M. D., 75, *80*
Puka, B., 21, *38*
Pukalos, J., 50, *62*
Putnam, L., 441, *444*

R

Ragan, S. L., 24, *38*, 378, *391*
Rakow, L., 387, *391*, 430, 441, *444*
Ransdell, H. J., 242, *253*
Rapson, R. L., 206, 207, *228*
Raven, B. H. , 296, *300*
Rawlins, W. K., 106, *123*
Read, S. J., 206, 208, *229*
Reed, C. E., 216, 229
Reis, H. T., 47, 53, *63*, 70, *80*, 112, 115,
    123, 124, 205, 207, 208, 209, 210,
    211, 215, 216, 219, 223, *227, 229*,
    230, 231, 304, *319*

Reisman, J. M., 42, 47, 52, *62*
Reitan, H.T., 271, *285*
Reynolds, R. A., 183, 185, 188, *200*
Rhodes, N., 161, *177*, 215, *231*
Ricci-Bitti, P. E., 235, *253*, 334, 338, *349*
Rice, R. W., 76, *80*
Richman, J., 112, *122*
Richmond, V. P., 401, *411*
Riessman, C. K., 20, *38*
Riggio, R. E., 321, 322, 327, 328, 329,
    344, *347, 349*, 352, 353, 354, *371*
Rime, B., 327, 328, *349*
Risman, B., 22, *38*, 73, *80*
Ritchie, J., 47, *61*, 112, *121*, 334, *346*
Robinson, D. T., 404, *412*
Robinson, N. S., 331, *350*
Robinson, W. P., 365, 367, *371*
Robison, J. T., 206, *227*
Roche, J. P., 415, *426*
Rockwell, P., 357, 358, *370*
Rodin, J., 342, *349*
Roesner, J. B., 179, *200*
Rogers, P. L., 87, 89, *100*, 158, 165, 167,
    168, 169, *172, 176*
Rogers, R. W., 296, *301*
Roggman, L. A., 238, *253*
Rohde, P., 335, 336, *349*
Roiger, J., 352, *369*
Roloff, M. E., 262, 271, *285*
Rosaldo, M. Z., 98, *100*
Rosario, M., 107, *124*
Rose, S., 424, *426*
Rosen, E., 209, 210, 211, *230*
Rosen, L. D., 160, *176*
Rosenberg, P. R., 264, *285*
Rosenblatt, J. S., 22, *38*
Rosenfeld, H. M., 164, *176*, 381, *392*
Rosenkrantz, J., 352, *370*
Rosenkrantz, P. S., 73, *78*, 394, *410*
Rosenthal, R., 87, 89, *100*, 156, 158,
    159, 161, 162, 165, 167, 168, 169,
    172, *176, 177*, 206, *231*, 245, *254*,
    352, 354, 365, 366, 367, *370, 372*,
    435, 436, *444*
Ross, L., 205, *226*
Ross, M., 208, *230*
Roter, D. L., 158, *174*
Rotter, G. S., 328, *349*
Rotter, N. G., 328, *349*
Roy, A. K., 390, *391*
Rubin, D. B., 156, *176*
Rubin, L. B., 203, 218, *230*, 288, 289,
    292, *301*
Rubin, R. B., 316, *319*
Ruble, D. N., 335, *349*
Ruble, T. L., 394, *412*
Ruch, W., 164, *176*
Rudd, M. J., 140, *153*

Ruddick, S., 20, *38*
Russel, L., 207, 219, *231*
Russell, D., 215, *230*
Rutt, D. J., 56, *61*, 221, *227*, 305, *319*,
Ryan, M., 160, *175*
Ryan, R. M., 279, *284*
Rytting, M. B., 249, *254*

S

Saal, F. E., 249, *254*
Saarni, C., 326, *349*
Sabatelli, R. M., 166, *176*, 327, *349*
Sacks, H., 380, 383, *392*
Sadalla, E.K., 238, 239, 240, 243, *253*,
    397, *412*
Sadker, D., 432, *444*
Sadker, M., 432, *444*
Sagrestano, L. M., 73, *80*, 290, 296, 297,
    301
Sahlstein, E., 432, *444*
Salovey, P., 342, *349*
Samter, W., 101, 110, 111, 113, 115,
    122, *124*, 219, *227*, 304, 305, 307,
    314, 316, *318*
Sandvik, E., 220, *228*
Sanford, N., 21, *38*
Sapadin, 48, 54, *62*
Sarason, I. G., 107, 113, 114, 117, 120,
    121
Saso, M., 180, 181, *200*
Sause, E. F., 150, 151, *153*
Scanlon, M. B., 45, 48, 51, *63*
Scanzoni, J. H., 264, *285*
Scardino, T J., 415, 418, *425*
Schaap, C., 7, *17*
Schaefer, R. E., 214, *229*
Schegloff, E., 380, 383, *392*
Scherer, K. R., 134, *152*, 235, *253*
Schloff, L., 102, *124*
Schlueter, D. W., 68, *80*
Schmidt, F., 430, *444*
Schmidt, G. W., 293, *302*
Schmidt, K. L., 181, *199*
Schmidt, S. M., 296, *301*
Schmitt, D. P., 241, 242, 243, *252*
Schmitt, D. R., 262, *285*
Schneider, D. J., 396, *412*
Schneider, F. W., 165, *173*
Schooler, C., 181, *200*
Schroeder, J. E., 166, *176*
Schumacher, A., 223, *230*
Schwartz, P., 72, *79*, 296, *301*, 374, 375,
    376, 377, 378, 379, 381, 385, 386,
    389, *391*
Schwarz, N., 208, *230*

Sedikides, C., 242, *254*
Seeley, j. R., 335, 336, *349*
Seesahai, M., 149, 150, *152*
Seibold, D., 262, *285*
Seligman, M. E. P., 335, 338, *348*
Semic, B. A., 332, *347*
Semin, G. R., 366, *372*
Semmelroth, J., 242, *252*
Senchak, M., 53, *62*, 70, *80*, 112, 115,
    124, 209, 210, 211, 219, 223, *230*,
    304, *319*
Serbin, L. A., 89, *100*
Shackelford, S. L., 279, *283*
Sharabany, R., 216, *230*
Shaver, P. R., 205, 207, 208, 209, 210,
    211, 218, 219, *228*, *230*
Shaw, M. E., 245, *252*, 271, *285*
Sheets, V. L., 244, *253*
Shelton, K., 151, *153*
Shenk, J. L., 292, 293, 295, *300*
Shepard, B., 325, *348*
Sherif, C. W., 290, *301*
Sherman, S. J., 262, *283*
Sherriffs, A.C., 394, *412*
Sherrod, D., 43, *63*
Shibley Hyde, J. S., 394, *412*
Shields, S. A., 331, *349*
Shinn, M., 107, *124*
Shipman, P., 98, *100*
Shotland, R. L., 249, *254*
Shulman, G. A., 326, *348*
Shumaker, S. A., 215, *230*
Siegel, H. I., 22, *38*
Siegelman, L., 164, *175*
Siegler, D. M., 74, *80*
Siegler, R. S., 74, *80*
Sigler, E., 164, *173*
Silbergeld, S., 71, *79*
Sillars, A. L., 377, 381, 383, *390*, *392*,
    436, *443*
Silva, P., 335, *345*
Silver, C. A., 251, *254*
Simon, H., 429, *443*
Simon, L. J., 159, 167, *176*
Simpson, J. A., 422, *426*
Singh, D., 238, *254*
Sinha, D., 180, *200*
Sink, C. R., 296, *301*
Sivacek, J., 279, *283*
Small, M. F., 244, 251, *254*
Smith, H. J., 167, *176*
Smith, J. S., 181, 192, 193, 196, *201*
Smith, K. C., 181, *200*, *201*
Smith, M., 434, *443*
Smith, P. A., 394, *412*
Smith, P. M., 134, *153*, 394, *412*
Smith-Lovin, L., 404, *412*
Smythe, M., 68, *80*

Snell, W. E., 334, 338, *349*
Snodgrass, S. E., 72, *80*
Solomon, B., 53, *62*, 70, *80*, 112, 115,
 124, 209, 210, 211, 219, 223, *230*,
 304, *319*
Sommer, C., 442, *444*
Spence, J. T., 71, *80*
Spender, D., 72, 73, *80*, 399, *412*
Spitzberg, B. H., 251, *254*, 332, 341, *347*,
 348, 406, *411*
Sprafkin, C. H., 89, *100*
Sprecher, S., 115, *124*, 420, 423, *426*
Stacks, D. W., 89, *100*
Stafford, L., 373, *392*
Staley, C. M., 151, *153*
Staneski, R. A., 334, 335, 338, *348*
Stapley, J.C., 334, *349*
Starr, D. P., 151, *153*
Steffan, V. J., 161, *173*, 291, *300*
Steil, J. M., 73, *80*, 183, 196, 197, *201*
Steinberg, L.D., 8, *17*
Stern, D. N., 206, *230*, 303, *319*
Sternberg, R. J., 165, *172*
Stevens, G., 97, *100*
Stewart, A. D., 325, *349*
Stewart, D. L., 259, 260, 263, *283*
Stewart, L. P., 90, *100*, 325, *349*
Stier, D. S., *38*, 84, 85, *100*, 214, 221,
 230
Stiver, I. P., 289, *301*
Stokes, J. P., 214, *228*, 399, *412*
Stone, J. I., 352, 366, *370*
Strathman, A. J., 167, *175*
Strayer, F. F., 303, *319*
Strayer, J., 321, *349*
Strejc, H., 56, *61*, 221, *227*, 305, *319*
Stringfield, D. O., 242, *253*
Stroeb, M. S., 216, *230*
Stroebe, W., 216, *230*
Strong, M. S., 54, *62*
Strzyzewski, K. D., 352, *369*
Stucky, N. P., 74, *79*
Studley, L. B., 130, *137*, 141, 142, 143,
 145, 149, 150, *153*
Stull, D. T., 70, *79*
Sturniolo, F., 164, *175*
Sudman, S., 208, *230*
Sullivan, H. S., 206, 211, *230*
Sunnafrank, M., 421, *426*
Surrey, J. L., 289, *301*
Susman, E., 323, *349*
Suttles, G. D., 57, *63*
Suzuki, A., 180, 197, 198, *201*
Swain, S., 20, *38*, 103, 119, *124*
Swedlund, A. C., 96, 97, *100*
Sweeney, L., 293, *302*
Swim, J. K., *38*, 74, *80*, 170, *176*
Symons, D., 89, 95, *100*, 238, 242, *254*

T

Talovic, S., 295, *301*
Tanaka, Y., 181, *201*
Tang, J., 366, *370*
Tannen, D. 2, *17*, 31, *38*, 76, *80*, 86, *100*,
 102, 103, 105, 107, 109, 118, 119,
 120, *124*, 136, *153*, 203, 221, *230*,
 289, *301*, 304, *319*, 354, 360, *372*,
 378, 379, 380, 386, *392*, 408, *412*
Tarule, J. M., 179, *199*, 289, *299*
Tavris, C., 21, 22, 30, 35, *38*
Taylor, D. A., 207, *226*
Taylor, D. M., 134, *152*
Taylor, S. E., 208, 220, *227*, *230*, 270,
 283, 397, *411*
Teitelbaum, M. A., 264, *285*
Tellegen, A., 401, *412*
Teng, G., 159, *175*
Terman, L. M., 291, *301*
Tesch, S. A., 48, *63*
Tesman, J., 325, *348*
Texter, L. A., 367, *370*
Theil, H., 144, *153*
Thelen, M., 325, *347*
Thoma, S. J., 160, *176*
Thomas, C. M., 416, *425*
Thomas, D. L., 327, *349*
Thompson, A., 115, *124*
Thompson, C. A., 183, 185, 187, 188,
 196, *199*, *201*
Thorne, B., 26, *38*, 72, 73, *81*, 116, 118,
 120, *124*, 291, *301*, 376, *392*
Thornhill, R., 237, 238, *252*, *254*
Throckmorton, B., 353, *371*
Tidwell, M., 209, 210, *230*
Tiger, L., 204, 216, *230*
Tillman, M. P., 207, 219, *231*
Tilson, M., 335, 336, *349*
Ting-Toomey, S., 136, *152*, 183, 184, 188,
 199, *201*
Todd-Mancillas, W., 383, *391*
Toffler, B. L., 278, *284*
Tomita, M., 235, *253*
Toner, B. B., 334, *348*
Tooke, W., 248, 249, *254*
Torres, L., 73, *81*
Tripathi, R. C., 180, *200*
Trivers, R. L., 236, 247, *255*
Trobst, K. K. , 101, 107, *124*
Tromel-Ploetz, S., 179, *201*
Trost, M. R., 234, 237, 238, 239, 240,
 242, 243, 244, 245, 246, 250, 251,
 253, *255*, 345, *348*
Tucker, J., 353, *371*
Turner, L. H., 86, *100*, 383, *391*
Tzavaras, A., 235, *253*

U

Uhl, S., 47, *63*
Ulman, K., 324, 326, *347*
Umberson, D., 215, *228*
Unger, R. K., 67, 72, *81*, 287, 290, *301*,
    302
Ura, M., 189, *200*
Utne Reader, 102, *124*

V

Vangelisti, A. L., 219, *230*
Vaux, A. C., 101, 107, 112, *121*, *124*,
    214, *230*
Veccia, E. M., 85, *99*
Verdi, A. F., 69, 70, 71, *81*
Vershure, B., 397, *412*
Vitters, A. G., 76, *80*
Vitulli, W. F., 249, *252*
Vogel, S. R., 73, *78*, 394, *410*
von Salisch, M., 214, *231*
Voyer, D., 160, *176*
Voyer, S., 160, *176*
Vrij, A., 366, *372*

W

Wada, M., 189, 190, 196, *201*
Wagenhals, W. L., 242, *253*
Wagner, F., 215, *228*
Wagner, H. L., 159, *176*, 327, 328, *349*
Wahrman, R., 75, *80*
Walcznski, P. T., 293, *302*
Waldrop, M. F., 216, *231*
Walker, K., 52, *63*
Wall, S. M., 48, *63*
Wallbott, H. G., 334, 338, *349*
Wallston, B. S., 290, *302*
Walsh, D. G., 247, 249, *255*
Walther, J. B., 354, *370*
Waring, E. M., 207, 219, *231*
Warner, R. M., 206, *231*
Warr, P. B., 161, *176*
Warren, M. P., 323, *346*
Warshay, D. W., 151, *153*
Wasserman, G. A., 303, *319*
Watson, D., 401, *412*
Watzlawick, P., 380, 383, *392*
Weber, N., 249, *254*
Weghorst, S. J., 340, 342, *350*
Weiner, E., 101, *123*
Weinstein, C. D., 295, *301*
Weisman, C. S., 264, *285*

Weiss, L., 42, 43, 53, *63*
Weiss, D. L., 246, 250, *254*
Weisz, G., 207, 219, *231*
Weitz, S., 88, *100*
Welch, B., 434, *444*
Wellman, B., 305, *319*
Werking, K. J., 101, 113, *122*, 219, 227,
    304, 305, 314, 316, *319*
Werner, P. D., 73, *81*, 394, *412*
West, C., 72, 77, *81*, 106, *124*, *125*, 304,
    319, 376, 379, 383, *392*, 441, *444*
West, R. L., 86, *100*
Westen, D., 242, *252*
Westmoreland, R., 151, *153*,
Wetzel, P. J., 180, 193, 194, 195, 196, *201*
Whaley, B. B., 110, 111, *124*
Wheelan, S. A., 69, 70, 71, *81*
Wheeler, L., *47*, *63*, 112, 115, *124*, 207,
    208, 209, 210, 211, 216, 223, *230*,
    231
Whelan, M., 161, *177*, 215, *231*
Whicker, M. L., 94, 96, *100*
White, C., 357, 358, 365, *369*, *370*, 406,
    411
White, G. L., 327, 339, 340, *349*, *350*
White, S. W., 216, *227*
Whitesell, N. R., 331, *350*
Whitley, B. E., 162, *174*, *176*
Whittaker, J., 271, *285*
Widenmann, S. J., 131, 132, 142, 149,
    150, 151, *153*
Wiemann, J. M, 131, 132, 142, 149, 150,
    151, *153*
Wigley, C. J., 264, *284*
Wiley, M. G., 75, *81*
Wilkins, B. M., 84, *100*, 179, *201*, 378,
    392, 432, *444*
Wilkinson, I., 296, *301*
Williams, G. C., 237, *255*
Williams, J. E., 73, *78*, 394, *412*
Williams, M., 164, *176*
Williams, S., 335, *345*
Williamson, G. M., 207, *231*
Wills, T. A., 215, *227*
Wilmot, W. W., 242, *252*, 414, *425*, *426*
Wilson, A., 367, *370*
Wilson, D. P., 291, *301*
Wilson, M., 236, 237, 242, 251, *252*
Wilson, T., 429, *444*
Winch, P., 198, *201*
Winstead, B. A., 43, *63*, 101, 107, 112,
    119, *121*, *122*, *124*, 271, *284*, 399,
    411
Wispé, L., 214, *231*
Witelson, S., 324, *350*
Witteman, H. , 296, *302*
Wittenberg, M., 216, *231*
Wong, P. T., 271, *284*, 399, *411*

Wood, J. T., 20, 21, 27, 28, 29, 30, *39*,
    46, 52, *63*, 102, 103, 104, 105,
    106, 107, 108, 109, 118, 119, 120,
    121, *124*, *125*, 151, *153*, 204, 215,
    216, 218, 221, 226, *231*, 304, *319*,
    412, 423, *426*
Wood, W., 75, *81*, 155, 161, *173*, *176*,
    177, 272, 279, *284*, 290, *300*, *302*
Woodall, G., 353, *370*
Woods, N., 72, *81*, 376, *392*
Wortman, C. B., 295, *299*
Wright, P. H., 20, *37*, *38*, 43, 44, 45, 48,
    50, 51, 53, 54, 55, 57, 60, *61*, *63*,
    120, *122*, *125*, 204, 218, 221, *227*,
    231, 305, 315, *319*
Wyer, M. M., 365, 367, *370*

Y

Yalom, G., 296, *301*

Yankeelov, P. A., 101, 107, 112, 119 ,
    121
Yeazell, M., 415, 417, *425*
Yoder, J. D., 8, *17*, 27, 32, *38*, *302*
Young, M. J., 365, 366, *371*
Yudkin, M., 102, *124*

Z

Zakahi, W. R., 401, 402, 403, *411*
Zanna, M., 398, *411*
Zelditch, M., 75, *78*
Zellner, W., 179, *201*
Zimmerman, D. H., 72, 77, *81*, 106, *124*,
    125, 304, *319*, 376, 379, *392*, 441,
    444
Zorn, T., 20, *38*, 395, *412*
Zuckerman, M., 159, 162, 164, 167, 170,
    172, *177*, 206, 209, 210, 211, *228*,
    231, 352, 365, 366, *372*

Subject Index

A

Acquaintance Description Form, 53
Affect, *see* Emotion
Affective orientation, 101
Agency, 43,46
Alpha bias, 2–3
American Psychologist, 3
Anger, *see* Emotion

B

Back channels, *see* Conversational maintenance
Beta bias, 3
Biological bases for sex differences, 18–20,
288
nonverbal sensitivity, 86–88
oppression, 88
political pressure to avoid discussion,
85
reproductive roles, 85
social and nonverbal sensitivity, 86
social sensitivity, 88–89
brain lateralization, 89
chromosomal evidence, 89
genetic predisposition, 88–89
hormonal evidence, 89
spatial skills, 90–93
ability to detect spatial relationships, 90–91
field independence, 91
mental strategies for performing, 91
rotation and visualization of objects, 90
spatial perception, 90–93
hemispheric lateralization, 92
hormones, 93

sex-linked chromosomes, 92
Biological determination, 98–99
weak determinism, 98
Biological perspective, *see* Emotion
Biological perspective, *see* Intimacy
Biological sex differences, origins of, 93–97
human mating patterns, 94–96
attraction, 96
dimorphism, 94
monogamy/polygamy, 94–96
parental investment and role differentiation, 96–97
Body Politics, 291
Bower birds, 235–236

C

Causal process model, 234, *see also* Interaction-based model of sex roles
Childhood sex roles, 31–32
Chronicle of Higher Education, 98
Comfort
value placed on provision and receipt
of, 113–114
affective goals, 114
cross-sex friendships, 113
instrumental goals, 114
opposite sex romances, 113
same-sex friendships, 113
Comfort providers, preference for gender
of, 112–113
Comforting behavior, 119
outcomes of, 114–116
marital commitment, 115
marital satisfaction, 115
person-centered comforting skills,
115
relationship commitment, 115

relationship satisfaction, 115
Comforting messages
    person-centered, 110
    sensitivity of, 111
Comforting strategies, person-centered,
    120
Communality, defined, 42
Communication
    defining, 4–5
    style, 77, 289
Communication Functions Questionnaire
    (CFQ), 113
Communicative competence, 407
Communicative Responses to Jealousy
    Scale, 341
Communion, 43, 46
Competence of men and women, 75
Conflict
    asymmetry of dependence, 293
    marital, 291–296
    process, 292
    social influence techniques, 296–298
        limitations of research, 298
        ongoing marital relationships,
            297–298
        power, 296–297
    structure, 292
    symmetrical dependence, 293
Conversation
    interaction, 10
    intimate, 70
    length, 308
        good friends vs. casual acquain-
            tances, 308
    objectives, 310–313, 315–318
        effect of satisfaction with friend-
            ships, 317–318
        entertainment function, 315–316
        fundamental objectives, 315
        pleasure, 316
    topic, 14, 308–310, 313–315
Conversational maintenance, 15, 373,
    378–381
    back channels, 374, 379, 382, 384, 386
    background research, 374–376
    interruptions, 379–380, 383, 386
        types of, 384
    limitations of study, 388
    perceived power balance, 375
    question asking, 380–381, 383–386
    talk time, 378–379, 382, 384–386
Courtship behaviors, 13
Courtship interaction, 243–250
    men's courtship behavior, 247–250
        immediacy of action, 249
        likelihood to approach women, 249
        research on, 248–250

status and dominance signals,
    248–249
women's courtship behavior, 244–247
    flirtation strategies, 245–246
    likelihood of approach, 246–247
    nonverbal behavior, 245
    rejection strategies, 246
    research on, 245–247
Critical scholarship, 35
Cross-cultural studies, *see* Friendship
Culture, *see also* Intimacy
    defined, 182
    Western perceptions of gender,
        181–182
        androgyny, 181
        depiction in popular literature, 181
        role of family, 181–182
Culture and sex differences, 12–13

D

Deception, 15
    decoding of, 364–367
        effect of sex composition of
            sender–receiver dyad,
            366–367
        overall accuracy, 365–366
    differences in nonverbal and verbal be-
        havior, 368–369
    during interviews, 354–361
    dyadic discussions, 361–363
    encoding of, 352–354
        preinteraction variables, 352–353
        sex difference effects, 363–364
        strategic and nonstrategic cues, 352
    influence of type during interview,
        358–361
    Interpersonal Deception Theory, 354
    nonverbal measures of, 355–357
Deception detection
    reaction to, 367
    training, 367
Deferential communication, 20
Demand–withdrawal interaction pattern,
    14, 291–296
    childrearing issues, 294
    intimacy, 292–293,
Different cultures perspective, 11, 31,
    102, 104–107, 117
    conversational maintenance, 387–388
    criteria for effective comforting mes-
        sages, 109–111
    feminist theory, 106–107
    intimacy, 217, 226
    language research, 105–106
    socialization research, 105

Differential parental investment model,
236–243
attractiveness, 239
evolution of a larger brain, 238
evolution of hunting, 238
implications for developing relationships, 241–243
sexual permissiveness, 243–244
tests of relational commitment, 242
monogamy, 237
pair bonding, 237
resource acquisition, 238–239
selfish gene, 237
Dominance, 65, 71–72
Dominance model, 376–378
conversation, gender inequality in,
376–377
conversational roles, 377
interruption behavior, 377–378
language, 376
marital communication, 377
Dynamism, 74

E

Elaboration likelihood model, 273
Emotion, 14–15
anger, sex differences in, 331–334
among children and adolescents,
331
support for predictions, 332–334
types of communicative responses,
331–332
biological and evolutionary perspective, 322–324
cerebral hemispheric processing,
322–324
hormones and temperament,
322–323
selection processes and evolution,
322–323
communicative responses to, 322
jealousy, sex differences in, 339–343
coping strategies, 339–341
emotional connection, 339
sexual infidelity, 339
support for predictions, 341–343
limitations to studies, 343–344
sadness, sex differences in, 334–339
support for predictions, 335–339
tactics for dealing with, 334
social skills, sex differences in, 326–331
Riggio's model of social skills, 328
support for predictions, 328–331
socialization perspective, 324–326
role of parents, 324–326

Emotional contagion, 207
Emotional sensitivity, 101
Emotional support, 101–102, 104, 117,
119
different cultures analysis of, 107–109
behavioral differences, 108
cognitive variables, 108
marital satisfaction, 115
Evolutionary framework (perspective), 11,
13, 235–243
sexual selection, 236
Expectancy violations theory, 418–419
communicator reward valence, 419
expectancies, 418
expectancy violations, 419
Expectancy violations, sexual
on first dates, 417–422, 419–422
interpretation and evaluation of,
420–421
outcomes, 421–422

F

Face, *see* Japanese and American sex differences in communication
Feminine bias in intimacy research, 103
Feminism, 28–29
radical difference, 28
revalorism, 29
First date initiation, 16, *see also* Sexual expectations, first date
Flirting, 13
Fried Green Tomatoes, 203
Friendship, 10, *see also* Comfort; Intimacy
communal–agentic dichotomy, 43–44
bimodal variation, 44
communality, 55–56
self-disclosure, 56
verbal expressions of, 56
communion and agency as separate
continua, 45–46
conceptions and values, 48
emotional expressiveness, 48
self-disclosure, 48
stimulation value, 49
utility value, 49
cross-cultural studies of sex differences
in, 47
future research relevance, 56
holistic and circumscribed, 53–54
influence of structural factors, 47
intimacy, 50–51, 56
close friendships, 53
defined, 50
potentially confounding variables in
research, 51
self-disclosure, 51–52

shared activities, 52
problems of research operationaliza-
        tion, 46–47
    dispositional bias, 46–47
    lopsided operationalization, 46
same sex, 106
sex-linked variations in, 42
    face-to-face, 43
    side-by-side, 43
structural factors, 57–58
    implications for communal and
            agentic friendships, 58–59
    implications for sex differences,
            59–60
    roles, 58
talk vs. activities, 49–50

G

Gender, *see* Sex and gender
Gender differences
    communication-related, 20
    degree vs. kind, 26
    magnitude of, 67–69
        effect size, 67–68
        sample sizes, 67
    pervasive, 20–21
    psychological, 25
    small, 23–26
        quantitative vs. observational re-
                search, 24–25
        within-sex variability and overlap,
                24
Gender polarity, 26–28
Gender schematicity, 408

H

*He and She Talk: How to Communicate with
    the Opposite Sex*, 102
Helping, *see* Intimacy

I

In a Different Voice, 29
Individual differences approach to sex dif-
        ferences, 288–290, *see also* Biologi-
        cal bases for sex differences;
        Biological sex differences, origins of
Influence, *see also* Conflict
    female persuasibility, 259
    gender differences in, 259–271
    susceptibility to attempts, 271–280
        existing research findings, 271–274

possible criticisms of, 272–274
resistance to persuasion paradigm,
        274–280
    boomerang effect, 278
    incentive-aroused ambivalence
            hypothesis, 279
    misanthropy, 276–277
    reactance, 277–279
Influenceability, 13–14
Instrumental orientation, 8–9, 101, 106
Interaction, sex differences in length of,
        70–71
Interaction style, 71
    differences in, 303–305
        adolescence, 303–304
        adulthood, 304
        childhood, 303
        underlying motivation, 304–305
Interaction-based model of sex roles
        (Causal process model), 395–396
    self concept, 395–396
    schema, 396
Interpersonal Attraction Scale, 401
Interpersonal Deception Theory, 354
Interpersonal process model, 205–208
Interpersonal sensitivity, 72
Interruption, 67, 69, 72
Interruption behavior, *see also* Dominance
        model
Intersexual choice, 236
Intimacy, 13, 20, 106, *see also* Conversa-
        tion; Demand–withdrawal interac-
        tion pattern; Friendship; Sexual
        expectations
    biological priming, 222–225
    coping styles, 215
    culture, 223
    definition, issues of, 218–221
    disruption of intimate relationships,
            216
    divorce, 216
    essential self, 205
    friendship style, 216–218
    giving and receiving social support,
            214–215
        structural vs. functional support,
                215
    helping, 215
    interpersonal context, 205–208
    Interpersonal process model, 205–208
    loneliness, 215–216
        bereavement, 216
    negative affect, 222
    nonverbal communication, 206,
            213–214, 221
        listening, 214
        smiling, 214

self-disclosure, 212–213
    within existing relationships, 213
sex-differentiated preferences for,
    217–218
social context of interaction, 222–225
spoken exchange, 221–222
    conversation, 221
    verbal content, 221
stress reactivity, 222
Intimate interaction
    characteristics
        caring, 207
        understanding, 206
        validation, 206–207
    event sampling approach, 208–212
    interpretative filters, 208
    involving opposite-sex others, 210–212
    involving same-sex others, 210–211
Intimate Strangers: Men and Women Together,
    203

J

Japanese and American sex differences in
        communication
    communication tactics, 183–184
        delivery of compliments, 184
        face-management tactics, 184
        persuasion and social influence tac-
            tics, 183–184
    different manifestation, 196
    face-threatening behavior, 187
    immediacy, verbal and nonverbal, 187
    limited research availability, 196
    linguistic structures and communica-
        tive styles, 195
    meanings associated with symbols and
        concepts, 186
    methodological problems, 197–198
        scale, 198
        self report, 197
    miscommunication, 193
    parallel linguistic constructs of Japa-
        nese men and women with
        American women, 194
    power, 193–194, 196
    relationships, 194
    speech characteristics and nonverbal be-
        havior, 185–186
        immediacy, 185–186
        language intensity, 185
        pitch and intonation, 185
        politeness, 185
        touch, 186, 196
    traits, tendencies, and styles, 186–187
        affect orientation, 186–187
        assertiveness, 187

    responsiveness, 187
    verbal aggressiveness, 187
Japanese communication styles
    power, features according to Western
        conception of, 194
        kenryoku, 194
        shihai, 194
    sex differences
        directives, 192
        forms of politeness, 195
        linguistic patterns, 190
        Motherese strategy, 192–193
        nonverbal behavior, 189–190
        politeness, 192
        politeness forms, 190
        rank terms, usage of, 193
        rules governing conversation, 189
        scarcity of studies, 195
        self-disclosure, 189–190
        sex vs. gender-based variability, 192
        social attractiveness, 189
        sociolinguistic behavior, 192, 195
    Western perceptions of, 196
Japanese culture
    jiritsu, 191
Jealousy, *see* Emotion

L

Language, 68, 119–120
    combinations, 128
    communication settings, 128
    features most often used by male/fe-
        male communicators,
        146–147
    forceful, 75
    gender differentiating, 129
    gender-linked language effect, 147
    judgments by observers, 128
    power, 291
    rater–speaker differences, 128
    sex differences research, 127
    word choice, 127–128
Language communities, 106
Language differences, 11–12, 133–138
    effect of, 139–146
        gender stereotypes, 145–146
        gender-linked language effect,
            139–143
            American dialects, 140–141
            dyadic interaction, 142
            written language, 141–142
            prediction from language fea-
                tures, 143–145
    multivariate assessment of, 136–138

patterns of gender-linked differences, 135–136
  dimensions of language style, 136
  intercultural style differences, 135–136
  review of research, 133–135
Language expectancy theory, 259–266
  fundamental propositions (modified), 261–263
    cultural and sociological expectations, 262
    normative expectations, 262
    source credibility, 262–263
    violations, 262
  gender and persuasion research, 263–266
  the general model, 259–261
  medical professionals, 264–266
Language similarities
  average language feature use, 131–132
  interruption, 131
  questions, 131
  sex guess accuracy, 130–131
Leadership, 68, 72
  emergence, 65, 68, 70, 74
  evaluation of, 75
  women's, 76
Lethal Weapon, 203
Listening, *see* Intimacy
Loneliness, 116, *see also* Intimacy

M

Management communication, 84
Marital communication, *see* Dominance
Marital conflict, 14
Mars and Venus in the Bedroom, 102
Martin's ratio measure of sex stereotyping, 401
Measurement in sex and gender research, 428–431
  biological sex vs. gender/socialization, 430
  sampling, 431
    bias in gender research, 66
    generalizability of college populations, 431
  size of sex/gender differences, 431–433
  understanding of sex/gender questions, 429
  use of biological indicators, 429
Men Are From Mars, Women Are From Venus, 27, 76, 83, 102, 203
Meta-analysis, 27, 68, 435
Muted group theory, 234

N

New York Rangers, 393
New York Times, 28
Newsweek, 85
Nonverbal behavior, *see* Courtship interaction; Deception
Nonverbal communication, *see* Intimacy
Nonverbal sensitivity
  age, 159
  amount learned, 168,
  cognitive complexity, 168
  comparison of effect sizes, 169–171
  correlates of, 163, 165–169
  to cues, 20
  empathic accuracy, 159
  sex differences, 158–159
Nonverbal sex differences, 12
Normal distribution assumption, implications for sex/gender research, 433–435

P

Paternity, certainty of, 236–237
Perception and evaluation, 74
Personal disclosures, 20
Persuasion, *see* Influenceability
Politeness, 72, *see also* Japanese and American sex differences in communication
Popular press, 27
Power, *see also* Language
Power and dominance, 72–73
  differences, 21
    career/professional, 22
    family, 22
  inequalities in, 21
  and prestige, 69
  social, 21
Problem talk, 118
Profile of Nonverbal Sensitivity (PONS), 87, 158–159
Psychodynamic theory, 288

R

Reinforcement Expectancy Theory, 266–271
  appropriate communication, 266
  compliance-gaining strategies in initial influence attempts, 266–268
  regard signal, 267
  sequential compliance-gaining attempts, 268–271

Relational maintenance, *373, see also* Conversational maintenance
Relationships, romantic, 106
Reproductive fitness, 236–237
Rochester Interaction Record, 2, 3, 13, 209
Role differentiation, 70
Romance, *see* Comfort

S

Sadness, *see* Emotion
Self-disclosure, 70–71, *see also* Intimacy
Sensitivity to nonverbal cues, 158–159
Sex and gender
    defining, 4, 290
        gender, 4
        sex, 4, 290
    link to communication
        biological factors, 8
        development and testing of theories of communication, 7
        gender as a social construction, 8
        sociological factors, 8
        stereotypes, 6
    theoretical explanations of, 6–8
Sex and gender research
    moderating, contextual factors, 5
Sex composition of speakers, 71–72
Sex differences
    comparison of magnitude of, 157
    extreme values, 436–438
    in gender self concepts, 170
    importance of, 435–436
    as a reflection of gender differences, 87–88
    size of, 12
    small differences, 19–20
    value of studying, 32–34
    versus similarities, 2–4
Sex role norm violation, perception of, 400–404
Sex role normative communication
    violation of, 404–408
        communicative competence, 405, 407–408
            social attractiveness, 405–408
Sex role norms during initial interaction, 398–400
    question asking, 398–399
    talking about the self, 399–400
Sex role stereotypes, 394–395
    agentic stereotype, 394–395
    communal stereotype, 394–395
Sex role violations, 15–16, 397–398
Sex/gender differences

need for theory, 34
    social structures, 34–35
Sex/gender differences and similarities in communication, 10
    key questions, 10
Sexual expectancy violations
    predicted outcome value, 421
Sexual expectations, *see also* Expectancy violations theory
    first date initiation and sexual evaluations, 414–417
        date rape, 416
        intimacy, 417
Sexual stereotypes, 438–440
    statistical fallacy, 439
Sexual strategies theory, 422–423
Situational context of interaction, 69–70
Situational variability in behavior, 77
Skill deficit/skill specialization account, 117–118
Smiling, 157–158, *see also* Intimacy
    comparison of effect sizes, 169–171
    correlates of, 163–165, 168
    sex differences, 157–158
Social role model, 291
Social role theory, 75–76
Social roles, 72–73
Social structural approach to sex differences, 287
Social structural approaches, 290–291
    transactional differences, 291
Socialization approach, 288–289
    child development, 288
Socialization perspective, *see also* Emotional communication
Socioemotional behavior, 69
Sociosexuality, 422
Speech accommodation theory, 142
Speech Dialect Attitudinal Scale (SDAS), 129, 139
Speech-qualifications of, 71
Standpoint theory, 29–30, 35–36
    goals in masculine vs. feminine communication culture, 29
Status, 72–73
Stereotypes, gender, 73–76
    lack of differences, 440–441
    social role interpretation of, 396–397
        cultural approaches, 396
        structural explanations, 397
Support, propensity to seek/provide, 101–102

T

Tag questions, use of, 73–74
Talk, amount of, 69

Talking from 9 to 5—Women and Men in the
        Workplace: Language, Sex, and Power,
        102
Task behavior, 69
    sex differences in, 70
Thelma and Louise, 203
Theories and measurement of gender,
        need for, 441–442
Theory of status characteristics and expec-
        tation states, 75–76
Theory–method link, 16
Touch, 84–85

U

UCLA Loneliness Scale, 216
Utne Reader, 102

V

Variance-accounted-for approach, 156

W

Wayne's World, 203
Who Stole Feminism?, 442
Women's intuition, 86
Women's language, 72–73, 106, 289
Women's ways of knowing, 289

Y

You Just Don't Understand: Women and Men
        in Conversation, 76, 102, 203